TWENTY YEARS AFTER

By
Alexandre Dumas, Père

Twenty Years After
by Alexandre Dumas, Père

Copyright © 2024

All Rights reserved.
No part of this publication may be reproduced,
stored in a retrieval system, or transmitted in any
form or by any means, electronic, mechanical,
photocopying or Otherwise, without the written
permission of the publisher.

The author/editor asserts the moral right to
be identified as the author/editor of this work.

ISBN: 978-93-56567-71-9

Published by

DOUBLE 9 BOOKS

2/13-B, Ansari Road
Daryaganj, New Delhi – 110002
info@double9books.com
www.double9books.com
Tel. 011-40042856

This book is under public domain

Printed in India.

About The Author

Alexandre Dumas pere was a French writer and dramatist, born on 24 July 1802. His father was a general in French army who fought in the French Revolution. Dumas father died in his early childhood so his mother brought him up in difficult conditions. Inspiring stories of his father's heroic military life gave him spectacular vision for historical, adventurous and heroic writing. Aristocratic background of his father helped him to get a job and he went Paris for employment. His interest in writing and theatre also evolved and he began his writing work with magazine article writing. In 1828, he wrote first solo play Henry III At The Court. His famous literary works - The Three Musketeers, Queen Margot, The Count of Monte Cristo, The Lady of the Camellias, Twenty Years After, etc. Alexandre Dumas has written on universal human themes of unity, faith, love, romance, loyalty, treachery, revenge and repossession. He died in 1870.

Contents

Chapter I. The Shade of Cardinal Richelieu. 9

Chapter II. A Nightly Patrol. 18

Chapter III. Dead Animosities. 27

Chapter IV. Anne of Austria at the Age of Forty-six. 40

Chapter V. The Gascon and the Italian. 49

Chapter VI. D'Artagnan in his Fortieth Year. 55

Chapter VII. Touches upon the Strange Effects a Half-pistole may have. 67

Chapter VIII. D'Artagnan, Going to a Distance to discover Aramis. 74

Chapter IX. The Abbé D'Herblay. 82

Chapter X. Monsieur Porthos du Vallon de Bracieux de Pierrefonds. 98

Chapter XI. Wealth does not necessarily produce Happiness. 104

Chapter XII. Porthos was Discontented with his Condition. 113

Chapter XIII. Two Angelic Faces. 118

Chapter XIV. The Castle of Bragelonne. 125

Chapter XV. Athos as a Diplomatist. 131

Chapter XVI. The Duc de Beaufort. 140

Chapter XVII. Duc de Beaufort amused his Leisure Hours
    in the Donjon of Vincennes. 145

Chapter XVIII. Grimaud begins his Functions. 152

Chapter XIX. Pâtés made by the Successor of Father
    Marteau are described. 162

Chapter XX. One of Marie Michon's Adventures. 170

Chapter XXI. The Abbé Scarron. 181

Chapter XXII. Saint Denis. 191

Chapter XXIII. One of the Forty Methods of Escape of the Duc de Beaufort... 198

Chapter XXIV. The timely Arrival of D'Artagnan in Paris. 208

Chapter XXV. An Adventure on the High Road. 216

Chapter XXVI. The Rencontre. 223

Chapter XXVII. The four old Friends prepare to meet again. 231

Chapter XXVIII. The Place Royale. 239

Chapter XXIX. The Ferry across the Oise. 244

Chapter XXX. Skirmishing. 252

Chapter XXXI. The Monk. 258

Chapter XXXII. The Absolution. 267

Chapter XXXIII. Grimaud Speaks. 273

Chapter XXXIV. On the Eve of Battle. 279

Chapter XXXV. A Dinner in the Old Style. 289

Chapter XXXVI. A Letter from Charles the First. 296

Chapter XXXVII. Cromwell's Letter. 301

Chapter XXXVIII. Henrietta Maria and Mazarin. 308

Chapter XXXIX. How, sometimes, the Unhappy mistake
    Chance for Providence. 313

Chapter XL. Uncle and Nephew. 320

Chapter XLI. Paternal Affection. 324

Chapter XLII. Another Queen in Want of Help. 332

Chapter XLIII. In which it is proved that first Impulses
    are oftentimes the best. 343

Chapter XLIV. Te Deum for the Victory of Lens. 350

Chapter XLV. The Beggar of St. Eustache. 364

Chapter XLVI. The Tower of St. Jacques de la Boucherie. 374

Chapter XLVII. The Riot. 381

Chapter XLVIII. The Riot becomes a Revolution. 388

Chapter XLIX. Misfortune refreshes the Memory. 400

Chapter L. The Interview. 407

Chapter LI. The Flight. 413

Chapter LII. The Carriage of Monsieur le Coadjuteur. 424

Chapter LIII. How D'Artagnan and Porthos earned by selling Straw. 437

Chapter LIV. In which we hear Tidings of Aramis. 446

Chapter LV. The Scotchman. 456

Chapter LVI. The Avenger. 465

Chapter LVII. Oliver Cromwell. 473

Chapter LVIII. Jesus Seigneur. 479

Chapter LIX. Noble Natures never lose Courage,
    nor good Stomachs their Appetites. 491

Chapter LX. Respect to Fallen Majesty. 499

Chapter LXI. D'Artagnan hits on a Plan. 506

Chapter LXII. London. 521

Chapter LXIII. The Trial. 526

Chapter LXIV. Whitehall. 534

Chapter LXV. The Workmen. 542

Chapter LXVI. Remember! 548

Chapter LXVII. The Man in the Mask. 553

Chapter LXVIII. Cromwell's House. 561

Chapter LXIX. Conversational. 567

Chapter LXX. The Skiff "Lightning." 574

Chapter LXXI. Port Wine. 583

Chapter LXXII. End of the Port Wine Mystery. 591

Chapter LXXIII. Fatality. 596

Chapter LXXIV. How Mousqueton had a Narrow Escape of being eaten. 602

Chapter LXXV. The Return. 608

Chapter LXXVI. The Ambassadors. 614

Chapter LXXVII. The three Lieutenants of the Generalissimo. 621

Chapter LXXVIII. The Battle of Charenton. 631
Chapter LXXIX. The Road to Picardy 638
Chapter LXXX. The Gratitude of Anne of Austria 645
Chapter LXXXI. Cardinal Mazarin as King. 650
Chapter LXXXII. Precautions. 654
Chapter LXXXIII. Strength and Sagacity 659
Chapter LXXXIV. Strength and Sagacity—Continued 668
Chapter LXXXV. The Oubliettes of Cardinal Mazarin. 677
Chapter LXXXVI. Conferences. 681
Chapter LXXXVII. Thinking that Porthos will be at last a Baron,
 and D'Artagnan a Captain. 687
Chapter LXXXVIII. Shows how with Threat and Pen more
 is effected than by the Sword. 695
Chapter LXXXIX. Difficult for Kings to return to the Capitals
 of their Kingdoms 707
Chapter XC. Conclusion. 717

Chapter I.

The Shade of Cardinal Richelieu.

In a splendid chamber of the Palais Royal, formerly styled the Palais Cardinal, a man was sitting in deep reverie, his head supported on his hands, leaning over a gilt and inlaid table which was covered with letters and papers. Behind this figure glowed a vast fireplace alive with leaping flames; great logs of oak blazed and crackled on the polished brass andirons whose flicker shone upon the superb habiliments of the lonely tenant of the room, which was illumined grandly by twin candelabra rich with wax-lights.

Any one who happened at that moment to contemplate that red simar—the gorgeous robe of office—and the rich lace, or who gazed on that pale brow, bent in anxious meditation, might, in the solitude of that apartment, combined with the silence of the ante-chambers and the measured paces of the guards upon the landing-place, have fancied that the shade of Cardinal Richelieu lingered still in his accustomed haunt.

It was, alas! the ghost of former greatness. France enfeebled, the authority of her sovereign contemned, her nobles returning to their former turbulence and insolence, her enemies within her frontiers—all proved the great Richelieu no longer in existence.

In truth, that the red simar which occupied the wonted place was his no longer, was still more strikingly obvious from the isolation which seemed, as we have observed, more appropriate to a phantom than a living creature—from the corridors deserted by courtiers, and courts crowded with guards—from that spirit of bitter ridicule, which, arising from the streets below, penetrated through the very casements of the room, which resounded with the murmurs of a whole city leagued against the minister; as well as from the distant and incessant sounds of guns firing—let off, happily, without other end or aim, except to show to the guards, the Swiss troops and the military who surrounded the Palais Royal, that the people were possessed of arms.

The shade of Richelieu was Mazarin. Now Mazarin was alone and defenceless, as he well knew.

"Foreigner!" he ejaculated, "Italian! that is their mean yet mighty byword of reproach—the watchword with which they assassinated, hanged, and made away with Concini; and if I gave them their way they would assassinate, hang, and make away with me in the same manner, although they have nothing to complain of except a tax or two now and then. Idiots! ignorant of their real enemies, they do not perceive that it is not the Italian who speaks French badly, but those who can say fine things to them in the purest Parisian accent, who are their real foes.

"Yes, yes," Mazarin continued, whilst his wonted smile, full of subtlety, lent a strange expression to his pale lips; "yes, these noises prove to me, indeed, that the destiny of favorites is precarious; but ye shall know I am no ordinary favorite. No! The Earl of Essex, 'tis true, wore a splendid ring, set with diamonds, given him by his royal mistress, whilst I—I have nothing but a simple circlet of gold, with a cipher on it and a date; but that ring has been blessed in the chapel of the Palais Royal,* so they will never ruin me, as they long to do, and whilst they shout, 'Down with Mazarin!' I, unknown, and unperceived by them, incite them to cry out, 'Long live the Duke de Beaufort' one day; another, 'Long live the Prince de Conde;' and again, 'Long live the parliament!'" And at this word the smile on the cardinal's lips assumed an expression of hatred, of which his mild countenance seemed incapable. "The parliament! We shall soon see how to dispose," he continued, "of the parliament! Both Orleans and Montargis are ours. It will be a work of time, but those who have begun by crying out: Down with Mazarin! will finish by shouting out, Down with all the people I have mentioned, each in his turn.

> * It is said that Mazarin, who, though a cardinal, had not taken such vows as to prevent it, was secretly married to Anne of Austria.—La Porte's Memoirs.

"Richelieu, whom they hated during his lifetime and whom they now praise after his death, was even less popular than I am. Often he was driven away, oftener still had he a dread of being sent away. The queen will never banish me, and even were I obliged to yield to the populace she would yield with me; if I fly, she will fly; and then we shall see how the rebels will get on without either king or queen.

"Oh, were I not a foreigner! were I but a Frenchman! were I but of gentle birth!"

The position of the cardinal was indeed critical, and recent events had added to his difficulties. Discontent had long pervaded the lower ranks of society in France. Crushed and impoverished by taxation—imposed by Mazarin, whose avarice impelled him to grind them down to the very dust—the people, as the Advocate-General Talon described it, had nothing left to them except their souls; and as those could not be sold by auction, they began to murmur. Patience had in vain been recommended to them by reports of brilliant victories gained by France; laurels, however, were not meat and drink, and the people had for some time been in a state of discontent.

Had this been all, it might not, perhaps, have greatly signified; for when the lower classes alone complained, the court of France, separated as it was from the poor by the intervening classes of the gentry and the *bourgeoisie*, seldom listened to their voice; but unluckily, Mazarin had had the imprudence to attack the magistrates and had sold no less than twelve appointments in the Court of Requests, at a high price; and as the officers of that court paid very dearly for their places, and as the addition of twelve new colleagues would necessarily lower the value of each place, the old functionaries formed a union amongst themselves, and, enraged, swore on the Bible not to allow of this addition to their number, but to resist all the persecutions which might ensue; and should any one of them chance to forfeit his post by this resistance, to combine to indemnify him for his loss.

Now the following occurrences had taken place between the two contending parties.

On the seventh of January between seven and eight hundred tradesmen had assembled in Paris to discuss a new tax which was to be levied on house property. They deputed ten of their number to wait upon the Duke of Orleans, who, according to his custom, affected popularity. The duke received them and they informed him that they were resolved not to pay this tax, even if they were obliged to defend themselves against its collectors by force of arms. They were listened to with great politeness by the duke, who held out hopes of easier measures, promised to speak in their behalf to the queen, and dismissed them with the ordinary expression of royalty, "We will see what we can do."

Two days afterward these same magistrates appeared before the cardinal and their spokesman addressed Mazarin with so much fearlessness and determination that the minister was astounded and sent the deputation away with the same answer as it had received from the Duke of Orleans—that he would see what could be done; and in accordance with that intention a council of state was assembled and the superintendent of finance was summoned.

This man, named Emery, was the object of popular detestation, in the first place because he *was* superintendent of finance, and every superintendent of finance deserved to be hated; in the second place, because he rather deserved the odium which he had incurred.

He was the son of a banker at Lyons named Particelli, who, after becoming a bankrupt, chose to change his name to Emery; and Cardinal Richelieu having discovered in him great financial aptitude, had introduced him with a strong recommendation to Louis XIII. under his assumed name, in order that he might be appointed to the post he subsequently held.

"You surprise me!" exclaimed the monarch. "I am rejoiced to hear you speak of Monsieur d'Emery as calculated for a post which requires a man of probity. I was really afraid that you were going to force that villain Particelli upon me."

"Sire," replied Richelieu, "rest assured that Particelli, the man to whom your majesty refers, has been hanged."

"Ah; so much the better!" exclaimed the king. "It is not for nothing that I am styled Louis the Just," and he signed Emery's appointment.

This was the same Emery who became eventually superintendent of finance.

He was sent for by the ministers and he came before them pale and trembling, declaring that his son had very nearly been assassinated the day before, near the palace. The mob had insulted him on account of the ostentatious luxury of his wife, whose house was hung with red velvet edged with gold fringe. This lady was the daughter of Nicholas de Camus, who arrived in Paris with twenty francs in his pocket, became secretary of state, and accumulated wealth enough to divide nine millions of francs among his children and to keep an income of forty thousand for himself.

The fact was that Emery's son had run a great chance of being suffocated, one of the rioters having proposed to squeeze him until he gave up all the gold he had swallowed. Nothing, therefore, was settled that day, as Emery's head was not steady enough for business after such an occurrence.

On the next day Mathieu Molé, the chief president, whose courage at this crisis, says the Cardinal de Retz, was equal to that of the Duc de Beaufort and the Prince de Condé—in other words, of the two men who were considered the bravest in France—had been attacked in his turn. The people threatened to hold him responsible for the evils that hung over them. But the chief president had replied with his habitual coolness, without betraying either disturbance or surprise, that should the agitators refuse obedience to the king's wishes he would have gallows erected in the public squares and proceed at once to hang the most active among them. To which the others had responded that they would be glad to see the gallows erected; they would serve for the hanging of those detestable judges who purchased favor at court at the price of the people's misery.

Nor was this all. On the eleventh the queen in going to mass at Notre Dame, as she always did on Saturdays, was followed by more than two hundred women demanding justice. These poor creatures had no bad intentions. They wished only to be allowed to fall on their knees before their sovereign, and that they might move her to compassion; but they were prevented by the royal guard and the queen proceeded on her way, haughtily disdainful of their entreaties.

At length parliament was convoked; the authority of the king was to be maintained.

One day—it was the morning of the day my story begins—the king, Louis XIV., then ten years of age, went in state, under pretext of returning thanks for his recovery from the small-pox, to Notre Dame. He took the opportunity of calling out his guard, the Swiss troops and the musketeers, and he had planted them round the Palais Royal, on the quays, and on the Pont Neuf. After mass the young monarch drove to the Parliament House, where, upon the throne, he hastily confirmed not only such edicts as he had already passed, but issued new ones, each one, according to Cardinal de Retz, more ruinous than the others—a proceeding which drew forth a strong remonstrance from the chief president, Molé—whilst President Blancmesnil and Councillor Broussel raised their voices in indignation against fresh taxes.

The king returned amidst the silence of a vast multitude to the Palais Royal. All minds were uneasy, most were foreboding, many of the people used threatening language.

At first, indeed, they were doubtful whether the king's visit to the parliament had been in order to lighten or increase their burdens; but scarcely was it known that the taxes were to be still further increased, when cries of "Down with Mazarin!" "Long live Broussel!" "Long live Blancmesnil!" resounded through the city. For the people had learned that Broussel and Blancmesnil had made speeches in their behalf, and, although the eloquence of these deputies had been without avail, it had none the less won for them the people's good-will. All attempts to disperse the groups collected in the streets, or silence their exclamations, were in vain. Orders had just been given to the royal guards and the Swiss guards, not only to stand firm, but to send out patrols to the streets of Saint Denis and Saint Martin, where the people thronged and where they were the most vociferous, when the mayor of Paris was announced at the Palais Royal.

He was shown in directly; he came to say that if these offensive precautions were not discontinued, in two hours Paris would be under arms.

Deliberations were being held when a lieutenant in the guards, named Comminges, made his appearance, with his clothes all torn, his face streaming with blood. The queen on seeing him uttered a cry of surprise and asked him what was going on.

As the mayor had foreseen, the sight of the guards had exasperated the mob. The tocsin was sounded. Comminges had arrested one of the ringleaders and had ordered him to be hanged near the cross of Du Trahoir; but in attempting to execute this command the soldiery were attacked in the marketplace with stones and halberds; the delinquent had escaped to the Rue des Lombards and rushed into a house. They broke open the doors and searched the dwelling, but in vain. Comminges, wounded by a stone which had struck him on the forehead, had left a picket in the street and returned to the Palais Royal, followed by a menacing crowd, to tell his story.

This account confirmed that of the mayor. The authorities were not in a condition to cope with serious revolt. Mazarin endeavored to circulate among the people a report that troops had only been stationed on the quays and on the Pont Neuf, on account of the ceremonial of the day, and that they would soon withdraw. In fact, about four o'clock they were all concentrated about the Palais Royal, the courts and ground floors of which were filled with musketeers and Swiss guards, and there awaited the outcome of all this disturbance.

Such was the state of affairs at the very moment we introduced our readers to the study of Cardinal Mazarin—once that of Cardinal Richelieu. We have seen in what state of mind he listened to the murmurs from below, which even reached him in his seclusion, and to the guns, the firing of which resounded through that room. All at once he raised his head; his brow slightly contracted like that of a man who has formed a resolution; he fixed his eyes upon an enormous clock that was about to strike ten, and taking up a whistle of silver gilt that stood upon the table near him, he shrilled it twice.

A door hidden in the tapestry opened noiselessly and a man in black silently advanced and stood behind the chair on which Mazarin sat.

"Bernouin," said the cardinal, not turning round, for having whistled, he knew that it was his *valet-de-chambre* who was behind him; "what musketeers are now within the palace?"

"The Black Musketeers, my lord."

"What company?"

"Tréville's company."

"Is there any officer belonging to this company in the ante-chamber?"

"Lieutenant d'Artagnan."

"A man on whom we can depend, I hope."

"Yes, my lord."

"Give me a uniform of one of these musketeers and help me to put it on."

The valet went out as silently as he had entered and appeared in a few minutes bringing the dress demanded.

The cardinal, in deep thought and in silence, began to take off the robes of state he had assumed in order to be present at the sitting of parliament, and to attire himself in the military coat, which he wore with a certain degree of easy grace, owing to his former campaigns in Italy. When he was completely dressed he said:

"Send hither Monsieur d'Artagnan."

The valet went out of the room, this time by the centre door, but still as silently as before; one might have fancied him an apparition.

When he was left alone the cardinal looked at himself in the glass with a feeling of self-satisfaction. Still young—for he was scarcely forty-six years of age—he possessed great elegance of form and was above the middle height; his complexion was brilliant and beautiful; his glance full of expression; his nose, though large, was well proportioned; his forehead broad and majestic; his hair, of a chestnut color, was curled slightly; his beard, which was darker than his hair, was turned carefully with a curling iron, a practice that greatly improved it. After a short time the cardinal arranged his shoulder belt, then looked with great complacency at his hands, which were most elegant and of which he took the greatest care; and throwing on one side the large kid gloves tried on at first, as belonging to the uniform, he put on others of silk only. At this instant the door opened.

"Monsieur d'Artagnan," said the *valet-de-chambre*.

An officer, as he spoke, entered the apartment. He was a man between thirty-nine and forty years of age, of medium height but a very well proportioned figure; with an intellectual and animated physiognomy; his beard black, and his hair turning gray, as often happens when people have found life either too gay or too sad, more especially when they happen to be of swart complexion.

D'Artagnan advanced a few steps into the apartment.

How perfectly he remembered his former entrance into that very room! Seeing, however, no one there except a musketeer of his own troop, he fixed his eyes upon the supposed soldier, in whose dress, nevertheless, he recognized at the first glance the cardinal.

The lieutenant remained standing in a dignified but respectful posture, such as became a man of good birth, who had in the course of his life been frequently in the society of the highest nobles.

The cardinal looked at him with a cunning rather than serious glance, yet he examined his countenance with attention and after a momentary silence said:

"You are Monsieur d'Artagnan?"

"I am that individual," replied the officer.

Mazarin gazed once more at a countenance full of intelligence, the play of which had been, nevertheless, subdued by age and experience; and D'Artagnan received the penetrating glance like one who had formerly sustained many a searching look, very different, indeed, from those which were inquiringly directed on him at that instant.

"Sir," resumed the cardinal, "you are to come with me, or rather, I am to go with you."

"I am at your command, my lord," returned D'Artagnan.

"I wish to visit in person the outposts which surround the Palais Royal; do you suppose that there is any danger in so doing?"

"Danger, my lord!" exclaimed D'Artagnan with a look of astonishment, "what danger?"

"I am told that there is a general insurrection."

"The uniform of the king's musketeers carries a certain respect with it, and even if that were not the case I would engage with four of my men to put to flight a hundred of these clowns."

"Did you witness the injury sustained by Comminges?"

"Monsieur de Comminges is in the guards and not in the musketeers——"

"Which means, I suppose, that the musketeers are better soldiers than the guards." The cardinal smiled as he spoke.

"Every one likes his own uniform best, my lord."

"Myself excepted," and again Mazarin smiled; "for you perceive that I have left off mine and put on yours."

"Lord bless us! this is modesty indeed!" cried D'Artagnan. "Had I such a uniform as your eminence possesses, I protest I should be mightily content, and I would take an oath never to wear any other costume——"

"Yes, but for to-night's adventure I don't suppose my dress would have been a very safe one. Give me my felt hat, Bernouin."

The valet instantly brought to his master a regimental hat with a wide brim. The cardinal put it on in military style.

"Your horses are ready saddled in their stables, are they not?" he said, turning to D'Artagnan.

"Yes, my lord."

"Well, let us set out."

"How many men does your eminence wish to escort you?"

"You say that with four men you will undertake to disperse a hundred low fellows; as it may happen that we shall have to encounter two hundred, take eight——"

"As many as my lord wishes."

"I will follow you. This way—light us downstairs Bernouin."

The valet held a wax-light; the cardinal took a key from his bureau and opening the door of a secret stair descended into the court of the Palais Royal.

Chapter II.

A Nightly Patrol.

In ten minutes Mazarin and his party were traversing the street "Les Bons Enfants" behind the theatre built by Richelieu expressly for the play of "Mirame," and in which Mazarin, who was an amateur of music, but not of literature, had introduced into France the first opera that was ever acted in that country.

The appearance of the town denoted the greatest agitation. Numberless groups paraded the streets and, whatever D'Artagnan might think of it, it was obvious that the citizens had for the night laid aside their usual forbearance, in order to assume a warlike aspect. From time to time noises came in the direction of the public markets. The report of firearms was heard near the Rue Saint Denis and occasionally church bells began to ring indiscriminately and at the caprice of the populace. D'Artagnan, meantime, pursued his way with the indifference of a man upon whom such acts of folly made no impression. When he approached a group in the middle of the street he urged his horse upon it without a word of warning; and the members of the group, whether rebels or not, as if they knew with what sort of a man they had to deal, at once gave place to the patrol. The cardinal envied that composure, which he attributed to the habit of meeting danger; but none the less he conceived for the officer under whose orders he had for the moment placed himself, that consideration which even prudence pays to careless courage. On approaching an outpost near the Barriere des Sergens, the sentinel cried out, "Who's there?" and D'Artagnan answered—having first asked the word of the cardinal— "Louis and Rocroy." After which he inquired if Lieutenant Comminges were not the commanding officer at the outpost. The soldier replied by pointing out to him an officer who was conversing, on foot, his hand upon the neck of a horse on which the individual to whom he was talking sat. Here was the officer D'Artagnan was seeking.

"Here is Monsieur Comminges," said D'Artagnan, returning to the cardinal. He instantly retired, from a feeling of respectful delicacy; it was, however, evident that the cardinal was recognized by both Comminges and the other officers on horseback.

"Well done, Guitant," cried the cardinal to the equestrian; "I see plainly that, notwithstanding the sixty-four years that have passed over your head, you are still the same man, active and zealous. What were you saying to this youngster?"

"My lord," replied Guitant, "I was observing that we live in troublous times and that to-day's events are very like those in the days of the Ligue, of which I heard so much in my youth. Are you aware that the mob have even suggested throwing up barricades in the Rue Saint Denis and the Rue Saint Antoine?"

"And what was Comminges saying to you in reply, my good Guitant?"

"My lord," said Comminges, "I answered that to compose a Ligue only one ingredient was wanting—in my opinion an essential one—a Duc de Guise; moreover, no generation ever does the same thing twice."

"No, but they mean to make a Fronde, as they call it," said Guitant.

"And what is a Fronde?" inquired Mazarin.

"My lord, Fronde is the name the discontented give to their party."

"And what is the origin of this name?"

"It seems that some days since Councillor Bachaumont remarked at the palace that rebels and agitators reminded him of schoolboys slinging—qui frondent—stones from the moats round Paris, young urchins who run off the moment the constable appears, only to return to their diversion the instant his back is turned. So they have picked up the word and the insurrectionists are called 'Frondeurs,' and yesterday every article sold was 'a la Fronde;' bread 'a la Fronde,' hats 'a la Fronde,' to say nothing of gloves, pocket-handkerchiefs, and fans; but listen——"

At that moment a window opened and a man began to sing:

"A tempest from the Fronde
Did blow to-day:
I think 'twill blow
Sieur Mazarin away."

"Insolent wretch!" cried Guitant.

"My lord," said Comminges, who, irritated by his wounds, wished for revenge and longed to give back blow for blow, "shall I fire off a ball to punish that jester, and to warn him not to sing so much out of tune in the future?"

And as he spoke he put his hand on the holster of his uncle's saddle-bow.

"Certainly not! certainly not," exclaimed Mazarin. "Diavolo! my dear friend, you are going to spoil everything—everything is going on famously. I know the French as well as if I had made them myself. They sing—let them pay the piper. During the Ligue, about which Guitant was speaking just now, the people chanted nothing except the mass, so everything went to destruction. Come, Guitant, come along, and let's see if they keep watch at the Quinze-Vingts as at the Barriere des Sergens."

And waving his hand to Comminges he rejoined D'Artagnan, who instantly put himself at the head of his troop, followed by the cardinal, Guitant and the rest of the escort.

"Just so," muttered Comminges, looking after Mazarin. "True, I forgot; provided he can get money out of the people, that is all he wants."

The street of Saint Honore, when the cardinal and his party passed through it, was crowded by an assemblage who, standing in groups, discussed the edicts of that memorable day. They pitied the young king, who was unconsciously ruining his country, and threw all the odium of his proceedings on Mazarin. Addresses to the Duke of Orleans and to Condé were suggested. Blancmesnil and Broussel seemed in the highest favor.

D'Artagnan passed through the very midst of this discontented mob just as if his horse and he had been made of iron. Mazarin and Guitant conversed together in whispers. The musketeers, who had already discovered who Mazarin was, followed in profound silence. In the street of Saint Thomas-du-Louvre they stopped at the barrier distinguished by the name of Quinze-Vingts. Here Guitant spoke to one of the subalterns, asking how matters were progressing.

"Ah, captain!" said the officer, "everything is quiet hereabout—if I did not know that something is going on in yonder house!"

And he pointed to a magnificent hotel situated on the very spot whereon the Vaudeville now stands.

"In that hotel? it is the Hotel Rambouillet," cried Guitant.

"I really don't know what hotel it is; all I do know is that I observed some suspicious looking people go in there——"

"Nonsense!" exclaimed Guitant, with a burst of laughter; "those men must be poets."

"Come, Guitant, speak, if you please, respectfully of these gentlemen," said Mazarin; "don't you know that I was in my youth a poet? I wrote verses in the style of Benserade——"

"You, my lord?"

"Yes, I; shall I repeat to you some of my verses?"

"Just as you please, my lord. I do not understand Italian."

"Yes, but you understand French," and Mazarin laid his hand upon Guitant's shoulder. "My good, my brave Guitant, whatsoever command I may give you in that language—in French—whatever I may order you to do, will you not perform it?"

"Certainly. I have already answered that question in the affirmative; but that command must come from the queen herself."

"Yes! ah yes!" Mazarin bit his lips as he spoke; "I know your devotion to her majesty."

"I have been a captain in the queen's guards for twenty years," was the reply.

"En route, Monsieur d'Artagnan," said the cardinal; "all goes well in this direction."

D'Artagnan, in the meantime, had taken the head of his detachment without a word and with that ready and profound obedience which marks the character of an old soldier.

He led the way toward the hill of Saint Roche. The Rue Richelieu and the Rue Villedot were then, owing to their vicinity to the ramparts, less frequented than any others in that direction, for the town was thinly inhabited thereabout.

"Who is in command here?" asked the cardinal.

"Villequier," said Guitant.

"Diavolo! Speak to him yourself, for ever since you were deputed by me to arrest the Duc de Beaufort, this officer and I have been on bad terms. He laid claim to that honor as captain of the royal guards."

"I am aware of that, and I have told him a hundred times that he was wrong. The king could not give that order, since at that time he was hardly four years old."

"Yes, but I could give him the order—I, Guitant—and I preferred to give it to you."

Guitant, without reply, rode forward and desired the sentinel to call Monsieur de Villequier.

"Ah! so you are here!" cried the officer, in the tone of ill-humor habitual to him; "what the devil are you doing here?"

"I wish to know—can you tell me, pray—is anything fresh occurring in this part of the town?"

"What do you mean? People cry out, 'Long live the king! down with Mazarin!' That's nothing new; no, we've been used to those acclamations for some time."

"And you sing chorus," replied Guitant, laughing.

"Faith, I've half a mind to do it. In my opinion the people are right; and cheerfully would I give up five years of my pay—which I am never paid, by the way—to make the king five years older."

"Really! And pray what would come to pass, supposing the king were five years older than he is?"

"As soon as ever the king comes of age he will issue his commands himself, and 'tis far pleasanter to obey the grandson of Henry IV. than the son of Peter Mazarin. 'Sdeath! I would die willingly for the king, but supposing I happened to be killed on account of Mazarin, as your nephew came near being to-day, there could be nothing in Paradise, however well placed I might be there, that could console me for it."

"Well, well, Monsieur de Villequier," Mazarin interposed, "I shall make it my care the king hears of your loyalty. Come, gentlemen," addressing the troop, "let us return."

"Stop," exclaimed Villequier, "so Mazarin was here! so much the better. I have been waiting for a long time to tell him what I think of him. I am obliged to you Guitant, although your intention was perhaps not very favorable to me, for such an opportunity."

He turned away and went off to his post, whistling a tune then popular among the party called the "Fronde," whilst Mazarin returned, in a pensive mood, toward the Palais Royal. All that he had heard from these three different men, Comminges, Guitant and Villequier, confirmed him in his conviction that in case of serious tumults there would be no one on his side except the queen; and then Anne of Austria had so often deserted her friends that her support seemed most precarious. During the whole of this nocturnal ride, during the whole time that he was endeavoring to understand the various characters of Comminges, Guitant and Villequier, Mazarin was, in truth, studying more especially one man. This man, who had remained immovable as bronze when menaced by the mob—not a muscle of whose face was stirred, either at Mazarin's witticisms or by the jests of the multitude—seemed to the cardinal a peculiar being, who, having participated in past events similar to those now occurring, was calculated to cope with those now on the eve of taking place.

The name of D'Artagnan was not altogether new to Mazarin, who, although he did not arrive in France before the year 1634 or 1635, that is to say, about eight or nine years after the events which we have related in a preceding narrative, * fancied he had heard it pronounced as that of one who was said to be a model of courage, address and loyalty.

* "The Three Musketeers."

Possessed by this idea, the cardinal resolved to know all about D'Artagnan immediately; of course he could not inquire from D'Artagnan himself who he was and what had been his career; he remarked, however, in the course of conversation that the lieutenant of musketeers spoke with a Gascon accent. Now the Italians and the Gascons are too much alike and know each other too well ever to trust what any one of them may say of himself; so in reaching the walls which surrounded the Palais Royal, the cardinal knocked at a little door, and after thanking D'Artagnan and requesting him to wait in the court of the Palais Royal, he made a sign to Guitant to follow him.

They both dismounted, consigned their horses to the lackey who had opened the door, and disappeared in the garden.

"My dear friend," said the cardinal, leaning, as they walked through the garden, on his friend's arm, "you told me just now that you had been twenty years in the queen's service."

"Yes, it's true. I have," returned Guitant.

"Now, my dear Guitant, I have often remarked that in addition to your courage, which is indisputable, and your fidelity, which is invincible, you possess an admirable memory."

"You have found that out, have you, my lord? Deuce take it—all the worse for me!"

"How?"

"There is no doubt but that one of the chief accomplishments of a courtier is to know when to forget."

"But you, Guitant, are not a courtier. You are a brave soldier, one of the few remaining veterans of the days of Henry IV. Alas! how few to-day exist!"

"Plague on't, my lord, have you brought me here to get my horoscope out of me?"

"No; I only brought you here to ask you," returned Mazarin, smiling, "if you have taken any particular notice of our lieutenant of musketeers?"

"Monsieur d'Artagnan? I have had no occasion to notice him particularly; he's an old acquaintance. He's a Gascon. De Tréville knows him and esteems him very highly, and De Tréville, as you know, is one of the queen's greatest friends. As a soldier the man ranks well; he did his whole duty and even more, at the siege of Rochelle—as at Suze and Perpignan."

"But you know, Guitant, we poor ministers often want men with other qualities besides courage; we want men of talent. Pray, was not Monsieur d'Artagnan, in the time of the cardinal, mixed up in some intrigue from which he came out, according to report, quite cleverly?"

"My lord, as to the report you allude to"—Guitant perceived that the cardinal wished to make him speak out—"I know nothing but what the public knows. I never meddle in intrigues, and if I occasionally become a confidant of the intrigues of others I am sure your eminence will approve of my keeping them secret."

Mazarin shook his head.

"Ah!" he said; "some ministers are fortunate and find out all that they wish to know."

"My lord," replied Guitant, "such ministers do not weigh men in the same balance; they get their information on war from warriors; on intrigues, from intriguers. Consult some politician of the period of which you speak, and if you pay well for it you will certainly get to know all you want."

"Eh, pardieu!" said Mazarin, with a grimace which he always made when spoken to about money. "They will be paid, if there is no way of getting out of it."

"Does my lord seriously wish me to name any one who was mixed up in the cabals of that day?"

"By Bacchus!" rejoined Mazarin, impatiently, "it's about an hour since I asked you for that very thing, wooden-head that you are."

"There is one man for whom I can answer, if he will speak out."

"That's my concern; I will make him speak."

"Ah, my lord, 'tis not easy to make people say what they don't wish to let out."

"Pooh! with patience one must succeed. Well, this man. Who is he?"

"The Comte de Rochefort."

"The Comte de Rochefort!"

"Unfortunately he has disappeared these four or five years and I don't know where he is."

"I know, Guitant," said Mazarin.

"Well, then, how is it that your eminence complained just now of want of information?"

"You think," resumed Mazarin, "that Rochefort——"

"He was Cardinal Richelieu's creature, my lord. I warn you, however, his services will cost you something. The cardinal was lavish to his underlings."

"Yes, yes, Guitant," said Mazarin; "Richelieu was a great man, a very great man, but he had that defect. Thanks, Guitant; I shall benefit by your advice this very evening."

Here they separated and bidding adieu to Guitant in the court of the Palais Royal, Mazarin approached an officer who was walking up and down within that inclosure.

It was D'Artagnan, who was waiting for him.

"Come hither," said Mazarin in his softest voice; "I have an order to give you."

D'Artagnan bent low and following the cardinal up the secret staircase, soon found himself in the study whence they had first set out.

The cardinal seated himself before his bureau and taking a sheet of paper wrote some lines upon it, whilst D'Artagnan stood imperturbable, without showing either impatience or curiosity. He was like a soldierly automaton, or rather, like a magnificent marionette.

The cardinal folded and sealed his letter.

"Monsieur d'Artagnan," he said, "you are to take this dispatch to the Bastile and bring back here the person it concerns. You must take a carriage and an escort, and guard the prisoner with the greatest care."

D'Artagnan took the letter, touched his hat with his hand, turned round upon his heel like a drill-sergeant, and a moment afterward was heard, in his dry and monotonous tone, commanding "Four men and an escort, a carriage and a horse." Five minutes afterward the wheels of the carriage and the horses' shoes were heard resounding on the pavement of the courtyard.

Chapter III.

Dead Animosities.

D'Artagnan arrived at the Bastile just as it was striking half-past eight. His visit was announced to the governor, who, on hearing that he came from the cardinal, went to meet him and received him at the top of the great flight of steps outside the door. The governor of the Bastile was Monsieur du Tremblay, the brother of the famous Capuchin, Joseph, that fearful favorite of Richelieu's, who went by the name of the Gray Cardinal.

During the period that the Duc de Bassompierre passed in the Bastile—where he remained for twelve long years—when his companions, in their dreams of liberty, said to each other: "As for me, I shall go out of the prison at such a time," and another, at such and such a time, the duke used to answer, "As for me, gentlemen, I shall leave only when Monsieur du Tremblay leaves;" meaning that at the death of the cardinal Du Tremblay would certainly lose his place at the Bastile and De Bassompierre regain his at court.

His prediction was nearly fulfilled, but in a very different way from that which De Bassompierre supposed; for after the death of Richelieu everything went on, contrary to expectation, in the same way as before; and Bassompierre had little chance of leaving his prison.

Monsieur du Tremblay received D'Artagnan with extreme politeness and invited him to sit down with him to supper, of which he was himself about to partake.

"I should be delighted to do so," was the reply; "but if I am not mistaken, the words 'In haste,' are written on the envelope of the letter which I brought."

"You are right," said Du Tremblay. "Halloo, major! tell them to order Number 25 to come downstairs."

The unhappy wretch who entered the Bastile ceased, as he crossed the threshold, to be a man—he became a number.

D'Artagnan shuddered at the noise of the keys; he remained on horseback, feeling no inclination to dismount, and sat looking at the bars, at the buttressed windows and the immense walls he had hitherto only seen from the other side of the moat, but by which he had for twenty years been awe-struck.

A bell resounded.

"I must leave you," said Du Tremblay; "I am sent for to sign the release of a prisoner. I shall be happy to meet you again, sir."

"May the devil annihilate me if I return thy wish!" murmured D'Artagnan, smiling as he pronounced the imprecation; "I declare I feel quite ill after only being five minutes in the courtyard. Go to! go to! I would rather die on straw than hoard up a thousand a year by being governor of the Bastile."

He had scarcely finished this soliloquy before the prisoner arrived. On seeing him D'Artagnan could hardly suppress an exclamation of surprise. The prisoner got into the carriage without seeming to recognize the musketeer.

"Gentlemen," thus D'Artagnan addressed the four musketeers, "I am ordered to exercise the greatest possible care in guarding the prisoner, and since there are no locks to the carriage, I shall sit beside him. Monsieur de Lillebonne, lead my horse by the bridle, if you please." As he spoke he dismounted, gave the bridle of his horse to the musketeer and placing himself by the side of the prisoner said, in a voice perfectly composed, "To the Palais Royal, at full trot."

The carriage drove on and D'Artagnan, availing himself of the darkness in the archway under which they were passing, threw himself into the arms of the prisoner.

"Rochefort!" he exclaimed; "you! is it you, indeed? I am not mistaken?"

"D'Artagnan!" cried Rochefort.

"Ah! my poor friend!" resumed D'Artagnan, "not having seen you for four or five years I concluded you were dead."

"I'faith," said Rochefort, "there's no great difference, I think, between a dead man and one who has been buried alive; now I have been buried alive, or very nearly so."

"And for what crime are you imprisoned in the Bastile."

"Do you wish me to speak the truth?"

"Yes."

"Well, then, I don't know."

"Have you any suspicion of me, Rochefort?"

"No! on the honor of a gentleman; but I cannot be imprisoned for the reason alleged; it is impossible."

"What reason?" asked D'Artagnan.

"For stealing."

"For stealing! you, Rochefort! you are laughing at me."

"I understand. You mean that this demands explanation, do you not?"

"I admit it."

"Well, this is what actually took place: One evening after an orgy in Reinard's apartment at the Tuileries with the Duc d'Harcourt, Fontrailles, De Rieux and others, the Duc d'Harcourt proposed that we should go and pull cloaks on the Pont Neuf; that is, you know, a diversion which the Duc d'Orleans made quite the fashion."

"Were you crazy, Rochefort? at your age!"

"No, I was drunk. And yet, since the amusement seemed to me rather tame, I proposed to Chevalier de Rieux that we should be spectators instead of actors, and, in order to see to advantage, that we should mount the bronze horse. No sooner said than done. Thanks to the spurs, which served as stirrups, in a moment we were perched upon the croupe; we were well placed and saw everything. Four or five cloaks had already been lifted, with a dexterity without parallel, and not one of the victims had dared to say a word, when some fool of a fellow, less patient than the others, took it into his head to cry out, 'Guard!' and drew upon us a patrol of archers. Duc d'Harcourt, Fontrailles, and the others escaped; De Rieux was inclined to do likewise, but I told him they wouldn't look for us where we were. He wouldn't listen, put his foot on the spur to get down, the spur broke, he fell with a broken leg, and, instead of keeping quiet, took to crying out like a gallows-bird. I then was ready to dismount, but it was too late; I descended into the arms of the archers. They conducted me to the Chatelet, where I slept soundly, being very sure that on the next day I should go forth free. The next day came and passed, the day after, a week; I then wrote to the cardinal. The same day they came for me and took me to the Bastile. That was five years ago. Do you believe it was because I committed the sacrilege of mounting en croupe behind Henry IV.?"

"No; you are right, my dear Rochefort, it couldn't be for that; but you will probably learn the reason soon."

"Ah, indeed! I forgot to ask you—where are you taking me?"

"To the cardinal."

"What does he want with me?"

"I do not know. I did not even know that you were the person I was sent to fetch."

"Impossible—you—a favorite of the minister!"

"A favorite! no, indeed!" cried D'Artagnan. "Ah, my poor friend! I am just as poor a Gascon as when I saw you at Meung, twenty-two years ago, you know; alas!" and he concluded his speech with a deep sigh.

"Nevertheless, you come as one in authority."

"Because I happened to be in the ante-chamber when the cardinal called me, by the merest chance. I am still a lieutenant in the musketeers and have been so these twenty years."

"Then no misfortune has happened to you?"

"And what misfortune could happen to me? To quote some Latin verses I have forgotten, or rather, never knew well, 'the thunderbolt never falls on the valleys,' and I am a valley, dear Rochefort,—one of the lowliest of the low."

"Then Mazarin is still Mazarin?"

"The same as ever, my friend; it is said that he is married to the queen."

"Married?"

"If not her husband, he is unquestionably her lover."

"You surprise me. Rebuff Buckingham and consent to Mazarin!"

"Just like the women," replied D'Artagnan, coolly.

"Like women, not like queens."

"Egad! queens are the weakest of their sex, when it comes to such things as these."

"And M. de Beaufort—is he still in prison?"

"Yes. Why?"

"Oh, nothing, but that he might get me out of this, if he were favorably inclined to me."

"You are probably nearer freedom than he is, so it will be your business to get him out."

"And," said the prisoner, "what talk is there of war with Spain?"

"With Spain, no," answered D'Artagnan; "but Paris."

"What do you mean?" cried Rochefort.

"Do you hear the guns, pray? The citizens are amusing themselves in the meantime."

"And you—do you really think that anything could be done with these bourgeois?"

"Yes, they might do well if they had any leader to unite them in one body."

"How miserable not to be free!"

"Don't be downcast. Since Mazarin has sent for you, it is because he wants you. I congratulate you! Many a long year has passed since any one has wanted to employ me; so you see in what a situation I am."

"Make your complaints known; that's my advice."

"Listen, Rochefort; let us make a compact. We are friends, are we not?"

"Egad! I bear the traces of our friendship—three slits or slashes from your sword."

"Well, if you should be restored to favor, don't forget me."

"On the honor of a Rochefort; but you must do the like for me."

"There's my hand,—I promise."

"Therefore, whenever you find any opportunity of saying something in my behalf——"

"I shall say it, and you?"

"I shall do the same."

"Apropos, are we to speak of your friends also, Athos, Porthos, and Aramis? or have you forgotten them?"

"Almost."

"What has become of them?"

"I don't know; we separated, as you know. They are alive, that's all that I can say about them; from time to time I hear of them indirectly, but in what part of the world they are, devil take me if I know, No, on my honor, I have not a friend in the world but you, Rochefort."

"And the illustrious—what's the name of the lad whom I made a sergeant in Piedmont's regiment?"

"Planchet!"

"The illustrious Planchet. What has become of him?"

"I shouldn't wonder if he were at the head of the mob at this very moment. He married a woman who keeps a confectioner's shop in the Rue des Lombards, for he's a lad who was always fond of sweetmeats; he's now a citizen of Paris. You'll see that that queer fellow will be a sheriff before I shall be a captain."

"Come, dear D'Artagnan, look up a little! Courage! It is when one is lowest on the wheel of fortune that the merry-go-round wheels and rewards us. This evening your destiny begins to change."

"Amen!" exclaimed D'Artagnan, stopping the carriage.

"What are you doing?" asked Rochefort.

"We are almost there and I want no one to see me getting out of your carriage; we are supposed not to know each other."

"You are right. Adieu."

"Au revoir. Remember your promise."

In five minutes the party entered the courtyard and D'Artagnan led the prisoner up the great staircase and across the corridor and ante-chamber.

As they stopped at the door of the cardinal's study, D'Artagnan was about to be announced when Rochefort slapped him on his shoulder.

"D'Artagnan, let me confess to you what I've been thinking about during the whole of my drive, as I looked out upon the parties of citizens who perpetually crossed our path and looked at you and your four men with fiery eyes."

"Speak out," answered D'Artagnan.

"I had only to cry out 'Help!' for you and for your companions to be cut to pieces, and then I should have been free."

"Why didn't you do it?" asked the lieutenant.

"Come, come!" cried Rochefort. "Did we not swear friendship? Ah! had any one but you been there, I don't say——"

D'Artagnan bowed. "Is it possible that Rochefort has become a better man than I am?" he said to himself. And he caused himself to be announced to the minister.

"Let M. de Rochefort enter," said Mazarin, eagerly, on hearing their names pronounced; "and beg M. d'Artagnan to wait; I shall have further need of him."

These words gave great joy to D'Artagnan. As he had said, it had been a long time since any one had needed him; and that demand for his services on the part of Mazarin seemed to him an auspicious sign.

Rochefort, rendered suspicious and cautious by these words, entered the apartment, where he found Mazarin sitting at the table, dressed in his ordinary garb and as one of the prelates of the Church, his costume being similar to that of the abbés in that day, excepting that his scarf and stockings were violet.

As the door was closed Rochefort cast a glance toward Mazarin, which was answered by one, equally furtive, from the minister.

There was little change in the cardinal; still dressed with sedulous care, his hair well arranged and curled, his person perfumed, he looked, owing to his extreme taste in dress, only half his age. But Rochefort, who had passed five years in prison, had become old in the lapse of a few years; the dark locks of this estimable friend of the defunct Cardinal Richelieu were now white; the deep bronze of his complexion had been succeeded by a mortal pallor which betokened debility. As he gazed at him Mazarin shook his head slightly, as much as to say, "This is a man who does not appear to me fit for much."

After a pause, which appeared an age to Rochefort, Mazarin took from a bundle of papers a letter, and showing it to the count, he said:

"I find here a letter in which you sue for liberty, Monsieur de Rochefort. You are in prison, then?"

Rochefort trembled in every limb at this question. "But I thought," he said, "that your eminence knew that circumstance better than any one——"

"I? Oh no! There is a congestion of prisoners in the Bastile, who were cooped up in the time of Monsieur de Richelieu; I don't even know their names."

"Yes, but in regard to myself, my lord, it cannot be so, for I was removed from the Chatelet to the Bastile owing to an order from your eminence."

"You think you were."

"I am certain of it."

"Ah, stay! I fancy I remember it. Did you not once refuse to undertake a journey to Brussels for the queen?"

"Ah! ah!" exclaimed Rochefort. "There is the true reason! Idiot that I am, though I have been trying to find it out for five years, I never found it out."

"But I do not say it was the cause of your imprisonment. I merely ask you, did you not refuse to go to Brussels for the queen, whilst you had consented to go there to do some service for the late cardinal?"

"That is the very reason I refused to go back to Brussels. I was there at a fearful moment. I was sent there to intercept a correspondence between

Chalais and the archduke, and even then, when I was discovered I was nearly torn to pieces. How could I, then, return to Brussels? I should injure the queen instead of serving her."

"Well, since the best motives are liable to misconstruction, the queen saw in your refusal nothing but a refusal—a distinct refusal she had also much to complain of you during the lifetime of the late cardinal; yes, her majesty the queen——"

Rochefort smiled contemptuously.

"Since I was a faithful servant, my lord, to Cardinal Richelieu during his life, it stands to reason that now, after his death, I should serve you well, in defiance of the whole world."

"With regard to myself, Monsieur de Rochefort," replied Mazarin, "I am not, like Monsieur de Richelieu, all-powerful. I am but a minister, who wants no servants, being myself nothing but a servant of the queen's. Now, the queen is of a sensitive nature. Hearing of your refusal to obey her she looked upon it as a declaration of war, and as she considers you a man of superior talent, and consequently dangerous, she desired me to make sure of you; that is the reason of your being shut up in the Bastile. But your release can be managed. You are one of those men who can comprehend certain matters and having understood them, can act with energy——"

"Such was Cardinal Richelieu's opinion, my lord."

"The cardinal," interrupted Mazarin, "was a great politician and therein shone his vast superiority over me. I am a straightforward, simple man; that's my great disadvantage. I am of a frankness of character quite French."

Rochefort bit his lips in order to prevent a smile.

"Now to the point. I want friends; I want faithful servants. When I say I want, I mean the queen wants them. I do nothing without her commands—pray understand that; not like Monsieur de Richelieu, who went on just as he pleased. So I shall never be a great man, as he was, but to compensate for that, I shall be a good man, Monsieur de Rochefort, and I hope to prove it to you."

Rochefort knew well the tones of that soft voice, in which sounded sometimes a sort of gentle lisp, like the hissing of young vipers.

"I am disposed to believe your eminence," he replied; "though I have had but little evidence of that good-nature of which your eminence speaks. Do not forget that I have been five years in the Bastile and that no medium of viewing things is so deceptive as the grating of a prison."

"Ah, Monsieur de Rochefort! have I not told you already that I had nothing to do with that? The queen—cannot you make allowances for the pettishness of a queen and a princess? But that has passed away as suddenly as it came, and is forgotten."

"I can easily suppose, sir, that her majesty has forgotten it amid the fetes and the courtiers of the Palais Royal, but I who have passed those years in the Bastile——"

"Ah! mon Dieu! my dear Monsieur de Rochefort! do you absolutely think that the Palais Royal is the abode of gayety? No. We have had great annoyances there. As for me, I play my game squarely, fairly, and above board, as I always do. Let us come to some conclusion. Are you one of us, Monsieur de Rochefort?"

"I am very desirous of being so, my lord, but I am totally in the dark about everything. In the Bastile one talks politics only with soldiers and jailers, and you have not an idea, my lord, how little is known of what is going on by people of that sort; I am of Monsieur de Bassompierre's party. Is he still one of the seventeen peers of France?"

"He is dead, sir; a great loss. His devotion to the queen was boundless; men of loyalty are scarce."

"I think so, forsooth," said Rochefort, "and when you find any of them, you march them off to the Bastile. However, there are plenty in the world, but you don't look in the right direction for them, my lord."

"Indeed! explain to me. Ah! my dear Monsieur de Rochefort, how much you must have learned during your intimacy with the late cardinal! Ah! he was a great man."

"Will your eminence be angry if I read you a lesson?"

"I! never! you know you may say anything to me. I try to be beloved, not feared."

"Well, there is on the wall of my cell, scratched with a nail, a proverb, which says, 'Like master, like servant.'"

"Pray, what does that mean?"

"It means that Monsieur de Richelieu was able to find trusty servants, dozens and dozens of them."

"He! the point aimed at by every poniard! Richelieu, who passed his life in warding off blows which were forever aimed at him!"

"But he did ward them off," said De Rochefort, "and the reason was, that though he had bitter enemies he possessed also true friends. I have known persons," he continued—for he thought he might avail himself of the opportunity of speaking of D'Artagnan—"who by their sagacity and address have deceived the penetration of Cardinal Richelieu; who by their valor have got the better of his guards and spies; persons without money, without support, without credit, yet who have preserved to the crowned head its crown and made the cardinal crave pardon."

"But those men you speak of," said Mazarin, smiling inwardly on seeing Rochefort approach the point to which he was leading him, "those men were not devoted to the cardinal, for they contended against him."

"No; in that case they would have met with more fitting reward. They had the misfortune to be devoted to that very queen for whom just now you were seeking servants."

"But how is it that you know so much of these matters?"

"I know them because the men of whom I speak were at that time my enemies; because they fought against me; because I did them all the harm I could and they returned it to the best of their ability; because one of them, with whom I had most to do, gave me a pretty sword-thrust, now about seven years ago, the third that I received from the same hand; it closed an old account."

"Ah!" said Mazarin, with admirable suavity, "could I but find such men!"

"My lord, there has stood for six years at your very door a man such as I describe, and during those six years he has been unappreciated and unemployed by you."

"Who is it?"

"It is Monsieur d'Artagnan."

"That Gascon!" cried Mazarin, with well acted surprise.

"'That Gascon' has saved a queen and made Monsieur de Richelieu confess that in point of talent, address and political skill, to him he was only a tyro."

"Really?"

"It is as I have the honor of telling it to your excellency."

"Tell me a little about it, my dear Monsieur de Rochefort."

"That is somewhat difficult, my lord," said Rochefort, with a smile.

"Then he will tell it me himself."

"I doubt it, my lord."

"Why do you doubt it?"

"Because the secret does not belong to him; because, as I have told you, it has to do with a great queen."

"And he was alone in achieving an enterprise like that?"

"No, my lord, he had three colleagues, three brave men, men such as you were wishing for just now."

"And were these four men attached to each other, true in heart, really united?"

"As if they had been one man—as if their four hearts had pulsated in one breast."

"You pique my curiosity, dear Rochefort; pray tell me the whole story."

"That is impossible; but I will tell you a true story, my lord."

"Pray do so, I delight in stories," cried the cardinal.

"Listen, then," returned Rochefort, as he spoke endeavoring to read in that subtle countenance the cardinal's motive. "Once upon a time there lived a queen—a powerful monarch—who reigned over one of the greatest kingdoms of the universe; and a minister; and this minister wished much to injure the queen, whom once he had loved too well. (Do not try, my lord, you cannot guess who it is; all this happened long before you came into the country where this queen reigned.) There came to the court an ambassador so brave, so magnificent, so elegant, that every woman lost her heart to him; and the queen had even the indiscretion to give him certain ornaments so rare that they could never be replaced by any like them.

"As these ornaments were given by the king the minister persuaded his majesty to insist upon the queen's appearing in them as part of her jewels at a ball which was soon to take place. There is no occasion to tell you, my lord, that the minister knew for a fact that these ornaments had sailed away with the ambassador, who was far away, beyond seas. This illustrious queen had fallen low as the least of her subjects—fallen from her high estate."

"Indeed!"

"Well, my lord, four men resolved to save her. These four men were not princes, neither were they dukes, neither were they men in power; they were not even rich. They were four honest soldiers, each with a good heart, a good arm and a sword at the service of those who wanted it. They set out. The minister knew of their departure and had planted people on the road to prevent them ever reaching their destination. Three of them were overwhelmed and disabled by numerous assailants; one of them alone arrived at the port, having either killed or wounded those who wished to stop him. He crossed the sea and brought back the set of ornaments to the great queen, who was able to wear them on her shoulder on the appointed day; and this very nearly ruined the minister. What do you think of that exploit, my lord?"

"It is magnificent!" said Mazarin, thoughtfully.

"Well, I know of ten such men."

Mazarin made no reply; he reflected.

Five or six minutes elapsed.

"You have nothing more to ask of me, my lord?" said Rochefort.

"Yes. And you say that Monsieur d'Artagnan was one of those four men?"

"He led the enterprise."

"And who were the others?"

"I leave it to Monsieur d'Artagnan to name them, my lord. They were his friends and not mine. He alone would have any influence with them; I do not even know them under their true names."

"You suspect me, Monsieur de Rochefort; I want him and you and all to aid me."

"Begin with me, my lord; for after five or six years of imprisonment it is natural to feel some curiosity as to one's destination."

"You, my dear Monsieur de Rochefort, shall have the post of confidence; you shall go to Vincennes, where Monsieur de Beaufort is confined; you will guard him well for me. Well, what is the matter?"

"The matter is that you have proposed to me what is impossible," said Rochefort, shaking his head with an air of disappointment.

"What! impossible? And why is it impossible?"

"Because Monsieur de Beaufort is one of my friends, or rather, I am one of his. Have you forgotten, my lord, that it is he who answered for me to the queen?"

"Since then Monsieur de Beaufort has become an enemy of the State."

"That may be, my lord; but since I am neither king nor queen nor minister, he is not my enemy and I cannot accept your offer."

"This, then, is what you call devotion! I congratulate you. Your devotion does not commit you too far, Monsieur de Rochefort."

"And then, my lord," continued Rochefort, "you understand that to emerge from the Bastile in order to enter Vincennes is only to change one's prison."

"Say at once that you are on the side of Monsieur de Beaufort; that will be the most sincere line of conduct," said Mazarin.

"My lord, I have been so long shut up, that I am only of one party—I am for fresh air. Employ me in any other way; employ me even actively, but let it be on the high roads."

"My dear Monsieur de Rochefort," Mazarin replied in a tone of raillery, "you think yourself still a young man; your spirit is that of the phoenix, but your strength fails you. Believe me, you ought now to take a rest. Here!"

"You decide, then, nothing about me, my lord?"

"On the contrary, I have come to a decision."

Bernouin came into the room.

"Call an officer of justice," he said; "and stay close to me," he added, in a low tone.

The officer entered. Mazarin wrote a few words, which he gave to this man; then he bowed.

"Adieu, Monsieur de Rochefort," he said.

Rochefort bent low.

"I see, my lord, I am to be taken back to the Bastile."

"You are sagacious."

"I shall return thither, my lord, but it is a mistake on your part not to employ me."

"You? the friend of my greatest foes? Don't suppose that you are the only person who can serve me, Monsieur de Rochefort. I shall find many men as able as you are."

"I wish you may, my lord," replied De Rochefort.

He was then reconducted by the little staircase, instead of passing through the ante-chamber where D'Artagnan was waiting. In the courtyard the carriage and the four musketeers were ready, but he looked around in vain for his friend.

"Ah!" he muttered to himself, "this changes the situation, and if there is still a crowd of people in the streets we will try to show Mazarin that we are still, thank God, good for something else than keeping guard over a prisoner;" and he jumped into the carriage with the alacrity of a man of five-and-twenty.

Chapter IV.

Anne of Austria at the Age of Forty-six.

When left alone with Bernouin, Mazarin was for some minutes lost in thought. He had gained much information, but not enough. Mazarin was a cheat at the card-table. This is a detail preserved to us by Brienne. He called it using his advantages. He now determined not to begin the game with D'Artagnan till he knew completely all his adversary's cards.

"My lord, have you any commands?" asked Bernouin.

"Yes, yes," replied Mazarin. "Light me; I am going to the queen."

Bernouin took up a candlestick and led the way.

There was a secret communication between the cardinal's apartments and those of the queen; and through this corridor* Mazarin passed whenever he wished to visit Anne of Austria.

*This secret passage is still to be seen in the Palais Royal.

In the bedroom in which this passage ended, Bernouin encountered Madame de Beauvais, like himself intrusted with the secret of these subterranean love affairs; and Madame de Beauvais undertook to prepare Anne of Austria, who was in her oratory with the young king, Louis XIV., to receive the cardinal.

Anne, reclining in a large easy-chair, her head supported by her hand, her elbow resting on a table, was looking at her son, who was turning over the leaves of a large book filled with pictures. This celebrated woman fully understood the art of being dull with dignity. It was her practice to pass hours either in her oratory or in her room, without either reading or praying.

When Madame de Beauvais appeared at the door and announced the cardinal, the child, who had been absorbed in the pages of Quintus Curtius, enlivened as they were by engravings of Alexander's feats of arms, frowned and looked at his mother.

"Why," he said, "does he enter without first asking for an audience?"

Anne colored slightly.

"The prime minister," she said, "is obliged in these unsettled days to inform the queen of all that is happening from time to time, without exciting the curiosity or remarks of the court."

"But Richelieu never came in this manner," said the pertinacious boy.

"How can you remember what Monsieur de Richelieu did? You were too young to know about such things."

"I do not remember what he did, but I have inquired and I have been told all about it."

"And who told you about it?" asked Anne of Austria, with a movement of impatience.

"I know that I ought never to name the persons who answer my questions," answered the child, "for if I do I shall learn nothing further."

At this very moment Mazarin entered. The king rose immediately, took his book, closed it and went to lay it down on the table, near which he continued standing, in order that Mazarin might be obliged to stand also.

Mazarin contemplated these proceedings with a thoughtful glance. They explained what had occurred that evening.

He bowed respectfully to the king, who gave him a somewhat cavalier reception, but a look from his mother reproved him for the hatred which, from his infancy, Louis XIV. had entertained toward Mazarin, and he endeavored to receive the minister's homage with civility.

Anne of Austria sought to read in Mazarin's face the occasion of this unexpected visit, since the cardinal usually came to her apartment only after every one had retired.

The minister made a slight sign with his head, whereupon the queen said to Madame Beauvais:

"It is time for the king to go to bed; call Laporte."

The queen had several times already told her son that he ought to go to bed, and several times Louis had coaxingly insisted on staying where he was; but now he made no reply, but turned pale and bit his lips with anger.

In a few minutes Laporte came into the room. The child went directly to him without kissing his mother.

"Well, Louis," said Anne, "why do you not kiss me?"

"I thought you were angry with me, madame; you sent me away."

"I do not send you away, but you have had the small-pox and I am afraid that sitting up late may tire you."

"You had no fears of my being tired when you ordered me to go to the palace to-day to pass the odious decrees which have raised the people to rebellion."

"Sire!" interposed Laporte, in order to turn the subject, "to whom does your majesty wish me to give the candle?"

"To any one, Laporte," the child said; and then added in a loud voice, "to any one except Mancini."

Now Mancini was a nephew of Mazarin's and was as much hated by Louis as the cardinal himself, although placed near his person by the minister.

And the king went out of the room without either embracing his mother or even bowing to the cardinal.

"Good," said Mazarin, "I am glad to see that his majesty has been brought up with a hatred of dissimulation."

"Why do you say that?" asked the queen, almost timidly.

"Why, it seems to me that the way in which he left us needs no explanation. Besides, his majesty takes no pains to conceal how little affection he has for me. That, however, does not hinder me from being entirely devoted to his service, as I am to that of your majesty."

"I ask your pardon for him, cardinal," said the queen; "he is a child, not yet able to understand his obligations to you."

The cardinal smiled.

"But," continued the queen, "you have doubtless come for some important purpose. What is it, then?"

Mazarin sank into a chair with the deepest melancholy painted on his countenance.

"It is likely," he replied, "that we shall soon be obliged to separate, unless you love me well enough to follow me to Italy."

"Why," cried the queen; "how is that?"

"Because, as they say in the opera of 'Thisbe,' 'The whole world conspires to break our bonds.'"

"You jest, sir!" answered the queen, endeavoring to assume something of her former dignity.

"Alas! I do not, madame," rejoined Mazarin. "Mark well what I say. The whole world conspires to break our bonds. Now as you are one of the whole world, I mean to say that you also are deserting me."

"Cardinal!"

"Heavens! did I not see you the other day smile on the Duke of Orleans? or rather at what he said?"

"And what was he saying?"

"He said this, madame: 'Mazarin is a stumbling-block. Send him away and all will then be well.'"

"What do you wish me to do?"

"Oh, madame! you are the queen!"

"Queen, forsooth! when I am at the mercy of every scribbler in the Palais Royal who covers waste paper with nonsense, or of every country squire in the kingdom."

"Nevertheless, you have still the power of banishing from your presence those whom you do not like!"

"That is to say, whom you do not like," returned the queen.

"I! persons whom I do not like!"

"Yes, indeed. Who sent away Madame de Chevreuse after she had been persecuted twelve years under the last reign?"

"A woman of intrigue, who wanted to keep up against me the spirit of cabal she had raised against M. de Richelieu."

"Who dismissed Madame de Hautefort, that friend so loyal that she refused the favor of the king that she might remain in mine?"

"A prude, who told you every night, as she undressed you, that it was a sin to love a priest, just as if one were a priest because one happens to be a cardinal."

"Who ordered Monsieur de Beaufort to be arrested?"

"An incendiary the burden of whose song was his intention to assassinate me."

"You see, cardinal," replied the queen, "that your enemies are mine."

"That is not enough madame, it is necessary that your friends should be also mine."

"My friends, monsieur?" The queen shook her head. "Alas, I have them no longer!"

"How is it that you have no friends in your prosperity when you had many in adversity?"

"It is because in my prosperity I forgot those old friends, monsieur; because I have acted like Queen Marie de Medicis, who, returning from her first exile, treated with contempt all those who had suffered for her and, being proscribed a second time, died at Cologne abandoned by every one, even by her own son."

"Well, let us see," said Mazarin; "isn't there still time to repair the evil? Search among your friends, your oldest friends."

"What do you mean, monsieur?"

"Nothing else than I say—search."

"Alas, I look around me in vain! I have no influence with any one. Monsieur is, as usual, led by his favorite; yesterday it was Choisy, to-day it is La Riviere, to-morrow it will be some one else. Monsieur le Prince is led by the coadjutor, who is led by Madame de Guemenee."

"Therefore, madame, I ask you to look, not among your friends of to-day, but among those of other times."

"Among my friends of other times?" said the queen.

"Yes, among your friends of other times; among those who aided you to contend against the Duc de Richelieu and even to conquer him."

"What is he aiming at?" murmured the queen, looking uneasily at the cardinal.

"Yes," continued his eminence; "under certain circumstances, with that strong and shrewd mind your majesty possesses, aided by your friends, you were able to repel the attacks of that adversary."

"I!" said the queen. "I suffered, that is all."

"Yes," said Mazarin, "as women suffer in avenging themselves. Come, let us come to the point. Do you know Monsieur de Rochefort?"

"One of my bitterest enemies—the faithful friend of Cardinal Richelieu."

"I know that, and we sent him to the Bastile," said Mazarin.

"Is he at liberty?" asked the queen.

"No; still there, but I only speak of him in order that I may introduce the name of another man. Do you know Monsieur d'Artagnan?" he added, looking steadfastly at the queen.

Anne of Austria received the blow with a beating heart.

"Has the Gascon been indiscreet?" she murmured to herself, then said aloud:

"D'Artagnan! stop an instant, the name seems certainly familiar. D'Artagnan! there was a musketeer who was in love with one of my women. Poor young creature! she was poisoned on my account."

"That's all you know of him?" asked Mazarin.

The queen looked at him, surprised.

"You seem, sir," she remarked, "to be making me undergo a course of cross-examination."

"Which you answer according to your fancy," replied Mazarin.

"Tell me your wishes and I will comply with them."

The queen spoke with some impatience.

"Well, madame," said Mazarin, bowing, "I desire that you give me a share in your friends, as I have shared with you the little industry and talent that Heaven has given me. The circumstances are grave and it will be necessary to act promptly."

"Still!" said the queen. "I thought that we were finally quit of Monsieur de Beaufort."

"Yes, you saw only the torrent that threatened to overturn everything and you gave no attention to the still water. There is, however, a proverb current in France relating to water which is quiet."

"Continue," said the queen.

"Well, then, madame, not a day passes in which I do not suffer affronts from your princes and your lordly servants, all of them automata who do not perceive that I wind up the spring that makes them move, nor do they see that beneath my quiet demeanor lies the still scorn of an injured, irritated man, who has sworn to himself to master them one of these days. We have arrested Monsieur de Beaufort, but he is the least dangerous among them. There is the Prince de Condé——"

"The hero of Rocroy. Do you think of him?"

"Yes, madame, often and often, but pazienza, as we say in Italy; next, after Monsieur de Condé, comes the Duke of Orleans."

"What are you saying? The first prince of the blood, the king's uncle!"

"No! not the first prince of the blood, not the king's uncle, but the base conspirator, the soul of every cabal, who pretends to lead the brave people who are weak enough to believe in the honor of a prince of the blood—not the prince nearest to the throne, not the king's uncle, I repeat, but the murderer of Chalais, of Montmorency and of Cinq-Mars, who is playing now the same game he played long ago and who thinks that he will win the game because he has a new adversary—instead of a man who threatened, a man who smiles. But he is mistaken; I shall not leave so near the queen that source of discord with which the deceased cardinal so often caused the anger of the king to rage above the boiling point."

Anne blushed and buried her face in her hands.

"What am I to do?" she said, bowed down beneath the voice of her tyrant.

"Endeavor to remember the names of those faithful servants who crossed the Channel, in spite of Monsieur de Richelieu, tracking the roads along which they passed by their blood, to bring back to your majesty certain jewels given by you to Buckingham."

Anne arose, full of majesty, and as if touched by a spring, and looking at the cardinal with the haughty dignity which in the days of her youth had made her so powerful: "You are insulting me!" she said.

"I wish," continued Mazarin, finishing, as it were, the speech this sudden movement of the queen had cut; "I wish, in fact, that you should now do for your husband what you formerly did for your lover."

"Again that accusation!" cried the queen. "I thought that calumny was stifled or extinct; you have spared me till now, but since you speak of it, once for all, I tell you——"

"Madame, I do not ask you to tell me," said Mazarin, astounded by this returning courage.

"I will tell you all," replied Anne. "Listen: there were in truth, at that epoch, four devoted hearts, four loyal spirits, four faithful swords, who saved more than my life—my honor——"

"Ah! you confess it!" exclaimed Mazarin.

"Is it only the guilty whose honor is at the sport of others, sir? and cannot women be dishonored by appearances? Yes, appearances were against me and I was about to suffer dishonor. However, I swear I was not guilty, I swear it by——"

The queen looked around her for some sacred object by which she could swear, and taking out of a cupboard hidden in the tapestry, a small coffer of rosewood set in silver, and laying it on the altar:

"I swear," she said, "by these sacred relics that Buckingham was not my lover."

"What relics are those by which you swear?" asked Mazarin, smiling. "I am incredulous."

The queen untied from around her throat a small golden key which hung there, and presented it to the cardinal.

"Open, sir," she said, "and look for yourself."

Mazarin opened the coffer; a knife, covered with rust, and two letters, one of which was stained with blood, alone met his gaze.

"What are these things?" he asked.

"What are these things?" replied Anne, with queen-like dignity, extending toward the open coffer an arm, despite the lapse of years, still beautiful. "These two letters are the only ones I ever wrote to him. This knife is the knife with which Felton stabbed him. Read the letters and see if I have lied or spoken the truth."

But Mazarin, notwithstanding this permission, instead of reading the letters, took the knife which the dying Buckingham had snatched out of the wound and sent by Laporte to the queen. The blade was red, for the blood had become rust; after a momentary examination during which the queen became as white as the cloth which covered the altar on which she was leaning, he put it back into the coffer with an involuntary shudder.

"It is well, madame, I believe your oath."

"No, no, read," exclaimed the queen, indignantly; "read, I command you, for I am resolved that everything shall be finished to-night and never will I recur to this subject again. Do you think," she said, with a ghastly smile, "that I shall be inclined to reopen this coffer to answer any future accusations?"

Mazarin, overcome by this determination, read the two letters. In one the queen asked for the ornaments back again. This letter had been conveyed by D'Artagnan and had arrived in time. The other was that which Laporte had placed in the hands of the Duke of Buckingham, warning him that he was about to be assassinated; that communication had arrived too late.

"It is well, madame," said Mazarin; "nothing can gainsay such testimony."

"Sir," replied the queen, closing the coffer and leaning her hand upon it, "if there is anything to be said, it is that I have always been ungrateful to the brave men who saved me—that I have given nothing to that gallant officer, D'Artagnan, you were speaking of just now, but my hand to kiss and this diamond."

As she spoke she extended her beautiful hand to the cardinal and showed him a superb diamond which sparkled on her finger.

"It appears," she resumed, "that he sold it—-he sold it in order to save me another time—to be able to send a messenger to the duke to warn him of his danger—he sold it to Monsieur des Essarts, on whose finger I remarked it. I bought it from him, but it belongs to D'Artagnan. Give it back to him, sir, and since you have such a man in your service, make him useful."

"Thank you, madame," said Mazarin. "I will profit by the advice."

"And now," added the queen, her voice broken by her emotion, "have you any other question to ask me?"

"Nothing,"—the cardinal spoke in his most conciliatory manner—"except to beg of you to forgive my unworthy suspicions. I love you so tenderly that I cannot help being jealous, even of the past."

A smile, which was indefinable, passed over the lips of the queen.

"Since you have no further interrogations to make, leave me, I beseech you," she said. "I wish, after such a scene, to be alone."

Mazarin bent low before her.

"I will retire, madame. Do you permit me to return?"

"Yes, to-morrow."

The cardinal took the queen's hand and pressed it with an air of gallantry to his lips.

Scarcely had he left her when the queen went into her son's room, and inquired from Laporte if the king was in bed. Laporte pointed to the child, who was asleep.

Anne ascended the steps side of the bed and softly kissed the placid forehead of her son; then she retired as silently as she had come, merely saying to Laporte:

"Try, my dear Laporte, to make the king more courteous to Monsieur le Cardinal, to whom both he and I are under such important obligations."

Chapter V.

The Gascon and the Italian.

Meanwhile the cardinal returned to his own room; and after asking Bernouin, who stood at the door, whether anything had occurred during his absence, and being answered in the negative, he desired that he might be left alone.

When he was alone he opened the door of the corridor and then that of the ante-chamber. There D'Artagnan was asleep upon a bench.

The cardinal went up to him and touched his shoulder. D'Artagnan started, awakened himself, and as he awoke, stood up exactly like a soldier under arms.

"Here I am," said he. "Who calls me?"

"I," said Mazarin, with his most smiling expression.

"I ask pardon of your eminence," said D'Artagnan, "but I was so fatigued——"

"Don't ask my pardon, monsieur," said Mazarin, "for you fatigued yourself in my service."

D'Artagnan admired Mazarin's gracious manner. "Ah," said he, between his teeth, "is there truth in the proverb that fortune comes while one sleeps?"

"Follow me, monsieur," said Mazarin.

"Come, come," murmured D'Artagnan, "Rochefort has kept his promise, but where in the devil is he?" And he searched the cabinet even to the smallest recesses, but there was no sign of Rochefort.

"Monsieur d'Artagnan," said the cardinal, sitting down on a fauteuil, "you have always seemed to me to be a brave and honorable man."

"Possibly," thought D'Artagnan, "but he has taken a long time to let me know his thoughts;" nevertheless, he bowed to the very ground in gratitude for Mazarin's compliment.

"Well," continued Mazarin, "the time has come to put to use your talents and your valor."

There was a sudden gleam of joy in the officer's eyes, which vanished immediately, for he knew nothing of Mazarin's purpose.

"Order, my lord," he said; "I am ready to obey your eminence."

"Monsieur d'Artagnan," continued the cardinal, "you performed sundry superb exploits in the last reign."

"Your eminence is too good to remember such trifles in my favor. It is true I fought with tolerable success."

"I don't speak of your warlike exploits, monsieur," said Mazarin; "although they gained you much reputation, they were surpassed by others."

D'Artagnan pretended astonishment.

"Well, you do not reply?" resumed Mazarin.

"I am waiting, my lord, till you tell me of what exploits you speak."

"I speak of the adventure—Eh, you know well what I mean."

"Alas, no, my lord!" replied D'Artagnan, surprised.

"You are discreet—so much the better. I speak of that adventure in behalf of the queen, of the ornaments, of the journey you made with three of your friends."

"Aha!" thought the Gascon; "is this a snare or not? Let me be on my guard."

And he assumed a look of stupidity which Mendori or Bellerose, two of the first actors of the day, might have envied.

"Bravo!" cried Mazarin; "they told me that you were the man I wanted. Come, let us see what you will do for me."

"Everything that your eminence may please to command me," was the reply.

"You will do for me what you have done for the queen?"

"Certainly," D'Artagnan said to himself, "he wishes to make me speak out. He's not more cunning than De Richelieu was! Devil take him!" Then he said aloud:

"The queen, my lord? I don't comprehend."

"You don't comprehend that I want you and your three friends to be of use to me?"

"Which of my friends, my lord?"

"Your three friends—the friends of former days."

"Of former days, my lord! In former days I had not only three friends, I had thirty; at two-and-twenty one calls every man one's friend."

"Well, sir," returned Mazarin, "prudence is a fine thing, but to-day you might regret having been too prudent."

"My lord, Pythagoras made his disciples keep silence for five years that they might learn to hold their tongues."

"But you have been silent for twenty years, sir. Speak, now the queen herself releases you from your promise."

"The queen!" said D'Artagnan, with an astonishment which this time was not pretended.

"Yes, the queen! And as a proof of what I say she commanded me to show you this diamond, which she thinks you know."

And so saying, Mazarin extended his hand to the officer, who sighed as he recognized the ring so gracefully given to him by the queen on the night of the ball at the Hotel de Ville and which she had repurchased from Monsieur des Essarts.

"'Tis true. I remember well that diamond, which belonged to the queen."

"You see, then, that I speak to you in the queen's name. Answer me without acting as if you were on the stage; your interests are concerned in your so doing."

"Faith, my lord, it is very necessary for me to make my fortune, your eminence has so long forgotten me."

"We need only a week to amend all that. Come, you are accounted for, you are here, but where are your friends?"

"I do not know, my lord. We have parted company this long time; all three have left the service."

"Where can you find them, then?"

"Wherever they are, that's my business."

"Well, now, what are your conditions, if I employ you?"

"Money, my lord, as much money as what you wish me to undertake will require. I remember too well how sometimes we were stopped for want of money, and but for that diamond, which I was obliged to sell, we should have remained on the road."

"The devil he does! Money! and a large sum!" said Mazarin. "Pray, are you aware that the king has no money in his treasury?"

"Do then as I did, my lord. Sell the crown diamonds. Trust me, don't let us try to do things cheaply. Great undertakings come poorly off with paltry means."

"Well," returned Mazarin, "we will satisfy you."

"Richelieu," thought D'Artagnan, "would have given me five hundred pistoles in advance."

"You will then be at my service?" asked Mazarin.

"Yes, if my friends agree."

"But if they refuse can I count on you?"

"I have never accomplished anything alone," said D'Artagnan, shaking his head.

"Go, then, and find them."

"What shall I say to them by way of inducement to serve your eminence?"

"You know them better than I. Adapt your promises to their respective characters."

"What shall I promise?"

"That if they serve me as well as they served the queen my gratitude shall be magnificent."

"But what are we to do?"

"Make your mind easy; when the time for action comes you shall be put in full possession of what I require from you; wait till that time arrives and find out your friends."

"My lord, perhaps they are not in Paris. It is even probable that I shall have to make a journey. I am only a lieutenant of musketeers, very poor, and journeys cost money."

"My intention," said Mazarin, "is not that you go with a great following; my plans require secrecy, and would be jeopardized by a too extravagant equipment."

"Still, my lord, I can't travel on my pay, for it is now three months behind; and I can't travel on my savings, for in my twenty-two years of service I have accumulated nothing but debts."

Mazarin remained some moments in deep thought, as if he were fighting with himself; then, going to a large cupboard closed with a triple lock, he took from it a bag of silver, and weighing it twice in his hands before he gave it to D'Artagnan:

"Take this," he said with a sigh, "'tis merely for your journey."

"If these are Spanish doubloons, or even gold crowns," thought D'Artagnan, "we shall yet be able to do business together." He saluted the cardinal and plunged the bag into the depths of an immense pocket.

"Well, then, all is settled; you are to set off," said the cardinal.

"Yes, my lord."

"Apropos, what are the names of your friends?"

"The Count de la Fere, formerly styled Athos; Monsieur du Vallon, whom we used to call Porthos; the Chevalier d'Herblay, now the Abbé d'Herblay, whom we styled Aramis——"

The cardinal smiled.

"Younger sons," he said, "who enlisted in the musketeers under feigned names in order not to lower their family names. Long swords but light purses. Was that it?"

"If, God willing, these swords should be devoted to the service of your eminence," said D'Artagnan, "I shall venture to express a wish, which is, that in its turn the purse of your eminence may become light and theirs heavy—for with these three men your eminence may rouse all Europe if you like."

"These Gascons," said the cardinal, laughing, "almost beat the Italians in effrontery."

"At all events," answered D'Artagnan, with a smile almost as crafty as the cardinal's, "they beat them when they draw their swords."

He then withdrew, and as he passed into the courtyard he stopped near a lamp and dived eagerly into the bag of money.

"Crown pieces only—silver pieces! I suspected it. Ah! Mazarin! Mazarin! thou hast no confidence in me! so much the worse for thee, for harm may come of it!"

Meanwhile the cardinal was rubbing his hands in great satisfaction.

"A hundred pistoles! a hundred pistoles! for a hundred pistoles I have discovered a secret for which Richelieu would have paid twenty thousand crowns; without reckoning the value of that diamond"—he cast a complacent look at the ring, which he had kept, instead of restoring to D'Artagnan—"which is worth, at least, ten thousand francs."

He returned to his room, and after depositing the ring in a casket filled with brilliants of every sort, for the cardinal was a connoisseur in precious stones, he called to Bernouin to undress him, regardless of the noises of gunfire that, though it was now near midnight, continued to resound through Paris.

In the meantime D'Artagnan took his way toward the Rue Tiquetonne, where he lived at the Hotel de la Chevrette.

We will explain in a few words how D'Artagnan had been led to choose that place of residence.

Chapter VI.

D'Artagnan in his Fortieth Year.

Years have elapsed, many events have happened, alas! since, in our romance of "The Three Musketeers," we took leave of D'Artagnan at No. 12 Rue des Fossoyeurs. D'Artagnan had not failed in his career, but circumstances had been adverse to him. So long as he was surrounded by his friends he retained his youth and the poetry of his character. He was one of those fine, ingenuous natures which assimilate themselves easily to the dispositions of others. Athos imparted to him his greatness of soul, Porthos his enthusiasm, Aramis his elegance. Had D'Artagnan continued his intimacy with these three men he would have become a superior character. Athos was the first to leave him, in order that he might retire to a little property he had inherited near Blois; Porthos, the second, to marry an attorney's wife; and lastly, Aramis, the third, to take orders and become an abbé. From that day D'Artagnan felt lonely and powerless, without courage to pursue a career in which he could only distinguish himself on condition that each of his three companions should endow him with one of the gifts each had received from Heaven.

Notwithstanding his commission in the musketeers, D'Artagnan felt completely solitary. For a time the delightful remembrance of Madame Bonancieux left on his character a certain poetic tinge, perishable indeed; for like all other recollections in this world, these impressions were, by degrees, effaced. A garrison life is fatal even to the most aristocratic organization; and imperceptibly, D'Artagnan, always in the camp, always on horseback, always in garrison, became (I know not how in the present age one would express it) a typical trooper. His early refinement of character was not only not lost, it grew even greater than ever; but it was now applied to the little, instead of to the great things of life—to the martial condition of the soldier—comprised under the head of a good lodging, a rich table, a congenial hostess. These important advantages D'Artagnan found to his own taste in the Rue Tiquetonne at the sign of the Roe.

From the time D'Artagnan took quarters in that hotel, the mistress of the house, a pretty and fresh looking Flemish woman, twenty-five or twenty-six years old, had been singularly interested in him; and after certain love passages, much obstructed by an inconvenient husband to whom a dozen times D'Artagnan had made a pretence of passing a sword through his body, that husband had disappeared one fine morning, after furtively selling certain choice lots of wine, carrying away with him money and jewels. He was thought to be dead; his wife, especially, who cherished the pleasing idea that she was a widow, stoutly maintained that death had taken him. Therefore, after the connection had continued three years, carefully fostered by D'Artagnan, who found his bed and his mistress more agreeable every year, each doing credit to the other, the mistress conceived the extraordinary desire of becoming a wife and proposed to D'Artagnan that he should marry her.

"Ah, fie!" D'Artagnan replied. "Bigamy, my dear! Come now, you don't really wish it?"

"But he is dead; I am sure of it."

"He was a very contrary fellow and might come back on purpose to have us hanged."

"All right; if he comes back you will kill him, you are so skillful and so brave."

"Peste! my darling! another way of getting hanged."

"So you refuse my request?"

"To be sure I do—furiously!"

The pretty landlady was desolate. She would have taken D'Artagnan not only as her husband, but as her God, he was so handsome and had so fierce a mustache.

Then along toward the fourth year came the expedition of Franche-Comte. D'Artagnan was assigned to it and made his preparations to depart. There were then great griefs, tears without end and solemn promises to remain faithful—all of course on the part of the hostess. D'Artagnan was too grand to promise anything; he purposed only to do all that he could to increase the glory of his name.

As to that, we know D'Artagnan's courage; he exposed himself freely to danger and while charging at the head of his company he received a ball through the chest which laid him prostrate on the field of battle. He had been seen falling from his horse and had not been seen to rise; every one, therefore, believed him to be dead, especially those to whom his death would give promotion. One believes readily what he wishes to believe. Now in the army, from the division-generals who desire the death of the general-in-chief, to the soldiers who desire the death of the corporals, all desire some one's death.

But D'Artagnan was not a man to let himself be killed like that. After he had remained through the heat of the day unconscious on the battle-field, the cool freshness of the night brought him to himself. He gained a village, knocked at the door of the finest house and was received as the wounded are always and everywhere received in France. He was petted, tended, cured; and one fine morning, in better health than ever before, he set out for France. Once in France he turned his course toward Paris, and reaching Paris went straight to Rue Tiquetonne.

But D'Artagnan found in his chamber the personal equipment of a man, complete, except for the sword, arranged along the wall.

"He has returned," said he. "So much the worse, and so much the better!"

It need not be said that D'Artagnan was still thinking of the husband. He made inquiries and discovered that the servants were new and that the mistress had gone for a walk.

"Alone?" asked D'Artagnan.

"With monsieur."

"Monsieur has returned, then?"

"Of course," naively replied the servant.

"If I had any money," said D'Artagnan to himself, "I would go away; but I have none. I must stay and follow the advice of my hostess, while thwarting the conjugal designs of this inopportune apparition."

He had just completed this monologue—which proves that in momentous circumstances nothing is more natural than the monologue—when the servant-maid, watching at the door, suddenly cried out:

"Ah! see! here is madame returning with monsieur."

D'Artagnan looked out and at the corner of Rue Montmartre saw the hostess coming along hanging to the arm of an enormous Swiss, who tiptoed in his walk with a magnificent air which pleasantly reminded him of his old friend Porthos.

"Is that monsieur?" said D'Artagnan to himself. "Oh! oh! he has grown a good deal, it seems to me." And he sat down in the hall, choosing a conspicuous place.

The hostess, as she entered, saw D'Artagnan and uttered a little cry, whereupon D'Artagnan, judging that he had been recognized, rose, ran to her and embraced her tenderly. The Swiss, with an air of stupefaction, looked at the hostess, who turned pale.

"Ah, it is you, monsieur! What do you want of me?" she asked, in great distress.

"Is monsieur your cousin? Is monsieur your brother?" said D'Artagnan, not in the slightest degree embarrassed in the role he was playing. And without waiting for her reply he threw himself into the arms of the Helvetian, who received him with great coldness.

"Who is that man?" he asked.

The hostess replied only by gasps.

"Who is that Swiss?" asked D'Artagnan.

"Monsieur is going to marry me," replied the hostess, between two gasps.

"Your husband, then, is at last dead?"

"How does that concern you?" replied the Swiss.

"It concerns me much," said D'Artagnan, "since you cannot marry madame without my consent and since——"

"And since?" asked the Swiss.

"And since—I do not give it," said the musketeer.

The Swiss became as purple as a peony. He wore his elegant uniform, D'Artagnan was wrapped in a sort of gray cloak; the Swiss was six feet high, D'Artagnan was hardly more than five; the Swiss considered himself on his own ground and regarded D'Artagnan as an intruder.

"Will you go away from here?" demanded the Swiss, stamping violently, like a man who begins to be seriously angry.

"I? By no means!" said D'Artagnan.

"Some one must go for help," said a lad, who could not comprehend that this little man should make a stand against that other man, who was so large.

D'Artagnan, with a sudden accession of wrath, seized the lad by the ear and led him apart, with the injunction:

"Stay you where you are and don't you stir, or I will pull this ear off. As for you, illustrious descendant of William Tell, you will straightway get together your clothes which are in my room and which annoy me, and go out quickly to another lodging."

The Swiss began to laugh boisterously. "I go out?" he said. "And why?"

"Ah, very well!" said D'Artagnan; "I see that you understand French. Come then, and take a turn with me and I will explain."

The hostess, who knew D'Artagnan's skill with the sword, began to weep and tear her hair. D'Artagnan turned toward her, saying, "Then send him away, madame."

"Pooh!" said the Swiss, who had needed a little time to take in D'Artagnan's proposal, "pooh! who are you, in the first place, to ask me to take a turn with you?"

"I am lieutenant in his majesty's musketeers," said D'Artagnan, "and consequently your superior in everything; only, as the question now is not of rank, but of quarters—you know the custom—come and seek for yours; the first to return will recover his chamber."

D'Artagnan led away the Swiss in spite of lamentations on the part of the hostess, who in reality found her heart inclining toward her former lover, though she would not have been sorry to give a lesson to that haughty musketeer who had affronted her by the refusal of her hand.

It was night when the two adversaries reached the field of battle. D'Artagnan politely begged the Swiss to yield to him the disputed chamber; the Swiss refused by shaking his head, and drew his sword.

"Then you will lie here," said D'Artagnan. "It is a wretched bed, but that is not my fault, and it is you who have chosen it." With these words he drew in his turn and crossed swords with his adversary.

He had to contend against a strong wrist, but his agility was superior to all force. The Swiss received two wounds and was not aware of it, by reason of the cold; but suddenly feebleness, occasioned by loss of blood, obliged him to sit down.

"There!" said D'Artagnan, "what did I tell you? Fortunately, you won't be laid up more than a fortnight. Remain here and I will send you your clothes by the boy. Good-by! Oh, by the way, you'd better take lodging in the Rue Montorgueil at the Chat Qui Pelote. You will be well fed there, if the hostess remains the same. Adieu."

Thereupon he returned in a lively mood to his room and sent to the Swiss the things that belonged to him. The boy found him sitting where D'Artagnan had left him, still overwhelmed by the coolness of his adversary.

The boy, the hostess, and all the house had the same regard for D'Artagnan that one would have for Hercules should he return to earth to repeat his twelve labors.

But when he was alone with the hostess he said: "Now, pretty Madeleine, you know the difference between a Swiss and a gentleman. As for you, you have acted like a barmaid. So much the worse for you, for by such conduct you have lost my esteem and my patronage. I have driven away the Swiss to humiliate you, but I shall lodge here no longer. I will not sleep where I must scorn. Ho, there, boy! Have my valise carried to the Muid d'Amour, Rue des Bourdonnais. Adieu, madame."

In saying these words D'Artagnan appeared at the same time majestic and grieved. The hostess threw herself at his feet, asked his pardon and held him back with a sweet violence. What more need be said? The spit turned, the stove roared, the pretty Madeleine wept; D'Artagnan felt himself invaded by hunger, cold and love. He pardoned, and having pardoned he remained.

And this explains how D'Artagnan had quarters in the Rue Tiquetonne, at the Hotel de la Chevrette.

D'Artagnan then returned home in thoughtful mood, finding a somewhat lively pleasure in carrying Mazarin's bag of money and thinking of that fine diamond which he had once called his own and which he had seen on the minister's finger that night.

"Should that diamond ever fall into my hands again," he reflected, "I would turn it at once into money; I would buy with the proceeds certain lands around my father's chateau, which is a pretty place, well enough, but with no land to it at all, except a garden about the size of the Cemetery des Innocents; and I should wait in all my glory till some rich heiress, attracted by my good looks, rode along to marry me. Then I should like to have three sons; I should make the first a nobleman, like Athos; the second a good soldier, like Porthos; the third an excellent abbé, like Aramis. Faith! that would be a far better life than I lead now; but Monsieur Mazarin is a mean wretch, who won't dispossess himself of his diamond in my favor."

On entering the Rue Tiquetonne he heard a tremendous noise and found a dense crowd near the house.

"Oho!" said he, "is the hotel on fire?" On approaching the hotel of the Roe he found, however, that it was in front of the next house the mob was collected. The people were shouting and running about with torches. By the light of one of these torches D'Artagnan perceived men in uniform.

He asked what was going on.

He was told that twenty citizens, headed by one man, had attacked a carriage which was escorted by a troop of the cardinal's bodyguard; but a reinforcement having come up, the assailants had been put to flight and the leader had taken refuge in the hotel next to his lodgings; the house was now being searched.

In his youth D'Artagnan had often headed the bourgeoisie against the military, but he was cured of all those hot-headed propensities; besides, he had the cardinal's hundred pistoles in his pocket, so he went into the hotel without a word. There he found Madeleine alarmed for his safety and anxious to tell him all the events of the evening, but he cut her short by ordering her to put his supper in his room and give him with it a bottle of good Burgundy.

He took his key and candle and went upstairs to his bedroom. He had been contented, for the convenience of the house, to lodge in the fourth story; and truth obliges us even to confess that his chamber was just above the gutter and below the roof. His first care on entering it was to lock up in an old bureau with a new lock his bag of money, and then as soon as supper was ready he sent away the waiter who brought it up and sat down to table.

Not to reflect on what had passed, as one might fancy. No, D'Artagnan considered that things are never well done when they are not reserved to their proper time. He was hungry; he supped, he went to bed. Neither was he one of those who think that the necessary silence of the night brings counsel with it. In the night he slept, but in the morning, refreshed and calm, he was inspired with his clearest views of everything. It was long since he had any reason for his morning's inspiration, but he always slept all night long. At daybreak he awoke and took a turn around his room.

"In '43," he said, "just before the death of the late cardinal, I received a letter from Athos. Where was I then? Let me see. Oh! at the siege of Besancon I was in the trenches. He told me—let me think—what was it? That he was living on a small estate—but where? I was just reading the name of the place when the wind blew my letter away, I suppose to the Spaniards; there's no use in thinking any more about Athos. Let me see: with regard to Porthos, I received a letter from him, too. He invited me to a hunting party on his property in the month of September, 1646. Unluckily, as I was then in Bearn, on account of my father's death, the letter followed me there. I had left Bearn when it arrived and I never received it until the month of April, 1647; and as the invitation was for September, 1646, I couldn't accept it. Let me look for this letter; it must be with my title deeds."

D'Artagnan opened an old casket which stood in a corner of the room, and which was full of parchments referring to an estate during a period of two hundred years lost to his family. He uttered an exclamation of delight, for the large handwriting of Porthos was discernible, and underneath some lines traced by his worthy spouse.

D'Artagnan eagerly searched for the heading of this letter; it was dated from the Chateau du Vallon.

Porthos had forgotten that any other address was necessary; in his pride he fancied that every one must know the Chateau du Vallon.

"Devil take the vain fellow," said D'Artagnan. "However, I had better find him out first, since he can't want money. Athos must have become an idiot by this time from drinking. Aramis must have worn himself to a shadow of his former self by constant genuflexion."

He cast his eyes again on the letter. There was a postscript:

"I write by the same courier to our worthy friend Aramis in his convent."

"In his convent! What convent? There are about two hundred in Paris and three thousand in France; and then, perhaps, on entering the convent he changed his name. Ah! if I were but learned in theology I should recollect what it was he used to dispute about with the curate of Montdidier and the superior of the Jesuits, when we were at Crevecoeur; I should know what doctrine he leans to and I should glean from that what saint he has adopted as his patron.

"Well, suppose I go back to the cardinal and ask him for a passport into all the convents one can find, even into the nunneries? It would be a curious idea, and maybe I should find my friend under the name of Achilles. But, no! I should lose myself in the cardinal's opinion. Great people only thank you for doing the impossible; what's possible, they say, they can effect themselves, and they are right. But let us wait a little and reflect. I received a letter from him, the dear fellow, in which he even asked me for some small service, which, in fact, I rendered him. Yes, yes; but now what did I do with that letter?"

D'Artagnan thought a moment and then went to the wardrobe in which hung his old clothes. He looked for his doublet of the year 1648 and as he had orderly habits, he found it hanging on its nail. He felt in the pocket and drew from it a paper; it was the letter of Aramis:

"Monsieur D'Artagnan: You know that I have had a quarrel with a certain gentleman, who has given me an appointment for this evening in the Place Royale. As I am of the church, and the affair might injure me if I should share it with any other than a sure friend like you, I write to beg that you will serve me as second.

"You will enter by the Rue Neuve Sainte Catherine; under the second lamp on the right you will find your adversary. I shall be with mine under the third.

"Wholly yours,

"Aramis."

D'Artagnan tried to recall his remembrances. He had gone to the rendezvous, had encountered there the adversary indicated, whose name he had never known, had given him a pretty sword-stroke on the arm, then had gone toward Aramis, who at the same time came to meet him, having already finished his affair. "It is over," Aramis had said. "I think I have killed the insolent fellow. But, dear friend, if you ever need me you know that I am entirely devoted to you." Thereupon Aramis had given him a clasp of the hand and had disappeared under the arcades.

So, then, he no more knew where Aramis was than where Athos and Porthos were, and the affair was becoming a matter of great perplexity, when he fancied he heard a pane of glass break in his room window. He thought directly of his bag and rushed from the inner room where he was sleeping. He was not mistaken; as he entered his bedroom a man was getting in by the window.

"Ah! you scoundrel!" cried D'Artagnan, taking the man for a thief and seizing his sword.

"Sir!" cried the man, "in the name of Heaven put your sword back into the sheath and don't kill me unheard. I'm no thief, but an honest citizen, well off in the world, with a house of my own. My name is—ah! but surely you are Monsieur d'Artagnan?"

"And thou—Planchet!" cried the lieutenant.

"At your service, sir," said Planchet, overwhelmed with joy; "if I were still capable of serving you."

"Perhaps so," replied D'Artagnan. "But why the devil dost thou run about the tops of houses at seven o'clock of the morning in the month of January?"

"Sir," said Planchet, "you must know; but, perhaps you ought not to know——"

"Tell us what," returned D'Artagnan, "but first put a napkin against the window and draw the curtains."

"Sir," said the prudent Planchet, "in the first place, are you on good terms with Monsieur de Rochefort?"

"Perfectly; one of my dearest friends."

"Ah! so much the better!"

"But what has De Rochefort to do with this manner you have of invading my room?"

"Ah, sir! I must first tell you that Monsieur de Rochefort is——"

Planchet hesitated.

"Egad, I know where he is," said D'Artagnan. "He's in the Bastile."

"That is to say, he was there," replied Planchet. "But in returning thither last night, when fortunately you did not accompany him, as his carriage was crossing the Rue de la Ferronnerie his guards insulted the people, who began to abuse them. The prisoner thought this a good opportunity for escape; he called out his name and cried for help. I was there. I heard the name of Rochefort. I remembered him well. I said in a loud voice that he was a prisoner, a friend of the Duc de Beaufort, who called for help. The people were infuriated; they stopped the horses and cut the escort to pieces, whilst I opened the doors of the carriage and Monsieur de Rochefort jumped out and soon was lost amongst the crowd. At this moment a patrol passed by. I was obliged to sound a retreat toward the Rue Tiquetonne; I was pursued and took refuge in the house next to this, where I have been concealed between two mattresses. This morning I ventured to run along the gutters and——"

"Well," interrupted D'Artagnan, "I am delighted that De Rochefort is free, but as for thee, if thou shouldst fall into the hands of the king's servants they will hang thee without mercy. Nevertheless, I promise thee thou shalt be hidden here, though I risk by concealing thee neither more nor less than my lieutenancy, if it was found out that I gave one rebel an asylum."

"Ah! sir, you know well I would risk my life for you."

"Thou mayst add that thou hast risked it, Planchet. I have not forgotten all I owe thee. Sit down there and eat in security. I see thee cast expressive glances at the remains of my supper."

"Yes, sir; for all I've had since yesterday was a slice of bread and butter, with preserves on it. Although I don't despise sweet things in proper time and place, I found the supper rather light."

"Poor fellow!" said D'Artagnan. "Well, come; set to."

"Ah, sir, you are going to save my life a second time!" cried Planchet.

And he seated himself at the table and ate as he did in the merry days of the Rue des Fossoyeurs, whilst D'Artagnan walked to and fro and thought how he could make use of Planchet under present circumstances. While he turned this over in his mind Planchet did his best to make up for lost time at table. At last he uttered a sigh of satisfaction and paused, as if he had partially appeased his hunger.

"Come," said D'Artagnan, who thought that it was now a convenient time to begin his interrogations, "dost thou know where Athos is?"

"No, sir," replied Planchet.

"The devil thou dost not! Dost know where Porthos is?"

"No—not at all."

"And Aramis?"

"Not in the least."

"The devil! the devil! the devil!"

"But, sir," said Planchet, with a look of shrewdness, "I know where Bazin is."

"Where is he?"

"At Notre Dame."

"What has he to do at Notre Dame?"

"He is beadle."

"Bazin beadle at Notre Dame! He must know where his master is!"

"Without a doubt he must."

D'Artagnan thought for a moment, then took his sword and put on his cloak to go out.

"Sir," said Planchet, in a mournful tone, "do you abandon me thus to my fate? Think, if I am found out here, the people of the house, who have not seen me enter it, will take me for a thief."

"True," said D'Artagnan. "Let's see. Canst thou speak any patois?"

"I can do something better than that, sir, I can speak Flemish."

"Where the devil didst thou learn it?"

"In Artois, where I fought for years. Listen, sir. Goeden morgen, mynheer, eth teen begeeray le weeten the ge sond heets omstand."

"Which means?"

"Good-day, sir! I am anxious to know the state of your health."

"He calls that a language! But never mind, that will do capitally."

D'Artagnan opened the door and called out to a waiter to desire Madeleine to come upstairs.

When the landlady made her appearance she expressed much astonishment at seeing Planchet.

"My dear landlady," said D'Artagnan, "I beg to introduce to you your brother, who is arrived from Flanders and whom I am going to take into my service."

"My brother?"

"Wish your sister good-morning, Master Peter."

"Wilkom, suster," said Planchet.

"Goeden day, broder," replied the astonished landlady.

"This is the case," said D'Artagnan; "this is your brother, Madeleine; you don't know him perhaps, but I know him; he has arrived from Amsterdam. You must dress him up during my absence. When I return, which will be in about an hour, you must offer him to me as a servant, and upon your recommendation, though he doesn't speak a word of French, I take him into my service. You understand?"

"That is to say, I guess your wishes, and that is all that's necessary," said Madeleine.

"You are a precious creature, my pretty hostess, and I am much obliged to you."

The next moment D'Artagnan was on his way to Notre Dame.

Chapter VII.

Touches upon the Strange Effects a Half-pistole may have.

D'Artagnan, as he crossed the Pont Neuf, congratulated himself on having found Planchet again, for at that time an intelligent servant was essential to him; nor was he sorry that through Planchet and the situation which he held in Rue des Lombards, a connection with the bourgeoisie might be commenced, at that critical period when that class were preparing to make war with the court party. It was like having a spy in the enemy's camp. In this frame of mind, grateful for the accidental meeting with Planchet, pleased with himself, D'Artagnan reached Notre Dame. He ran up the steps, entered the church, and addressing a verger who was sweeping the chapel, asked him if he knew Monsieur Bazin.

"Monsieur Bazin, the beadle?" said the verger. "Yes. There he is, attending mass, in the chapel of the Virgin."

D'Artagnan nearly jumped for joy; he had despaired of finding Bazin, but now, he thought, since he held one end of the thread he would be pretty sure to reach the other end.

He knelt down just opposite the chapel in order not to lose sight of his man; and as he had almost forgotten his prayers and had omitted to take a book with him, he made use of his time in gazing at Bazin.

Bazin wore his dress, it may be observed, with equal dignity and saintly propriety. It was not difficult to understand that he had gained the crown of his ambition and that the silver-mounted wand he brandished was in his eyes as honorable a distinction as the marshal's baton which Condé threw, or did not throw, into the enemy's line of battle at Fribourg. His person had undergone a change, analogous to the change in his dress; his figure had grown rotund and, as it were, canonical. The striking points of his face were effaced; he had still a nose, but his cheeks, fattened out, each took a portion of it unto themselves; his chin had joined his throat; his eyes were swelled up with the puffiness of his cheeks; his hair, cut straight in holy guise, covered his forehead as far as his eyebrows.

The officiating priest was just finishing mass whilst D'Artagnan was looking at Bazin; he pronounced the words of the holy Sacrament and retired, giving the benediction, which was received by the kneeling communicants, to the astonishment of D'Artagnan, who recognized in the priest the coadjutor* himself, the famous Jean Francois Gondy, who at that time, having a presentiment of the part he was to play, was beginning to court popularity by almsgiving. It was to this end that he performed from time to time some of those early masses which the common people, generally, alone attended.

* A sacerdotal officer.

D'Artagnan knelt as well as the rest, received his share of the benediction and made the sign of the cross; but when Bazin passed in his turn, with his eyes raised to Heaven and walking, in all humility, the very last, D'Artagnan pulled him by the hem of his robe.

Bazin looked down and started, as if he had seen a serpent.

"Monsieur d'Artagnan!" he cried; "Vade retro Satanas!"

"So, my dear Bazin!" said the officer, laughing, "this is the way you receive an old friend."

"Sir," replied Bazin, "the true friends of a Christian are those who aid him in working out his salvation, not those who hinder him in doing so."

"I don't understand you, Bazin; nor can I see how I can be a stumbling-block in the way of your salvation," said D'Artagnan.

"You forget, sir, that you very nearly ruined forever that of my master; and that it was owing to you that he was very nearly being damned eternally for remaining a musketeer, whilst all the time his true vocation was the church."

"My dear Bazin, you ought to perceive," said D'Artagnan, "from the place in which you find me, that I am greatly changed in everything. Age produces good sense, and, as I doubt not but that your master is on the road to salvation, I want you to tell me where he is, that he may help me to mine."

"Rather say, to take him back with you into the world. Fortunately, I don't know where he is."

"How!" cried D'Artagnan; "you don't know where Aramis is?"

"Formerly," replied Bazin, "Aramis was his name of perdition. By Aramis is meant Simara, which is the name of a demon. Happily for him he has ceased to bear that name."

"And therefore," said D'Artagnan, resolved to be patient to the end, "it is not Aramis I seek, but the Abbé d'Herblay. Come, my dear Bazin, tell me where he is."

"Didn't you hear me tell you, Monsieur d'Artagnan, that I don't know where he is?"

"Yes, certainly; but to that I answer that it is impossible."

"It is, nevertheless, the truth, monsieur—the pure truth, the truth of the good God."

D'Artagnan saw clearly that he would get nothing out of this man, who was evidently telling a falsehood in his pretended ignorance of the abode of Aramis, but whose lies were bold and decided.

"Well, Bazin," said D'Artagnan, "since you do not know where your master lives, let us speak of it no more; let us part good friends. Accept this half-pistole to drink to my health."

"I do not drink"—Bazin pushed away with dignity the officer's hand—"'tis good only for the laity."

"Incorruptible!" murmured D'Artagnan; "I am unlucky;" and whilst he was lost in thought Bazin retreated toward the sacristy, and even there he could not think himself safe until he had shut and locked the door behind him.

D'Artagnan was still in deep thought when some one touched him on the shoulder. He turned and was about to utter an exclamation of surprise when the other made to him a sign of silence.

"You here, Rochefort?" he said, in a low voice.

"Hush!" returned Rochefort. "Did you know that I am at liberty?"

"I knew it from the fountain-head—from Planchet. And what brought you here?"

"I came to thank God for my happy deliverance," said Rochefort.

"And nothing more? I suppose that is not all."

"To take my orders from the coadjutor and to see if we cannot wake up Mazarin a little."

"A bad plan; you'll be shut up again in the Bastile."

"Oh, as to that, I shall take care, I assure you. The air, the fresh, free air is so good; besides," and Rochefort drew a deep breath as he spoke, "I am going into the country to make a tour."

"Stop," cried D'Artagnan; "I, too, am going."

"And if I may without impertinence ask—where are you going?"

"To seek my friends."

"What friends?"

"Those that you asked about yesterday."

"Athos, Porthos and Aramis—you are looking for them?"

"Yes."

"On honor?"

"What, then, is there surprising in that?"

"Nothing. Queer, though. And in whose behalf are you looking for them?"

"You are in no doubt on that score."

"That is true."

"Unfortunately, I have no idea where they are."

"And you have no way to get news of them? Wait a week and I myself will give you some."

"A week is too long. I must find them within three days."

"Three days are a short time and France is large."

"No matter; you know the word must; with that word great things are done."

"And when do you set out?"

"I am now on my road."

"Good luck to you."

"And to you—a good journey."

"Perhaps we shall meet on our road."

"That is not probable."

"Who knows? Chance is so capricious. Adieu, till we meet again! Apropos, should Mazarin speak to you about me, tell him that I should have requested you to acquaint him that in a short time he will see whether I am, as he says, too old for action."

And Rochefort went away with one of those diabolical smiles which used formerly to make D'Artagnan shudder, but D'Artagnan could now see it without alarm, and smiling in his turn, with an expression of melancholy which the recollections called up by that smile could, perhaps, alone give to his countenance, he said:

"Go, demon, do what thou wilt! It matters little now to me. There's no second Constance in the world."

On his return to the cathedral, D'Artagnan saw Bazin, who was conversing with the sacristan. Bazin was making, with his spare little short arms, ridiculous gestures. D'Artagnan perceived that he was enforcing prudence with respect to himself.

D'Artagnan slipped out of the cathedral and placed himself in ambuscade at the corner of the Rue des Canettes; it was impossible that Bazin should go out of the cathedral without his seeing him.

In five minutes Bazin made his appearance, looking in every direction to see if he were observed, but he saw no one. Calmed by appearances he ventured to walk on through the Rue Notre Dame. Then D'Artagnan rushed out of his hiding place and arrived in time to see Bazin turn down the Rue de la Juiverie and enter, in the Rue de la Calandre, a respectable looking house; and this D'Artagnan felt no doubt was the habitation of the worthy beadle. Afraid of making any inquiries at this house, D'Artagnan entered a small tavern at the corner of the street and asked for a cup of hypocras. This beverage required a good half-hour to prepare. And D'Artagnan had time, therefore, to watch Bazin unsuspected.

He perceived in the tavern a pert boy between twelve and fifteen years of age whom he fancied he had seen not twenty minutes before under the guise of a chorister. He questioned him, and as the boy had no interest in deceiving, D'Artagnan learned that he exercised, from six o'clock in the morning until nine, the office of chorister, and from nine o'clock till midnight that of a waiter in the tavern.

Whilst he was talking to this lad a horse was brought to the door of Bazin's house. It was saddled and bridled. Almost immediately Bazin came downstairs.

"Look!" said the boy, "there's our beadle, who is going a journey."

"And where is he going?" asked D'Artagnan.

"Forsooth, I don't know."

"Half a pistole if you can find out," said D'Artagnan.

"For me?" cried the boy, his eyes sparkling with joy, "if I can find out where Bazin is going? That is not difficult. You are not joking, are you?"

"No, on the honor of an officer; there is the half-pistole;" and he showed him the seductive coin, but did not give it him.

"I shall ask him."

"Just the very way not to know. Wait till he is set out and then, marry, come up, ask, and find out. The half-pistole is ready," and he put it back again into his pocket.

"I understand," said the child, with that jeering smile which marks especially the "gamin de Paris." "Well, we must wait."

They had not long to wait. Five minutes afterward Bazin set off on a full trot, urging on his horse by the blows of a parapluie, which he was in the habit of using instead of a riding whip.

Scarcely had he turned the corner of the Rue de la Juiverie when the boy rushed after him like a bloodhound on full scent.

Before ten minutes had elapsed the child returned.

"Well!" said D'Artagnan.

"Well!" answered the boy, "the thing is done."

"Where is he gone?"

"The half-pistole is for me?"

"Doubtless, answer me."

"I want to see it. Give it me, that I may see it is not false."

"There it is."

The child put the piece of money into his pocket.

"And now, where is he gone?" inquired D'Artagnan.

"He is gone to Noisy."

"How dost thou know?"

"Ah, faith! there was no great cunning necessary. I knew the horse he rode; it belonged to the butcher, who lets it out now and then to M. Bazin. Now I thought that the butcher would not let his horse out like that without knowing where it was going. And he answered 'that Monsieur Bazin went to Noisy.' 'Tis his custom. He goes two or three times a week."

"Dost thou know Noisy well?"

"I think so, truly; my nurse lives there."

"Is there a convent at Noisy?"

"Isn't there a great and grand one—the convent of Jesuits?"

"What is thy name?"

"Friquet."

D'Artagnan wrote the child's name in his tablets.

"Please, sir," said the boy, "do you think I can gain any more half-pistoles in any way?"

"Perhaps," replied D'Artagnan.

And having got out all he wanted, he paid for the hypocras, which he did not drink, and went quickly back to the Rue Tiquetonne.

Chapter VIII.

D'Artagnan, Going to a Distance to discover Aramis.

On entering the hotel D'Artagnan saw a man sitting in a corner by the fire. It was Planchet, but so completely transformed, thanks to the old clothes that the departing husband had left behind, that D'Artagnan himself could hardly recognize him. Madeleine introduced him in presence of all the servants. Planchet addressed the officer with a fine Flemish phrase; the officer replied in words that belonged to no language at all, and the bargain was concluded; Madeleine's brother entered D'Artagnan's service.

The plan adopted by D'Artagnan was soon perfected. He resolved not to reach Noisy in the day, for fear of being recognized; he had therefore plenty of time before him, for Noisy is only three or four leagues from Paris, on the road to Meaux.

He began his day by breakfasting substantially—a bad beginning when one wants to employ the head, but an excellent precaution when one wants to work the body; and about two o'clock he had his two horses saddled, and followed by Planchet he quitted Paris by the Barriere de la Villete. A most active search was still prosecuted in the house near the Hotel de la Chevrette for the discovery of Planchet.

At about a league and a half from the city, D'Artagnan, finding that in his impatience he had set out too soon, stopped to give the horses breathing time. The inn was full of disreputable looking people, who seemed as if they were on the point of commencing some nightly expedition. A man, wrapped in a cloak, appeared at the door, but seeing a stranger he beckoned to his companions, and two men who were drinking in the inn went out to speak to him.

D'Artagnan, on his side, went up to the landlady, praised her wine—which was a horrible production from the country of Montreuil—and heard from her that there were only two houses of importance in the village; one of these belonged to the Archbishop of Paris, and was at that time the abode of his niece the Duchess of Longueville; the other was a convent of Jesuits and was the property—a by no means unusual circumstance—of these worthy fathers.

At four o'clock D'Artagnan recommenced his journey. He proceeded slowly and in deep reverie. Planchet also was lost in thought, but the subject of their reflections was not the same.

One word which their landlady had pronounced had given a particular turn to D'Artagnan's deliberations; this was the name of Madame de Longueville.

That name was indeed one to inspire imagination and produce thought. Madame de Longueville was one of the highest ladies in the realm; she was also one of the greatest beauties at court. She had formerly been suspected of an intimacy of too tender a nature with Coligny, who, for her sake, had been killed in a duel, in the Place Royale, by the Duc de Guise. She was now connected by bonds of a political nature with the Prince de Marsillac, the eldest son of the old Duc de Rochefoucauld, whom she was trying to inspire with an enmity toward the Duc de Condé, her brother-in-law, whom she now hated mortally.

D'Artagnan thought of all these matters. He remembered how at the Louvre he had often seen, as she passed by him in the full radiance of her dazzling charms, the beautiful Madame de Longueville. He thought of Aramis, who, without possessing any greater advantages than himself, had formerly been the lover of Madame de Chevreuse, who had been to a former court what Madame de Longueville was in that day; and he wondered how it was that there should be in the world people who succeed in every wish, some in ambition, others in love, whilst others, either from chance, or from ill-luck, or from some natural defect or impediment, remain half-way upon the road toward fulfilment of their hopes and expectations.

He was confessing to himself that he belonged to the latter unhappy class, when Planchet approached and said:

"I will lay a wager, your honor, that you and I are thinking of the same thing."

"I doubt it, Planchet," replied D'Artagnan, "but what are you thinking of?"

"I am thinking, sir, of those desperate looking men who were drinking in the inn where we rested."

"Always cautious, Planchet."

"'Tis instinct, your honor."

"Well, what does your instinct tell you now?"

"Sir, my instinct told me that those people were assembled there for some bad purpose; and I was reflecting on what my instinct had told me, in the darkest corner of the stable, when a man wrapped in a cloak and followed by two other men, came in."

"Ah ah!" said D'Artagnan, Planchet's recital agreeing with his own observations. "Well?"

"One of these two men said, 'He must certainly be at Noisy, or be coming there this evening, for I have seen his servant.'

"'Art thou sure?' said the man in the cloak.

"'Yes, my prince.'"

"My prince!" interrupted D'Artagnan.

"Yes, 'my prince;' but listen. 'If he is here'—this is what the other man said—'let's see decidedly what to do with him.'

"'What to do with him?' answered the prince.

"'Yes, he's not a man to allow himself to be taken anyhow; he'll defend himself.'

"'Well, we must try to take him alive. Have you cords to bind him with and a gag to stop his mouth?'

"'We have.'

"'Remember that he will most likely be disguised as a horseman.'

"'Yes, yes, my lord; don't be uneasy.'

"'Besides, I shall be there.'

"'You will assure us that justice——'

"'Yes, yes! I answer for all that,' the prince said.

"'Well, then, we'll do our best.' Having said that, they went out of the stable."

"Well, what matters all that to us?" said D'Artagnan. "This is one of those attempts that happen every day."

"Are you sure that we are not its objects?"

"We? Why?"

"Just remember what they said. 'I have seen his servant,' said one, and that applies very well to me."

"Well?"

"'He must certainly be at Noisy, or be coming there this evening,' said the other; and that applies very well to you."

"What else?"

"Then the prince said: 'Take notice that in all probability he will be disguised as a cavalier;' which seems to me to leave no room for doubt, since you are dressed as a cavalier and not as an officer of musketeers. Now then, what do you say to that?"

"Alas! my dear Planchet," said D'Artagnan, sighing, "we are unfortunately no longer in those times in which princes would care to assassinate me. Those were good old days; never fear—these people owe us no grudge."

"Is your honor sure?"

"I can answer for it they do not."

"Well, we won't speak of it any more, then;" and Planchet took his place in D'Artagnan's suite with that sublime confidence he had always had in his master, which even fifteen years of separation had not destroyed.

They had traveled onward about half a mile when Planchet came close up to D'Artagnan.

"Stop, sir, look yonder," he whispered; "don't you see in the darkness something pass by, like shadows? I fancy I hear horses' feet."

"Impossible!" returned D'Artagnan. "The ground is soaking wet; yet I fancy, as thou sayest, that I see something."

At this moment the neighing of a horse struck his ear, coming through darkness and space.

"There are men somewhere about, but that's of no consequence to us," said D'Artagnan; "let us ride onward."

At about half-past eight o'clock they reached the first houses in Noisy; every one was in bed and not a light was to be seen in the village. The obscurity was broken only now and then by the still darker lines of the roofs of houses. Here and there a dog barked behind a door or an affrighted cat fled precipitately from the midst of the pavement to take refuge behind a pile of faggots, from which retreat her eyes would shine like peridores. These were the only living creatures that seemed to inhabit the village.

Toward the middle of the town, commanding the principal open space, rose a dark mass, separated from the rest of the world by two lanes and overshadowed in the front by enormous lime-trees. D'Artagnan looked attentively at the building.

"This," he said to Planchet, "must be the archbishop's chateau, the abode of the fair Madame de Longueville; but the convent, where is that?"

"The convent, your honor, is at the other end of the village; I know it well."

"Well, then, Planchet, gallop up to it whilst I tighten my horse's girth, and come back and tell me if there is a light in any of the Jesuits' windows."

In about five minutes Planchet returned.

"Sir," he said, "there is one window of the convent lighted up."

"Hem! If I were a 'Frondeur,'" said D'Artagnan, "I should knock here and should be sure of a good supper. If I were a monk I should knock yonder and should have a good supper there, too; whereas, 'tis very possible that between the castle and the convent we shall sleep on hard beds, dying with hunger and thirst."

"Yes," added Planchet, "like the famous ass of Buridan. Shall I knock?"

"Hush!" replied D'Artagnan; "the light no longer burns in yonder window."

"Do you hear nothing?" whispered Planchet.

"What is that noise?"

There came a sound like a whirlwind, at the same time two troops of horsemen, each composed of ten men, sallied forth from each of the lanes which encompassed the house and surrounded D'Artagnan and Planchet.

"Heyday!" cried D'Artagnan, drawing his sword and taking refuge behind his horse; "are you not mistaken? is it really for us that you mean your attack?"

"Here he is! we have him!" cried the horsemen, rushing on D'Artagnan with naked swords.

"Don't let him escape!" said a loud voice.

"No, my lord; be assured we shall not."

D'Artagnan thought it was now time for him to join in the conversation.

"Halloo, gentlemen!" he called out in his Gascon accent, "what do you want? what do you demand?"

"That thou shalt soon know," shouted a chorus of horsemen.

"Stop, stop!" cried he whom they had addressed as "my lord;" "'tis not his voice."

"Ah! just so, gentlemen! pray, do people get into a passion at random at Noisy? Take care, for I warn you that the first man that comes within the length of my sword—and my sword is long—I rip him up."

The chieftain of the party drew near.

"What are you doing here?" he asked in a lofty tone, as that of one accustomed to command.

"And you—what are you doing here?" replied D'Artagnan.

"Be civil, or I shall beat you; for although one may not choose to proclaim oneself, one insists on respect suitable to one's rank."

"You don't choose to discover yourself, because you are the leader of an ambuscade," returned D'Artagnan; "but with regard to myself, who am traveling quietly with my own servant, I have not the same reasons as you have to conceal my name."

"Enough! enough! what is your name?"

"I shall tell you my name in order that you may know where to find me, my lord, or my prince, as it may suit you best to be called," said our Gascon, who did not choose to seem to yield to a threat. "Do you know Monsieur d'Artagnan?"

"Lieutenant in the king's musketeers?" said the voice; "you are Monsieur d'Artagnan?"

"I am."

"Then you came here to defend him?"

"Him? whom?"

"The man we are seeking."

"It seems," said D'Artagnan, "that whilst I thought I was coming to Noisy I have entered, without suspecting it, into the kingdom of mysteries."

"Come," replied the same lofty tone, "answer! Are you waiting for him underneath these windows? Did you come to Noisy to defend him?"

"I am waiting for no one," replied D'Artagnan, who was beginning to be angry. "I propose to defend no one but myself, and I shall defend myself vigorously, I give you warning."

"Very well," said the voice; "go away from here and leave the place to us."

"Go away from here!" said D'Artagnan, whose purposes were in conflict with that order, "that is not so easy, since I am on the point of falling, and my horse, too, through fatigue; unless, indeed, you are disposed to offer me a supper and a bed in the neighborhood."

"Rascal!"

"Eh! monsieur!" said D'Artagnan, "I beg you will have a care what you say; for if you utter another word like that, be you marquis, duke, prince or king, I will thrust it down your throat! do you hear?"

"Well, well," rejoined the leader, "there's no doubt 'tis a Gascon who is speaking, and therefore not the man we are looking for. Our blow has failed for to-night; let us withdraw. We shall meet again, Master d'Artagnan," continued the leader, raising his voice.

"Yes, but never with the same advantages," said D'Artagnan, in a tone of raillery; "for when you meet me again you will perhaps be alone and there will be daylight."

"Very good, very good," said the voice. "En route, gentlemen."

And the troop, grumbling angrily, disappeared in the darkness and took the road to Paris. D'Artagnan and Planchet remained for some moments still on the defensive; then, as the noise of the horsemen became more and more distant, they sheathed their swords.

"Thou seest, simpleton," said D'Artagnan to his servant, "that they wished no harm to us."

"But to whom, then?"

"I'faith! I neither know nor care. What I do care for now, is to make my way into the Jesuits' convent; so to horse and let us knock at their door. Happen what will, the devil take them, they can't eat us."

And he mounted his horse. Planchet had just done the same when an unexpected weight fell upon the back of the horse, which sank down.

"Hey! your honor!" cried Planchet, "I've a man behind me."

D'Artagnan turned around and plainly saw two human forms on Planchet's horse.

"'Tis then the devil that pursues!" he cried; drawing his sword and preparing to attack the new foe.

"No, no, dear D'Artagnan," said the figure, "'tis not the devil, 'tis Aramis; gallop fast, Planchet, and when you come to the end of the village turn swiftly to the left."

And Planchet, with Aramis behind him, set off at full gallop, followed by D'Artagnan, who began to think he was in the merry maze of some fantastic dream.

Chapter IX.

The Abbé D'Herblay.

At the extremity of the village Planchet turned to the left in obedience to the orders of Aramis, and stopped underneath the window which had light in it. Aramis alighted and clapped his hands three times. Immediately the window was opened and a ladder of rope was let down from it.

"My friend," said Aramis, "if you like to ascend I shall be delighted to receive you."

"Ah," said D'Artagnan, "is that the way you return to your apartment?"

"After nine at night, pardieu!" said Aramis, "the rule of the convent is very severe."

"Pardon me, my dear friend," said D'Artagnan, "I think you said 'pardieu!'"

"Do you think so?" said Aramis, smiling; "it is possible. You have no idea, my dear fellow, how one acquires bad habits in these cursed convents, or what evil ways all these men of the church have, with whom I am obliged to live. But will you not go up?"

"Pass on before me, I beg of you."

"As the late cardinal used to say to the late king, 'only to show you the way, sire.'" And Aramis ascended the ladder quickly and reached the window in an instant.

D'Artagnan followed, but less nimbly, showing plainly that this mode of ascent was not one to which he was accustomed.

"I beg your pardon," said Aramis, noticing his awkwardness; "if I had known that I was to have the honor of your visit I should have procured the gardener's ladder; but for me alone this is good enough."

"Sir," said Planchet when he saw D'Artagnan on the summit of the ladder, "this way is easy for Monsieur Aramis and even for you; in case of necessity I might also climb up, but my two horses cannot mount the ladder."

"Take them to yonder shed, my friend," said Aramis, pointing to a low building on the plain; "there you will find hay and straw for them; then come back here and clap your hands three times, and we will give you wine and food. Marry, forsooth, people don't die of hunger here."

And Aramis, drawing in the ladder, closed the window. D'Artagnan then looked around attentively.

Never was there an apartment at the same time more warlike and more elegant. At each corner were arranged trophies, presenting to view swords of all sorts, and on the walls hung four great pictures representing in their ordinary military costume the Cardinal de Lorraine, the Cardinal de Richelieu, the Cardinal de la Valette, and the Archbishop of Bordeaux. Exteriorly, nothing in the room showed that it was the habitation of an abbé. The hangings were of damask, the carpets from Alencon, and the bed, especially, had more the look of a fine lady's couch, with its trimmings of fine lace and its embroidered counterpane, than that of a man who had made a vow that he would endeavor to gain Heaven by fasting and mortification.

"You are examining my den," said Aramis. "Ah, my dear fellow, excuse me; I am lodged like a Chartreux. But what are you looking for?"

"I am looking for the person who let down the ladder. I see no one and yet the ladder didn't come down of itself."

"No, it is Bazin."

"Ah! ah!" said D'Artagnan.

"But," continued Aramis, "Bazin is a well trained servant, and seeing that I was not alone he discreetly retired. Sit down, my dear friend, and let us talk." And Aramis pushed forward a large easy-chair, in which D'Artagnan stretched himself out.

"In the first place, you will sup with me, will you not?" asked Aramis.

"Yes, if you really wish it," said D'Artagnan, "and even with great pleasure, I confess; the journey has given me a devil of an appetite."

"Ah, my poor friend!" said Aramis, "you will find meagre fare; you were not expected."

"Am I then threatened with the omelet of Crevecoeur?"

"Oh, let us hope," said Aramis, "that with the help of God and of Bazin we shall find something better than that in the larder of the worthy Jesuit fathers. Bazin, my friend, come here."

The door opened and Bazin entered; on perceiving the musketeer he uttered an exclamation that was almost a cry of despair.

"My dear Bazin," said D'Artagnan, "I am delighted to see with what wonderful composure you can tell a lie even in church!"

"Sir," replied Bazin, "I have been taught by the good Jesuit fathers that it is permitted to tell a falsehood when it is told in a good cause."

"So far well," said Aramis; "we are dying of hunger. Serve us up the best supper you can, and especially give us some good wine."

Bazin bowed low, sighed, and left the room.

"Now we are alone, dear Aramis," said D'Artagnan, "tell me how the devil you managed to alight upon the back of Planchet's horse."

"I'faith!" answered Aramis, "as you see, from Heaven."

"From Heaven," replied D'Artagnan, shaking his head; "you have no more the appearance of coming from thence than you have of going there."

"My friend," said Aramis, with a look of imbecility on his face which D'Artagnan had never observed whilst he was in the musketeers, "if I did not come from Heaven, at least I was leaving Paradise, which is almost the same."

"Here, then, is a puzzle for the learned," observed D'Artagnan, "until now they have never been able to agree as to the situation of Paradise; some place it on Mount Ararat, others between the rivers Tigris and Euphrates; it seems that they have been looking very far away for it, while it was actually very near. Paradise is at Noisy le Sec, upon the site of the archbishop's chateau. People do not go out from it by the door, but by the window; one doesn't descend here by the marble steps of a peristyle, but by the branches of a lime-tree; and the angel with a flaming sword who guards this elysium seems to have changed his celestial name of Gabriel into that of the more terrestrial one of the Prince de Marsillac."

Aramis burst into a fit of laughter.

"You were always a merry companion, my dear D'Artagnan," he said, "and your witty Gascon fancy has not deserted you. Yes, there is something in what you say; nevertheless, do not believe that it is Madame de Longueville with whom I am in love."

"A plague on't! I shall not do so. After having been so long in love with Madame de Chevreuse, you would hardly lay your heart at the feet of her mortal enemy!"

"Yes," replied Aramis, with an absent air; "yes, that poor duchess! I once loved her much, and to do her justice, she was very useful to us. Eventually she was obliged to leave France. He was a relentless enemy, that damned cardinal," continued Aramis, glancing at the portrait of the old minister. "He had even given orders to arrest her and would have cut off her head had she not escaped with her waiting-maid—poor Kitty! I have heard that she met with a strange adventure in I don't know what village, with I don't know what curé, of whom she asked hospitality and who, having but one chamber, and taking her for a cavalier, offered to share it with her. For she had a wonderful way of dressing as a man, that dear Marie; I know only one other woman who can do it as well. So they made this song about her: '*Laboissiere, dis moi.*' You know it, don't you?"

"No, sing it, please."

Aramis immediately complied, and sang the song in a very lively manner.

"Bravo!" cried D'Artagnan, "you sing charmingly, dear Aramis. I do not perceive that singing masses has spoiled your voice."

"My dear D'Artagnan," replied Aramis, "you understand, when I was a musketeer I mounted guard as seldom as I could; now when I am an abbé I say as few masses as I can. But to return to our duchess."

"Which—the Duchess de Chevreuse or the Duchess de Longueville?"

"Have I not already told you that there is nothing between me and the Duchess de Longueville? Little flirtations, perhaps, and that's all. No, I spoke of the Duchess de Chevreuse; did you see her after her return from Brussels, after the king's death?"

"Yes, she is still beautiful."

"Yes," said Aramis, "I saw her also at that time. I gave her good advice, by which she did not profit. I ventured to tell her that Mazarin was the lover of Anne of Austria. She wouldn't believe me, saying that she knew Anne of Austria, who was too proud to love such a worthless coxcomb. After that she plunged into the cabal headed by the Duke of Beaufort; and the 'coxcomb' arrested De Beaufort and banished Madame de Chevreuse."

"You know," resumed D'Artagnan, "that she has had leave to return to France?"

"Yes she is come back and is going to commit some fresh folly or another."

"Oh, but this time perhaps she will follow your advice."

"Oh, this time," returned Aramis, "I haven't seen her; she is much changed."

"In that respect unlike you, my dear Aramis, for you are still the same; you have still your beautiful dark hair, still your elegant figure, still your feminine hands, which are admirably suited to a prelate."

"Yes," replied Aramis, "I am extremely careful of my appearance. Do you know that I am growing old? I am nearly thirty-seven."

"Mind, Aramis"—D'Artagnan smiled as he spoke—"since we are together again, let us agree on one point: what age shall we be in future?"

"How?"

"Formerly I was your junior by two or three years, and if I am not mistaken I am turned forty years old."

"Indeed! Then 'tis I who am mistaken, for you have always been a good chronologist. By your reckoning I must be forty-three at least. The devil I am! Don't let it out at the Hotel Rambouillet; it would ruin me," replied the abbé.

"Don't be afraid," said D'Artagnan. "I never go there."

"Why, what in the world," cried Aramis, "is that animal Bazin doing? Bazin! Hurry up there, you rascal; we are mad with hunger and thirst!"

Bazin entered at that moment carrying a bottle in each hand.

"At last," said Aramis, "we are ready, are we?"

"Yes, monsieur, quite ready," said Bazin; "but it took me some time to bring up all the——"

"Because you always think you have on your shoulders your beadle's robe, and spend all your time reading your breviary. But I give you warning that if in polishing your chapel utensils you forget how to brighten up my sword, I will make a great fire of your blessed images and will see that you are roasted on it."

Bazin, scandalized, made a sign of the cross with the bottle in his hand. D'Artagnan, more surprised than ever at the tone and manners of the Abbé d'Herblay, which contrasted so strongly with those of the Musketeer Aramis, remained staring with wide-open eyes at the face of his friend.

Bazin quickly covered the table with a damask cloth and arranged upon it so many things, gilded, perfumed, appetizing, that D'Artagnan was quite overcome.

"But you expected some one then?" asked the officer.

"Oh," said Aramis, "I always try to be prepared; and then I knew you were seeking me."

"From whom?"

"From Master Bazin, to be sure; he took you for the devil, my dear fellow, and hastened to warn me of the danger that threatened my soul if I should meet again a companion so wicked as an officer of musketeers."

"Oh, monsieur!" said Bazin, clasping his hands supplicatingly.

"Come, no hypocrisy! you know that I don't like it. You will do much better to open the window and let down some bread, a chicken and a bottle of wine to your friend Planchet, who has been this last hour killing himself clapping his hands."

Planchet, in fact, had bedded and fed his horses, and then coming back under the window had repeated two or three times the signal agreed upon.

Bazin obeyed, fastened to the end of a cord the three articles designated and let them down to Planchet, who then went satisfied to his shed.

"Now to supper," said Aramis.

The two friends sat down and Aramis began to cut up fowls, partridges and hams with admirable skill.

"The deuce!" cried D'Artagnan; "do you live in this way always?"

"Yes, pretty well. The coadjutor has given me dispensations from fasting on the jours maigres, on account of my health; then I have engaged as my cook the cook who lived with Lafollone—you know the man I mean?—the friend of the cardinal, and the famous epicure whose grace after dinner used to be, 'Good Lord, do me the favor to cause me to digest what I have eaten.'"

"Nevertheless he died of indigestion, in spite of his grace," said D'Artagnan.

"What can you expect?" replied Aramis, in a tone of resignation. "Every man that's born must fulfil his destiny."

"If it be not an indelicate question," resumed D'Artagnan, "have you grown rich?"

"Oh, Heaven! no. I make about twelve thousand francs a year, without counting a little benefice of a thousand crowns the prince gave me."

"And how do you make your twelve thousand francs? By your poems?"

"No, I have given up poetry, except now and then to write a drinking song, some gay sonnet or some innocent epigram; I compose sermons, my friend."

"What! sermons? Do you preach them?"

"No; I sell them to those of my cloth who wish to become great orators."

"Ah, indeed! and you have not been tempted by the hopes of reputation yourself?"

"I should, my dear D'Artagnan, have been so, but nature said 'No.' When I am in the pulpit, if by chance a pretty woman looks at me, I look at her again: if she smiles, I smile too. Then I speak at random; instead of preaching about the torments of hell I talk of the joys of Paradise. An event took place in the Church of St. Louis au Marais. A gentleman laughed in my face. I stopped short to tell him that he was a fool; the congregation went out to get stones to stone me with, but whilst they were away I found means to conciliate the priests who were present, so that my foe was pelted instead of me. 'Tis true that he came the next morning to my house, thinking that he had to do with an abbé—like all other abbés."

"And what was the end of the affair?"

"We met in the Place Royale—Egad! you know about it."

"Was I not your second?" cried D'Artagnan.

"You were; you know how I settled the matter."

"Did he die?"

"I don't know. But, at all events, I gave him absolution in articulo mortis. 'Tis enough to kill the body, without killing the soul."

Bazin made a despairing sign which meant that while perhaps he approved the moral he altogether disapproved the tone in which it was uttered.

"Bazin, my friend," said Aramis, "you don't seem to be aware that I can see you in that mirror, and you forget that once for all I have forbidden all signs of approbation or disapprobation. You will do me the favor to bring us some Spanish wine and then to withdraw. Besides, my friend D'Artagnan has something to say to me privately, have you not, D'Artagnan?"

D'Artagnan nodded his head and Bazin retired, after placing on the table the Spanish wine.

The two friends, left alone, remained silent, face to face. Aramis seemed to await a comfortable digestion; D'Artagnan, to be preparing his exordium. Each of them, when the other was not looking, hazarded a sly glance. It was Aramis who broke the silence.

"What are you thinking of, D'Artagnan?" he began.

"I was thinking, my dear old friend, that when you were a musketeer you turned your thoughts incessantly to the church, and now that you are an abbé you are perpetually longing to be once more a musketeer."

"'Tis true; man, as you know," said Aramis, "is a strange animal, made up of contradictions. Since I became an abbé I dream of nothing but battles."

"That is apparent in your surroundings; you have rapiers here of every form and to suit the most exacting taste. Do you still fence well?"

"I—I fence as well as you did in the old time—better still, perhaps; I do nothing else all day."

"And with whom?"

"With an excellent master-at-arms that we have here."

"What! here?"

"Yes, here, in this convent, my dear fellow. There is everything in a Jesuit convent."

"Then you would have killed Monsieur de Marsillac if he had come alone to attack you, instead of at the head of twenty men?"

"Undoubtedly," said Aramis, "and even at the head of his twenty men, if I could have drawn without being recognized."

"God pardon me!" said D'Artagnan to himself, "I believe he has become more Gascon than I am!" Then aloud: "Well, my dear Aramis, do you ask me why I came to seek you?"

"No, I have not asked you that," said Aramis, with his subtle manner; "but I have expected you to tell me."

"Well, I sought you for the single purpose of offering you a chance to kill Monsieur de Marsillac whenever you please, prince though he is."

"Hold on! wait!" said Aramis; "that is an idea!"

"Of which I invite you to take advantage, my friend. Let us see; with your thousand crowns from the abbey and the twelve thousand francs you make by selling sermons, are you rich? Answer frankly."

"I? I am as poor as Job, and were you to search my pockets and my boxes I don't believe you would find a hundred pistoles."

"Peste! a hundred pistoles!" said D'Artagnan to himself; "he calls that being as poor as Job! If I had them I should think myself as rich as Croesus." Then aloud: "Are you ambitious?"

"As Enceladus."

"Well, my friend, I bring you the means of becoming rich, powerful, and free to do whatever you wish."

The shadow of a cloud passed over Aramis's face as quickly as that which in August passes over the field of grain; but quick as it was, it did not escape D'Artagnan's observation.

"Speak on," said Aramis.

"One question first. Do you take any interest in politics?"

A gleam of light shone in Aramis's eyes, as brief as the shadow that had passed over his face, but not so brief but that it was seen by D'Artagnan.

"No," Aramis replied.

"Then proposals from any quarter will be agreeable to you, since for the moment you have no master but God?"

"It is possible."

"Have you, my dear Aramis, thought sometimes of those happy, happy, happy days of youth we passed laughing, drinking, and fighting each other for play?"

"Certainly, and more than once regretted them; it was indeed a glorious time."

"Well, those splendidly wild days may chance to come again; I am commissioned to find out my companions and I began by you, who were the very soul of our society."

Aramis bowed, rather with respect than pleasure at the compliment.

"To meddle in politics," he exclaimed, in a languid voice, leaning back in his easy-chair. "Ah! dear D'Artagnan! see how regularly I live and how easy I am here. We have experienced the ingratitude of 'the great,' as you well know."

"'Tis true," replied D'Artagnan. "Yet the great sometimes repent of their ingratitude."

"In that case it would be quite another thing. Come! let's be merciful to every sinner! Besides, you are right in another respect, which is in thinking that if we were to meddle in politics there could not be a better time than the present."

"How can you know that? You who never interest yourself in politics?"

"Ah! without caring about them myself, I live among those who are much occupied in them. Poet as I am, I am intimate with Sarazin, who is devoted to the Prince de Conti, and with Monsieur de Bois-Robert, who, since the death of Cardinal Richelieu, is of all parties or any party; so that political discussions have not altogether been uninteresting to me."

"I have no doubt of it," said D'Artagnan.

"Now, my dear friend, look upon all I tell you as merely the statement of a monk—of a man who resembles an echo—repeating simply what he hears. I understand that Mazarin is at this very moment extremely uneasy as to the state of affairs; that his orders are not respected like those of our former bugbear, the deceased cardinal, whose portrait as you see hangs yonder—for whatever may be thought of him, it must be allowed that Richelieu was great."

"I will not contradict you there," said D'Artagnan.

"My first impressions were favorable to the minister; I said to myself that a minister is never loved, but that with the genius this one was said to have he would eventually triumph over his enemies and would make himself feared, which in my opinion is much more to be desired than to be loved——"

D'Artagnan made a sign with his head which indicated that he entirely approved that doubtful maxim.

"This, then," continued Aramis, "was my first opinion; but as I am very ignorant in matters of this kind and as the humility which I profess obliges me not to rest on my own judgment, but to ask the opinion of others, I have inquired—Eh!—my friend——"

Aramis paused.

"Well? what?" asked his friend.

"Well, I must mortify myself. I must confess that I was mistaken. Monsieur de Mazarin is not a man of genius, as I thought, he is a man of no origin—once a servant of Cardinal Bentivoglio, and he got on by intrigue. He is an upstart, a man of no name, who will only be the tool of a party in France. He will amass wealth, he will injure the king's revenue and pay to himself the pensions which Richelieu paid to others. He is neither a gentleman in manner nor in feeling, but a sort of buffoon, a punchinello, a pantaloon. Do you know him? I do not."

"Hem!" said D'Artagnan, "there is some truth in what you say."

"Ah! it fills me with pride to find that, thanks to a common sort of penetration with which I am endowed, I am approved by a man like you, fresh from the court."

"But you speak of him, not of his party, his resources."

"It is true—the queen is for him."

"Something in his favor."

"But he will never have the king."

"A mere child."

"A child who will be of age in four years. Then he has neither the parliament nor the people with him—they represent the wealth of the country; nor the nobles nor the princes, who are the military power of France."

D'Artagnan scratched his ear. He was forced to confess to himself that this reasoning was not only comprehensive, but just.

"You see, my poor friend, that I am sometimes bereft of my ordinary thoughtfulness; perhaps I am wrong in speaking thus to you, who have evidently a leaning to Mazarin."

"I!" cried D'Artagnan, "not in the least."

"You spoke of a mission."

"Did I? I was wrong then, no, I said what you say—there is a crisis at hand. Well! let's fly the feather before the wind; let us join with that side to which the wind will carry it and resume our adventurous life. We were once four valiant knights—four hearts fondly united; let us unite again, not our hearts, which have never been severed, but our courage and our fortunes. Here's a good opportunity for getting something better than a diamond."

"You are right, D'Artagnan; I held a similar project, but as I had not nor ever shall have your fruitful, vigorous imagination, the idea was suggested to me. Every one nowadays wants auxiliaries; propositions have been made to me and I confess to you frankly that the coadjutor has made me speak out."

"Monsieur de Gondy! the cardinal's enemy?"

"No; the king's friend," said Aramis; "the king's friend, you understand. Well, it is a question of serving the king, the gentleman's duty."

"But the king is with Mazarin."

"He is, but not willingly; in appearance, not heart; and that is exactly the snare the king's enemies are preparing for the poor child."

"Ah! but this is, indeed, civil war which you propose to me, dear Aramis."

"War for the king."

"Yet the king will be at the head of the army on Mazarin's side."

"But his heart will be in the army commanded by the Duc de Beaufort."

"Monsieur de Beaufort? He is at Vincennes."

"Did I say Monsieur de Beaufort? Monsieur de Beaufort or another. Monsieur de Beaufort or Monsieur le Prince."

"But Monsieur le Prince is to set out for the army; he is entirely devoted to the cardinal."

"Oh oh!" said Aramis, "there are questions between them at this very moment. And besides, if it is not the prince, then Monsieur de Gondy——"

"But Monsieur de Gondy is to be made a cardinal; they are soliciting the hat for him."

"And are there no cardinals that can fight? Come now, recall the four cardinals that at the head of armies have equalled Monsieur de Guebriant and Monsieur de Gassion."

"But a humpbacked general!

"Under the cuirass the hump will not be seen. Besides, remember that Alexander was lame and Hannibal had but one eye."

"Do you see any great advantage in adhering to this party?" asked D'Artagnan.

"I foresee in it the aid of powerful princes."

"With the enmity of the government."

"Counteracted by parliament and insurrections."

"That may be done if they can separate the king from his mother."

"That may be done," said Aramis.

"Never!" cried D'Artagnan. "You, Aramis, know Anne of Austria better than I do. Do you think she will ever forget that her son is her safeguard, her shield, the pledge for her dignity, for her fortune and her life? Should she forsake Mazarin she must join her son and go over to the princes' side; but you know better than I do that there are certain reasons why she can never abandon Mazarin."

"Perhaps you are right," said Aramis, thoughtfully; "therefore I shall not pledge myself."

"To them or to us, do you mean, Aramis?"

"To no one. I am a priest," resumed Aramis. "What have I to do with politics? I am not obliged to read any breviary. I have a jolly little circle of witty abbés and pretty women; everything goes on smoothly, so certainly, dear friend, I shall not meddle in politics."

"Well, listen, my dear Aramis," said D'Artagnan; "your philosophy convinces me, on my honor. I don't know what devil of an insect stung me and made me ambitious. I have a post by which I live; at the death of Monsieur de Tréville, who is old, I may be a captain, which is a very snug berth for a once penniless Gascon. Instead of running after adventures I shall accept an invitation from Porthos; I shall go and shoot on his estate. You know he has estates—Porthos?"

"I should think so, indeed. Ten leagues of wood, of marsh land and valleys; he is lord of the hill and the plain and is now carrying on a suit for his feudal rights against the Bishop of Noyon!"

"Good," said D'Artagnan to himself. "That's what I wanted to know. Porthos is in Picardy."

Then aloud:

"And he has taken his ancient name of Vallon?"

"To which he adds that of Bracieux, an estate which has been a barony, by my troth."

"So that Porthos will be a baron."

"I don't doubt it. The 'Baroness Porthos' will sound particularly charming."

And the two friends began to laugh.

"So," D'Artagnan resumed, "you will not become a partisan of Mazarin's?"

"Nor you of the Prince de Condé?"

"No, let us belong to no party, but remain friends; let us be neither Cardinalists nor Frondists."

"Adieu, then." And D'Artagnan poured out a glass of wine.

"To old times," he said.

"Yes," returned Aramis. "Unhappily, those times are past."

"Nonsense! They will return," said D'Artagnan. "At all events, if you want me, remember the Rue Tiquetonne, Hotel de la Chevrette."

"And I shall be at the convent of Jesuits; from six in the morning to eight at night come by the door. From eight in the evening until six in the morning come in by the window."

"Adieu, dear friend."

"Oh, I can't let you go so! I will go with you." And he took his sword and cloak.

"He wants to be sure that I go away," said D'Artagnan to himself.

Aramis whistled for Bazin, but Bazin was asleep in the ante-chamber, and Aramis was obliged to shake him by the ear to awake him.

Bazin stretched his arms, rubbed his eyes, and tried to go to sleep again.

"Come, come, sleepy head; quick, the ladder!"

"But," said Bazin, yawning portentously, "the ladder is still at the window."

"The other one, the gardener's. Didn't you see that Monsieur d'Artagnan mounted with difficulty? It will be even more difficult to descend."

D'Artagnan was about to assure Aramis that he could descend easily, when an idea came into his head which silenced him.

Bazin uttered a profound sigh and went out to look for the ladder. Presently a good, solid, wooden ladder was placed against the window.

"Now then," said D'Artagnan, "this is something like; this is a means of communication. A woman could go up a ladder like that."

Aramis's searching look seemed to seek his friend's thought even at the bottom of his heart, but D'Artagnan sustained the inquisition with an air of admirable simplicity. Besides, at that moment he put his foot on the first step of the ladder and began his descent. In a moment he was on the ground. Bazin remained at the window.

"Stay there," said Aramis; "I shall return immediately."

The two friends went toward the shed. At their approach Planchet came out leading the two horses.

"That is good to see," said Aramis. "There is a servant active and vigilant, not like that lazy fellow Bazin, who is no longer good for anything since he became connected with the church. Follow us, Planchet; we shall continue our conversation to the end of the village."

They traversed the width of the village, talking of indifferent things, then as they reached the last houses:

"Go, then, dear friend," said Aramis, "follow your own career. Fortune lavishes her smiles upon you; do not let her flee from your embrace. As for me, I remain in my humility and indolence. Adieu!"

"Thus 'tis quite decided," said D'Artagnan, "that what I have to offer to you does not tempt you?"

"On the contrary, it would tempt me were I any other man," rejoined Aramis; "but I repeat, I am made up of contradictions. What I hate to-day I adore to-morrow, and vice versa. You see that I cannot, like you, for instance, settle on any fixed plan."

"Thou liest, subtile one," said D'Artagnan to himself. "Thou alone, on the contrary, knowest how to choose thy object and to gain it stealthily."

The friends embraced. They descended into the plain by the ladder. Planchet met them hard by the shed. D'Artagnan jumped into the saddle, then the old companions in arms again shook hands. D'Artagnan and Planchet spurred their steeds and took the road to Paris.

But after he had gone about two hundred steps D'Artagnan stopped short, alighted, threw the bridle of his horse over the arm of Planchet and took the pistols from his saddle-bow to fasten them to his girdle.

"What's the matter?" asked Planchet.

"This is the matter: be he ever so cunning he shall never say I was his dupe. Stand here, don't stir, turn your back to the road and wait for me."

Having thus spoken, D'Artagnan cleared the ditch by the roadside and crossed the plain so as to wind around the village. He had observed between the house that Madame de Longueville inhabited and the convent of the Jesuits, an open space surrounded by a hedge.

The moon had now risen and he could see well enough to retrace his road.

He reached the hedge and hid himself behind it; in passing by the house where the scene which we have related took place, he remarked that the window was again lighted up and he was convinced that Aramis had not yet returned to his own apartment and that when he did it would not be alone.

In truth, in a few minutes he heard steps approaching and low whispers.

Close to the hedge the steps stopped.

D'Artagnan knelt down near the thickest part of the hedge.

Two men, to the astonishment of D'Artagnan, appeared shortly; soon, however, his surprise vanished, for he heard the murmurs of a soft, harmonious voice; one of these two men was a woman disguised as a cavalier.

"Calm yourself, dear Rene," said the soft voice, "the same thing will never happen again. I have discovered a sort of subterranean passage which runs beneath the street and we shall only have to raise one of the marble slabs before the door to open you an entrance and an outlet."

"Oh!" answered another voice, which D'Artagnan instantly recognized as that of Aramis. "I swear to you, princess, that if your reputation did not depend on precautions and if my life alone were jeopardized——"

"Yes, yes! I know you are as brave and venturesome as any man in the world, but you do not belong to me alone; you belong to all our party. Be prudent! sensible!"

"I always obey, madame, when I am commanded by so gentle a voice."

He kissed her hand tenderly.

"Ah!" exclaimed the cavalier with a soft voice.

"What's the matter?" asked Aramis.

"Do you not see that the wind has blown off my hat?"

Aramis rushed after the fugitive hat. D'Artagnan took advantage of the circumstance to find a place in the hedge not so thick, where his glance could penetrate to the supposed cavalier. At that instant, the moon, inquisitive, perhaps, like D'Artagnan, came from behind a cloud and by her light D'Artagnan recognized the large blue eyes, the golden hair and the classic head of the Duchess de Longueville.

Aramis returned, laughing, one hat on his head and the other in his hand; and he and his companion resumed their walk toward the convent.

"Good!" said D'Artagnan, rising and brushing his knees; "now I have thee—thou art a Frondeur and the lover of Madame de Longueville."

Chapter X.

Monsieur Porthos du Vallon de Bracieux de Pierrefonds.

Thanks to what Aramis had told him, D'Artagnan, who knew already that Porthos called himself Du Vallon, was now aware that he styled himself, from his estate, De Bracieux; and that he was, on account of this estate, engaged in a lawsuit with the Bishop of Noyon. It was, then, in the neighborhood of Noyon that he must seek that estate. His itinerary was promptly determined: he would go to Dammartin, from which place two roads diverge, one toward Soissons, the other toward Compiegne; there he would inquire concerning the Bracieux estate and go to the right or to the left according to the information obtained.

Planchet, who was still a little concerned for his safety after his recent escapade, declared that he would follow D'Artagnan even to the end of the world, either by the road to the right or by that to the left; only he begged his former master to set out in the evening, for greater security to himself. D'Artagnan suggested that he should send word to his wife, so that she might not be anxious about him, but Planchet replied with much sagacity that he was very sure his wife would not die of anxiety through not knowing where he was, while he, Planchet, remembering her incontinence of tongue, would die of anxiety if she did know.

This reasoning seemed to D'Artagnan so satisfactory that he no further insisted; and about eight o'clock in the evening, the time when the vapors of night begin to thicken in the streets, he left the Hotel de la Chevrette, and followed by Planchet set forth from the capital by way of the Saint Denis gate.

At midnight the two travelers were at Dammartin, but it was then too late to make inquiries—the host of the Cygne de la Croix had gone to bed.

The next morning D'Artagnan summoned the host, one of those sly Normans who say neither yes nor no and fear to commit themselves by giving a direct answer. D'Artagnan, however, gathered from his equivocal replies that the road to the right was the one he ought to take, and on that uncertain information he resumed his journey. At nine in the morning he reached Nanteuil and stopped for breakfast. His host here was a good fellow from Picardy, who gave him all the information he needed. The Bracieux estate was a few leagues from Villars-Cotterets.

D'Artagnan was acquainted with Villars-Cotterets, having gone thither with the court on several occasions; for at that time Villars-Cotterets was a royal residence. He therefore shaped his course toward that place and dismounted at the Dauphin d'Or. There he ascertained that the Bracieux estate was four leagues distant, but that Porthos was not at Bracieux. Porthos had, in fact, been involved in a dispute with the Bishop of Noyon in regard to the Pierrefonds property, which adjoined his own, and weary at length of a legal controversy which was beyond his comprehension, he put an end to it by purchasing Pierrefonds and added that name to his others. He now called himself Du Vallon de Bracieux de Pierrefonds, and resided on his new estate.

The travelers were therefore obliged to stay at the hotel until the next day; the horses had done ten leagues that day and needed rest. It is true they might have taken others, but there was a great forest to pass through and Planchet, as we have seen, had no liking for forests after dark.

There was another thing that Planchet had no liking for and that was starting on a journey with a hungry stomach. Accordingly, D'Artagnan, on awaking, found his breakfast waiting for him. It need not be said that Planchet in resuming his former functions resumed also his former humility and was not ashamed to make his breakfast on what was left by D'Artagnan.

It was nearly eight o'clock when they set out again. Their course was clearly defined: they were to follow the road toward Compiegne and on emerging from the forest turn to the right.

The morning was beautiful, and in this early springtime the birds sang on the trees and the sunbeams shone through the misty glades, like curtains of golden gauze.

In other parts of the forest the light could scarcely penetrate through the foliage, and the stems of two old oak trees, the refuge of the squirrel, startled by the travelers, were in deep shadow.

There came up from all nature in the dawn of day a perfume of herbs, flowers and leaves, which delighted the heart. D'Artagnan, sick of the closeness of Paris, thought that when a man had three names of his different estates joined one to another, he ought to be very happy in such a paradise; then he shook his head, saying, "If I were Porthos and D'Artagnan came to make me such a proposition as I am going to make to him, I know what I should say to it."

As to Planchet, he thought of little or nothing, but was happy as a hunting-hound in his old master's company.

At the extremity of the wood D'Artagnan perceived the road that had been described to him, and at the end of the road he saw the towers of an immense feudal castle.

"Oh! oh!" he said, "I fancied this castle belonged to the ancient branch of Orleans. Can Porthos have negotiated for it with the Duc de Longueville?"

"Faith!" exclaimed Planchet, "here's land in good condition; if it belongs to Monsieur Porthos I wish him joy."

"Zounds!" cried D'Artagnan, "don't call him Porthos, nor even Vallon; call him De Bracieux or De Pierrefonds; thou wilt knell out damnation to my mission otherwise."

As he approached the castle which had first attracted his eye, D'Artagnan was convinced that it could not be there that his friend dwelt; the towers, though solid and as if built yesterday, were open and broken. One might have fancied that some giant had cleaved them with blows from a hatchet.

On arriving at the extremity of the castle D'Artagnan found himself overlooking a beautiful valley, in which, at the foot of a charming little lake, stood several scattered houses, which, humble in their aspect, and covered, some with tiles, others with thatch, seemed to acknowledge as their sovereign lord a pretty chateau, built about the beginning of the reign of Henry IV., and surmounted by four stately, gilded weather-cocks. D'Artagnan no longer doubted that this was Porthos's pleasant dwelling place.

The road led straight up to the chateau which, compared to its ancestor on the hill, was exactly what a fop of the coterie of the Duc d'Enghein would have been beside a knight in steel armor in the time of Charles VII. D'Artagnan spurred his horse on and pursued his road, followed by Planchet at the same pace.

In ten minutes D'Artagnan reached the end of an alley regularly planted with fine poplars and terminating in an iron gate, the points and crossed bars of which were gilt. In the midst of this avenue was a nobleman, dressed in green and with as much gilding about him as the iron gate, riding on a tall horse. On his right hand and his left were two footmen, with the seams of their dresses laced. A considerable number of clowns were assembled and rendered homage to their lord.

"Ah!" said D'Artagnan to himself, "can this be the Seigneur du Vallon de Bracieux de Pierrefonds? Well-a-day! how he has shrunk since he gave up the name of Porthos!"

"This cannot be Monsieur Porthos," observed Planchet replying, as it were, to his master's thoughts. "Monsieur Porthos was six feet high; this man is scarcely five."

"Nevertheless," said D'Artagnan, "the people are bowing very low to this person."

As he spoke, he rode toward the tall horse—to the man of importance and his valets. As he approached he seemed to recognize the features of this individual.

"Jesu!" cried Planchet, "can it be?"

At this exclamation the man on horseback turned slowly and with a lofty air, and the two travelers could see, displayed in all their brilliancy, the large eyes, the vermilion visage, and the eloquent smile of—Mousqueton.

It was indeed Mousqueton—Mousqueton, as fat as a pig, rolling about with rude health, puffed out with good living, who, recognizing D'Artagnan and acting very differently from the hypocrite Bazin, slipped off his horse and approached the officer with his hat off, so that the homage of the assembled crowd was turned toward this new sun, which eclipsed the former luminary.

"Monsieur d'Artagnan! Monsieur d'Artagnan!" cried Mousqueton, his fat cheeks swelling out and his whole frame perspiring with joy; "Monsieur d'Artagnan! oh! what joy for my lord and master, Du Vallon de Bracieux de Pierrefonds!"

"Thou good Mousqueton! where is thy master?"

"You stand upon his property!"

"But how handsome thou art—how fat! thou hast prospered and grown stout!" and D'Artagnan could not restrain his astonishment at the change good fortune had produced on the once famished one.

"Hey, yes, thank God, I am pretty well," said Mousqueton.

"But hast thou nothing to say to thy friend Planchet?"

"How, my friend Planchet? Planchet—art thou there?" cried Mousqueton, with open arms and eyes full of tears.

"My very self," replied Planchet; "but I wanted first to see if thou wert grown proud."

"Proud toward an old friend? never, Planchet! thou wouldst not have thought so hadst thou known Mousqueton well."

"So far so well," answered Planchet, alighting, and extending his arms to Mousqueton, the two servants embraced with an emotion which touched those who were present and made them suppose that Planchet was a great lord in disguise, so highly did they estimate the position of Mousqueton.

"And now, sir," resumed Mousqueton, when he had rid himself of Planchet, who had in vain tried to clasp his hands behind his friend's fat back, "now, sir, allow me to leave you, for I could not permit my master to hear of your arrival from any but myself; he would never forgive me for not having preceded you."

"This dear friend," said D'Artagnan, carefully avoiding to utter either the former name borne by Porthos or his new one, "then he has not forgotten me?"

"Forgotten—he!" cried Mousqueton; "there's not a day, sir, that we don't expect to hear that you were made marshal either instead of Monsieur de Gassion, or of Monsieur de Bassompierre."

On D'Artagnan's lips there played one of those rare and melancholy smiles which seemed to emanate from the depth of his soul—the last trace of youth and happiness that had survived life's disillusions.

"And you—fellows," resumed Mousqueton, "stay near Monsieur le Comte d'Artagnan and pay him every attention in your power whilst I go to prepare my lord for his visit."

And mounting his horse Mousqueton rode off down the avenue on the grass at a hand gallop.

"Ah, there! there's something promising," said D'Artagnan. "No mysteries, no cloak to hide one's self in, no cunning policy here; people laugh outright, they weep for joy here. I see nothing but faces a yard broad; in short, it seems to me that nature herself wears a holiday garb, and that the trees, instead of leaves and flowers, are covered with red and green ribbons as on gala days."

"As for me," said Planchet, "I seem to smell, from this place, even, a most delectable perfume of fine roast meat, and to see the scullions in a row by the hedge, hailing our approach. Ah! sir, what a cook must Monsieur Pierrefonds have, when he was so fond of eating and drinking, even whilst he was only called Monsieur Porthos!"

"Say no more!" cried D'Artagnan. "If the reality corresponds with appearances I am lost; for a man so well off will never change his happy condition, and I shall fail with him, as I have already done with Aramis."

Chapter XI.

Wealth does not necessarily produce Happiness.

D'Artagnan passed through the iron gate and arrived in front of the chateau. He alighted as he saw a species of giant on the steps. Let us do justice to D'Artagnan. Independently of every selfish wish, his heart palpitated with joy when he saw that tall form and martial demeanor, which recalled to him a good and brave man.

He ran to Porthos and threw himself into his arms; the whole body of servants, arranged in a semi-circle at a respectful distance, looked on with humble curiosity. Mousqueton, at the head of them, wiped his eyes. Porthos linked his arm in that of his friend.

"Ah! how delightful to see you again, dear friend!" he cried, in a voice which was now changed from a baritone into a bass, "you've not then forgotten me?"

"Forget you! oh! dear Du Vallon, does one forget the happiest days of flowery youth, one's dearest friends, the dangers we have dared together? On the contrary, there is not an hour we have passed together that is not present to my memory."

"Yes, yes," said Porthos, trying to give to his mustache a curl which it had lost whilst he had been alone. "Yes, we did some fine things in our time and we gave that poor cardinal a few threads to unravel."

And he heaved a sigh.

"Under any circumstances," he resumed, "you are welcome, my dear friend; you will help me to recover my spirits; to-morrow we will hunt the hare on my plain, which is a superb tract of land, or pursue the deer in my woods, which are magnificent. I have four harriers which are considered the swiftest in the county, and a pack of hounds which are unequalled for twenty leagues around."

And Porthos heaved another sigh.

"But, first," interposed D'Artagnan, "you must present me to Madame du Vallon."

A third sigh from Porthos.

"I lost Madame du Vallon two years ago," he said, "and you find me still in affliction on that account. That was the reason why I left my Chateau du Vallon near Corbeil, and came to my estate, Bracieux. Poor Madame du Vallon! her temper was uncertain, but she came at last to accustom herself to my little ways and understand my little wishes."

"So you are free now, and rich?"

"Alas!" groaned Porthos, "I am a widower and have forty thousand francs a year. Let us go to breakfast."

"I shall be happy to do so; the morning air has made me hungry."

"Yes," said Porthos; "my air is excellent."

They went into the chateau; there was nothing but gilding, high and low; the cornices were gilt, the mouldings were gilt, the legs and arms of the chairs were gilt. A table, ready set out, awaited them.

"You see," said Porthos, "this is my usual style."

"Devil take me!" answered D'Artagnan, "I wish you joy of it. The king has nothing like it."

"No," answered Porthos, "I hear it said that he is very badly fed by the cardinal, Monsieur de Mazarin. Taste this cutlet, my dear D'Artagnan; 'tis off one of my sheep."

"You have very tender mutton and I wish you joy of it." said D'Artagnan.

"Yes, the sheep are fed in my meadows, which are excellent pasture."

"Give me another cutlet."

"No, try this hare, which I had killed yesterday in one of my warrens."

"Zounds! what a flavor!" cried D'Artagnan; "ah! they are fed on thyme only, your hares."

"And how do you like my wine?" asked Porthos; "it is pleasant, isn't it?"

"Capital!"

"It is nothing, however, but a wine of the country."

"Really?"

"Yes, a small declivity to the south, yonder on my hill, gives me twenty hogsheads."

"Quite a vineyard, hey?"

Porthos sighed for the fifth time—D'Artagnan had counted his sighs. He became curious to solve the problem.

"Well now," he said, "it seems, my dear friend, that something vexes you; you are ill, perhaps? That health, which——"

"Excellent, my dear friend; better than ever. I could kill an ox with a blow of my fist."

"Well, then, family affairs, perhaps?"

"Family! I have, happily, only myself in the world to care for."

"But what makes you sigh?"

"My dear fellow," replied Porthos, "to be candid with you, I am not happy."

"You are not happy, Porthos? You who have chateau, meadows, mountains, woods—you who have forty thousand francs a year—you—are—not—happy?"

"My dear friend, all those things I have, but I am a hermit in the midst of superfluity."

"Surrounded, I suppose, only by clodhoppers, with whom you could not associate."

Porthos turned rather pale and drank off a large glass of wine.

"No; but just think, there are paltry country squires who have all some title or another and pretend to go back as far as Charlemagne, or at least to Hugh Capet. When I first came here; being the last comer, it was for me to make the first advances. I made them, but you know, my dear friend, Madame du Vallon——"

Porthos, in pronouncing these words, seemed to gulp down something.

"Madame du Vallon was of doubtful gentility. She had, in her first marriage—I don't think, D'Artagnan, I am telling you anything new—married a lawyer; they thought that 'nauseous;' you can understand that's a word bad enough to make one kill thirty thousand men. I have killed two, which has made people hold their tongues, but has not made me their friend. So that I have no society; I live alone; I am sick of it—my mind preys on itself."

D'Artagnan smiled. He now saw where the breastplate was weak, and prepared the blow.

"But now," he said, "that you are a widower, your wife's connection cannot injure you."

"Yes, but understand me; not being of a race of historic fame, like the De Courcys, who were content to be plain sirs, or the Rohans, who didn't wish to be dukes, all these people, who are all either vicomtes or comtes go before me at church in all the ceremonies, and I can say nothing to them. Ah! If I only were a——"

"A baron, don't you mean?" cried D'Artagnan, finishing his friend's sentence.

"Ah!" cried Porthos; "would I were but a baron!"

"Well, my friend, I am come to give you this very title which you wish for so much."

Porthos gave a start that shook the room; two or three bottles fell and were broken. Mousqueton ran thither, hearing the noise.

Porthos waved his hand to Mousqueton to pick up the bottles.

"I am glad to see," said D'Artagnan, "that you have still that honest lad with you."

"He is my steward," replied Porthos; "he will never leave me. Go away now, Mouston."

"So he's called Mouston," thought D'Artagnan; "'tis too long a word to pronounce 'Mousqueton.'"

"Well," he said aloud, "let us resume our conversation later, your people may suspect something; there may be spies about. You can suppose, Porthos, that what I have to say relates to most important matters."

"Devil take them; let us walk in the park," answered Porthos, "for the sake of digestion."

"Egad," said D'Artagnan, "the park is like everything else and there are as many fish in your pond as rabbits in your warren; you are a happy man, my friend since you have not only retained your love of the chase, but acquired that of fishing."

"My friend," replied Porthos, "I leave fishing to Mousqueton,—it is a vulgar pleasure,—but I shoot sometimes; that is to say, when I am dull, and I sit on one of those marble seats, have my gun brought to me, my favorite dog, and I shoot rabbits."

"Really, how very amusing!"

"Yes," replied Porthos, with a sigh, "it is amusing."

D'Artagnan now no longer counted the sighs. They were innumerable.

"However, what had you to say to me?" he resumed; "let us return to that subject."

"With pleasure," replied D'Artagnan; "I must, however, first frankly tell you that you must change your mode of life."

"How?"

"Go into harness again, gird on your sword, run after adventures, and leave as in old times a little of your fat on the roadside."

"Ah! hang it!" said Porthos.

"I see you are spoiled, dear friend; you are corpulent, your arm has no longer that movement of which the late cardinal's guards have so many proofs."

"Ah! my fist is strong enough I swear," cried Porthos, extending a hand like a shoulder of mutton.

"So much the better."

"Are we then to go to war?"

"By my troth, yes."

"Against whom?"

"Are you a politician, friend?"

"Not in the least."

"Are you for Mazarin or for the princes?"

"I am for no one."

"That is to say, you are for us. Well, I tell you that I come to you from the cardinal."

This speech was heard by Porthos in the same sense as if it had still been in the year 1640 and related to the true cardinal.

"Ho! ho! What are the wishes of his eminence?"

"He wishes to have you in his service."

"And who spoke to him of me?"

"Rochefort—you remember him?"

"Yes, pardieu! It was he who gave us so much trouble and kept us on the road so much; you gave him three sword-wounds in three separate engagements."

"But you know he is now our friend?"

"No, I didn't know that. So he cherishes no resentment?"

"You are mistaken, Porthos," said D'Artagnan. "It is I who cherish no resentment."

Porthos didn't understand any too clearly; but then we know that understanding was not his strong point. "You say, then," he continued, "that the Count de Rochefort spoke of me to the cardinal?"

"Yes, and the queen, too."

"The queen, do you say?"

"To inspire us with confidence she has even placed in Mazarin's hands that famous diamond—you remember all about it—that I once sold to Monsieur des Essarts and of which, I don't know how, she has regained possession."

"But it seems to me," said Porthos, "that she would have done much better if she had given it back to you."

"So I think," replied D'Artagnan; "but kings and queens are strange beings and have odd fancies; nevertheless, since they are the ones who have riches and honors, we are devoted to them."

"Yes, we are devoted to them," repeated Porthos; "and you—to whom are you devoted now?"

"To the king, the queen, and to the cardinal; moreover, I have answered for your devotion also."

"And you say that you have made certain conditions on my behalf?"

"Magnificent, my dear fellow, magnificent! In the first place you have plenty of money, haven't you? forty thousand francs income, I think you said."

Porthos began to be suspicious. "Eh! my friend," said he, "one never has too much money. Madame du Vallon left things in much disorder; I am not much of a hand at figures, so that I live almost from hand to mouth."

"He is afraid I have come to borrow money," thought D'Artagnan. "Ah, my friend," said he, "it is all the better if you are in difficulties."

"How is it all the better?"

"Yes, for his eminence will give you all that you want—land, money, and titles."

"Ah! ah! ah!" said Porthos, opening his eyes at that last word.

"Under the other cardinal," continued D'Artagnan, "we didn't know enough to make our profits; this, however, doesn't concern you, with your forty thousand francs income, the happiest man in the world, it seems to me."

Porthos sighed.

"At the same time," continued D'Artagnan, "notwithstanding your forty thousand francs a year, and perhaps even for the very reason that you have forty thousand francs a year, it seems to me that a little coronet would do well on your carriage, hey?"

"Yes indeed," said Porthos.

"Well, my dear friend, win it—it is at the point of your sword. We shall not interfere with each other—your object is a title; mine, money. If I can get enough to rebuild Artagnan, which my ancestors, impoverished by the Crusades, allowed to fall into ruins, and to buy thirty acres of land about it, that is all I wish. I shall retire and die tranquilly—at home."

"For my part," said Porthos, "I desire to be made a baron."

"You shall be one."

"And have you not seen any of our other friends?"

"Yes, I have seen Aramis."

"And what does he wish? To be a bishop?"

"Aramis," answered D'Artagnan, who did not wish to undeceive Porthos, "Aramis, fancy, has become a monk and a Jesuit, and lives like a bear. My offers did not arouse him,—did not even tempt him."

"So much the worse! He was a clever man. And Athos?"

"I have not yet seen him. Do you know where I shall find him?"

"Near Blois. He is called Bragelonne. Only imagine, my dear friend. Athos, who was of as high birth as the emperor and who inherits one estate which gives him the title of comte, what is he to do with all those dignities—the Comte de la Fere, Comte de Bragelonne?"

"And he has no children with all these titles?"

"Ah!" said Porthos, "I have heard that he had adopted a young man who resembles him greatly."

"What, Athos? Our Athos, who was as virtuous as Scipio? Have you seen him?

"No."

"Well, I shall see him to-morrow and tell him about you; but I'm afraid, entre nous, that his liking for wine has aged and degraded him."

"Yes, he used to drink a great deal," replied Porthos.

"And then he was older than any of us," added D'Artagnan.

"Some years only. His gravity made him look older than he was."

"Well then, if we can get Athos, all will be well. If we cannot, we will do without him. We two are worth a dozen."

"Yes," said Porthos, smiling at the remembrance of his former exploits; "but we four, altogether, would be equal to thirty-six, more especially as you say the work will not be child's play. Will it last long?"

"By'r Lady! two or three years perhaps."

"So much the better," cried Porthos. "You have no idea, my friend, how my bones ache since I came here. Sometimes on a Sunday, I take a ride in the fields and on the property of my neighbours, in order to pick up a nice little quarrel, which I am really in want of, but nothing happens. Either they respect or they fear me, which is more likely, but they let me trample down the clover with my dogs, insult and obstruct every one, and I come back still more weary and low-spirited, that's all. At any rate, tell me: there's more chance of fighting in Paris, is there not?"

"In that respect, my dear friend, it's delightful. No more edicts, no more of the cardinal's guards, no more De Jussacs, nor other bloodhounds. I'Gad! underneath a lamp in an inn, anywhere, they ask 'Are you one of the Fronde?' They unsheathe, and that's all that is said. The Duke de Guise killed Monsieur de Coligny in the Place Royale and nothing was said of it."

"Ah, things go on gaily, then," said Porthos.

"Besides which, in a short time," resumed D'Artagnan, "We shall have set battles, cannonades, conflagrations and there will be great variety."

"Well, then, I decide."

"I have your word, then?"

"Yes, 'tis given. I shall fight heart and soul for Mazarin; but——"

"But?"

"But he must make me a baron."

"Zounds!" said D'Artagnan, "that's settled already; I will be responsible for the barony."

On this promise being given, Porthos, who had never doubted his friend's assurance, turned back with him toward the castle.

Chapter XII.

Porthos was Discontented with his Condition.

As they returned toward the castle, D'Artagnan thought of the miseries of poor human nature, always dissatisfied with what it has, ever desirous of what it has not.

In the position of Porthos, D'Artagnan would have been perfectly happy; and to make Porthos contented there was wanting—what? five letters to put before his three names, a tiny coronet to paint upon the panels of his carriage!

"I shall pass all my life," thought D'Artagnan, "in seeking for a man who is really contented with his lot."

Whilst making this reflection, chance seemed, as it were, to give him the lie direct. When Porthos had left him to give some orders he saw Mousqueton approaching. The face of the steward, despite one slight shade of care, light as a summer cloud, seemed a physiognomy of absolute felicity.

"Here is what I am looking for," thought D'Artagnan; "but alas! the poor fellow does not know the purpose for which I am here."

He then made a sign for Mousqueton to come to him.

"Sir," said the servant, "I have a favour to ask you."

"Speak out, my friend."

"I am afraid to do so. Perhaps you will think, sir, that prosperity has spoiled me?"

"Art thou happy, friend?" asked D'Artagnan.

"As happy as possible; and yet, sir, you may make me even happier than I am."

"Well, speak, if it depends on me."

"Oh, sir! it depends on you only."

"I listen—I am waiting to hear."

"Sir, the favor I have to ask of you is, not to call me 'Mousqueton' but 'Mouston.' Since I have had the honor of being my lord's steward I have taken the last name as more dignified and calculated to make my inferiors respect me. You, sir, know how necessary subordination is in any large establishment of servants."

D'Artagnan smiled; Porthos wanted to lengthen out his names, Mousqueton to cut his short.

"Well, my dear Mouston," he said, "rest satisfied. I will call thee Mouston; and if it makes thee happy I will not 'tutoyer' you any longer."

"Oh!" cried Mousqueton, reddening with joy; "if you do me, sir, such honor, I shall be grateful all my life; it is too much to ask."

"Alas!" thought D'Artagnan, "it is very little to offset the unexpected tribulations I am bringing to this poor devil who has so warmly welcomed me."

"Will monsieur remain long with us?" asked Mousqueton, with a serene and glowing countenance.

"I go to-morrow, my friend," replied D'Artagnan.

"Ah, monsieur," said Mousqueton, "then you have come here only to awaken our regrets."

"I fear that is true," said D'Artagnan, in a low tone.

D'Artagnan was secretly touched with remorse, not at inducing Porthos to enter into schemes in which his life and fortune would be in jeopardy, for Porthos, in the title of baron, had his object and reward; but poor Mousqueton, whose only wish was to be called Mouston—was it not cruel to snatch him from the delightful state of peace and plenty in which he was?

He was thinking of these matters when Porthos summoned him to dinner.

"What! to dinner?" said D'Artagnan. "What time is it, then?"

"Eh! why, it is after one o'clock."

"Your home is a paradise, Porthos; one takes no note of time. I follow you, though I am not hungry."

"Come, if one can't always eat, one can always drink—a maxim of poor Athos, the truth of which I have discovered since I began to be lonely."

D'Artagnan, who as a Gascon, was inclined to sobriety, seemed not so sure as his friend of the truth of Athos's maxim, but he did his best to keep up with his host. Meanwhile his misgivings in regard to Mousqueton recurred to his mind and with greater force because Mousqueton, though he did not himself wait on the table, which would have been beneath him in his new position, appeared at the door from time to time and evinced his gratitude to D'Artagnan by the quality of the wine he directed to be served. Therefore, when, at dessert, upon a sign from D'Artagnan, Porthos had sent away his servants and the two friends were alone:

"Porthos," said D'Artagnan, "who will attend you in your campaigns?"

"Why," replied Porthos, "Mouston, of course."

This was a blow to D'Artagnan. He could already see the intendant's beaming smile change to a contortion of grief. "But," he said, "Mouston is not so young as he was, my dear fellow; besides, he has grown fat and perhaps has lost his fitness for active service."

"That may be true," replied Porthos; "but I am used to him, and besides, he wouldn't be willing to let me go without him, he loves me so much."

"Oh, blind self-love!" thought D'Artagnan.

"And you," asked Porthos, "haven't you still in your service your old lackey, that good, that brave, that intelligent—-what, then, is his name?"

"Planchet—yes, I have found him again, but he is lackey no longer."

"What is he, then?"

"With his sixteen hundred francs—you remember, the sixteen hundred francs he earned at the siege of La Rochelle by carrying a letter to Lord de Winter—he has set up a little shop in the Rue des Lombards and is now a confectioner."

"Ah, he is a confectioner in the Rue des Lombards! How does it happen, then, that he is in your service?"

"He has been guilty of certain escapades and fears he may be disturbed." And the musketeer narrated to his friend Planchet's adventure.

"Well," said Porthos, "if any one had told you in the old times that the day would come when Planchet would rescue Rochefort and that you would protect him in it——"

"I should not have believed him; but men are changed by events."

"There is nothing truer than that," said Porthos; "but what does not change, or changes for the better, is wine. Taste of this; it is a Spanish wine which our friend Athos thought much of."

At that moment the steward came in to consult his master upon the proceedings of the next day and also with regard to the shooting party which had been proposed.

"Tell me, Mouston," said Porthos, "are my arms in good condition?"

"Your arms, my lord—what arms?"

"Zounds! my weapons."

"What weapons?"

"My military weapons."

"Yes, my lord; at any rate, I think so."

"Make sure of it, and if they want it, have them burnished up. Which is my best cavalry horse?"

"Vulcan."

"And the best hack?"

"Bayard."

"What horse dost thou choose for thyself?"

"I like Rustaud, my lord; a good animal, whose paces suit me."

"Strong, thinkest thou?"

"Half Norman, half Mecklenburger; will go night and day."

"That will do for us. See to these horses. Polish up or make some one else polish my arms. Then take pistols with thee and a hunting-knife."

"Are we then going to travel, my lord?" asked Mousqueton, rather uneasy.

"Something better still, Mouston."

"An expedition, sir?" asked the steward, whose roses began to change into lilies.

"We are going to return to the service, Mouston," replied Porthos, still trying to restore his mustache to the military curl it had long lost.

"Into the service—the king's service?" Mousqueton trembled; even his fat, smooth cheeks shook as he spoke, and he looked at D'Artagnan with an air of reproach; he staggered, and his voice was almost choked.

"Yes and no. We shall serve in a campaign, seek out all sorts of adventures—return, in short, to our former life."

These last words fell on Mousqueton like a thunderbolt. It was those very terrible old days that made the present so excessively delightful, and the blow was so great he rushed out, overcome, and forgot to shut the door.

The two friends remained alone to speak of the future and to build castles in the air. The good wine which Mousqueton had placed before them traced out in glowing drops to D'Artagnan a fine perspective, shining with quadruples and pistoles, and showed to Porthos a blue ribbon and a ducal mantle; they were, in fact, asleep on the table when the servants came to light them to their bed.

Mousqueton was, however, somewhat consoled by D'Artagnan, who the next day told him that in all probability war would always be carried on in the heart of Paris and within reach of the Chateau du Vallon, which was near Corbeil, or Bracieux, which was near Melun, and of Pierrefonds, which was between Compiegne and Villars-Cotterets.

"But—formerly—it appears," began Mousqueton timidly.

"Oh!" said D'Artagnan, "we don't now make war as we did formerly. To-day it's a sort of diplomatic arrangement; ask Planchet."

Mousqueton inquired, therefore, the state of the case of his old friend, who confirmed the statement of D'Artagnan. "But," he added, "in this war prisoners stand a chance of being hung."

"The deuce they do!" said Mousqueton; "I think I should like the siege of Rochelle better than this war, then!"

Porthos, meantime, asked D'Artagnan to give him his instructions how to proceed on his journey.

"Four days," replied his friend, "are necessary to reach Blois; one day to rest there; three or four days to return to Paris. Set out, therefore, in a week, with your suite, and go to the Hotel de la Chevrette, Rue Tiquetonne, and there await me."

"That's agreed," said Porthos.

"As to myself, I shall go around to see Athos; for though I don't think his aid worth much, one must with one's friends observe all due politeness," said D'Artagnan.

The friends then took leave of each other on the very border of the estate of Pierrefonds, to which Porthos escorted his friend.

"At least," D'Artagnan said to himself, as he took the road to Villars-Cotterets, "at least I shall not be alone in my undertaking. That devil, Porthos, is a man of prodigious strength; still, if Athos joins us, well, we shall be three of us to laugh at Aramis, that little coxcomb with his too good luck."

At Villars-Cotterets he wrote to the cardinal:

"My Lord,—I have already one man to offer to your eminence, and he is well worth twenty men. I am just setting out for Blois. The Comte de la Fere inhabits the Castle of Bragelonne, in the environs of that city."

Chapter XIII.

Two Angelic Faces.

The road was long, but the horses upon which D'Artagnan and Planchet rode had been refreshed in the well supplied stables of the Lord of Bracieux; the master and servant rode side by side, conversing as they went, for D'Artagnan had by degrees thrown off the master and Planchet had entirely ceased to assume the manners of a servant. He had been raised by circumstances to the rank of a confidant to his master. It was many years since D'Artagnan had opened his heart to any one; it happened, however, that these two men, on meeting again, assimilated perfectly. Planchet was in truth no vulgar companion in these new adventures; he was a man of uncommonly sound sense. Without courting danger he never shrank from an encounter; in short, he had been a soldier and arms ennoble a man; it was, therefore, on the footing of friends that D'Artagnan and Planchet arrived in the neighborhood of Blois.

Going along, D'Artagnan, shaking his head, said:

"I know that my going to Athos is useless and absurd; but still I owe this courtesy to my old friend, a man who had in him material for the most noble and generous of characters."

"Oh, Monsieur Athos was a noble gentleman," said Planchet, "was he not? Scattering money round about him as Heaven sprinkles rain. Do you remember, sir, that duel with the Englishman in the inclosure des Carmes? Ah! how lofty, how magnificent Monsieur Athos was that day, when he said to his adversary: 'You have insisted on knowing my name, sir; so much the worse for you, since I shall be obliged to kill you.' I was near him, those were his exact words, when he stabbed his foe as he said he would, and his adversary fell without saying, 'Oh!' 'Tis a noble gentleman—Monsieur Athos."

"Yes, true as Gospel," said D'Artagnan; "but one single fault has swallowed up all these fine qualities."

"I remember well," said Planchet, "he was fond of drinking—in truth, he drank, but not as other men drink. One seemed, as he raised the wine to his lips, to hear him say, 'Come, juice of the grape, and chase away my sorrows.' And how he used to break the stem of a glass or the neck of a bottle! There was no one like him for that."

"And now," replied D'Artagnan, "behold the sad spectacle that awaits us. This noble gentleman with his lofty glance, this handsome cavalier, so brilliant in feats of arms that every one was surprised that he held in his hand a sword only instead of a baton of command! Alas! we shall find him changed into a broken down old man, with garnet nose and eyes that slobber; we shall find him extended on some lawn, whence he will look at us with a languid eye and peradventure will not recognize us. God knows, Planchet, that I should fly from a sight so sad if I did not wish to show my respect for the illustrious shadow of what was once the Comte de la Fere, whom we loved so much."

Planchet shook his head and said nothing. It was evident that he shared his master's apprehensions.

"And then," resumed D'Artagnan, "to this decrepitude is probably added poverty, for he must have neglected the little that he had, and the dirty scoundrel, Grimaud, more taciturn than ever and still more drunken than his master—stay, Planchet, it breaks my heart to merely think of it."

"I fancy myself there and that I see him staggering and hear him stammering," said Planchet, in a piteous tone, "but at all events we shall soon know the real state of things, for I imagine that those lofty walls, now turning ruby in the setting sun, are the walls of Blois."

"Probably; and those steeples, pointed and sculptured, that we catch a glimpse of yonder, are similar to those that I have heard described at Chambord."

At this moment one of those heavy wagons, drawn by bullocks, which carry the wood cut in the fine forests of the country to the ports of the Loire, came out of a byroad full of ruts and turned on that which the two horsemen were following. A man carrying a long switch with a nail at the end of it, with which he urged on his slow team, was walking with the cart.

"Ho! friend," cried Planchet.

"What's your pleasure, gentlemen?" replied the peasant, with a purity of accent peculiar to the people of that district and which might have put to shame the cultured denizens of the Sorbonne and the Rue de l'Universite.

"We are looking for the house of Monsieur de la Fere," said D'Artagnan.

The peasant took off his hat on hearing this revered name.

"Gentlemen," he said, "the wood that I am carting is his; I cut it in his copse and I am taking it to the chateau."

D'Artagnan determined not to question this man; he did not wish to hear from another what he had himself said to Planchet.

"The chateau!" he said to himself, "what chateau? Ah, I understand! Athos is not a man to be thwarted; he, like Porthos, has obliged his peasantry to call him 'my lord,' and to dignify his pettifogging place by the name of chateau. He had a heavy hand—dear old Athos—after drinking."

D'Artagnan, after asking the man the right way, continued his route, agitated in spite of himself at the idea of seeing once more that singular man whom he had so truly loved and who had contributed so much by advice and example to his education as a gentleman. He checked by degrees the speed of his horse and went on, his head drooping as if in deep thought.

Soon, as the road turned, the Chateau de la Valliere appeared in view; then, a quarter of a mile beyond, a white house, encircled in sycamores, was visible at the farther end of a group of trees, which spring had powdered with a snow of flowers.

On beholding this house, D'Artagnan, calm as he was in general, felt an unusual disturbance within his heart—so powerful during the whole course of life are the recollections of youth. He proceeded, nevertheless, and came opposite to an iron gate, ornamented in the taste of the period.

Through the gate was seen kitchen-gardens, carefully attended to, a spacious courtyard, in which neighed several horses held by valets in various liveries, and a carriage, drawn by two horses of the country.

"We are mistaken," said D'Artagnan. "This cannot be the establishment of Athos. Good heavens! suppose he is dead and that this property now belongs to some one who bears his name. Alight, Planchet, and inquire, for I confess that I have scarcely courage so to do."

Planchet alighted.

"Thou must add," said D'Artagnan, "that a gentleman who is passing by wishes to have the honor of paying his respects to the Comte de la Fere, and if thou art satisfied with what thou hearest, then mention my name!"

Planchet, leading his horse by the bridle, drew near to the gate and rang the bell, and immediately a servant-man with white hair and of erect stature, notwithstanding his age, presented himself.

"Does Monsieur le Comte de la Fere live here?" asked Planchet.

"Yes, monsieur, it is here he lives," the servant replied to Planchet, who was not in livery.

"A nobleman retired from service, is he not?"

"Yes."

"And who had a lackey named Grimaud?" persisted Planchet, who had prudently considered that he couldn't have too much information.

"Monsieur Grimaud is absent from the chateau for the time being," said the servitor, who, little used as he was to such inquiries, began to examine Planchet from head to foot.

"Then," cried Planchet joyously, "I see well that it is the same Comte de la Fere whom we seek. Be good enough to open to me, for I wish to announce to monsieur le comte that my master, one of his friends, is here, and wishes to greet him."

"Why didn't you say so?" said the servitor, opening the gate. "But where is your master?"

"He is following me."

The servitor opened the gate and walked before Planchet, who made a sign to D'Artagnan. The latter, his heart palpitating more than ever, entered the courtyard without dismounting.

Whilst Planchet was standing on the steps before the house he heard a voice say:

"Well, where is this gentleman and why do they not bring him here?"

This voice, the sound of which reached D'Artagnan, reawakened in his heart a thousand sentiments, a thousand recollections that he had forgotten. He vaulted hastily from his horse, whilst Planchet, with a smile on his lips, advanced toward the master of the house.

"But I know you, my lad," said Athos, appearing on the threshold.

"Oh, yes, monsieur le comte, you know me and I know you. I am Planchet—Planchet, whom you know well." But the honest servant could say no more, so much was he overcome by this unexpected interview.

"What, Planchet, is Monsieur d'Artagnan here?"

"Here I am, my friend, dear Athos!" cried D'Artagnan, in a faltering voice and almost staggering from agitation.

At these words a visible emotion was expressed on the beautiful countenance and calm features of Athos. He rushed toward D'Artagnan with eyes fixed upon him and clasped him in his arms. D'Artagnan, equally moved, pressed him also closely to him, whilst tears stood in his eyes. Athos then took him by the hand and led him into the drawing-room, where there were several people. Every one arose.

"I present to you," he said, "Monsieur le Chevalier D'Artagnan, lieutenant of his majesty's musketeers, a devoted friend and one of the most excellent, brave gentlemen that I have ever known."

D'Artagnan received the compliments of those who were present in his own way, and whilst the conversation became general he looked earnestly at Athos.

Strange! Athos was scarcely aged at all! His fine eyes, no longer surrounded by that dark line which nights of dissipation pencil too infallibly, seemed larger, more liquid than ever. His face, a little elongated, had gained in calm dignity what it had lost in feverish excitement. His hand, always wonderfully beautiful and strong, was set off by a ruffle of lace, like certain hands by Titian and Vandyck. He was less stiff than formerly. His long, dark hair, softly powdered here and there with silver tendrils, fell elegantly over his shoulders in wavy curls; his voice was still youthful, as if belonging to a Hercules of twenty-five, and his magnificent teeth, which he had preserved white and sound, gave an indescribable charm to his smile.

Meanwhile the guests, seeing that the two friends were longing to be alone, prepared to depart, when a noise of dogs barking resounded through the courtyard and many persons said at the same moment:

"Ah! 'tis Raoul, who is come home."

Athos, as the name of Raoul was pronounced, looked inquisitively at D'Artagnan, in order to see if any curiosity was painted on his face. But D'Artagnan was still in confusion and turned around almost mechanically when a fine young man of fifteen years of age, dressed simply, but in perfect taste, entered the room, raising, as he came, his hat, adorned with a long plume of scarlet feathers.

Nevertheless, D'Artagnan was struck by the appearance of this new personage. It seemed to explain to him the change in Athos; a resemblance between the boy and the man explained the mystery of this regenerated existence. He remained listening and gazing.

"Here you are, home again, Raoul," said the comte.

"Yes, sir," replied the youth, with deep respect, "and I have performed the commission that you gave me."

"But what's the matter, Raoul?" said Athos, very anxiously. "You are pale and agitated."

"Sir," replied the young man, "it is on account of an accident which has happened to our little neighbor."

"To Mademoiselle de la Vallière?" asked Athos, quickly.

"What is it?" cried many persons present.

"She was walking with her nurse Marceline, in the place where the woodmen cut the wood, when, passing on horseback, I stopped. She saw me also and in trying to jump from the end of a pile of wood on which she had mounted, the poor child fell and was not able to rise again. I fear that she has badly sprained her ankle."

"Oh, heavens!" cried Athos. "And her mother, Madame de Saint-Remy, have they yet told her of it?"

"No, sir, Madame de Saint-Remy is at Blois with the Duchess of Orleans. I am afraid that what was first done was unskillful, if not worse than useless. I am come, sir, to ask your advice."

"Send directly to Blois, Raoul; or, rather, take horse and ride immediately yourself."

Raoul bowed.

"But where is Louise?" asked the comte.

"I have brought her here, sir, and I have deposited her in charge of Charlotte, who, till better advice comes, has bathed the foot in cold well-water."

The guests now all took leave of Athos, excepting the old Duc de Barbe, who, as an old friend of the family of La Vallière, went to see little Louise and offered to take her to Blois in his carriage.

"You are right, sir," said Athos. "She will be the sooner with her mother. As for you, Raoul, I am sure it is your fault, some giddiness or folly."

"No, sir, I assure you," muttered Raoul, "it is not."

"Oh, no, no, I declare it is not!" cried the young girl, while Raoul turned pale at the idea of his being perhaps the cause of her disaster.

"Nevertheless, Raoul, you must go to Blois and you must make your excuses and mine to Madame de Saint-Remy."

The youth looked pleased. He again took in his strong arms the little girl, whose pretty golden head and smiling face rested on his shoulder, and placed her gently in the carriage; then jumping on his horse with the elegance of a first-rate esquire, after bowing to Athos and D'Artagnan, he went off close by the door of the carriage, on somebody inside of which his eyes were riveted.

Chapter XIV.

The Castle of Bragelonne.

Whilst this scene was going on, D'Artagnan remained with open mouth and a confused gaze. Everything had turned out so differently from what he expected that he was stupefied with wonder.

Athos, who had been observing him and guessing his thoughts, took his arm and led him into the garden.

"Whilst supper is being prepared," he said, smiling, "you will not, my friend, be sorry to have the mystery which so puzzles you cleared up."

"True, monsieur le comte," replied D'Artagnan, who felt that by degrees Athos was resuming that great influence which aristocracy had over him.

Athos smiled.

"First and foremost, dear D'Artagnan, we have no title such as count here. When I call you 'chevalier,' it is in presenting you to my guests, that they may know who you are. But to you, D'Artagnan, I am, I hope, still dear Athos, your comrade, your friend. Do you intend to stand on ceremony because you are less attached to me than you were?"

"Oh! God forbid!"

"Then let us be as we used to be; let us be open with each other. You are surprised at what you see here?"

"Extremely."

"But above all things, I am a marvel to you?"

"I confess it."

"I am still young, am I not? Should you not have known me again, in spite of my eight-and-forty years of age?"

"On the contrary, I do not find you the same person at all."

"I understand," cried Athos, with a gentle blush. "Everything, D'Artagnan, even folly, has its limit."

"Then your means, it appears, are improved; you have a capital house—your own, I presume? You have a park, and horses, servants."

Athos smiled.

"Yes, I inherited this little property when I quitted the army, as I told you. The park is twenty acres—twenty, comprising kitchen-gardens and a common. I have two horses,—I do not count my servant's bobtailed nag. My sporting dogs consist of two pointers, two harriers and two setters. But then all this extravagance is not for myself," added Athos, laughing.

"Yes, I see, for the young man Raoul," said D'Artagnan.

"You guess aright, my friend; this youth is an orphan, deserted by his mother, who left him in the house of a poor country priest. I have brought him up. It is Raoul who has worked in me the change you see; I was dried up like a miserable tree, isolated, attached to nothing on earth; it was only a deep affection that could make me take root again and drag me back to life. This child has caused me to recover what I had lost. I had no longer any wish to live for myself, I have lived for him. I have corrected the vices that I had; I have assumed the virtues that I had not. Precept something, but example more. I may be mistaken, but I believe that Raoul will be as accomplished a gentleman as our degenerate age could display."

The remembrance of Milady recurred to D'Artagnan.

"And you are happy?" he said to his friend.

"As happy as it is allowed to one of God's creatures to be on this earth; but say out all you think, D'Artagnan, for you have not yet done so."

"You are too bad, Athos; one can hide nothing from you," answered D'Artagnan. "I wished to ask you if you ever feel any emotions of terror resembling——"

"Remorse! I finish your phrase. Yes and no. I do not feel remorse, because that woman, I profoundly hold, deserved her punishment. Had she one redeeming trait? I doubt it. I do not feel remorse, because had we allowed her to live she would have persisted in her work of destruction. But I do not mean, my friend that we were right in what we did. Perhaps all blood demands some expiation. Hers had been accomplished; it remains, possibly, for us to accomplish ours."

"I have sometimes thought as you do, Athos."

"She had a son, that unhappy woman?"

"Yes."

"Have you ever heard of him?"

"Never."

"He must be about twenty-three years of age," said Athos, in a low tone. "I often think of that young man, D'Artagnan."

"Strange! for I had forgotten him," said the lieutenant.

Athos smiled; the smile was melancholy.

"And Lord de Winter—do you know anything about him?"

"I know that he is in high favor with Charles I."

"The fortunes of that monarch now are at low water. He shed the blood of Strafford; that confirms what I said just now—blood will have blood. And the queen?"

"What queen?"

"Madame Henrietta of England, daughter of Henry IV."

"She is at the Louvre, as you know."

"Yes, and I hear in bitter poverty. Her daughter, during the severest cold, was obliged for want of fire to remain in bed. Do you grasp that?" said Athos, shrugging his shoulders; "the daughter of Henry IV. shivering for want of a fagot! Why did she not ask from any one of us a home instead of from Mazarin? She should have wanted nothing."

"Have you ever seen the queen of England?" inquired D'Artagnan.

"No; but my mother, as a child, saw her. Did I ever tell you that my mother was lady of honor to Marie de Medici?"

"Never. You know, Athos, you never spoke much of such matters."

"Ah, mon Dieu, yes, you are right," Athos replied; "but then there must be some occasion for speaking."

"Porthos wouldn't have waited for it so patiently," said D'Artagnan, with a smile.

"Every one according to his nature, my dear D'Artagnan. Porthos, in spite of a touch of vanity, has many excellent qualities. Have you seen him?"

"I left him five days ago," said D'Artagnan, and he portrayed with Gascon wit and sprightliness the magnificence of Porthos in his Chateau of Pierrefonds; nor did he neglect to launch a few arrows of wit at the excellent Monsieur Mouston.

"I sometimes wonder," replied Athos, smiling at that gayety which recalled the good old days, "that we could form an association of men who would be, after twenty years of separation, still so closely bound together. Friendship throws out deep roots in honest hearts, D'Artagnan. Believe me, it is only the evil-minded who deny friendship; they cannot understand it. And Aramis?"

"I have seen him also," said D'Artagnan; "but he seemed to me cold."

"Ah, you have seen Aramis?" said Athos, turning on D'Artagnan a searching look. "Why, it is a veritable pilgrimage, my dear friend, that you are making to the Temple of Friendship, as the poets would say."

"Why, yes," replied D'Artagnan, with embarrassment.

"Aramis, you know," continued Athos, "is naturally cold, and then he is always involved in intrigues with women."

"I believe he is at this moment in a very complicated one," said D'Artagnan.

Athos made no reply.

"He is not curious," thought D'Artagnan.

Athos not only failed to reply, he even changed the subject of conversation.

"You see," said he, calling D'Artagnan's attention to the fact that they had come back to the chateau after an hour's walk, "we have made a tour of my domains."

"All is charming and everything savors of nobility," replied D'Artagnan.

At this instant they heard the sound of horses' feet.

"'Tis Raoul who has come back," said Athos; "and we can now hear how the poor child is."

In fact, the young man appeared at the gate, covered with dust, entered the courtyard, leaped from his horse, which he consigned to the charge of a groom, and then went to greet the count and D'Artagnan.

"Monsieur," said Athos, placing his hand on D'Artagnan's shoulder, "monsieur is the Chevalier D'Artagnan of whom you have often heard me speak, Raoul."

"Monsieur," said the young man, saluting again and more profoundly, "monsieur le comte has pronounced your name before me as an example whenever he wished to speak of an intrepid and generous gentleman."

That little compliment could not fail to move D'Artagnan. He extended a hand to Raoul and said:

"My young friend, all the praises that are given me should be passed on to the count here; for he has educated me in everything and it is not his fault that his pupil profited so little from his instructions. But he will make it up in you I am sure. I like your manner, Raoul, and your politeness has touched me."

Athos was more delighted than can be told. He looked at D'Artagnan with an expression of gratitude and then bestowed on Raoul one of those strange smiles, of which children are so proud when they receive them.

"Now," said D'Artagnan to himself, noticing that silent play of countenance, "I am sure of it."

"I hope the accident has been of no consequence?"

"They don't yet know, sir, on account of the swelling; but the doctor is afraid some tendon has been injured."

At this moment a little boy, half peasant, half foot-boy, came to announce supper.

Athos led his guest into a dining-room of moderate size, the windows of which opened on one side on a garden, on the other on a hot-house full of magnificent flowers.

D'Artagnan glanced at the dinner service. The plate was magnificent, old, and appertaining to the family. D'Artagnan stopped to look at a sideboard on which was a superb ewer of silver.

"That workmanship is divine!" he exclaimed.

"Yes, a chef d'oeuvre of the great Florentine sculptor, Benvenuto Cellini," replied Athos.

"What battle does it represent?"

"That of Marignan, just at the point where one of my forefathers is offering his sword to Francis I., who has broken his. It was on that occasion that my ancestor, Enguerrand de la Fere, was made a knight of the Order of St. Michael; besides which, the king, fifteen years afterward, gave him also this ewer and a sword which you may have seen formerly in my house, also a lovely specimen of workmanship. Men were giants in those times," said Athos; "now we are pigmies in comparison. Let us sit down to supper. Call Charles," he added, addressing the boy who waited.

"My good Charles, I particularly recommend to your care Planchet, the laquais of Monsieur D'Artagnan. He likes good wine; now you have the key of the cellar. He has slept a long time on a hard bed, so he won't object to a soft one; take every care of him, I beg of you." Charles bowed and retired.

"You think of everything," said D'Artagnan; "and I thank you for Planchet, my dear Athos."

Raoul stared on hearing this name and looked at the count to be quite sure that it was he whom the lieutenant thus addressed.

"That name sounds strange to you," said Athos, smiling; "it was my nom de guerre when Monsieur D'Artagnan, two other gallant friends and myself performed some feats of arms at the siege of La Rochelle, under the deceased cardinal and Monsieur de Bassompierre. My friend is still so kind as to address me by that old and well beloved appellation, which makes my heart glad when I hear it."

"'Tis an illustrious name," said the lieutenant, "and had one day triumphal honors paid to it."

"What do you mean, sir?" inquired Raoul.

"You have not forgotten St. Gervais, Athos, and the napkin which was converted into a banner?" and he then related to Raoul the story of the bastion, and Raoul fancied he was listening to one of those deeds of arms belonging to days of chivalry, so gloriously recounted by Tasso and Ariosto.

"D'Artagnan does not tell you, Raoul," said Athos, in his turn, "that he was reckoned one of the finest swordsmen of his time—a knuckle of iron, a wrist of steel, a sure eye and a glance of fire; that's what his adversary met with. He was eighteen, only three years older than you are, Raoul, when I saw him set to work, pitted against tried men."

"And did Monsieur D'Artagnan come off the conqueror?" asked the young man, with glistening eye.

"I killed one man, if I recollect rightly," replied D'Artagnan, with a look of inquiry directed to Athos; "another I disarmed or wounded, I don't remember which."

"Wounded!" said Athos; "it was a phenomenon of skill."

The young man would willingly have prolonged this conversation far into the night, but Athos pointed out to him that his guest must need repose. D'Artagnan would fain have declared that he was not fatigued, but Athos insisted on his retiring to his chamber, conducted thither by Raoul.

Chapter XV.

Athos as a Diplomatist.

D'Artagnan retired to bed—not to sleep, but to think over all he had heard that evening. Being naturally goodhearted, and having had once a liking for Athos, which had grown into a sincere friendship, he was delighted at thus meeting a man full of intelligence and moral strength, instead of a drunkard. He admitted without annoyance the continued superiority of Athos over himself, devoid as he was of that jealousy which might have saddened a less generous disposition; he was delighted also that the high qualities of Athos appeared to promise favorably for his mission. Nevertheless, it seemed to him that Athos was not in all respects sincere and frank. Who was the youth he had adopted and who bore so striking a resemblance to him? What could explain Athos's having re-entered the world and the extreme sobriety he had observed at table? The absence of Grimaud, whose name had never once been uttered by Athos, gave D'Artagnan uneasiness. It was evident either that he no longer possessed the confidence of his friend, or that Athos was bound by some invisible chain, or that he had been forewarned of the lieutenant's visit.

He could not help thinking of M. Rochefort, whom he had seen in Notre Dame; could De Rochefort have forestalled him with Athos? Again, the moderate fortune which Athos possessed, concealed as it was, so skillfully, seemed to show a regard for appearances and to betray a latent ambition which might be easily aroused. The clear and vigorous intellect of Athos would render him more open to conviction than a less able man would be. He would enter into the minister's schemes with the more ardor, because his natural activity would be doubled by necessity.

Resolved to seek an explanation on all these points on the following day, D'Artagnan, in spite of his fatigue, prepared for an attack and determined that it should take place after breakfast. He determined to cultivate the good-will of the youth Raoul and, either whilst fencing with him or when out shooting, to extract from his simplicity some information which would connect the Athos of old times with the Athos of the present. But D'Artagnan at the same time, being a man of extreme caution, was quite aware what injury he should do himself, if by any indiscretion or awkwardness he should betray has manoeuvering to the experienced eye of Athos. Besides, to tell truth, whilst D'Artagnan was quite disposed to adopt a subtle course against the cunning of Aramis or the vanity of Porthos, he was ashamed to equivocate with Athos, true-hearted, open Athos. It seemed to him that if Porthos and Aramis deemed him superior to them in the arts of diplomacy, they would like him all the better for it; but that Athos, on the contrary, would despise him.

"Ah! why is not Grimaud, the taciturn Grimaud, here?" thought D'Artagnan, "there are so many things his silence would have told me; with Grimaud silence was another form of eloquence!"

There reigned a perfect stillness in the house. D'Artagnan had heard the door shut and the shutters barred; the dogs became in their turn silent. At last a nightingale, lost in a thicket of shrubs, in the midst of its most melodious cadences had fluted low and lower into stillness and fallen asleep. Not a sound was heard in the castle, except of a footstep up and down, in the chamber above—as he supposed, the bedroom of Athos.

"He is walking about and thinking," thought D'Artagnan; "but of what? It is impossible to know; everything else might be guessed, but not that."

At length Athos went to bed, apparently, for the noise ceased.

Silence and fatigue together overcame D'Artagnan and sleep overtook him also. He was not, however, a good sleeper. Scarcely had dawn gilded his window curtains when he sprang out of bed and opened the windows. Somebody, he perceived, was in the courtyard, moving stealthily. True to his custom of never passing anything over that it was within his power to know, D'Artagnan looked out of the window and perceived the close red coat and brown hair of Raoul.

The young man was opening the door of the stable. He then, with noiseless haste, took out the horse that he had ridden on the previous evening, saddled and bridled it himself and led the animal into the alley to the right of the kitchen-garden, opened a side door which conducted him to a bridle road, shut it after him, and D'Artagnan saw him pass by like a dart, bending, as he went, beneath the pendent flowery branches of maple and acacia. The road, as D'Artagnan had observed, was the way to Blois.

"So!" thought the Gascon "here's a young blade who has already his love affair, who doesn't at all agree with Athos in his hatred to the fair sex. He's not going to hunt, for he has neither dogs nor arms; he's not going on a message, for he goes secretly. Why does he go in secret? Is he afraid of me or of his father? for I am sure the count is his father. By Jove! I shall know about that soon, for I shall soon speak out to Athos."

Day was now advanced; all the noises that had ceased the night before reawakened, one after the other. The bird on the branch, the dog in his kennel, the sheep in the field, the boats moored in the Loire, even, became alive and vocal. The latter, leaving the shore, abandoned themselves gaily to the current. The Gascon gave a last twirl to his mustache, a last turn to his hair, brushed, from habit, the brim of his hat with the sleeve of his doublet, and went downstairs. Scarcely had he descended the last step of the threshold when he saw Athos bent down toward the ground, as if he were looking for a crown-piece in the dust.

"Good-morning, my dear host," cried D'Artagnan.

"Good-day to you; have you slept well?"

"Excellently, Athos, but what are you looking for? You are perhaps a tulip fancier?"

"My dear friend, if I am, you must not laugh at me for being so. In the country people alter; one gets to like, without knowing it, all those beautiful objects that God causes to spring from the earth, which are despised in cities. I was looking anxiously for some iris roots I planted here, close to this reservoir, and which some one has trampled upon this morning. These gardeners are the most careless people in the world; in bringing the horse out to the water they've allowed him to walk over the border."

D'Artagnan began to smile.

"Ah! you think so, do you?"

And he took his friend along the alley, where a number of tracks like those which had trampled down the flowerbeds, were visible.

"Here are the horse's hoofs again, it seems, Athos," he said carelessly.

"Yes, indeed, the marks are recent."

"Quite so," replied the lieutenant.

"Who went out this morning?" Athos asked, uneasily. "Has any horse got loose?"

"Not likely," answered the Gascon; "these marks are regular."

"Where is Raoul?" asked Athos; "how is it that I have not seen him?"

"Hush!" exclaimed D'Artagnan, putting his finger on his lips; and he related what he had seen, watching Athos all the while.

"Ah, he's gone to Blois; the poor boy——"

"Wherefore?"

"Ah, to inquire after the little La Valliere; she has sprained her foot, you know."

"You think he has?"

"I am sure of it," said Athos; "don't you see that Raoul is in love?"

"Indeed! with whom—with a child seven years old?"

"Dear friend, at Raoul's age the heart is so expansive that it must encircle one object or another, fancied or real. Well, his love is half real, half fanciful. She is the prettiest little creature in the world, with flaxen hair, blue eyes,—at once saucy and languishing."

"But what say you to Raoul's fancy?"

"Nothing—I laugh at Raoul; but this first desire of the heart is imperious. I remember, just at his age, how deep in love I was with a Grecian statue which our good king, then Henry IV., gave my father, insomuch that I was mad with grief when they told me that the story of Pygmalion was nothing but a fable."

"It is mere want of occupation. You do not make Raoul work, so he takes his own way of employing himself."

"Exactly; therefore I think of sending him away from here."

"You will be wise to do so."

"No doubt of it; but it will break his heart. So long as three or four years ago he used to adorn and adore his little idol, whom he will some day fall in love with in right earnest if he remains here. The parents of little La Valliere have for a long time perceived and been amused at it; now they begin to look concerned."

"Nonsense! However, Raoul must be diverted from this fancy. Send him away or you will never make a man of him."

"I think I shall send him to Paris."

"So!" thought D'Artagnan, and it seemed to him that the moment for attack had arrived.

"Suppose," he said, "we roughly chalk out a career for this young man. I wish to consult you about some thing."

"Do so."

"Do you think it is time for us to enter the service?"

"But are you not still in the service—you, D'Artagnan?"

"I mean active service. Our former life, has it still no attractions for you? would you not be happy to begin anew in my society and in that of Porthos, the exploits of our youth?"

"Do you propose to me to do so, D'Artagnan?"

"Decidedly and honestly."

"On whose side?" asked Athos, fixing his clear, benevolent glance on the countenance of the Gascon.

"Ah, devil take it, you speak in earnest——"

"And must have a definite answer. Listen, D'Artagnan. There is but one person, or rather, one cause, to whom a man like me can be useful—that of the king."

"Exactly," answered the musketeer.

"Yes, but let us understand each other," returned Athos, seriously. "If by the cause of the king you mean that of Monsieur de Mazarin, we do not understand each other."

"I don't say exactly," answered the Gascon, confused.

"Come, D'Artagnan, don't let us play a sidelong game; your hesitation, your evasion, tells me at once on whose side you are; for that party no one dares openly to recruit, and when people recruit for it, it is with averted eyes and humble voice."

"Ah! my dear Athos!"

"You know that I am not alluding to you; you are the pearl of brave, bold men. I speak of that spiteful and intriguing Italian—of the pedant who has tried to put on his own head a crown which he stole from under a pillow—of the scoundrel who calls his party the party of the king—who wants to send the princes of the blood to prison, not daring to kill them, as our great cardinal— our cardinal did—of the miser, who weighs his gold pieces and keeps the clipped ones for fear, though he is rich, of losing them at play next morning— of the impudent fellow who insults the queen, as they say—so much the worse for her—and who is going in three months to make war upon us, in order that he may retain his pensions; is that the master whom you propose to me? I thank you, D'Artagnan."

"You are more impetuous than you were," returned D'Artagnan. "Age has warmed, not chilled your blood. Who informed you this was the master I propose to you? Devil take it," he muttered to himself, "don't let me betray my secrets to a man not inclined to entertain them."

"Well, then," said Athos, "what are your schemes? what do you propose?"

"Zounds! nothing more than natural. You live on your estate, happy in golden mediocrity. Porthos has, perhaps, sixty thousand francs income. Aramis has always fifty duchesses quarreling over the priest, as they quarreled formerly over the musketeer; but I—what have I in the world? I have worn my cuirass these twenty years, kept down in this inferior rank, without going forward or backward, hardly half living. In fact, I am dead. Well! when there is some idea of being resuscitated, you say he's a scoundrel, an impudent fellow, a miser, a bad master! By Jove! I am of your opinion, but find me a better one or give me the means of living."

Athos was for a few moments thoughtful.

"Good! D'Artagnan is for Mazarin," he said to himself.

From that moment he grew very guarded.

On his side D'Artagnan became more cautious also.

"You spoke to me," Athos resumed, "of Porthos; have you persuaded him to seek his fortune? But he has wealth, I believe, already."

"Doubtless he has. But such is man, we always want something more than we already have."

"What does Porthos wish for?"

"To be a baron."

"Ah, true! I forgot," said Athos, laughing.

"'Tis true!" thought the Gascon, "where has he heard it? Does he correspond with Aramis? Ah! if I knew that he did I should know all."

The conversation was interrupted by the entrance of Raoul.

"Is our little neighbor worse?" asked D'Artagnan, seeing a look of vexation on the face of the youth.

"Ah, sir!" replied Raoul, "her fall is a very serious one, and without any ostensible injury, the physician fears she will be lame for life."

"This is terrible," said Athos.

"And what makes me all the more wretched, sir, is, that I was the cause of this misfortune."

"How so?" asked Athos.

"It was to run to meet me that she leaped from that pile of wood."

"There's only one remedy, dear Raoul—that is, to marry her as a compensation." remarked D'Artagnan.

"Ah, sir!" answered Raoul, "you joke about a real misfortune; that is cruel, indeed."

The good understanding between the two friends was not in the least altered by the morning's skirmish. They breakfasted with a good appetite, looking now and then at poor Raoul, who with moist eyes and a full heart, scarcely ate at all.

After breakfast two letters arrived for Athos, who read them with profound attention, whilst D'Artagnan could not restrain himself from jumping up several times on seeing him read these epistles, in one of which, there being at the time a very strong light, he perceived the fine writing of Aramis. The other was in a feminine hand, long, and crossed.

"Come," said D'Artagnan to Raoul, seeing that Athos wished to be alone, "come, let us take a turn in the fencing gallery; that will amuse you."

And they both went into a low room where there were foils, gloves, masks, breastplates, and all the accessories for a fencing match.

In a quarter of an hour Athos joined them and at the same moment Charles brought in a letter for D'Artagnan, which a messenger had just desired might be instantly delivered.

It was now Athos's turn to take a sly look.

D'Artagnan read the letter with apparent calmness and said, shaking his head:

"See, dear friend, what it is to belong to the army. Faith, you are indeed right not to return to it. Monsieur de Tréville is ill, so my company can't do without me; there! my leave is at an end!"

"Do you return to Paris?" asked Athos, quickly.

"Egad! yes; but why don't you come there also?"

Athos colored a little and answered:

"Should I go, I shall be delighted to see you there."

"Halloo, Planchet!" cried the Gascon from the door, "we must set out in ten minutes; give the horses some hay."

Then turning to Athos he added:

"I seem to miss something here. I am really sorry to go away without having seen Grimaud."

"Grimaud!" replied Athos. "I'm surprised you have never so much as asked after him. I have lent him to a friend——"

"Who will understand the signs he makes?" returned D'Artagnan.

"I hope so."

The friends embraced cordially; D'Artagnan pressed Raoul's hand.

"Will you not come with me?" he said; "I shall pass by Blois."

Raoul turned toward Athos, who showed him by a secret sign that he did not wish him to go.

"No, monsieur," replied the young man; "I will remain with monsieur le comte."

"Adieu, then, to both, my good friends," said D'Artagnan; "may God preserve you! as we used to say when we said good-bye to each other in the late cardinal's time."

Athos waved his hand, Raoul bowed, and D'Artagnan and Planchet set out.

The count followed them with his eyes, his hands resting on the shoulders of the youth, whose height was almost equal to his own; but as soon as they were out of sight he said:

"Raoul, we set out to-night for Paris."

"Eh?" cried the young man, turning pale.

"You may go and offer your adieus and mine to Madame de Saint-Remy. I shall wait for you here till seven."

The young man bent low, with an expression of sorrow and gratitude mingled, and retired in order to saddle his horse.

As to D'Artagnan, scarcely, on his side, was he out of sight when he drew from his pocket a letter, which he read over again:

"Return immediately to Paris.—J. M——."

"The epistle is laconic," said D'Artagnan; "and if there had not been a postscript, probably I should not have understood it; but happily there is a postscript."

And he read that welcome postscript, which made him forget the abruptness of the letter.

"P. S.—Go to the king's treasurer, at Blois; tell him your name and show him this letter; you will receive two hundred pistoles."

"Assuredly," said D'Artagnan, "I admire this piece of prose. The cardinal writes better than I thought. Come, Planchet, let us pay a visit to the king's treasurer and then set off."

"Toward Paris, sir?"

"Toward Paris."

And they set out at as hard a canter as their horses could maintain.

Chapter XVI.

The Duc de Beaufort.

The circumstances that had hastened the return of D'Artagnan to Paris were as follows:

One evening, when Mazarin, according to custom, went to visit the queen, in passing the guard-chamber he heard loud voices; wishing to know on what topic the soldiers were conversing, he approached with his wonted wolf-like step, pushed open the door and put his head close to the chink.

There was a dispute among the guards.

"I tell you," one of them was saying, "that if Coysel predicted that, 'tis as good as true; I know nothing about it, but I have heard say that he's not only an astrologer, but a magician."

"Deuce take it, friend, if he's one of thy friends thou wilt ruin him in saying so."

"Why?"

"Because he may be tried for it."

"Ah! absurd! they don't burn sorcerers nowadays."

"No? 'Tis not a long time since the late cardinal burnt Urban Grandier, though."

"My friend, Urban Grandier wasn't a sorcerer, he was a learned man. He didn't predict the future, he knew the past—often a more dangerous thing."

Mazarin nodded an assent, but wishing to know what this prediction was, about which they disputed, he remained in the same place.

"I don't say," resumed the guard, "that Coysel is not a sorcerer, but I say that if his prophecy gets wind, it's a sure way to prevent it's coming true."

"How so?"

"Why, in this way: if Coysel says loud enough for the cardinal to hear him, on such or such a day such a prisoner will escape, 'tis plain that the cardinal will take measures of precaution and that the prisoner will not escape."

"Good Lord!" said another guard, who might have been thought asleep on a bench, but who had lost not a syllable of the conversation, "do you suppose that men can escape their destiny? If it is written yonder, in Heaven, that the Duc de Beaufort is to escape, he will escape; and all the precautions of the cardinal will not prevent it."

Mazarin started. He was an Italian and therefore superstitious. He walked straight into the midst of the guards, who on seeing him were silent.

"What were you saying?" he asked with his flattering manner; "that Monsieur de Beaufort had escaped, were you not?"

"Oh, no, my lord!" said the incredulous soldier. "He's well guarded now; we only said he would escape."

"Who said so?"

"Repeat your story, Saint Laurent," replied the man, turning to the originator of the tale.

"My lord," said the guard, "I have simply mentioned the prophecy I heard from a man named Coysel, who believes that, be he ever so closely watched and guarded, the Duke of Beaufort will escape before Whitsuntide."

"Coysel is a madman!" returned the cardinal.

"No," replied the soldier, tenacious in his credulity; "he has foretold many things which have come to pass; for instance, that the queen would have a son; that Monsieur Coligny would be killed in a duel with the Duc de Guise; and finally, that the coadjutor would be made cardinal. Well! the queen has not only one son, but two; then, Monsieur de Coligny was killed, and——"

"Yes," said Mazarin, "but the coadjutor is not yet made cardinal!"

"No, my lord, but he will be," answered the guard.

Mazarin made a grimace, as if he meant to say, "But he does not wear the cardinal's cap;" then he added:

"So, my friend, it's your opinion that Monsieur de Beaufort will escape?"

"That's my idea, my lord; and if your eminence were to offer to make me at this moment governor of the castle of Vincennes, I should refuse it. After Whitsuntide it would be another thing."

There is nothing so convincing as a firm conviction. It has its own effect upon the most incredulous; and far from being incredulous, Mazarin was superstitious. He went away thoughtful and anxious and returned to his own room, where he summoned Bernouin and desired him to fetch thither in the morning the special guard he had placed over Monsieur de Beaufort and to awaken him whenever he should arrive.

The guard had, in fact, touched the cardinal in the tenderest point. During the whole five years in which the Duc de Beaufort had been in prison not a day had passed in which the cardinal had not felt a secret dread of his escape. It was not possible, as he knew well, to confine for the whole of his life the grandson of Henry IV., especially when this young prince was scarcely thirty years of age. But however and whensoever he did escape, what hatred he must cherish against him to whom he owed his long imprisonment; who had taken him, rich, brave, glorious, beloved by women, feared by men, to cut off his life's best, happiest years; for it is not life, it is merely existence, in prison! Meantime, Mazarin redoubled his surveillance over the duke. But like the miser in the fable, he could not sleep for thinking of his treasure. Often he awoke in the night, suddenly, dreaming that he had been robbed of Monsieur de Beaufort. Then he inquired about him and had the vexation of hearing that the prisoner played, drank, sang, but that whilst playing, drinking, singing, he often stopped short to vow that Mazarin should pay dear for all the amusements he had forced him to enter into at Vincennes.

So much did this one idea haunt the cardinal even in his sleep, that when at seven in the morning Bernouin came to arouse him, his first words were: "Well, what's the matter? Has Monsieur de Beaufort escaped from Vincennes?"

"I do not think so, my lord," said Bernouin; "but you will hear about him, for La Ramee is here and awaits the commands of your eminence."

"Tell him to come in," said Mazarin, arranging his pillows, so that he might receive the visitor sitting up in bed.

The officer entered, a large fat man, with an open physiognomy. His air of perfect serenity made Mazarin uneasy.

"Approach, sir," said the cardinal.

The officer obeyed.

"Do you know what they are saying here?"

"No, your eminence."

"Well, they say that Monsieur de Beaufort is going to escape from Vincennes, if he has not done so already."

The officer's face expressed complete stupefaction. He opened at once his little eyes and his great mouth, to inhale better the joke his eminence deigned to address to him, and ended by a burst of laughter, so violent that his great limbs shook in hilarity as they would have done in an ague.

"Escape! my lord—escape! Your eminence does not then know where Monsieur de Beaufort is?"

"Yes, I do, sir; in the donjon of Vincennes."

"Yes, sir; in a room, the walls of which are seven feet thick, with grated windows, each bar as thick as my arm."

"Sir," replied Mazarin, "with perseverance one may penetrate through a wall; with a watch-spring one may saw through an iron bar."

"Then my lord does not know that there are eight guards about him, four in his chamber, four in the antechamber, and that they never leave him."

"But he leaves his room, he plays at tennis at the Mall?"

"Sir, those amusements are allowed; but if your eminence wishes it, we will discontinue the permission."

"No, no!" cried Mazarin, fearing that should his prisoner ever leave his prison he would be the more exasperated against him if he thus retrenched his amusement. He then asked with whom he played.

"My lord, either with the officers of the guard, with the other prisoners, or with me."

"But does he not approach the walls while playing?"

"Your eminence doesn't know those walls; they are sixty feet high and I doubt if Monsieur de Beaufort is sufficiently weary of life to risk his neck by jumping off."

"Hum!" said the cardinal, beginning to feel more comfortable. "You mean to say, then, my dear Monsieur la Ramee——"

"That unless Monsieur de Beaufort can contrive to metamorphose himself into a little bird, I will continue answerable for him."

"Take care! you assert a great deal," said Mazarin. "Monsieur de Beaufort told the guards who took him to Vincennes that he had often thought what he should do in case he were put into prison, and that he had found out forty ways of escaping."

"My lord, if among these forty there had been one good way he would have been out long ago."

"Come, come; not such a fool as I fancied!" thought Mazarin.

"Besides, my lord must remember that Monsieur de Chavigny is governor of Vincennes," continued La Ramee, "and that Monsieur de Chavigny is not friendly to Monsieur de Beaufort."

"Yes, but Monsieur de Chavigny is sometimes absent."

"When he is absent I am there."

"But when you leave him, for instance?"

"Oh! when I leave him, I place in my stead a bold fellow who aspires to be his majesty's special guard. I promise you he keeps a good watch over the prisoner. During the three weeks that he has been with me, I have only had to reproach him with one thing—being too severe with the prisoners."

"And who is this Cerberus?"

"A certain Monsieur Grimaud, my lord."

"And what was he before he went to Vincennes?"

"He was in the country, as I was told by the person who recommended him to me."

"And who recommended this man to you?"

"The steward of the Duc de Grammont."

"He is not a gossip, I hope?"

"Lord a mercy, my lord! I thought for a long time that he was dumb; he answers only by signs. It seems his former master accustomed him to that."

"Well, dear Monsieur la Ramee," replied the cardinal "let him prove a true and thankful keeper and we will shut our eyes upon his rural misdeeds and put on his back a uniform to make him respectable, and in the pockets of that uniform some pistoles to drink to the king's health."

Mazarin was large in promises,—quite unlike the virtuous Monsieur Grimaud so bepraised by La Ramee; for he said nothing and did much.

It was now nine o'clock. The cardinal, therefore, got up, perfumed himself, dressed, and went to the queen to tell her what had detained him. The queen, who was scarcely less afraid of Monsieur de Beaufort than the cardinal himself, and who was almost as superstitious as he was, made him repeat word for word all La Ramee's praises of his deputy. Then, when the cardinal had ended:

"Alas, sir! why have we not a Grimaud near every prince?"

"Patience!" replied Mazarin, with his Italian smile; "that may happen one day; but in the meantime——"

"Well, in the meantime?"

"I shall still take precautions."

And he wrote to D'Artagnan to hasten his return.

Chapter XVII.

Duc de Beaufort amused his Leisure Hours in the Donjon of Vincennes.

The captive who was the source of so much alarm to the cardinal and whose means of escape disturbed the repose of the whole court, was wholly unconscious of the terror he caused at the Palais Royal.

He had found himself so strictly guarded that he soon perceived the fruitlessness of any attempt at escape. His vengeance, therefore, consisted in coining curses on the head of Mazarin; he even tried to make some verses on him, but soon gave up the attempt, for Monsieur de Beaufort had not only not received from Heaven the gift of versifying, he had the greatest difficulty in expressing himself in prose.

The duke was the grandson of Henry IV. and Gabrielle d'Estrees—as good-natured, as brave, as proud, and above all, as Gascon as his ancestor, but less elaborately educated. After having been for some time after the death of Louis XIII. the favorite, the confidant, the first man, in short, at the court, he had been obliged to yield his place to Mazarin and so became the second in influence and favor; and eventually, as he was stupid enough to be vexed at this change of position, the queen had had him arrested and sent to Vincennes in charge of Guitant, who made his appearance in these pages in the beginning of this history and whom we shall see again. It is understood, of course, that when we say "the queen," Mazarin is meant.

During the five years of this seclusion, which would have improved and matured the intellect of any other man, M. de Beaufort, had he not affected to brave the cardinal, despise princes, and walk alone without adherents or disciples, would either have regained his liberty or made partisans. But these considerations never occurred to the duke and every day the cardinal received fresh accounts of him which were as unpleasant as possible to the minister.

After having failed in poetry, Monsieur de Beaufort tried drawing. He drew portraits, with a piece of coal, of the cardinal; and as his talents did not enable him to produce a very good likeness, he wrote under the picture that there might be little doubt regarding the original: "Portrait of the Illustrious Coxcomb, Mazarin." Monsieur de Chavigny, the governor of Vincennes, waited upon the duke to request that he would amuse himself in some other way, or that at all events, if he drew likenesses, he would not put mottoes underneath them. The next day the prisoner's room was full of pictures and mottoes. Monsieur de Beaufort, in common with many other prisoners, was bent upon doing things that were prohibited; and the only resource the governor had was, one day when the duke was playing at tennis, to efface all these drawings, consisting chiefly of profiles. M. de Beaufort did not venture to draw the cardinal's fat face.

The duke thanked Monsieur de Chavigny for having, as he said, cleaned his drawing-paper for him; he then divided the walls of his room into compartments and dedicated each of these compartments to some incident in Mazarin's life. In one was depicted the "Illustrious Coxcomb" receiving a shower of blows from Cardinal Bentivoglio, whose servant he had been; another, the "Illustrious Mazarin" acting the part of Ignatius Loyola in a tragedy of that name; a third, the "Illustrious Mazarin" stealing the portfolio of prime minister from Monsieur de Chavigny, who had expected to have it; a fourth, the "Illustrious Coxcomb Mazarin" refusing to give Laporte, the young king's valet, clean sheets, and saving that "it was quite enough for the king of France to have clean sheets every three months."

The governor, of course, thought proper to threaten his prisoner that if he did not give up drawing such pictures he should be obliged to deprive him of all the means of amusing himself in that manner. To this Monsieur de Beaufort replied that since every opportunity of distinguishing himself in arms was taken from him, he wished to make himself celebrated in the arts; since he could not be a Bayard, he would become a Raphael or a Michael Angelo. Nevertheless, one day when Monsieur de Beaufort was walking in the meadow his fire was put out, his charcoal all removed, taken away; and thus his means of drawing utterly destroyed.

The poor duke swore, fell into a rage, yelled, and declared that they wished to starve him to death as they had starved the Marechal Ornano and the Grand Prior of Vendome; but he refused to promise that he would not make any more drawings and remained without any fire in the room all the winter.

His next act was to purchase a dog from one of his keepers. With this animal, which he called Pistache, he was often shut up for hours alone, superintending, as every one supposed, its education. At last, when Pistache was sufficiently well trained, Monsieur de Beaufort invited the governor and officers of Vincennes to attend a representation which he was going to have in his apartment.

The party assembled, the room was lighted with waxlights, and the prisoner, with a bit of plaster he had taken out of the wall of his room, had traced a long white line, representing a cord, on the floor. Pistache, on a signal from his master, placed himself on this line, raised himself on his hind paws, and holding in his front paws a wand with which clothes used to be beaten, he began to dance upon the line with as many contortions as a rope-dancer. Having been several times up and down it, he gave the wand back to his master and began without hesitation to perform the same evolutions over again.

The intelligent creature was received with loud applause.

The first part of the entertainment being concluded Pistache was desired to say what o'clock it was; he was shown Monsieur de Chavigny's watch; it was then half-past six; the dog raised and dropped his paw six times; the seventh he let it remain upraised. Nothing could be better done; a sun-dial could not have shown the hour with greater precision.

Then the question was put to him who was the best jailer in all the prisons in France.

The dog performed three evolutions around the circle and laid himself, with the deepest respect, at the feet of Monsieur de Chavigny, who at first seemed inclined to like the joke and laughed long and loud, but a frown succeeded, and he bit his lips with vexation.

Then the duke put to Pistache this difficult question, who was the greatest thief in the world?

Pistache went again around the circle, but stopped at no one, and at last went to the door and began to scratch and bark.

"See, gentlemen," said M. de Beaufort, "this wonderful animal, not finding here what I ask for, seeks it out of doors; you shall, however, have his answer. Pistache, my friend, come here. Is not the greatest thief in the world, Monsieur (the king's secretary) Le Camus, who came to Paris with twenty francs in his pocket and who now possesses ten millions?"

The dog shook his head.

"Then is it not," resumed the duke, "the Superintendent Emery, who gave his son, when he was married, three hundred thousand francs and a house, compared to which the Tuileries are a heap of ruins and the Louvre a paltry building?"

The dog again shook his head as if to say "no."

"Then," said the prisoner, "let's think who it can be. Can it be, can it possibly be, the 'Illustrious Coxcomb, Mazarin de Piscina,' hey?"

Pistache made violent signs that it was, by raising and lowering his head eight or ten times successively.

"Gentlemen, you see," said the duke to those present, who dared not even smile, "that it is the 'Illustrious Coxcomb' who is the greatest thief in the world; at least, according to Pistache."

"Let us go on to another of his exercises."

"Gentlemen!"—there was a profound silence in the room when the duke again addressed them—"do you not remember that the Duc de Guise taught all the dogs in Paris to jump for Mademoiselle de Pons, whom he styled 'the fairest of the fair?' Pistache is going to show you how superior he is to all other dogs. Monsieur de Chavigny, be so good as to lend me your cane."

Monsieur de Chavigny handed his cane to Monsieur de Beaufort. Monsieur de Beaufort placed it horizontally at the height of one foot.

"Now, Pistache, my good dog, jump the height of this cane for Madame de Montbazon."

"But," interposed Monsieur de Chavigny, "it seems to me that Pistache is only doing what other dogs have done when they jumped for Mademoiselle de Pons."

"Stop," said the duke, "Pistache, jump for the queen." And he raised his cane six inches higher.

The dog sprang, and in spite of the height jumped lightly over it.

"And now," said the duke, raising it still six inches higher, "jump for the king."

The dog obeyed and jumped quickly over the cane.

"Now, then," said the duke, and as he spoke, lowered the cane almost level with the ground; "Pistache, my friend, jump for the 'Illustrious Coxcomb, Mazarin de Piscina.'"

The dog turned his back to the cane.

"What," asked the duke, "what do you mean?" and he gave him the cane again, first making a semicircle from the head to the tail of Pistache. "Jump then, Monsieur Pistache."

But Pistache, as at first, turned round on his legs and stood with his back to the cane.

Monsieur de Beaufort made the experiment a third time, but by this time Pistache's patience was exhausted; he threw himself furiously upon the cane, wrested it from the hands of the prince and broke it with his teeth.

Monsieur de Beaufort took the pieces out of his mouth and presented them with great formality to Monsieur de Chavigny, saying that for that evening the entertainment was ended, but in three months it should be repeated, when Pistache would have learned a few new tricks.

Three days afterward Pistache was found dead—poisoned.

Then the duke said openly that his dog had been killed by a drug with which they meant to poison him; and one day after dinner he went to bed, calling out that he had pains in his stomach and that Mazarin had poisoned him.

This fresh impertinence reached the ears of the cardinal and alarmed him greatly. The donjon of Vincennes was considered very unhealthy and Madame de Rambouillet had said that the room in which the Marechal Ornano and the Grand Prior de Vendome had died was worth its weight in arsenic—a bon mot which had great success. So it was ordered the prisoner was henceforth to eat nothing that had not previously been tasted, and La Ramee was in consequence placed near him as taster.

Every kind of revenge was practiced upon the duke by the governor in return for the insults of the innocent Pistache. De Chavigny, who, according to report, was a son of Richelieu's, and had been a creature of the late cardinal's, understood tyranny. He took from the duke all the steel knives and silver forks and replaced them with silver knives and wooden forks, pretending that as he had been informed that the duke was to pass all his life at Vincennes, he was afraid of his prisoner attempting suicide. A fortnight afterward the duke, going to the tennis court, found two rows of trees about the size of his little finger planted by the roadside; he asked what they were for and was told that they were to shade him from the sun on some future day. One morning the gardener went to him and told him, as if to please him, that he was going to plant a bed of asparagus for his especial use. Now, since, as every one knows, asparagus takes four years in coming to perfection, this civility infuriated Monsieur de Beaufort.

At last his patience was exhausted. He assembled his keepers, and notwithstanding his well-known difficulty of utterance, addressed them as follows:

"Gentlemen! will you permit a grandson of Henry IV. to be overwhelmed with insults and ignominy?

"Odds fish! as my grandfather used to say, I once reigned in Paris! do you know that? I had the king and Monsieur the whole of one day in my care. The queen at that time liked me and called me the most honest man in the kingdom. Gentlemen and citizens, set me free; I shall go to the Louvre and strangle Mazarin. You shall be my body-guard. I will make you all captains, with good pensions! Odds fish! On! march forward!"

But eloquent as he might be, the eloquence of the grandson of Henry IV. did not touch those hearts of stone; not one man stirred, so Monsieur de Beaufort was obliged to be satisfied with calling them all kinds of rascals underneath the sun.

Sometimes, when Monsieur de Chavigny paid him a visit, the duke used to ask him what he should think if he saw an army of Parisians, all fully armed, appear at Vincennes to deliver him from prison.

"My lord," answered De Chavigny, with a low bow, "I have on the ramparts twenty pieces of artillery and in my casemates thirty thousand guns. I should bombard the troops till not one grain of gunpowder was unexploded."

"Yes, but after you had fired off your thirty thousand guns they would take the donjon; the donjon being taken, I should be obliged to let them hang you—at which I should be most unhappy, certainly."

And in his turn the duke bowed low to Monsieur de Chavigny.

"For myself, on the other hand, my lord," returned the governor, "when the first rebel should pass the threshold of my postern doors I should be obliged to kill you with my own hand, since you were confided peculiarly to my care and as I am obliged to give you up, dead or alive."

And once more he bowed low before his highness.

These bitter-sweet pleasantries lasted ten minutes, sometimes longer, but always finished thus:

Monsieur de Chavigny, turning toward the door, used to call out: "Halloo! La Ramee!"

La Ramee came into the room.

"La Ramee, I recommend Monsieur le Duc to you, particularly; treat him as a man of his rank and family ought to be treated; that is, never leave him alone an instant."

La Ramee became, therefore, the duke's dinner guest by compulsion—an eternal keeper, the shadow of his person; but La Ramee—gay, frank, convivial, fond of play, a great hand at tennis, had one defect in the duke's eyes—his incorruptibility.

Now, although La Ramee appreciated, as of a certain value, the honor of being shut up with a prisoner of so great importance, still the pleasure of living in intimacy with the grandson of Henry IV. hardly compensated for the loss of that which he had experienced in going from time to time to visit his family.

One may be a jailer or a keeper and at the same time a good father and husband. La Ramee adored his wife and children, whom now he could only catch a glimpse of from the top of the wall, when in order to please him they used to walk on the opposite side of the moat. 'Twas too brief an enjoyment, and La Ramee felt that the gayety of heart he had regarded as the cause of health (of which it was perhaps rather the result) would not long survive such a mode of life.

He accepted, therefore, with delight, an offer made to him by his friend the steward of the Duc de Grammont, to give him a substitute; he also spoke of it to Monsieur de Chavigny, who promised that he would not oppose it in any way—that is, if he approved of the person proposed.

We consider it useless to draw a physical or moral portrait of Grimaud; if, as we hope, our readers have not wholly forgotten the first part of this work, they must have preserved a clear idea of that estimable individual, who is wholly unchanged, except that he is twenty years older, an advance in life that has made him only more silent; although, since the change that had been working in himself, Athos had given Grimaud permission to speak.

But Grimaud had for twelve or fifteen years preserved habitual silence, and a habit of fifteen or twenty years' duration becomes second nature.

Chapter XVIII.

Grimaud begins his Functions.

Grimaud thereupon presented himself with his smooth exterior at the donjon of Vincennes. Now Monsieur de Chavigny piqued himself on his infallible penetration; for that which almost proved that he was the son of Richelieu was his everlasting pretension; he examined attentively the countenance of the applicant for place and fancied that the contracted eyebrows, thin lips, hooked nose, and prominent cheek-bones of Grimaud were favorable signs. He addressed about twelve words to him; Grimaud answered in four.

"Here's a promising fellow and it is I who have found out his merits," said Monsieur de Chavigny. "Go," he added, "and make yourself agreeable to Monsieur la Ramee, and tell him that you suit me in all respects."

Grimaud had every quality that could attract a man on duty who wishes to have a deputy. So, after a thousand questions which met with only a word in reply, La Ramee, fascinated by this sobriety in speech, rubbed his hands and engaged Grimaud.

"My orders?" asked Grimaud.

"They are these; never to leave the prisoner alone; to keep away from him every pointed or cutting instrument, and to prevent his conversing any length of time with the keepers."

"Those are all?" asked Grimaud.

"All now," replied La Ramee.

"Good," answered Grimaud; and he went right to the prisoner.

The duke was in the act of combing his beard, which he had allowed to grow, as well as his hair, in order to reproach Mazarin with his wretched appearance and condition. But having some days previously seen from the top of the donjon Madame de Montbazon pass in her carriage, and still cherishing an affection for that beautiful woman, he did not wish to be to her what he wished to be to Mazarin, and in the hope of seeing her again, had asked for a leaden comb, which was allowed him. The comb was to be a leaden one, because his beard, like that of most fair people, was rather red; he therefore dyed it thus whilst combing it.

As Grimaud entered he saw this comb on the tea-table; he took it up, and as he took it he made a low bow.

The duke looked at this strange figure with surprise. The figure put the comb in its pocket.

"Ho! hey! what's that?" cried the duke. "Who is this creature?"

Grimaud did not answer, but bowed a second time.

"Art thou dumb?" cried the duke.

Grimaud made a sign that he was not.

"What art thou, then? Answer! I command thee!" said the duke.

"A keeper," replied Grimaud.

"A keeper!" reiterated the duke; "there was nothing wanting in my collection, except this gallows-bird. Halloo! La Ramee! some one!"

La Ramee ran in haste to obey the call.

"Who is this wretch who takes my comb and puts it in his pocket?" asked the duke.

"One of your guards, my prince; a man of talent and merit, whom you will like, as I and Monsieur de Chavigny do, I am sure."

"Why does he take my comb?"

"Why do you take my lord's comb?" asked La Ramee.

Grimaud drew the comb from his pocket and passing his fingers over the largest teeth, pronounced this one word, "Pointed."

"True," said La Ramee.

"What does the animal say?" asked the duke.

"That the king has forbidden your lordship to have any pointed instrument."

"Are you mad, La Ramee? You yourself gave me this comb."

"I was very wrong, my lord, for in giving it to you I acted in opposition to my orders."

The duke looked furiously at Grimaud.

"I perceive that this creature will be my particular aversion," he muttered.

Grimaud, nevertheless, was resolved for certain reasons not at once to come to a full rupture with the prisoner; he wanted to inspire, not a sudden repugnance, but a good, sound, steady hatred; he retired, therefore, and gave place to four guards, who, having breakfasted, could attend on the prisoner.

A fresh practical joke now occurred to the duke. He had asked for crawfish for his breakfast on the following morning; he intended to pass the day in making a small gallows and hang one of the finest of these fish in the middle of his room—the red color evidently conveying an allusion to the cardinal—so that he might have the pleasure of hanging Mazarin in effigy without being accused of having hung anything more significant than a crawfish.

The day was employed in preparations for the execution. Every one grows childish in prison, but the character of Monsieur de Beaufort was particularly disposed to become so. In the course of his morning's walk he collected two or three small branches from a tree and found a small piece of broken glass, a discovery that quite delighted him. When he came home he formed his handkerchief into a loop.

Nothing of all this escaped Grimaud, but La Ramee looked on with the curiosity of a father who thinks that he may perhaps get a cheap idea concerning a new toy for his children. The guards looked on it with indifference. When everything was ready, the gallows hung in the middle of the room, the loop made, and when the duke had cast a glance upon the plate of crawfish, in order to select the finest specimen among them, he looked around for his piece of glass; it had disappeared.

"Who has taken my piece of glass?" asked the duke, frowning. Grimaud made a sign to denote that he had done so.

"What! thou again! Why didst thou take it?"

"Yes—why?" asked La Ramee.

Grimaud, who held the piece of glass in his hand, said: "Sharp."

"True, my lord!" exclaimed La Ramee. "Ah! deuce take it! we have a precious fellow here!"

"Monsieur Grimaud!" said the duke, "for your sake I beg of you, never come within the reach of my fist!"

"Hush! hush!" cried La Ramee, "give me your gibbet, my lord. I will shape it out for you with my knife."

And he took the gibbet and shaped it out as neatly as possible.

"That's it," said the duke, "now make me a little hole in the floor whilst I go and fetch the culprit."

La Ramee knelt down and made a hole in the floor; meanwhile the duke hung the crawfish up by a thread. Then he placed the gibbet in the middle of the room, bursting with laughter.

La Ramee laughed also and the guards laughed in chorus; Grimaud, however, did not even smile. He approached La Ramee and showing him the crawfish hung up by the thread:

"Cardinal," he said.

"Hung by order of his Highness the Duc de Beaufort!" cried the prisoner, laughing violently, "and by Master Jacques Chrysostom La Ramee, the king's commissioner."

La Ramee uttered a cry of horror and rushed toward the gibbet, which he broke at once and threw the pieces out of the window. He was going to throw the crawfish out also, when Grimaud snatched it from his hands.

"Good to eat!" he said, and put it in his pocket.

This scene so enchanted the duke that at the moment he forgave Grimaud for his part in it; but on reflection he hated him more and more, being convinced he had some evil motive for his conduct.

But the story of the crab made a great noise through the interior of the donjon and even outside. Monsieur de Chavigny, who at heart detested the cardinal, took pains to tell the story to two or three friends, who put it into immediate circulation.

The prisoner happened to remark among the guards one man with a very good countenance; and he favored this man the more as Grimaud became the more and more odious to him. One morning he took this man on one side and had succeeded in speaking to him, when Grimaud entered and seeing what was going on approached the duke respectfully, but took the guard by the arm.

"Go away," he said.

The guard obeyed.

"You are insupportable!" cried the duke; "I shall beat you."

Grimaud bowed.

"I will break every bone in your body!" cried the duke.

Grimaud bowed, but stepped back.

"Mr. Spy," cried the duke, more and more enraged, "I will strangle you with my own hands."

And he extended his hands toward Grimaud, who merely thrust the guard out and shut the door behind him. At the same time he felt the duke's arms on his shoulders like two iron claws; but instead either of calling out or defending himself, he placed his forefinger on his lips and said in a low tone:

"Hush!" smiling as he uttered the word.

A gesture, a smile and a word from Grimaud, all at once, were so unusual that his highness stopped short, astounded.

Grimaud took advantage of that instant to draw from his vest a charming little note with an aristocratic seal, and presented it to the duke without a word.

The duke, more and more bewildered, let Grimaud loose and took the note.

"From Madame de Montbazon?" he cried.

Grimaud nodded assent.

The duke tore open the note, passed his hands over his eyes, for he was dazzled and confused, and read:

"My Dear Duke,—You may entirely confide in the brave lad who will give you this note; he has consented to enter the service of your keeper and to shut himself up at Vincennes with you, in order to prepare and assist your escape, which we are contriving. The moment of your deliverance is at hand; have patience and courage and remember that in spite of time and absence all your friends continue to cherish for you the sentiments they have so long professed and truly entertained.

"Yours wholly and most affectionately

"Marie de Montbazon.

"P.S.—I sign my full name, for I should be vain if I could suppose that after five years of absence you would remember my initials."

The poor duke became perfectly giddy. What for five years he had been wanting—a faithful servant, a friend, a helping hand—seemed to have fallen from Heaven just when he expected it the least.

"Oh, dearest Marie! she thinks of me, then, after five years of separation! Heavens! there is constancy!" Then turning to Grimaud, he said:

"And thou, my brave fellow, thou consentest thus to aid me?"

Grimaud signified his assent.

"And you have come here with that purpose?"

Grimaud repeated the sign.

"And I was ready to strangle you!" cried the duke.

Grimaud smiled.

"Wait, then," said the duke, fumbling in his pocket. "Wait," he continued, renewing his fruitless search; "it shall not be said that such devotion to a grandson of Henry IV. went without recompense."

The duke's endeavors evinced the best intention in the world, but one of the precautions taken at Vincennes was that of allowing prisoners to keep no money. Whereupon Grimaud, observing the duke's disappointment, drew from his pocket a purse filled with gold and handed it to him.

"Here is what you are looking for," he said.

The duke opened the purse and wanted to empty it into Grimaud's hands, but Grimaud shook his head.

"Thank you, monseigneur," he said, drawing back; "I am paid."

The duke went from one surprise to another. He held out his hand. Grimaud drew near and kissed it respectfully. The grand manner of Athos had left its mark on Grimaud.

"What shall we do? and when? and how proceed?"

"It is now eleven," answered Grimaud. "Let my lord at two o'clock ask leave to make up a game at tennis with La Ramee and let him send two or three balls over the ramparts."

"And then?"

"Your highness will approach the walls and call out to a man who works in the moat to send them back again."

"I understand," said the duke.

Grimaud made a sign that he was going away.

"Ah!" cried the duke, "will you not accept any money from me?"

"I wish my lord would make me one promise."

"What! speak!"

"'Tis this: when we escape together, that I shall go everywhere and be always first; for if my lord should be overtaken and caught, there's every chance of his being brought back to prison, whereas if I am caught the least that can befall me is to be—hung."

"True, on my honor as a gentleman it shall be as thou dost suggest."

"Now," resumed Grimaud, "I've only one thing more to ask—that your highness will continue to detest me."

"I'll try," said the duke.

At this moment La Ramee, after the interview we have described with the cardinal, entered the room. The duke had thrown himself, as he was wont to do in moments of dullness and vexation, on his bed. La Ramee cast an inquiring look around him and observing the same signs of antipathy between the prisoner and his guardian he smiled in token of his inward satisfaction. Then turning to Grimaud:

"Very good, my friend, very good. You have been spoken of in a promising quarter and you will soon, I hope, have news that will be agreeable to you."

Grimaud saluted in his politest manner and withdrew, as was his custom on the entrance of his superior.

"Well, my lord," said La Ramee, with his rude laugh, "you still set yourself against this poor fellow?"

"So! 'tis you, La Ramee; in faith, 'tis time you came back again. I threw myself on the bed and turned my nose to the wall, that I mightn't break my promise and strangle Grimaud."

"I doubt, however," said La Ramee, in sprightly allusion to the silence of his subordinate, "if he has said anything disagreeable to your highness."

"Pardieu! you are right—a mute from the East! I swear it was time for you to come back, La Ramee, and I was eager to see you again."

"Monseigneur is too good," said La Ramee, flattered by the compliment.

"Yes," continued the duke, "really, I feel bored today beyond the power of description."

"Then let us have a match in the tennis court," exclaimed La Ramee.

"If you wish it."

"I am at your service, my lord."

"I protest, my dear La Ramee," said the duke, "that you are a charming fellow and that I would stay forever at Vincennes to have the pleasure of your society."

"My lord," replied La Ramee, "I think if it depended on the cardinal your wishes would be fulfilled."

"What do you mean? Have you seen him lately?"

"He sent for me to-day."

"Really! to speak to you about me?"

"Of what else do you imagine he would speak to me? Really, my lord, you are his nightmare."

The duke smiled with bitterness.

"Ah, La Ramee! if you would but accept my offers! I would make your fortune."

"How? you would no sooner have left prison than your goods would be confiscated."

"I shall no sooner be out of prison than I shall be master of Paris."

"Pshaw! pshaw! I cannot hear such things said as that; this is a fine conversation with an officer of the king! I see, my lord, I shall be obliged to fetch a second Grimaud!"

"Very well, let us say no more about it. So you and the cardinal have been talking about me? La Ramee, some day when he sends for you, you must let me put on your clothes; I will go in your stead; I will strangle him, and upon my honor, if that is made a condition I will return to prison."

"Monseigneur, I see well that I must call Grimaud."

"Well, I am wrong. And what did the cuistre [pettifogger] say about me?"

"I admit the word, monseigneur, because it rhymes with ministre [minister]. What did he say to me? He told me to watch you."

"And why so? why watch me?" asked the duke uneasily.

"Because an astrologer had predicted that you would escape."

"Ah! an astrologer predicted that?" said the duke, starting in spite of himself.

"Oh, mon Dieu! yes! those imbeciles of magicians can only imagine things to torment honest people."

"And what did you reply to his most illustrious eminence?"

"That if the astrologer in question made almanacs I would advise him not to buy one."

"Why not?"

"Because before you could escape you would have to be turned into a bird."

"Unfortunately, that is true. Let us go and have a game at tennis, La Ramee."

"My lord—I beg your highness's pardon—but I must beg for half an hour's leave of absence."

"Why?"

"Because Monseigneur Mazarin is a prouder man than his highness, though not of such high birth: he forgot to ask me to breakfast."

"Well, shall I send for some breakfast here?"

"No, my lord; I must tell you that the confectioner who lived opposite the castle—Daddy Marteau, as they called him——"

"Well?"

"Well, he sold his business a week ago to a confectioner from Paris, an invalid, ordered country air for his health."

"Well, what have I to do with that?"

"Why, good Lord! this man, your highness, when he saw me stop before his shop, where he has a display of things which would make your mouth water, my lord, asked me to get him the custom of the prisoners in the donjon. 'I bought,' said he, 'the business of my predecessor on the strength of his assurance that he supplied the castle; whereas, on my honor, Monsieur de Chavigny, though I've been here a week, has not ordered so much as a tartlet.' 'But,' I then replied, 'probably Monsieur de Chavigny is afraid your pastry is not good.' 'My pastry not good! Well, Monsieur La Ramee, you shall judge of it yourself and at once.' 'I cannot,' I replied; 'it is absolutely necessary for me to return to the chateau.' 'Very well,' said he, 'go and attend to your affairs, since you seem to be in a hurry, but come back in half an hour.' 'In half an hour?' 'Yes, have you breakfasted?' 'Faith, no.' 'Well, here is a pate that will be ready for you, with a bottle of old Burgundy.' So, you see, my lord, since I am hungry, I would, with your highness's leave——" And La Ramee bent low.

"Go, then, animal," said the duke; "but remember, I only allow you half an hour."

"May I promise your custom to the successor of Father Marteau, my lord?"

"Yes, if he does not put mushrooms in his pies; thou knowest that mushrooms from the wood of Vincennes are fatal to my family."

La Ramee went out, but in five minutes one of the officers of the guard entered in compliance with the strict orders of the cardinal that the prisoner should never be left alone a moment.

But during these five minutes the duke had had time to read again the note from Madame de Montbazon, which proved to the prisoner that his friends were concerting plans for his deliverance, but in what way he knew not.

But his confidence in Grimaud, whose petty persecutions he now perceived were only a blind, increased, and he conceived the highest opinion of his intellect and resolved to trust entirely to his guidance.

Chapter XIX.

Pâtés made by the Successor of Father Marteau are described.

In half an hour La Ramee returned, full of glee, like most men who have eaten, and more especially drank to their heart's content. The pates were excellent, the wine delicious.

The weather was fine and the game at tennis took place in the open air.

At two o'clock the tennis balls began, according to Grimaud's directions, to take the direction of the moat, much to the joy of La Ramee, who marked fifteen whenever the duke sent a ball into the moat; and very soon balls were wanting, so many had gone over. La Ramee then proposed to send some one to pick them up, but the duke remarked that it would be losing time; and going near the rampart himself and looking over, he saw a man working in one of the numerous little gardens cleared out by the peasants on the opposite side of the moat.

"Hey, friend!" cried the duke.

The man raised his head and the duke was about to utter a cry of surprise. The peasant, the gardener, was Rochefort, whom he believed to be in the Bastile.

"Well? Who's up there?" said the man.

"Be so good as to collect and throw us back our balls," said the duke.

The gardener nodded and began to fling up the balls, which were picked up by La Ramee and the guard. One, however, fell at the duke's feet, and seeing that it was intended for him, he put it into his pocket.

La Ramee was in ecstasies at having beaten a prince of the blood.

The duke went indoors and retired to bed, where he spent, indeed, the greater part of every day, as they had taken his books away. La Ramee carried off all his clothes, in order to be certain that the duke would not stir. However, the duke contrived to hide the ball under his bolster and as soon as the door was closed he tore off the cover of the ball with his teeth and found underneath the following letter:

My Lord,—Your friends are watching over you and the hour of your deliverance is at hand. Ask day after to-morrow to have a pie supplied you by the new confectioner opposite the castle, and who is no other than Noirmont, your former maitre d'hotel. Do not open the pie till you are alone. I hope you will be satisfied with its contents.

"Your highness's most devoted servant,

"In the Bastile, as elsewhere,

"Comte de Rochefort."

The duke, who had latterly been allowed a fire, burned the letter, but kept the ball, and went to bed, hiding the ball under his bolster. La Ramee entered; he smiled kindly on the prisoner, for he was an excellent man and had taken a great liking for the captive prince. He endeavored to cheer him up in his solitude.

"Ah, my friend!" cried the duke, "you are so good; if I could but do as you do, and eat pates and drink Burgundy at the house of Father Marteau's successor."

"'Tis true, my lord," answered La Ramee, "that his pates are famous and his wine magnificent."

"In any case," said the duke, "his cellar and kitchen might easily excel those of Monsieur de Chavigny."

"Well, my lord," said La Ramee, falling into the trap, "what is there to prevent your trying them? Besides, I have promised him your patronage."

"You are right," said the duke. "If I am to remain here permanently, as Monsieur Mazarin has kindly given me to understand, I must provide myself with a diversion for my old age, I must turn gourmand."

"My lord," said La Ramee, "if you will take a bit of good advice, don't put that off till you are old."

"Good!" said the Duc de Beaufort to himself, "every man in order that he may lose his heart and soul, must receive from celestial bounty one of the seven capital sins, perhaps two; it seems that Master La Ramee's is gluttony. Let us then take advantage of it." Then, aloud:

"Well, my dear La Ramee! the day after to-morrow is a holiday."

"Yes, my lord—Pentecost."

"Will you give me a lesson the day after to-morrow?"

"In what?"

"In gastronomy?"

"Willingly, my lord."

"But tete-a-tete. Send the guards to take their meal in the canteen of Monsieur de Chavigny; we'll have a supper here under your direction."

"Hum!" said La Ramee.

The proposal was seductive, but La Ramee was an old stager, acquainted with all the traps a prisoner was likely to set. Monsieur de Beaufort had said that he had forty ways of getting out of prison. Did this proposed breakfast cover some stratagem? He reflected, but he remembered that he himself would have charge of the food and the wine and therefore that no powder could be mixed with the food, no drug with the wine. As to getting him drunk, the duke couldn't hope to do that, and he laughed at the mere thought of it. Then an idea came to him which harmonized everything.

The duke had followed with anxiety La Ramee's unspoken soliloquy, reading it from point to point upon his face. But presently the exempt's face suddenly brightened.

"Well," he asked, "that will do, will it not?"

"Yes, my lord, on one condition."

"What?"

"That Grimaud shall wait on us at table."

Nothing could be more agreeable to the duke, however, he had presence of mind enough to exclaim:

"To the devil with your Grimaud! He will spoil the feast."

"I will direct him to stand behind your chair, and since he doesn't speak, your highness will neither see nor hear him and with a little effort can imagine him a hundred miles away."

"Do you know, my friend, I find one thing very evident in all this, you distrust me."

"My lord, the day after to-morrow is Pentecost."

"Well, what is Pentecost to me? Are you afraid that the Holy Spirit will come as a tongue of fire to open the doors of my prison?"

"No, my lord; but I have already told you what that damned magician predicted."

"And what was it?"

"That the day of Pentecost would not pass without your highness being out of Vincennes."

"You believe in sorcerers, then, you fool?"

"I—-I mind them no more than that——" and he snapped his fingers; "but it is my Lord Giulio who cares about them; as an Italian he is superstitious."

The duke shrugged his shoulders.

"Well, then," with well acted good-humor, "I allow Grimaud, but no one else; you must manage it all. Order whatever you like for supper—the only thing I specify is one of those pies; and tell the confectioner that I will promise him my custom if he excels this time in his pies—not only now, but when I leave my prison."

"Then you think you will some day leave it?" said La Ramee.

"The devil!" replied the prince; "surely, at the death of Mazarin. I am fifteen years younger than he is. At Vincennes, 'tis true, one lives faster——"

"My lord," replied La Ramee, "my lord——"

"Or dies sooner, for it comes to the same thing."

La Ramee was going out. He stopped, however, at the door for an instant.

"Whom does your highness wish me to send to you?"

"Any one, except Grimaud."

"The officer of the guard, then, with his chessboard?"

"Yes."

Five minutes afterward the officer entered and the duke seemed to be immersed in the sublime combinations of chess.

A strange thing is the mind, and it is wonderful what revolutions may be wrought in it by a sign, a word, a hope. The duke had been five years in prison, and now to him, looking back upon them, those five years, which had passed so slowly, seemed not so long a time as were the two days, the forty-eight hours, which still parted him from the time fixed for his escape. Besides, there was one thing that engaged his most anxious thought—in what way was the escape to be effected? They had told him to hope for it, but had not told him what was to be hidden in the mysterious pate. And what friends awaited him without? He had friends, then, after five years in prison? If that were so he was indeed a highly favored prince. He forgot that besides his friends of his own sex, a woman, strange to say, had remembered him. It is true that she had not, perhaps, been scrupulously faithful to him, but she had remembered him; that was something.

So the duke had more than enough to think about; accordingly he fared at chess as he had fared at tennis; he made blunder upon blunder and the officer with whom he played found him easy game.

But his successive defeats did service to the duke in one way—they killed time for him till eight o'clock in the evening; then would come night, and with night, sleep. So, at least, the duke believed; but sleep is a capricious fairy, and it is precisely when one invokes her presence that she is most likely to keep him waiting. The duke waited until midnight, turning on his mattress like St. Laurence on his gridiron. Finally he slept.

But at daybreak he awoke. Wild dreams had disturbed his repose. He dreamed that he was endowed with wings—he wished to fly away. For a time these wings supported him, but when he reached a certain height this new aid failed him. His wings were broken and he seemed to sink into a bottomless abyss, whence he awoke, bathed in perspiration and nearly as much overcome as if he had really fallen. He fell asleep again and another vision appeared. He was in a subterranean passage by which he was to leave Vincennes. Grimaud was walking before him with a lantern. By degrees the passage narrowed, yet the duke continued his course. At last it became so narrow that the fugitive tried in vain to proceed. The sides of the walls seem to close in, even to press against him. He made fruitless efforts to go on; it was impossible. Nevertheless, he still saw Grimaud with his lantern in front, advancing. He wished to call out to him but could not utter a word. Then at the other extremity he heard the footsteps of those who were pursuing him. These steps came on, came fast. He was discovered; all hope of flight was gone. Still the walls seemed to be closing on him; they appeared to be in concert with his enemies. At last he heard the voice of La Ramee. La Ramee took his hand and laughed aloud. He was captured again, and conducted to the low and vaulted chamber, in which Ornano, Puylaurens, and his uncle had died. Their three graves were there, rising above the ground, and a fourth was also there, yawning for its ghastly tenant.

The duke was obliged to make as many efforts to awake as he had done to go to sleep; and La Ramee found him so pale and fatigued that he inquired whether he was ill.

"In fact," said one of the guards who had remained in the chamber and had been kept awake by a toothache, brought on by the dampness of the atmosphere, "my lord has had a very restless night and two or three times, while dreaming, he called for help."

"What is the matter with your highness?" asked La Ramee.

"'Tis your fault, you simpleton," answered the duke. "With your idle nonsense yesterday about escaping, you worried me so that I dreamed that I was trying to escape and broke my neck in doing so."

La Ramee laughed.

"Come," he said, "'tis a warning from Heaven. Never commit such an imprudence as to try to escape, except in your dreams."

"And you are right, my dear La Ramee," said the duke, wiping away the sweat that stood on his brow, wide awake though he was; "after this I will think of nothing but eating and drinking."

"Hush!" said La Ramee; and one by one he sent away the guards, on various pretexts.

"Well?" asked the duke when they were alone.

"Well!" replied La Ramee, "your supper is ordered."

"Ah! and what is it to be? Monsieur, my majordomo, will there be a pie?"

"I should think so, indeed—almost as high as a tower."

"You told him it was for me?"

"Yes, and he said he would do his best to please your highness."

"Good!" exclaimed the duke, rubbing his hands.

"Devil take it, my lord! what a gourmand you are growing; I haven't seen you with so cheerful a face these five years."

The duke saw that he had not controlled himself as he ought, but at that moment, as if he had listened at the door and comprehended the urgent need of diverting La Ramee's ideas, Grimaud entered and made a sign to La Ramee that he had something to say to him.

La Ramee drew near to Grimaud, who spoke to him in a low voice.

The duke meanwhile recovered his self-control.

"I have already forbidden that man," he said, "to come in here without my permission."

"You must pardon him, my lord," said La Ramee, "for I directed him to come."

"And why did you so direct when you know that he displeases me?"

"My lord will remember that it was agreed between us that he should wait upon us at that famous supper. My lord has forgotten the supper."

"No, but I have forgotten Monsieur Grimaud."

"My lord understands that there can be no supper unless he is allowed to be present."

"Go on, then; have it your own way."

"Come here, my lad," said La Ramee, "and hear what I have to say."

Grimaud approached, with a very sullen expression on his face.

La Ramee continued: "My lord has done me the honor to invite me to a supper to-morrow en tete-a-tete."

Grimaud made a sign which meant that he didn't see what that had to do with him.

"Yes, yes," said La Ramee, "the matter concerns you, for you will have the honor to serve us; and besides, however good an appetite we may have and however great our thirst, there will be something left on the plates and in the bottles, and that something will be yours."

Grimaud bowed in thanks.

"And now," said La Ramee, "I must ask your highness's pardon, but it seems that Monsieur de Chavigny is to be away for a few days and he has sent me word that he has certain directions to give me before his departure."

The duke tried to exchange a glance with Grimaud, but there was no glance in Grimaud's eyes.

"Go, then," said the duke, "and return as soon as possible."

"Does your highness wish to take revenge for the game of tennis yesterday?"

Grimaud intimated by a scarcely perceptible nod that he should consent.

"Yes," said the duke, "but take care, my dear La Ramee, for I propose to beat you badly."

La Ramee went out. Grimaud looked after him, and when the door was closed he drew out of his pocket a pencil and a sheet of paper.

"Write, my lord," he said.

"And what?"

Grimaud dictated.

"All is ready for to-morrow evening. Keep watch from seven to nine. Have two riding horses ready. We shall descend by the first window in the gallery."

"What next?"

"Sign your name, my lord."

The duke signed.

"Now, my lord, give me, if you have not lost it, the ball—that which contained the letter."

The duke took it from under his pillow and gave it to Grimaud. Grimaud gave a grim smile.

"Well?" asked the duke.

"Well, my lord, I sew up the paper in the ball and you, in your game of tennis, will send the ball into the ditch."

"But will it not be lost?"

"Oh no; there will be some one at hand to pick it up."

"A gardener?"

Grimaud nodded.

"The same as yesterday?"

Another nod on the part of Grimaud.

"The Count de Rochefort?"

Grimaud nodded the third time.

"Come, now," said the duke, "give some particulars of the plan for our escape."

"That is forbidden me," said Grimaud, "until the last moment."

"Who will be waiting for me beyond the ditch?"

"I know nothing about it, my lord."

"But at least, if you don't want to see me turn crazy, tell what that famous pate will contain."

"Two poniards, a knotted rope and a poire d'angoisse." *

* This poire d'angoisse was a famous gag, in the form of a pear, which, being thrust into the mouth, by the aid of a spring, dilated, so as to distend the jaws to their greatest width.

"Yes, I understand."

"My lord observes that there will be enough to go around."

"We shall take to ourselves the poniards and the rope," replied the duke.

"And make La Ramee eat the pear," answered Grimaud.

"My dear Grimaud, thou speakest seldom, but when thou dost, one must do thee justice—thy words are words of gold."

Chapter XX.

One of Marie Michon's Adventures.

Whilst these projects were being formed by the Duc de Beaufort and Grimaud, the Comte de la Fere and the Vicomte de Bragelonne were entering Paris by the Rue du Faubourg Saint Marcel.

They stopped at the sign of the Fox, in the Rue du Vieux Colombier, a tavern known for many years by Athos, and asked for two bedrooms.

"You must dress yourself, Raoul," said Athos, "I am going to present you to some one."

"To-day, monsieur?" asked the young man.

"In half an hour."

The young man bowed. Perhaps, not being endowed with the endurance of Athos, who seemed to be made of iron, he would have preferred a bath in the river Seine of which he had heard so much, and afterward his bed; but the Comte de la Fere had spoken and he had no thought but to obey.

"By the way," said Athos, "take some pains with your toilet, Raoul; I want you to be approved."

"I hope, sir," replied the youth, smiling, "that there's no idea of a marriage for me; you know of my engagement to Louise?"

Athos, in his turn, smiled also.

"No, don't be alarmed, although it is to a lady that I am going to present you, and I am anxious that you should love her———"

The young man looked at the count with a certain uneasiness, but at a smile from Athos he was quickly reassured.

"How old is she?" inquired the Vicomte de Bragelonne.

"My dear Raoul, learn, once for all, that that is a question which is never asked. When you can find out a woman's age by her face, it is useless to ask it; when you cannot do so, it is indiscreet."

"Is she beautiful?"

"Sixteen years ago she was deemed not only the prettiest, but the most graceful woman in France."

This reply reassured the vicomte. A woman who had been a reigning beauty a year before he was born could not be the subject of any scheme for him. He retired to his toilet. When he reappeared, Athos received him with the same paternal smile as that which he had often bestowed on D'Artagnan, but a more profound tenderness for Raoul was now visibly impressed upon his face.

Athos cast a glance at his feet, hands and hair—those three marks of race. The youth's dark hair was neatly parted and hung in curls, forming a sort of dark frame around his face; such was the fashion of the day. Gloves of gray kid, matching the hat, well displayed the form of a slender and elegant hand; whilst his boots, similar in color to the hat and gloves, confined feet small as those of a boy twelve years old.

"Come," murmured Athos, "if she is not proud of him, she must be hard to please."

It was three o'clock in the afternoon. The two travelers proceeded to the Rue Saint Dominique and stopped at the door of a magnificent hotel, surmounted with the arms of De Luynes.

"'Tis here," said Athos.

He entered the hotel and ascended the front steps, and addressing a footman who waited there in a grand livery, asked if the Duchess de Chevreuse was visible and if she could receive the Comte de la Fere?

The servant returned with a message to say, that, though the duchess had not the honor of knowing Monsieur de la Fere, she would receive him.

Athos followed the footman, who led him through a long succession of apartments and paused at length before a closed door. Athos made a sign to the Vicomte de Bragelonne to remain where he was.

The footman opened the door and announced Monsieur le Comte de la Fere.

Madame de Chevreuse, whose name appears so often in our story "The Three Musketeers," without her actually having appeared in any scene, was still a beautiful woman. Although about forty-four or forty-five years old, she might have passed for thirty-five. She still had her rich fair hair; her large, animated, intelligent eyes, so often opened by intrigue, so often closed by the blindness of love. She had still her nymph-like form, so that when her back was turned she still was not unlike the girl who had jumped, with Anne of Austria, over the moat of the Tuileries in 1563. In all other respects she was the same mad creature who threw over her amours such an air of originality as to make them proverbial for eccentricity in her family.

She was in a little boudoir, hung with blue damask, adorned by red flowers, with a foliage of gold, looking upon a garden; and reclined upon a sofa, her head supported on the rich tapestry which covered it. She held a book in her hand and her arm was supported by a cushion.

At the footman's announcement she raised herself a little and peeped out, with some curiosity.

Athos appeared.

He was dressed in violet-tinted velvet, trimmed with silk of the same color. His shoulder-knots were of burnished silver, his mantle had no gold nor embroidery on it; a simple plume of violet feathers adorned his hat; his boots were of black leather, and at his girdle hung that sword with a magnificent hilt that Porthos had so often admired in the Rue Feron. Splendid lace adorned the falling collar of his shirt, and lace fell also over the top of his boots.

In his whole person he bore such an impress of high degree, that Madame de Chevreuse half rose from her seat when she saw him and made him a sign to sit down near her.

Athos bowed and obeyed. The footman was withdrawing, but Athos stopped him by a sign.

"Madame," he said to the duchess, "I have had the boldness to present myself at your hotel without being known to you; it has succeeded, since you deign to receive me. I have now the boldness to ask you for an interview of half an hour."

"I grant it, monsieur," replied Madame de Chevreuse with her most gracious smile.

"But that is not all, madame. Oh, I am very presuming, I am aware. The interview for which I ask is of us two alone, and I very earnestly wish that it may not be interrupted."

"I am not at home to any one," said the Duchess de Chevreuse to the footman. "You may go."

The footman went out.

There ensued a brief silence, during which these two persons, who at first sight recognized each other so clearly as of noble race, examined each other without embarrassment on either side.

The duchess was the first to speak.

"Well, sir, I am waiting with impatience to hear what you wish to say to me."

"And I, madame," replied Athos, "am looking with admiration."

"Sir," said Madame de Chevreuse, "you must excuse me, but I long to know to whom I am talking. You belong to the court, doubtless, yet I have never seen you at court. Have you, by any chance, been in the Bastile?"

"No, madame, I have not; but very likely I am on the road to it."

"Ah! then tell me who you are, and get along with you upon your journey," replied the duchess, with the gayety which made her so charming, "for I am sufficiently in bad odor already, without compromising myself still more."

"Who I am, madame? My name has been mentioned to you—the Comte de la Fere; you do not know that name. I once bore another, which you knew, but you have certainly forgotten it."

"Tell it me, sir."

"Formerly," said the count, "I was Athos."

Madame de Chevreuse looked astonished. The name was not wholly forgotten, but mixed up and confused with ancient recollections.

"Athos?" said she; "wait a moment."

And she placed her hands on her brow, as if to force the fugitive ideas it contained to concentration in a moment.

"Shall I help you, madame?" asked Athos.

"Yes, do," said the duchess.

"This Athos was connected with three young musketeers, named Porthos, D'Artagnan, and——"

He stopped short.

"And Aramis," said the duchess, quickly.

"And Aramis; I see you have not forgotten the name."

"No," she said; "poor Aramis; a charming man, elegant, discreet, and a writer of poetical verses. I am afraid he has turned out ill," she added.

"He has; he is an abbé."

"Ah, what a misfortune!" exclaimed the duchess, playing carelessly with her fan. "Indeed, sir, I thank you; you have recalled one of the most agreeable recollections of my youth."

"Will you permit me, then, to recall another to you?"

"Relating to him?"

"Yes and no."

"Faith!" said Madame de Chevreuse, "say on. With a man like you I fear nothing."

Athos bowed. "Aramis," he continued, "was intimate with a young needlewoman from Tours, a cousin of his, named Marie Michon."

"Ah, I knew her!" cried the duchess. "It was to her he wrote from the siege of Rochelle, to warn her of a plot against the Duke of Buckingham."

"Exactly so; will you allow me to speak to you of her?"

"If," replied the duchess, with a meaning look, "you do not say too much against her."

"I should be ungrateful," said Athos, "and I regard ingratitude, not as a fault or a crime, but as a vice, which is much worse."

"You ungrateful to Marie Michon, monsieur?" said Madame de Chevreuse, trying to read in Athos's eyes. "But how can that be? You never knew her."

"Eh, madame, who knows?" said Athos. "There is a popular proverb to the effect that it is only mountains that never meet; and popular proverbs contain sometimes a wonderful amount of truth."

"Oh, go on, monsieur, go on!" said Madame de Chevreuse eagerly; "you can't imagine how much this conversation interests me."

"You encourage me," said Athos, "I will continue, then. That cousin of Aramis, that Marie Michon, that needlewoman, notwithstanding her low condition, had acquaintances in the highest rank; she called the grandest ladies of the court her friend, and the queen—proud as she is, in her double character as Austrian and as Spaniard—called her her sister."

"Alas!" said Madame de Chevreuse, with a slight sigh and a little movement of her eyebrows that was peculiarly her own, "since that time everything has changed."

"And the queen had reason for her affection, for Marie was devoted to her—devoted to that degree that she served her as medium of intercourse with her brother, the king of Spain."

"Which," interrupted the duchess, "is now brought up against her as a great crime."

"And therefore," continued Athos, "the cardinal—the true cardinal, the other one—determined one fine morning to arrest poor Marie Michon and send her to the Chateau de Loches. Fortunately the affair was not managed so secretly but that it became known to the queen. The case had been provided for: if Marie Michon should be threatened with any danger the queen was to send her a prayer-book bound in green velvet."

"That is true, monsieur, you are well informed."

"One morning the green book was brought to her by the Prince de Marsillac. There was no time to lose. Happily Marie and a follower of hers named Kitty could disguise themselves admirably in men's clothes. The prince procured for Marie Michon the dress of a cavalier and for Kitty that of a lackey; he sent them two excellent horses, and the fugitives went out hastily from Tours, shaping their course toward Spain, trembling at the least noise, following unfrequented roads, and asking for hospitality when they found themselves where there was no inn."

"Why, really, it was all exactly as you say!" cried Madame de Chevreuse, clapping her hands. "It would indeed be strange if——" she checked herself.

"If I should follow the two fugitives to the end of their journey?" said Athos. "No, madame, I will not thus waste your time. We will accompany them only to a little village in Limousin, lying between Tulle and Angouleme—a little village called Roche-l'Abeille."

Madame de Chevreuse uttered a cry of surprise, and looked at Athos with an expression of astonishment that made the old musketeer smile.

"Wait, madame," continued Athos, "what remains for me to tell you is even more strange than what I have narrated."

"Monsieur," said Madame de Chevreuse, "I believe you are a sorcerer; I am prepared for anything. But really—No matter, go on."

"The journey of that day had been long and wearing; it was a cold day, the eleventh of October, there was no inn or chateau in the village and the homes of the peasants were poor and unattractive. Marie Michon was a very aristocratic person; like her sister the queen, she had been accustomed to pleasing perfumes and fine linen; she resolved, therefore, to seek hospitality of the priest."

Athos paused.

"Oh, continue!" said the duchess. "I have told you that I am prepared for anything."

"The two travelers knocked at the door. It was late; the priest, who had gone to bed, cried out to them to come in. They entered, for the door was not locked—there is much confidence among villagers. A lamp burned in the chamber occupied by the priest. Marie Michon, who made the most charming cavalier in the world, pushed open the door, put her head in and asked for hospitality. 'Willingly, my young cavalier,' said the priest, 'if you will be content with the remains of my supper and with half my chamber.'

"The two travelers consulted for a moment. The priest heard a burst of laughter and then the master, or rather, the mistress, replied: 'Thank you, monsieur le curé, I accept.' 'Sup, then, and make as little noise as possible,' said the priest, 'for I, too, have been on the go all day and shall not be sorry to sleep to-night.'"

Madame de Chevreuse evidently went from surprise to astonishment, and from astonishment to stupefaction. Her face, as she looked at Athos, had taken on an expression that cannot be described. It could be seen that she had wished to speak, but she had remained silent through fear of losing one of her companion's words.

"What happened then?" she asked.

"Then?" said Athos. "Ah, I have come now to what is most difficult."

"Speak, speak! One can say anything to me. Besides, it doesn't concern me; it relates to Mademoiselle Marie Michon."

"Ah, that is true," said Athos. "Well, then, Marie Michon had supper with her follower, and then, in accordance with the permission given her, she entered the chamber of her host, Kitty meanwhile taking possession of an armchair in the room first entered, where they had taken their supper."

"Really, monsieur," said Madame de Chevreuse, "unless you are the devil in person I don't know how you could become acquainted with all these details."

"A charming woman was that Marie Michon," resumed Athos, "one of those wild creatures who are constantly conceiving the strangest ideas. Now, thinking that her host was a priest, that coquette took it into her head that it would be a happy souvenir for her old age, among the many happy souvenirs she already possessed, if she could win that of having damned an abbé."

"Count," said the duchess, "upon my word, you frighten me."

"Alas!" continued Athos, "the poor abbé was not a St. Ambroise, and I repeat, Marie Michon was an adorable creature."

"Monsieur!" cried the duchess, seizing Athos's hands, "tell me this moment how you know all these details, or I will send to the convent of the Vieux Augustins for a monk to come and exorcise you."

Athos laughed. "Nothing is easier, madame. A cavalier, charged with an important mission, had come an hour before your arrival, seeking hospitality, at the very moment that the curé, summoned to the bedside of a dying person, left not only his house but the village, for the entire night. The priest having all confidence in his guest, who, besides, was a nobleman, had left to him his house, his supper and his chamber. And therefore Marie came seeking hospitality from the guest of the good abbé and not from the good abbé himself."

"And that cavalier, that guest, that nobleman who arrived before she came?"

"It was I, the Comte de la Fere," said Athos, rising and bowing respectfully to the Duchess de Chevreuse.

The duchess remained a moment stupefied; then, suddenly bursting into laughter:

"Ah! upon my word," said she, "it is very droll, and that mad Marie Michon fared better than she expected. Sit down, dear count, and go on with your story."

"At this point I have to accuse myself of a fault, madame. I have told you that I was traveling on an important mission. At daybreak I left the chamber without noise, leaving my charming companion asleep. In the front room the follower was also still asleep, her head leaning back on the chair, in all respects worthy of her mistress. Her pretty face arrested my attention; I approached and recognized that little Kitty whom our friend Aramis had placed with her. In that way I discovered that the charming traveler was——"

"Marie Michon!" said Madame de Chevreuse, hastily.

"Marie Michon," continued Athos. "Then I went out of the house; I proceeded to the stable and found my horse saddled and my lackey ready. We set forth on our journey."

"And have you never revisited that village?" eagerly asked Madame de Chevreuse.

"A year after, madame."

"Well?"

"I wanted to see the good curé again. I found him much preoccupied with an event that he could not at all comprehend. A week before he had received, in a cradle, a beautiful little boy three months old, with a purse filled with gold and a note containing these simple words: '11 October, 1633.'"

"It was the date of that strange adventure," interrupted Madame de Chevreuse.

"Yes, but he couldn't understand what it meant, for he had spent that night with a dying person and Marie Michon had left his house before his return."

"You must know, monsieur, that Marie Michon, when she returned to France in 1643, immediately sought for information about that child; as a fugitive she could not take care of it, but on her return she wished to have it near her."

"And what said the abbé?" asked Athos.

"That a nobleman whom he did not know had wished to take charge of it, had answered for its future, and had taken it away."

"That was true."

"Ah! I see! That nobleman was you; it was his father!"

"Hush! do not speak so loud, madame; he is there."

"He is there! my son! the son of Marie Michon! But I must see him instantly."

"Take care, madame," said Athos, "for he knows neither his father nor his mother."

"You have kept the secret! you have brought him to see me, thinking to make me happy. Oh, thanks! sir, thanks!" cried Madame de Chevreuse, seizing his hand and trying to put it to her lips; "you have a noble heart."

"I bring him to you, madame," said Athos, withdrawing his hand, "hoping that in your turn you will do something for him; till now I have watched over his education and I have made him, I hope, an accomplished gentleman; but I am now obliged to return to the dangerous and wandering life of party faction. To-morrow I plunge into an adventurous affair in which I may be killed. Then it will devolve on you to push him on in that world where he is called on to occupy a place."

"Rest assured," cried the duchess, "I shall do what I can. I have but little influence now, but all that I have shall most assuredly be his. As to his title and fortune——"

"As to that, madame, I have made over to him the estate of Bragelonne, my inheritance, which will give him ten thousand francs a year and the title of vicomte."

"Upon my soul, monsieur," said the duchess, "you are a true nobleman! But I am eager to see our young vicomte. Where is he?"

"There, in the salon. I will have him come in, if you really wish it."

Athos moved toward the door; the duchess held him back.

"Is he handsome?" she asked.

Athos smiled.

"He resembles his mother."

So he opened the door and beckoned the young man in.

The duchess could not restrain a cry of joy on seeing so handsome a young cavalier, so far surpassing all that her maternal pride had been able to conceive.

"Vicomte, come here," said Athos; "the duchess permits you to kiss her hand."

The youth approached with his charming smile and his head bare, and kneeling down, kissed the hand of the Duchess de Chevreuse.

"Sir," he said, turning to Athos, "was it not in compassion to my timidity that you told me that this lady was the Duchess de Chevreuse, and is she not the queen?"

"No, vicomte," said Madame de Chevreuse, taking his hand and making him sit near her, while she looked at him with eyes sparkling with pleasure; "no, unhappily, I am not the queen. If I were I should do for you at once the most that you deserve. But let us see; whatever I may be," she added, hardly restraining herself from kissing that pure brow, "let us see what profession you wish to follow."

Athos, standing, looked at them both with indescribable pleasure.

"Madame," answered the youth in his sweet voice, "it seems to me that there is only one career for a gentleman—that of the army. I have been brought up by monsieur le comte with the intention, I believe, of making me a soldier; and he gave me reason to hope that at Paris he would present me to some one who would recommend me to the favor of the prince."

"Yes, I understand it well. Personally, I am on bad terms with him, on account of the quarrels between Madame de Montbazon, my mother-in-law, and Madame de Longueville. But the Prince de Marsillac! Yes, indeed, that's the right thing. The Prince de Marsillac—my old friend—will recommend our young friend to Madame de Longueville, who will give him a letter to her brother, the prince, who loves her too tenderly not to do what she wishes immediately."

"Well, that will do charmingly," said the count; "but may I beg that the greatest haste may be made, for I have reasons for wishing the vicomte not to sleep longer than to-morrow night in Paris!"

"Do you wish it known that you are interested about him, monsieur le comte?"

"Better for him in future that he should be supposed never to have seen me."

"Oh, sir!" cried Raoul.

"You know, Bragelonne," said Athos, "I never speak without reflection."

"Well, comte, I am going instantly," interrupted the duchess, "to send for the Prince de Marsillac, who is happily, in Paris just now. What are you going to do this evening?"

"We intend to visit the Abbé Scarron, for whom I have a letter of introduction and at whose house I expect to meet some of my friends."

"'Tis well; I will go there also, for a few minutes," said the duchess; "do not quit his salon until you have seen me."

Athos bowed and prepared to leave.

"Well, monsieur le comte," said the duchess, smiling, "does one leave so solemnly his old friends?"

"Ah," murmured Athos, kissing her hand, "had I only sooner known that Marie Michon was so charming a creature!" And he withdrew, sighing.

Chapter XXI.

The Abbé Scarron.

There was once in the Rue des Tournelles a house known by all the sedan chairmen and footmen of Paris, and yet, nevertheless, this house was neither that of a great lord nor of a rich man. There was neither dining, nor playing at cards, nor dancing in that house. Nevertheless, it was the rendezvous of the great world and all Paris went there. It was the abode of the little Abbé Scarron.

In the home of the witty abbé dwelt incessant laughter; there all the items of the day had their source and were so quickly transformed, misrepresented, metamorphosed, some into epigrams, some into falsehoods, that every one was anxious to pass an hour with little Scarron, listening to what he said, reporting it to others.

The diminutive Abbé Scarron, who, however, was an abbé only because he owned an abbey, and not because he was in orders, had formerly been one of the gayest prebendaries in the town of Mans, which he inhabited. On a day of the carnival he had taken a notion to provide an unusual entertainment for that good town, of which he was the life and soul. He had made his valet cover him with honey; then, opening a feather bed, he had rolled in it and had thus become the most grotesque fowl it is possible to imagine. He then began to visit his friends of both sexes, in that strange costume. At first he had been followed through astonishment, then with derisive shouts, then the porters had insulted him, then children had thrown stones at him, and finally he was obliged to run, to escape the missiles. As soon as he took to flight every one pursued him, until, pressed on all sides, Scarron found no way of escaping his escort, except by throwing himself into the river; but the water was icy cold. Scarron was heated, the cold seized on him, and when he reached the farther bank he found himself crippled.

Every means had been employed in vain to restore the use of his limbs. He had been subjected to a severe disciplinary course of medicine, at length he sent away all his doctors, declaring that he preferred the disease to the treatment, and came to Paris, where the fame of his wit had preceded him. There he had a chair made on his own plan, and one day, visiting Anne of Austria in this chair, she asked him, charmed as she was with his wit, if he did not wish for a title.

"Yes, your majesty, there is a title which I covet much," replied Scarron.

"And what is that?"

"That of being your invalid," answered Scarron.

So he was called the queen's invalid, with a pension of fifteen hundred francs.

From that lucky moment Scarron led a happy life, spending both income and principal. One day, however, an emissary of the cardinal's gave him to understand that he was wrong in receiving the coadjutor so often.

"And why?" asked Scarron; "is he not a man of good birth?"

"Certainly."

"Agreeable?"

"Undeniably."

"Witty?"

"He has, unfortunately, too much wit."

"Well, then, why do you wish me to give up seeing such a man?"

"Because he is an enemy."

"Of whom?"

"Of the cardinal."

"What?" answered Scarron, "I continue to receive Monsieur Gilles Despreaux, who thinks ill of me, and you wish me to give up seeing the coadjutor, because he thinks ill of another man. Impossible!"

The conversation had rested there and Scarron, through sheer obstinacy, had seen Monsieur de Gondy only the more frequently.

Now, the very morning of which we speak was that of his quarter-day payment, and Scarron, as usual, had sent his servant to get his money at the pension-office, but the man had returned and said that the government had no more money to give Monsieur Scarron.

It was on Thursday, the abbé's reception day; people went there in crowds. The cardinal's refusal to pay the pension was known about the town in half an hour and he was abused with wit and vehemence.

In the Rue Saint Honore Athos fell in with two gentlemen whom he did not know, on horseback like himself, followed by a lackey like himself, and going in the same direction that he was. One of them, hat in hand, said to him:

"Would you believe it, monsieur? that contemptible Mazarin has stopped poor Scarron's pension."

"That is unreasonable," said Athos, saluting in his turn the two cavaliers. And they separated with courteous gestures.

"It happens well that we are going there this evening," said Athos to the vicomte; "we will pay our compliments to that poor man."

"What, then, is this Monsieur Scarron, who thus puts all Paris in commotion? Is he some minister out of office?"

"Oh, no, not at all, vicomte," Athos replied; "he is simply a gentleman of great genius who has fallen into disgrace with the cardinal through having written certain verses against him."

"Do gentlemen, then, make verses?" asked Raoul, naively, "I thought it was derogatory."

"So it is, my dear vicomte," said Athos, laughing, "to make bad ones; but to make good ones increases fame—witness Monsieur de Rotrou. Nevertheless," he continued, in the tone of one who gives wholesome advice, "I think it is better not to make them."

"Then," said Raoul, "this Monsieur Scarron is a poet?"

"Yes; you are warned, vicomte. Consider well what you do in that house. Talk only by gestures, or rather always listen."

"Yes, monsieur," replied Raoul.

"You will see me talking with one of my friends, the Abbé d'Herblay, of whom you have often heard me speak."

"I remember him, monsieur."

"Come near to us from time to time, as if to speak; but do not speak, and do not listen. That little stratagem may serve to keep off interlopers."

"Very well, monsieur; I will obey you at all points."

Athos made two visits in Paris; at seven o'clock he and Raoul directed their steps to the Rue des Tournelles; it was stopped by porters, horses and footmen. Athos forced his way through and entered, followed by the young man. The first person that struck him on his entrance was Aramis, planted near a great chair on castors, very large, covered with a canopy of tapestry, under which there moved, enveloped in a quilt of brocade, a little face, youngish, very merry, somewhat pallid, whilst its eyes never ceased to express a sentiment at once lively, intellectual, and amiable. This was the Abbé Scarron, always laughing, joking, complimenting—yet suffering—and toying nervously with a small switch.

Around this kind of rolling tent pressed a crowd of gentlemen and ladies. The room was neatly, comfortably furnished. Large valances of silk, embroidered with flowers of gay colors, which were rather faded, fell from the wide windows; the fittings of the room were simple, but in excellent taste. Two well trained servingmen were in attendance on the company. On perceiving Athos, Aramis advanced toward him, took him by the hand and presented him to Scarron. Raoul remained silent, for he was not prepared for the dignity of the bel esprit.

After some minutes the door opened and a footman announced Mademoiselle Paulet.

Athos touched the shoulder of the vicomte.

"Look at this lady, Raoul, she is an historic personage; it was to visit her King Henry IV. was going when he was assassinated."

Every one thronged around Mademoiselle Paulet, for she was always very much the fashion. She was a tall woman, with a slender figure and a forest of golden curls, such as Raphael was fond of and Titian has painted all his Magdalens with. This fawn-colored hair, or, perhaps the sort of ascendancy which she had over other women, gave her the name of "La Lionne." Mademoiselle Paulet took her accustomed seat, but before sitting down, she cast, in all her queen-like grandeur, a look around the room, and her eyes rested on Raoul.

Athos smiled.

"Mademoiselle Paulet has observed you, vicomte; go and bow to her; don't try to appear anything but what you are, a true country youth; on no account speak to her of Henry IV."

"When shall we two walk together?" Athos then said to Aramis.

"Presently—there are not a sufficient number of people here yet; we shall be remarked."

At this moment the door opened and in walked the coadjutor.

At this name every one looked around, for his was already a very celebrated name. Athos did the same. He knew the Abbé de Gondy only by report.

He saw a little dark man, ill made and awkward with his hands in everything—except drawing a sword and firing a pistol—with something haughty and contemptuous in his face.

Scarron turned around toward him and came to meet him in his chair.

"Well," said the coadjutor, on seeing him, "you are in disgrace, then, abbé?"

This was the orthodox phrase. It had been said that evening a hundred times—and Scarron was at his hundredth bon mot on the subject; he was very nearly at the end of his humoristic tether, but one despairing effort saved him.

"Monsieur, the Cardinal Mazarin has been so kind as to think of me," he said.

"But how can you continue to receive us?" asked the coadjutor; "if your income is lessened I shall be obliged to make you a canon of Notre Dame."

"Oh, no!" cried Scarron, "I should compromise you too much."

"Perhaps you have resources of which we are ignorant?"

"I shall borrow from the queen."

"But her majesty has no property," interposed Aramis.

At this moment the door opened and Madame de Chevreuse was announced. Every one arose. Scarron turned his chair toward the door, Raoul blushed, Athos made a sign to Aramis, who went and hid himself in the enclosure of a window.

In the midst of all the compliments that awaited her on her entrance, the duchess seemed to be looking for some one; at last she found out Raoul and her eyes sparkled; she perceived Athos and became thoughtful; she saw Aramis in the seclusion of the window and gave a start of surprise behind her fan.

"Apropos," she said, as if to drive away thoughts that pursued her in spite of herself, "how is poor Voiture, do you know, Scarron?"

"What, is Monsieur Voiture ill?" inquired a gentleman who had spoken to Athos in the Rue Saint Honore; "what is the matter with him?"

"He was acting, but forgot to take the precaution to have a change of linen ready after the performance," said the coadjutor, "so he took cold and is about to die."

"Is he then so ill, dear Voiture?" asked Aramis, half hidden by the window curtain.

"Die!" cried Mademoiselle Paulet, bitterly, "he! Why, he is surrounded by sultanas, like a Turk. Madame de Saintot has hastened to him with broth; La Renaudot warms his sheets; the Marquise de Rambouillet sends him his tisanes."

"You don't like him, my dear Parthenie," said Scarron.

"What an injustice, my dear invalid! I hate him so little that I should be delighted to order masses for the repose of his soul."

"You are not called 'Lionne' for nothing," observed Madame de Chevreuse, "your teeth are terrible."

"You are unjust to a great poet, it seems to me," Raoul ventured to say.

"A great poet! come, one may easily see, vicomte, that you are lately from the provinces and have never so much as seen him. A great poet! he is scarcely five feet high."

"Bravo bravo!" cried a tall man with an enormous mustache and a long rapier, "bravo, fair Paulet, it is high time to put little Voiture in his right place. For my part, I always thought his poetry detestable, and I think I know something about poetry."

"Who is this officer," inquired Raoul of Athos, "who is speaking?"

"Monsieur de Scudery, the author of 'Clelie,' and of 'Le Grand Cyrus,' which were composed partly by him and partly by his sister, who is now talking to that pretty person yonder, near Monsieur Scarron."

Raoul turned and saw two faces just arrived. One was perfectly charming, delicate, pensive, shaded by beautiful dark hair, and eyes soft as velvet, like those lovely flowers, the heartsease, in which shine out the golden petals. The other, of mature age, seemed to have the former one under her charge, and was cold, dry and yellow—the true type of a duenna or a devotee.

Raoul resolved not to quit the room without having spoken to the beautiful girl with the soft eyes, who by a strange fancy, although she bore no resemblance, reminded him of his poor little Louise, whom he had left in the Chateau de la Valliere and whom, in the midst of all the party, he had never for one moment quite forgotten. Meantime Aramis had drawn near to the coadjutor, who, smiling all the while, contrived to drop some words into his ear. Aramis, notwithstanding his self-control, could not refrain from a slight movement of surprise.

"Laugh, then," said Monsieur de Retz; "they are looking at us." And leaving Aramis he went to talk with Madame de Chevreuse, who was in the midst of a large group.

Aramis affected a laugh, to divert the attention of certain curious listeners, and perceiving that Athos had betaken himself to the embrasure of a window and remained there, he proceeded to join him, throwing out a few words carelessly as he moved through the room.

As soon as the two friends met they began a conversation which was emphasized by frequent gesticulation.

Raoul then approached them as Athos had directed him to do.

"'Tis a rondeau by Monsieur Voiture that monsieur l'abbé is repeating to me." said Athos in a loud voice, "and I confess I think it incomparable."

Raoul stayed only a few minutes near them and then mingled with the group round Madame de Chevreuse.

"Well, then?" asked Athos, in a low tone.

"It is to be to-morrow," said Aramis hastily.

"At what time?"

"Six o'clock."

"Where?"

"At Saint Mande."

"Who told you?"

"The Count de Rochefort."

Some one drew near.

"And then philosophic ideas are wholly wanting in Voiture's works, but I am of the same opinion as the coadjutor—he is a poet, a true poet." Aramis spoke so as to be heard by everybody.

"And I, too," murmured the young lady with the velvet eyes. "I have the misfortune also to admire his poetry exceedingly."

"Monsieur Scarron, do me the honor," said Raoul, blushing, "to tell me the name of that young lady whose opinion seems so different from that of others of the company."

"Ah! my young vicomte," replied Scarron, "I suppose you wish to propose to her an alliance offensive and defensive."

Raoul blushed again.

"You asked the name of that young lady. She is called the fair Indian."

"Excuse me, sir," returned Raoul, blushing still more deeply, "I know no more than I did before. Alas! I am from the country."

"Which means that you know very little about the nonsense which here flows down our streets. So much the better, young man! so much the better! Don't try to understand it—you will only lose your time."

"You forgive me, then, sir," said Raoul, "and you will deign to tell me who is the person that you call the young Indian?"

"Certainly; one of the most charming persons that lives—Mademoiselle Frances d'Aubigne."

"Does she belong to the family of the celebrated Agrippa, the friend of Henry IV.?"

"His granddaughter. She comes from Martinique, so I call her the beautiful Indian."

Raoul looked surprised and his eyes met those of the young lady, who smiled.

The company went on speaking of the poet Voiture.

"Monsieur," said Mademoiselle d'Aubigne to Scarron, as if she wished to join in the conversation he was engaged in with Raoul, "do you not admire Monsieur Voiture's friends? Listen how they pull him to pieces even whilst they praise him; one takes away from him all claim to good sense, another robs him of his poetry, a third of his originality, another of his humor, another of his independence of character, a sixth—but, good heavens! what will they leave him? as Mademoiselle de Scudery remarks."

Scarron and Raoul laughed. The fair Indian, astonished at the sensation her observation produced, looked down and resumed her air of naivete.

Athos, still within the inclosure of the window, watched this scene with a smile of disdain on his lips.

"Tell the Comte de la Fere to come to me," said Madame de Chevreuse, "I want to speak to him."

"And I," said the coadjutor, "want it to be thought that I do not speak to him. I admire, I love him—for I know his former adventures—but I shall not speak to him until the day after to-morrow."

"And why day after to-morrow?" asked Madame de Chevreuse.

"You will know that to-morrow evening," said the coadjutor, smiling.

"Really, my dear Gondy," said the duchess, "you remind one of the Apocalypse. Monsieur d'Herblay," she added, turning toward Aramis, "will you be my servant once more this evening?"

"How can you doubt it?" replied Aramis; "this evening, to-morrow, always; command me."

"I will, then. Go and look for the Comte de la Fere; I wish to speak with him."

Aramis found Athos and brought him.

"Monsieur le comte," said the duchess, giving him a letter, "here is what I promised you; our young friend will be extremely well received."

"Madame, he is very happy in owing any obligation to you."

"You have no reason to envy him on that score, for I owe to you the pleasure of knowing him," replied the witty woman, with a smile which recalled Marie Michon to Aramis and to Athos.

As she uttered that bon mot, she arose and asked for her carriage. Mademoiselle Paulet had already gone; Mademoiselle de Scudery was going.

"Vicomte," said Athos to Raoul, "follow the duchess; beg her to do you the favor to take your arm in going downstairs, and thank her as you descend."

The fair Indian approached Scarron.

"You are going already?" he said.

"One of the last, as you see; if you hear anything of Monsieur Voiture, be so kind as to send me word to-morrow."

"Oh!" said Scarron, "he may die now."

"Why?" asked the young girl with the velvet eyes.

"Certainly; his panegyric has been uttered."

They parted, laughing, she turning back to gaze at the poor paralytic man with interest, he looking after her with eyes of love.

One by one the several groups broke up. Scarron seemed not to observe that certain of his guests had talked mysteriously, that letters had passed from hand to hand and that the assembly had seemed to have a secret purpose quite apart from the literary discussion carried on with so much ostentation. What was all that to Scarron? At his house rebellion could be planned with impunity, for, as we have said, since that morning he had ceased to be "the queen's invalid."

As to Raoul, he had attended the duchess to her carriage, where, as she took her seat, she gave him her hand to kiss; then, by one of those wild caprices which made her so adorable and at the same time so dangerous, she had suddenly put her arm around his neck and kissed his forehead, saying:

"Vicomte, may my good wishes and this kiss bring you good fortune!"

Then she had pushed him away and directed the coachman to stop at the Hotel de Luynes. The carriage had started, Madame de Chevreuse had made a parting gesture to the young man, and Raoul had returned in a state of stupefaction.

Athos surmised what had taken place and smiled. "Come, vicomte," he said, "it is time for you to go to bed; you will start in the morning for the army of monsieur le prince. Sleep well your last night as citizen."

"I am to be a soldier then?" said the young man. "Oh, monsieur, I thank you with all my heart."

"Adieu, count," said the Abbé d'Herblay; "I return to my convent."

"Adieu, abbé," said the coadjutor, "I am to preach to-morrow and have twenty texts to examine this evening."

"Adieu, gentlemen," said the count; "I am going to sleep twenty-four hours; I am just falling down with fatigue."

The three men saluted one another, whilst exchanging a last look.

Scarron followed their movements with a glance from the corner of his eye.

"Not one of them will do as he says," he murmured, with his little monkey smile; "but they may do as they please, the brave gentlemen! Who knows if they will not manage to restore to me my pension? They can move their arms, they can, and that is much. Alas, I have only my tongue, but I will try to show that it is good for something. Ho, there, Champenois! here, it is eleven o'clock. Come and roll me to bed. Really, that Demoiselle d'Aubigne is very charming!"

So the invalid disappeared soon afterward and went into his sleeping-room; and one by one the lights in the salon of the Rue des Tournelles were extinguished.

Chapter XXII.

Saint Denis.

The day had begun to break when Athos arose and dressed himself. It was plain, by a paleness still greater than usual, and by those traces which loss of sleep leaves on the face, that he must have passed almost the whole of the night without sleeping. Contrary to the custom of a man so firm and decided, there was this morning in his personal appearance something tardy and irresolute.

He was occupied with the preparations for Raoul's departure and was seeking to gain time. In the first place he himself furbished a sword, which he drew from its perfumed leather sheath; he examined it to see if its hilt was well guarded and if the blade was firmly attached to the hilt. Then he placed at the bottom of the valise belonging to the young man a small bag of louis, called Olivain, the lackey who had followed him from Blois, and made him pack the valise under his own eyes, watchful to see that everything should be put in which might be useful to a young man entering on his first campaign.

At length, after occupying about an hour in these preparations, he opened the door of the room in which the vicomte slept, and entered.

The sun, already high, penetrated into the room through the window, the curtains of which Raoul had neglected to close on the previous evening. He was still sleeping, his head gracefully reposing on his arm.

Athos approached and hung over the youth in an attitude full of tender melancholy; he looked long on this young man, whose smiling mouth and half closed eyes bespoke soft dreams and lightest slumber, as if his guardian angel watched over him with solicitude and affection. By degrees Athos gave himself up to the charms of his reverie in the proximity of youth, so pure, so fresh. His own youth seemed to reappear, bringing with it all those savoury remembrances, which are like perfumes more than thoughts. Between the past and the present was an ineffable abyss. But imagination has the wings of an angel of light and travels safely through or over the seas where we have been almost shipwrecked, the darkness in which our illusions are lost, the precipice whence our happiness has been hurled and swallowed up. He remembered that all the first part of his life had been embittered by a woman and he thought with alarm of the influence love might assume over so fine, and at the same time so vigorous an organization as that of Raoul.

In recalling all he had been through, he foresaw all that Raoul might suffer; and the expression of the deep and tender compassion which throbbed in his heart was pictured in the moist eye with which he gazed on the young man.

At this moment Raoul awoke, without a cloud on his face without weariness or lassitude; his eyes were fixed on those of Athos and perhaps he comprehended all that passed in the heart of the man who was awaiting his awakening as a lover awaits the awakening of his mistress, for his glance, in return, had all the tenderness of love.

"You are there, sir?" he said, respectfully.

"Yes, Raoul," replied the count.

"And you did not awaken me?"

"I wished to leave you still to enjoy some moments of sleep, my child; you must be fatigued from yesterday."

"Oh, sir, how good you are!"

Athos smiled.

"How do you feel this morning?" he inquired.

"Perfectly well; quite rested, sir."

"You are still growing," Athos continued, with that charming and paternal interest felt by a grown man for a youth.

"Oh, sir, I beg your pardon!" exclaimed Raoul, ashamed of so much attention; "in an instant I shall be dressed."

Athos then called Olivain.

"Everything," said Olivain to Athos, "has been done according to your directions; the horses are waiting."

"And I was asleep," cried Raoul, "whilst you, sir, you had the kindness to attend to all these details. Truly, sir, you overwhelm me with benefits!"

"Therefore you love me a little, I hope," replied Athos, in a tone of emotion.

"Oh, sir! God knows how much I love, revere you."

"See that you forget nothing," said Athos, appearing to look about him, that he might hide his emotion.

"No, indeed, sir," answered Raoul.

The servant then approached Athos and said, hesitatingly:

"Monsieur le vicomte has no sword."

"'Tis well," said Athos, "I will take care of that."

They went downstairs, Raoul looking every now and then at the count to see if the moment of farewell was at hand, but Athos was silent. When they reached the steps Raoul saw three horses.

"Oh, sir! then you are going with me?"

"I will accompany you a portion of the way," said Athos.

Joy shone in Raoul's eyes and he leaped lightly to his saddle.

Athos mounted more slowly, after speaking in a low voice to the lackey, who, instead of following them immediately, returned to their rooms. Raoul, delighted at the count's companionship, perceived, or affected to perceive nothing of this byplay.

They set out, passing over the Pont Neuf; they pursued their way along the quay then called L'Abreuvoir Pepin, and went along by the walls of the Grand Chatelet. They proceeded to the Rue Saint Denis.

After passing through the Porte Saint Denis, Athos looked at Raoul's way of riding and observed:

"Take care, Raoul! I have already often told you of this; you must not forget it, for it is a great defect in a rider. See! your horse is tired already, he froths at the mouth, whilst mine looks as if he had only just left the stable. You hold the bit too tight and so make his mouth hard, so that you will not be able to make him manoeuvre quickly. The safety of a cavalier often depends on the prompt obedience of his horse. In a week, remember, you will no longer be performing your manoeuvres for practice, but on a field of battle."

Then suddenly, in order not to give too uncomfortable an importance to this observation:

"See, Raoul!" he resumed; "what a fine plain for partridge shooting."

The young man stored in his mind the admonition whilst he admired the delicate tenderness with which it was bestowed.

"I have remarked also another thing," said Athos, "which is, that in firing off your pistol you hold your arm too far outstretched. This tension lessens the accuracy of the aim. So in twelve times you thrice missed the mark."

"Which you, sir, struck twelve times," answered Raoul, smiling.

"Because I bent my arm and rested my hand on my elbow—so; do you understand what I mean?"

"Yes, sir. I have fired since in that manner and have been quite successful."

"What a cold wind!" resumed Athos; "a wintry blast. Apropos, if you fire—and you will do so, for you are recommended to a young general who is very fond of powder—remember that in single combat, which often takes place in the cavalry, never to fire the first shot. He who fires the first shot rarely hits his man, for he fires with the apprehension of being disarmed, before an armed foe; then, whilst he fires, make your horse rear; that manoeuvre has saved my life several times."

"I shall do so, if only in gratitude——"

"Eh!" cried Athos, "are not those fellows poachers they have arrested yonder? They are. Then another important thing, Raoul: should you be wounded in a battle, and fall from your horse, if you have any strength left, disentangle yourself from the line that your regiment has formed; otherwise, it may be driven back and you will be trampled to death by the horses. At all events, should you be wounded, write to me that very instant, or get some one at once to write to me. We are judges of wounds, we old soldiers," Athos added, smiling.

"Thank you, sir," answered the young man, much moved.

They arrived that very moment at the gate of the town, guarded by two sentinels.

"Here comes a young gentleman," said one of them, "who seems as if he were going to join the army."

"How do you make that out?" inquired Athos.

"By his manner, sir, and his age; he's the second to-day."

"Has a young man, such as I am, gone through this morning, then?" asked Raoul.

"Faith, yes, with a haughty presence, a fine equipage; such as the son of a noble house would have."

"He will be my companion on the journey, sir," cried Raoul. "Alas! he cannot make me forget what I shall have lost!"

Thus talking, they traversed the streets, full of people on account of the fete, and arrived opposite the old cathedral, where first mass was going on.

"Let us alight; Raoul," said Athos. "Olivain, take care of our horses and give me my sword."

The two gentlemen then went into the church. Athos gave Raoul some of the holy water. A love as tender as that of a lover for his mistress dwells, undoubtedly, in some paternal hearts toward a son.

Athos said a word to one of the vergers, who bowed and proceeded toward the basement.

"Come, Raoul," he said, "let us follow this man."

The verger opened the iron grating that guarded the royal tombs and stood on the topmost step, whilst Athos and Raoul descended. The sepulchral depths of the descent were dimly lighted by a silver lamp on the lowest step; and just below this lamp there was laid, wrapped in a flowing mantle of violet velvet, worked with fleurs-de-lis of gold, a catafalque resting on trestles of oak. The young man, prepared for this scene by the state of his own feelings, which were mournful, and by the majesty of the cathedral which he had passed through, descended in a slow and solemn manner and stood with head uncovered before these mortal spoils of the last king, who was not to be placed by the side of his forefathers until his successor should take his place there; and who appeared to abide on that spot, that he might thus address human pride, so sure to be exalted by the glories of a throne: "Dust of the earth! Here I await thee!"

There was profound silence.

Then Athos raised his hand and pointing to the coffin:

"This temporary sepulture is," he said, "that of a man who was of feeble mind, yet one whose reign was full of great events; because over this king watched the spirit of another man, even as this lamp keeps vigil over this coffin and illumines it. He whose intellect was thus supreme, Raoul, was the actual sovereign; the other, nothing but a phantom to whom he lent a soul; and yet, so powerful is majesty amongst us, this man has not even the honor of a tomb at the feet of him in whose service his life was worn away. Remember, Raoul, this! If Richelieu made the king, by comparison, seem small, he made royalty great. The Palace of the Louvre contains two things—the king, who must die, and royalty, which never dies. The minister, so feared, so hated by his master, has descended into the tomb, drawing after him the king, whom he would not leave alone on earth, lest his work should be destroyed. So blind were his contemporaries that they regarded the cardinal's death as a deliverance; and I, even I, opposed the designs of the great man who held the destinies of

France within the hollow of his hand. Raoul, learn how to distinguish the king from royalty; the king is but a man; royalty is the gift of God. Whenever you hesitate as to whom you ought to serve, abandon the exterior, the material appearance for the invisible principle, for the invisible principle is everything. Raoul, I seem to read your future destiny as through a cloud. It will be happier, I think, than ours has been. Different in your fate from us, you will have a king without a minister, whom you may serve, love, respect. Should the king prove a tyrant, for power begets tyranny, serve, love, respect royalty, that Divine right, that celestial spark which makes this dust still powerful and holy, so that we—gentlemen, nevertheless, of rank and condition—are as nothing in comparison with the cold corpse there extended."

"I shall adore God, sir," said Raoul, "respect royalty and ever serve the king. And if death be my lot, I hope to die for the king, for royalty and for God. Have I, sir, comprehended your instructions?"

Athos smiled.

"Yours is a noble nature." he said; "here is your sword."

Raoul bent his knee to the ground.

"It was worn by my father, a loyal gentleman. I have worn it in my turn and it has sometimes not been disgraced when the hilt was in my hand and the sheath at my side. Should your hand still be too weak to use this sword, Raoul, so much the better. You will have the more time to learn to draw it only when it ought to be used."

"Sir," replied Raoul, putting the sword to his lips as he received it from the count, "I owe you everything and yet this sword is the most precious gift you have yet made me. I will wear it, I swear to you, as a grateful man should do."

"'Tis well; arise, vicomte, embrace me."

Raoul arose and threw himself with emotion into the count's arms.

"Adieu," faltered the count, who felt his heart die away within him; "adieu, and think of me."

"Oh! for ever and ever!" cried the youth; "oh! I swear to you, sir, should any harm befall me, your name will be the last name that I shall utter, the remembrance of you my last thought."

Athos hastened upstairs to conceal his emotion, and regained with hurried steps the porch where Olivain was waiting with the horses.

"Olivain," said Athos, showing the servant Raoul's shoulder-belt, "tighten the buckle of the sword, it falls too low. You will accompany monsieur le vicomte till Grimaud rejoins you. You know, Raoul, Grimaud is an old and zealous servant; he will follow you."

"Yes, sir," answered Raoul.

"Now to horse, that I may see you depart!"

Raoul obeyed.

"Adieu, Raoul," said the count; "adieu, my dearest boy!"

"Adieu, sir, adieu, my beloved protector."

Athos waved his hand—he dared not trust himself to speak: and Raoul went away, his head uncovered. Athos remained motionless, looking after him until he turned the corner of the street.

Then the count threw the bridle of his horse into the hands of a peasant, remounted the steps, went into the cathedral, there to kneel down in the darkest corner and pray.

Chapter XXIII.

One of the Forty Methods of Escape of the Duc de Beaufort.

Meanwhile time was passing on for the prisoner, as well as for those who were preparing his escape; only for him it passed more slowly. Unlike other men, who enter with ardor upon a perilous resolution and grow cold as the moment of execution approaches, the Duc de Beaufort, whose buoyant courage had become a proverb, seemed to push time before him and sought most eagerly to hasten the hour of action. In his escape alone, apart from his plans for the future, which, it must be admitted, were for the present sufficiently vague and uncertain, there was a beginning of vengeance which filled his heart. In the first place his escape would be a serious misfortune to Monsieur de Chavigny, whom he hated for the petty persecutions he owed to him. It would be a still worse affair for Mazarin, whom he execrated for the greater offences he had committed. It may be observed that there was a proper proportion in his sentiments toward the governor of the prison and the minister—toward the subordinate and the master.

Then Monsieur de Beaufort, who was so familiar with the interior of the Palais Royal, though he did not know the relations existing between the queen and the cardinal, pictured to himself, in his prison, all that dramatic excitement which would ensue when the rumor should run from the minister's cabinet to the chamber of Anne of Austria: "Monsieur de Beaufort has escaped!" Whilst saying that to himself, Monsieur de Beaufort smiled pleasantly and imagined himself already outside, breathing the air of the plains and the forests, pressing a strong horse between his knees and crying out in a loud voice, "I am free!"

It is true that on coming to himself he found that he was still within four walls; he saw La Ramee twirling his thumbs ten feet from him, and his guards laughing and drinking in the ante-chamber. The only thing that was pleasant to him in that odious tableau—such is the instability of the human mind—was the sullen face of Grimaud, for whom he had at first conceived such a hatred and who now was all his hope. Grimaud seemed to him an Antinous. It is needless to say that this transformation was visible only to the prisoner's feverish imagination. Grimaud was still the same, and therefore he retained the entire confidence of his superior, La Ramee, who now relied upon him more than he did upon himself, for, as we have said, La Ramee felt at the bottom of his heart a certain weakness for Monsieur de Beaufort.

And so the good La Ramee made a festivity of the little supper with his prisoner. He had but one fault—he was a gourmand; he had found the pates good, the wine excellent. Now the successor of Pere Marteau had promised him a pate of pheasant instead of a pate of fowl, and Chambertin wine instead of Macon. All this, set off by the presence of that excellent prince, who was so good-natured, who invented so droll tricks against Monsieur de Chavigny and so fine jokes against Mazarin, made for La Ramee the approaching Pentecost one of the four great feasts of the year. He therefore looked forward to six o'clock with as much impatience as the duke himself.

Since daybreak La Ramee had been occupied with the preparations, and trusting no one but himself, he had visited personally the successor of Pere Marteau. The latter had surpassed himself; he showed La Ramee a monstrous pate, ornamented with Monsieur de Beaufort's coat-of-arms. It was empty as yet, but a pheasant and two partridges were lying near it. La Ramee's mouth watered and he returned to the duke's chamber rubbing his hands. To crown his happiness, Monsieur de Chavigny had started on a journey that morning and in his absence La Ramee was deputy-governor of the chateau.

As for Grimaud, he seemed more sullen than ever.

In the course of the forenoon Monsieur de Beaufort had a game of tennis with La Ramee; a sign from Grimaud put him on the alert. Grimaud, going in advance, followed the course which they were to take in the evening. The game was played in an inclosure called the little court of the chateau, a place quite deserted except when Monsieur de Beaufort was playing; and even then the precaution seemed superfluous, the wall was so high.

There were three gates to open before reaching the inclosure, each by a different key. When they arrived Grimaud went carelessly and sat down by a loophole in the wall, letting his legs dangle outside. It was evident that there the rope ladder was to be attached.

This manoeuvre, transparent to the Duc de Beaufort, was quite unintelligible to La Ramee.

The game at tennis, which, upon a sign from Grimaud, Monsieur de Beaufort had consented to play, began in the afternoon. The duke was in full strength and beat La Ramee completely.

Four of the guards, who were constantly near the prisoner, assisted in picking up the tennis balls. When the game was over, the duke, laughing at La Ramee for his bad play, offered these men two louis d'or to go and drink his health, with their four other comrades.

The guards asked permission of La Ramee, who gave it to them, but not till the evening, however; until then he had business and the prisoner was not to be left alone.

Six o'clock came and, although they were not to sit down to table until seven o'clock, dinner was ready and served up. Upon a sideboard appeared the colossal pie with the duke's arms on it, and seemingly cooked to a turn, as far as one could judge by the golden color which illuminated the crust.

The rest of the dinner was to come.

Every one was impatient, La Ramee to sit down to table, the guards to go and drink, the duke to escape.

Grimaud alone was calm as ever. One might have fancied that Athos had educated him with the express forethought of such a great event.

There were moments when, looking at Grimaud, the duke asked himself if he was not dreaming and if that marble figure was really at his service and would grow animated when the moment came for action.

La Ramee sent away the guards, desiring them to drink to the duke's health, and as soon as they were gone shut all the doors, put the keys in his pocket and showed the table to the prince with an air that signified:

"Whenever my lord pleases."

The prince looked at Grimaud, Grimaud looked at the clock; it was hardly a quarter-past six. The escape was fixed to take place at seven o'clock; there was therefore three-quarters of an hour to wait.

The duke, in order to pass away another quarter of an hour, pretended to be reading something that interested him and muttered that he wished they would allow him to finish his chapter. La Ramee went up to him and looked over his shoulder to see what sort of a book it was that had so singular an influence over the prisoner as to make him put off taking his dinner.

It was "Caesar's Commentaries," which La Ramee had lent him, contrary to the orders of the governor; and La Ramee resolved never again to disobey these injunctions.

Meantime he uncorked the bottles and went to smell if the pie was good.

At half-past six the duke arose and said very gravely:

"Certainly, Caesar was the greatest man of ancient times."

"You think so, my lord?" answered La Ramee.

"Yes."

"Well, as for me, I prefer Hannibal."

"And why, pray, Master La Ramee?" asked the duke.

"Because he left no Commentaries," replied La Ramee, with his coarse laugh.

The duke vouchsafed no reply, but sitting down at the table made a sign that La Ramee should seat himself opposite. There is nothing so expressive as the face of an epicure who finds himself before a well spread table, so La Ramee, when receiving his plate of soup from Grimaud, presented a type of perfect bliss.

The duke smiled.

"Zounds!" he said; "I don't suppose there is a more contented man at this moment in all the kingdom than yourself!"

"You are right, my lord duke," answered the officer; "I don't know any pleasanter sight on earth than a well covered table; and when, added to that, he who does the honors is the grandson of Henry IV., you will, my lord duke, easily comprehend that the honor fairly doubles the pleasure one enjoys."

The duke, in his turn, bowed, and an imperceptible smile appeared on the face of Grimaud, who kept behind La Ramee.

"My dear La Ramee," said the duke, "you are the only man to turn such faultless compliments."

"No, my lord duke," replied La Ramee, in the fullness of his heart; "I say what I think; there is no compliment in what I say to you——"

"Then you are attached to me?" asked the duke.

"To own the truth, I should be inconsolable if you were to leave Vincennes."

"A droll way of showing your affliction." The duke meant to say "affection."

"But, my lord," returned La Ramee, "what would you do if you got out? Every folly you committed would embroil you with the court and they would put you into the Bastile, instead of Vincennes. Now, Monsieur de Chavigny is not amiable, I allow, but Monsieur du Tremblay is considerably worse."

"Indeed!" exclaimed the duke, who from time to time looked at the clock, the fingers of which seemed to move with sickening slowness.

"But what can you expect from the brother of a capuchin monk, brought up in the school of Cardinal Richelieu? Ah, my lord, it is a great happiness that the queen, who always wished you well, had a fancy to send you here, where there's a promenade and a tennis court, good air, and a good table."

"In short," answered the duke, "if I comprehend you aright, La Ramee, I am ungrateful for having ever thought of leaving this place?"

"Oh! my lord duke, 'tis the height of ingratitude; but your highness has never seriously thought of it?"

"Yes," returned the duke, "I must confess I sometimes think of it."

"Still by one of your forty methods, your highness?"

"Yes, yes, indeed."

"My lord," said La Ramee, "now we are quite at our ease and enjoying ourselves, pray tell me one of those forty ways invented by your highness."

"Willingly," answered the duke, "give me the pie!"

"I am listening," said La Ramee, leaning back in his armchair and raising his glass of Madeira to his lips, and winking his eye that he might see the sun through the rich liquid that he was about to taste.

The duke glanced at the clock. In ten minutes it would strike seven.

Grimaud placed the pie before the duke, who took a knife with a silver blade to raise the upper crust; but La Ramee, who was afraid of any harm happening to this fine work of art, passed his knife, which had an iron blade, to the duke.

"Thank you, La Ramee," said the prisoner.

"Well, my lord! this famous invention of yours?"

"Must I tell you," replied the duke, "on what I most reckon and what I determine to try first?"

"Yes, that's the thing, my lord!" cried his custodian, gaily.

"Well, I should hope, in the first instance, to have for keeper an honest fellow like you."

"And you have me, my lord. Well?"

"Having, then, a keeper like La Ramee, I should try also to have introduced to him by some friend or other a man who would be devoted to me, who would assist me in my flight."

"Come, come," said La Ramee, "that's not a bad idea."

"Capital, isn't it? for instance, the former servingman of some brave gentleman, an enemy himself to Mazarin, as every gentleman ought to be."

"Hush! don't let us talk politics, my lord."

"Then my keeper would begin to trust this man and to depend upon him, and I should have news from those without the prison walls."

"Ah, yes! but how can the news be brought to you?"

"Nothing easier; in a game of tennis, for example."

"In a game of tennis?" asked La Ramee, giving more serious attention to the duke's words.

"Yes; see, I send a ball into the moat; a man is there who picks it up; the ball contains a letter. Instead of returning the ball to me when I call for it from the top of the wall, he throws me another; that other ball contains a letter. Thus we have exchanged ideas and no one has seen us do it."

"The devil it does! The devil it does!" said La Ramee, scratching his head; "you are in the wrong to tell me that, my lord. I shall have to watch the men who pick up balls."

The duke smiled.

"But," resumed La Ramee, "that is only a way of corresponding."

"And that is a great deal, it seems to me."

"But not enough."

"Pardon me; for instance, I say to my friends, Be on a certain day, on a certain hour, at the other side of the moat with two horses."

"Well, what then?" La Ramee began to be uneasy; "unless the horses have wings to mount the ramparts and come and fetch you."

"That's not needed. I have," replied the duke, "a way of descending from the ramparts."

"What?"

"A rope ladder."

"Yes, but," answered La Ramee, trying to laugh, "a ladder of ropes can't be sent around a ball, like a letter."

"No, but it may be sent in something else."

"In something else—in something else? In what?"

"In a pate, for example."

"In a pate?" said La Ramee.

"Yes. Let us suppose one thing," replied the duke "let us suppose, for instance, that my maitre d'hotel, Noirmont, has purchased the shop of Pere Marteau——"

"Well?" said La Ramee, shuddering.

"Well, La Ramee, who is a gourmand, sees his pates, thinks them more attractive than those of Pere Marteau and proposes to me that I shall try them. I consent on condition that La Ramee tries them with me. That we may be more at our ease, La Ramee removes the guards, keeping only Grimaud to wait on us. Grimaud is the man whom a friend has sent to second me in everything. The moment for my escape is fixed—seven o'clock. Well, at a few minutes to seven——"

"At a few minutes to seven?" cried La Ramee, cold sweat upon his brow.

"At a few minutes to seven," returned the duke (suiting the action to the words), "I raise the crust of the pie; I find in it two poniards, a ladder of rope, and a gag. I point one of the poniards at La Ramee's breast and I say to him, 'My friend, I am sorry for it, but if thou stirrest, if thou utterest one cry, thou art a dead man!'"

The duke, in pronouncing these words, suited, as we have said, the action to the words. He was standing near the officer and he directed the point of the poniard in such a manner, close to La Ramee's heart, that there could be no doubt in the mind of that individual as to his determination. Meanwhile, Grimaud, still mute as ever, drew from the pie the other poniard, the rope ladder and the gag.

La Ramee followed all these objects with his eyes, his alarm every moment increasing.

"Oh, my lord," he cried, with an expression of stupefaction in his face; "you haven't the heart to kill me!"

"No; not if thou dost not oppose my flight."

"But, my lord, if I allow you to escape I am a ruined man."

"I will compensate thee for the loss of thy place."

"You are determined to leave the chateau?"

"By Heaven and earth! This night I am determined to be free."

"And if I defend myself, or call, or cry out?"

"I will kill thee, on the honor of a gentleman."

At this moment the clock struck.

"Seven o'clock!" said Grimaud, who had not spoken a word.

La Ramee made one movement, in order to satisfy his conscience. The duke frowned, the officer felt the point of the poniard, which, having penetrated through his clothes, was close to his heart.

"Let us dispatch," said the duke.

"My lord, one last favor."

"What? speak, make haste."

"Bind my arms, my lord, fast."

"Why bind thee?"

"That I may not be considered as your accomplice."

"Your hands?" asked Grimaud.

"Not before me, behind me."

"But with what?" asked the duke.

"With your belt, my lord!" replied La Ramee.

The duke undid his belt and gave it to Grimaud, who tied La Ramee in such a way as to satisfy him.

"Your feet, too," said Grimaud.

La Ramee stretched out his legs, Grimaud took a table-cloth, tore it into strips and tied La Ramee's feet together.

"Now, my lord," said the poor man, "let me have the poire d'angoisse. I ask for it; without it I should be tried in a court of justice because I did not raise the alarm. Thrust it into my mouth, my lord, thrust it in."

Grimaud prepared to comply with this request, when the officer made a sign as if he had something to say.

"Speak," said the duke.

"Now, my lord, do not forget, if any harm happens to me on your account, that I have a wife and four children."

"Rest assured; put the gag in, Grimaud."

In a second La Ramee was gagged and laid prostrate. Two or three chairs were thrown down as if there had been a struggle. Grimaud then took from the pocket of the officer all the keys it contained and first opened the door of the room in which they were, then shut it and double-locked it, and both he and the duke proceeded rapidly down the gallery which led to the little inclosure. At last they reached the tennis court. It was completely deserted. No sentinels, no one at any of the windows. The duke ran to the rampart and perceived on the other side of the ditch, three cavaliers with two riding horses. The duke exchanged a signal with them. It was indeed for him that they were there.

Grimaud, meantime, undid the means of escape.

This was not, however, a rope ladder, but a ball of silk cord, with a narrow board which was to pass between the legs, the ball to unwind itself by the weight of the person who sat astride upon the board.

"Go!" said the duke.

"First, my lord?" inquired Grimaud.

"Certainly. If I am caught, I risk nothing but being taken back again to prison. If they catch thee, thou wilt be hung."

"True," replied Grimaud.

And instantly, Grimaud, sitting upon the board as if on horseback, commenced his perilous descent.

The duke followed him with his eyes, with involuntary terror. He had gone down about three-quarters of the length of the wall when the cord broke. Grimaud fell—precipitated into the moat.

The duke uttered a cry, but Grimaud did not give a single moan. He must have been dreadfully hurt, for he did not stir from the place where he fell.

Immediately one of the men who were waiting slipped down into the moat, tied under Grimaud's shoulders the end of a cord, and the remaining two, who held the other end, drew Grimaud to them.

"Descend, my lord," said the man in the moat. "There are only fifteen feet more from the top down here, and the grass is soft."

The duke had already begun to descend. His task was the more difficult, as there was no board to support him. He was obliged to let himself down by his hands and from a height of fifty feet. But as we have said he was active, strong, and full of presence of mind. In less than five minutes he arrived at the end of the cord. He was then only fifteen feet from the ground, as the gentlemen below had told him. He let go the rope and fell upon his feet, without receiving any injury.

He instantly began to climb up the slope of the moat, on the top of which he met De Rochefort. The other two gentlemen were unknown to him. Grimaud, in a swoon, was tied securely to a horse.

"Gentlemen," said the duke, "I will thank you later; now we have not a moment to lose. On, then! on! those who love me, follow me!"

And he jumped on his horse and set off at full gallop, snuffing the fresh air in his triumph and shouting out, with an expression of face which it would be impossible to describe:

"Free! free! free!"

Chapter XXIV.

The timely Arrival of D'Artagnan in Paris.

At Blois, D'Artagnan received the money paid to him by Mazarin for any future service he might render the cardinal.

From Blois to Paris was a journey of four days for ordinary travelers, but D'Artagnan arrived on the third day at the Barriere Saint Denis. In turning the corner of the Rue Montmartre, in order to reach the Rue Tiquetonne and the Hotel de la Chevrette, where he had appointed Porthos to meet him, he saw at one of the windows of the hotel, that friend himself dressed in a sky-blue waistcoat, embroidered with silver, and gaping, till he showed every one of his white teeth; whilst the people passing by admiringly gazed at this gentleman, so handsome and so rich, who seemed to weary of his riches and his greatness.

D'Artagnan and Planchet had hardly turned the corner when Porthos recognized them.

"Eh! D'Artagnan!" he cried. "Thank God you have come!"

"Eh! good-day, dear friend!" replied D'Artagnan.

Porthos came down at once to the threshold of the hotel.

"Ah, my dear friend!" he cried, "what bad stabling for my horses here."

"Indeed!" said D'Artagnan; "I am most unhappy to hear it, on account of those fine animals."

"And I, also—I was also wretchedly off," he answered, moving backward and forward as he spoke; "and had it not been for the hostess," he added, with his air of vulgar self-complacency, "who is very agreeable and understands a joke, I should have got a lodging elsewhere."

The pretty Madeleine, who had approached during this colloquy, stepped back and turned pale as death on hearing Porthos's words, for she thought the scene with the Swiss was about to be repeated. But to her great surprise D'Artagnan remained perfectly calm, and instead of being angry he laughed, and said to Porthos:

"Yes, I understand, the air of La Rue Tiquetonne is not like that of Pierrefonds; but console yourself, I will soon conduct you to one much better."

"When will you do that?"

"Immediately, I hope."

"Ah! so much the better!"

To that exclamation of Porthos's succeeded a groaning, low and profound, which seemed to come from behind a door. D'Artagnan, who had just dismounted, then saw, outlined against the wall, the enormous stomach of Mousqueton, whose down-drawn mouth emitted sounds of distress.

"And you, too, my poor Monsieur Mouston, are out of place in this poor hotel, are you not?" asked D'Artagnan, in that rallying tone which may indicate either compassion or mockery.

"He finds the cooking detestable," replied Porthos.

"Why, then, doesn't he attend to it himself, as at Chantilly?"

"Ah, monsieur, I have not here, as I had there, the ponds of monsieur le prince, where I could catch those beautiful carp, nor the forests of his highness to provide me with partridges. As for the cellar, I have searched every part and poor stuff I found."

"Monsieur Mouston," said D'Artagnan, "I should indeed condole with you had I not at this moment something very pressing to attend to."

Then taking Porthos aside:

"My dear Du Vallon," he said, "here you are in full dress most fortunately, for I am going to take you to the cardinal's."

"Gracious me! really!" exclaimed Porthos, opening his great wondering eyes.

"Yes, my friend."

"A presentation? indeed!"

"Does that alarm you?"

"No, but it agitates me."

"Oh! don't be distressed; you have to deal with a cardinal of another kind. This one will not oppress you by his dignity."

"'Tis the same thing—you understand me, D'Artagnan—a court."

"There's no court now. Alas!"

"The queen!"

"I was going to say, there's no longer a queen. The queen! Rest assured, we shall not see her."

"And you say that we are going from here to the Palais Royal?"

"Immediately. Only, that there may be no delay, I shall borrow one of your horses."

"Certainly; all the four are at your service."

"Oh, I need only one of them for the time being."

"Shall we take our valets?"

"Yes, you may as well take Mousqueton. As to Planchet, he has certain reasons for not going to court."

"And what are they?"

"Oh, he doesn't stand well with his eminence."

"Mouston," said Porthos, "saddle Vulcan and Bayard."

"And for myself, monsieur, shall I saddle Rustaud?"

"No, take a more stylish horse, Phoebus or Superbe; we are going with some ceremony."

"Ah," said Mousqueton, breathing more freely, "you are only going, then, to make a visit?"

"Oh! yes, of course, Mouston; nothing else. But to avoid risk, put the pistols in the holsters. You will find mine on my saddle, already loaded."

Mouston breathed a sigh; he couldn't understand visits of ceremony made under arms.

"Indeed," said Porthos, looking complacently at his old lackey as he went away, "you are right, D'Artagnan; Mouston will do; Mouston has a very fine appearance."

D'Artagnan smiled.

"But you, my friend—are you not going to change your dress?"

"No, I shall go as I am. This traveling dress will serve to show the cardinal my haste to obey his commands."

They set out on Vulcan and Bayard, followed by Mousqueton on Phoebus, and arrived at the Palais Royal at about a quarter to seven. The streets were crowded, for it was the day of Pentecost, and the crowd looked in wonder at these two cavaliers; one as fresh as if he had come out of a bandbox, the other so covered with dust that he looked as if he had but just come off a field of battle.

Mousqueton also attracted attention; and as the romance of Don Quixote was then the fashion, they said that he was Sancho, who, after having lost one master, had found two.

On reaching the palace, D'Artagnan sent to his eminence the letter in which he had been ordered to return without delay. He was soon ordered to the presence of the cardinal.

"Courage!" he whispered to Porthos, as they proceeded. "Do not be intimidated. Believe me, the eye of the eagle is closed forever. We have only the vulture to deal with. Hold yourself as bolt upright as on the day of the bastion of St. Gervais, and do not bow too low to this Italian; that might give him a poor idea of you."

"Good!" answered Porthos. "Good!"

Mazarin was in his study, working at a list of pensions and benefices, of which he was trying to reduce the number. He saw D'Artagnan and Porthos enter with internal pleasure, yet showed no joy in his countenance.

"Ah! you, is it? Monsieur le lieutenant, you have been very prompt. 'Tis well. Welcome to ye."

"Thanks, my lord. Here I am at your eminence's service, as well as Monsieur du Vallon, one of my old friends, who used to conceal his nobility under the name of Porthos."

Porthos bowed to the cardinal.

"A magnificent cavalier," remarked Mazarin.

Porthos turned his head to the right and to the left, and drew himself up with a movement full of dignity.

"The best swordsman in the kingdom, my lord," said D'Artagnan.

Porthos bowed to his friend.

Mazarin was as fond of fine soldiers as, in later times, Frederick of Prussia used to be. He admired the strong hands, the broad shoulders and the steady eye of Porthos. He seemed to see before him the salvation of his administration and of the kingdom, sculptured in flesh and bone. He remembered that the old association of musketeers was composed of four persons.

"And your two other friends?" he asked.

Porthos opened his mouth, thinking it a good opportunity to put in a word in his turn; D'Artagnan checked him by a glance from the corner of his eye.

"They are prevented at this moment, but will join us later."

Mazarin coughed a little.

"And this gentleman, being disengaged, takes to the service willingly?" he asked.

"Yes, my lord, and from pure devotion to the cause, for Monsieur de Bracieux is rich."

"Rich!" said Mazarin, whom that single word always inspired with a great respect.

"Fifty thousand francs a year," said Porthos.

These were the first words he had spoken.

"From pure zeal?" resumed Mazarin, with his artful smile; "from pure zeal and devotion then?"

"My lord has, perhaps, no faith in those words?" said D'Artagnan.

"Have you, Monsieur le Gascon?" asked Mazarin, supporting his elbows on his desk and his chin on his hands.

"I," replied the Gascon, "I believe in devotion as a word at one's baptism, for instance, which naturally comes before one's proper name; every one is naturally more or less devout, certainly; but there should be at the end of one's devotion something to gain."

"And your friend, for instance; what does he expect to have at the end of his devotion?"

"Well, my lord, my friend has three magnificent estates: that of Vallon, at Corbeil; that of Bracieux, in the Soissonais; and that of Pierrefonds, in the Valois. Now, my lord, he would like to have one of his three estates erected into a barony."

"Only that?" said Mazarin, his eyes twinkling with joy on seeing that he could pay for Porthos's devotion without opening his purse; "only that? That can be managed."

"I shall be baron!" explained Porthos, stepping forward.

"I told you so," said D'Artagnan, checking him with his hand; "and now his eminence confirms it."

"And you, Monsieur D'Artagnan, what do you want?"

"My lord," said D'Artagnan, "it is twenty years since Cardinal de Richelieu made me lieutenant."

"Yes, and you would be gratified if Cardinal Mazarin should make you captain."

D'Artagnan bowed.

"Well, that is not impossible. We will see, gentlemen, we will see. Now, Monsieur de Vallon," said Mazarin, "what service do you prefer, in the town or in the country?"

Porthos opened his mouth to reply.

"My lord," said D'Artagnan, "Monsieur de Vallon is like me, he prefers service extraordinary—that is to say, enterprises that are considered mad and impossible."

That boastfulness was not displeasing to Mazarin; he fell into meditation.

"And yet," he said, "I must admit that I sent for you to appoint you to quiet service; I have certain apprehensions—well, what is the meaning of that?"

In fact, a great noise was heard in the ante-chamber; at the same time the door of the study was burst open and a man, covered with dust, rushed into it, exclaiming:

"My lord the cardinal! my lord the cardinal!"

Mazarin thought that some one was going to assassinate him and he drew back, pushing his chair on the castors. D'Artagnan and Porthos moved so as to plant themselves between the person entering and the cardinal.

"Well, sir," exclaimed Mazarin, "what's the matter? and why do you rush in here, as if you were about to penetrate a crowded market-place?"

"My lord," replied the messenger, "I wish to speak to your eminence in secret. I am Monsieur du Poins, an officer in the guards, on duty at the donjon of Vincennes."

Mazarin, perceiving by the paleness and agitation of the messenger that he had something of importance to say, made a sign that D'Artagnan and Porthos should give place.

D'Artagnan and Porthos withdrew to a corner of the cabinet.

"Speak, monsieur, speak at once!" said Mazarin "What is the matter?"

"The matter is, my lord, that the Duc de Beaufort has contrived to escape from the Chateau of Vincennes."

Mazarin uttered a cry and became paler than the man who had brought the news. He fell back, almost fainting, in his chair.

"Escaped? Monsieur de Beaufort escaped?"

"My lord, I saw him run off from the top of the terrace."

"And you did not fire on him?"

"He was out of range."

"Monsieur de Chavigny—where was he?"

"Absent."

"And La Ramee?"

"Was found locked up in the prisoner's room, a gag in his mouth and a poniard near him."

"But the man who was under him?"

"Was an accomplice of the duke's and escaped along with him."

Mazarin groaned.

"My lord," said D'Artagnan, advancing toward the cardinal, "it seems to me that your eminence is losing precious time. It may still be possible to overtake the prisoner. France is large; the nearest frontier is sixty leagues distant."

"And who is to pursue him?" cried Mazarin.

"I, pardieu!"

"And you would arrest him?"

"Why not?"

"You would arrest the Duc de Beaufort, armed, in the field?"

"If your eminence should order me to arrest the devil, I would seize him by the horns and would bring him in."

"So would I," said Porthos.

"So would you!" said Mazarin, looking with astonishment at those two men. "But the duke will not yield himself without a furious battle."

"Very well," said D'Artagnan, his eyes aflame, "battle! It is a long time since we have had a battle, eh, Porthos?"

"Battle!" cried Porthos.

"And you think you can catch him?"

"Yes, if we are better mounted than he."

"Go then, take what guards you find here, and pursue him."

"You command us, my lord, to do so?"

"And I sign my orders," said Mazarin, taking a piece of paper and writing some lines; "Monsieur du Vallon, your barony is on the back of the Duc de Beaufort's horse; you have nothing to do but to overtake it. As for you, my dear lieutenant, I promise you nothing; but if you bring him back to me, dead or alive, you may ask all you wish."

"To horse, Porthos!" said D'Artagnan, taking his friend by the hand.

"Here I am," smiled Porthos, with his sublime composure.

They descended the great staircase, taking with them all the guards they found on their road, and crying out, "To arms! To arms!" and immediately put spur to horse, which set off along the Rue Saint Honore with the speed of the whirlwind.

"Well, baron, I promise you some good exercise!" said the Gascon.

"Yes, my captain."

As they went, the citizens, awakened, left their doors and the street dogs followed the cavaliers, barking. At the corner of the Cimetiere Saint Jean, D'Artagnan upset a man; it was too insignificant an occurrence to delay people so eager to get on. The troop continued its course as though their steeds had wings.

Alas! there are no unimportant events in this world and we shall see that this apparently slight incident came near endangering the monarchy.

Chapter XXV.

An Adventure on the High Road.

The musketeers rode the whole length of the Faubourg Saint Antoine and of the road to Vincennes, and soon found themselves out of the town, then in a forest and then within sight of a village.

The horses seemed to become more lively with each successive step; their nostrils reddened like glowing furnaces. D'Artagnan, freely applying his spurs, was in advance of Porthos two feet at the most; Mousqueton followed two lengths behind; the guards were scattered according to the varying excellence of their respective mounts.

From the top of an eminence D'Artagnan perceived a group of people collected on the other side of the moat, in front of that part of the donjon which looks toward Saint Maur. He rode on, convinced that in this direction he would gain intelligence of the fugitive. In five minutes he had arrived at the place, where the guards joined him, coming up one by one.

The several members of that group were much excited. They looked at the cord, still hanging from the loophole and broken at about twenty feet from the ground. Their eyes measured the height and they exchanged conjectures. On the top of the wall sentinels went and came with a frightened air.

A few soldiers, commanded by a sergeant, drove away idlers from the place where the duke had mounted his horse. D'Artagnan went straight to the sergeant.

"My officer," said the sergeant, "it is not permitted to stop here."

"That prohibition is not for me," said D'Artagnan. "Have the fugitives been pursued?"

"Yes, my officer; unfortunately, they are well mounted."

"How many are there?"

"Four, and a fifth whom they carried away wounded."

"Four!" said D'Artagnan, looking at Porthos. "Do you hear, baron? They are only four!"

A joyous smile lighted Porthos's face.

"How long a start have they?"

"Two hours and a quarter, my officer."

"Two hours and a quarter—that is nothing; we are well mounted, are we not, Porthos?"

Porthos breathed a sigh; he thought of what was in store for his poor horses.

"Very good," said D'Artagnan; "and now in what direction did they set out?"

"That I am forbidden to tell."

D'Artagnan drew from his pocket a paper. "Order of the king," he said.

"Speak to the governor, then."

"And where is the governor?"

"In the country."

Anger mounted to D'Artagnan's face; he frowned and his cheeks were colored.

"Ah, you scoundrel!" he said to the sergeant, "I believe you are impudent to me! Wait!"

He unfolded the paper, presented it to the sergeant with one hand and with the other took a pistol from his holsters and cocked it.

"Order of the king, I tell you. Read and answer, or I will blow out your brains!"

The sergeant saw that D'Artagnan was in earnest. "The Vendomois road," he replied.

"And by what gate did they go out?"

"By the Saint Maur gate."

"If you are deceiving me, rascal, you will be hanged to-morrow."

"And if you catch up with them you won't come back to hang me," murmured the sergeant.

D'Artagnan shrugged his shoulders, made a sign to his escort and started.

"This way, gentlemen, this way!" he cried, directing his course toward the gate that had been pointed out.

But, now that the duke had escaped, the concierge had seen fit to fasten the gate with a double lock. It was necessary to compel him to open it, as the sergeant had been compelled to speak, and this took another ten minutes. This last obstacle having been overcome, the troop pursued their course with their accustomed ardor; but some of the horses could no longer sustain this pace; three of them stopped after an hour's gallop, and one fell down.

D'Artagnan, who never turned his head, did not perceive it. Porthos told him of it in his calm manner.

"If only we two arrive," said D'Artagnan, "it will be enough, since the duke's troop are only four in number."

"That is true," said Porthos

And he spurred his courser on.

At the end of another two hours the horses had gone twelve leagues without stopping; their legs began to tremble, and the foam they shed whitened the doublets of their masters.

"Let us rest here an instant to give these poor creatures breathing time," said Porthos.

"Let us rather kill them! yes, kill them!" cried D'Artagnan; "I see fresh tracks; 'tis not a quarter of an hour since they passed this place."

In fact, the road was trodden by horses' feet, visible even in the approaching gloom of evening.

They set out; after a run of two leagues, Mousqueton's horse sank.

"Gracious me!" said Porthos, "there's Phoebus ruined."

"The cardinal will pay you a hundred pistoles."

"I'm above that."

"Let us set out again, at full gallop."

"Yes, if we can."

But at last the lieutenant's horse refused to go on; he could not breathe; one last spur, instead of making him advance, made him fall.

"The devil!" exclaimed Porthos; "there's Vulcan foundered."

"Zounds!" cried D'Artagnan, "then we must stop! Give me your horse, Porthos. What the devil are you doing?"

"By Jove, I am falling, or rather, Bayard is falling," answered Porthos.

All three then cried: "All's over."

"Hush!" said D'Artagnan.

"What is it?"

"I hear a horse."

"It belongs to one of our companions, who is overtaking us."

"No," said D'Artagnan, "it is in advance."

"That is another thing," said Porthos; and he listened toward the quarter indicated by D'Artagnan.

"Monsieur," said Mousqueton, who, abandoning his horse on the high road, had come on foot to rejoin his master, "Phoebus could no longer hold out and——"

"Silence!" said Porthos.

In fact, at that moment a second neighing was borne to them on the night wind.

"It is five hundred feet from here, in advance," said D'Artagnan.

"True, monsieur," said Mousqueton; "and five hundred feet from here is a small hunting-house."

"Mousqueton, thy pistols," said D'Artagnan.

"I have them at hand, monsieur."

"Porthos, take yours from your holsters."

"I have them."

"Good!" said D'Artagnan, seizing his own; "now you understand, Porthos?"

"Not too well."

"We are out on the king's service."

"Well?"

"For the king's service we need horses."

"That is true," said Porthos.

"Then not a word, but set to work!"

They went on through the darkness, silent as phantoms; they saw a light glimmering in the midst of some trees.

"Yonder is the house, Porthos," said the Gascon; "let me do what I please and do you what I do."

They glided from tree to tree till they arrived at twenty steps from the house unperceived and saw by means of a lantern suspended under a hut, four fine horses. A groom was rubbing them down; near them were saddles and bridles.

D'Artagnan approached quickly, making a sign to his two companions to remain a few steps behind.

"I buy those horses," he said to the groom.

The groom turned toward him with a look of surprise, but made no reply.

"Didn't you hear, fellow?"

"Yes, I heard."

"Why, then, didn't you reply?"

"Because these horses are not to be sold," was the reply.

"I take them, then," said the lieutenant.

And he took hold of one within his reach; his two companions did the same thing.

"Sir," cried the groom, "they have traversed six leagues and have only been unsaddled half an hour."

"Half an hour's rest is enough," replied the Gascon.

The groom cried aloud for help. A kind of steward appeared, just as D'Artagnan and his companions were prepared to mount. The steward attempted to expostulate.

"My dear friend," cried the lieutenant, "if you say a word I will blow out your brains."

"But, sir," answered the steward, "do you know that these horses belong to Monsieur de Montbazon?"

"So much the better; they must be good animals, then."

"Sir, I shall call my people."

"And I, mine; I've ten guards behind me, don't you hear them gallop? and I'm one of the king's musketeers. Come, Porthos; come, Mousqueton."

They all mounted the horses as quickly as possible.

"Halloo! hi! hi!" cried the steward; "the house servants, with the carbines!"

"On! on!" cried D'Artagnan; "there'll be firing! on!"

They all set off, swift as the wind.

"Here!" cried the steward, "here!" whilst the groom ran to a neighboring building.

"Take care of your horses!" cried D'Artagnan to him.

"Fire!" replied the steward.

A gleam, like a flash of lightning, illumined the road, and with the flash was heard the whistling of balls, which were fired wildly in the air.

"They fire like grooms," said Porthos. "In the time of the cardinal people fired better than that, do you remember the road to Crevecoeur, Mousqueton?"

"Ah, sir! my left side still pains me!"

"Are you sure we are on the right track, lieutenant?"

"Egad, didn't you hear? these horses belong to Monsieur de Montbazon; well, Monsieur de Montbazon is the husband of Madame de Montbazon——"

"And——"

"And Madame de Montbazon is the mistress of the Duc de Beaufort."

"Ah! I understand," replied Porthos; "she has ordered relays of horses."

"Exactly so."

"And we are pursuing the duke with the very horses he has just left?"

"My dear Porthos, you are really a man of most superior understanding," said D'Artagnan, with a look as if he spoke against his conviction.

"Pooh!" replied Porthos, "I am what I am."

They rode on for an hour, till the horses were covered with foam and dust.

"Zounds! what is yonder?" cried D'Artagnan.

"You are very lucky if you see anything such a night as this," said Porthos.

"Something bright."

"I, too," cried Mousqueton, "saw them also."

"Ah! ah! have we overtaken them?"

"Good! a dead horse!" said D'Artagnan, pulling up his horse, which shied; "it seems their horses, too, are breaking down, as well as ours."

"I seem to hear the noise of a troop of horsemen," exclaimed Porthos, leaning over his horse's mane.

"Impossible."

"They appear to be numerous."

"Then 'tis something else."

"Another horse!" said Porthos.

"Dead?"

"No, dying."

"Saddled?"

"Yes, saddled and bridled."

"Then we are upon the fugitives."

"Courage, we have them!"

"But if they are numerous," observed Mousqueton, "'tis not we who have them, but they who have us."

"Nonsense!" cried D'Artagnan, "they'll suppose us to be stronger than themselves, as we're in pursuit; they'll be afraid and will disperse."

"Certainly," remarked Porthos.

"Ah! do you see?" cried the lieutenant.

"The lights again! this time I, too, saw them," said Porthos.

"On! on! forward! forward!" cried D'Artagnan, in his stentorian voice; "we shall laugh over all this in five minutes."

And they darted on anew. The horses, excited by pain and emulation, raced over the dark road, in the midst of which was now seen a moving mass, denser and more obscure than the rest of the horizon.

Chapter XXVI.

The Rencontre.

They rode on in this way for ten minutes. Suddenly two dark forms seemed to separate from the mass, advanced, grew in size, and as they loomed up larger and larger, assumed the appearance of two horsemen.

"Aha!" cried D'Artagnan, "they're coming toward us."

"So much the worse for them," said Porthos.

"Who goes there?" cried a hoarse voice.

The three horsemen made no reply, stopped not, and all that was heard was the noise of swords drawn from the scabbards and the cocking of the pistols with which the two phantoms were armed.

"Bridle in mouth!" said D'Artagnan.

Porthos understood him and he and the lieutenant each drew with the left hand a pistol from their bolsters and cocked it in their turn.

"Who goes there?" was asked a second time. "Not a step forward, or you're dead men."

"Stuff!" cried Porthos, almost choked with dust and chewing his bridle as a horse chews his bit. "Stuff and nonsense; we have seen plenty of dead men in our time."

Hearing these words, the two shadows blockaded the road and by the light of the stars might be seen the shining of their arms.

"Back!" shouted D'Artagnan, "or you are dead!"

Two shots were the reply to this threat; but the assailants attacked their foes with such velocity that in a moment they were upon them; a third pistol-shot was heard, aimed by D'Artagnan, and one of his adversaries fell. As for Porthos, he assaulted the foe with such violence that, although his sword was thrust aside, the enemy was thrown off his horse and fell about ten steps from it.

"Finish, Mouston, finish the work!" cried Porthos. And he darted on beside his friend, who had already begun a fresh pursuit.

"Well?" said Porthos.

"I've broken my man's skull," cried D'Artagnan. "And you——"

"I've only thrown the fellow down, but hark!"

Another shot of a carbine was heard. It was Mousqueton, who was obeying his master's command.

"On! on!" cried D'Artagnan; "all goes well! we have the first throw."

"Ha! ha!" answered Porthos, "behold, other players appear."

And in fact, two other cavaliers made their appearance, detached, as it seemed, from the principal group; they again disputed the road.

This time the lieutenant did not wait for the opposite party to speak.

"Stand aside!" he cried; "stand off the road!"

"What do you want?" asked a voice.

"The duke!" Porthos and D'Artagnan roared out both at once.

A burst of laughter was the answer, but finished with a groan. D'Artagnan had, with his sword, cut in two the poor wretch who had laughed.

At the same time Porthos and his adversary fired on each other and D'Artagnan turned to him.

"Bravo! you've killed him, I think."

"No, wounded his horse only."

"What would you have, my dear fellow? One doesn't hit the bull's-eye every time; it is something to hit inside the ring. Ho! parbleu! what is the matter with my horse?"

"Your horse is falling," said Porthos, reining in his own.

In truth, the lieutenant's horse stumbled and fell on his knees; then a rattling in his throat was heard and he lay down to die. He had received in the chest the bullet of D'Artagnan's first adversary. D'Artagnan swore loud enough to be heard in the skies.

"Does your honor want a horse?" asked Mousqueton.

"Zounds! want one!" cried the Gascon.

"Here's one, your honor——"

"How the devil hast thou two horses?" asked D'Artagnan, jumping on one of them.

"Their masters are dead! I thought they might be useful, so I took them."

Meantime Porthos had reloaded his pistols.

"Be on the qui vive!" cried D'Artagnan. "Here are two other cavaliers."

As he spoke, two horsemen advanced at full speed.

"Ho! your honor!" cried Mousqueton, "the man you upset is getting up."

"Why didn't thou do as thou didst to the first man?" said Porthos.

"I held the horses, my hands were full, your honor."

A shot was fired that moment; Mousqueton shrieked with pain.

"Ah, sir! I'm hit in the other side! exactly opposite the other! This hurt is just the fellow of the one I had on the road to Amiens."

Porthos turned around like a lion, plunged on the dismounted cavalier, who tried to draw his sword; but before it was out of the scabbard, Porthos, with the hilt of his had struck him such a terrible blow on the head that he fell like an ox beneath the butcher's knife.

Mousqueton, groaning, slipped from his horse, his wound not allowing him to keep the saddle.

On perceiving the cavaliers, D'Artagnan had stopped and charged his pistol afresh; besides, his horse, he found, had a carbine on the bow of the saddle.

"Here I am!" exclaimed Porthos. "Shall we wait, or shall we charge?"

"Let us charge them," answered the Gascon.

"Charge!" cried Porthos.

They spurred on their horses; the other cavaliers were only twenty steps from them.

"For the king!" cried D'Artagnan.

"The king has no authority here!" answered a deep voice, which seemed to proceed from a cloud, so enveloped was the cavalier in a whirlwind of dust.

"'Tis well, we will see if the king's name is not a passport everywhere," replied the Gascon.

"See!" answered the voice.

Two shots were fired at once, one by D'Artagnan, the other by the adversary of Porthos. D'Artagnan's ball took off his enemy's hat. The ball fired by Porthos's foe went through the throat of his horse, which fell, groaning.

"For the last time, where are you going?"

"To the devil!" answered D'Artagnan.

"Good! you may be easy, then—you'll get there."

D'Artagnan then saw a musket-barrel leveled at him; he had no time to draw from his holsters. He recalled a bit of advice which Athos had once given him, and made his horse rear.

The ball struck the animal full in front. D'Artagnan felt his horse giving way under him and with his wonderful agility threw himself to one side.

"Ah! this," cried the voice, the tone of which was at once polished and jeering, "this is nothing but a butchery of horses and not a combat between men. To the sword, sir! the sword!"

And he jumped off his horse.

"To the swords! be it so!" replied D'Artagnan; "that is exactly what I want."

D'Artagnan, in two steps, was engaged with the foe, whom, according to custom, he attacked impetuously, but he met this time with a skill and a strength of arm that gave him pause. Twice he was obliged to step back; his opponent stirred not one inch. D'Artagnan returned and again attacked him.

Twice or thrice thrusts were attempted on both sides, without effect; sparks were emitted from the swords like water spouting forth.

At last D'Artagnan thought it was time to try one of his favorite feints in fencing. He brought it to bear, skillfully executed it with the rapidity of lightning, and struck the blow with a force which he fancied would prove irresistible.

The blow was parried.

"'Sdeath!" he cried, with his Gascon accent.

At this exclamation his adversary bounded back and, bending his bare head, tried to distinguish in the gloom the features of the lieutenant.

As to D'Artagnan, afraid of some feint, he still stood on the defensive.

"Have a care," cried Porthos to his opponent; "I've still two pistols charged."

"The more reason you should fire the first!" cried his foe.

Porthos fired; the flash threw a gleam of light over the field of battle.

As the light shone on them a cry was heard from the other two combatants.

"Athos!" exclaimed D'Artagnan.

"D'Artagnan!" ejaculated Athos.

Athos raised his sword; D'Artagnan lowered his.

"Aramis!" cried Athos, "don't fire!"

"Ah! ha! is it you, Aramis?" said Porthos.

And he threw away his pistol.

Aramis pushed his back into his saddle-bags and sheathed his sword.

"My son!" exclaimed Athos, extending his hand to D'Artagnan.

This was the name which he gave him in former days, in their moments of tender intimacy.

"Athos!" cried D'Artagnan, wringing his hands. "So you defend him! And I, who have sworn to take him dead or alive, I am dishonored—and by you!"

"Kill me!" replied Athos, uncovering his breast, "if your honor requires my death."

"Oh! woe is me! woe is me!" cried the lieutenant; "there's only one man in the world who could stay my hand; by a fatality that very man bars my way. What shall I say to the cardinal?"

"You can tell him, sir," answered a voice which was the voice of high command in the battle-field, "that he sent against me the only two men capable of getting the better of four men; of fighting man to man, without discomfiture, against the Comte de la Fere and the Chevalier d'Herblay, and of surrendering only to fifty men!

"The prince!" exclaimed at the same moment Athos and Aramis, unmasking as they addressed the Duc de Beaufort, whilst D'Artagnan and Porthos stepped backward.

"Fifty cavaliers!" cried the Gascon and Porthos.

"Look around you, gentlemen, if you doubt the fact," said the duke.

The two friends looked to the right, to the left; they were encompassed by a troop of horsemen.

"Hearing the noise of the fight," resumed the duke, "I fancied you had about twenty men with you, so I came back with those around me, tired of always running away, and wishing to draw my sword in my own cause; but you are only two."

"Yes, my lord; but, as you have said, two that are a match for twenty," said Athos.

"Come, gentlemen, your swords," said the duke.

"Our swords!" cried D'Artagnan, raising his head and regaining his self-possession. "Never!"

"Never!" added Porthos.

Some of the men moved toward them.

"One moment, my lord," whispered Athos, and he said something in a low voice.

"As you will," replied the duke. "I am too much indebted to you to refuse your first request. Gentlemen," he said to his escort, "withdraw. Monsieur d'Artagnan, Monsieur du Vallon, you are free."

The order was obeyed; D'Artagnan and Porthos then found themselves in the centre of a large circle.

"Now, D'Herblay," said Athos, "dismount and come here."

Aramis dismounted and went to Porthos, whilst Athos approached D'Artagnan.

All four once more together.

"Friends!" said Athos, "do you regret you have not shed our blood?"

"No," replied D'Artagnan; "I regret to see that we, hitherto united, are opposed to each other. Ah! nothing will ever go well with us hereafter!"

"Oh, Heaven! No, all is over!" said Porthos.

"Well, be on our side now," resumed Aramis.

"Silence, D'Herblay!" cried Athos; "such proposals are not to be made to gentlemen such as these. 'Tis a matter of conscience with them, as with us."

"Meantime, here we are, enemies!" said Porthos. "Gramercy! who would ever have thought it?"

D'Artagnan only sighed.

Athos looked at them both and took their hands in his.

"Gentlemen," he said, "this is a serious business and my heart bleeds as if you had pierced it through and through. Yes, we are severed; there is the great, the distressing truth! But we have not as yet declared war; perhaps we shall have to make certain conditions, therefore a solemn conference is indispensable."

"For my own part, I demand it," said Aramis.

"I accept it," interposed D'Artagnan, proudly.

Porthos bowed, as if in assent.

"Let us choose a place of rendezvous," continued Athos, "and in a last interview arrange our mutual position and the conduct we are to maintain toward each other."

"Good!" the other three exclaimed.

"Well, then, the place?"

"Will the Place Royale suit you?" asked D'Artagnan.

"In Paris?"

"Yes."

Athos and Aramis looked at each other.

"The Place Royale—be it so!" replied Athos.

"When?"

"To-morrow evening, if you like!"

"At what hour?"

"At ten in the evening, if that suits you; by that time we shall have returned."

"Good."

"There," continued Athos, "either peace or war will be decided; honor, at all events, will be maintained!"

"Alas!" murmured D'Artagnan, "our honor as soldiers is lost to us forever!"

"D'Artagnan," said Athos, gravely, "I assure you that you do me wrong in dwelling so upon that. What I think of is, that we have crossed swords as enemies. Yes," he continued, sadly shaking his head, "Yes, it is as you said, misfortune, indeed, has overtaken us. Come, Aramis."

"And we, Porthos," said D'Artagnan, "will return, carrying our shame to the cardinal."

"And tell him," cried a voice, "that I am not too old yet for a man of action."

D'Artagnan recognized the voice of De Rochefort.

"Can I do anything for you, gentlemen?" asked the duke.

"Bear witness that we have done all that we could."

"That shall be testified to, rest assured. Adieu! we shall meet soon, I trust, in Paris, where you shall have your revenge." The duke, as he spoke, kissed his hand, spurred his horse into a gallop and disappeared, followed by his troop, who were soon lost in distance and darkness.

D'Artagnan and Porthos were now alone with a man who held by the bridles two horses; they thought it was Mousqueton and went up to him.

"What do I see?" cried the lieutenant. "Grimaud, is it thou?"

Grimaud signified that he was not mistaken.

"And whose horses are these?" cried D'Artagnan.

"Who has given them to us?" said Porthos.

"The Comte de la Fere."

"Athos! Athos!" muttered D'Artagnan; "you think of every one; you are indeed a nobleman! Whither art thou going, Grimaud?"

"To join the Vicomte de Bragelonne in Flanders, your honor."

They were taking the road toward Paris, when groans, which seemed to proceed from a ditch, attracted their attention.

"What is that?" asked D'Artagnan.

"It is I—Mousqueton," said a mournful voice, whilst a sort of shadow arose out of the side of the road.

Porthos ran to him. "Art thou dangerously wounded, my dear Mousqueton?" he said.

"No, sir, but I am severely."

"What can we do?" said D'Artagnan; "we must return to Paris."

"I will take care of Mousqueton," said Grimaud; and he gave his arm to his old comrade, whose eyes were full of tears, nor could Grimaud tell whether the tears were caused by wounds or by the pleasure of seeing him again.

D'Artagnan and Porthos went on, meantime, to Paris. They were passed by a sort of courier, covered with dust, the bearer of a letter from the duke to the cardinal, giving testimony to the valor of D'Artagnan and Porthos.

Mazarin had passed a very bad night when this letter was brought to him, announcing that the duke was free and that he would henceforth raise up mortal strife against him.

"What consoles me," said the cardinal after reading the letter, "is that, at least, in this chase, D'Artagnan has done me one good turn—he has destroyed Broussel. This Gascon is a precious fellow; even his misadventures are of use."

The cardinal referred to that man whom D'Artagnan upset at the corner of the Cimetiere Saint Jean in Paris, and who was no other than the Councillor Broussel.

Chapter XXVII.

The four old Friends prepare to meet again.

"Well," said Porthos, seated in the courtyard of the Hotel de la Chevrette, to D'Artagnan, who, with a long and melancholy face, had returned from the Palais Royal; "did he receive you ungraciously, my dear friend?"

"I'faith, yes! a brute, that cardinal. What are you eating there, Porthos?"

"I am dipping a biscuit in a glass of Spanish wine; do the same."

"You are right. Gimblou, a glass of wine."

"Well, how has all gone off?"

"Zounds! you know there's only one way of saying things, so I went in and said, 'My lord, we were not the strongest party.'

"'Yes, I know that,' he said, 'but give me the particulars.'

"You know, Porthos, I could not give him the particulars without naming our friends; to name them would be to commit them to ruin, so I merely said they were fifty and we were two.

"'There was firing, nevertheless, I heard,' he said; 'and your swords—they saw the light of day, I presume?'

"'That is, the night, my lord,' I answered.

"'Ah!' cried the cardinal, 'I thought you were a Gascon, my friend?'

"'I am a Gascon,' said I, 'only when I succeed.' The answer pleased him and he laughed.

"'That will teach me,' he said, 'to have my guards provided with better horses; for if they had been able to keep up with you and if each one of them had done as much as you and your friend, you would have kept your word and would have brought him back to me dead or alive.'"

"Well, there's nothing bad in that, it seems to me," said Porthos.

"Oh, mon Dieu! no, nothing at all. It was the way in which he spoke. It is incredible how these biscuit soak up wine! They are veritable sponges! Gimblou, another bottle."

The bottle was brought with a promptness which showed the degree of consideration D'Artagnan enjoyed in the establishment. He continued:

"So I was going away, but he called me back.

"'You have had three horses foundered or killed?' he asked me.

"'Yes, my lord.'

"'How much were they worth?'"

"Why," said Porthos, "that was very good of him, it seems to me."

"'A thousand pistoles,' I said."

"A thousand pistoles!" Porthos exclaimed. "Oh! oh! that is a large sum. If he knew anything about horses he would dispute the price."

"Faith! he was very much inclined to do so, the contemptible fellow. He made a great start and looked at me. I also looked at him; then he understood, and putting his hand into a drawer, he took from it a quantity of notes on a bank in Lyons."

"For a thousand pistoles?"

"For a thousand pistoles—just that amount, the beggar; not one too many."

"And you have them?"

"They are here."

"Upon my word, I think he acted very generously."

"Generously! to men who had risked their lives for him, and besides had done him a great service?"

"A great service—what was that?"

"Why, it seems that I crushed for him a parliament councillor."

"What! that little man in black that you upset at the corner of Saint Jean Cemetery?"

"That's the man, my dear fellow; he was an annoyance to the cardinal. Unfortunately, I didn't crush him flat. It seems that he came to himself and that he will continue to be an annoyance."

"See that, now!" said Porthos; "and I turned my horse aside from going plump on to him! That will be for another time."

"He owed me for the councillor, the pettifogger!"

"But," said Porthos, "if he was not crushed completely——"

"Ah! Monsieur de Richelieu would have said, 'Five hundred crowns for the councillor.' Well, let's say no more about it. How much were your animals worth, Porthos?"

"Ah, if poor Mousqueton were here he could tell you to a fraction."

"No matter; you can tell within ten crowns."

"Why, Vulcan and Bayard cost me each about two hundred pistoles, and putting Phoebus at a hundred and fifty, we should be pretty near the amount."

"There will remain, then, four hundred and fifty pistoles," said D'Artagnan, contentedly.

"Yes," said Porthos, "but there are the equipments."

"That is very true. Well, how much for the equipments?"

"If we say one hundred pistoles for the three——"

"Good for the hundred pistoles; there remains, then, three hundred and fifty."

Porthos made a sign of assent.

"We will give the fifty pistoles to the hostess for our expenses," said D'Artagnan, "and share the three hundred."

"We will share," said Porthos.

"A paltry piece of business!" murmured D'Artagnan crumpling his note.

"Pooh!" said Porthos, "it is always that. But tell me——"

"What?"

"Didn't he speak of me in any way?"

"Ah! yes, indeed!" cried D'Artagnan, who was afraid of disheartening his friend by telling him that the cardinal had not breathed a word about him; "yes, surely, he said——"

"He said?" resumed Porthos.

"Stop, I want to remember his exact words. He said, 'As to your friend, tell him he may sleep in peace.'"

"Good, very good," said Porthos; "that signified as clear as daylight that he still intends to make me a baron."

At this moment nine o'clock struck. D'Artagnan started.

"Ah, yes," said Porthos, "there is nine o'clock. We have a rendezvous, you remember, at the Place Royale."

"Ah! stop! hold your peace, Porthos, don't remind me of it; 'tis that which has made me so cross since yesterday. I shall not go."

"Why?" asked Porthos.

"Because it is a grievous thing for me to meet again those two men who caused the failure of our enterprise."

"And yet," said Porthos, "neither of them had any advantage over us. I still had a loaded pistol and you were in full fight, sword in hand."

"Yes," said D'Artagnan; "but what if this rendezvous had some hidden purpose?"

"Oh!" said Porthos, "you can't think that, D'Artagnan!"

D'Artagnan did not believe Athos to be capable of a deception, but he sought an excuse for not going to the rendezvous.

"We must go," said the superb lord of Bracieux, "lest they should say we were afraid. We who have faced fifty foes on the high road can well meet two in the Place Royale."

"Yes, yes, but they took part with the princes without apprising us of it. Athos and Aramis have played a game with me which alarms me. We discovered yesterday the truth; what is the use of going to-day to learn something else?"

"You really have some distrust, then?" said Porthos.

"Of Aramis, yes, since he has become an abbé. You can't imagine, my dear fellow, the sort of man he is. He sees us on the road which leads him to a bishopric, and perhaps will not be sorry to get us out of his way."

"Ah, as regards Aramis, that is another thing," said Porthos, "and it wouldn't surprise me at all."

"Perhaps Monsieur de Beaufort will try, in his turn, to lay hands on us."

"Nonsense! He had us in his power and he let us go. Besides we can be on our guard; let us take arms, let Planchet post himself behind us with his carbine."

"Planchet is a Frondeur," answered D'Artagnan.

"Devil take these civil wars! one can no more now reckon on one's friends than on one's footmen," said Porthos. "Ah! if Mousqueton were here! there's a fellow who will never desert me!"

"So long as you are rich! Ah! my friend! 'tis not civil war that disunites us. It is that we are each of us twenty years older; it is that the honest emotions of youth have given place to suggestions of interest, whispers of ambition, counsels of selfishness. Yes, you are right; let us go, Porthos, but let us go well armed; were we not to keep the rendezvous, they would declare we were afraid. Halloo! Planchet! here! saddle our horses, take your carbine."

"Whom are we going to attack, sir?"

"No one; a mere matter of precaution," answered the Gascon.

"You know, sir, that they wished to murder that good councillor, Broussel, the father of the people?"

"Really, did they?" said D'Artagnan.

"Yes, but he has been avenged. He was carried home in the arms of the people. His house has been full ever since. He has received visits from the coadjutor, from Madame de Longueville, and the Prince de Conti; Madame de Chevreuse and Madame de Vendome have left their names at his door. And now, whenever he wishes——"

"Well, whenever he wishes?"

Planchet began to sing:

"Un vent de fronde S'est leve ce matin; Je crois qu'il gronde Contre le Mazarin. Un vent de fronde S'est leve ce matin."

"It doesn't surprise me," said D'Artagnan, in a low tone to Porthos, "that Mazarin would have been much better satisfied had I crushed the life out of his councillor."

"You understand, then, monsieur," resumed Planchet, "that if it were for some enterprise like that undertaken against Monsieur Broussel that you should ask me to take my carbine——"

"No, don't be alarmed; but where did you get all these details?"

"From a good source, sir; I heard it from Friquet."

"From Friquet? I know that name——"

"A son of Monsieur de Broussel's servant, and a lad that, I promise you, in a revolt will not give away his share to the dogs."

"Is he not a singing boy at Notre Dame?" asked D'Artagnan.

"Yes, that is the very boy; he's patronized by Bazin."

"Ah, yes, I know."

"Of what importance is this little reptile to you?" asked Porthos.

"Gad!" replied D'Artagnan; "he has already given me good information and he may do the same again."

Whilst all this was going on, Athos and Aramis were entering Paris by the Faubourg St. Antoine. They had taken some refreshment on the road and hastened on, that they might not fail at the appointed place. Bazin was their only attendant, for Grimaud had stayed behind to take care of Mousqueton. As they were passing onward, Athos proposed that they should lay aside their arms and military costume, and assume a dress more suited to the city.

"Oh, no, dear count!" cried Aramis, "is it not a warlike encounter that we are going to?"

"What do you mean, Aramis?"

"That the Place Royale is the termination to the main road to Vendomois, and nothing else."

"What! our friends?"

"Are become our most dangerous enemies, Athos. Let us be on our guard."

"Oh! my dear D'Herblay!"

"Who can say whether D'Artagnan may not have betrayed us to the cardinal? who can tell whether Mazarin may not take advantage of this rendezvous to seize us?"

"What! Aramis, you think that D'Artagnan, that Porthos, would lend their hands to such an infamy?"

"Among friends, my dear Athos, no, you are right; but among enemies it would be only a stratagem."

Athos crossed his arms and bowed his noble head.

"What can you expect, Athos? Men are so made; and we are not always twenty years old. We have cruelly wounded, as you know, that personal pride by which D'Artagnan is blindly governed. He has been beaten. Did you not observe his despair on the journey? As to Porthos, his barony was perhaps dependent on that affair. Well, he found us on his road and will not be baron this time. Perhaps that famous barony will have something to do with our interview this evening. Let us take our precautions, Athos."

"But suppose they come unarmed? What a disgrace to us."

"Oh, never fear! besides, if they do, we can easily make an excuse; we came straight off a journey and are insurgents, too."

"An excuse for us! to meet D'Artagnan with a false excuse! to have to make a false excuse to Porthos! Oh, Aramis!" continued Athos, shaking his head mournfully, "upon my soul, you make me the most miserable of men; you disenchant a heart not wholly dead to friendship. Go in whatever guise you choose; for my part, I shall go unarmed."

"No, for I will not allow you to do so. 'Tis not one man, not Athos only, not the Comte de la Fere whom you will ruin by this amiable weakness, but a whole party to whom you belong and who depend upon you."

"Be it so then," replied Athos, sorrowfully.

And they pursued their road in mournful silence.

Scarcely had they reached by the Rue de la Mule the iron gate of the Place Royale, when they perceived three cavaliers, D'Artagnan, Porthos, and Planchet, the two former wrapped up in their military cloaks under which their swords were hidden, and Planchet, his musket by his side. They were waiting at the entrance of the Rue Sainte Catharine, and their horses were fastened to the rings of the arcade. Athos, therefore, commanded Bazin to fasten up his horse and that of Aramis in the same manner.

They then advanced two and two, and saluted each other politely.

"Now where will it be agreeable to you that we hold our conference?" inquired Aramis, perceiving that people were stopping to look at them, supposing that they were going to engage in one of those far-famed duels still extant in the memory of the Parisians, and especially the inhabitants of the Place Royale.

"The gate is shut," said Aramis, "but if these gentlemen like a cool retreat under the trees, and perfect seclusion, I will get the key from the Hotel de Rohan and we shall be well suited."

D'Artagnan darted a look into the obscurity of the Place. Porthos ventured to put his head between the railings, to try if his glance could penetrate the gloom.

"If you prefer any other place," said Athos, in his persuasive voice, "choose for yourselves."

"This place, if Monsieur d'Herblay can procure the key, is the best that we can have," was the answer.

Aramis went off at once, begging Athos not to remain alone within reach of D'Artagnan and Porthos; a piece of advice which was received with a contemptuous smile.

Aramis returned soon with a man from the Hotel de Rohan, who was saying to him:

"You swear, sir, that it is not so?"

"Stop," and Aramis gave him a louis d'or.

"Ah! you will not swear, my master," said the concierge, shaking his head.

"Well, one can never say what may happen; at present we and these gentlemen are excellent friends."

"Yes, certainly," added Athos and the other two.

D'Artagnan had heard the conversation and had understood it.

"You see?" he said to Porthos.

"What do I see?"

"That he wouldn't swear."

"Swear what?"

"That man wanted Aramis to swear that we are not going to the Place Royale to fight."

"And Aramis wouldn't swear?"

"No."

"Attention, then!"

Athos did not lose sight of the two speakers. Aramis opened the gate and faced around in order that D'Artagnan and Porthos might enter. In passing through the gate, the hilt of the lieutenant's sword was caught in the grating and he was obliged to pull off his cloak; in doing so he showed the butt end of his pistols and a ray of the moon was reflected on the shining metal.

"Do you see?" whispered Aramis to Athos, touching his shoulder with one hand and pointing with the other to the arms which the Gascon wore under his belt.

"Alas! I do!" replied Athos, with a deep sigh.

He entered third, and Aramis, who shut the gate after him, last. The two serving-men waited without; but as if they likewise mistrusted each other, they kept their respective distances.

Chapter XXVIII.

The Place Royale.

They proceeded silently to the centre of the Place, but as at this very moment the moon had just emerged from behind a cloud, they thought they might be observed if they remained on that spot and therefore regained the shade of the lime-trees.

There were benches here and there; the four gentlemen stopped near them; at a sign from Athos, Porthos and D'Artagnan sat down, the two others stood in front of them.

After a few minutes of silent embarrassment, Athos spoke.

"Gentlemen," he said, "our presence here is the best proof of former friendship; not one of us has failed the others at this rendezvous; not one has, therefore, to reproach himself."

"Hear me, count," replied D'Artagnan; "instead of making compliments to each other, let us explain our conduct to each other, like men of right and honest hearts."

"I wish for nothing more; have you any cause of complaint against me or Monsieur d'Herblay? If so, speak out," answered Athos.

"I have," replied D'Artagnan. "When I saw you at your chateau at Bragelonne, I made certain proposals to you which you perfectly understood; instead of answering me as a friend, you played with me as a child; the friendship, therefore, that you boast of was not broken yesterday by the shock of swords, but by your dissimulation at your castle."

"D'Artagnan!" said Athos, reproachfully.

"You asked for candor and you have it. You ask what I have against you; I tell you. And I have the same sincerity to show you, if you wish, Monsieur d'Herblay; I acted in a similar way to you and you also deceived me."

"Really, monsieur, you say strange things," said Aramis. "You came seeking me to make to me certain proposals, but did you make them? No, you sounded me, nothing more. Very well what did I say to you? that Mazarin was contemptible and that I wouldn't serve Mazarin. But that is all. Did I tell you that I wouldn't serve any other? On the contrary, I gave you to understand, I think, that I adhered to the princes. We even joked very pleasantly, if I remember rightly, on the very probable contingency of your being charged by the cardinal with my arrest. Were you a party man? There is no doubt of that. Well, why should not we, too, belong to a party? You had your secret and we had ours; we didn't exchange them. So much the better; it proves that we know how to keep our secrets."

"I do not reproach you, monsieur," said D'Artagnan; "'tis only because Monsieur de la Fere has spoken of friendship that I question your conduct."

"And what do you find in it that is worthy of blame?" asked Aramis, haughtily.

The blood mounted instantly to the temples of D'Artagnan, who arose, and replied:

"I consider it worthy conduct of a pupil of Jesuits."

On seeing D'Artagnan rise, Porthos rose also; these four men were therefore all standing at the same time, with a menacing aspect, opposite to each other.

Upon hearing D'Artagnan's reply, Aramis seemed about to draw his sword, when Athos prevented him.

"D'Artagnan," he said, "you are here to-night, still infuriated by yesterday's adventure. I believed your heart noble enough to enable a friendship of twenty years to overcome an affront of a quarter of an hour. Come, do you really think you have anything to say against me? Say it then; if I am in fault I will avow the error."

The grave and harmonious tones of that beloved voice seemed to have still its ancient influence, whilst that of Aramis, which had become harsh and tuneless in his moments of ill-humor, irritated him. He answered therefore:

"I think, monsieur le comte, that you had something to communicate to me at your chateau of Bragelonne, and that gentleman"—he pointed to Aramis—"had also something to tell me when I was in his convent. At that time I was not concerned in the adventure, in the course of which you have so successfully estopped me! However, because I was prudent you must not take me for a fool. If I had wished to widen the breach between those whom

Monsieur d'Herblay chooses to receive with a rope ladder and those whom he receives with a wooden ladder, I could have spoken out."

"What are you meddling with?" cried Aramis, pale with anger, suspecting that D'Artagnan had acted as a spy on him and had seen him with Madame de Longueville.

"I never meddle save with what concerns me, and I know how to make believe that I haven't seen what does not concern me; but I hate hypocrites, and among that number I place musketeers who are abbés and abbés who are musketeers; and," he added, turning to Porthos "here's a gentleman who's of the same opinion as myself."

Porthos, who had not spoken one word, answered merely by a word and a gesture.

He said "yes" and he put his hand on his sword.

Aramis started back and drew his. D'Artagnan bent forward, ready either to attack or to stand on his defense.

Athos at that moment extended his hand with the air of supreme command which characterized him alone, drew out his sword and the scabbard at the same time, broke the blade in the sheath on his knee and threw the pieces to his right. Then turning to Aramis:

"Aramis," he said, "break your sword."

Aramis hesitated.

"It must be done," said Athos; then in a lower and more gentle voice, he added. "I wish it."

Then Aramis, paler than before, but subdued by these words, snapped the serpent blade between his hands, and then folding his arms, stood trembling with rage.

These proceedings made D'Artagnan and Porthos draw back. D'Artagnan did not draw his sword; Porthos put his back into the sheath.

"Never!" exclaimed Athos, raising his right hand to Heaven, "never! I swear before God, who seeth us, and who, in the darkness of this night heareth us, never shall my sword cross yours, never my eye express a glance of anger, nor my heart a throb of hatred, at you. We lived together, we loved, we hated together; we shed, we mingled our blood together, and too probably, I may still add, that there may be yet a bond between us closer even than that of friendship; perhaps there may be the bond of crime; for we four, we once did condemn, judge and slay a human being whom we had not any right to cut off from this world, although apparently fitter for hell than for this life. D'Artagnan, I have always loved you as my son; Porthos, we slept six years side by side; Aramis is your brother as well as mine, and Aramis has once loved you, as I love you now and as I have ever loved you. What can Cardinal Mazarin be to us, to four men who compelled such a man as Richelieu to act as we pleased? What is such or such a prince to us, who fixed the diadem upon a great queen's head? D'Artagnan, I ask your pardon for having yesterday crossed swords with you; Aramis does the same to Porthos; now hate me if you can; but for my own part, I shall ever, even if you do hate me, retain esteem and friendship for you. I repeat my words, Aramis, and then, if you desire it, and if they desire it, let us separate forever from our old friends."

There was a solemn, though momentary silence, which was broken by Aramis.

"I swear," he said, with a calm brow and kindly glance, but in a voice still trembling with recent emotion, "I swear that I no longer bear animosity to those who were once my friends. I regret that I ever crossed swords with you, Porthos; I swear not only that it shall never again be pointed at your breast, but that in the bottom of my heart there will never in future be the slightest hostile sentiment; now, Athos, come."

Athos was about to retire.

"Oh! no! no! do not go away!" exclaimed D'Artagnan, impelled by one of those irresistible impulses which showed the nobility of his nature, the native brightness of his character; "I swear that I would give the last drop of my blood and the last fragment of my limbs to preserve the friendship of such a friend as you, Athos—of such a man as you, Aramis." And he threw himself into the arms of Athos.

"My son!" exclaimed Athos, pressing him in his arms.

"And as for me," said Porthos, "I swear nothing, but I'm choked. Forsooth! If I were obliged to fight against you, I think I should allow myself to be pierced through and through, for I never loved any one but you in the wide world;" and honest Porthos burst into tears as he embraced Athos.

"My friends," said Athos, "this is what I expected from such hearts as yours. Yes, I have said it and I now repeat it: our destinies are irrevocably united, although we now pursue divergent roads. I respect your convictions, and whilst we fight for opposite sides, let us remain friends. Ministers, princes, kings, will pass away like mountain torrents; civil war, like a forest flame; but we—we shall remain; I have a presentiment that we shall."

"Yes," replied D'Artagnan, "let us still be musketeers, and let us retain as our battle-standard that famous napkin of the bastion St. Gervais, on which the great cardinal had three fleurs-de-lis embroidered."

"Be it so," cried Aramis. "Cardinalists or Frondeurs, what matters it? Let us meet again as capital seconds in a duel, devoted friends in business, merry companions in our ancient pleasures."

"And whenever," added Athos, "we meet in battle, at this word, 'Place Royale!' let us put our swords into our left hands and shake hands with the right, even in the very lust and music of the hottest carnage."

"You speak charmingly," said Porthos.

"And are the first of men!" added D'Artagnan. "You excel us all."

Athos smiled with ineffable pleasure.

"'Tis then all settled. Gentlemen, your hands; are we not pretty good Christians?"

"Egad!" said D'Artagnan, "by Heaven! yes."

"We should be so on this occasion, if only to be faithful to our oath," said Aramis.

"Ah, I'm ready to do what you will," cried Porthos; "even to swear by Mahomet. Devil take me if I've ever been so happy as at this moment."

And he wiped his eyes, still moist.

"Has not one of you a cross?" asked Athos.

Aramis smiled and drew from his vest a cross of diamonds, which was hung around his neck by a chain of pearls. "Here is one," he said.

"Well," resumed Athos, "swear on this cross, which, in spite of its magnificent material, is still a cross; swear to be united in spite of everything, and forever, and may this oath bind us to each other, and even, also, our descendants! Does this oath satisfy you?"

"Yes," said they all, with one accord.

"Ah, traitor!" muttered D'Artagnan, leaning toward Aramis and whispering in his ear, "you have made us swear on the crucifix of a Frondeuse."

Chapter XXIX.

The Ferry across the Oise.

We hope that the reader has not quite forgotten the young traveler whom we left on the road to Flanders.

In losing sight of his guardian, whom he had quitted, gazing after him in front of the royal basilican, Raoul spurred on his horse, in order not only to escape from his own melancholy reflections, but also to hide from Olivain the emotion his face might betray.

One hour's rapid progress, however, sufficed to disperse the gloomy fancies that had clouded the young man's bright anticipations; and the hitherto unfelt pleasure of freedom—a pleasure which is sweet even to those who have never known dependence—seemed to Raoul to gild not only Heaven and earth, but especially that blue but dim horizon of life we call the future.

Nevertheless, after several attempts at conversation with Olivain he foresaw that many days passed thus would prove exceedingly dull; and the count's agreeable voice, his gentle and persuasive eloquence, recurred to his mind at the various towns through which they journeyed and about which he had no longer any one to give him those interesting details which he would have drawn from Athos, the most amusing and the best informed of guides. Another recollection contributed also to sadden Raoul: on their arrival at Sonores he had perceived, hidden behind a screen of poplars, a little chateau which so vividly recalled that of La Valliere to his mind that he halted for nearly ten minutes to gaze at it, and resumed his journey with a sigh too abstracted even to reply to Olivain's respectful inquiry about the cause of so much fixed attention. The aspect of external objects is often a mysterious guide communicating with the fibres of memory, which in spite of us will arouse them at times; this thread, like that of Ariadne, when once unraveled will conduct one through a labyrinth of thought, in which one loses one's self in endeavoring to follow that phantom of the past which is called recollection.

Now the sight of this chateau had taken Raoul back fifty leagues westward and had caused him to review his life from the moment when he had taken leave of little Louise to that in which he had seen her for the first time; and every branch of oak, every gilded weathercock on roof of slates, reminded him that, instead of returning to the friends of his childhood, every instant estranged him further and that perhaps he had even left them forever.

With a full heart and burning head he desired Olivain to lead on the horses to a wayside inn, which he observed within gunshot range, a little in advance of the place they had reached.

As for himself, he dismounted and remained under a beautiful group of chestnuts in flower, amidst which were murmuring a multitude of happy bees, and bade Olivain send the host to him with writing paper and ink, to be placed on a table which he found there, conveniently ready. Olivain obeyed and continued on his way, whilst Raoul remained sitting, with his elbow leaning on the table, from time to time gently shaking the flowers from his head, which fell upon him like snow, and gazing vaguely on the charming landscape spread out before him, dotted over with green fields and groups of trees. Raoul had been there about ten minutes, during five of which he was lost in reverie, when there appeared within the circle comprised in his rolling gaze a man with a rubicund face, who, with a napkin around his body, another under his arm, and a white cap upon his head, approached him, holding paper, pen and ink in hand.

"Ha! ha!" laughed the apparition, "every gentleman seems to have the same fancy, for not a quarter of an hour ago a young lad, well mounted like you, as tall as you and of about your age, halted before this clump of trees and had this table and this chair brought here, and dined here, with an old gentleman who seemed to be his tutor, upon a pie, of which they haven't left a mouthful, and two bottles of Macon wine, of which they haven't left a drop, but fortunately we have still some of the same wine and some of the same pies left, and if your worship will but give your orders——"

"No, friend," replied Raoul, smiling, "I am obliged to you, but at this moment I want nothing but the things for which I have asked—only I shall be very glad if the ink prove black and the pen good; upon these conditions I will pay for the pen the price of the bottle, and for the ink the price of the pie."

"Very well, sir," said the host, "I'll give the pie and the bottle of wine to your servant, and in this way you will have the pen and ink into the bargain."

"Do as you like," said Raoul, who was beginning his apprenticeship with that particular class of society, who, when there were robbers on the highroads, were connected with them, and who, since highwaymen no longer exist, have advantageously and aptly filled their vacant place.

The host, his mind at ease about his bill, placed pen, ink and paper upon the table. By a lucky chance the pen was tolerably good and Raoul began to write. The host remained standing in front of him, looking with a kind of involuntary admiration at his handsome face, combining both gravity and sweetness of expression. Beauty has always been and always will be all-powerful.

"He's not a guest like the other one here just now," observed mine host to Olivain, who had rejoined his master to see if he wanted anything, "and your young master has no appetite."

"My master had appetite enough three days ago, but what can one do? he lost it the day before yesterday."

And Olivain and the host took their way together toward the inn, Olivain, according to the custom of serving-men well pleased with their place, relating to the tavern-keeper all that he could say in favor of the young gentleman; whilst Raoul wrote on thus:

"Sir,—After a four hours' march I stop to write to you, for I miss you every moment, and I am always on the point of turning my head as if to reply when you speak to me. I was so bewildered by your departure and so overcome with grief at our separation, that I am sure I was able to but very feebly express all the affection and gratitude I feel toward you. You will forgive me, sir, for your heart is of such a generous nature that you can well understand all that has passed in mine. I entreat you to write to me, for you form a part of my existence, and, if I may venture to tell you so, I also feel anxious. It seemed to me as if you were yourself preparing for some dangerous undertaking, about which I did not dare to question you, since you told me nothing. I have, therefore, as you see, great need of hearing from you. Now that you are no longer beside me I am afraid every moment of erring. You sustained me powerfully, sir, and I protest to you that to-day I feel very lonely. Will you have the goodness, sir, should you receive news from Blois, to send me a few lines about my little friend Mademoiselle de la Valliere, about whose health, when we left, so much anxiety was felt? You can understand, honored and dear guardian, how precious and indispensable to me is the remembrance of the years that I have passed with you. I hope that you will sometimes, too, think of me, and if at certain hours you should miss me, if you should feel any slight regret at my absence, I shall be overwhelmed with joy at the thought that you appreciate my affection for and my devotion to yourself, and that I have been able to prove them to you whilst I had the happiness of living with you."

After finishing this letter Raoul felt more composed; he looked well around him to see if Olivain and the host might not be watching him, whilst he impressed a kiss upon the paper, a mute and touching caress, which the heart of Athos might well divine on opening the letter.

During this time Olivain had finished his bottle and eaten his pie; the horses were also refreshed. Raoul motioned to the host to approach, threw a crown upon the table, mounted his horse, and posted his letter at Senlis. The rest that had been thus afforded to men and horses enabled them to continue their journey at a good round pace. At Verberie, Raoul desired Olivain to make some inquiry about the young man who was preceding them; he had been observed to pass only three-quarters of an hour previously, but he was well mounted, as the tavern-keeper had already said, and rode at a rapid pace.

"Let us try and overtake this gentleman," said Raoul to Olivain; "like ourselves he is on his way to join the army and may prove agreeable company."

It was about four o'clock in the afternoon when Raoul arrived at Compiegne; there he dined heartily and again inquired about the young gentleman who was in advance of them. He had stopped, like Raoul, at the Hotel of the Bell and Bottle, the best at Compiegne; and had started again on his journey, saying that he should sleep at Noyon.

"Well, let us sleep at Noyon," said Raoul.

"Sir," replied Olivain, respectfully, "allow me to remark that we have already much fatigued the horses this morning. I think it would be well to sleep here and to start again very early to-morrow. Eighteen leagues is enough for the first stage."

"The Comte de la Fere wished me to hasten on," replied Raoul, "that I might rejoin the prince on the morning of the fourth day; let us push on, then, to Noyon; it will be a stage similar to those we traveled from Blois to Paris. We shall arrive at eight o'clock. The horses will have a long night's rest, and at five o'clock to-morrow morning we can be again on the road."

Olivain dared offer no opposition to this determination but he followed his master, grumbling.

"Go on, go on," said he, between his teeth, "expend your ardor the first day; to-morrow, instead of journeying twenty leagues, you will travel ten, the day after to-morrow, five, and in three days you will be in bed. There you must rest; young people are such braggarts."

It was easy to see that Olivain had not been taught in the school of the Planchets and the Grimauds. Raoul really felt tired, but he was desirous of testing his strength, and, brought up in the principles of Athos and certain of having heard him speak a thousand times of stages of twenty-five leagues, he did not wish to fall far short of his model. D'Artagnan, that man of iron, who seemed to be made of nerve and muscle only, had struck him with admiration. Therefore, in spite of Olivain's remarks, he continued to urge his steed more and more, and following a pleasant little path, leading to a ferry, and which he had been assured shortened the journey by the distance of one league, he arrived at the summit of a hill and perceived the river flowing before him. A little troop of men on horseback were waiting on the edge of the stream, ready to embark. Raoul did not doubt this was the gentleman and his escort; he called out to him, but they were too distant to be heard; then, in spite of the weariness of his beast, he made it gallop but the rising ground soon deprived him of all sight of the travelers, and when he had again attained a new height, the ferryboat had left the shore and was making for the opposite bank. Raoul, seeing that he could not arrive in time to cross the ferry with the travelers, halted to wait for Olivain. At this moment a shriek was heard that seemed to come from the river. Raoul turned toward the side whence the cry had sounded, and shaded his eyes from the glare of the setting sun with his hand.

"Olivain!" he exclaimed, "what do I see below there?"

A second scream, more piercing than the first, now sounded.

"Oh, sir!" cried Olivain, "the rope which holds the ferryboat has broken and the boat is drifting. But what do I see in the water—something struggling?"

"Oh, yes," exclaimed Raoul, fixing his glance on one point in the stream, splendidly illumined by the setting sun, "a horse, a rider!"

"They are sinking!" cried Olivain in his turn.

It was true, and Raoul was convinced that some accident had happened and that a man was drowning; he gave his horse its head, struck his spurs into its sides, and the animal, urged by pain and feeling that he had space open before him, bounded over a kind of paling which inclosed the landing place, and fell into the river, scattering to a distance waves of white froth.

"Ah, sir!" cried Olivain, "what are you doing? Good God!"

Raoul was directing his horse toward the unhappy man in danger. This was, in fact, a custom familiar to him. Having been brought up on the banks of the Loire, he might have been said to have been cradled on its waves; a hundred times he had crossed it on horseback, a thousand times had swum across. Athos, foreseeing the period when he should make a soldier of the viscount, had inured him to all kinds of arduous undertakings.

"Oh, heavens!" continued Olivain, in despair, "what would the count say if he only saw you now!"

"The count would do as I do," replied Raoul, urging his horse vigorously forward.

"But I—but I," cried Olivain, pale and disconsolate rushing about on the shore, "how shall I cross?"

"Leap, coward!" cried Raoul, swimming on; then addressing the traveler, who was struggling twenty yards in front of him: "Courage, sir!" said he, "courage! we are coming to your aid."

Olivain advanced, retired, then made his horse rear—turned it and then, struck to the core by shame, leaped, as Raoul had done, only repeating:

"I am a dead man! we are lost!"

In the meantime, the ferryboat had floated away, carried down by the stream, and the shrieks of those whom it contained resounded more and more. A man with gray hair had thrown himself from the boat into the river and was swimming vigorously toward the person who was drowning; but being obliged to go against the current he advanced but slowly. Raoul continued his way and was visibly gaining ground; but the horse and its rider, of whom he did not lose sight, were evidently sinking. The nostrils of the horse were no longer above water, and the rider, who had lost the reins in struggling, fell with his head back and his arms extended. One moment longer and all would disappear.

"Courage!" cried Raoul, "courage!"

"Too late!" murmured the young man, "too late!"

The water closed above his head and stifled his voice.

Raoul sprang from his horse, to which he left the charge of its own preservation, and in three or four strokes was at the gentleman's side; he seized the horse at once by the curb and raised its head above water; the animal began to breathe again and, as if he comprehended that they had come to his aid, redoubled his efforts. Raoul at the same time seized one of the young man's hands and placed it on the mane, which it grasped with the tenacity of a drowning man. Thus, sure that the rider would not release his hold, Raoul now only directed his attention to the horse, which he guided to the opposite bank, helping it to cut through the water and encouraging it with words.

All at once the horse stumbled against a ridge and then placed its foot on the sand.

"Saved!" exclaimed the man with gray hair, who also touched bottom.

"Saved!" mechanically repeated the young gentleman, releasing the mane and sliding from the saddle into Raoul's arms; Raoul was but ten yards from the shore; there he bore the fainting man, and laying him down upon the grass, unfastened the buttons of his collar and unhooked his doublet. A moment later the gray-headed man was beside him. Olivain managed in his turn to land, after crossing himself repeatedly; and the people in the ferryboat guided themselves as well as they were able toward the bank, with the aid of a pole which chanced to be in the boat.

Thanks to the attentions of Raoul and the man who accompanied the young gentleman, the color gradually returned to the pale cheeks of the dying man, who opened his eyes, at first entirely bewildered, but who soon fixed his gaze upon the person who had saved him.

"Ah, sir," he exclaimed, "it was you! Without you I was a dead man—thrice dead."

"But one recovers, sir, as you perceive," replied Raoul, "and we have but had a little bath."

"Oh! sir, what gratitude I feel!" exclaimed the man with gray hair.

"Ah, there you are, my good D'Arminges; I have given you a great fright, have I not? but it is your own fault. You were my tutor, why did you not teach me to swim?"

"Oh, monsieur le comte," replied the old man, "had any misfortune happened to you, I should never have dared to show myself to the marshal again."

"But how did the accident happen?" asked Raoul.

"Oh, sir, in the most natural way possible," replied he to whom they had given the title of count. "We were about a third of the way across the river when the cord of the ferryboat broke. Alarmed by the cries and gestures of the boatmen, my horse sprang into the water. I cannot swim, and dared not throw myself into the river. Instead of aiding the movements of my horse, I paralyzed them; and I was just going to drown myself with the best grace in the world, when you arrived just in time to pull me out of the water; therefore, sir, if you will agree, henceforward we are friends until death."

"Sir," replied Raoul, bowing, "I am entirely at your service, I assure you."

"I am called the Count de Guiche," continued the young man; "my father is the Marechal de Grammont; and now that you know who I am, do me the honor to inform me who you are."

"I am the Viscount de Bragelonne," answered Raoul, blushing at being unable to name his father, as the Count de Guiche had done.

"Viscount, your countenance, your goodness and your courage incline me toward you; my gratitude is already due. Shake hands—I crave your friendship."

"Sir," said Raoul, returning the count's pressure of the hand, "I like you already, from my heart; pray regard me as a devoted friend, I beseech you."

"And now, where are you going, viscount?" inquired De Guiche.

"To join the army, under the prince, count."

"And I, too!" exclaimed the young man, in a transport of joy. "Oh, so much the better, we will fire the first shot together."

"It is well; be friends," said the tutor; "young as you both are, you were perhaps born under the same star and were destined to meet. And now," continued he, "you must change your clothes; your servants, to whom I gave directions the moment they had left the ferryboat, ought to be already at the inn. Linen and wine are both being warmed; come."

The young men had no objection to this proposition; on the contrary, they thought it very timely.

They mounted again at once, whilst looks of admiration passed between them. They were indeed two elegant horsemen, with figures slight and upright, noble faces, bright and proud looks, loyal and intelligent smiles.

De Guiche might have been about eighteen years of age, but he was scarcely taller than Raoul, who was only fifteen.

Chapter XXX.

Skirmishing.

The halt at Noyon was but brief, every one there being wrapped in profound sleep. Raoul had desired to be awakened should Grimaud arrive, but Grimaud did not arrive. Doubtless, too, the horses on their part appreciated the eight hours of repose and the abundant stabling which was granted them. The Count de Guiche was awakened at five o'clock in the morning by Raoul, who came to wish him good-day. They breakfasted in haste, and at six o'clock had already gone ten miles.

The young count's conversation was most interesting to Raoul, therefore he listened much, whilst the count talked well and long. Brought up in Paris, where Raoul had been but once; at the court, which Raoul had never seen; his follies as page; two duels, which he had already found the means of fighting, in spite of the edicts against them and, more especially, in spite of his tutor's vigilance—these things excited the greatest curiosity in Raoul. Raoul had only been at M. Scarron's house; he named to Guiche the people whom he had seen there. Guiche knew everybody—Madame de Neuillan, Mademoiselle d'Aubigne, Mademoiselle de Scudery, Mademoiselle Paulet, Madame de Chevreuse. He criticised everybody humorously. Raoul trembled, lest he should laugh among the rest at Madame de Chevreuse, for whom he entertained deep and genuine sympathy, but either instinctively, or from affection for the duchess, he said everything in her favor. His praises increased Raoul's friendship twofold. Then came the question of gallantry and love affairs. Under this head, also, Bragelonne had much more to hear than to tell. He listened attentively and fancied that he discovered through three or four rather frivolous adventures, that the count, like himself, had a secret to hide in the depths of his heart.

De Guiche, as we have said before, had been educated at the court, and the intrigues of this court were not unknown to him. It was the same court of which Raoul had so often heard the Comte de la Fere speak, except that its aspect had much changed since the period when Athos had himself been part of it; therefore everything which the Count de Guiche related was new to his traveling companion. The young count, witty and caustic, passed all the world in review; the queen herself was not spared, and Cardinal Mazarin came in for his share of ridicule.

The day passed away as rapidly as an hour. The count's tutor, a man of the world and a bon vivant, up to his eyes in learning, as his pupil described him, often recalled the profound erudition, the witty and caustic satire of Athos to Raoul; but as regarded grace, delicacy, and nobility of external appearance, no one in these points was to be compared to the Comte de la Fere.

The horses, which were more kindly used than on the previous day, stopped at Arras at four o'clock in the evening. They were approaching the scene of war; and as bands of Spaniards sometimes took advantage of the night to make expeditions even as far as the neighborhood of Arras, they determined to remain in the town until the morrow. The French army held all between Pont-a-Marc as far as Valenciennes, falling back upon Douai. The prince was said to be in person at Bethune.

The enemy's army extended from Cassel to Courtray; and as there was no species of violence or pillage it did not commit, the poor people on the frontier quitted their isolated dwellings and fled for refuge into the strong cities which held out a shelter to them. Arras was encumbered with fugitives. An approaching battle was much spoken of, the prince having manoeuvred, until that movement, only in order to await a reinforcement that had just reached him.

The young men congratulated themselves on having arrived so opportunely. The evening was employed in discussing the war; the grooms polished their arms; the young men loaded the pistols in case of a skirmish, and they awoke in despair, having both dreamed that they had arrived too late to participate in the battle. In the morning it was rumored that Prince de Condé had evacuated Bethune and fallen back on Carvin, leaving, however, a strong garrison in the former city.

But as there was nothing positively certain in this report, the young warriors decided to continue their way toward Bethune, free on the road to diverge to the right and march to Carvin if necessary.

The count's tutor was well acquainted with the country; he consequently proposed to take a crossroad, which lay between that of Lens and that of Bethune. They obtained information at Ablain, and a statement of their route was left for Grimaud. About seven o'clock in the morning they set out. De Guiche, who was young and impulsive, said to Raoul, "Here we are, three masters and three servants. Our valets are well armed and yours seems to be tough enough."

"I have never seen him put to the test," replied Raoul, "but he is a Breton, which promises something."

"Yes, yes," resumed De Guiche; "I am sure he can fire a musket when required. On my side I have two sure men, who have been in action with my father. We therefore represent six fighting men; if we should meet a little troop of enemies, equal or even superior in number to our own, shall we charge them, Raoul?"

"Certainly, sir," replied the viscount.

"Holloa! young people—stop there!" said the tutor, joining in the conversation. "Zounds! how you manoeuvre my instructions, count! You seem to forget the orders I received to conduct you safe and sound to his highness the prince! Once with the army you may be killed at your good pleasure; but until that time, I warn you that in my capacity of general of the army I shall order a retreat and turn my back on the first red coat we come across." De Guiche and Raoul glanced at each other, smiling.

They arrived at Ablain without accident. There they inquired and learned that the prince had in reality quitted Bethune and stationed himself between Cambria and La Venthie. Therefore, leaving directions at every place for Grimaud, they took a crossroad which conducted the little troop by the bank of a small stream flowing into the Lys. The country was beautiful, intersected by valleys as green as the emerald. Here and there they passed little copses crossing the path which they were following. In anticipation of some ambuscade in each of these little woods the tutor placed his two servants at the head of the band, thus forming the advance guard. Himself and the two young men represented the body of the army, whilst Olivain, with his rifle upon his knee and his eyes upon the watch, protected the rear.

They had observed for some time before them, on the horizon, a rather thick wood; and when they had arrived at a distance of a hundred steps from it, Monsieur d'Arminges took his usual precautions and sent on in advance the count's two grooms. The servants had just disappeared under the trees, followed by the tutor, and the young men were laughing and talking about a hundred yards off. Olivain was at the same distance in the rear, when suddenly there resounded five or six musket-shots. The tutor cried halt; the young men obeyed, pulling up their steeds, and at the same moment the two valets were seen returning at a gallop.

The young men, impatient to learn the cause of the firing, spurred on toward the servants. The tutor followed them.

"Were you stopped?" eagerly inquired the two youths.

"No," replied the servants, "it is even probable that we have not been seen; the shots were fired about a hundred paces in advance of us, in the thickest part of the wood, and we returned to ask your advice."

"My advice is this," said Monsieur d'Arminges, "and if needs be, my will, that we beat a retreat. There may be an ambuscade concealed in this wood."

"Did you see nothing there?" asked the count.

"I thought I saw," said one of the servants, "horsemen dressed in yellow, creeping along the bed of the stream.

"That's it," said the tutor. "We have fallen in with a party of Spaniards. Come back, sirs, back."

The two youths looked at each other, and at this moment a pistol-shot and cries for help were heard. Another glance between the young men convinced them both that neither had any wish to go back, and as the tutor had already turned his horse's head, they both spurred forward, Raoul crying: "Follow me, Olivain!" and the Count de Guiche: "Follow, Urban and Planchet!" And before the tutor could recover from his surprise they had both disappeared into the forest. Whilst they spurred their steeds they held their pistols ready also. In five minutes they arrived at the spot whence the noise had proceeded, and then restraining their horses, they advanced cautiously.

"Hush," whispered De Guiche, "these are cavaliers."

"Yes, three on horseback and three who have dismounted."

"Can you see what they are doing?"

"Yes, they appear to be searching a wounded or dead man."

"It is some cowardly assassination," said De Guiche.

"They are soldiers, though," resumed De Bragelonne.

"Yes, skirmishers; that is to say, highway robbers."

"At them!" cried Raoul. "At them!" echoed De Guiche.

"Oh! gentlemen! gentlemen! in the name of Heaven!" cried the poor tutor.

But he was not listened to, and his cries only served to arouse the attention of the Spaniards.

The men on horseback at once rushed at the two youths, leaving the three others to complete the plunder of the dead or wounded travelers; for on approaching nearer, instead of one extended figure, the young men discovered two. De Guiche fired the first shot at ten paces and missed his man; and the Spaniard, who had advanced to meet Raoul, aimed in his turn, and Raoul felt a pain in the left arm, similar to that of a blow from a whip. He let off his fire at but four paces. Struck in the breast and extending his arms, the Spaniard fell back on the crupper, and the terrified horse, turning around, carried him off.

Raoul at this moment perceived the muzzle of a gun pointed at him, and remembering the recommendation of Athos, he, with the rapidity of lightning, made his horse rear as the shot was fired. His horse bounded to one side, losing its footing, and fell, entangling Raoul's leg under its body. The Spaniard sprang forward and seized the gun by its muzzle, in order to strike Raoul on the head with the butt. In the position in which Raoul lay, unfortunately, he could neither draw his sword from the scabbard, nor his pistols from their holsters. The butt end of the musket hovered over his head, and he could scarcely restrain himself from closing his eyes, when with one bound Guiche reached the Spaniard and placed a pistol at his throat. "Yield!" he cried, "or you are a dead man!" The musket fell from the soldier's hands, who yielded on the instant. Guiche summoned one of his grooms, and delivering the prisoner into his charge, with orders to shoot him through the head if he attempted to escape, he leaped from his horse and approached Raoul.

"Faith, sir," said Raoul, smiling, although his pallor betrayed the excitement consequent on a first affair, "you are in a great hurry to pay your debts and have not been long under any obligation to me. Without your aid," continued he, repeating the count's words "I should have been a dead man—thrice dead."

"My antagonist took flight," replied De Guiche "and left me at liberty to come to your assistance. But are you seriously wounded? I see you are covered with blood!"

"I believe," said Raoul, "that I have got something like a scratch on the arm. If you will help me to drag myself from under my horse I hope nothing need prevent us continuing our journey."

Monsieur d'Arminges and Olivain had already dismounted and were attempting to raise the struggling horse. At last Raoul succeeded in drawing his foot from the stirrup and his leg from under the animal, and in a second he was on his feet again.

"Nothing broken?" asked De Guiche.

"Faith, no, thank Heaven!" replied Raoul; "but what has become of the poor wretches whom these scoundrels were murdering?"

"I fear we arrived too late. They have killed them, I think, and taken flight, carrying off their booty. My servants are examining the bodies."

"Let us go and see whether they are quite dead, or if they can still be helped," suggested Raoul. "Olivain, we have come into possession of two horses, but I have lost my own. Take for yourself the better of the two and give me yours."

They approached the spot where the unfortunate victims lay.

Chapter XXXI.

The Monk.

Two men lay prone upon the ground, one bathed in blood and motionless, with his face toward the earth; this one was dead. The other leaned against a tree, supported there by the two valets, and was praying fervently, with clasped hands and eyes raised to Heaven. He had received a ball in his thigh, which had broken the bone. The young men first approached the dead man.

"He is a priest," said Bragelonne, "he has worn the tonsure. Oh, the scoundrels! to lift their hands against a minister of God."

"Come here, sir," said Urban, an old soldier who had served under the cardinal duke in all his campaigns; "come here, there is nothing to be done with him, whilst we may perhaps be able to save the other."

The wounded man smiled sadly. "Save me! Oh, no!" said he, "but help me to die, if you can."

"Are you a priest?" asked Raoul.

"No sir."

"I ask, as your unfortunate companion appeared to me to belong to the church."

"He is the curate of Bethune, sir, and was carrying the holy vessels belonging to his church, and the treasure of the chapter, to a safe place, the prince having abandoned our town yesterday; and as it was known that bands of the enemy were prowling about the country, no one dared to accompany the good man, so I offered to do so.

"And, sir," continued the wounded man, "I suffer much and would like, if possible, to be carried to some house."

"Where you can be relieved?" asked De Guiche.

"No, where I can confess."

"But perhaps you are not so dangerously wounded as you think," said Raoul.

"Sir," replied the wounded man, "believe me, there is no time to lose; the ball has broken the thigh bone and entered the intestines."

"Are you a surgeon?" asked De Guiche.

"No, but I know a little about wounds, and mine, I know, is mortal. Try, therefore, either to carry me to some place where I may see a priest or take the trouble to send one to me here. It is my soul that must be saved; as for my body, it is lost."

"To die whilst doing a good deed! It is impossible. God will help you."

"Gentlemen, in the name of Heaven!" said the wounded man, collecting all his forces, as if to get up, "let us not lose time in useless words. Either help me to gain the nearest village or swear to me on your salvation that you will send me the first monk, the first curé, the first priest you may meet. But," he added in a despairing tone, "perhaps no one will dare to come for it is known that the Spaniards are ranging through the country, and I shall die without absolution. My God! my God! Good God! good God!" added the wounded man, in an accent of terror which made the young men shudder; "you will not allow that? that would be too terrible!"

"Calm yourself, sir," replied De Guiche. "I swear to you, you shall receive the consolation that you ask. Only tell us where we shall find a house at which we can demand aid and a village from which we can fetch a priest."

"Thank you, and God reward you! About half a mile from this, on the same road, there is an inn, and about a mile further on, after leaving the inn, you will reach the village of Greney. There you must find the curate, or if he is not at home, go to the convent of the Augustines, which is the last house on the right, and bring me one of the brothers. Monk or priest, it matters not, provided only that he has received from holy church the power of absolving in articulo mortis."

"Monsieur d'Arminges," said De Guiche, "remain beside this unfortunate man and see that he is removed as gently as possible. The vicomte and myself will go and find a priest."

"Go, sir," replied the tutor; "but in Heaven's name do not expose yourself to danger!"

"Do not fear. Besides, we are safe for to-day; you know the axiom, 'Non bis in idem.'"

"Courage, sir," said Raoul to the wounded man. "We are going to execute your wishes."

"May Heaven prosper you!" replied the dying man, with an accent of gratitude impossible to describe.

The two young men galloped off in the direction mentioned and in ten minutes reached the inn. Raoul, without dismounting, called to the host and announced that a wounded man was about to be brought to his house and begged him in the meantime to prepare everything needful. He desired him also, should he know in the neighborhood any doctor or chirurgeon, to fetch him, taking on himself the payment of the messenger.

The host, who saw two young noblemen, richly clad, promised everything they required, and our two cavaliers, after seeing that preparations for the reception were actually begun, started off again and proceeded rapidly toward Greney.

They had gone rather more than a league and had begun to descry the first houses of the village, the red-tiled roofs of which stood out from the green trees which surrounded them, when, coming toward them mounted on a mule, they perceived a poor monk, whose large hat and gray worsted dress made them take him for an Augustine brother. Chance for once seemed to favor them in sending what they were so assiduously seeking. He was a man about twenty-two or twenty-three years old, but who appeared much older from ascetic exercises. His complexion was pale, not of that deadly pallor which is a kind of neutral beauty, but of a bilious, yellow hue; his colorless hair was short and scarcely extended beyond the circle formed by the hat around his head, and his light blue eyes seemed destitute of any expression.

"Sir," began Raoul, with his usual politeness, "are you an ecclesiastic?"

"Why do you ask me that?" replied the stranger, with a coolness which was barely civil.

"Because we want to know," said De Guiche, haughtily.

The stranger touched his mule with his heel and continued his way.

In a second De Guiche had sprung before him and barred his passage. "Answer, sir," exclaimed he; "you have been asked politely, and every question is worth an answer."

"I suppose I am free to say or not to say who I am to two strangers who take a fancy to ask me."

It was with difficulty that De Guiche restrained the intense desire he had of breaking the monk's bones.

"In the first place," he said, making an effort to control himself, "we are not people who may be treated anyhow; my friend there is the Viscount of Bragelonne and I am the Count de Guiche. Nor was it from caprice we asked the question, for there is a wounded and dying man who demands the succor of the church. If you be a priest, I conjure you in the name of humanity to follow me to aid this man; if you be not, it is a different matter, and I warn you in the name of courtesy, of which you appear profoundly ignorant, that I shall chastise you for your insolence."

The pale face of the monk became so livid and his smile so strange, that Raoul, whose eyes were still fixed upon him, felt as if this smile had struck to his heart like an insult.

"He is some Spanish or Flemish spy," said he, putting his hand to his pistol. A glance, threatening and transient as lightning, replied to Raoul.

"Well, sir," said De Guiche, "are you going to reply?"

"I am a priest," said the young man.

"Then, father," said Raoul, forcing himself to convey a respect by speech that did not come from his heart, "if you are a priest you have an opportunity, as my friend has told you, of exercising your vocation. At the next inn you will find a wounded man, now being attended by our servants, who has asked the assistance of a minister of God."

"I will go," said the monk.

And he touched his mule.

"If you do not go, sir," said De Guiche, "remember that we have two steeds able to catch your mule and the power of having you seized wherever you may be; and then I swear your trial will be summary; one can always find a tree and a cord."

The monk's eye again flashed, but that was all; he merely repeated his phrase, "I will go,"—and he went.

"Let us follow him," said De Guiche; "it will be the surest plan."

"I was about to propose so doing," answered De Bragelonne.

In the space of five minutes the monk turned around to ascertain whether he was followed or not.

"You see," said Raoul, "we have done wisely."

"What a horrible face that monk has," said De Guiche.

"Horrible!" replied Raoul, "especially in expression."

"Yes, yes," said De Guiche, "a strange face; but these monks are subject to such degrading practices; their fasts make them pale, the blows of the discipline make them hypocrites, and their eyes become inflamed through weeping for the good things of this life we common folk enjoy, but they have lost."

"Well," said Raoul, "the poor man will get his priest, but, by Heaven, the penitent appears to me to have a better conscience than the confessor. I confess I am accustomed to priests of a very different appearance."

"Ah!" exclaimed De Guiche, "you must understand that this is one of those wandering brothers, who go begging on the high road until some day a benefice falls down from Heaven on them; they are mostly foreigners—Scotch, Irish or Danish. I have seen them before."

"As ugly?"

"No, but reasonably hideous."

"What a misfortune for the wounded man to die under the hands of such a friar!"

"Pshaw!" said De Guiche. "Absolution comes not from him who administers it, but from God. However, for my part, I would rather die unshriven than have anything to say to such a confessor. You are of my opinion, are you not, viscount? and I see you playing with the pommel of your sword, as if you had a great inclination to break the holy father's head."

"Yes, count, it is a strange thing and one which might astonish you, but I feel an indescribable horror at the sight of yonder man. Have you ever seen a snake rise up on your path?"

"Never," answered De Guiche.

"Well, it has happened to me to do so in our Blaisois forests, and I remember that the first time I encountered one with its eyes fixed upon me, curled up, swinging its head and pointing its tongue, I remained fixed, pale and as though fascinated, until the moment when the Comte de la Fere——"

"Your father?" asked De Guiche.

"No, my guardian," replied Raoul, blushing.

"Very well——"

"Until the moment when the Comte de la Fere," resumed Raoul, "said, 'Come, Bragelonne, draw your sword;' then only I rushed upon the reptile and cut it in two, just at the moment when it was rising on its tail and hissing, ere it sprang upon me. Well, I vow I felt exactly the same sensation at sight of that man when he said, 'Why do you ask me that?' and looked so strangely at me."

"Then you regret that you did not cut your serpent in two morsels?"

"Faith, yes, almost," said Raoul.

They had now arrived within sight of the little inn and could see on the opposite side the procession bearing the wounded man and guided by Monsieur d'Arminges. The youths spurred on.

"There is the wounded man," said De Guiche, passing close to the Augustine brother. "Be good enough to hurry yourself a little, monsieur monk."

As for Raoul, he avoided the monk by the whole width of the road and passed him, turning his head away in repulsion.

The young men rode up to the wounded man to announce that they were followed by the priest. He raised himself to glance in the direction which they pointed out, saw the monk, and fell back upon the litter, his face illumined by joy.

"And now," said the youths, "we have done all we can for you; and as we are in haste to rejoin the prince's army we must continue our journey. You will excuse us, sir, but we are told that a battle is expected and we do not wish to arrive the day after it."

"Go, my young sirs," said the sick man, "and may you both be blessed for your piety. You have done for me, as you promised, all that you could do. As for me I can only repeat, may God protect you and all dear to you!"

"Sir," said De Guiche to his tutor, "we will precede you, and you can rejoin us on the road to Cambrin."

The host was at his door and everything was prepared—bed, bandages, and lint; and a groom had gone to Lens, the nearest village, for a doctor.

"Everything," said he to Raoul, "shall be done as you desire; but you will not stop to have your wound dressed?"

"Oh, my wound—mine—'tis nothing," replied the viscount; "it will be time to think about it when we next halt; only have the goodness, should you see a cavalier who makes inquiries about a young man on a chestnut horse followed by a servant, to tell him, in fact, that you have seen me, but that I have continued my journey and intend to dine at Mazingarbe and to stop at Cambrin. This cavalier is my attendant."

"Would it not be safer and more certain if I should ask him his name and tell him yours?" demanded the host.

"There is no harm in over-precaution. I am the Viscount de Bragelonne and he is called Grimaud."

At this moment the wounded man arrived from one direction and the monk from the other, the latter dismounting from his mule and desiring that it should be taken to the stables without being unharnessed.

"Sir monk," said De Guiche, "confess well that brave man; and be not concerned for your expenses or for those of your mule; all is paid."

"Thanks, monsieur," said the monk, with one of those smiles that made Bragelonne shudder.

"Come, count," said Raoul, who seemed instinctively to dislike the vicinity of the Augustine; "come, I feel ill here," and the two young men spurred on.

The litter, borne by two servants, now entered the house. The host and his wife were standing on the steps, whilst the unhappy man seemed to suffer dreadful pain and yet to be concerned only to know if he was followed by the monk. At sight of this pale, bleeding man, the wife grasped her husband's arm.

"Well, what's the matter?" asked the latter, "are you going to be ill just now?"

"No, but look," replied the hostess, pointing to the wounded man; "I ask you if you recognize him?"

"That man—wait a bit."

"Ah! I see you know him," exclaimed the wife; "for you have become pale in your turn."

"Truly," cried the host, "misfortune is coming on our house; it is the former executioner of Bethune."

"The former executioner of Bethune!" murmured the young monk, shrinking back and showing on his countenance the feeling of repugnance which his penitent inspired.

Monsieur d'Arminges, who was at the door, perceived his hesitation.

"Sir monk," said he, "whether he is now or has been an executioner, this unfortunate being is none the less a man. Render to him, then, the last service he can by any possibility ask of you, and your work will be all the more meritorious."

The monk made no reply, but silently wended his way to the room where the two valets had deposited the dying man on a bed. D'Arminges and Olivain and the two grooms then mounted their horses, and all four started off at a quick trot to rejoin Raoul and his companion. Just as the tutor and his escort disappeared in their turn, a new traveler stopped on the threshold of the inn.

"What does your worship want?" demanded the host, pale and trembling from the discovery he had just made.

The traveler made a sign as if he wished to drink, and then pointed to his horse and gesticulated like a man who is brushing something.

"Ah, diable!" said the host to himself; "this man seems dumb. And where will your worship drink?"

"There," answered the traveler, pointing to the table.

"I was mistaken," said the host, "he's not quite dumb. And what else does your worship wish for?"

"To know if you have seen a young man pass, fifteen years of age, mounted on a chestnut horse and followed by a groom?"

"The Viscount de Bragelonne?

"Just so."

"Then you are called Monsieur Grimaud?"

The traveler made a sign of assent.

"Well, then," said the host, "your young master was here a quarter of an hour ago; he will dine at Mazingarbe and sleep at Cambrin."

"How far is Mazingarbe?"

"Two miles and a half."

"Thank you."

Grimaud was drinking his wine silently and had just placed his glass on the table to be filled a second time, when a terrific scream resounded from the room occupied by the monk and the dying man. Grimaud sprang up.

"What is that?" said he; "whence comes that cry?"

"From the wounded man's room," replied the host.

"What wounded man?"

"The former executioner of Bethune, who has just been brought in here, assassinated by Spaniards, and who is now being confessed by an Augustine friar."

"The old executioner of Bethune," muttered Grimaud; "a man between fifty-five and sixty, tall, strong, swarthy, black hair and beard?"

"That is he, except that his beard has turned gray and his hair is white; do you know him?" asked the host.

"I have seen him once," replied Grimaud, a cloud darkening his countenance at the picture so suddenly summoned to the bar of recollection.

At this instant a second cry, less piercing than the first, but followed by prolonged groaning, was heard.

The three listeners looked at one another in alarm.

"We must see what it is," said Grimaud.

"It sounds like the cry of one who is being murdered," murmured the host.

"Mon Dieu!" said the woman, crossing herself.

If Grimaud was slow in speaking, we know that he was quick to act; he sprang to the door and shook it violently, but it was bolted on the other side.

"Open the door!" cried the host; "open it instantly, sir monk!"

No reply.

"Unfasten it, or I will break it in!" said Grimaud.

The same silence, and then, ere the host could oppose his design, Grimaud seized a pair of pincers he perceived in a corner and forced the bolt. The room was inundated with blood, dripping from the mattresses upon which lay the wounded man, speechless; the monk had disappeared.

"The monk!" cried the host; "where is the monk?"

Grimaud sprang toward an open window which looked into the courtyard.

"He has escaped by this means," exclaimed he.

"Do you think so?" said the host, bewildered; "boy, see if the mule belonging to the monk is still in the stable."

"There is no mule," cried he to whom this question was addressed.

The host clasped his hands and looked around him suspiciously, whilst Grimaud knit his brows and approached the wounded man, whose worn, hard features awoke in his mind such awful recollections of the past.

"There can be no longer any doubt but that it is himself," said he.

"Does he still live?" inquired the innkeeper.

Making no reply, Grimaud opened the poor man's jacket to feel if the heart beat, whilst the host approached in his turn; but in a moment they both fell back, the host uttering a cry of horror and Grimaud becoming pallid. The blade of a dagger was buried up to the hilt in the left side of the executioner.

"Run! run for help!" cried Grimaud, "and I will remain beside him here."

The host quitted the room in agitation, and as for his wife, she had fled at the sound of her husband's cries.

Chapter XXXII.

The Absolution.

This is what had taken place: We have seen that it was not of his own free will, but, on the contrary, very reluctantly, that the monk attended the wounded man who had been recommended to him in so strange a manner. Perhaps he would have sought to escape by flight had he seen any possibility of doing so. He was restrained by the threats of the two gentlemen and by the presence of their attendants, who doubtless had received their instructions. And besides, he considered it most expedient, without exhibiting too much ill-will, to follow to the end his role as confessor.

The monk entered the chamber and approached the bed of the wounded man. The executioner searched his face with the quick glance peculiar to those who are about to die and have no time to lose. He made a movement of surprise and said:

"Father, you are very young."

"Men who bear my robe have no age," replied the monk, dryly.

"Alas, speak to me more gently, father; in my last moments I need a friend."

"Do you suffer much?" asked the monk.

"Yes, but in my soul much more than in my body."

"We will save your soul," said the young man; "but are you really the executioner of Bethune, as these people say?"

"That is to say," eagerly replied the wounded man, who doubtless feared that the name of executioner would take from him the last help that he could claim—"that is to say, I was, but am no longer; it is fifteen years since I gave up the office. I still assist at executions, but no longer strike the blow myself—no, indeed."

"You have, then, a repugnance to your profession?"

"So long as I struck in the name of the law and of justice my profession allowed me to sleep quietly, sheltered as I was by justice and law; but since that terrible night when I became an instrument of private vengeance and when with personal hatred I raised the sword over one of God's creatures—since that day——"

The executioner paused and shook his head with an expression of despair.

"Tell me about it," said the monk, who, sitting on the foot of the bed, began to be interested in a story so strangely introduced.

"Ah!" cried the dying man, with all the effusiveness of a grief declared after long suppression, "ah! I have sought to stifle remorse by twenty years of good deeds; I have assuaged the natural ferocity of those who shed blood; on every occasion I have exposed my life to save those who were in danger, and I have preserved lives in exchange for that I took away. That is not all; the money gained in the exercise of my profession I have distributed to the poor; I have been assiduous in attending church and those who formerly fled from me have become accustomed to seeing me. All have forgiven me, some have even loved me; but I think that God has not pardoned me, for the memory of that execution pursues me constantly and every night I see that woman's ghost rising before me."

"A woman! You have assassinated a woman, then?" cried the monk.

"You also!" exclaimed the executioner, "you use that word which sounds ever in my ears—'assassinated!' I have assassinated, then, and not executed! I am an assassin, then, and not an officer of justice!" and he closed his eyes with a groan.

The monk doubtless feared that he would die without saying more, for he exclaimed eagerly:

"Go on, I know nothing, as yet; when you have finished your story, God and I will judge."

"Oh, father," continued the executioner, without opening his eyes, as if he feared on opening them to see some frightful object, "it is especially when night comes on and when I have to cross a river, that this terror which I have been unable to conquer comes upon me; it then seems as if my hand grew heavy, as if the cutlass was still in its grasp, as if the water had the color of blood, and all the voices of nature—the whispering of the trees, the murmur of the wind, the lapping of the wave—united in a voice tearful, despairing, terrible, crying to me, 'Place for the justice of God!'"

"Delirium!" murmured the monk, shaking his head.

The executioner opened his eyes, turned toward the young man and grasped his arm.

"'Delirium,'" he repeated; "'delirium,' do you say? Oh, no! I remember too well. It was evening; I had thrown the body into the river and those words which my remorse repeats to me are those which I in my pride pronounced. After being the instrument of human justice I aspired to be that of the justice of God."

"But let me see, how was it done? Speak," said the monk.

"It was at night. A man came to me and showed me an order and I followed him. Four other noblemen awaited me. They led me away masked. I reserved the right of refusing if the office they required of me should seem unjust. We traveled five or six leagues, serious, silent, and almost without speaking. At length, through the window of a little hut, they showed me a woman sitting, leaning on a table, and said, 'there is the person to be executed.'"

"Horrible!" said the monk. "And you obeyed?"

"Father, that woman was a monster. It was said that she had poisoned her second husband; she had tried to assassinate her brother-in-law; she had just poisoned a young woman who was her rival, and before leaving England she had, it was believed, caused the favorite of the king to be murdered."

"Buckingham?" cried the monk.

"Yes, Buckingham."

"The woman was English, then?"

"No, she was French, but she had married in England."

The monk turned pale, wiped his brow and went and bolted the door. The executioner thought that he had abandoned him and fell back, groaning, upon his bed.

"No, no; I am here," said the monk, quickly coming back to him. "Go on; who were those men?"

"One of them was a foreigner, English, I think. The four others were French and wore the uniform of musketeers."

"Their names?" asked the monk.

"I don't know them, but the four other noblemen called the Englishman 'my lord.'"

"Was the woman handsome?"

"Young and beautiful. Oh, yes, especially beautiful. I see her now, as on her knees at my feet, with her head thrown back, she begged for life. I have never understood how I could have laid low a head so beautiful, with a face so pale."

The monk seemed agitated by a strange emotion; he trembled all over; he seemed eager to put a question which yet he dared not ask. At length, with a violent effort at self-control:

"The name of that woman?" he said.

"I don't know what it was. As I have said, she was twice married, once in France, the second time in England."

"She was young, you say?"

"Twenty-five years old."

"Beautiful?"

"Ravishingly."

"Blond?"

"Yes."

"Abundance of hair—falling over her shoulders?"

"Yes."

"Eyes of an admirable expression?"

"When she chose. Oh, yes, it is she!"

"A voice of strange sweetness?"

"How do you know it?"

The executioner raised himself on his elbow and gazed with a frightened air at the monk, who became livid.

"And you killed her?" the monk exclaimed. "You were the tool of those cowards who dared not kill her themselves? You had no pity for that youthfulness, that beauty, that weakness? you killed that woman?"

"Alas! I have already told you, father, that woman, under that angelic appearance, had an infernal soul, and when I saw her, when I recalled all the evil she had done to me——"

"To you? What could she have done to you? Come, tell me!"

"She had seduced and ruined my brother, a priest. She had fled with him from her convent."

"With your brother?"

"Yes, my brother was her first lover, and she caused his death. Oh, father, do not look in that way at me! Oh, I am guilty, then; you will not pardon me?"

The monk recovered his usual expression.

"Yes, yes," he said, "I will pardon you if you tell me all."

"Oh!" cried the executioner, "all! all! all!"

"Answer, then. If she seduced your brother—you said she seduced him, did you not?"

"Yes."

"If she caused his death—you said that she caused his death?"

"Yes," repeated the executioner.

"Then you must know what her name was as a young girl."

"Oh, mon Dieu!" cried the executioner, "I think I am dying. Absolution, father! absolution."

"Tell me her name and I will give it."

"Her name was——My God, have pity on me!" murmured the executioner; and he fell back on the bed, pale, trembling, and apparently about to die.

"Her name!" repeated the monk, bending over him as if to tear from him the name if he would not utter it; "her name! Speak, or no absolution!"

The dying man collected all his forces.

The monk's eyes glittered.

"Anne de Bueil," murmured the wounded man.

"Anne de Bueil!" cried the monk, standing up and lifting his hands to Heaven. "Anne de Bueil! You said Anne de Bueil, did you not?"

"Yes, yes, that was her name; and now absolve me, for I am dying."

"I, absolve you!" cried the priest, with a laugh which made the dying man's hair stand on end; "I, absolve you? I am not a priest."

"You are not a priest!" cried the executioner. "What, then, are you?"

"I am about to tell you, wretched man."

"Oh, mon Dieu!"

"I am John Francis de Winter."

"I do not know you," said the executioner.

"Wait, wait; you are going to know me. I am John Francis de Winter," he repeated, "and that woman——"

"Well, that woman?"

"Was my mother!"

The executioner uttered the first cry, that terrible cry which had been first heard.

"Oh, pardon me, pardon me!" he murmured; "if not in the name of God, at least in your own name; if not as priest, then as son."

"Pardon you!" cried the pretended monk, "pardon you! Perhaps God will pardon you, but I, never!"

"For pity's sake," said the executioner, extending his arms.

"No pity for him who had no pity! Die, impenitent, die in despair, die and be damned!" And drawing a poniard from beneath his robe he thrust it into the breast of the wounded man, saying, "Here is my absolution!"

Then was heard that second cry, not so loud as the first and followed by a long groan.

The executioner, who had lifted himself up, fell back upon his bed. As to the monk, without withdrawing the poniard from the wound, he ran to the window, opened it, leaped out into the flowers of a small garden, glided onward to the stable, took out his mule, went out by a back gate, ran to a neighbouring thicket, threw off his monkish garb, took from his valise the complete habiliment of a cavalier, clothed himself in it, went on foot to the first post, secured there a horse and continued with a loose rein his journey to Paris.

Chapter XXXIII.

Grimaud Speaks.

Grimaud was left alone with the executioner, who in a few moments opened his eyes.

"Help, help," he murmured; "oh, God! have I not a single friend in the world who will aid me either to live or to die?"

"Take courage," said Grimaud; "they are gone to find assistance."

"Who are you?" asked the wounded man, fixing his half opened eyes on Grimaud.

"An old acquaintance," replied Grimaud.

"You?" and the wounded man sought to recall the features of the person now before him.

"Under what circumstances did we meet?" he asked again.

"One night, twenty years ago, my master fetched you from Bethune and conducted you to Armentieres."

"I know you well now," said the executioner; "you were one of the four grooms."

"Just so."

"Where do you come from now?"

"I was passing by and drew up at this inn to rest my horse. They told me the executioner of Bethune was here and wounded, when you uttered two piercing cries. At the first we ran to the door and at the second forced it open."

"And the monk?" exclaimed the executioner, "did you see the monk?"

"What monk?"

"The monk that was shut in with me."

"No, he was no longer here; he appears to have fled by the window. Was he the man that stabbed you?"

"Yes," said the executioner.

Grimaud moved as if to leave the room.

"What are you going to do?" asked the wounded man.

"He must be apprehended."

"Do not attempt it; he has revenged himself and has done well. Now I may hope that God will forgive me, since my crime is expiated."

"Explain yourself." said Grimaud.

"The woman whom you and your masters commanded me to kill——"

"Milady?"

"Yes, Milady; it is true you called her thus."

"What has the monk to do with this Milady?"

"She was his mother."

Grimaud trembled and stared at the dying man in a dull and leaden manner.

"His mother!" he repeated.

"Yes, his mother."

"But does he know this secret, then?"

"I mistook him for a monk and revealed it to him in confession."

"Unhappy man!" cried Grimaud, whose face was covered with sweat at the bare idea of the evil results such a revelation might cause; "unhappy man, you named no one, I hope?"

"I pronounced no name, for I knew none, except his mother's, as a young girl, and it was by this name that he recognized her, but he knows that his uncle was among her judges."

Thus speaking, he fell back exhausted. Grimaud, wishing to relieve him, advanced his hand toward the hilt of the dagger.

"Touch me not!" said the executioner; "if this dagger is withdrawn I shall die."

Grimaud remained with his hand extended; then, striking his forehead, he exclaimed:

"Oh! if this man should ever discover the names of the others, my master is lost."

"Haste! haste to him and warn him," cried the wounded man, "if he still lives; warn his friends, too. My death, believe me, will not be the end of this atrocious misadventure."

"Where was the monk going?" asked Grimaud.

"Toward Paris."

"Who stopped him?"

"Two young gentlemen, who were on their way to join the army and the name of one of whom I heard his companion mention—the Viscount de Bragelonne."

"And it was this young man who brought the monk to you? Then it was the will of God that it should be so and this it is which makes it all so awful," continued Grimaud. "And yet that woman deserved her fate; do you not think so?"

"On one's death-bed the crimes of others appear very small in comparison with one's own," said the executioner; and falling back exhausted he closed his eyes.

Grimaud was reluctant to leave the man alone and yet he perceived the necessity of starting at once to bear these tidings to the Comte de la Fere. Whilst he thus hesitated the host re-entered the room, followed not only by a surgeon, but by many other persons, whom curiosity had attracted to the spot. The surgeon approached the dying man, who seemed to have fainted.

"We must first extract the steel from the side," said he, shaking his head in a significant manner.

The prophecy which the wounded man had just uttered recurred to Grimaud, who turned away his head. The weapon, as we have already stated, was plunged into the body to the hilt, and as the surgeon, taking it by the end, drew it forth, the wounded man opened his eyes and fixed them on him in a manner truly frightful. When at last the blade had been entirely withdrawn, a red froth issued from the mouth of the wounded man and a stream of blood spouted afresh from the wound when he at length drew breath; then, fixing his eyes upon Grimaud with a singular expression, the dying man uttered the last death-rattle and expired.

Then Grimaud, lifting the dagger from the pool of blood which was gliding along the room, to the horror of all present, made a sign to the host to follow him, paid him with a generosity worthy of his master and again mounted his horse. Grimaud's first intention had been to return to Paris, but he remembered the anxiety which his prolonged absence might occasion Raoul, and reflecting that there were now only two miles between the vicomte and himself and a quarter of an hour's riding would unite them, and that the going, returning and explanation would not occupy an hour, he put spurs to his horse and a few minutes after had reached the only inn of Mazingarbe.

Raoul was seated at table with the Count de Guiche and his tutor, when all at once the door opened and Grimaud presented himself, travel-stained, dirty, and sprinkled with the blood of the unhappy executioner.

"Grimaud, my good Grimaud!" exclaimed Raoul "here you are at last! Excuse me, sirs, this is not a servant, but a friend. How did you leave the count?" continued he. "Does he regret me a little? Have you seen him since I left him? Answer, for I have many things to tell you, too; indeed, the last three days some odd adventures have happened—but what is the matter? how pale you are! and blood, too! What is this?"

"It is the blood of the unfortunate man whom you left at the inn and who died in my arms."

"In your arms?—that man! but know you who he was?"

"He used to be the headsman of Bethune."

"You knew him? and he is dead?"

"Yes."

"Well, sir," said D'Arminges, "it is the common lot; even an executioner is not exempted. I had a bad opinion of him the moment I saw his wound, and since he asked for a monk you know that it was his opinion, too, that death would follow."

At the mention of the monk, Grimaud became pale.

"Come, come," continued D'Arminges, "to dinner;" for like most men of his age and generation he did not allow sentiment or sensibility to interfere with a repast.

"You are right, sir," said Raoul. "Come, Grimaud, order dinner for yourself and when you have rested a little we can talk."

"No, sir, no," said Grimaud. "I cannot stop a moment; I must start for Paris again immediately."

"What? You start for Paris? You are mistaken; it is Olivain who leaves me; you are to remain."

"On the contrary, Olivain is to stay and I am to go. I have come for nothing else but to tell you so."

"But what is the meaning of this change?"

"I cannot tell you."

"Explain yourself."

"I cannot explain myself."

"Come, tell me, what is the joke?"

"Monsieur le vicomte knows that I never joke."

"Yes, but I know also that Monsieur le Comte de la Fere arranged that you were to remain with me and that Olivain should return to Paris. I shall follow the count's directions."

"Not under present circumstances, monsieur."

"Perhaps you mean to disobey me?"

"Yes, monsieur, I must."

"You persist, then?"

"Yes, I am going; may you be happy, monsieur," and Grimaud saluted and turned toward the door to go out.

Raoul, angry and at the same time uneasy, ran after him and seized him by the arm. "Grimaud!" he cried; "remain; I wish it."

"Then," replied Grimaud, "you wish me to allow monsieur le comte to be killed." He saluted and made a movement to depart.

"Grimaud, my friend," said the viscount, "will you leave me thus, in such anxiety? Speak, speak, in Heaven's name!" And Raoul fell back trembling upon his chair.

"I can tell you but one thing, sir, for the secret you wish to know is not my own. You met a monk, did you not?"

"Yes."

The young men looked at each other with an expression of fear.

"You conducted him to the wounded man and you had time to observe him, and perhaps you would know him again were you to meet him."

"Yes, yes!" cried both young men.

"Very well; if ever you meet him again, wherever it may be, whether on the high road or in the street or in a church, anywhere that he or you may be, put your foot on his neck and crush him without pity, without mercy, as you would crush a viper or a scorpion! destroy him utterly and quit him not until he is dead; the lives of five men are not safe, in my opinion, as long as he is on the earth."

And without adding another word, Grimaud, profiting by the astonishment and terror into which he had thrown his auditors, rushed from the room. Two minutes later the thunder of a horse's hoofs was heard upon the road; it was Grimaud, on his way to Paris. When once in the saddle Grimaud reflected on two things; first, that at the pace he was going his horse would not carry him ten miles, and secondly, that he had no money. But Grimaud's ingenuity was more prolific than his speech, and therefore at the first halt he sold his steed and with the money obtained from the purchase took post horses.

Chapter XXXIV.

On the Eve of Battle.

Raoul was aroused from his sombre reflections by his host, who rushed into the apartment crying out, "The Spaniards! the Spaniards!"

That cry was of such importance as to overcome all preoccupation. The young men made inquiries and ascertained that the enemy was advancing by way of Houdin and Bethune.

While Monsieur d'Arminges gave orders for the horses to be made ready for departure, the two young men ascended to the upper windows of the house and saw in the direction of Marsin and of Lens a large body of infantry and cavalry. This time it was not a wandering troop of partisans; it was an entire army. There was therefore nothing for them to do but to follow the prudent advice of Monsieur d'Arminges and beat a retreat. They quickly went downstairs. Monsieur d'Arminges was already mounted. Olivain had ready the horses of the young men, and the lackeys of the Count de Guiche guarded carefully between them the Spanish prisoner, mounted on a pony which had been bought for his use. As a further precaution they had bound his hands.

The little company started off at a trot on the road to Cambrin, where they expected to find the prince. But he was no longer there, having withdrawn on the previous evening to La Bassee, misled by false intelligence of the enemy's movements. Deceived by this intelligence he had concentrated his forces between Vieille-Chapelle and La Venthie; and after a reconnoissance along the entire line, in company with Marshal de Grammont, he had returned and seated himself before a table, with his officers around him. He questioned them as to the news they had each been charged to obtain, but nothing positive had been learned. The hostile army had disappeared two days before and seemed to have gone out of existence.

Now an enemy is never so near and consequently so threatening, as when he has completely disappeared. The prince was, therefore, contrary to his custom, gloomy and anxious, when an officer entered and announced to Marshal de Grammont that some one wished to see him.

The Duc de Grammont received permission from the prince by a glance and went out. The prince followed him with his eyes and continued looking at the door; no one ventured to speak, for fear of disturbing him.

Suddenly a dull and heavy noise was heard. The prince leaped to his feet, extending his hand in the direction whence came the sound, there was no mistaking it—it was the noise of cannon. Every one stood up.

At that moment the door opened.

"Monseigneur," said Marshal de Grammont, with a radiant face, "will your highness permit my son, Count de Guiche, and his traveling companion, Viscount de Bragelonne, to come in and give news of the enemy, whom they have found while we were looking for him?"

"What!" eagerly replied the prince, "will I permit? I not only permit, I desire; let them come in."

The marshal introduced the two young men and placed them face to face with the prince.

"Speak, gentlemen," said the prince, saluting them; "first speak; we shall have time afterward for the usual compliments. The most urgent thing now is to learn where the enemy is and what he is doing."

It fell naturally to the Count de Guiche to make reply; not only was he the elder, but he had been presented to the prince by his father. Besides, he had long known the prince, whilst Raoul now saw him for the first time. He therefore narrated to the prince what they had seen from the inn at Mazingarbe.

Meanwhile Raoul closely observed the young general, already made so famous by the battles of Rocroy, Fribourg, and Nordlingen.

Louis de Bourbon, Prince de Condé, who, since the death of his father, Henri de Bourbon, was called, in accordance with the custom of that period, Monsieur le Prince, was a young man, not more than twenty-six or twenty-seven years old, with the eye of an eagle—agl' occhi grifani, as Dante says—aquiline nose, long, waving hair, of medium height, well formed, possessed of all the qualities essential to the successful soldier—that is to say, the rapid glance, quick decision, fabulous courage. At the same time he was a man of elegant manners and strong mind, so that in addition to the revolution he had made in war, by his new contributions to its methods, he had also made a revolution at Paris, among the young noblemen of the court, whose natural chief he was and who, in distinction from the social leaders of the ancient court, modeled after Bassompierre, Bellegarde and the Duke d'Angouleme, were called the petits-maitres.

At the first words of the Count de Guiche, the prince, having in mind the direction whence came the sound of cannon, had understood everything. The enemy was marching upon Lens, with the intention, doubtless, of securing possession of that town and separating from France the army of France. But in what force was the enemy? Was it a corps sent out to make a diversion? Was it an entire army? To this question De Guiche could not respond.

Now, as these questions involved matters of gravest consequence, it was these to which the prince had especially desired an answer, exact, precise, positive.

Raoul conquered the very natural feeling of timidity he experienced and approaching the prince:

"My lord," he said, "will you permit me to hazard a few words on that subject, which will perhaps relieve you of your uncertainty?"

The prince turned and seemed to cover the young man with a single glance; he smiled on perceiving that he was a child hardly fifteen years old.

"Certainly, monsieur, speak," he said, softening his stern, accented tones, as if he were speaking to a woman.

"My lord," said Raoul, blushing, "might examine the Spanish prisoner."

"Have you a Spanish prisoner?" cried the prince.

"Yes, my lord."

"Ah, that is true," said De Guiche; "I had forgotten it."

"That is easily understood; it was you who took him, count," said Raoul, smiling.

The old marshal turned toward the viscount, grateful for that praise of his son, whilst the prince exclaimed:

"The young man is right; let the prisoner be brought in."

Meanwhile the prince took De Guiche aside and asked him how the prisoner had been taken and who this young man was.

"Monsieur," said the prince, turning toward Raoul, "I know that you have a letter from my sister, Madame de Longueville; but I see that you have preferred commending yourself to me by giving me good counsel."

"My lord," said Raoul, coloring up, "I did not wish to interrupt your highness in a conversation so important as that in which you were engaged with the count. But here is the letter."

"Very well," said the prince; "give it to me later. Here is the prisoner; let us attend to what is most pressing."

The prisoner was one of those military adventurers who sold their blood to whoever would buy, and grew old in stratagems and spoils. Since he had been taken he had not uttered a word, so that it was not known to what country he belonged. The prince looked at him with unspeakable distrust.

"Of what country are you?" asked the prince.

The prisoner muttered a few words in a foreign tongue.

"Ah! ah! it seems that he is a Spaniard. Do you speak Spanish, Grammont?"

"Faith, my lord, but indifferently."

"And I not at all," said the prince, laughing. "Gentlemen," he said, turning to those who were near him "can any one of you speak Spanish and serve me as interpreter?"

"I can, my lord," said Raoul.

"Ah, you speak Spanish?"

"Enough, I think, to fulfill your highness's wishes on this occasion."

Meanwhile the prisoner had remained impassive and as if he had no understanding of what was taking place.

"My lord asks of what country you are," said the young man, in the purest Castilian.

"Ich bin ein Deutscher," replied the prisoner.

"What in the devil does he say?" asked the prince. "What new gibberish is that?"

"He says he is German, my lord," replied Raoul; "but I doubt it, for his accent is bad and his pronunciation defective."

"Then you speak German, also?" asked the prince.

"Yes, my lord."

"Well enough to question him in that language?"

"Yes, my lord."

"Question him, then."

Raoul began the examination, but the result justified his opinion. The prisoner did not understand, or seemed not to understand, what Raoul said to him; and Raoul could hardly understand his replies, containing a mixture of Flemish and Alsatian. However, amidst all the prisoner's efforts to elude a systematic examination, Raoul had recognized his natural accent.

"Non siete Spagnuolo," he said; "non siete Tedesco; siete Italiano."

The prisoner started and bit his lips.

"Ah, that," said the prince, "I understand that language thoroughly; and since he is Italian I will myself continue the examination. Thank you, viscount," continued the prince, laughing, "and I appoint you from this moment my interpreter."

But the prisoner was not less unwilling to respond in Italian than in the other languages; his aim was to elude the examination. Therefore, he knew nothing either of the enemy's numbers, or of those in command, or of the purpose of the army.

"Very good," said the prince, understanding the reason of that ignorance; "the man was caught in the act of assassination and robbery; he might have purchased his life by speaking; he doesn't wish to speak. Take him out and shoot him."

The prisoner turned pale. The two soldiers who had brought him in took him, each by one arm, and led him toward the door, whilst the prince, turning to Marshal de Grammont, seemed to have already forgotten the order he had given.

When he reached the threshold of the door the prisoner stopped. The soldiers, who knew only their orders, attempted to force him along.

"One moment," said the prisoner, in French. "I am ready to speak, my lord."

"Ah! ah!" said the prince, laughing, "I thought we should come to that. I have a sure method of limbering tongues. Young men, take advantage of it against the time when you may be in command."

"But on condition," continued the prisoner, "that your highness will swear that my life shall be safe."

"Upon my honor," said the prince.

"Question, then, my lord."

"Where did the army cross the Lys?"

"Between Saint-Venant and Aire."

"By whom is it commanded?"

"By Count de Fuonsaldagna, General Beck and the archduke."

"Of how many does it consist?"

"Eighteen thousand men and thirty-six cannon."

"And its aim is?"

"Lens."

"You see; gentlemen!" said the prince, turning with a triumphant air toward Marshal de Grammont and the other officers.

"Yes, my lord," said the marshal, "you have divined all that was possible to human genius."

"Recall Le Plessis, Bellievre, Villequier and D'Erlac," said the prince, "recall all the troops that are on this side of the Lys. Let them hold themselves in readiness to march to-night. To-morrow, according to all probability, we shall attack the enemy."

"But, my lord," said Marshal de Grammont, "consider that when we have collected all our forces we shall have hardly thirteen thousand men."

"Monsieur le marechal," said the prince, with that wonderful glance that was peculiar to him, "it is with small armies that great battles are won."

Then turning toward the prisoner, "Take away that man," he said, "and keep him carefully in sight. His life is dependent on the information he has given us; if it is true, he shall be free; if false, let him be shot."

The prisoner was led away.

"Count de Guiche," said the prince, "it is a long time since you saw your father, remain here with him. Monsieur," he continued, addressing Raoul, "if you are not too tired, follow me."

"To the end of the world, my lord!" cried Raoul, feeling an unknown enthusiasm for that young general, who seemed to him so worthy of his renown.

The prince smiled; he despised flatterers, but he appreciated enthusiasts.

"Come, monsieur," he said, "you are good in council, as we have already discovered; to-morrow we shall know if you are good in action."

"And I," said the marshal, "what am I to do?"

"Wait here to receive the troops. I shall either return for them myself or shall send a courier directing you to bring them to me. Twenty guards, well mounted, are all that I shall need for my escort."

"That is very few," said the marshal.

"It is enough," replied the prince. "Have you a good horse, Monsieur de Bragelonne?"

"My horse was killed this morning, my lord, and I am mounted provisionally on my lackey's."

"Choose for yourself in my stables the horse you like best. No false modesty; take the best horse you can find. You will need it this evening, perhaps; you will certainly need it to-morrow."

Raoul didn't wait to be told twice; he knew that with superiors, especially when those superiors are princes, the highest politeness is to obey without delay or argument; he went down to the stables, picked out a pie-bald Andalusian horse, saddled and bridled it himself, for Athos had advised him to trust no one with those important offices at a time of danger, and went to rejoin the prince, who at that moment mounted his horse.

"Now, monsieur," he said to Raoul, "will you give me the letter you have brought?"

Raoul handed the letter to the prince.

"Keep near me," said the latter.

The prince threw his bridle over the pommel of the saddle, as he was wont to do when he wished to have both hands free, unsealed the letter of Madame de Longueville and started at a gallop on the road to Lens, attended by Raoul and his small escort, whilst messengers sent to recall the troops set out with a loose rein in other directions. The prince read as he hastened on.

"Monsieur," he said, after a moment, "they tell me great things of you. I have only to say, after the little that I have seen and heard, that I think even better of you than I have been told."

Raoul bowed.

Meanwhile, as the little troop drew nearer to Lens, the noise of the cannon sounded louder. The prince kept his gaze fixed in the direction of the sound with the steadfastness of a bird of prey. One would have said that his gaze could pierce the branches of trees which limited his horizon. From time to time his nostrils dilated as if eager for the smell of powder, and he panted like a horse.

At length they heard the cannon so near that it was evident they were within a league of the field of battle, and at a turn of the road they perceived the little village of Aunay.

The peasants were in great commotion. The report of Spanish cruelty had gone out and every one was frightened. The women had already fled, taking refuge in Vitry; only a few men remained. On seeing the prince they hastened to meet him. One of them recognized him.

"Ah, my lord," he said, "have you come to drive away those rascal Spaniards and those Lorraine robbers?"

"Yes," said the prince, "if you will serve me as guide."

"Willingly, my lord. Where does your highness wish to go?"

"To some elevated spot whence I can look down on Lens and the surrounding country——"

"In that case, I'm your man."

"I can trust you—you are a true Frenchman?"

"I am an old soldier of Rocroy, my lord."

"Here," said the prince, handing him a purse, "here is for Rocroy. Now, do you want a horse, or will you go afoot?"

"Afoot, my lord; I have served always in the infantry. Besides, I expect to lead your highness into places where you will have to walk."

"Come, then," said the prince; "let us lose no time."

The peasant started off, running before the prince's horse; then, a hundred steps from the village, he took a narrow road hidden at the bottom of the valley. For a half league they proceeded thus, the cannon-shot sounding so near that they expected at each discharge to hear the hum of the balls. At length they entered a path which, going out from the road, skirted the mountainside. The prince dismounted, ordered one of his aids and Raoul to follow his example, and directed the others to await his orders, keeping themselves meanwhile on the alert. He then began to ascend the path.

In about ten minutes they reached the ruins of an old chateau; those ruins crowned the summit of a hill which overlooked the surrounding country. At a distance of hardly a quarter of a league they looked down on Lens, at bay, and before Lens the enemy's entire army.

With a single glance the prince took in the extent of country that lay before him, from Lens as far as Vimy. In a moment the plan of the battle which on the following day was to save France the second time from invasion was unrolled in his mind. He took a pencil, tore a page from his tablets and wrote:

"My Dear Marshal,—In an hour Lens will be in the enemy's possession. Come and rejoin me; bring with you the whole army. I shall be at Vendin to place it in position. To-morrow we shall retake Lens and beat the enemy."

Then, turning toward Raoul: "Go, monsieur," he said; "ride fast and give this letter to Monsieur de Grammont."

Raoul bowed, took the letter, went hastily down the mountain, leaped on his horse and set out at a gallop. A quarter of an hour later he was with the marshal.

A portion of the troops had already arrived and the remainder was expected from moment to moment. Marshal de Grammont put himself at the head of all the available cavalry and infantry and took the road to Vendin, leaving the Duc de Chatillon to await and bring on the rest. All the artillery was ready to move, and started off at a moment's notice.

It was seven o'clock in the evening when the marshal arrived at the appointed place. The prince awaited him there. As he had foreseen, Lens had fallen into the hands of the enemy immediately after Raoul's departure. The event was announced by the cessation of the firing.

As the shadows of night deepened the troops summoned by the prince arrived in successive detachments. Orders were given that no drum should be beaten, no trumpet sounded.

At nine o'clock the night had fully come. Still a last ray of twilight lighted the plain. The army marched silently, the prince at the head of the column. Presently the army came in sight of Lens; two or three houses were in flames and a dull noise was heard which indicated what suffering was endured by a town taken by assault.

The prince assigned to every one his post. Marshal de Grammont was to hold the extreme left, resting on Mericourt. The Duc de Chatillon commanded the centre. Finally, the prince led the right wing, resting on Aunay. The order of battle on the morrow was to be that of the positions taken in the evening. Each one, on awaking, would find himself on the field of battle.

The movement was executed in silence and with precision. At ten o'clock every one was in his appointed position; at half-past ten the prince visited the posts and gave his final orders for the following day.

Three things were especially urged upon the officers, who were to see that the soldiers observed them scrupulously: the first, that the different corps should so march that cavalry and infantry should be on the same line and that each body should protect its gaps; the second, to go to the charge no faster than a walk; the third, to let the enemy fire first.

The prince assigned the Count de Guiche to his father and kept Bragelonne near his own person; but the two young men sought the privilege of passing the night together and it was accorded them. A tent was erected for them near that of the marshal.

Although the day had been fatiguing, neither of them was inclined to sleep. And besides, even for old soldiers the evening before a battle is a serious time; it was so with greater reason to two young men who were about to witness for the first time that terrible spectacle. On the evening before a battle one thinks of a thousand things forgotten till then; those who are indifferent to one another become friends and those who are friends become brothers. It need not be said that if in the depths of the heart there is a sentiment more tender, it reaches then, quite naturally, the highest exaltation of which it is capable. Some sentiment of this kind must have been cherished by each one of these two friends, for each of them almost immediately sat down by himself at an end of the tent and began to write.

The letters were long—the four pages were covered with closely written words. The writers sometimes looked up at each other and smiled; they understood without speaking, their organizations were so delicate and sympathetic. The letters being finished, each put his own into two envelopes, so that no one, without tearing the first envelope, could discover to whom the second was addressed; then they drew near to each other and smilingly exchanged their letters.

"In case any evil should happen to me," said Bragelonne.

"In case I should be killed," said De Guiche.

They then embraced each other like two brothers, and each wrapping himself in his cloak they soon passed into that kindly sleep of youth which is the prerogative of birds, flowers and infants.

Chapter XXXV.

A Dinner in the Old Style.

The second interview between the former musketeers was not so formal and threatening as the first. Athos, with his superior understanding, wisely deemed that the supper table would be the most complete and satisfactory point of reunion, and at the moment when his friends, in deference to his deportment and sobriety, dared scarcely speak of some of their former good dinners, he was the first to propose that they should all assemble around some well spread table and abandon themselves unreservedly to their own natural character and manners—a freedom which had formerly contributed so much to that good understanding between them which gave them the name of the inseparables. For different reasons this was an agreeable proposition to them all, and it was therefore agreed that each should leave a very exact address and that upon the request of any of the associates a meeting should be convoked at a famous eating house in the Rue de la Monnaie, of the sign of the Hermitage. The first rendezvous was fixed for the following Wednesday, at eight o'clock in the evening precisely.

On that day, in fact, the four friends arrived punctually at the hour, each from his own abode or occupation. Porthos had been trying a new horse; D'Artagnan was on guard at the Louvre; Aramis had been to visit one of his penitents in the neighborhood; and Athos, whose domicile was established in the Rue Guenegaud, found himself close at hand. They were, therefore, somewhat surprised to meet altogether at the door of the Hermitage, Athos starting out from the Pont Neuf, Porthos by the Rue de la Roule, D'Artagnan by the Rue des Fosse Saint Germain l'Auxerrois, and Aramis by the Rue de Bethisy.

The first words exchanged between the four friends, on account of the ceremony which each of them mingled with their demonstration, were somewhat forced and even the repast began with a kind of stiffness. Athos perceived this embarrassment, and by way of supplying an effectual remedy, called for four bottles of champagne.

At this order, given in Athos's habitually calm manner, the face of the Gascon relaxed and Porthos's brow grew smooth. Aramis was astonished. He knew that Athos not only never drank, but more, that he had a kind of repugnance to wine. This astonishment was doubled when Aramis saw Athos fill a bumper and toss it off with all his former enthusiasm. His companions followed his example. In a very few minutes the four bottles were empty and this excellent specific succeeded in dissipating even the slightest cloud that might have rested on their spirits. Now the four friends began to speak loud, scarcely waiting till one had finished before another began, and each assumed his favorite attitude on or at the table. Soon—strange fact—Aramis undid two buttons of his doublet, seeing which, Porthos unfastened his entirely.

Battles, long journeys, blows given and received, sufficed for the first themes of conversation, which turned upon the silent struggles sustained against him who was now called the great cardinal.

"Faith," said Aramis, laughing, "we have praised the dead enough, let us revile the living a little; I should like to say something evil of Mazarin; is it permissible?"

"Go on, go on," replied D'Artagnan, laughing heartily; "relate your story and I will applaud it if it is a good one."

"A great prince," said Aramis, "with whom Mazarin sought an alliance, was invited by him to send him a list of the conditions on which he would do him the honor to negotiate with him. The prince, who had a great repugnance to treat with such an ill-bred fellow, made out a list, against the grain, and sent it. In this list there were three conditions which displeased Mazarin and he offered the prince ten thousand crowns to renounce them."

"Ah, ha, ha!" laughed the three friends, "not a bad bargain; and there was no fear of being taken at his word; what did the prince do then?"

"The prince immediately sent fifty thousand francs to Mazarin, begging him never to write to him again, and offered twenty thousand francs more, on condition that he would never speak to him. What did Mazarin do?"

"Stormed!" suggested Athos.

"Beat the messenger!" cried Porthos.

"Accepted the money!" said D'Artagnan.

"You have guessed it," answered Aramis; and they all laughed so heartily that the host appeared in order to inquire whether the gentlemen wanted anything; he thought they were fighting.

At last their hilarity calmed down and:

"Faith!" exclaimed D'Artagnan to the two friends, "you may well wish ill to Mazarin; for I assure you, on his side he wishes you no good."

"Pooh! really?" asked Athos. "If I thought the fellow knew me by my name I would be rebaptized, for fear it might be thought I knew him."

"He knows you better by your actions than your name; he is quite aware that there are two gentlemen who greatly aided the escape of Monsieur de Beaufort, and he has instigated an active search for them, I can answer for it."

"By whom?"

"By me; and this morning he sent for me to ask me if I had obtained any information."

"And what did you reply?"

"That I had none as yet; but that I was to dine to-day with two gentlemen, who would be able to give me some."

"You told him that?" said Porthos, a broad smile spreading over his honest face. "Bravo! and you are not afraid of that, Athos?"

"No," replied Athos, "it is not the search of Mazarin that I fear."

"Now," said Aramis, "tell me a little what you do fear."

"Nothing for the present; at least, nothing in good earnest."

"And with regard to the past?" asked Porthos.

"Oh! the past is another thing," said Athos, sighing; "the past and the future."

"Are you afraid for your young Raoul?" asked Aramis.

"Well," said D'Artagnan, "one is never killed in a first engagement."

"Nor in the second," said Aramis

"Nor in the third," returned Porthos; "and even when one is killed, one rises again, the proof of which is, that here we are!"

"No," said Athos, "it is not Raoul about whom I am anxious, for I trust he will conduct himself like a gentleman; and if he is killed—well, he will die bravely; but hold—should such a misfortune happen—well—" Athos passed his hand across his pale brow.

"Well?" asked Aramis.

"Well, I shall look upon it as an expiation."

"Ah!" said D'Artagnan; "I know what you mean."

"And I, too," added Aramis; "but you must not think of that, Athos; what is past, is past."

"I don't understand," said Porthos.

"The affair at Armentieres," whispered D'Artagnan.

"The affair at Armentieres?" asked he again.

"Milady."

"Oh, yes!" said Porthos; "true, I had forgotten it!"

Athos looked at him intently.

"You have forgotten it, Porthos?" said he.

"Faith! yes, it is so long ago," answered Porthos.

"This affair does not, then, weigh upon your conscience?"

"Faith, no."

"And you, D'Artagnan?"

"I—I own that when my mind returns to that terrible period I have no recollection of anything but the rigid corpse of poor Madame Bonancieux. Yes, yes," murmured he, "I have often felt regret for the victim, but never the very slightest remorse for the assassin."

Athos shook his dead doubtfully.

"Consider," said Aramis, "if you admit divine justice and its participation in the things of this world, that woman was punished by the will of heaven. We were but the instruments, that is all."

"But as to free will, Aramis?"

"How acts the judge? He has a free will, yet he fearlessly condemns. What does the executioner? He is master of his arm, yet he strikes without remorse."

"The executioner!" muttered Athos, as if arrested by some recollection.

"I know that it is terrible," said D'Artagnan; "but when I reflect that we have killed English, Rochellais, Spaniards, nay, even French, who never did us any other harm but to aim at and to miss us, whose only fault was to cross swords with us and to be unable to ward off our blows—I can, on my honor, find an excuse for my share in the murder of that woman."

"As for me," said Porthos, "now that you have reminded me of it, Athos, I have the scene again before me, as if I now were there. Milady was there, as it were, where you sit." (Athos changed color.) "I—I was where D'Artagnan stands. I wore a long sword which cut like a Damascus—you remember it, Aramis for you always called it Balizarde. Well, I swear to you, all three, that had the executioner of Bethune—was he not of Bethune?—yes, egad! of Bethune!—not been there, I would have cut off the head of that infamous being without thinking of it, or even after thinking of it. She was a most atrocious woman."

"And then," said Aramis, with the tone of philosophical indifference which he had assumed since he had belonged to the church and in which there was more atheism than confidence in God, "what is the use of thinking of it all? At the last hour we must confess this action and God knows better than we can whether it is a crime, a fault, or a meritorious deed. I repent of it? Egad! no. Upon my honor and by the holy cross; I only regret it because she was a woman."

"The most satisfactory part of the matter," said D'Artagnan, "is that there remains no trace of it."

"She had a son," observed Athos.

"Oh! yes, I know that," said D'Artagnan, "and you mentioned it to me; but who knows what has become of him? If the serpent be dead, why not its brood? Do you think his uncle De Winter would have brought up that young viper? De Winter probably condemned the son as he had done the mother."

"Then," said Athos, "woe to De Winter, for the child had done no harm."

"May the devil take me, if the child be not dead," said Porthos. "There is so much fog in that detestable country, at least so D'Artagnan declares."

Just as the quaint conclusion reached by Porthos was about to bring back hilarity to faces now more or less clouded, hasty footsteps were heard upon the stair and some one knocked at the door.

"Come in," cried Athos.

"Please your honors," said the host, "a person in a great hurry wishes to speak to one of you."

"To which of us?" asked all the four friends.

"To him who is called the Comte de la Fere."

"It is I," said Athos, "and what is the name of the person?"

"Grimaud."

"Ah!" exclaimed Athos, turning pale. "Back already! What can have happened, then, to Bragelonne?"

"Let him enter," cried D'Artagnan; "let him come up."

But Grimaud had already mounted the staircase and was waiting on the last step; so springing into the room he motioned the host to leave it. The door being closed, the four friends waited in expectation. Grimaud's agitation, his pallor, the sweat which covered his face, the dust which soiled his clothes, all indicated that he was the messenger of some important and terrible news.

"Your honors," said he, "that woman had a child; that child has become a man; the tigress had a little one, the tiger has roused himself; he is ready to spring upon you—beware!"

Athos glanced around at his friends with a melancholy smile. Porthos turned to look at his sword, which was hanging on the wall; Aramis seized his knife; D'Artagnan arose.

"What do you mean, Grimaud?" he exclaimed.

"That Milady's son has left England, that he is in France, on his road to Paris, if he be not here already."

"The devil he is!" said Porthos. "Are you sure of it?"

"Certain," replied Grimaud.

This announcement was received in silence. Grimaud was so breathless, so exhausted, that he had fallen back upon a chair. Athos filled a beaker with champagne and gave it to him.

"Well, after all," said D'Artagnan, "supposing that he lives, that he comes to Paris; we have seen many other such. Let him come."

"Yes," echoed Porthos, glancing affectionately at his sword, still hanging on the wall; "we can wait for him; let him come."

"Moreover, he is but a child," said Aramis.

Grimaud rose.

"A child!" he exclaimed. "Do you know what he has done, this child? Disguised as a monk he discovered the whole history in confession from the executioner of Bethune, and having confessed him, after having learned everything from him, he gave him absolution by planting this dagger into his heart. See, it is on fire yet with his hot blood, for it is not thirty hours since it was drawn from the wound."

And Grimaud threw the dagger on the table.

D'Artagnan, Porthos and Aramis rose and in one spontaneous motion rushed to their swords. Athos alone remained seated, calm and thoughtful.

"And you say he is dressed as a monk, Grimaud?"

"Yes, as an Augustine monk."

"What sized man is he?"

"About my height; thin, pale, with light blue eyes and tawny flaxen hair."

"And he did not see Raoul?" asked Athos.

"Yes, on the contrary, they met, and it was the viscount himself who conducted him to the bed of the dying man."

Athos, in his turn, rising without speaking, went and unhooked his sword.

"Heigh, sir," said D'Artagnan, trying to laugh, "do you know we look very much like a flock of silly, mouse-evading women! How is it that we, four men who have faced armies without blinking, begin to tremble at the mention of a child?"

"It is true," said Athos, "but this child comes in the name of Heaven."

And very soon they left the inn.

Chapter XXXVI.

A Letter from Charles the First.

The reader must now cross the Seine with us and follow us to the door of the Carmelite Convent in the Rue Saint Jacques. It is eleven o'clock in the morning and the pious sisters have just finished saying mass for the success of the armies of King Charles I. Leaving the church, a woman and a young girl dressed in black, the one as a widow and the other as an orphan, have re-entered their cell.

The woman kneels on a prie-dieu of painted wood and at a short distance from her stands the young girl, leaning against a chair, weeping.

The woman must have once been handsome, but traces of sorrow have aged her. The young girl is lovely and her tears only embellish her; the lady appears to be about forty years of age, the girl about fourteen.

"Oh, God!" prayed the kneeling suppliant, "protect my husband, guard my son, and take my wretched life instead!"

"Oh, God!" murmured the girl, "leave me my mother!"

"Your mother can be of no use to you in this world, Henrietta," said the lady, turning around. "Your mother has no longer either throne or husband; she has neither son, money nor friends; the whole world, my poor child, has abandoned your mother!" And she fell back, weeping, into her daughter's arms.

"Courage, take courage, my dear mother!" said the girl.

"Ah! 'tis an unfortunate year for kings," said the mother. "And no one thinks of us in this country, for each must think about his own affairs. As long as your brother was with me he kept me up; but he is gone and can no longer send us news of himself, either to me or to your father. I have pledged my last jewels, sold your clothes and my own to pay his servants, who refused to accompany him unless I made this sacrifice. We are now reduced to live at the expense of these daughters of Heaven; we are the poor, succored by God."

"But why not address yourself to your sister, the queen?" asked the girl.

"Alas! the queen, my sister, is no longer queen, my child. Another reigns in her name. One day you will be able to understand how all this is."

"Well, then, to the king, your nephew. Shall I speak to him? You know how much he loves me, my mother.

"Alas! my nephew is not yet king, and you know Laporte has told us twenty times that he himself is in need of almost everything."

"Then let us pray to Heaven," said the girl.

The two women who thus knelt in united prayer were the daughter and grand-daughter of Henry IV., the wife and daughter of Charles I.

They had just finished their double prayer, when a nun softly tapped at the door of the cell.

"Enter, my sister," said the queen.

"I trust your majesty will pardon this intrusion on her meditations, but a foreign lord has arrived from England and waits in the parlor, demanding the honor of presenting a letter to your majesty."

"Oh, a letter! a letter from the king, perhaps. News from your father, do you hear, Henrietta? And the name of this lord?"

"Lord de Winter."

"Lord de Winter!" exclaimed the queen, "the friend of my husband. Oh, bid him enter!"

And the queen advanced to meet the messenger, whose hand she seized affectionately, whilst he knelt down and presented a letter to her, contained in a case of gold.

"Ah! my lord!" said the queen, "you bring us three things which we have not seen for a long time. Gold, a devoted friend, and a letter from the king, our husband and master."

De Winter bowed again, unable to reply from excess of emotion.

On their side the mother and daughter retired into the embrasure of a window to read eagerly the following letter:

"Dear Wife,—We have now reached the moment of decision. I have concentrated here at Naseby camp all the resources Heaven has left me, and I write to you in haste from thence. Here I await the army of my rebellious subjects. I am about to struggle for the last time with them. If victorious, I shall continue the struggle; if beaten, I am lost. I shall try, in the latter case (alas! in our position, one must provide for everything), I shall try to gain the coast of

France. But can they, will they receive an unhappy king, who will bring such a sad story into a country already agitated by civil discord? Your wisdom and your affection must serve me as guides. The bearer of this letter will tell you, madame, what I dare not trust to pen and paper and the risks of transit. He will explain to you the steps that I expect you to pursue. I charge him also with my blessing for my children and with the sentiments of my soul for yourself, my dearest sweetheart."

The letter bore the signature, not of "Charles, King," but of "Charles—still king."

"And let him be no longer king," cried the queen. "Let him be conquered, exiled, proscribed, provided he still lives. Alas! in these days the throne is too dangerous a place for me to wish him to retain it. But my lord, tell me," she continued, "hide nothing from me—what is, in truth, the king's position? Is it as hopeless as he thinks?"

"Alas! madame, more hopeless than he thinks. His majesty has so good a heart that he cannot understand hatred; is so loyal that he does not suspect treason! England is torn in twain by a spirit of disturbance which, I greatly fear, blood alone can exorcise."

"But Lord Montrose," replied the queen, "I have heard of his great and rapid successes of battles gained. I heard it said that he was marching to the frontier to join the king."

"Yes, madame; but on the frontier he was met by Lesly; he had tried victory by means of superhuman undertakings. Now victory has abandoned him. Montrose, beaten at Philiphaugh, was obliged to disperse the remains of his army and to fly, disguised as a servant. He is at Bergen, in Norway."

"Heaven preserve him!" said the queen. "It is at least a consolation to know that some who have so often risked their lives for us are safe. And now, my lord, that I see how hopeless the position of the king is, tell me with what you are charged on the part of my royal husband."

"Well, then, madame," said De Winter, "the king wishes you to try and discover the dispositions of the king and queen toward him."

"Alas! you know that even now the king is but a child and the queen a woman weak enough. Here, Monsieur Mazarin is everything."

"Does he desire to play the part in France that Cromwell plays in England?"

"Oh, no! He is a subtle, conscienceless Italian, who though he very likely dreams of crime, dares not commit it; and unlike Cromwell, who disposes of both Houses, Mazarin has had the queen to support him in his struggle with the parliament."

"More reason, then, he should protect a king pursued by parliament."

The queen shook her head despairingly.

"If I judge for myself, my lord," she said, "the cardinal will do nothing, and will even, perhaps, act against us. The presence of my daughter and myself in France is already irksome to him; much more so would be that of the king. My lord," added Henrietta, with a melancholy smile, "it is sad and almost shameful to be obliged to say that we have passed the winter in the Louvre without money, without linen, almost without bread, and often not rising from bed because we wanted fire."

"Horrible!" cried De Winter; "the daughter of Henry IV., and the wife of King Charles! Wherefore did you not apply, then, madame, to the first person you saw from us?"

"Such is the hospitality shown to a queen by the minister from whom a king demands it."

"But I heard that a marriage between the Prince of Wales and Mademoiselle d'Orleans was spoken of," said De Winter.

"Yes, for an instant I hoped it was so. The young people felt a mutual esteem; but the queen, who at first sanctioned their affection, changed her mind, and Monsieur, the Duc d'Orleans, who had encouraged the familiarity between them, has forbidden his daughter to think any more about the union. Oh, my lord!" continued the queen, without restraining her tears, "it is better to fight as the king has done, and to die, as perhaps he will, than live in beggary like me."

"Courage, madame! courage! Do not despair! The interests of the French crown, endangered at this moment, are to discountenance rebellion in a neighboring nation. Mazarin, as a statesman, will understand the politic necessity."

"Are you sure," said the queen doubtfully, "that you have not been forestalled?"

"By whom?"

"By the Joices, the Prinns, the Cromwells?"

"By a tailor, a coachmaker, a brewer! Ah! I hope, madame, that the cardinal will not enter into negotiations with such men!"

"Ah! what is he himself?" asked Madame Henrietta.

"But for the honor of the king—of the queen."

"Well, let us hope he will do something for the sake of their honor," said the queen. "A true friend's eloquence is so powerful, my lord, that you have reassured me. Give me your hand and let us go to the minister; and yet," she added, "suppose he should refuse and that the king loses the battle?"

"His majesty will then take refuge in Holland, where I hear his highness the Prince of Wales now is."

"And can his majesty count upon many such subjects as yourself for his flight?"

"Alas! no, madame," answered De Winter; "but the case is provided for and I am come to France to seek allies."

"Allies!" said the queen, shaking her head.

"Madame," replied De Winter, "provided I can find some of my good old friends of former times I will answer for anything."

"Come then, my lord," said the queen, with the painful doubt that is felt by those who have suffered much; "come, and may Heaven hear you."

Chapter XXXVII.

Cromwell's Letter.

At the very moment when the queen quitted the convent to go to the Palais Royal, a young man dismounted at the gate of this royal abode and announced to the guards that he had something of importance to communicate to Cardinal Mazarin. Although the cardinal was often tormented by fear, he was more often in need of counsel and information, and he was therefore sufficiently accessible. The true difficulty of being admitted was not to be found at the first door, and even the second was passed easily enough; but at the third watched, besides the guard and the doorkeepers, the faithful Bernouin, a Cerberus whom no speech could soften, no wand, even of gold, could charm.

It was therefore at the third door that those who solicited or were bidden to an audience underwent their formal interrogatory.

The young man having left his horse tied to the gate in the court, mounted the great staircase and addressed the guard in the first chamber.

"Cardinal Mazarin?" said he.

"Pass on," replied the guard.

The cavalier entered the second hall, which was guarded by the musketeers and doorkeepers.

"Have you a letter of audience?" asked a porter, advancing to the new arrival.

"I have one, but not one from Cardinal Mazarin."

"Enter, and ask for Monsieur Bernouin," said the porter, opening the door of the third room. Whether he only held his usual post or whether it was by accident, Monsieur Bernouin was found standing behind the door and must have heard all that had passed.

"You seek me, sir," said he. "From whom may the letter be you bear to his eminence?"

"From General Oliver Cromwell," said the new comer. "Be so good as to mention this name to his eminence and to bring me word whether he will receive me—yes or no."

Saying which, he resumed the proud and sombre bearing peculiar at that time to Puritans. Bernouin cast an inquisitorial glance at the person of the young man and entered the cabinet of the cardinal, to whom he transmitted the messenger's words.

"A man bringing a letter from Oliver Cromwell?" said Mazarin. "And what kind of a man?"

"A genuine Englishman, your eminence. Hair sandy-red—more red than sandy; gray-blue eyes—more gray than blue; and for the rest, stiff and proud."

"Let him give in his letter."

"His eminence asks for the letter," said Bernouin, passing back into the ante-chamber.

"His eminence cannot see the letter without the bearer of it," replied the young man; "but to convince you that I am really the bearer of a letter, see, here it is; and kindly add," continued he, "that I am not a simple messenger, but an envoy extraordinary."

Bernouin re-entered the cabinet, returning in a few seconds. "Enter, sir," said he.

The young man appeared on the threshold of the minister's closet, in one hand holding his hat, in the other the letter. Mazarin rose. "Have you, sir," asked he, "a letter accrediting you to me?"

"There it is, my lord," said the young man.

Mazarin took the letter and read it thus:

"Mr. Mordaunt, one of my secretaries, will remit this letter of introduction to His Eminence, the Cardinal Mazarin, in Paris. He is also the bearer of a second confidential epistle for his eminence.

"Oliver Cromwell."

"Very well, Monsieur Mordaunt," said Mazarin, "give me this second letter and sit down."

The young man drew from his pocket a second letter, presented it to the cardinal, and took his seat. The cardinal, however, did not unseal the letter at once, but continued to turn it again and again in his hand; then, in accordance with his usual custom and judging from experience that few people could hide anything from him when he began to question them, fixing his eyes upon them at the same time, he thus addressed the messenger:

"You are very young, Monsieur Mordaunt, for this difficult task of ambassador, in which the oldest diplomatists often fail."

"My lord, I am twenty-three years of age; but your eminence is mistaken in saying that I am young. I am older than your eminence, although I possess not your wisdom. Years of suffering, in my opinion, count double, and I have suffered for twenty years."

"Ah, yes, I understand," said Mazarin; "want of fortune, perhaps. You are poor, are you not?" Then he added to himself: "These English Revolutionists are all beggars and ill-bred."

"My lord, I ought to have a fortune of six millions, but it has been taken from me."

"You are not, then, a man of the people?" said Mazarin, astonished.

"If I bore my proper title I should be a lord. If I bore my name you would have heard one of the most illustrious names of England."

"What is your name, then?" asked Mazarin.

"My name is Mordaunt," replied the young man, bowing.

Mazarin now understood that Cromwell's envoy desired to retain his incognito. He was silent for an instant, and during that time he scanned the young man even more attentively than he had done at first. The messenger was unmoved.

"Devil take these Puritans," said Mazarin aside; "they are carved from granite." Then he added aloud, "But you have relations left you?"

"I have one remaining. Three times I presented myself to ask his support and three times he ordered his servants to turn me away."

"Oh, mon Dieu! my dear Mr. Mordaunt," said Mazarin, hoping by a display of affected pity to catch the young man in a snare, "how extremely your history interests me! You know not, then, anything of your birth—you have never seen your mother?"

"Yes, my lord; she came three times, whilst I was a child, to my nurse's house; I remember the last time she came as well as if it were to-day."

"You have a good memory," said Mazarin.

"Oh! yes, my lord," said the young man, with such peculiar emphasis that the cardinal felt a shudder run through every vein.

"And who brought you up?" he asked again.

"A French nurse, who sent me away when I was five years old because no one paid her for me, telling me the name of a relation of whom she had heard my mother often speak."

"What became of you?"

"As I was weeping and begging on the high road, a minister from Kingston took me in, instructed me in the Calvinistic faith, taught me all he knew himself and aided me in my researches after my family."

"And these researches?"

"Were fruitless; chance did everything."

"You discovered what had become of your mother?"

"I learned that she had been assassinated by my relation, aided by four friends, but I was already aware that I had been robbed of my wealth and degraded from my nobility by King Charles I."

"Oh! I now understand why you are in the service of Cromwell; you hate the king."

"Yes, my lord, I hate him!" said the young man.

Mazarin marked with surprise the diabolical expression with which the young man uttered these words. Just as, ordinarily, faces are colored by blood, his face seemed dyed by hatred and became livid.

"Your history is a terrible one, Mr. Mordaunt, and touches me keenly; but happily for you, you serve an all-powerful master; he ought to aid you in your search; we have so many means of gaining information."

"My lord, to a well-bred dog it is only necessary to show one end of a track; he is certain to reach the other."

"But this relation you mentioned—do you wish me to speak to him?" said Mazarin, who was anxious to make a friend about Cromwell's person.

"Thanks, my lord, I will speak to him myself. He will treat me better the next time I see him."

"You have the means, then, of touching him?"

"I have the means of making myself feared."

Mazarin looked at the young man, but at the fire which shot from his glance he bent his head; then, embarrassed how to continue such a conversation, he opened Cromwell's letter.

The young man's eyes gradually resumed their dull and glassy appearance and he fell into a profound reverie. After reading the first lines of the letter Mazarin gave a side glance at him to see if he was watching the expression of his face as he read. Observing his indifference, he shrugged his shoulders, saying:

"Send on your business those who do theirs at the same time! Let us see what this letter contains."

We here present the letter verbatim:

"To his Eminence, Monseigneur le Cardinal Mazarini:

"I have wished, monseigneur, to learn your intentions relating to the existing state of affairs in England. The two kingdoms are so near that France must be interested in our situation, as we are interested in that of France. The English are almost of one mind in contending against the tyranny of Charles and his adherents. Placed by popular confidence at the head of that movement, I can appreciate better than any other its significance and its probable results. I am at present in the midst of war, and am about to deliver a decisive battle against King Charles. I shall gain it, for the hope of the nation and the Spirit of the Lord are with me. This battle won by me, the king will have no further resources in England or in Scotland; and if he is not captured or killed, he will endeavor to pass over into France to recruit soldiers and to refurnish himself with arms and money. France has already received Queen Henrietta, and, unintentionally, doubtless, has maintained a centre of inextinguishable civil war in my country. But Madame Henrietta is a daughter of France and was entitled to the hospitality of France. As to King Charles, the question must be viewed differently; in receiving and aiding him, France will censure the acts of the English nation, and thus so essentially harm England, and especially the well-being of the government, that such a proceeding will be equivalent to pronounced hostilities."

At this moment Mazarin became very uneasy at the turn which the letter was taking and paused to glance under his eyes at the young man. The latter continued in thought. Mazarin resumed his reading:

"It is important, therefore, monseigneur, that I should be informed as to the intentions of France. The interests of that kingdom and those of England, though taking now diverse directions, are very nearly the same. England needs tranquillity at home, in order to consummate the expulsion of her king; France needs tranquillity to establish on solid foundations the throne of her young monarch. You need, as much as we do, that interior condition of repose which, thanks to the energy of our government, we are about to attain.

"Your quarrels with the parliament, your noisy dissensions with the princes, who fight for you to-day and to-morrow will fight against you, the popular following directed by the coadjutor, President Blancmesnil, and Councillor Broussel—all that disorder, in short, which pervades the several departments of the state, must lead you to view with uneasiness the possibility of a foreign war; for in that event England, exalted by the enthusiasm of new ideas, will ally herself with Spain, already seeking that alliance. I have therefore believed, monseigneur, knowing your prudence and your personal relation to the events of the present time, that you will choose to hold your forces concentrated in the interior of the French kingdom and leave to her own the new government of England. That neutrality consists simply in excluding King Charles from the territory of France and in refraining from helping him—a stranger to your country—with arms, with money or with troops.

"My letter is private and confidential, and for that reason I send it to you by a man who shares my most intimate counsels. It anticipates, through a sentiment which your eminence will appreciate, measures to be taken after the events. Oliver Cromwell considered it more expedient to declare himself to a mind as intelligent as Mazarin's than to a queen admirable for firmness, without doubt, but too much guided by vain prejudices of birth and of divine right.

"Farewell, monseigneur; should I not receive a reply in the space of fifteen days, I shall presume my letter will have miscarried.

"Oliver Cromwell."

"Mr. Mordaunt," said the cardinal, raising his voice, as if to arouse the dreamer, "my reply to this letter will be more satisfactory to General Cromwell if I am convinced that all are ignorant of my having given one; go, therefore, and await it at Boulogne-sur-Mer, and promise me to set out to-morrow morning."

"I promise, my lord," replied Mordaunt; "but how many days does your eminence expect me to await your reply?"

"If you do not receive it in ten days you can leave."

Mordaunt bowed.

"That is not all, sir," continued Mazarin; "your private adventures have touched me to the quick; besides, the letter from Mr. Cromwell makes you an important person as ambassador; come, tell me, what can I do for you?"

Mordaunt reflected a moment and, after some hesitation, was about to speak, when Bernouin entered hastily and bending down to the ear of the cardinal, whispered:

"My lord, the Queen Henrietta Maria, accompanied by an English noble, is entering the Palais Royal at this moment."

Mazarin made a bound from his chair, which did not escape the attention of the young man and suppressed the confidence he was about to make.

"Sir," said the cardinal, "you have heard me? I fix on Boulogne because I presume that every town in France is indifferent to you; if you prefer another, name it; but you can easily conceive that, surrounded as I am by influences I can only muzzle by discretion, I desire your presence in Paris to be unknown."

"I go, sir," said Mordaunt, advancing a few steps to the door by which he had entered.

"No, not that way, I beg, sir," quickly exclaimed the cardinal, "be so good as to pass by yonder gallery, by which you can regain the hall. I do not wish you to be seen leaving; our interview must be kept secret."

Mordaunt followed Bernouin, who led him through the adjacent chamber and left him with a doorkeeper, showing him the way out.

Chapter XXXVIII.

Henrietta Maria and Mazarin.

The cardinal rose, and advanced in haste to receive the queen of England. He showed the more respect to this queen, deprived of every mark of pomp and stripped of followers, as he felt some self-reproach for his own want of heart and his avarice. But supplicants for favor know how to accommodate the expression of their features, and the daughter of Henry IV. smiled as she advanced to meet a man she hated and despised.

"Ah!" said Mazarin to himself, "what a sweet face; does she come to borrow money of me?"

And he threw an uneasy glance at his strong box; he even turned inside the bevel of the magnificent diamond ring, the brilliancy of which drew every eye upon his hand, which indeed was white and handsome.

"Your eminence," said the august visitor, "it was my first intention to speak of the matters that have brought me here to the queen, my sister, but I have reflected that political affairs are more especially the concern of men."

"Madame," said Mazarin, "your majesty overwhelms me with flattering distinction."

"He is very gracious," thought the queen; "can he have guessed my errand?"

"Give," continued the cardinal, "your commands to the most respectful of your servants."

"Alas, sir," replied the queen, "I have lost the habit of commanding and have adopted instead that of making petitions. I am here to petition you, too happy should my prayer be favorably heard."

"I am listening, madame, with the greatest interest," said Mazarin.

"Your eminence, it concerns the war which the king, my husband, is now sustaining against his rebellious subjects. You are perhaps ignorant that they are fighting in England," added she, with a melancholy smile, "and that in a short time they will fight in a much more decided fashion than they have done hitherto."

"I am completely ignorant of it, madame," said the cardinal, accompanying his words with a slight shrug of the shoulders; "alas, our own wars quite absorb the time and the mind of a poor, incapable, infirm old minister like me."

"Well, then, your eminence," said the queen, "I must inform you that Charles I., my husband, is on the eve of a decisive engagement. In case of a check" (Mazarin made a slight movement), "one must foresee everything; in the case of a check, he desires to retire into France and to live here as a private individual. What do you say to this project?"

The cardinal had listened without permitting a single fibre of his face to betray what he felt, and his smile remained as it ever was—false and flattering; and when the queen finished speaking, he said:

"Do you think, madame, that France, agitated and disturbed as it is, would be a safe retreat for a dethroned king? How will the crown, which is scarce firmly set on the head of Louis XIV., support a double weight?"

"The weight was not so heavy when I was in peril," interrupted the queen, with a sad smile, "and I ask no more for my husband than has been done for me; you see that we are very humble monarchs, sir."

"Oh, you, madame," the cardinal hastened to say, in order to cut short the explanation he foresaw was coming, "with regard to you, that is another thing. A daughter of Henry IV., of that great, that sublime sovereign——"

"All which does not prevent you refusing hospitality to his son-in-law, sir! Nevertheless, you ought to remember that that great, that sublime monarch, when proscribed at one time, as my husband may be, demanded aid from England and England accorded it to him; and it is but just to say that Queen Elizabeth was not his niece."

"Peccato!" said Mazarin, writhing beneath this simple eloquence, "your majesty does not understand me; you judge my intentions wrongly, and that is partly because, doubtless, I explain myself in French."

"Speak Italian, sir. Ere the cardinal, your predecessor, sent our mother, Marie de Medicis, to die in exile, she taught us that language. If anything yet remains of that great, that sublime king, Henry, of whom you have just spoken, he would be much surprised at so little pity for his family being united to such a profound admiration of himself."

The perspiration stood in large drops on Mazarin's brow.

"That admiration is, on the contrary, so great, so real, madame," returned Mazarin, without noticing the change of language offered to him by the queen, "that if the king, Charles I.—whom Heaven protect from evil!—came into France, I would offer him my house—my own house; but, alas! it would be but an unsafe retreat. Some day the people will burn that house, as they burned that of the Marechal d'Ancre. Poor Concino Concini! And yet he but desired the good of the people."

"Yes, my lord, like yourself!" said the queen, ironically.

Mazarin pretended not to understand the double meaning of his own sentence, but continued to compassionate the fate of Concino Concini.

"Well then, your eminence," said the queen, becoming impatient, "what is your answer?"

"Madame," cried Mazarin, more and more moved, "will your majesty permit me to give you counsel?"

"Speak, sir," replied the queen; "the counsels of so prudent a man as yourself ought certainly to be available."

"Madame, believe me, the king ought to defend himself to the last."

"He has done so, sir, and this last battle, which he encounters with resources much inferior to those of the enemy, proves that he will not yield without a struggle; but in case he is beaten?"

"Well, madame, in that case, my advice—I know that I am very bold to offer advice to your majesty—my advice is that the king should not leave his kingdom. Absent kings are very soon forgotten; if he passes over into France his cause is lost."

"But," persisted the queen, "if such be your advice and you have his interest at heart, send him help of men and money, for I can do nothing for him; I have sold even to my last diamond to aid him. If I had had a single ornament left, I should have bought wood this winter to make a fire for my daughter and myself."

"Oh, madame," said Mazarin, "your majesty knows not what you ask. On the day when foreign succor follows in the train of a king to replace him on his throne, it is an avowal that he no longer possesses the help and love of his own subjects."

"To the point, sir," said the queen, "to the point, and answer me, yes or no; if the king persists in remaining in England will you send him succor? If he comes to France will you accord him hospitality? What do you intend to do? Speak."

"Madame," said the cardinal, affecting an effusive frankness of speech, "I shall convince your majesty, I trust, of my devotion to you and my desire to terminate an affair which you have so much at heart. After which your majesty will, I think, no longer doubt my zeal in your behalf."

The queen bit her lips and moved impatiently on her chair.

"Well, what do you propose to do?" she, said at length; "come, speak."

"I will go this instant and consult the queen, and we will refer the affair at once to parliament."

"With which you are at war—is it not so? You will charge Broussel to report it. Enough, sir, enough. I understand you or rather, I am wrong. Go to the parliament, for it was from this parliament, the enemy of monarchs, that the daughter of the great, the sublime Henry IV., whom you so much admire, received the only relief this winter which prevented her from dying of hunger and cold!"

And with these words Henrietta rose in majestic indignation, whilst the cardinal, raising his hands clasped toward her, exclaimed, "Ah, madame, madame, how little you know me, mon Dieu!"

But Queen Henrietta, without even turning toward him who made these hypocritical pretensions, crossed the cabinet, opened the door for herself and passing through the midst of the cardinal's numerous guards, courtiers eager to pay homage, the luxurious show of a competing royalty, she went and took the hand of De Winter, who stood apart in isolation. Poor queen, already fallen! Though all bowed before her, as etiquette required, she had now but a single arm on which she could lean.

"It signifies little," said Mazarin, when he was alone. "It gave me pain and it was an ungracious part to play, but I have said nothing either to the one or to the other. Bernouin!"

Bernouin entered.

"See if the young man with the black doublet and the short hair, who was with me just now, is still in the palace."

Bernouin went out and soon returned with Comminges, who was on guard.

"Your eminence," said Comminges, "as I was re-conducting the young man for whom you have asked, he approached the glass door of the gallery, and gazed intently upon some object, doubtless the picture by Raphael, which is opposite the door. He reflected for a second and then descended the stairs. I believe I saw him mount a gray horse and leave the palace court. But is not your eminence going to the queen?"

"For what purpose?"

"Monsieur de Guitant, my uncle, has just told me that her majesty had received news of the army."

"It is well; I will go."

Comminges had seen rightly, and Mordaunt had really acted as he had related. In crossing the gallery parallel to the large glass gallery, he perceived De Winter, who was waiting until the queen had finished her negotiation.

At this sight the young man stopped short, not in admiration of Raphael's picture, but as if fascinated at the sight of some terrible object. His eyes dilated and a shudder ran through his body. One would have said that he longed to break through the wall of glass which separated him from his enemy; for if Comminges had seen with what an expression of hatred the eyes of this young man were fixed upon De Winter, he would not have doubted for an instant that the Englishman was his eternal foe.

But he stopped, doubtless to reflect; for instead of allowing his first impulse, which had been to go straight to Lord de Winter, to carry him away, he leisurely descended the staircase, left the palace with his head down, mounted his horse, which he reined in at the corner of the Rue Richelieu, and with his eyes fixed on the gate, waited until the queen's carriage had left the court.

He had not long to wait, for the queen scarcely remained a quarter of an hour with Mazarin, but this quarter of an hour of expectation appeared a century to him. At last the heavy machine, which was called a chariot in those days, came out, rumbling against the gates, and De Winter, still on horseback, bent again to the door to converse with her majesty.

The horses started on a trot and took the road to the Louvre, which they entered. Before leaving the convent of the Carmelites, Henrietta had desired her daughter to attend her at the palace, which she had inhabited for a long time and which she had only left because their poverty seemed to them more difficult to bear in gilded chambers.

Mordaunt followed the carriage, and when he had watched it drive beneath the sombre arches he went and stationed himself under a wall over which the shadow was extended, and remained motionless, amidst the moldings of Jean Goujon, like a bas-relievo, representing an equestrian statue.

Chapter XXXIX.

How, sometimes, the Unhappy mistake Chance for Providence.

"Well, madame," said De Winter, when the queen had dismissed her attendants.

"Well, my lord, what I foresaw has come to pass."

"What? does the cardinal refuse to receive the king? France refuse hospitality to an unfortunate prince? Ay, but it is for the first time, madame!"

"I did not say France, my lord; I said the cardinal, and the cardinal is not even a Frenchman."

"But did you see the queen?"

"It is useless," replied Henrietta, "the queen will not say yes when the cardinal says no. Are you not aware that this Italian directs everything, both indoors and out? And moreover, I should not be surprised had we been forestalled by Cromwell. He was embarrassed whilst speaking to me and yet quite firm in his determination to refuse. Then did you not observe the agitation in the Palais Royal, the passing to and fro of busy people? Can they have received any news, my lord?"

"Not from England, madame. I made such haste that I am certain of not having been forestalled. I set out three days ago, passing miraculously through the Puritan army, and I took post horses with my servant Tony; the horses upon which we were mounted were bought in Paris. Besides, the king, I am certain, awaits your majesty's reply before risking anything."

"You will tell him, my lord," resumed the queen, despairingly, "that I can do nothing; that I have suffered as much as himself—more than he has—obliged as I am to eat the bread of exile and to ask hospitality from false friends who smile at my tears; and as regards his royal person, he must sacrifice it generously and die like a king. I shall go and die by his side."

"Madame, madame," exclaimed De Winter, "your majesty abandons yourself to despair; and yet, perhaps, there still remains some hope."

"No friends left, my lord; no other friends left in the wide world but yourself! Oh, God!" exclaimed the poor queen, raising her eyes to Heaven, "have You indeed taken back all the generous hearts that once existed in the world?"

"I hope not, madame," replied De Winter, thoughtfully; "I once spoke to you of four men."

"What can be done with four?"

"Four devoted, resolute men can do much, assure yourself, madame; and those of whom I speak performed great things at one time."

"And where are these four men?"

"Ah, that is what I do not know. It is twenty years since I saw them, and yet whenever I have seen the king in danger I have thought of them."

"And these men were your friends?"

"One of them held my life in his hands and gave it to me. I know not whether he is still my friend, but since that time I have remained his."

"And these men are in France, my lord?"

"I believe so."

"Tell me their names; perhaps I may have heard them mentioned and might be able to aid you in finding them."

"One of them was called the Chevalier d'Artagnan."

"Ah, my lord, if I mistake not, the Chevalier d'Artagnan is lieutenant of royal guards; but take care, for I fear that this man is entirely devoted to the cardinal."

"That would be a misfortune," said De Winter, "and I shall begin to think that we are really doomed."

"But the others," said the queen, who clung to this last hope as a shipwrecked man clings to the hull of his vessel. "The others, my lord!"

"The second—I heard his name by chance; for before fighting us, these four gentlemen told us their names; the second was called the Comte de la Fere. As for the two others, I had so much the habit of calling them by nicknames that I have forgotten their real ones."

"Oh, mon Dieu, it is a matter of the greatest urgency to find them out," said the queen, "since you think these worthy gentlemen might be so useful to the king."

"Oh, yes," said De Winter, "for they are the same men. Listen, madame, and recall your remembrances. Have you never heard that Queen Anne of Austria was once saved from the greatest danger ever incurred by a queen?"

"Yes, at the time of her relations with Monsieur de Buckingham; it had to do in some way with certain studs and diamonds."

"Well, it was that affair, madame; these men are the ones who saved her; and I smile with pity when I reflect that if the names of those gentlemen are unknown to you it is because the queen has forgotten them, who ought to have made them the first noblemen of the realm."

"Well, then, my lord, they must be found; but what can four men, or rather three men do—for I tell you, you must not count on Monsieur d'Artagnan."

"It will be one valiant sword the less, but there will remain still three, without reckoning my own; now four devoted men around the king to protect him from his enemies, to be at his side in battle, to aid him with counsel, to escort him in flight, are sufficient, not to make the king a conqueror, but to save him if conquered; and whatever Mazarin may say, once on the shores of France your royal husband may find as many retreats and asylums as the seabird finds in a storm."

"Seek, then, my lord, seek these gentlemen; and if they will consent to go with you to England, I will give to each a duchy the day that we reascend the throne, besides as much gold as would pave Whitehall. Seek them, my lord, and find them, I conjure you."

"I will search for them, madame," said De Winter "and doubtless I shall find them; but time fails me. Has your majesty forgotten that the king expects your reply and awaits it in agony?"

"Then indeed we are lost!" cried the queen, in the fullness of a broken heart.

At this moment the door opened and the young Henrietta appeared; then the queen, with that wonderful strength which is the privilege of parents, repressed her tears and motioned to De Winter to change the subject.

But that act of self-control, effective as it was, did not escape the eyes of the young princess. She stopped on the threshold, breathed a sigh, and addressing the queen:

"Why, then, do you always weep, mother, when I am away from you?" she said.

The queen smiled, but instead of answering:

"See, De Winter," she said, "I have at least gained one thing in being only half a queen; and that is that my children call me 'mother' instead of 'madame.'"

Then turning toward her daughter:

"What do you want, Henrietta?" she demanded.

"My mother," replied the young princess, "a cavalier has just entered the Louvre and wishes to present his respects to your majesty; he arrives from the army and has, he says, a letter to remit to you, on the part of the Marechal de Grammont, I think."

"Ah!" said the queen to De Winter, "he is one of my faithful adherents; but do you not observe, my dear lord, that we are so poorly served that it is left to my daughter to fill the office of doorkeeper?"

"Madame, have pity on me," exclaimed De Winter; "you wring my heart!"

"And who is this cavalier, Henrietta?" asked the queen.

"I saw him from the window, madame; he is a young man that appears scarce sixteen years of age, and is called the Viscount de Bragelonne."

The queen, smiling, made a sign with her head; the young princess opened the door and Raoul appeared on the threshold.

Advancing a few steps toward the queen, he knelt down.

"Madame," said he, "I bear to your majesty a letter from my friend the Count de Guiche, who told me he had the honor of being your servant; this letter contains important news and the expression of his respect."

At the name of the Count de Guiche a blush spread over the cheeks of the young princess and the queen glanced at her with some degree of severity.

"You told me that the letter was from the Marechal de Grammont, Henrietta!" said the queen.

"I thought so, madame," stammered the young girl.

"It is my fault, madame," said Raoul. "I did announce myself, in truth, as coming on the part of the Marechal de Grammont; but being wounded in the right arm he was unable to write and therefore the Count de Guiche acted as his secretary."

"There has been fighting, then?" asked the queen, motioning to Raoul to rise.

"Yes, madame," said the young man.

At this announcement of a battle having taken place, the princess opened her mouth as though to ask a question of interest; but her lips closed again without articulating a word, while the color gradually faded from her cheeks.

The queen saw this, and doubtless her maternal heart translated the emotion, for addressing Raoul again:

"And no evil has happened to the young Count de Guiche?" she asked; "for not only is he our servant, as you say, sir, but more—he is one of our friends."

"No, madame," replied Raoul; "on the contrary, he gained great glory and had the honor of being embraced by his highness, the prince, on the field of battle."

The young princess clapped her hands; and then, ashamed of having been betrayed into such a demonstration of joy, she half turned away and bent over a vase of roses, as if to inhale their odor.

"Let us see," said the queen, "what the count says." And she opened the letter and read:

"Madame,—Being unable to have the honor of writing to you myself, by reason of a wound I have received in my right hand, I have commanded my son, the Count de Guiche, who, with his father, is equally your humble servant, to write to tell you that we have just gained the battle of Lens, and that this victory cannot fail to give great power to Cardinal Mazarin and to the queen over the affairs of Europe. If her majesty will have faith in my counsels she ought to profit by this event to address at this moment, in favor of her august husband, the court of France. The Vicomte de Bragelonne, who will have the honor of remitting this letter to your majesty, is the friend of my son, who owes to him his life; he is a gentleman in whom your majesty may confide entirely, in case your majesty may have some verbal or written order to remit to me.

"I have the honor to be, with respect, etc.,

"Marechal de Grammont."

At the moment mention occurred of his having rendered a service to the count, Raoul could not help turning his glance toward the young princess, and then he saw in her eyes an expression of infinite gratitude to the young man; he no longer doubted that the daughter of King Charles I. loved his friend.

"The battle of Lens gained!" said the queen; "they are lucky here indeed; they can gain battles! Yes, the Marechal de Grammont is right; this will change the aspect of French affairs, but I much fear it will do nothing for English, even if it does not harm them. This is recent news, sir," continued she, "and I thank you for having made such haste to bring it to me; without this letter I should not have heard till to-morrow, perhaps after to-morrow—the last of all Paris."

"Madame," said Raoul, "the Louvre is but the second palace this news has reached; it is as yet unknown to all, and I had sworn to the Count de Guiche to remit this letter to your majesty before even I should embrace my guardian."

"Your guardian! is he, too, a Bragelonne?" asked Lord de Winter. "I once knew a Bragelonne—is he still alive?"

"No, sir, he is dead; and I believe it is from him my guardian, whose near relation he was, inherited the estate from which I take my name."

"And your guardian, sir," asked the queen, who could not help feeling some interest in the handsome young man before her, "what is his name?"

"The Comte de la Fere, madame," replied the young man, bowing.

De Winter made a gesture of surprise and the queen turned to him with a start of joy.

"The Comte de la Fere!" she cried. "Have you not mentioned that name to me?"

As for De Winter he could scarcely believe that he had heard aright. "The Comte de la Fere!" he cried in his turn. "Oh, sir, reply, I entreat you—is not the Comte de la Fere a noble whom I remember, handsome and brave, a musketeer under Louis XIII., who must be now about forty-seven or forty-eight years of age?"

"Yes, sir, you are right in every particular!"

"And who served under an assumed name?"

"Under the name of Athos. Latterly I heard his friend, Monsieur d'Artagnan, give him that name."

"That is it, madame, that is the same. God be praised! And he is in Paris?" continued he, addressing Raoul; then turning to the queen: "We may still hope. Providence has declared for us, since I have found this brave man again in so miraculous a manner. And, sir, where does he reside, pray?"

"The Comte de la Fere lodges in the Rue Guenegaud, Hotel du Grand Roi Charlemagne."

"Thanks, sir. Inform this dear friend that he may remain within, that I shall go and see him immediately."

"Sir, I obey with pleasure, if her majesty will permit me to depart."

"Go, Monsieur de Bragelonne," said the queen, "and rest assured of our affection."

Raoul bent respectfully before the two princesses, and bowing to De Winter, departed.

The queen and De Winter continued to converse for some time in low voices, in order that the young princess should not overhear them; but the precaution was needless: she was in deep converse with her own thoughts.

Then, when De Winter rose to take leave:

"Listen, my lord," said the queen; "I have preserved this diamond cross which came from my mother, and this order of St. Michael which came from my husband. They are worth about fifty thousand pounds. I had sworn to die of hunger rather than part with these precious pledges; but now that this ornament may be useful to him or his defenders, everything must be sacrificed. Take them, and if you need money for your expedition, sell them fearlessly, my lord. But should you find the means of retaining them, remember, my lord, that I shall esteem you as having rendered the greatest service that a gentleman can render to a queen; and in the day of my prosperity he who brings me this order and this cross shall be blessed by me and my children."

"Madame," replied De Winter, "your majesty will be served by a man devoted to you. I hasten to deposit these two objects in a safe place, nor should I accept them if the resources of our ancient fortune were left to us, but our estates are confiscated, our ready money is exhausted, and we are reduced to turn to service everything we possess. In an hour hence I shall be with the Comte de la Fere, and to-morrow your majesty shall have a definite reply."

The queen tendered her hand to Lord de Winter, who, kissing it respectfully, went out and traversed alone and unconducted those large, dark and deserted apartments, brushing away tears which, blase as he was by fifty years spent as a courtier, he could not withhold at the spectacle of royal distress so dignified, yet so intense.

Chapter XL.

Uncle and Nephew.

The horse and servant belonging to De Winter were waiting for him at the door; he proceeded toward his abode very thoughtfully, looking behind him from time to him to contemplate the dark and silent frontage of the Louvre. It was then that he saw a horseman, as it were, detach himself from the wall and follow him at a little distance. In leaving the Palais Royal he remembered to have observed a similar shadow.

"Tony," he said, motioning to his groom to approach.

"Here I am, my lord."

"Did you remark that man who is following us?"

"Yes, my lord."

"Who is he?"

"I do not know, only he has followed your grace from the Palais Royal, stopped at the Louvre to wait for you, and now leaves the Louvre with you."

"Some spy of the cardinal," said De Winter to him, aside. "Let us pretend not to notice that he is watching us."

And spurring on he plunged into the labyrinth of streets which led to his hotel, situated near the Marais, for having for so long a time lived near the Place Royale, Lord de Winter naturally returned to lodge near his ancient dwelling.

The unknown spurred his horse to a gallop.

De Winter dismounted at his hotel and went up into his apartment, intending to watch the spy; but as he was about to place his gloves and hat on a table, he saw reflected in a glass opposite to him a figure which stood on the threshold of the room. He turned around and Mordaunt stood before him.

There was a moment of frozen silence between these two.

"Sir," said De Winter, "I thought I had already made you aware that I am weary of this persecution; withdraw, then, or I shall call and have you turned out as you were in London. I am not your uncle, I know you not."

"My uncle," replied Mordaunt, with his harsh and bantering tone, "you are mistaken; you will not have me turned out this time as you did in London—you dare not. As for denying that I am your nephew, you will think twice about it, now that I have learned some things of which I was ignorant a year ago."

"And how does it concern me what you have learned?" said De Winter.

"Oh, it concerns you very closely, my uncle, I am sure, and you will soon be of my opinion," added he, with a smile which sent a shudder through the veins of him he thus addressed. "When I presented myself before you for the first time in London, it was to ask you what had become of my fortune; the second time it was to demand who had sullied my name; and this time I come before you to ask a question far more terrible than any other, to say to you as God said to the first murderer: 'Cain, what hast thou done to thy brother Abel?' My lord, what have you done with your sister—your sister, who was my mother?"

De Winter shrank back from the fire of those scorching eyes.

"Your mother?" he said.

"Yes, my lord, my mother," replied the young man, advancing into the room until he was face to face with Lord de Winter, and crossing his arms. "I have asked the headsman of Bethune," he said, his voice hoarse and his face livid with passion and grief. "And the headsman of Bethune gave me a reply."

De Winter fell back in a chair as though struck by a thunderbolt and in vain attempted a reply.

"Yes," continued the young man; "all is now explained; with this key I open the abyss. My mother inherited an estate from her husband, you have assassinated her; my name would have secured me the paternal estate, you have deprived me of it; you have despoiled me of my fortune. I am no longer astonished that you knew me not. I am not surprised that you refused to recognize me. When a man is a robber it is hard to call him nephew whom he has impoverished; when one is a murderer, to recognize the man whom one has made an orphan."

These words produced a contrary effect to that which Mordaunt had anticipated. De Winter remembered the monster that Milady had been; he rose, dignified and calm, restraining by the severity of his look the wild glance of the young man.

"You desire to fathom this horrible secret?" said De Winter; "well, then, so be it. Know, then, what manner of woman it was for whom to-day you call me to account. That woman had, in all probability, poisoned my brother, and in order to inherit from me she was about to assassinate me in my turn. I have proof of it. What say you to that?"

"I say that she was my mother."

"She caused the unfortunate Duke of Buckingham to be stabbed by a man who was, ere that, honest, good and pure. What say you to that crime, of which I have the proof?"

"She was my mother."

"On our return to France she had a young woman who was attached to one of her opponents poisoned in the convent of the Augustines at Bethune. Will this crime persuade you of the justice of her punishment—for of all this I have the proofs?"

"She was my mother!" cried the young man, who uttered these three successive exclamations with constantly increasing force.

"At last, charged with murders, with debauchery, hated by every one and yet threatening still, like a panther thirsting for blood, she fell under the blows of men whom she had rendered desperate, though they had never done her the least injury; she met with judges whom her hideous crimes had evoked; and that executioner you saw—that executioner who you say told you everything—that executioner, if he told you everything, told you that he leaped with joy in avenging on her his brother's shame and suicide. Depraved as a girl, adulterous as a wife, an unnatural sister, homicide, poisoner, execrated by all who knew her, by every nation that had been visited by her, she died accursed by Heaven and earth."

A sob which Mordaunt could not repress burst from his throat and his livid face became suffused with blood; he clenched his fists, sweat covered his face, his hair, like Hamlet's, stood on end, and racked with fury he cried out:

"Silence, sir! she was my mother! Her crimes, I know them not; her disorders, I know them not; her vices, I know them not. But this I know, that I had a mother, that five men leagued against one woman, murdered her clandestinely by night—silently—like cowards. I know that you were one of them, my uncle, and that you cried louder than the others: 'She must die.' Therefore I warn you, and listen well to my words, that they may be engraved upon your memory, never to be forgotten: this murder, which has robbed me of everything—this murder, which has deprived me of my name—this murder, which has impoverished me—this murder, which has made me corrupt, wicked, implacable—I shall summon you to account for it first and then those who were your accomplices, when I discover them!"

With hatred in his eyes, foaming at his mouth, and his fist extended, Mordaunt had advanced one more step, a threatening, terrible step, toward De Winter. The latter put his hand to his sword, and said, with the smile of a man who for thirty years has jested with death:

"Would you assassinate me, sir? Then I shall recognize you as my nephew, for you would be a worthy son of such a mother."

"No," replied Mordaunt, forcing his features and the muscles of his body to resume their usual places and be calm; "no, I shall not kill you; at least not at this moment, for without you I could not discover the others. But when I have found them, then tremble, sir. I stabbed to the heart the headsman of Bethune, without mercy or pity, and he was the least guilty of you all."

With these words the young man went out and descended the stairs with sufficient calmness to pass unobserved; then upon the lowest landing place he passed Tony, leaning over the balustrade, waiting only for a call from his master to mount to his room.

But De Winter did not call; crushed, enfeebled, he remained standing and with listening ear; then only when he had heard the step of the horse going away he fell back on a chair, saying:

"My God, I thank Thee that he knows me only."

Chapter XLI.

Paternal Affection.

Whilst this terrible scene was passing at Lord de Winter's, Athos, seated near his window, his elbow on the table and his head supported on his hand, was listening intently to Raoul's account of the adventures he met with on his journey and the details of the battle.

Listening to the relation of those emotions so fresh and pure, the fine, noble face of Athos betrayed indescribable pleasure; he inhaled the tones of that young voice, as harmonious music. He forgot all that was dark in the past and that was cloudy in the future. It almost seemed as if the return of this much loved boy had changed his fears to hopes. Athos was happy—happy as he had never been before.

"And you assisted and took part in this great battle, Bragelonne!" cried the former musketeer.

"Yes, sir."

"And it was a fierce one?"

"His highness the prince charged eleven times in person."

"He is a great commander, Bragelonne."

"He is a hero, sir. I did not lose sight of him for an instant. Oh! how fine it is to be called Condé and to be so worthy of such a name!"

"He was calm and radiant, was he not?"

"As calm as at parade, radiant as at a fete. When we went up to the enemy it was slowly; we were forbidden to draw first and we were marching toward the Spaniards, who were on a height with lowered muskets. When we arrived about thirty paces from them the prince turned around to the soldiers: 'Comrades,' he said, 'you are about to suffer a furious discharge; but after that you will make short work with those fellows.' There was such dead silence that friends and enemies could have heard these words; then raising his sword, 'Sound trumpets!' he cried."

"Well, very good; you will do as much when the opportunity occurs, will you, Raoul?"

"I know not, sir, but I thought it really very fine and grand!"

"Were you afraid, Raoul?" asked the count.

"Yes, sir," replied the young man naively; "I felt a great chill at my heart, and at the word 'fire,' which resounded in Spanish from the enemy's ranks, I closed my eyes and thought of you."

"In honest truth, Raoul?" said Athos, pressing his hand.

"Yes, sir; at that instant there was such a rataplan of musketry that one might have imagined the infernal regions had opened. Those who were not killed felt the heat of the flames. I opened my eyes, astonished to find myself alive and even unhurt; a third of the squadron were lying on the ground, wounded, dead or dying. At that moment I encountered the eye of the prince. I had but one thought and that was that he was observing me. I spurred on and found myself in the enemy's ranks."

"And the prince was pleased with you?"

"He told me so, at least, sir, when he desired me to return to Paris with Monsieur de Chatillon, who was charged to carry the news to the queen and to bring the colors we had taken. 'Go,' said he; 'the enemy will not rally for fifteen days and until that time I have no need of your service. Go and see those whom you love and who love you, and tell my sister De Longueville that I thank her for the present that she made me of you.' And I came, sir," added Raoul, gazing at the count with a smile of real affection, "for I thought you would be glad to see me again."

Athos drew the young man toward him and pressed his lips to his brow, as he would have done to a young daughter.

"And now, Raoul," said he, "you are launched; you have dukes for friends, a marshal of France for godfather, a prince of the blood as commander, and on the day of your return you have been received by two queens; it is not so bad for a novice."

"Oh sir," said Raoul, suddenly, "you recall something, which, in my haste to relate my exploits, I had forgotten; it is that there was with Her Majesty the Queen of England, a gentleman who, when I pronounced your name, uttered a cry of surprise and joy; he said he was a friend of yours, asked your address, and is coming to see you."

"What is his name?"

"I did not venture to ask, sir; he spoke elegantly, although I thought from his accent he was an Englishman."

"Ah!" said Athos, leaning down his head as if to remember who it could be. Then, when he raised it again, he was struck by the presence of a man who was standing at the open door and was gazing at him with a compassionate air.

"Lord de Winter!" exclaimed the count.

"Athos, my friend!"

And the two gentlemen were for an instant locked in each other's arms; then Athos, looking into his friend's face and taking him by both hands, said:

"What ails you, my lord? you appear as unhappy as I am the reverse."

"Yes, truly, dear friend; and I may even say the sight of you increases my dismay."

And De Winter glancing around him, Raoul quickly understood that the two friends wished to be alone and he therefore left the room unaffectedly.

"Come, now that we are alone," said Athos, "let us talk of yourself."

"Whilst we are alone let us speak of ourselves," replied De Winter. "He is here."

"Who?"

"Milady's son."

Athos, again struck by this name, which seemed to pursue him like an echo, hesitated for a moment, then slightly knitting his brows, he calmly said:

"I know it, Grimaud met him between Bethune and Arras and then came here to warn me of his presence."

"Does Grimaud know him, then?"

"No; but he was present at the deathbed of a man who knew him."

"The headsman of Bethune?" exclaimed De Winter.

"You know about that?" cried Athos, astonished.

"He has just left me," replied De Winter, "after telling me all. Ah! my friend! what a horrible scene! Why did we not destroy the child with the mother?"

"What need you fear?" said Athos, recovering from the instinctive fear he had at first experienced, by the aid of reason; "are we not men accustomed to defend ourselves? Is this young man an assassin by profession—a murderer in cold blood? He has killed the executioner of Bethune in an access of passion, but now his fury is assuaged."

De Winter smiled sorrowfully and shook his head.

"Do you not know the race?" said he.

"Pooh!" said Athos, trying to smile in his turn. "It must have lost its ferocity in the second generation. Besides, my friend, Providence has warned us, that we may be on our guard. All we can now do is to wait. Let us wait; and, as I said before, let us speak of yourself. What brings you to Paris?"

"Affairs of importance which you shall know later. But what is this that I hear from Her Majesty the Queen of England? Monsieur d'Artagnan sides with Mazarin! Pardon my frankness, dear friend. I neither hate nor blame the cardinal, and your opinions will be held ever sacred by me. But do you happen to belong to him?"

"Monsieur d'Artagnan," replied Athos, "is in the service; he is a soldier and obeys all constitutional authority. Monsieur d'Artagnan is not rich and has need of his position as lieutenant to enable him to live. Millionaires like yourself, my lord, are rare in France."

"Alas!" said De Winter, "I am at this moment as poor as he is, if not poorer. But to return to our subject."

"Well, then, you wish to know if I am of Mazarin's party? No. Pardon my frankness, too, my lord."

"I am obliged to you, count, for this pleasing intelligence! You make me young and happy again by it. Ah! so you are not a Mazarinist? Delightful! Indeed, you could not belong to him. But pardon me, are you free? I mean to ask if you are married?"

"Ah! as to that, no," replied Athos, laughing.

"Because that young man, so handsome, so elegant, so polished——"

"Is a child I have adopted and who does not even know who was his father."

"Very well; you are always the same, Athos, great and generous. Are you still friends with Monsieur Porthos and Monsieur Aramis?"

"Add Monsieur d'Artagnan, my lord. We still remain four friends devoted to each other; but when it becomes a question of serving the cardinal or of fighting him, of being Mazarinists or Frondists, then we are only two."

"Is Monsieur Aramis with D'Artagnan?" asked Lord de Winter.

"No," said Athos; "Monsieur Aramis does me the honor to share my opinions."

"Could you put me in communication with your witty and agreeable friend? Is he much changed?"

"He has become an abbé, that is all."

"You alarm me; his profession must have made him renounce any great undertakings."

"On the contrary," said Athos, smiling, "he has never been so much a musketeer as since he became an abbé, and you will find him a veritable soldier."

"Could you engage to bring him to me to-morrow morning at ten o'clock, on the Pont du Louvre?"

"Oh, oh!" exclaimed Athos, smiling, "you have a duel in prospect."

"Yes, count, and a splendid duel, too; a duel in which I hope you will take your part."

"Where are we to go, my lord?"

"To Her Majesty the Queen of England, who has desired me to present you to her."

"This is an enigma," said Athos, "but it matters not; since you know the solution of it I ask no further. Will your lordship do me the honor to sup with me?"

"Thanks, count, no," replied De Winter. "I own to you that that young man's visit has subdued my appetite and probably will rob me of my sleep. What undertaking can have brought him to Paris? It was not to meet me that he came, for he was ignorant of my journey. This young man terrifies me, my lord; there lies in him a sanguinary predisposition."

"What occupies him in England?"

"He is one of Cromwell's most enthusiastic disciples."

"But what attached him to the cause? His father and mother were Catholics, I believe?"

"His hatred of the king, who deprived him of his estates and forbade him to bear the name of De Winter."

"And what name does he now bear?"

"Mordaunt."

"A Puritan, yet disguised as a monk he travels alone in France."

"Do you say as a monk?"

"It was thus, and by mere accident—may God pardon me if I blaspheme—that he heard the confession of the executioner of Bethune."

"Then I understand it all! he has been sent by Cromwell to Mazarin, and the queen guessed rightly; we have been forestalled. Everything is clear to me now. Adieu, count, till to-morrow."

"But the night is dark," said Athos, perceiving that Lord de Winter seemed more uneasy than he wished to appear; "and you have no servant."

"I have Tony, a safe if simple youth."

"Halloo, there, Grimaud, Olivain, and Blaisois! call the viscount and take the musket with you."

Blaisois was the tall youth, half groom, half peasant, whom we saw at the Chateau de Bragelonne, whom Athos had christened by the name of his province.

"Viscount," said Athos to Raoul, as he entered, "you will conduct my lord as far as his hotel and permit no one to approach him."

"Oh! count," said De Winter, "for whom do you take me?"

"For a stranger who does not know Paris," said Athos, "and to whom the viscount will show the way."

De Winter shook him by the hand.

"Grimaud," said Athos, "put yourself at the head of the troop and beware of the monk."

Grimaud shuddered, and nodding, awaited the departure, regarding the butt of his musket with silent eloquence. Then obeying the orders given him by Athos, he headed the small procession, bearing the torch in one hand and the musket in the other, until it reached De Winter's inn, when pounding on the portal with his fist, he bowed to my lord and faced about without a word.

The same order was followed in returning, nor did Grimaud's searching glance discover anything of a suspicious appearance, save a dark shadow, as it were, in ambuscade, at the corner of the Rue Guenegaud and of the Quai. He fancied, also, that in going he had already observed the street watcher who had attracted his attention. He pushed on toward him, but before he could reach it the shadow had disappeared into an alley, into which Grimaud deemed it scarcely prudent to pursue it.

The next day, on awaking, the count perceived Raoul by his bedside. The young man was already dressed and was reading a new book by M. Chapelain.

"Already up, Raoul?" exclaimed the count.

"Yes, sir," replied Raoul, with slight hesitation; "I did not sleep well."

"You, Raoul, not sleep well! then you must have something on your mind!" said Athos.

"Sir, you will perhaps think that I am in a great hurry to leave you when I have only just arrived, but——"

"Have you only two days of leave, Raoul?"

"On the contrary, sir, I have ten; nor is it to the camp I wish to go."

"Where, then?" said Athos, smiling, "if it be not a secret. You are now almost a man, since you have made your first passage of arms, and have acquired the right to go where you will without consulting me."

"Never, sir," said Raoul, "as long as I possess the happiness of having you for a protector, shall I deem I have the right of freeing myself from a guardianship so valuable to me. I have, however, a wish to go and pass a day at Blois. You look at me and you are going to laugh at me."

"No, on the contrary, I am not inclined to laugh," said Athos, suppressing a sigh. "You wish to see Blois again; it is but natural."

"Then you permit me to go, you are not angry in your heart?" exclaimed Raoul, joyously.

"Certainly; and why should I regret what gives you pleasure?"

"Oh! how kind you are," exclaimed the young man, pressing his guardian's hand; "and I can set out immediately?"

"When you like, Raoul."

"Sir," said Raoul, as he turned to leave the room, "I have thought of one thing, and that is about the Duchess of Chevreuse, who was so kind to me and to whom I owe my introduction to the prince."

"And you ought to thank her, Raoul. Well, try the Hotel de Luynes, Raoul, and ask if the duchess can receive you. I am glad to see you pay attention to the usages of the world. You must take Grimaud and Olivain."

"Both, sir?" asked Raoul, astonished.

"Both."

Raoul went out, and when Athos heard his young, joyous voice calling to Grimaud and Olivain, he sighed.

"It is very soon to leave me," he thought, "but he follows the common custom. Nature has made us thus; she makes the young look ever forward, not behind. He certainly likes the child, but will he love me less as his affection grows for her?"

And Athos confessed to himself that, he was unprepared for so prompt a departure; but Raoul was so happy that this reflection effaced everything else from the consideration of his guardian.

Everything was ready at ten o'clock for the departure, and as Athos was watching Raoul mount, a groom rode up from the Duchess de Chevreuse. He was charged to tell the Comte de la Fere, that she had learned of the return of her youthful protege, and also the manner he had conducted himself on the field, and she added that she should be very glad to offer him her congratulations.

"Tell her grace," replied Athos, "that the viscount has just mounted his horse to proceed to the Hotel de Luynes."

Then, with renewed instructions to Grimaud, Athos signified to Raoul that he could set out, and ended by reflecting that it was perhaps better that Raoul should be away from Paris at that moment.

Chapter XLII.

Another Queen in Want of Help.

Athos had not failed to send early to Aramis and had given his letter to Blaisois, the only serving-man whom he had left. Blaisois found Bazin donning his beadle's gown, his services being required that day at Notre Dame.

Athos had desired Blaisois to try to speak to Aramis himself. Blaisois, a tall, simple youth, who understood nothing but what he was expressly told, asked, therefore for the Abbé d'Herblay, and in spite of Bazin's assurances that his master was not at home, he persisted in such a manner as to put Bazin into a passion. Blaisois seeing Bazin in clerical guise, was a little discomposed at his denials and wanted to pass at all risks, believing too, that the man with whom he had to do was endowed with the virtues of his cloth, namely, patience and Christian charity.

But Bazin, still the servant of a musketeer, when once the blood mounted to his fat cheeks, seized a broomstick and began belaboring Blaisois, saying:

"You have insulted the church, my friend, you have insulted the church!"

At this moment Aramis, aroused by this unusual disturbance, cautiously opened the door of his room; and Blaisois, looking reproachfully at the Cerberus, drew the letter from his pocket and presented it to Aramis.

"From the Comte de la Fere," said Aramis. "All right." And he retired into his room without even asking the cause of so much noise.

Blaisois returned disconsolate to the Hotel of the Grand Roi Charlemagne and when Athos inquired if his commission was executed, he related his adventure.

"You foolish fellow!" said Athos, laughing. "And you did not tell him that you came from me?"

"No, sir."

At ten o'clock Athos, with his habitual exactitude, was waiting on the Pont du Louvre and was almost immediately joined by Lord de Winter.

They waited ten minutes and then his lordship began to fear Aramis was not coming to join them.

"Patience," said Athos, whose eyes were fixed in the direction of the Rue du Bac, "patience; I see an abbé cuffing a man, then bowing to a woman; it must be Aramis."

It was indeed Aramis. Having run against a young shopkeeper who was gaping at the crows and who had splashed him, Aramis with one blow of his fist had distanced him ten paces.

At this moment one of his penitents passed, and as she was young and pretty Aramis took off his cap to her with his most gracious smile.

A most affectionate greeting, as one can well believe took place between him and Lord de Winter.

"Where are we going?" inquired Aramis; "are we going to fight, perchance? I carry no sword this morning and cannot return home to procure one."

"No," said Lord de Winter, "we are going to pay a visit to Her Majesty the Queen of England."

"Oh, very well," replied Aramis; then bending his face down to Athos's ear, "what is the object of this visit?" continued he.

"Nay, I know not; some evidence required from us, perhaps."

"May it not be about that cursed affair?" asked Aramis, "in which case I do not greatly care to go, for it will be to pocket a lecture; and since it is my function to give them to others I am rather averse to receiving them myself."

"If it were so," answered Athos, "we should not be taken there by Lord de Winter, for he would come in for his share; he was one of us."

"You're right; yes, let us go."

On arriving at the Louvre Lord de Winter entered first; indeed, there was but one porter there to receive them at the gate.

It was impossible in daylight for the impoverished state of the habitation grudging charity had conceded to an unfortunate queen to pass unnoticed by Athos, Aramis, and even the Englishman. Large rooms, completely stripped of furniture, bare walls upon which, here and there, shone the old gold moldings which had resisted time and neglect, windows with broken panes (impossible to close), no carpets, neither guards nor servants: this is what first met the eyes of Athos, to which he, touching his companion's elbow, directed his attention by his glances.

"Mazarin is better lodged," said Aramis.

"Mazarin is almost king," answered Athos; "Madame Henrietta is almost no longer queen."

"If you would condescend to be clever, Athos," observed Aramis, "I really do think you would be wittier than poor Monsieur de Voiture."

Athos smiled.

The queen appeared to be impatiently expecting them, for at the first slight noise she heard in the hall leading to her room she came herself to the door to receive these courtiers in the corridors of Misfortune.

"Enter. You are welcome, gentlemen," she said.

The gentlemen entered and remained standing, but at a motion from the queen they seated themselves. Athos was calm and grave, but Aramis was furious; the sight of such royal misery exasperated him and his eyes examined every new trace of poverty that presented itself.

"You are examining the luxury I enjoy," said the queen, glancing sadly around her.

"Madame," replied Aramis, "I must ask your pardon, but I know not how to hide my indignation at seeing how a daughter of Henry IV. is treated at the court of France."

"Monsieur Aramis is not an officer?" asked the queen of Lord de Winter.

"That gentleman is the Abbé d'Herblay," replied he.

Aramis blushed. "Madame," he said, "I am an abbé, it is true, but I am so against my will. I never had a vocation for the bands; my cassock is fastened by one button only, and I am always ready to become a musketeer once more. This morning, being ignorant that I should have the honor of seeing your majesty, I encumbered myself with this dress, but you will find me none the less a man devoted to your majesty's service, in whatever way you may see fit to use me."

"The Abbé d'Herblay," resumed De Winter, "is one of those gallant musketeers formerly belonging to His Majesty King Louis XIII., of whom I have spoken to you, madame." Then turning to Athos, he continued, "And this gentleman is that noble Comte de la Fere, whose high reputation is so well known to your majesty."

"Gentlemen," said the queen, "a few years ago I had around me ushers, treasures, armies; and by the lifting of a finger all these were busied in my service. To-day, look around you, and it may astonish you, that in order to accomplish a plan which is dearer to me than life I have only Lord de Winter, the friend of twenty years, and you, gentlemen, whom I see for the first time and whom I know but as my countrymen."

"It is enough," said Athos, bowing low, "if the lives of three men can purchase yours, madame."

"I thank you, gentlemen. But hear me," continued she. "I am not only the most miserable of queens, but the most unhappy of mothers, the most wretched of wives. My children, two of them, at least, the Duke of York and the Princess Elizabeth, are far away from me, exposed to the blows of the ambitious and our foes; my husband, the king, is leading in England so wretched an existence that it is no exaggeration to aver that he seeks death as a thing to be desired. Hold! gentlemen, here is the letter conveyed to me by Lord de Winter. Read it."

Obeying the queen, Athos read aloud the letter which we have already seen, in which King Charles demanded to know whether the hospitality of France would be accorded him.

"Well?" asked Athos, when he had closed the letter.

"Well," said the queen, "it has been refused."

The two friends exchanged a smile of contempt.

"And now," said Athos, "what is to be done? I have the honor to inquire from your majesty what you desire Monsieur d'Herblay and myself to do in your service. We are ready."

"Ah, sir, you have a noble heart!" exclaimed the queen, with a burst of gratitude; whilst Lord de Winter turned to her with a glance which said, "Did I not answer for them?"

"But you, sir?" said the queen to Aramis.

"I, madame," replied he, "follow Monsieur de la Fere wherever he leads, even were it on to death, without demanding wherefore; but when it concerns your majesty's service, then," added he, looking at the queen with all the grace of former days, "I precede the count."

"Well, then, gentlemen," said the queen, "since it is thus, and since you are willing to devote yourselves to the service of a poor princess whom the whole world has abandoned, this is what is required to be done for me. The king is alone with a few gentlemen, whom he fears to lose every day; surrounded by the Scotch, whom he distrusts, although he be himself a Scotchman. Since Lord de Winter left him I am distracted, sirs. I ask much, too much, perhaps, for I have no title to request it. Go to England, join the king, be his friends, protectors, march to battle at his side, and be near him in his house, where conspiracies, more dangerous than the perils of war, are hatching every day. And in exchange for the sacrifice that you make, gentlemen, I promise—not to reward you, I believe that word would offend you—but to love you as a sister, to prefer you, next to my husband and my children, to every one. I swear it before Heaven."

And the queen raised her eyes solemnly upward.

"Madame," said Athos, "when must we set out?"

"You consent then?" exclaimed the queen, joyfully.

"Yes, madame; only it seems to me that your majesty goes too far in engaging to load us with a friendship so far above our merit. We render service to God, madame, in serving a prince so unfortunate, a queen so virtuous. Madame, we are yours, body and soul."

"Oh, sirs," said the queen, moved even to tears, "this is the first time for five years I have felt the least approach to joy or hope. God, who can read my heart, all the gratitude I feel, will reward you! Save my husband! Save the king, and although you care not for the price that is placed upon a good action in this world, leave me the hope that we shall meet again, when I may be able to thank you myself. In the meantime, I remain here. Have you anything to ask of me? From this moment I become your friend, and since you are engaged in my affairs I ought to occupy myself in yours."

"Madame," replied Athos, "I have only to ask your majesty's prayers."

"And I," said Aramis, "I am alone in the world and have only your majesty to serve."

The queen held out her hand, which they kissed, and she said in a low tone to De Winter:

"If you need money, my lord, separate the jewels I have given you; detach the diamonds and sell them to some Jew. You will receive for them fifty or sixty thousand francs; spend them if necessary, but let these gentlemen be treated as they deserve, that is to say, like kings."

The queen had two letters ready, one written by herself, the other by her daughter, the Princess Henrietta. Both were addressed to King Charles.

She gave the first to Athos and the other to Aramis, so that should they be separated by chance they might make themselves known to the king; after which they withdrew.

At the foot of the staircase De Winter stopped.

"Not to arouse suspicions, gentlemen," said he, "go your way and I will go mine, and this evening at nine o'clock we will assemble again at the Gate Saint Denis. We will travel on horseback as far as our horses can go and afterward we can take the post. Once more, let me thank you, my good friends, both in my own name and the queen's."

The three gentlemen then shook hands, Lord de Winter taking the Rue Saint Honore, and Athos and Aramis remaining together.

"Well," said Aramis, when they were alone, "what do you think of this business, my dear count?"

"Bad," replied Athos, "very bad."

"But you received it with enthusiasm."

"As I shall ever receive the defense of a great principle, my dear D'Herblay. Monarchs are only strong by the assistance of the aristocracy, but aristocracy cannot survive without the countenance of monarchs. Let us, then, support monarchy, in order to support ourselves.

"We shall be murdered there," said Aramis. "I hate the English—they are coarse, like every nation that swills beer."

"Would it be better to remain here," said Athos, "and take a turn in the Bastile or the dungeon of Vincennes for having favored the escape of Monsieur de Beaufort? I'faith, Aramis, believe me, there is little left to regret. We avoid imprisonment and we play the part of heroes; the choice is easy."

"It is true; but in everything, friend, one must always return to the same question—a stupid one, I admit, but very necessary—have you any money?"

"Something like a hundred pistoles, that my farmer sent to me the day before I left Bragelonne; but out of that sum I ought to leave fifty for Raoul—a young man must live respectably. I have then about fifty pistoles. And you?"

"As for me, I am quite sure that after turning out all my pockets and emptying my drawers I shall not find ten louis at home. Fortunately Lord de Winter is rich."

"Lord de Winter is ruined for the moment; Oliver Cromwell has annexed his income resources."

"Now is the time when Baron Porthos would be useful."

"Now it is that I regret D'Artagnan."

"Let us entice them away."

"This secret, Aramis, does not belong to us; take my advice, then, and let no one into our confidence. And moreover, in taking such a step we should appear to be doubtful of ourselves. Let us regret their absence to ourselves for our own sakes, but not speak of it."

"You are right; but what are you going to do until this evening? I have two things to postpone."

"And what are they?"

"First, a thrust with the coadjutor, whom I met last night at Madame de Rambouillet's and whom I found particular in his remarks respecting me."

"Oh, fie—a quarrel between priests, a duel between allies!"

"What can I do, friend? he is a bully and so am I; his cassock is a burden to him and I imagine I have had enough of mine; in fact, there is so much resemblance between us that I sometimes believe he is Aramis and I am the coadjutor. This kind of life fatigues and oppresses me; besides, he is a turbulent fellow, who will ruin our party. I am convinced that if I gave him a box on the ear, such as I gave this morning to the little citizen who splashed me, it would change the appearance of things."

"And I, my dear Aramis," quietly replied Athos, "I think it would only change Monsieur de Retz's appearance. Take my advice, leave things just as they are; besides, you are neither of you now your own masters; he belongs to the Fronde and you to the queen of England. So, if the second matter which you regret being unable to attend to is not more important than the first——"

"Oh! that is of the first importance."

"Attend to it, then, at once."

"Unfortunately, it is a thing that I can't perform at any time I choose. It was arranged for the evening and no other time will serve."

"I understand," said Athos smiling, "midnight."

"About that time."

"But, my dear fellow, those are things that bear postponement and you must put it off, especially with so good an excuse to give on your return——"

"Yes, if I return."

"If you do not return, how does it concern you? Be reasonable. Come, you are no longer twenty years old."

"To my great regret, mordieu! Ah, if I were but twenty years old!"

"Yes," said Athos, "doubtless you would commit great follies! But now we must part. I have one or two visits to make and a letter yet to write. Call for me at eight o'clock or shall I wait supper for you at seven?"

"That will do very well," said Aramis. "I have twenty visits to make and as many letters to write."

They then separated. Athos went to pay a visit to Madame de Vendome, left his name at Madame de Chevreuse's and wrote the following letter to D'Artagnan:

"Dear Friend,—I am about to set off with Aramis on important business. I wished to make my adieux to you, but time does not permit. Remember that I write to you now to repeat how much affection for you I still cherish.

"Raoul is gone to Blois and is ignorant of my departure; watch over him in my absence as much as you possibly can; and if by chance you receive no news of me three months hence, tell him to open a packet which he will find addressed to him in my bronze casket at Blois, of which I send you now the key.

"Embrace Porthos from Aramis and myself. Adieu, perhaps farewell."

At the hour agreed upon Aramis arrived; he was dressed as an officer and had the old sword at his side which he had drawn so often and which he was more than ever ready to draw.

"By-the-bye," he said, "I think that we are decidedly wrong to depart thus, without leaving a line for Porthos and D'Artagnan."

"The thing is done, dear friend," said Athos; "I foresaw that and have embraced them both from you and myself."

"You are a wonderful man, my dear count," said Aramis; "you think of everything."

"Well, have you made up your mind to this journey?"

"Quite; and now that I reflect about it, I am glad to leave Paris at this moment."

"And so am I," replied Athos; "my only regret is not having seen D'Artagnan; but the rascal is so cunning, he might have guessed our project."

When supper was over Blaisois entered. "Sir," said he, "here is Monsieur d'Artagnan's answer."

"But I did not tell you there would be an answer, stupid!" said Athos.

"And I set off without waiting for one, but he called me back and gave me this;" and he presented a little leather bag, plump and giving out a golden jingle.

Athos opened it and began by drawing forth a little note, written in these terms:

"My dear Count,—When one travels, and especially for three months, one never has a superfluity of money. Now, recalling former times of mutual distress, I send you half my purse; it is money to obtain which I made Mazarin sweat. Don't make a bad use of it, I entreat you.

"As to what you say about not seeing you again, I believe not a word of it; with such a heart as yours—and such a sword—one passes through the valley of the shadow of death a dozen times, unscathed and unalarmed. Au revoir, not farewell.

"It is unnecessary to say that from the day I saw Raoul I loved him; nevertheless, believe that I heartily pray that I may not become to him a father, however much I might be proud of such a son.

"Your

"D'Artagnan.

"P.S.—Be it well understood that the fifty louis which I send are equally for Aramis as for you—for you as Aramis."

Athos smiled, and his fine eye was dimmed by a tear. D'Artagnan, who had loved him so tenderly, loved him still, although a Mazarinist.

"There are the fifty louis, i'faith," said Aramis, emptying the purse on the table, all bearing the effigy of Louis XIII. "Well, what shall you do with this money, count? Shall you keep it or send it back?"

"I shall keep it, Aramis, and even though I had no need of it I still should keep it. What is offered from a generous heart should be accepted generously. Take twenty-five of them, Aramis, and give me the remaining twenty-five."

"All right; I am glad to see you are of my opinion. There now, shall we start?"

"When you like; but have you no groom?"

"No; that idiot Bazin had the folly to make himself verger, as you know, and therefore cannot leave Notre Dame.

"Very well, take Blaisois, with whom I know not what to do, since I already have Grimaud."

"Willingly," said Aramis.

At this moment Grimaud appeared at the door. "Ready," said he, with his usual curtness.

"Let us go, then," said Athos.

The two friends mounted, as did their servants. At the corner of the Quai they encountered Bazin, who was running breathlessly.

"Oh, sir!" exclaimed he, "thank Heaven I have arrived in time. Monsieur Porthos has just been to your house and has left this for you, saying that the letter was important and must be given to you before you left."

"Good," said Aramis, taking a purse which Bazin presented to him. "What is this?"

"Wait, your reverence, there is a letter."

"You know I have already told you that if you ever call me anything but chevalier I will break every bone in your body. Give me the letter."

"How can you read?" asked Athos, "it is as dark as a cold oven."

"Wait," said Bazin, striking a flint, and setting afire a twisted wax-light, with which he started the church candles. Thus illumined, Aramis read the following epistle:

"My dear D'Herblay,—I learned from D'Artagnan who has embraced me on the part of the Comte de la Fere and yourself, that you are setting out on a journey which may perhaps last two or three months; as I know that you do not like to ask money of your friends I offer you some of my own accord. Here are two hundred pistoles, which you can dispose of as you wish and return to me when opportunity occurs. Do not fear that you put me to inconvenience; if I want money I can send for some to any of my chateaux; at Bracieux alone, I have twenty thousand francs in gold. So, if I do not send you more it is because I fear you would not accept a larger sum.

"I address you, because you know, that although I esteem him from my heart I am a little awed by the Comte de la Fere; but it is understood that what I offer you I offer him at the same time.

"I am, as I trust you do not doubt, your devoted

"Du Vallon de Bracieux de Pierrefonds."

"Well," said Aramis, "what do you say to that?"

"I say, my dear D'Herblay, that it is almost sacrilege to distrust Providence when one has such friends, and therefore we will divide the pistoles from Porthos, as we divided the louis sent by D'Artagnan."

The division being made by the light of Bazin's taper, the two friends continued their road and a quarter of an hour later they had joined De Winter at the Porte Saint Denis.

Chapter XLIII.

In which it is proved that first Impulses are oftentimes the best.

The three gentlemen took the road to Picardy, a road so well known to them and which recalled to Athos and Aramis some of the most picturesque adventures of their youth.

"If Mousqueton were with us," observed Athos, on reaching the spot where they had had a dispute with the paviers, "how he would tremble at passing this! Do you remember, Aramis, that it was here he received that famous bullet wound?"

"By my faith, 'twould be excusable in him to tremble," replied Aramis, "for even I feel a shudder at the recollection; hold, just above that tree is the little spot where I thought I was killed."

It was soon time for Grimaud to recall the past. Arriving before the inn at which his master and himself had made such an enormous repast, he approached Athos and said, showing him the airhole of the cellar:

"Sausages!"

Athos began to laugh, for this juvenile escapade of his appeared to be as amusing as if some one had related it of another person.

At last, after traveling two days and a night, they arrived at Boulogne toward the evening, favored by magnificent weather. Boulogne was a strong position, then almost a deserted town, built entirely on the heights; what is now called the lower town did not then exist.

"Gentlemen," said De Winter, on reaching the gate of the town, "let us do here as at Paris—let us separate to avoid suspicion. I know an inn, little frequented, but of which the host is entirely devoted to me. I will go there, where I expect to find letters, and you go to the first tavern in the town, to

L'Epee du Grand Henri for instance, refresh yourselves, and in two hours be upon the jetty; our boat is waiting for us there."

The matter being thus decided, the two friends found, about two hundred paces further, the tavern indicated. Their horses were fed, but not unsaddled; the grooms supped, for it was already late, and their two masters, impatient to return, appointed a place of meeting with them on the jetty and desired them on no account to exchange a word with any one. It is needless to say that this caution concerned Blaisois alone—long enough since it had been a useless one to Grimaud.

Athos and Aramis walked down toward the port. From their dress, covered with dust, and from a certain easy manner by means of which a man accustomed to travel is always recognizable, the two friends excited the attention of a few promenaders. There was more especially one upon whom their arrival had produced a decided impression. This man, whom they had noticed from the first for the same reason they had themselves been remarked by others, was walking in a listless way up and down the jetty. From the moment he perceived them he did not cease to look at them and seemed to burn with the wish to speak to them.

On reaching the jetty Athos and Aramis stopped to look at a little boat made fast to a pile and ready rigged as if waiting to start.

"That is doubtless our boat," said Athos.

"Yes," replied Aramis, "and the sloop out there making ready to sail must be that which is to take us to our destination; now," continued he, "if only De Winter does not keep us waiting. It is not at all amusing here; there is not a single woman passing."

"Hush!" said Athos, "we are overheard."

In truth, the walker, who, during the observations of the two friends, had passed and repassed behind them several times, stopped at the name of De Winter; but as his face betrayed no emotion at mention of this name, it might have been by chance he stood so still.

"Gentlemen," said the man, who was young and pale, bowing with ease and courtesy, "pardon my curiosity, but I see you come from Paris, or at least that you are strangers at Boulogne."

"We come from Paris, yes," replied Athos, with the same courtesy; "what is there we can do for you?"

"Sir," said the young man, "will you be so good as to tell me if it be true that Cardinal Mazarin is no longer minister?"

"That is a strange question," said Aramis.

"He is and he is not," replied Athos; "that is to say, he is dismissed by one-half of France, but by intrigues and promises he makes the other half sustain him; you will perceive that this may last a long time."

"However, sir," said the stranger, "he has neither fled nor is in prison?"

"No, sir, not at this moment at least."

"Sirs, accept my thanks for your politeness," said the young man, retreating.

"What do you think of that interrogator?" asked Aramis.

"I think he is either a dull provincial person or a spy in search of information."

"And you replied to him with that notion?"

"Nothing warranted me to answer him otherwise; he was polite to me and I was so to him."

"But if he be a spy——"

"What do you think a spy would be about here? We are not living in the time of Cardinal Richelieu, who would have closed the ports on bare suspicion."

"It matters not; you were wrong to reply to him as you did," continued Aramis, following with his eyes the young man, now vanishing behind the cliffs.

"And you," said Athos, "you forget that you committed a very different kind of imprudence in pronouncing Lord de Winter's name. Did you not see that at that name the young man stopped?"

"More reason, then, when he spoke to you, for sending him about his business."

"A quarrel?" asked Athos.

"And since when have you become afraid of a quarrel?"

"I am always afraid of a quarrel when I am expected at any place and when such a quarrel might possibly prevent my reaching it. Besides, let me own something to you. I am anxious to see that young man nearer."

"And wherefore?"

"Aramis, you will certainly laugh at me, you will say that I am always repeating the same thing, you will call me the most timorous of visionaries; but to whom do you see a resemblance in that young man?"

"In beauty or on the contrary?" asked Aramis, laughing.

"In ugliness, in so far as a man can resemble a woman."

"Ah! Egad!" cried Aramis, "you set me thinking. No, in truth you are no visionary, my dear friend, and now I think of it—you—yes, i'faith, you're right—those delicate, yet firm-set lips, those eyes which seem always at the command of the intellect and never of the heart! Yes, it is one of Milady's bastards!"

"You laugh Aramis."

"From habit, that is all. I swear to you, I like no better than yourself to meet that viper in my path."

"Ah! here is De Winter coming," said Athos.

"Good! one thing now is only awanting and that is, that our grooms should not keep us waiting."

"No," said Athos. "I see them about twenty paces behind my lord. I recognize Grimaud by his long legs and his determined slouch. Tony carries our muskets."

"Then we set sail to-night?" asked Aramis, glancing toward the west, where the sun had left a single golden cloud, which, dipping into the ocean, appeared by degrees to be extinguished.

"Probably," said Athos.

"Diable!" resumed Aramis, "I have little fancy for the sea by day, still less at night; the sounds of wind and wave, the frightful movements of the vessel; I confess I prefer the convent of Noisy."

Athos smiled sadly, for it was evident that he was thinking of other things as he listened to his friend and moved toward De Winter.

"What ails our friend?" said Aramis, "he resembles one of Dante's damned, whose neck Apollyon has dislocated and who are ever looking at their heels. What the devil makes him glower thus behind him?"

When De Winter perceived them, in his turn he advanced toward them with surprising rapidity.

"What is the matter, my lord?" said Athos, "and what puts you out of breath thus?"

"Nothing," replied De Winter; "nothing; and yet in passing the heights it seemed to me——" and he again turned round.

Athos glanced at Aramis.

"But let us go," continued De Winter; "let us be off; the boat must be waiting for us and there is our sloop at anchor—do you see it there? I wish I were on board already," and he looked back again.

"He has seen him," said Athos, in a low tone, to Aramis.

They had reached the ladder which led to the boat. De Winter made the grooms who carried the arms and the porters with the luggage descend first and was about to follow them.

At this moment Athos perceived a man walking on the seashore parallel to the jetty, and hastening his steps, as if to reach the other side of the port, scarcely twenty steps from the place of embarking. He fancied in the darkness that he recognized the young man who had questioned him. Athos now descended the ladder in his turn, without losing sight of the young man. The latter, to make a short cut, had appeared on a sluice.

"He certainly bodes us no good," said Athos; "but let us embark; once out at sea, let him come."

And Athos sprang into the boat, which was immediately pushed off and which soon sped seawards under the efforts of four stalwart rowers.

But the young man had begun to follow, or rather to advance before the boat. She was obliged to pass between the point of the jetty, surmounted by a beacon just lighted, and a rock which jutted out. They saw him in the distance climbing the rock in order to look down upon the boat as it passed.

"Ay, but," said Aramis, "that young fellow is decidedly a spy."

"Which is the young man?" asked De Winter, turning around.

"He who followed us and spoke to us awaits us there; behold!"

De Winter turned and followed the direction of Aramis's finger. The beacon bathed with light the little strait through which they were about to pass and the rock where the young man stood with bare head and crossed arms.

"It is he!" exclaimed De Winter, seizing the arm of Athos; "it is he! I thought I recognized him and I was not mistaken."

"Whom do you mean?" asked Aramis.

"Milady's son," replied Athos.

"The monk!" exclaimed Grimaud.

The young man heard these words and bent so forward over the rock that one might have supposed he was about to precipitate himself from it.

"Yes, it is I, my uncle—I, the son of Milady—I, the monk—I, the secretary and friend of Cromwell—I know you now, both you and your companions."

In that boat sat three men, unquestionably brave, whose courage no man would have dared dispute; nevertheless, at that voice, that accent and those gestures, they felt a chill access of terror cramp their veins. As for Grimaud, his hair stood on end and drops of sweat ran down his brow.

"Ah!" exclaimed Aramis, "that is the nephew, the monk, and the son of Milady, as he says himself."

"Alas, yes," murmured De Winter.

"Then wait," said Aramis; and with the terrible coolness which on important occasions he showed, he took one of the muskets from Tony, shouldered and aimed it at the young man, who stood, like the accusing angel, upon the rock.

"Fire!" cried Grimaud, unconsciously.

Athos threw himself on the muzzle of the gun and arrested the shot which was about to be fired.

"The devil take you," said Aramis. "I had him so well at the point of my gun I should have sent a ball into his breast."

"It is enough to have killed the mother," said Athos, hoarsely.

"The mother was a wretch, who struck at us all and at those dear to us."

"Yes, but the son has done us no harm."

Grimaud, who had risen to watch the effect of the shot, fell back hopeless, wringing his hands.

The young man burst into a laugh.

"Ah, it is certainly you!" he cried. "I know you even better now."

His mocking laugh and threatening words passed over their heads, carried by the breeze, until lost in the depths of the horizon. Aramis shuddered.

"Be calm," exclaimed Athos, "for Heaven's sake! have we ceased to be men?"

"No," said Aramis, "but that fellow is a fiend; and ask the uncle whether I was wrong to rid him of his dear nephew."

De Winter only replied by a groan.

"It was all up with him," continued Aramis; "ah I much fear that with all your wisdom such mercy yet will prove supernal folly."

Athos took Lord de Winter's hand and tried to turn the conversation.

"When shall we land in England?" he asked; but De Winter seemed not to hear his words and made no reply.

"Hold, Athos," said Aramis, "perhaps there is yet time. See if he is still in the same place."

Athos turned around with an effort; the sight of the young man was evidently painful to him, and there he still was, in fact, on the rock, the beacon shedding around him, as it were, a doubtful aureole.

"Decidedly, Aramis," said Athos, "I think I was wrong not to let you fire."

"Hold your tongue," replied Aramis; "you would make me weep, if such a thing were possible."

At this moment they were hailed by a voice from the sloop and a few seconds later men, servants and baggage were aboard. The captain was only waiting for his passengers; hardly had they put foot on deck ere her head was turned towards Hastings, where they were to disembark. At this instant the three friends turned, in spite of themselves, a last look on the rock, upon the menacing figure which pursued them and now stood out with a distinctness still. Then a voice reached them once more, sending this threat: "To our next meeting, sirs, in England."

Chapter XLIV.

Te Deum for the Victory of Lens.

The bustle which had been observed by Henrietta Maria and for which she had vainly sought to discover a reason, was occasioned by the battle of Lens, announced by the prince's messenger, the Duc de Chatillon, who had taken such a noble part in the engagement; he was, besides, charged to hang five and twenty flags, taken from the Lorraine party, as well as from the Spaniards, upon the arches of Notre Dame.

Such news was decisive; it destroyed, in favor of the court, the struggle commenced with parliament. The motive given for all the taxes summarily imposed and to which the parliament had made opposition, was the necessity of sustaining the honor of France and the uncertain hope of beating the enemy. Now, since the affair of Nordlingen, they had experienced nothing but reverses; the parliament had a plea for calling Mazarin to account for imaginary victories, always promised, ever deferred; but this time there really had been fighting, a triumph and a complete one. And this all knew so well that it was a double victory for the court, a victory at home and abroad; so that even when the young king learned the news he exclaimed, "Ah, gentlemen of the parliament, we shall see what you will say now!" Upon which the queen had pressed the royal child to her heart, whose haughty and unruly sentiments were in such harmony with her own. A council was called on the same evening, but nothing transpired of what had been decided on. It was only known that on the following Sunday a Te Deum would be sung at Notre Dame in honor of the victory of Lens.

The following Sunday, then, the Parisians arose with joy; at that period a Te Deum was a grand affair; this kind of ceremony had not then been abused and it produced a great effect. The shops were deserted, houses closed; every one wished to see the young king with his mother, and the famous Cardinal Mazarin whom they hated so much that no one wished to be deprived of his presence. Moreover, great liberty prevailed throughout the immense crowd; every opinion was openly expressed and chorused, so to speak, of coming insurrection, as the thousand bells of all the Paris churches rang out the Te Deum. The police belonging to the city being formed by the city itself, nothing threatening presented itself to disturb this concert of universal hatred or freeze the frequent scoffs of slanderous lips.

Nevertheless, at eight o'clock in the morning the regiment of the queen's guards, commanded by Guitant, under whom was his nephew Comminges, marched publicly, preceded by drums and trumpets, filing off from the Palais Royal as far as Notre Dame, a manoeuvre which the Parisians witnessed tranquilly, delighted as they were with military music and brilliant uniforms.

Friquet had put on his Sunday clothes, under the pretext of having a swollen face which he had managed to simulate by introducing a handful of cherry kernels into one side of his mouth, and had procured a whole holiday from Bazin. On leaving Bazin, Friquet started off to the Palais Royal, where he arrived at the moment of the turning out of the regiment of guards; and as he had only gone there for the enjoyment of seeing it and hearing the music, he took his place at their head, beating the drum on two pieces of slate and passing from that exercise to that of the trumpet, which he counterfeited quite naturally with his mouth in a manner which had more than once called forth the praises of amateurs of imitative harmony.

This amusement lasted from the Barriere des Sergens to the place of Notre Dame, and Friquet found in it very real enjoyment; but when at last the regiment separated, penetrated the heart of the city and placed itself at the extremity of the Rue Saint Christophe, near the Rue Cocatrix, in which Broussel lived, then Friquet remembered that he had not had breakfast; and after thinking in which direction he had better turn his steps in order to accomplish this important act of the day, he reflected deeply and decided that Councillor Broussel should bear the cost of this repast.

In consequence he took to his heels, arrived breathlessly at the councillor's door, and knocked violently.

His mother, the councillor's old servant, opened it.

"What doest thou here, good-for-nothing?" she said, "and why art thou not at Notre Dame?"

"I have been there, mother," said Friquet, "but I saw things happen of which Master Broussel ought to be warned, and so with Monsieur Bazin's permission—you know, mother, Monsieur Bazin, the verger—I came to speak to Monsieur Broussel."

"And what hast thou to say, boy, to Monsieur Broussel?"

"I wish to tell him," replied Friquet, screaming with all his might, "that there is a whole regiment of guards coming this way. And as I hear everywhere that at the court they are ill-disposed to him, I wish to warn him, that he may be on his guard."

Broussel heard the scream of the young oddity, and, enchanted with this excess of zeal, came down to the first floor, for he was, in truth, working in his room on the second.

"Well," said he, "friend, what matters the regiment of guards to us, and art thou not mad to make such a disturbance? Knowest thou not that it is the custom of these soldiers to act thus and that it is usual for the regiment to form themselves into two solid walls when the king goes by?"

Friquet counterfeited surprise, and twisting his new cap around in his fingers, said:

"It is not astonishing for you to know it, Monsieur Broussel, who knows everything; but as for me, by holy truth, I did not know it and I thought I would give you good advice; you must not be angry with me for that, Monsieur Broussel."

"On the contrary, my boy, on the contrary, I am pleased with your zeal. Dame Nanette, look for those apricots which Madame de Longueville sent to us yesterday from Noisy and give half a dozen of them to your son, with a crust of new bread."

"Oh, thank you, sir, thank you, Monsieur Broussel," said Friquet; "I am so fond of apricots!"

Broussel then proceeded to his wife's room and asked for breakfast; it was nine o'clock. The councillor placed himself at the window; the street was completely deserted, but in the distance was heard, like the noise of the tide rushing in, the deep hum of the populous waves increasing now around Notre Dame.

This noise redoubled when D'Artagnan, with a company of musketeers, placed himself at the gates of Notre Dame to secure the service of the church. He had instructed Porthos to profit by this opportunity to see the ceremony; and Porthos, in full dress, mounted his finest horse, taking the part of supernumerary musketeer, as D'Artagnan had so often done formerly. The sergeant of this company, a veteran of the Spanish wars, had recognized Porthos, his old companion, and very soon all those who served under him were placed in possession of startling facts concerning the honor of the ancient musketeers of Tréville. Porthos had not only been well received by the company, but he was moreover looked on with great admiration.

At ten o'clock the guns of the Louvre announced the departure of the king, and then a movement, similar to that of trees in a stormy wind that bend and writhe with agitated tops, ran though the multitude, which was compressed behind the immovable muskets of the guard. At last the king appeared with the queen in a gilded chariot. Ten other carriages followed, containing the ladies of honor, the officers of the royal household, and the court.

"God save the king!" was the cry in every direction; the young monarch gravely put his head out of the window, looked sufficiently grateful and even bowed; at which the cries of the multitude were renewed.

Just as the court was settling down in the cathedral, a carriage, bearing the arms of Comminges, quitted the line of the court carriages and proceeded slowly to the end of the Rue Saint Christophe, now entirely deserted. When it arrived there, four guards and a police officer, who accompanied it, mounted into the heavy machine and closed the shutters; then through an opening cautiously made, the policeman began to watch the length of the Rue Cocatrix, as if he was waiting for some one.

All the world was occupied with the ceremony, so that neither the chariot nor the precautions taken by those who were within it had been observed. Friquet, whose eye, ever on the alert, could alone have discovered them, had gone to devour his apricots upon the entablature of a house in the square of Notre Dame. Thence he saw the king, the queen and Monsieur Mazarin, and heard the mass as well as if he had been on duty.

Toward the end of the service, the queen, seeing Comminges standing near her, waiting for a confirmation of the order she had given him before quitting the Louvre, said in a whisper:

"Go, Comminges, and may God aid you!"

Comminges immediately left the church and entered the Rue Saint Christophe. Friquet, seeing this fine officer thus walk away, followed by two guards, amused himself by pursuing them and did this so much the more gladly as the ceremony ended at that instant and the king remounted his carriage.

Hardly had the police officer observed Comminges at the end of the Rue Cocatrix when he said one word to the coachman, who at once put his vehicle into motion and drove up before Broussel's door. Comminges knocked at the door at the same moment, and Friquet was waiting behind Comminges until the door should be opened.

"What dost thou there, rascal?" asked Comminges.

"I want to go into Master Broussel's house, captain," replied Friquet, in that wheedling way the "gamins" of Paris know so well how to assume when necessary.

"And on what floor does he live?" asked Comminges.

"In the whole house," said Friquet; "the house belongs to him; he occupies the second floor when he works and descends to the first to take his meals; he must be at dinner now; it is noon."

"Good," said Comminges.

At this moment the door was opened, and having questioned the servant the officer learned that Master Broussel was at home and at dinner.

Broussel was seated at the table with his family, having his wife opposite to him, his two daughters by his side, and his son, Louvieres, whom we have already seen when the accident happened to the councillor—an accident from which he had quite recovered—at the bottom of the table. The worthy man, restored to perfect health, was tasting the fine fruit which Madame de Longueville had sent to him.

At sight of the officer Broussel was somewhat moved, but seeing him bow politely he rose and bowed also. Still, in spite of this reciprocal politeness, the countenances of the women betrayed a certain amount of uneasiness; Louvieres became very pale and waited impatiently for the officer to explain himself.

"Sir," said Comminges, "I am the bearer of an order from the king."

"Very well, sir," replied Broussel, "what is this order?" And he held out his hand.

"I am commissioned to seize your person, sir," said Comminges, in the same tone and with the same politeness; "and if you will believe me you had better spare yourself the trouble of reading that long letter and follow me."

A thunderbolt falling in the midst of these good people, so peacefully assembled there, would not have produced a more appalling effect. It was a horrible thing at that period to be imprisoned by the enmity of the king. Louvieres sprang forward to snatch his sword, which stood against a chair in a corner of the room; but a glance from the worthy Broussel, who in the midst of it all did not lose his presence of mind, checked this foolhardy action of despair. Madame Broussel, separated by the width of the table from her husband, burst into tears, and the young girls clung to their father's arms.

"Come, sir," said Comminges, "make haste; you must obey the king."

"Sir," said Broussel, "I am in bad health and cannot give myself up a prisoner in this state; I must have time."

"It is impossible," said Comminges; "the order is strict and must be put into execution this instant."

"Impossible!" said Louvieres; "sir, beware of driving us to despair."

"Impossible!" cried a shrill voice from the end of the room.

Comminges turned and saw Dame Nanette, her eyes flashing with anger and a broom in her hand.

"My good Nanette, be quiet, I beseech you," said Broussel.

"Me! keep quiet while my master is being arrested! he, the support, the liberator, the father of the people! Ah! well, yes; you have to know me yet. Are you going?" added she to Comminges.

The latter smiled.

"Come, sir," said he, addressing Broussel, "silence that woman and follow me."

"Silence me! me! me!" said Nanette. "Ah! yet one wants some one besides you for that, my fine king's cockatoo! You shall see." And Dame Nanette sprang to the window, threw it open, and in such a piercing voice that it might have been heard in the square of Notre Dame:

"Help!" she screamed, "my master is being arrested; the Councillor Broussel is being arrested! Help!"

"Sir," said Comminges, "declare yourself at once; will you obey or do you intend to rebel against the king?"

"I obey, I obey, sir!" cried Broussel, trying to disengage himself from the grasp of his two daughters and by a look restrain his son, who seemed determined to dispute authority.

"In that case," commanded Comminges, "silence that old woman."

"Ah! old woman!" screamed Nanette.

And she began to shriek more loudly, clinging to the bars of the window:

"Help! help! for Master Broussel, who is arrested because he has defended the people! Help!"

Comminges seized the servant around the waist and would have dragged her from her post; but at that instant a treble voice, proceeding from a kind of entresol, was heard screeching:

"Murder! fire! assassins! Master Broussel is being killed! Master Broussel is being strangled."

It was Friquet's voice; and Dame Nanette, feeling herself supported, recommenced with all her strength to sound her shrilly squawk.

Many curious faces had already appeared at the windows and the people attracted to the end of the street began to run, first men, then groups, and then a crowd of people; hearing cries and seeing a chariot they could not understand it; but Friquet sprang from the entresol on to the top of the carriage.

"They want to arrest Master Broussel!" he cried; "the guards are in the carriage and the officer is upstairs!"

The crowd began to murmur and approached the house. The two guards who had remained in the lane mounted to the aid of Comminges; those who were in the chariot opened the doors and presented arms.

"Don't you see them?" cried Friquet, "don't you see? there they are!"

The coachman turning around, gave Friquet a slash with his whip which made him scream with pain.

"Ah! devil's coachman!" cried Friquet, "you're meddling too! Wait!"

And regaining his entresol he overwhelmed the coachman with every projectile he could lay hands on.

The tumult now began to increase; the street was not able to contain the spectators who assembled from every direction; the crowd invaded the space which the dreaded pikes of the guards had till then kept clear between them and the carriage. The soldiers, pushed back by these living walls, were in danger of being crushed against the spokes of the wheels and the panels of the carriages. The cries which the police officer repeated twenty times: "In the king's name," were powerless against this formidable multitude—seemed, on the contrary, to exasperate it still more; when, at the shout, "In the name of the king," an officer ran up, and seeing the uniforms ill-treated, he sprang into the scuffle sword in hand, and brought unexpected help to the guards. This gentleman was a young man, scarcely sixteen years of age, now white with anger. He leaped from his charger, placed his back against the shaft of the carriage, making a rampart of his horse, drew his pistols from their holsters and fastened them to his belt, and began to fight with the back sword, like a man accustomed to the handling of his weapon.

During ten minutes he alone kept the crowd at bay; at last Comminges appeared, pushing Broussel before him.

"Let us break the carriage!" cried the people.

"In the king's name!" cried Comminges.

"The first who advances is a dead man!" cried Raoul, for it was in fact he, who, feeling himself pressed and almost crushed by a gigantic citizen, pricked him with the point of his sword and sent him howling back.

Comminges, so to speak, threw Broussel into the carriage and sprang in after him. At this moment a shot was fired and a ball passed through the hat of Comminges and broke the arm of one of the guards. Comminges looked up and saw amidst the smoke the threatening face of Louvieres appearing at the window of the second floor.

"Very well, sir," said Comminges, "you shall hear of this anon."

"And you of me, sir," said Louvieres; "and we shall see then who can speak the loudest."

Friquet and Nanette continued to shout; the cries, the noise of the shot and the intoxicating smell of powder produced their usual maddening effects.

"Down with the officer! down with him!" was the cry.

"One step nearer," said Comminges, putting down the sashes, that the interior of the carriage might be well seen, and placing his sword on his prisoner's breast, "one step nearer, and I kill the prisoner; my orders were to carry him off alive or dead. I will take him dead, that's all."

A terrible cry was heard, and the wife and daughters of Broussel held up their hands in supplication to the people; the latter knew that this officer, who was so pale, but who appeared so determined, would keep his word; they continued to threaten, but they began to disperse.

"Drive to the palace," said Comminges to the coachman, who was by then more dead than alive.

The man whipped his animals, which cleared a way through the crowd; but on arriving on the Quai they were obliged to stop; the carriage was upset, the horses carried off, stifled, mangled by the crowd. Raoul, on foot, for he had not time to mount his horse again, tired, like the guards, of distributing blows with the flat of his sword, had recourse to its point. But this last and dreaded resource served only to exasperate the multitude. From time to time a shot from a musket or the blade of a rapier flashed among the crowd; projectiles continued to hail down from the windows and some shots were heard, the echo of which, though they were probably fired in the air, made all hearts vibrate. Voices, unheard except on days of revolution, were distinguished;

faces were seen that only appeared on days of bloodshed. Cries of "Death! death to the guards! to the Seine with the officer!" were heard above all the noise, deafening as it was. Raoul, his hat in ribbons, his face bleeding, felt not only his strength but also his reason going; a red mist covered his sight, and through this mist he saw a hundred threatening arms stretched over him, ready to seize upon him when he fell. The guards were unable to help any one—each one was occupied with his self-preservation. All was over; carriages, horses, guards, and perhaps even the prisoner were about to be torn to shreds, when all at once a voice well known to Raoul was heard, and suddenly a great sword glittered in the air; at the same time the crowd opened, upset, trodden down, and an officer of the musketeers, striking and cutting right and left, rushed up to Raoul and took him in his arms just as he was about to fall.

"God's blood!" cried the officer, "have they killed him? Woe to them if it be so!"

And he turned around, so stern with anger, strength and threat, that the most excited rebels hustled back on one another, in order to escape, and some of them even rolled into the Seine.

"Monsieur d'Artagnan!" murmured Raoul.

"Yes, 'sdeath! in person, and fortunately it seems for you, my young friend. Come on, here, you others," he continued, rising in his stirrups, raising his sword, and addressing those musketeers who had not been able to follow his rapid onslaught. "Come, sweep away all that for me! Shoulder muskets! Present arms! Aim——"

At this command the mountain of populace thinned so suddenly that D'Artagnan could not repress a burst of Homeric laughter.

"Thank you, D'Artagnan," said Comminges, showing half of his body through the window of the broken vehicle, "thanks, my young friend; your name—that I may mention it to the queen."

Raoul was about to reply when D'Artagnan bent down to his ear.

"Hold your tongue," said he, "and let me answer. Do not lose time, Comminges," he continued; "get out of the carriage if you can and make another draw up; be quick, or in five minutes the mob will be on us again with swords and muskets and you will be killed. Hold! there's a carriage coming over yonder."

Then bending again to Raoul, he whispered: "Above all things do not divulge your name."

"That's right. I will go," said Comminges; "and if they come back, fire!"

"Not at all—not at all," replied D'Artagnan; "let no one move. On the contrary, one shot at this moment would be paid for dearly to-morrow."

Comminges took his four guards and as many musketeers and ran to the carriage, from which he made the people inside dismount, and brought them to the vehicle which had upset. But when it was necessary to convey the prisoner from one carriage to the other, the people, catching sight of him whom they called their liberator, uttered every imaginable cry and knotted themselves once more around the vehicle.

"Start, start!" said D'Artagnan. "There are ten men to accompany you. I will keep twenty to hold in check the mob; go, and lose not a moment. Ten men for Monsieur de Comminges."

As the carriage started off the cries were redoubled and more than ten thousand people thronged the Quai and overflowed the Pont Neuf and adjacent streets. A few shots were fired and one musketeer was wounded.

"Forward!" cried D'Artagnan, driven to extremities, biting his moustache; and then he charged with his twenty men and dispersed them in fear. One man alone remained in his place, gun in hand.

"Ah!" he exclaimed, "it is thou who wouldst have him assassinated? Wait an instant." And he pointed his gun at D'Artagnan, who was riding toward him at full speed. D'Artagnan bent down to his horse's neck, the young man fired, and the ball severed the feathers from the hat. The horse started, brushed against the imprudent man, who thought by his strength alone to stay the tempest, and he fell against the wall. D'Artagnan pulled up his horse, and whilst his musketeers continued to charge, he returned and bent with drawn sword over the man he had knocked down.

"Oh, sir!" exclaimed Raoul, recognizing the young man as having seen him in the Rue Cocatrix, "spare him! it is his son!"

D'Artagnan's arm dropped to his side. "Ah, you are his son!" he said; "that is a different thing."

"Sir, I surrender," said Louvieres, presenting his unloaded musket to the officer.

"Eh, no! do not surrender, egad! On the contrary, be off, and quickly. If I take you, you will be hung!"

The young man did not wait to be told twice, but passing under the horse's head disappeared at the corner of the Rue Guenegaud.

"I'faith!" said D'Artagnan to Raoul, "you were just in time to stay my hand. He was a dead man; and on my honor, if I had discovered that it was his son, I should have regretted having killed him."

"Ah! sir!" said Raoul, "allow me, after thanking you for that poor fellow's life, to thank you on my own account. I too, sir, was almost dead when you arrived."

"Wait, wait, young man; do not fatigue yourself with speaking. We can talk of it afterward."

Then seeing that the musketeers had cleared the Quai from the Pont Neuf to the Quai Saint Michael, he raised his sword for them to double their speed. The musketeers trotted up, and at the same time the ten men whom D'Artagnan had given to Comminges appeared.

"Halloo!" cried D'Artagnan; "has something fresh happened?"

"Eh, sir!" replied the sergeant, "their vehicle has broken down a second time; it really must be doomed."

"They are bad managers," said D'Artagnan, shrugging his shoulders. "When a carriage is chosen, it ought to be strong. The carriage in which a Broussel is to be arrested ought to be able to bear ten thousand men."

"What are your commands, lieutenant?"

"Take the detachment and conduct him to his place."

"But you will be left alone?"

"Certainly. So you suppose I have need of an escort? Go."

The musketeers set off and D'Artagnan was left alone with Raoul.

"Now," he said, "are you in pain?"

"Yes; my head is not only swimming but burning."

"What's the matter with this head?" said D'Artagnan, raising the battered hat. "Ah! ah! a bruise."

"Yes, I think I received a flower-pot upon my head."

"Brutes!" said D'Artagnan. "But were you not on horseback? you have spurs."

"Yes, but I got down to defend Monsieur de Comminges and my horse was taken away. Here it is, I see."

At this very moment Friquet passed, mounted on Raoul's horse, waving his parti-colored cap and crying, "Broussel! Broussel!"

"Halloo! stop, rascal!" cried D'Artagnan. "Bring hither that horse."

Friquet heard perfectly, but he pretended not to do so and tried to continue his road. D'Artagnan felt inclined for an instant to pursue Master Friquet, but not wishing to leave Raoul alone he contented himself with taking a pistol from the holster and cocking it.

Friquet had a quick eye and a fine ear. He saw D'Artagnan's movement, heard the sound of the click, and stopped at once.

"Ah! it is you, your honor," he said, advancing toward D'Artagnan; "and I am truly pleased to meet you."

D'Artagnan looked attentively at Friquet and recognized the little chorister of the Rue de la Calandre.

"Ah! 'tis thou, rascal!" said he, "come here: so thou hast changed thy trade; thou art no longer a choir boy nor a tavern boy; thou hast become a horse stealer?"

"Ah, your honor, how can you say so?" exclaimed Friquet. "I was seeking the gentleman to whom this horse belongs—an officer, brave and handsome as a youthful Caesar;" then, pretending to see Raoul for the first time:

"Ah! but if I mistake not," continued he, "here he is; you won't forget the boy, sir."

Raoul put his hand in his pocket.

"What are you about?" asked D'Artagnan.

"To give ten francs to this honest fellow," replied Raoul, taking a pistole from his pocket.

"Ten kicks on his back!" said D'Artagnan; "be off, you little villain, and forget not that I have your address."

Friquet, who did not expect to be let off so cheaply, bounded off like a gazelle up the Quai a la Rue Dauphine, and disappeared. Raoul mounted his horse, and both leisurely took their way to the Rue Tiquetonne.

D'Artagnan watched over the youth as if he had been his own son.

They arrived without accident at the Hotel de la Chevrette.

The handsome Madeleine announced to D'Artagnan that Planchet had returned, bringing Mousqueton with him, who had heroically borne the extraction of the ball and was as well as his state would permit.

D'Artagnan desired Planchet to be summoned, but he had disappeared.

"Then bring some wine," said D'Artagnan. "You are much pleased with yourself," said he to Raoul when they were alone, "are you not?"

"Well, yes," replied Raoul. "It seems to me I did my duty. I defended the king."

"And who told you to defend the king?"

"The Comte de la Fere himself."

"Yes, the king; but to-day you have not fought for the king, you have fought for Mazarin; which is not quite the same thing."

"But you yourself?"

"Oh, for me; that is another matter. I obey my captain's orders. As for you, your captain is the prince, understand that rightly; you have no other. But has one ever seen such a wild fellow," continued he, "making himself a Mazarinist and helping to arrest Broussel! Breathe not a word of that, or the Comte de la Fere will be furious."

"You think the count will be angry with me?"

"Think it? I'm certain of it; were it not for that, I should thank you, for you have worked for us. However, I scold you instead of him, and in his place; the storm will blow over more easily, believe me. And moreover, my dear child," continued D'Artagnan, "I am making use of the privilege conceded to me by your guardian."

"I do not understand you, sir," said Raoul.

D'Artagnan rose, and taking a letter from his writing-desk, presented it to Raoul. The face of the latter became serious when he had cast his eyes upon the paper.

"Oh, mon Dieu!" he said, raising his fine eyes to D'Artagnan, moist with tears, "the count has left Paris without seeing me?"

"He left four days ago," said D'Artagnan.

"But this letter seems to intimate that he is about to incur danger, perhaps death."

"He—he—incur danger of death! No, be not anxious; he is traveling on business and will return ere long. I hope you have no repugnance to accept me as your guardian in the interim."

"Oh, no, Monsieur d'Artagnan," said Raoul, "you are such a brave gentleman and the Comte de la Fere has so much affection for you!"

"Eh! Egad! love me too; I will not torment you much, but only on condition that you become a Frondist, my young friend, and a hearty Frondist, too."

"But can I continue to visit Madame de Chevreuse?"

"I should say you could! and the coadjutor and Madame de Longueville; and if the worthy Broussel were there, whom you so stupidly helped arrest, I should tell you to excuse yourself to him at once and kiss him on both cheeks."

"Well, sir, I will obey you, although I do not understand you."

"It is unnecessary for you to understand. Hold," continued D'Artagnan, turning toward the door, which had just opened, "here is Monsieur du Vallon, who comes with his coat torn."

"Yes, but in exchange," said Porthos, covered with perspiration and soiled by dust, "in exchange, I have torn many skins. Those wretches wanted to take away my sword! Deuce take 'em, what a popular commotion!" continued the giant, in his quiet manner; "but I knocked down more than twenty with the hilt of Balizarde. A draught of wine, D'Artagnan."

"Oh, I'll answer for you," said the Gascon, filling Porthos's glass to the brim; "but when you have drunk, give me your opinion."

"Upon what?" asked Porthos.

"Look here," resumed D'Artagnan; "here is Monsieur de Bragelonne, who determined at all risks to aid the arrest of Broussel and whom I had great difficulty to prevent defending Monsieur de Comminges."

"The devil!" said Porthos; "and his guardian, what would he have said to that?"

"Do you hear?" interrupted D'Artagnan; "become a Frondist, my friend, belong to the Fronde, and remember that I fill the count's place in everything;" and he jingled his money.

"Will you come?" said he to Porthos.

"Where?" asked Porthos, filling a second glass of wine.

"To present our respects to the cardinal."

Porthos swallowed the second glass with the same grace with which he had imbibed the first, took his beaver and followed D'Artagnan. As for Raoul, he remained bewildered with what he had seen, having been forbidden by D'Artagnan to leave the room until the tumult was over.

Chapter XLV.

The Beggar of St. Eustache.

D'Artagnan had calculated that in not going at once to the Palais Royal he would give Comminges time to arrive before him, and consequently to make the cardinal acquainted with the eminent services which he, D'Artagnan, and his friend had rendered to the queen's party in the morning.

They were indeed admirably received by Mazarin, who paid them numerous compliments, and announced that they were more than half on their way to obtain what they desired, namely, D'Artagnan his captaincy, Porthos his barony.

D'Artagnan would have preferred money in hand to all that fine talk, for he knew well that to Mazarin it was easy to promise and hard to perform. But, though he held the cardinal's promises as of little worth, he affected to be completely satisfied, for he was unwilling to discourage Porthos.

Whilst the two friends were with the cardinal, the queen sent for him. Mazarin, thinking that it would be the means of increasing the zeal of his two defenders if he procured them personal thanks from the queen, motioned them to follow him. D'Artagnan and Porthos pointed to their dusty and torn dresses, but the cardinal shook his head.

"Those costumes," he said, "are of more worth than most of those which you will see on the backs of the queen's courtiers; they are costumes of battle."

D'Artagnan and Porthos obeyed. The court of Anne of Austria was full of gayety and animation; for, after having gained a victory over the Spaniard, it had just gained another over the people. Broussel had been conducted out of Paris without further resistance, and was at this time in the prison of Saint Germain; while Blancmesnil, who was arrested at the same time, but whose arrest had been made without difficulty or noise, was safe in the Castle of Vincennes.

Comminges was near the queen, who was questioning him upon the details of his expedition, and every one was listening to his account, when D'Artagnan and Porthos were perceived at the door, behind the cardinal.

"Ah, madame," said Comminges, hastening to D'Artagnan, "here is one who can tell you better than myself, for he was my protector. Without him I should probably at this moment be a dead fish in the nets at Saint Cloud, for it was a question of nothing less than throwing me into the river. Speak, D'Artagnan, speak."

D'Artagnan had been a hundred times in the same room with the queen since he had become lieutenant of the musketeers, but her majesty had never once spoken to him.

"Well, sir," at last said Anne of Austria, "you are silent, after rendering such a service?"

"Madame," replied D'Artagnan, "I have nought to say, save that my life is ever at your majesty's service, and that I shall only be happy the day I lose it for you."

"I know that, sir; I have known that," said the queen, "a long time; therefore I am delighted to be able thus publicly to mark my gratitude and my esteem."

"Permit me, madame," said D'Artagnan, "to reserve a portion for my friend; like myself" (he laid an emphasis on these words) "an ancient musketeer of the company of Tréville; he has done wonders."

"His name?" asked the queen.

"In the regiment," said D'Artagnan, "he is called Porthos" (the queen started), "but his true name is the Chevalier du Vallon."

"De Bracieux de Pierrefonds," added Porthos.

"These names are too numerous for me to remember them all, and I will content myself with the first," said the queen, graciously. Porthos bowed. At this moment the coadjutor was announced; a cry of surprise ran through the royal assemblage. Although the coadjutor had preached that same morning it was well known that he leaned much to the side of the Fronde; and Mazarin, in requesting the archbishop of Paris to make his nephew preach, had evidently had the intention of administering to Monsieur de Retz one of those Italian kicks he so much enjoyed giving.

The fact was, in leaving Notre Dame the coadjutor had learned the event of the day. Although almost engaged to the leaders of the Fronde he had not gone so far but that retreat was possible should the court offer him the advantages for which he was ambitious and to which the coadjutorship was but a stepping-stone. Monsieur de Retz wished to become archbishop in his uncle's place, and cardinal, like Mazarin; and the popular party could with difficulty accord him favors so entirely royal. He therefore hastened to the palace to congratulate the queen on the battle of Lens, determined beforehand to act with or against the court, as his congratulations were well or ill received.

The coadjutor possessed, perhaps, as much wit as all those put together who were assembled at the court to laugh at him. His speech, therefore, was so well turned, that in spite of the great wish felt by the courtiers to laugh, they could find no point on which to vent their ridicule. He concluded by saying that he placed his feeble influence at her majesty's command.

During the whole time he was speaking, the queen appeared to be well pleased with the coadjutor's harangue; but terminating as it did with such a phrase, the only one which could be caught at by the jokers, Anne turned around and directed a glance toward her favorites, which announced that she delivered up the coadjutor to their tender mercies. Immediately the wits of the court plunged into satire. Nogent-Beautin, the fool of the court, exclaimed that "the queen was very happy to have the succor of religion at such a moment." This caused a universal burst of laughter. The Count de Villeroy said that "he did not know how any fear could be entertained for a moment, when the court had, to defend itself against the parliament and the citizens of Paris, his holiness the coadjutor, who by a signal could raise an army of curates, church porters and vergers."

The Marechal de la Meilleraie added that in case the coadjutor should appear on the field of battle it would be a pity that he should not be distinguished in the melee by wearing a red hat, as Henry IV. had been distinguished by his white plume at the battle of Ivry.

During this storm, Gondy, who had it in his power to make it most unpleasant for the jesters, remained calm and stern. The queen at last asked him if he had anything to add to the fine discourse he had just made to her.

"Yes, madame," replied the coadjutor; "I have to beg you to reflect twice ere you cause a civil war in the kingdom."

The queen turned her back and the laughing recommenced.

The coadjutor bowed and left the palace, casting upon the cardinal such a glance as is best understood by mortal foes. That glance was so sharp that it penetrated the heart of Mazarin, who, reading in it a declaration of war, seized D'Artagnan by the arm and said:

"If occasion requires, monsieur, you will remember that man who has just gone out, will you not?"

"Yes, my lord," he replied. Then, turning toward Porthos, "The devil!" said he, "this has a bad look. I dislike these quarrels among men of the church."

Gondy withdrew, distributing benedictions on his way, and finding a malicious satisfaction in causing the adherents of his foes to prostrate themselves at his feet.

"Oh!" he murmured, as he left the threshold of the palace: "ungrateful court! faithless court! cowardly court! I will teach you how to laugh to-morrow—but in another manner."

But whilst they were indulging in extravagant joy at the Palais Royal, to increase the hilarity of the queen, Mazarin, a man of sense, and whose fear, moreover, gave him foresight, lost no time in making idle and dangerous jokes; he went out after the coadjutor, settled his account, locked up his gold, and had confidential workmen to contrive hiding places in his walls.

On his return home the coadjutor was informed that a young man had come in after his departure and was waiting for him; he started with delight when, on demanding the name of this young man, he learned that it was Louvieres. He hastened to his cabinet. Broussel's son was there, still furious, and still bearing bloody marks of his struggle with the king's officers. The only precaution he had taken in coming to the archbishopric was to leave his arquebuse in the hands of a friend.

The coadjutor went to him and held out his hand. The young man gazed at him as if he would have read the secret of his heart.

"My dear Monsieur Louvieres," said the coadjutor, "believe me, I am truly concerned for the misfortune which has happened to you."

"Is that true, and do you speak seriously?" asked Louvieres.

"From the depth of my heart," said Gondy.

"In that case, my lord, the time for words has passed and the hour for action is at hand; my lord, in three days, if you wish it, my father will be out of prison and in six months you may be cardinal."

The coadjutor started.

"Oh! let us speak frankly," continued Louvieres, "and act in a straightforward manner. Thirty thousand crowns in alms is not given, as you have done for the last six months, out of pure Christian charity; that would be too grand. You are ambitious—it is natural; you are a man of genius and you know your worth. As for me, I hate the court and have but one desire at this moment—vengeance. Give us the clergy and the people, of whom you can dispose, and I will bring you the citizens and the parliament; with these four elements Paris is ours in a week; and believe me, monsieur coadjutor, the court will give from fear what it will not give from good-will."

It was now the coadjutor's turn to fix his piercing eyes on Louvieres.

"But, Monsieur Louvieres, are you aware that it is simply civil war you are proposing to me?"

"You have been preparing long enough, my lord, for it to be welcome to you now."

"Never mind," said the coadjutor; "you must be well aware that this requires reflection."

"And how many hours of reflection do you ask?"

"Twelve hours, sir; is it too long?"

"It is now noon; at midnight I will be at your house."

"If I should not be in, wait for me."

"Good! at midnight, my lord."

"At midnight, my dear Monsieur Louvieres."

When once more alone Gondy sent to summon all the curates with whom he had any connection to his house. Two hours later, thirty officiating ministers from the most populous, and consequently the most disturbed parishes of Paris had assembled there. Gondy related to them the insults he had received at the Palais Royal and retailed the jests of Beautin, the Count de Villeroy and Marechal de la Meilleraie. The curates asked him what was to be done.

"Simply this," said the coadjutor. "You are the directors of all consciences. Well, undermine in them the miserable prejudice of respect and fear of kings; teach your flocks that the queen is a tyrant; and repeat often and loudly, so that all may know it, that the misfortunes of France are caused by Mazarin, her lover and her destroyer; begin this work to-day, this instant even, and in three days I shall expect the result. For the rest, if any one of you have further or better counsel to expound, I will listen to him with the greatest pleasure."

Three curates remained—those of St. Merri, St. Sulpice and St. Eustache. The others withdrew.

"You think, then, that you can help me more efficaciously than your brothers?" said Gondy.

"We hope so," answered the curates.

"Let us hear. Monsieur de St. Merri, you begin."

"My lord, I have in my parish a man who might be of the greatest use to you."

"Who and what is this man?"

"A shopkeeper in the Rue des Lombards, who has great influence upon the commerce of his quarter."

"What is his name?"

"He is named Planchet, who himself also caused a rising about six weeks ago; but as he was searched for after this emeute he disappeared."

"And can you find him?"

"I hope so. I think he has not been arrested, and as I am his wife's confessor, if she knows where he is I shall know it too."

"Very well, sir, find this man, and when you have found him bring him to me."

"We will be with you at six o'clock, my lord."

"Go, my dear curate, and may God assist you!"

"And you, sir?" continued Gondy, turning to the curate of St. Sulpice.

"I, my lord," said the latter, "I know a man who has rendered great services to a very popular prince and who would make an excellent leader of revolt. Him I can place at your disposal; it is Count de Rochefort."

"I know him also, but unfortunately he is not in Paris."

"My lord, he has been for three days at the Rue Cassette."

"And wherefore has he not been to see me?"

"He was told—my lord will pardon me——"

"Certainly, speak."

"That your lordship was about to treat with the court."

Gondy bit his lips.

"They are mistaken; bring him here at eight o'clock, sir, and may Heaven bless you as I bless you!"

"And now 'tis your turn," said the coadjutor, turning to the last that remained; "have you anything as good to offer me as the two gentlemen who have left us?"

"Better, my lord."

"Diable! think what a solemn engagement you are making; one has offered a wealthy shopkeeper, the other a count; you are going, then, to offer a prince, are you?"

"I offer you a beggar, my lord."

"Ah! ah!" said Gondy, reflecting, "you are right, sir; some one who could raise the legion of paupers who choke up the crossings of Paris; some one who would know how to cry aloud to them, that all France might hear it, that it is Mazarin who has reduced them to poverty."

"Exactly your man."

"Bravo! and the man?"

"A plain and simple beggar, as I have said, my lord, who asks for alms, as he gives holy water; a practice he has carried on for six years on the steps of St. Eustache."

"And you say that he has a great influence over his compeers?"

"Are you aware, my lord, that mendicity is an organized body, a kind of association of those who have nothing against those who have everything; an association in which every one takes his share; one that elects a leader?"

"Yes, I have heard it said," replied the coadjutor.

"Well, the man whom I offer you is a general syndic."

"And what do you know of him?"

"Nothing, my lord, except that he is tormented with remorse."

"What makes you think so?"

"On the twenty-eighth of every month he makes me say a mass for the repose of the soul of one who died a violent death; yesterday I said this mass again."

"And his name?"

"Maillard; but I do not think it is his right one."

"And think you that we should find him at this hour at his post?"

"Certainly."

"Let us go and see your beggar, sir, and if he is such as you describe him, you are right—it will be you who have discovered the true treasure."

Gondy dressed himself as an officer, put on a felt cap with a red feather, hung on a long sword, buckled spurs to his boots, wrapped himself in an ample cloak and followed the curate.

The coadjutor and his companion passed through all the streets lying between the archbishopric and the St. Eustache Church, watching carefully to ascertain the popular feeling. The people were in an excited mood, but, like a swarm of frightened bees, seemed not to know at what point to concentrate; and it was very evident that if leaders of the people were not provided all this agitation would pass off in idle buzzing.

On arriving at the Rue des Prouvaires, the curate pointed toward the square before the church.

"Stop!" he said, "there he is at his post."

Gondy looked at the spot indicated and perceived a beggar seated in a chair and leaning against one of the moldings; a little basin was near him and he held a holy water brush in his hand.

"Is it by permission that he remains there?" asked Gondy.

"No, my lord; these places are bought. I believe this man paid his predecessor a hundred pistoles for his."

"The rascal is rich, then?"

"Some of those men sometimes die worth twenty thousand and twenty-five and thirty thousand francs and sometimes more."

"Hum!" said Gondy, laughing; "I was not aware my alms were so well invested."

In the meantime they were advancing toward the square, and the moment the coadjutor and the curate put their feet on the first church step the mendicant arose and proffered his brush.

He was a man between sixty-six and sixty-eight years of age, little, rather stout, with gray hair and light eyes. His countenance denoted the struggle between two opposite principles—a wicked nature, subdued by determination, perhaps by repentance.

He started on seeing the cavalier with the curate. The latter and the coadjutor touched the brush with the tips of their fingers and made the sign of the cross; the coadjutor threw a piece of money into the hat, which was on the ground.

"Maillard," began the curate, "this gentleman and I have come to talk with you a little."

"With me!" said the mendicant; "it is a great honor for a poor distributor of holy water."

There was an ironical tone in his voice which he could not quite disguise and which astonished the coadjutor.

"Yes," continued the curate, apparently accustomed to this tone, "yes, we wish to know your opinion of the events of to-day and what you have heard said by people going in and out of the church."

The mendicant shook his head.

"These are melancholy doings, your reverence, which always fall again upon the poor. As to what is said, everybody is discontented, everybody complains, but 'everybody' means 'nobody.'"

"Explain yourself, my good friend," said the coadjutor.

"I mean that all these cries, all these complaints, these curses, produce nothing but storms and flashes and that is all; but the lightning will not strike until there is a hand to guide it."

"My friend," said Gondy, "you seem to be a clever and a thoughtful man; are you disposed to take a part in a little civil war, should we have one, and put at the command of the leader, should we find one, your personal influence and the influence you have acquired over your comrades?"

"Yes, sir, provided this war were approved of by the church and would advance the end I wish to attain—I mean, the remission of my sins."

"The war will not only be approved of, but directed by the church. As for the remission of your sins, we have the archbishop of Paris, who has the very greatest power at the court of Rome, and even the coadjutor, who possesses some plenary indulgences; we will recommend you to him."

"Consider, Maillard," said the curate, "that I have recommended you to this gentleman, who is a powerful lord, and that I have made myself responsible for you."

"I know, monsieur le curé," said the beggar, "that you have always been very kind to me, and therefore I, in my turn, will be serviceable to you."

"And do you think your power as great with the fraternity as monsieur le curé told me it was just now?"

"I think they have some esteem for me," said the mendicant with pride, "and that not only will they obey me, but wherever I go they will follow me."

"And could you count on fifty resolute men, good, unemployed, but active souls, brawlers, capable of bringing down the walls of the Palais Royal by crying, 'Down with Mazarin,' as fell those at Jericho?"

"I think," said the beggar, "I can undertake things more difficult and more important than that."

"Ah, ah," said Gondy, "you will undertake, then, some night, to throw up some ten barricades?"

"I will undertake to throw up fifty, and when the day comes, to defend them."

"I'faith!" exclaimed Gondy, "you speak with a certainty that gives me pleasure; and since monsieur le curé can answer for you——"

"I answer for him," said the curate.

"Here is a bag containing five hundred pistoles in gold; make all your arrangements, and tell me where I shall be able to find you this evening at ten o'clock."

"It must be on some elevated place, whence a given signal may be seen in every part of Paris."

"Shall I give you a line for the vicar of St. Jacques de la Boucherie? he will let you into the rooms in his tower," said the curate.

"Capital," answered the mendicant.

"Then," said the coadjutor, "this evening, at ten o'clock, and if I am pleased with you another bag of five hundred pistoles will be at your disposal."

The eyes of the mendicant dashed with cupidity, but he quickly suppressed his emotion.

"This evening, sir," he replied, "all will be ready."

Chapter XLVI.

The Tower of St. Jacques de la Boucherie.

At a quarter to six o'clock, Monsieur de Gondy, having finished his business, returned to the archiepiscopal palace.

At six o'clock the curate of St. Merri was announced.

The coadjutor glanced rapidly behind and saw that he was followed by another man. The curate then entered, followed by Planchet.

"Your holiness," said the curate, "here is the person of whom I had the honor to speak to you."

Planchet saluted in the manner of one accustomed to fine houses.

"And you are disposed to serve the cause of the people?" asked Gondy.

"Most undoubtedly," said Planchet. "I am a Frondist from my heart. You see in me, such as I am, a person sentenced to be hung."

"And on what account?"

"I rescued from the hands of Mazarin's police a noble lord whom they were conducting back to the Bastile, where he had been for five years."

"Will you name him?"

"Oh, you know him well, my lord—it is Count de Rochefort."

"Ah! really, yes," said the coadjutor, "I have heard this affair mentioned. You raised the whole district, so they told me!"

"Very nearly," replied Planchet, with a self-satisfied air.

"And your business is——"

"That of a confectioner, in the Rue des Lombards."

"Explain to me how it happens that, following so peaceful a business, you had such warlike inclinations."

"Why does my lord, belonging to the church, now receive me in the dress of an officer, with a sword at his side and spurs to his boots?"

"Not badly answered, i'faith," said Gondy, laughing; "but I have, you must know, always had, in spite of my bands, warlike inclinations."

"Well, my lord, before I became a confectioner I myself was three years sergeant in the Piedmontese regiment, and before I became sergeant I was for eighteen months the servant of Monsieur d'Artagnan."

"The lieutenant of musketeers?" asked Gondy.

"Himself, my lord."

"But he is said to be a furious Mazarinist."

"Phew!" whistled Planchet.

"What do you mean by that?"

"Nothing, my lord; Monsieur d'Artagnan belongs to the service; Monsieur d'Artagnan makes it his business to defend the cardinal, who pays him, as much as we make it ours, we citizens, to attack him, whom he robs."

"You are an intelligent fellow, my friend; can we count upon you?"

"You may count upon me, my lord, provided you want to make a complete upheaval of the city."

"'Tis that exactly. How many men, think you, you could collect together to-night?"

"Two hundred muskets and five hundred halberds."

"Let there be only one man in every district who can do as much and by to-morrow we shall have quite a powerful army. Are you disposed to obey Count de Rochefort?"

"I would follow him to hell, and that is saying not a little, as I believe him entirely capable of the descent."

"Bravo!"

"By what sign to-morrow shall we be able to distinguish friends from foes?"

"Every Frondist must put a knot of straw in his hat."

"Good! Give the watchword."

"Do you want money?"

"Money never comes amiss at any time, my lord; if one has it not, one must do without it; with it, matters go on much better and more rapidly."

Gondy went to a box and drew forth a bag.

"Here are five hundred pistoles," he said; "and if the action goes off well you may reckon upon a similar sum to-morrow."

"I will give a faithful account of the sum to your lordship," said Planchet, putting the bag under his arm.

"That is right; I recommend the cardinal to your attention."

"Make your mind easy, he is in good hands."

Planchet went out, the curate remaining for a moment.

"Are you satisfied, my lord?" he asked.

"Yes; he appears to be a resolute fellow."

"Well, he will do more than he has promised."

"He will do wonders then."

The curate rejoined Planchet, who was waiting for him on the stairs. Ten minutes later the curate of St. Sulpice was announced. As soon as the door of Gondy's study was opened a man rushed in. It was the Count de Rochefort.

"'Tis you, then, my dear count," cried Gondy, offering his hand.

"You have made up your mind at last, my lord?" said Rochefort.

"It has been made up a long time," said Gondy.

"Let us say no more on the subject; you tell me so, I believe you. Well, we are going to give a ball to Mazarin."

"I hope so."

"And when will the dance begin?"

"The invitations are given for this evening," said the coadjutor, "but the violins will not begin to play until to-morrow morning."

"You may reckon upon me and upon fifty soldiers which the Chevalier d'Humieres has promised me whenever I need them."

"Upon fifty soldiers?"

"Yes, he is making recruits and he will lend them to me; if any are missing when the fete is over, I shall replace them."

"Good, my dear Rochefort; but that is not all. What have you done with Monsieur de Beaufort?"

"He is in Vendome, where he will wait until I write to him to return to Paris."

"Write to him; now's the time."

"You are sure of your enterprise?"

"Yes, but he must make haste; for hardly will the people of Paris have revolted before we shall have a score of princes begging to lead them. If he defers he will find the place of honor taken."

"Shall I send word to him as coming from you?"

"Yes certainly."

"Shall I tell him that he can count on you?"

"To the end."

"And you will leave the command to him?"

"Of the war, yes, but in politics——"

"You must know it is not his element."

"He must leave me to negotiate for my cardinal's hat in my own fashion."

"You care about it, then, so much?"

"Since they force me to wear a hat of a form which does not become me," said Gondy, "I wish at least that the hat should be red."

"One must not dispute matters of taste and colors," said Rochefort, laughing. "I answer for his consent."

"How soon can he be here?"

"In five days."

"Let him come and he will find a change, I will answer for it."

"Therefore, go and collect your fifty men and hold yourself in readiness."

"For what?"

"For everything."

"Is there any signal for the general rally?"

"A knot of straw in the hat."

"Very good. Adieu, my lord."

"Adieu, my dear Rochefort."

"Ah, Monsieur Mazarin, Monsieur Mazarin," said Rochefort, leading off his curate, who had not found an opportunity of uttering a single word during the foregoing dialogue, "you will see whether I am too old to be a man of action."

It was half-past nine o'clock and the coadjutor required half an hour to go from the archbishop's palace to the tower of St. Jacques de la Boucherie. He remarked that a light was burning in one of the highest windows of the tower. "Good," said he, "our syndic is at his post."

He knocked and the door was opened. The vicar himself awaited him, conducted him to the top of the tower, and when there pointed to a little door, placed the light which he had brought with him in a corner of the wall, that the coadjutor might be able to find it on his return, and went down again. Although the key was in the door the coadjutor knocked.

"Come in," said a voice which he recognized as that of the mendicant, whom he found lying on a kind of truckle bed. He rose on the entrance of the coadjutor, and at that moment ten o'clock struck.

"Well," said Gondy, "have you kept your word with me?"

"Not exactly," replied the mendicant.

"How is that?"

"You asked me for five hundred men, did you not? Well, I have ten thousand for you."

"You are not boasting?"

"Do you wish for a proof?"

"Yes."

There were three candles alight, each of which burnt before a window, one looking upon the city, the other upon the Palais Royal, and a third upon the Rue Saint Denis.

The man went silently to each of the candles and blew them out one after the other.

"What are you doing?" asked the coadjutor.

"I have given the signal."

"For what?"

"For the barricades. When you leave this you will behold my men at work. Only take care you do not break your legs in stumbling over some chain or your neck by falling in a hole."

"Good! there is your money, the same sum as that you have received already. Now remember that you are a general and do not go and drink."

"For twenty years I have tasted nothing but water."

The man took the bag from the hands of the coadjutor, who heard the sound of his fingers counting and handling the gold pieces.

"Ah! ah!" said the coadjutor, "you are avaricious, my good fellow."

The mendicant sighed and threw down the bag.

"Must I always be the same?" said he, "and shall I never succeed in overcoming the old leaven? Oh, misery, oh, vanity!"

"You take it, however."

"Yes, but I make hereby a vow in your presence, to employ all that remains to me in pious works."

His face was pale and drawn, like that of a man who had just undergone some inward struggle.

"Singular man!" muttered Gondy, taking his hat to go away; but on turning around he saw the beggar between him and the door. His first idea was that this man intended to do him some harm, but on the contrary he saw him fall on his knees before him with his hands clasped.

"Your blessing, your holiness, before you go, I beseech you!" he cried.

"Your holiness!" said Gondy; "my friend, you take me for some one else."

"No, your holiness, I take you for what you are, that is to say, the coadjutor; I recognized you at the first glance."

Gondy smiled. "And you want my blessing?" he said.

"Yes, I have need of it."

The mendicant uttered these words in a tone of such humility, such earnest repentance, that Gondy placed his hand upon him and gave him his benediction with all the unction of which he was capable.

"Now," said Gondy, "there is a communion between us. I have blessed you and you are sacred to me. Come, have you committed some crime, pursued by human justice, from which I can protect you?"

The beggar shook his head. "The crime which I have committed, my lord, has no call upon human justice, and you can only deliver me from it by blessing me frequently, as you have just done."

"Come, be candid," said the coadjutor, "you have not all your life followed the trade which you do now?"

"No, my lord. I have pursued it for six years only."

"And previously, where were you?"

"In the Bastile."

"And before you went to the Bastile?"

"I will tell you, my lord, on the day when you are willing to hear my confession."

"Good! At whatsoever hour of the day or night you may present yourself, remember that I shall be ready to give you absolution."

"Thank you, my lord," said the mendicant in a hoarse voice. "But I am not yet ready to receive it."

"Very well. Adieu."

"Adieu, your holiness," said the mendicant, opening the door and bending low before the prelate.

Chapter XLVII.

The Riot.

It was about eleven o'clock at night. Gondy had not walked a hundred steps ere he perceived the strange change which had been made in the streets of Paris.

The whole city seemed peopled with fantastic beings; silent shadows were seen unpaving the streets and others dragging and upsetting great wagons, whilst others again dug ditches large enough to ingulf whole regiments of horsemen. These active beings flitted here and there like so many demons completing some unknown labor; these were the beggars of the Court of Miracles—the agents of the giver of holy water in the Square of Saint Eustache, preparing barricades for the morrow.

Gondy gazed on these deeds of darkness, on these nocturnal laborers, with a kind of fear; he asked himself, if, after having called forth these foul creatures from their dens, he should have the power of making them retire again. He felt almost inclined to cross himself when one of these beings happened to approach him. He reached the Rue Saint Honore and went up it toward the Rue de la Ferronnerie; there the aspect changed; here it was the tradesmen who were running from shop to shop; their doors seemed closed like their shutters, but they were only pushed to in such a manner as to open and allow the men, who seemed fearful of showing what they carried, to enter, closing immediately. These men were shopkeepers, who had arms to lend to those who had none.

One individual went from door to door, bending under the weight of swords, guns, muskets and every kind of weapon, which he deposited as fast as he could. By the light of a lantern the coadjutor recognized Planchet.

The coadjutor proceeded onward to the quay by way of the Rue de la Monnaie; there he found groups of bourgeois clad in black cloaks or gray, according as they belonged to the upper or lower bourgeoisie. They were standing motionless, while single men passed from one group to another. All these cloaks, gray or black, were raised behind by the point of a sword, or before by the barrel of an arquebuse or a musket.

On reaching the Pont Neuf the coadjutor found it strictly guarded and a man approached him.

"Who are you?" asked the man. "I do not know you for one of us."

"Then it is because you do not know your friends, my dear Monsieur Louvieres," said the coadjutor, raising his hat.

Louvieres recognized him and bowed.

Gondy continued his way and went as far as the Tour de Nesle. There he saw a lengthy chain of people gliding under the walls. They might be said to be a procession of ghosts, for they were all wrapped in white cloaks. When they reached a certain spot these men appeared to be annihilated, one after the other, as if the earth had opened under their feet. Gondy, edged into a corner, saw them vanish from the first until the last but one. The last raised his eyes, to ascertain, doubtless, that neither his companions nor himself had been watched, and, in spite of the darkness, he perceived Gondy. He walked straight up to him and placed a pistol to his throat.

"Halloo! Monsieur de Rochefort," said Gondy, laughing, "are you a boy to play with firearms?"

Rochefort recognized the voice.

"Ah, it is you, my lord!" said he.

"The very same. What people are you leading thus into the bowels of the earth?"

"My fifty recruits from the Chevalier d'Humieres, who are destined to enter the light cavalry and who have only received as yet for their equipment their white cloaks."

"And where are you going?"

"To the house of one of my friends, a sculptor, only we enter by the trap through which he lets down his marble."

"Very good," said Gondy, shaking Rochefort by the hand, who descended in his turn and closed the trap after him.

It was now one o'clock in the morning and the coadjutor returned home. He opened a window and leaned out to listen. A strange, incomprehensible, unearthly sound seemed to pervade the whole city; one felt that something unusual and terrible was happening in all the streets, now dark as ocean's most unfathomable caves. From time to time a dull sound was heard, like that of a rising tempest or a billow of the sea; but nothing clear, nothing distinct, nothing intelligible; it was like those mysterious subterraneous noises that precede an earthquake.

The work of revolt continued the whole night thus. The next morning, on awaking, Paris seemed to be startled at her own appearance. It was like a besieged town. Armed men, shouldering muskets, watched over the barricades with menacing looks; words of command, patrols, arrests, executions, even, were encountered at every step. Those bearing plumed hats and gold swords were stopped and made to cry, "Long live Broussel!" "Down with Mazarin!" and whoever refused to comply with this ceremony was hooted at, spat upon and even beaten. They had not yet begun to slay, but it was well felt that the inclination to do so was not wanting.

The barricades had been pushed as far as the Palais Royal. From the Rue de Bons Enfants to that of the Ferronnerie, from the Rue Saint Thomas-du-Louvre to the Pont Neuf, from the Rue Richelieu to the Porte Saint Honore, there were more than ten thousand armed men; those who were at the front hurled defiance at the impassive sentinels of the regiment of guards posted around the Palais Royal, the gates of which were closed behind them, a precaution which made their situation precarious. Among these thousands moved, in bands numbering from one hundred to two hundred, pale and haggard men, clothed in rags, who bore a sort of standard on which was inscribed these words: "Behold the misery of the people!" Wherever these men passed, frenzied cries were heard; and there were so many of these bands that the cries were to be heard in all directions.

The astonishment of Mazarin and of Anne of Austria was great when it was announced to them that the city, which the previous evening they had left entirely tranquil, had awakened to such feverish commotion; nor would either the one or the other believe the reports that were brought to them, declaring they would rather rely on the evidence of their own eyes and ears. Then a window was opened and when they saw and heard they were convinced.

Mazarin shrugged his shoulders and pretended to despise the populace; but he turned visibly pale and ran to his closet, trembling all over, locked up his gold and jewels in his caskets and put his finest diamonds on his fingers. As for the queen, furious, and left to her own guidance, she went for the Marechal de la Meilleraie and desired him to take as many men as he pleased and to go and see what was the meaning of this pleasantry.

The marshal was ordinarily very adventurous and was wont to hesitate at nothing; and he had that lofty contempt for the populace which army officers usually profess. He took a hundred and fifty men and attempted to go out by the Pont du Louvre, but there he met Rochefort and his fifty horsemen, attended by more than five hundred men. The marshal made no attempt to force that barrier and returned up the quay. But at Pont Neuf he found Louvieres and his bourgeois. This time the marshal charged, but he was welcomed by musket shots, while stones fell like hail from all the windows. He left there three men.

He beat a retreat toward the market, but there he met Planchet with his halberdiers; their halberds were leveled at him threateningly. He attempted to ride over those gray cloaks, but the gray cloaks held their ground and the marshal retired toward the Rue Saint Honore, leaving four of his guards dead on the field of battle.

The marshal then entered the Rue Saint Honore, but there he was opposed by the barricades of the mendicant of Saint Eustache. They were guarded, not only by armed men, but even by women and children. Master Friquet, the owner of a pistol and of a sword which Louvieres had given him, had organized a company of rogues like himself and was making a tremendous racket.

The marshal thought this barrier not so well fortified as the others and determined to break through it. He dismounted twenty men to make a breach in the barricade, whilst he and others, remaining on their horses, were to protect the assailants. The twenty men marched straight toward the barrier, but from behind the beams, from among the wagon-wheels and from the heights of the rocks a terrible fusillade burst forth and at the same time Planchet's halberdiers appeared at the corner of the Cemetery of the Innocents, and Louvieres's bourgeois at the corner of the Rue de la Monnaie.

The Marechal de la Meilleraie was caught between two fires, but he was brave and made up his mind to die where he was. He returned blow for blow and cries of pain began to be heard in the crowd. The guards, more skillful, did greater execution; but the bourgeois, more numerous, overwhelmed them with a veritable hurricane of iron. Men fell around him as they had fallen at Rocroy or at Lerida. Fontrailles, his aide-de-camp, had an arm broken; his horse had received a bullet in his neck and he had difficulty in controlling him, maddened by pain. In short, he had reached that supreme moment when the bravest feel a shudder in their veins, when suddenly, in the direction of the Rue de l'Arbre-Sec, the crowd opened, crying: "Long live the coadjutor!" and Gondy, in surplice and cloak, appeared, moving tranquilly in the midst of the fusillade and bestowing his benedictions to the right and left, as undisturbed as if he were leading a procession of the Fete Dieu.

All fell to their knees. The marshal recognized him and hastened to meet him.

"Get me out of this, in Heaven's name!" he said, "or I shall leave my carcass here and those of all my men."

A great tumult arose, in the midst of which even the noise of thunder could not have been heard. Gondy raised his hand and demanded silence. All were still.

"My children," he said, "this is the Marechal de la Meilleraie, as to whose intentions you have been deceived and who pledges himself, on returning to the Louvre, to demand of the queen, in your name, our Broussel's release. You pledge yourself to that, marshal?" added Gondy, turning to La Meilleraie.

"Morbleu!" cried the latter, "I should say that I do pledge myself to it! I had no hope of getting off so easily."

"He gives you his word of honor," said Gondy.

The marshal raised his hand in token of assent.

"Long live the coadjutor!" cried the crowd. Some voices even added: "Long live the marshal!" But all took up the cry in chorus: "Down with Mazarin!"

The crowd gave place, the barricade was opened, and the marshal, with the remnant of his company, retreated, preceded by Friquet and his bandits, some of them making a presence of beating drums and others imitating the sound of the trumpet. It was almost a triumphal procession; only, behind the guards the barricades were closed again. The marshal bit his fingers.

In the meantime, as we have said, Mazarin was in his closet, putting his affairs in order. He called for D'Artagnan, but in the midst of such tumult he little expected to see him, D'Artagnan not being on service. In about ten minutes D'Artagnan appeared at the door, followed by the inseparable Porthos.

"Ah, come in, come in, Monsieur d'Artagnan!" cried the cardinal, "and welcome your friend too. But what is going on in this accursed Paris?"

"What is going on, my lord? nothing good," replied D'Artagnan, shaking his head. "The town is in open revolt, and just now, as I was crossing the Rue Montorgueil with Monsieur du Vallon, who is here, and is your humble servant, they wanted in spite of my uniform, or perhaps because of my uniform, to make us cry 'Long live Broussel!' and must I tell you, my lord what they wished us to cry as well?"

"Speak, speak."

"'Down with Mazarin!' I'faith, the treasonable word is out."

Mazarin smiled, but became very pale.

"And you did cry?" he asked.

"I'faith, no," said D'Artagnan; "I was not in voice; Monsieur du Vallon has a cold and did not cry either. Then, my lord——"

"Then what?" asked Mazarin.

"Look at my hat and cloak."

And D'Artagnan displayed four gunshot holes in his cloak and two in his beaver. As for Porthos's coat, a blow from a halberd had cut it open on the flank and a pistol shot had cut his feather in two.

"Diavolo!" said the cardinal, pensively gazing at the two friends with lively admiration; "I should have cried, I should."

At this moment the tumult was heard nearer.

Mazarin wiped his forehead and looked around him. He had a great desire to go to the window, but he dared not.

"See what is going on, Monsieur D'Artagnan," said he.

D'Artagnan went to the window with his habitual composure. "Oho!" said he, "what is this? Marechal de la Meilleraie returning without a hat—Fontrailles with his arm in a sling—wounded guards—horses bleeding; eh, then, what are the sentinels about? They are aiming—they are going to fire!"

"They have received orders to fire on the people if the people approach the Palais Royal!" exclaimed Mazarin.

"But if they fire, all is lost!" cried D'Artagnan.

"We have the gates."

"The gates! to hold for five minutes—the gates, they will be torn down, twisted into iron wire, ground to powder! God's death, don't fire!" screamed D'Artagnan, throwing open the window.

In spite of this recommendation, which, owing to the noise, could scarcely have been heard, two or three musket shots resounded, succeeded by a terrible discharge. The balls might be heard peppering the facade of the Palais Royal, and one of them, passing under D'Artagnan's arm, entered and broke a mirror, in which Porthos was complacently admiring himself.

"Alack! alack!" cried the cardinal, "a Venetian glass!"

"Oh, my lord," said D'Artagnan, quietly shutting the window, "it is not worth while weeping yet, for probably an hour hence there will not be one of your mirrors remaining in the Palais Royal, whether they be Venetian or Parisian."

"But what do you advise, then?" asked Mazarin, trembling.

"Eh, egad, to give up Broussel as they demand! What the devil do you want with a member of the parliament? He is of no earthly use to anybody."

"And you, Monsieur du Vallon, is that your advice? What would you do?"

"I should give up Broussel," said Porthos.

"Come, come with me, gentlemen!" exclaimed Mazarin. "I will go and discuss the matter with the queen."

He stopped at the end of the corridor and said:

"I can count upon you, gentlemen, can I not?"

"We do not give ourselves twice over," said D'Artagnan; "we have given ourselves to you; command, we shall obey."

"Very well, then," said Mazarin; "enter this cabinet and wait till I come back."

And turning off he entered the drawing-room by another door.

Chapter XLVIII.

The Riot becomes a Revolution.

The closet into which D'Artagnan and Porthos had been ushered was separated from the drawing-room where the queen was by tapestried curtains only, and this thin partition enabled them to hear all that passed in the adjoining room, whilst the aperture between the two hangings, small as it was, permitted them to see.

The queen was standing in the room, pale with anger; her self-control, however, was so great that it might have been imagined that she was calm. Comminges, Villequier and Guitant were behind her and the women again were behind the men. The Chancellor Sequier, who twenty years previously had persecuted her so ruthlessly, stood before her, relating how his carriage had been smashed, how he had been pursued and had rushed into the Hotel d'O——, that the hotel was immediately invaded, pillaged and devastated; happily he had time to reach a closet hidden behind tapestry, in which he was secreted by an old woman, together with his brother, the Bishop of Meaux. Then the danger was so imminent, the rioters came so near, uttering such threats, that the chancellor thought his last hour had come and confessed himself to his brother priest, so as to be all ready to die in case he was discovered. Fortunately, however, he had not been taken; the people, believing that he had escaped by some back entrance, retired and left him at liberty to retreat. Then, disguised in the clothes of the Marquis d'O——, he had left the hotel, stumbling over the bodies of an officer and two guards who had been killed whilst defending the street door.

During the recital Mazarin entered and glided noiselessly up to the queen to listen.

"Well," said the queen, when the chancellor had finished speaking; "what do you think of it all?"

"I think that matters look very gloomy, madame."

"But what step would you propose to me?"

"I could propose one to your majesty, but I dare not."

"You may, you may, sir," said the queen with a bitter smile; "you were not so timid once."

The chancellor reddened and stammered some words.

"It is not a question of the past, but of the present," said the queen; "you said you could give me advice—what is it?"

"Madame," said the chancellor, hesitating, "it would be to release Broussel."

The queen, although already pale, became visibly paler and her face was contracted.

"Release Broussel!" she cried, "never!"

At this moment steps were heard in the ante-room and without any announcement the Marechal de la Meilleraie appeared at the door.

"Ah, there you are, marechal," cried Anne of Austria joyfully. "I trust you have brought this rabble to reason."

"Madame," replied the marechal, "I have left three men on the Pont Neuf, four at the Halle, six at the corner of the Rue de l'Arbre-Sec and two at the door of your palace—fifteen in all. I have brought away ten or twelve wounded. I know not where I have left my hat, and in all probability I should have been left with my hat, had the coadjutor not arrived in time to rescue me."

"Ah, indeed," said the queen, "it would have much astonished me if that low cur, with his distorted legs, had not been mixed up with all this."

"Madame," said La Meilleraie, "do not say too much against him before me, for the service he rendered me is still fresh."

"Very good," said the queen, "be as grateful as you like, it does not implicate me; you are here safe and sound, that is all I wished for; you are not only welcome, but welcome back."

"Yes, madame; but I only came back on one condition—that I would transmit to your majesty the will of the people."

"The will!" exclaimed the queen, frowning. "Oh! oh! monsieur marechal, you must indeed have found yourself in wondrous peril to have undertaken so strange a commission!"

The irony with which these words were uttered did not escape the marechal.

"Pardon, madame," he said, "I am not a lawyer, I am a mere soldier, and probably, therefore, I do not quite comprehend the value of certain words; I ought to have said the wishes, and not the will, of the people. As for what you do me the honor to say, I presume you mean I was afraid?"

The queen smiled.

"Well, then, madame, yes, I did feel fear; and though I have been through twelve pitched battles and I cannot count how many charges and skirmishes, I own for the third time in my life I was afraid. Yes, and I would rather face your majesty, however threatening your smile, than face those demons who accompanied me hither and who sprung from I know not whence, unless from deepest hell."

("Bravo," said D'Artagnan in a whisper to Porthos; "well answered.")

"Well," said the queen, biting her lips, whilst her courtiers looked at each other with surprise, "what is the desire of my people?"

"That Broussel shall be given up to them, madame."

"Never!" said the queen, "never!"

"Your majesty is mistress," said La Meilleraie, retreating a few steps.

"Where are you going, marechal?" asked the queen.

"To give your majesty's reply to those who await it."

"Stay, marechal; I will not appear to parley with rebels."

"Madame, I have pledged my word, and unless you order me to be arrested I shall be forced to return."

Anne of Austria's eyes shot glances of fire.

"Oh! that is no impediment, sir," said she; "I have had greater men than you arrested—Guitant!"

Mazarin sprang forward.

"Madame," said he, "if I dared in my turn advise——"

"Would it be to give up Broussel, sir? If so, you can spare yourself the trouble."

"No," said Mazarin; "although, perhaps, that counsel is as good as any other."

"Then what may it be?"

"To call for monsieur le coadjuteur."

"The coadjutor!" cried the queen, "that dreadful mischief maker! It is he who has raised all this revolt."

"The more reason," said Mazarin; "if he has raised it he can put it down."

"And hold, madame," suggested Comminges, who was near a window, out of which he could see; "hold, the moment is a happy one, for there he is now, giving his blessing in the square of the Palais Royal."

The queen sprang to the window.

"It is true," she said, "the arch hypocrite—see!"

"I see," said Mazarin, "that everybody kneels before him, although he be but coadjutor, whilst I, were I in his place, though I am cardinal, should be torn to pieces. I persist, then, madame, in my wish" (he laid an emphasis on the word), "that your majesty should receive the coadjutor."

"And wherefore do you not say, like the rest, your will?" replied the queen, in a low voice.

Mazarin bowed.

"Monsieur le marechal," said the queen, after a moment's reflection, "go and find the coadjutor and bring him to me."

"And what shall I say to the people?"

"That they must have patience," said Anne, "as I have."

The fiery Spanish woman spoke in a tone so imperative that the marechal made no reply; he bowed and went out.

(D'Artagnan turned to Porthos. "How will this end?" he said.

"We shall soon see," said Porthos, in his tranquil way.)

In the meantime Anne of Austria approached Comminges and conversed with him in a subdued tone, whilst Mazarin glanced uneasily at the corner occupied by D'Artagnan and Porthos. Ere long the door opened and the marechal entered, followed by the coadjutor.

"There, madame," he said, "is Monsieur Gondy, who hastens to obey your majesty's summons."

The queen advanced a few steps to meet him, and then stopped, cold, severe, unmoved, with her lower lip scornfully protruded.

Gondy bowed respectfully.

"Well, sir," said the queen, "what is your opinion of this riot?"

"That it is no longer a riot, madame," he replied, "but a revolt."

"The revolt is at the door of those who think my people can rebel," cried Anne, unable to dissimulate before the coadjutor, whom she looked upon, and probably with reason, as the promoter of the tumult. "Revolt! thus it is called by those who have wished for this demonstration and who are, perhaps, the cause of it; but, wait, wait! the king's authority will put all this to rights."

"Was it to tell me that, madame," coldly replied Gondy, "that your majesty admitted me to the honor of entering your presence?"

"No, my dear coadjutor," said Mazarin; "it was to ask your advice in the unhappy dilemma in which we find ourselves."

"Is it true," asked Gondy, feigning astonishment, "that her majesty summoned me to ask for my opinion?"

"Yes," said the queen, "it is requested."

The coadjutor bowed.

"Your majesty wishes, then——"

"You to say what you would do in her place," Mazarin hastened to reply.

The coadjutor looked at the queen, who replied by a sign in the affirmative.

"Were I in her majesty's place," said Gondy, coldly, "I should not hesitate; I should release Broussel."

"And if I do not give him up, what think you will be the result?" exclaimed the queen.

"I believe that not a stone in Paris will remain unturned," put in the marechal.

"It was not your opinion that I asked," said the queen, sharply, without even turning around.

"If it is I whom your majesty interrogates," replied the coadjutor in the same calm manner, "I reply that I hold monsieur le marechal's opinion in every respect."

The color mounted to the queen's face; her fine blue eyes seemed to start out of her head and her carmine lips, compared by all the poets of the day to a pomegranate in flower, were trembling with anger. Mazarin himself, who was well accustomed to the domestic outbreaks of this disturbed household, was alarmed.

"Give up Broussel!" she cried; "fine counsel, indeed. Upon my word! one can easily see it comes from a priest."

Gondy remained firm, and the abuse of the day seemed to glide over his head as the sarcasms of the evening before had done; but hatred and revenge were accumulating in his heart silently and drop by drop. He looked coldly at the queen, who nudged Mazarin to make him say something in his turn.

Mazarin, according to his custom, was thinking much and saying little.

"Ho! ho!" said he, "good advice, advice of a friend. I, too, would give up that good Monsieur Broussel, dead or alive, and all would be at an end."

"If you yield him dead, all will indeed be at an end, my lord, but quite otherwise than you mean."

"Did I say 'dead or alive?'" replied Mazarin. "It was only a way of speaking. You know I am not familiar with the French language, which you, monsieur le coadjuteur, both speak and write so well."

("This is a council of state," D'Artagnan remarked to Porthos; "but we held better ones at La Rochelle, with Athos and Aramis."

"At the Saint Gervais bastion," said Porthos.

"There and elsewhere.")

The coadjutor let the storm pass over his head and resumed, still with the same tranquillity:

"Madame, if the opinion I have submitted to you does not please you it is doubtless because you have better counsels to follow. I know too well the wisdom of the queen and that of her advisers to suppose that they will leave the capital long in trouble that may lead to a revolution."

"Thus, then, it is your opinion," said Anne of Austria, with a sneer and biting her lips with rage, "that yesterday's riot, which to-day is already a rebellion, to-morrow may become a revolution?"

"Yes, madame," replied the coadjutor, gravely.

"But if I am to believe you, sir, the people seem to have thrown off all restraint."

"It is a bad year for kings," said Gondy, shaking his head; "look at England, madame."

"Yes; but fortunately we have no Oliver Cromwell in France," replied the queen.

"Who knows?" said Gondy; "such men are like thunderbolts—one recognizes them only when they have struck."

Every one shuddered and there was a moment of silence, during which the queen pressed her hand to her side, evidently to still the beatings of her heart.

("Porthos," murmured D'Artagnan, "look well at that priest."

"Yes," said Porthos, "I see him. What then?"

"Well, he is a man."

Porthos looked at D'Artagnan in astonishment. Evidently he did not understand his meaning.)

"Your majesty," continued the coadjutor, pitilessly, "is about to take such measures as seem good to you, but I foresee that they will be violent and such as will still further exasperate the rioters."

"In that case, you, monsieur le coadjuteur, who have such power over them and are at the same time friendly to us," said the queen, ironically, "will quiet them by bestowing your blessing upon them."

"Perhaps it will be too late," said Gondy, still unmoved; "perhaps I shall have lost all influence; while by giving up Broussel your majesty will strike at the root of the sedition and will gain the right to punish severely any revival of the revolt."

"Have I not, then, that right?" cried the queen.

"If you have it, use it," replied Gondy.

("Peste!" said D'Artagnan to Porthos. "There is a man after my own heart. Oh! if he were minister and I were his D'Artagnan, instead of belonging to that beast of a Mazarin, mordieu! what fine things we would do together!"

"Yes," said Porthos.)

The queen made a sign for every one, except Mazarin, to quit the room; and Gondy bowed, as if to leave with the rest.

"Stay, sir," said Anne to him.

"Good," thought Gondy, "she is going to yield."

("She is going to have him killed," said D'Artagnan to Porthos, "but at all events it shall not be by me. I swear to Heaven, on the contrary, that if they fall upon him I will fall upon them."

"And I, too," said Porthos.)

"Good," muttered Mazarin, sitting down, "we shall soon see something startling."

The queen's eyes followed the retreating figures and when the last had closed the door she turned away. It was evident that she was making unnatural efforts to subdue her anger; she fanned herself, smelled at her vinaigrette and walked up and down. Gondy, who began to feel uneasy, examined the tapestry with his eyes, touched the coat of mail which he wore under his long gown and felt from time to time to see if the handle of a good Spanish dagger, which was hidden under his cloak, was well within reach.

"And now," at last said the queen, "now that we are alone, repeat your counsel, monsieur le coadjuteur."

"It is this, madame: that you should appear to have reflected, and publicly acknowledge an error, which constitutes the extra strength of a strong government; release Broussel from prison and give him back to the people."

"Oh!" cried Anne, "to humble myself thus! Am I, or am I not, the queen? This screaming mob, are they, or are they not, my subjects? Have I friends? Have I guards? Ah! by Notre Dame! as Queen Catherine used to say," continued she, excited by her own words, "rather than give up this infamous Broussel to them I will strangle him with my own hands!"

And she sprang toward Gondy, whom assuredly at that moment she hated more than Broussel, with outstretched arms. The coadjutor remained immovable and not a muscle of his face was discomposed; only his glance flashed like a sword in returning the furious looks of the queen.

("He were a dead man" said the Gascon, "if there were still a Vitry at the court and if Vitry entered at this moment; but for my part, before he could reach the good prelate I would kill Vitry at once; the cardinal would be infinitely pleased with me."

"Hush!" said Porthos; "listen.")

"Madame," cried the cardinal, seizing hold of Anne and drawing her back, "Madame, what are you about?"

Then he added in Spanish, "Anne, are you mad? You, a queen to quarrel like a washerwoman! And do you not perceive that in the person of this priest is represented the whole people of Paris and that it is dangerous to insult him at this moment, and if this priest wished it, in an hour you would be without a crown? Come, then, on another occasion you can be firm and strong; but to-day is not the proper time; to-day, flatter and caress, or you are only a common woman."

(At the first words of this address D'Artagnan had seized Porthos's arm, which he pressed with gradually increasing force. When Mazarin ceased speaking he said to Porthos in a low tone:

"Never tell Mazarin that I understand Spanish, or I am a lost man and you are also."

"All right," said Porthos.)

This rough appeal, marked by the eloquence which characterized Mazarin when he spoke in Italian or Spanish and which he lost entirely in speaking French, was uttered with such impenetrable expression that Gondy, clever physiognomist as he was, had no suspicion of its being more than a simple warning to be more subdued.

The queen, on her part, thus chided, softened immediately and sat down, and in an almost weeping voice, letting her arms fall by her side, said:

"Pardon me, sir, and attribute this violence to what I suffer. A woman, and consequently subject to the weaknesses of my sex, I am alarmed at the idea of civil war; a queen, accustomed to be obeyed, I am excited at the first opposition."

"Madame," replied Gondy, bowing, "your majesty is mistaken in qualifying my sincere advice as opposition. Your majesty has none but submissive and respectful subjects. It is not the queen with whom the people are displeased; they ask for Broussel and are only too happy, if you release him to them, to live under your government."

Mazarin, who at the words, "It is not the queen with whom the people are displeased," had pricked up his ears, thinking that the coadjutor was about to speak of the cries, "Down with Mazarin," and pleased with Gondy's suppression of this fact, he said with his sweetest voice and his most gracious expression:

"Madame, credit the coadjutor, who is one of the most able politicians we have; the first available cardinal's hat seems to belong already to his noble brow."

"Ah! how much you have need of me, cunning rogue!" thought Gondy.

("And what will he promise us?" said D'Artagnan. "Peste, if he is giving away hats like that, Porthos, let us look out and both demand a regiment to-morrow. Corbleu! let the civil war last but one year and I will have a constable's sword gilt for me.")

"And for me?" put in Porthos.

"For you? I will give you the baton of the Marechal de la Meilleraie, who does not seem to be much in favor just now.")

"And so, sir," said the queen, "you are seriously afraid of a public tumult."

"Seriously," said Gondy, astonished at not having further advanced; "I fear that when the torrent has broken its embankment it will cause fearful destruction."

"And I," said the queen, "think that in such a case other embankments should be raised to oppose it. Go; I will reflect."

Gondy looked at Mazarin, astonished, and Mazarin approached the queen to speak to her, but at this moment a frightful tumult arose from the square of the Palais Royal.

Gondy smiled, the queen's color rose and Mazarin grew even paler.

"What is that again?" he asked.

At this moment Comminges rushed into the room.

"Pardon, your majesty," he cried, "but the people have dashed the sentinels against the gates and they are now forcing the doors; what are your commands?"

"Listen, madame," said Gondy.

The moaning of waves, the noise of thunder, the roaring of a volcano, cannot be compared with the tempest of cries heard at that moment.

"What are my commands?" said the queen.

"Yes, for time presses."

"How many men have you about the Palais Royal?"

"Six hundred."

"Place a hundred around the king and with the remainder sweep away this mob for me."

"Madame," cried Mazarin, "what are you about?"

"Go!" said the queen.

Comminges went out with a soldier's passive obedience.

At this moment a monstrous battering was heard. One of the gates began to yield.

"Oh! madame," cried Mazarin, "you have ruined us all—the king, yourself and me."

At this cry from the soul of the frightened cardinal, Anne became alarmed in her turn and would have recalled Comminges.

"It is too late," said Mazarin, tearing his hair, "too late!"

The gale had given way. Hoarse shouts were heard from the excited mob. D'Artagnan put his hand to his sword, motioning to Porthos to follow his example.

"Save the queen!" cried Mazarin to the coadjutor.

Gondy sprang to the window and threw it open; he recognized Louvieres at the head of a troop of about three or four thousand men.

"Not a step further," he shouted, "the queen is signing!"

"What are you saying?" asked the queen.

"The truth, madame," said Mazarin, placing a pen and a paper before her, "you must;" then he added: "Sign, Anne, I implore you—I command you."

The queen fell into a chair, took the pen and signed.

The people, kept back by Louvieres, had not made another step forward; but the awful murmuring, which indicates an angry people, continued.

The queen had written, "The keeper of the prison at Saint Germain will set Councillor Broussel at liberty;" and she had signed it.

The coadjutor, whose eyes devoured her slightest movements, seized the paper immediately the signature had been affixed to it, returned to the window and waved it in his hand.

"This is the order," he said.

All Paris seemed to shout with joy, and then the air resounded with the cries of "Long live Broussel!" "Long live the coadjutor!"

"Long live the queen!" cried De Gondy; but the cries which replied to his were poor and few, and perhaps he had but uttered it to make Anne of Austria sensible of her weakness.

"And now that you have obtained what you want, go," said she, "Monsieur de Gondy."

"Whenever her majesty has need of me," replied the coadjutor, bowing, "her majesty knows I am at her command."

"Ah, cursed priest!" cried Anne, when he had retired, stretching out her arm to the scarcely closed door, "one day I will make you drink the dregs of the atrocious gall you have poured out on me to-day."

Mazarin wished to approach her. "Leave me!" she exclaimed; "you are not a man!" and she went out of the room.

"It is you who are not a woman," muttered Mazarin.

Then, after a moment of reverie, he remembered where he had left D'Artagnan and Porthos and that they must have overheard everything. He knit his brows and went direct to the tapestry, which he pushed aside. The closet was empty.

At the queen's last word, D'Artagnan had dragged Porthos into the gallery. Thither Mazarin went in his turn and found the two friends walking up and down.

"Why did you leave the closet, Monsieur d'Artagnan?" asked the cardinal.

"Because," replied D'Artagnan, "the queen desired every one to leave and I thought that this command was intended for us as well as for the rest."

"And you have been here since——"

"About a quarter of an hour," said D'Artagnan, motioning to Porthos not to contradict him.

Mazarin saw the sign and remained convinced that D'Artagnan had seen and heard everything; but he was pleased with his falsehood.

"Decidedly, Monsieur d'Artagnan, you are the man I have been seeking. You may reckon upon me and so may your friend." Then bowing to the two musketeers with his most gracious smile, he re-entered his closet more calmly, for on the departure of De Gondy the uproar had ceased as though by enchantment.

Chapter XLIX.

Misfortune refreshes the Memory.

Anne of Austria returned to her oratory, furious.

"What!" she cried, wringing her beautiful hands, "What! the people have seen Monsieur de Condé, a prince of the blood royal, arrested by my mother-in-law, Maria de Medicis; they saw my mother-in-law, their former regent, expelled by the cardinal; they saw Monsieur de Vendome, that is to say, the son of Henry IV., a prisoner at Vincennes; and whilst these great personages were imprisoned, insulted and threatened, they said nothing; and now for a Broussel—good God! what, then, is to become of royalty?"

The queen unconsciously touched here upon the exciting question. The people had made no demonstration for the princes, but they had risen for Broussel; they were taking the part of a plebeian and in defending Broussel they instinctively felt they were defending themselves.

During this time Mazarin walked up and down the study, glancing from time to time at his beautiful Venetian mirror, starred in every direction. "Ah!" he said, "it is sad, I know well, to be forced to yield thus; but, pshaw! we shall have our revenge. What matters it about Broussel—it is a name, not a thing."

Mazarin, clever politician as he was, was for once mistaken; Broussel was a thing, not a name.

The next morning, therefore, when Broussel made his entrance into Paris in a large carriage, having his son Louvieres at his side and Friquet behind the vehicle, the people threw themselves in his way and cries of "Long live Broussel!" "Long live our father!" resounded from all parts and was death to Mazarin's ears; and the cardinal's spies brought bad news from every direction, which greatly agitated the minister, but was calmly received by the queen. The latter seemed to be maturing in her mind some great stroke, a fact which increased the uneasiness of the cardinal, who knew the proud princess and dreaded much the determination of Anne of Austria.

The coadjutor returned to parliament more a monarch than king, queen, and cardinal, all three together. By his advice a decree from parliament summoned the citizens to lay down their arms and demolish the barricades. They now knew that it required but one hour to take up arms again and one night to reconstruct the barricades.

Rochefort had returned to the Chevalier d'Humieres his fifty horsemen, less two, missing at roll call. But the chevalier was himself at heart a Frondist and would hear nothing said of compensation.

The mendicant had gone to his old place on the steps of Saint Eustache and was again distributing holy water with one hand and asking alms with the other. No one could suspect that those two hands had been engaged with others in drawing out from the social edifice the keystone of royalty.

Louvieres was proud and satisfied; he had taken revenge on Mazarin and had aided in his father's deliverance from prison. His name had been mentioned as a name of terror at the Palais Royal. Laughingly he said to the councillor, restored to his family:

"Do you think, father, that if now I should ask for a company the queen would give it to me?"

D'Artagnan profited by this interval of calm to send away Raoul, whom he had great difficulty in keeping shut up during the riot, and who wished positively to strike a blow for one party or the other. Raoul had offered some opposition at first; but D'Artagnan made use of the Comte de la Fere's name, and after paying a visit to Madame de Chevreuse, Raoul started to rejoin the army.

Rochefort alone was dissatisfied with the termination of affairs. He had written to the Duc de Beaufort to come and the duke was about to arrive, and he would find Paris tranquil. He went to the coadjutor to consult with him whether it would not be better to send word to the duke to stop on the road, but Gondy reflected for a moment, and then said:

"Let him continue his journey."

"All is not then over?" asked Rochefort.

"My dear count, we have only just begun."

"What induces you to think so?"

"The knowledge that I have of the queen's heart; she will not rest contented beaten."

"Is she, then, preparing for a stroke?"

"I hope so."

"Come, let us see what you know."

"I know that she has written to the prince to return in haste from the army."

"Ah! ha!" said Rochefort, "you are right. We must let Monsieur de Beaufort come."

In fact, the evening after this conversation the report was circulated that the Prince de Condé had arrived. It was a very simple, natural circumstance and yet it created a profound sensation. It was said that Madame de Longueville, for whom the prince had more than a brother's affection and in whom he had confided, had been indiscreet. His confidence had unveiled the sinister project of the queen.

Even on the night of the prince's return, some citizens, bolder than the rest, such as the sheriffs, captains and the quartermaster, went from house to house among their friends, saying:

"Why do we not take the king and place him in the Hotel de Ville? It is a shame to leave him to be educated by our enemies, who will give him evil counsel; whereas, brought up by the coadjutor, for instance, he would imbibe national principles and love his people."

That night the question was secretly agitated and on the morrow the gray and black cloaks, the patrols of armed shop-people, and the bands of mendicants reappeared.

The queen had passed the night in lonely conference with the prince, who had entered the oratory at midnight and did not leave till five o'clock in the morning.

At five o'clock Anne went to the cardinal's room. If she had not yet taken any repose, he at least was already up. Six days had already passed out of the ten he had asked from Mordaunt; he was therefore occupied in revising his reply to Cromwell, when some one knocked gently at the door of communication with the queen's apartments. Anne of Austria alone was permitted to enter by that door. The cardinal therefore rose to open it.

The queen was in a morning gown, but it became her still; for, like Diana of Poictiers and Ninon, Anne of Austria enjoyed the privilege of remaining ever beautiful; nevertheless, this morning she looked handsomer than usual, for her eyes had all the sparkle inward satisfaction adds to expression.

"What is the matter, madame?" said Mazarin, uneasily. "You seem secretly elated."

"Yes, Giulio," she said, "proud and happy; for I have found the means of strangling this hydra."

"You are a great politician, my queen," said Mazarin; "let us hear the means." And he hid what he had written by sliding the letter under a folio of blank paper.

"You know," said the queen, "that they want to take the king away from me?"

"Alas! yes, and to hang me."

"They shall not have the king."

"Nor hang me."

"Listen. I want to carry off my son from them, with yourself. I wish that this event, which on the day it is known will completely change the aspect of affairs, should be accomplished without the knowledge of any others but yourself, myself, and a third person."

"And who is this third person?"

"Monsieur le Prince."

"He has come, then, as they told me?"

"Last evening."

"And you have seen him?"

"He has just left me."

"And will he aid this project?"

"The plan is his own."

"And Paris?"

"He will starve it out and force it to surrender at discretion."

"The plan is not wanting in grandeur; I see but one impediment."

"What is it?"

"Impossibility."

"A senseless word. Nothing is impossible."

"On paper."

"In execution. We have money?"

"A little," said Mazarin, trembling, lest Anne should ask to draw upon his purse.

"Troops?"

"Five or six thousand men."

"Courage?"

"Plenty."

"Then the thing is easy. Oh! do think of it, Giulio! Paris, this odious Paris, waking up one morning without queen or king, surrounded, besieged, famished—having for its sole resource its stupid parliament and their coadjutor with crooked limbs!"

"Charming! charming!" said Mazarin. "I can imagine the effect, I do not see the means."

"I will find the means myself."

"You are aware it will be war, civil war, furious, devouring, implacable?"

"Oh! yes, yes, war," said Anne of Austria. "Yes, I will reduce this rebellious city to ashes. I will extinguish the fire with blood! I will perpetuate the crime and punishment by making a frightful example. Paris!; I—I detest, I loathe it!"

"Very fine, Anne. You are now sanguinary; but take care. We are not in the time of Malatesta and Castruccio Castracani. You will get yourself decapitated, my beautiful queen, and that would be a pity."

"You laugh."

"Faintly. It is dangerous to go to war with a nation. Look at your brother monarch, Charles I. He is badly off, very badly."

"We are in France, and I am Spanish."

"So much the worse; I had much rather you were French and myself also; they would hate us both less."

"Nevertheless, you consent?"

"Yes, if the thing be possible."

"It is; it is I who tell you so; make preparations for departure."

"I! I am always prepared to go, only, as you know, I never do go, and perhaps shall go this time as little as before."

"In short, if I go, will you go too?"

"I will try."

"You torment me, Giulio, with your fears; and what are you afraid of, then?"

"Of many things."

"What are they?"

Mazarin's face, smiling as it was, became clouded.

"Anne," said he, "you are but a woman and as a woman you may insult men at your ease, knowing that you can do it with impunity. You accuse me of fear; I have not so much as you have, since I do not fly as you do. Against whom do they cry out? is it against you or against myself? Whom would they hang, yourself or me? Well, I can weather the storm—I, whom, notwithstanding, you tax with fear—not with bravado, that is not my way; but I am firm. Imitate me. Make less hubbub and think more deeply. You cry very loud, you end by doing nothing; you talk of flying——"

Mazarin shrugged his shoulders and taking the queen's hand led her to the window.

"Look!" he said.

"Well?" said the queen, blinded by her obstinacy.

"Well, what do you see from this window? If I am not mistaken those are citizens, helmeted and mailed, armed with good muskets, as in the time of the League, and whose eyes are so intently fixed on this window that they will see you if you raise that curtain much; and now come to the other side—what do you see? Creatures of the people, armed with halberds, guarding your doors. You will see the same at every opening from this palace to which I should lead you. Your doors are guarded, the airholes of your cellars are guarded, and I could say to you, as that good La Ramee said to me of the Duc de Beaufort, you must be either bird or mouse to get out."

"He did get out, nevertheless."

"Do you think of escaping in the same way?"

"I am a prisoner, then?"

"Parbleu!" said Mazarin, "I have been proving it to you this last hour."

And he quietly resumed his dispatch at the place where he had been interrupted.

Anne, trembling with anger and scarlet with humiliation, left the room, shutting the door violently after her. Mazarin did not even turn around. When once more in her own apartment Anne fell into a chair and wept; then suddenly struck with an idea:

"I am saved!" she exclaimed, rising; "oh, yes! yes! I know a man who will find the means of taking me from Paris, a man I have too long forgotten." Then falling into a reverie, she added, however, with an expression of joy, "Ungrateful woman that I am, for twenty years I have forgotten this man, whom I ought to have made a marechal of France. My mother-in-law expended gold, caresses, dignities on Concini, who ruined her; the king made Vitry marechal of France for an assassination: while I have left in obscurity, in poverty, the noble D'Artagnan, who saved me!"

And running to a table, on which were paper, pens and ink, she hastily began to write.

Chapter L.

The Interview.

It had been D'Artagnan's practice, ever since the riots, to sleep in the same room as Porthos, and on this eventful morning he was still there, sleeping, and dreaming that a yellow cloud had overspread the sky and was raining gold pieces into his hat, which he held out till it was overflowing with pistoles. As for Porthos, he dreamed that the panels of his carriage were not capacious enough to contain the armorial bearings he had ordered to be painted on them. They were both aroused at seven o'clock by the entrance of an unliveried servant, who brought a letter for D'Artagnan.

"From whom?" asked the Gascon.

"From the queen," replied the servant.

"Ho!" said Porthos, raising himself in his bed; "what does she say?"

D'Artagnan requested the servant to wait in the next room and when the door was closed he sprang up from his bed and read rapidly, whilst Porthos looked at him with starting eyes, not daring to ask a single question.

"Friend Porthos," said D'Artagnan, handing the letter to him, "this time, at least, you are sure of your title of baron, and I of my captaincy. Read for yourself and judge."

Porthos took the letter and with a trembling voice read the following words:

"The queen wishes to speak to Monsieur d'Artagnan, who must follow the bearer."

"Well!" exclaimed Porthos; "I see nothing in that very extraordinary."

"But I see much that is very extraordinary in it," replied D'Artagnan. "It is evident, by their sending for me, that matters are becoming complicated. Just reflect a little what an agitation the queen's mind must be in for her to have remembered me after twenty years."

"It is true," said Porthos.

"Sharpen your sword, baron, load your pistols, and give some corn to the horses, for I will answer for it, something lightning-like will happen ere to-morrow."

"But, stop; do you think it can be a trap that they are laying for us?" suggested Porthos, incessantly thinking how his greatness must be irksome to inferior people.

"If it is a snare," replied D'Artagnan, "I shall scent it out, be assured. If Mazarin is an Italian, I am a Gascon."

And D'Artagnan dressed himself in an instant.

Whilst Porthos, still in bed, was hooking on his cloak for him, a second knock at the door was heard.

"Come in," exclaimed D'Artagnan; and another servant entered.

"From His Eminence, Cardinal Mazarin," presenting a letter.

D'Artagnan looked at Porthos.

"A complicated affair," said Porthos; "where will you begin?"

"It is arranged capitally; his eminence expects me in half an hour."

"Good."

"My friend," said D'Artagnan, turning to the servant, "tell his eminence that in half an hour I shall be at his command."

"It is very fortunate," resumed the Gascon, when the valet had retired, "that he did not meet the other one."

"Do you not think that they have sent for you, both for the same thing?"

"I do not think it, I am certain of it."

"Quick, quick, D'Artagnan. Remember that the queen awaits you, and after the queen, the cardinal, and after the cardinal, myself."

D'Artagnan summoned Anne of Austria's servant and signified that he was ready to follow him into the queen's presence.

The servant conducted him by the Rue des Petits Champs and turning to the left entered the little garden gate leading into the Rue Richelieu; then they gained the private staircase and D'Artagnan was ushered into the oratory. A certain emotion, for which he could not account, made the lieutenant's heart beat: he had no longer the assurance of youth; experience had taught him the importance of past events. Formerly he would have approached the queen as a young man who bends before a woman; but now it was a different thing; he answered her summons as an humble soldier obeys an illustrious general.

The silence of the oratory was at last disturbed by the slight rustling of silk, and D'Artagnan started when he perceived the tapestry raised by a white hand, which, by its form, its color and its beauty he recognized as that royal hand which had one day been presented to him to kiss. The queen entered.

"It is you, Monsieur d'Artagnan," she said, fixing a gaze full of melancholy interest on the countenance of the officer, "and I know you well. Look at me well in your turn. I am the queen; do you recognize me?"

"No, madame," replied D'Artagnan.

"But are you no longer aware," continued Anne, giving that sweet expression to her voice which she could do at will, "that in former days the queen had once need of a young, brave and devoted cavalier—that she found this cavalier—and that, although he might have thought that she had forgotten him, she had kept a place for him in the depths of her heart?"

"No, madame, I was ignorant of that," said the musketeer.

"So much the worse, sir," said Anne of Austria; "so much the worse, at least for the queen, for to-day she has need of the same courage and the same devotion."

"What!" exclaimed D'Artagnan, "does the queen, surrounded as she is by such devoted servants, such wise counselors, men, in short, so great by merit or position—does she deign to cast her eyes on an obscure soldier?"

Anne understood this covert reproach and was more moved than irritated by it. She had many a time felt humiliated by the self-sacrifice and disinterestedness shown by the Gascon gentleman. She had allowed herself to be exceeded in generosity.

"All that you tell me of those by whom I am surrounded, Monsieur d'Artagnan, is doubtless true," said the queen, "but I have confidence in you alone. I know that you belong to the cardinal, but belong to me as well, and I will take upon myself the making of your fortune. Come, will you do to-day what formerly the gentleman you do not know did for the queen?"

"I will do everything your majesty commands," replied D'Artagnan.

The queen reflected for a moment and then, seeing the cautious demeanor of the musketeer:

"Perhaps you like repose?" she said.

"I do not know, for I have never had it, madame."

"Have you any friends?"

"I had three, two of whom have left Paris, to go I know not where. One alone is left to me, but he is one of those known, I believe, to the cavalier of whom your majesty did me the honor to speak."

"Very good," said the queen; "you and your friend are worth an army."

"What am I to do, madame?"

"Return at five o'clock and I will tell you; but do not breathe to a living soul, sir, the rendezvous which I give you."

"No, madame."

"Swear it upon the cross."

"Madame, I have never been false to my word; when I say I will not do a thing, I mean it."

The queen, although astonished at this language, to which she was not accustomed from her courtiers, argued from it a happy omen of the zeal with which D'Artagnan would serve her in the accomplishment of her project. It was one of the Gascon's artifices to hide his deep cunning occasionally under an appearance of rough loyalty.

"Has the queen any further commands for me now?" asked D'Artagnan.

"No, sir," replied Anne of Austria, "and you may retire until the time that I mentioned to you."

D'Artagnan bowed and went out.

"Diable!" he exclaimed when the door was shut, "they seem to have the greatest need of me just now."

Then, as the half hour had already glided by, he crossed the gallery and knocked at the cardinal's door.

Bernouin introduced him.

"I come for your commands, my lord," he said.

And according to his custom D'Artagnan glanced rapidly around and remarked that Mazarin had a sealed letter before him. But it was so placed on the desk that he could not see to whom it was addressed.

"You come from the queen?" said Mazarin, looking fixedly at D'Artagnan.

"I! my lord—who told you that?"

"Nobody, but I know it."

"I regret infinitely to tell you, my lord, that you are mistaken," replied the Gascon, impudently, firm to the promise he had just made to Anne of Austria.

"I opened the door of the ante-room myself and I saw you enter at the end of the corridor."

"Because I was shown up the private stairs."

"How so?"

"I know not; it must have been a mistake."

Mazarin was aware that it was not easy to make D'Artagnan reveal anything he was desirous of hiding, so he gave up, for the time, the discovery of the mystery the Gascon was concealing.

"Let us speak of my affairs," said Mazarin, "since you will tell me naught of yours. Are you fond of traveling?"

"My life has been passed on the high road."

"Would anything retain you particularly in Paris?"

"Nothing but an order from a superior would retain me in Paris."

"Very well. Here is a letter, which must be taken to its address."

"To its address, my lord? But it has none."

In fact, the side of the letter opposite the seal was blank.

"I must tell you," resumed Mazarin, "that it is in a double envelope."

"I understand; and I am to take off the first one when I have reached a certain place?"

"Just so, take it and go. You have a friend, Monsieur du Vallon, whom I like much; let him accompany you."

"The devil!" said D'Artagnan to himself. "He knows that we overheard his conversation yesterday and he wants to get us away from Paris."

"Do you hesitate?" asked Mazarin.

"No, my lord, and I will set out at once. There is one thing only which I must request."

"What is it? Speak."

"That your eminence will go at once to the queen."

"What for?"

"Merely to say these words: 'I am going to send Monsieur d'Artagnan away and I wish him to set out directly.'"

"I told you," said Mazarin, "that you had seen the queen."

"I had the honor of saying to your eminence that there had been some mistake."

"What is the meaning of that?"

"May I venture to repeat my prayer to your eminence?"

"Very well; I will go. Wait here for me." And looking attentively around him, to see if he had left any of his keys in his closets, Mazarin went out. Ten minutes elapsed, during which D'Artagnan made every effort to read through the first envelope what was written on the second. But he did not succeed.

Mazarin returned, pale, and evidently thoughtful. He seated himself at his desk and D'Artagnan proceeded to examine his face, as he had just examined the letter he held, but the envelope which covered his countenance appeared as impenetrable as that which covered the letter.

"Ah!" thought the Gascon; "he looks displeased. Can it be with me? He meditates. Is it about sending me to the Bastile? All very fine, my lord, but at the very first hint you give of such a thing I will strangle you and become Frondist. I should be carried home in triumph like Monsieur Broussel and Athos would proclaim me the French Brutus. It would be exceedingly droll."

The Gascon, with his vivid imagination, had already seen the advantage to be derived from his situation. Mazarin gave, however, no order of the kind, but on the contrary began to be insinuating.

"You were right," he said, "my dear Monsieur d'Artagnan, and you cannot set out yet. I beg you to return me that dispatch."

D'Artagnan obeyed, and Mazarin ascertained that the seal was intact.

"I shall want you this evening," he said "Return in two hours."

"My lord," said D'Artagnan, "I have an appointment in two hours which I cannot miss."

"Do not be uneasy," said Mazarin; "it is the same."

"Good!" thought D'Artagnan; "I fancied it was so."

"Return, then, at five o'clock and bring that worthy Monsieur du Vallon with you. Only, leave him in the ante-room, as I wish to speak to you alone."

D'Artagnan bowed, and thought: "Both at the same hour; both commands alike; both at the Palais Royal. Monsieur de Gondy would pay a hundred thousand francs for such a secret!"

"You are thoughtful," said Mazarin, uneasily.

"Yes, I was thinking whether we ought to come armed or not."

"Armed to the teeth!" replied Mazarin.

"Very well, my lord; it shall be so."

D'Artagnan saluted, went out and hastened to repeat to his friend Mazarin's flattering promises, which gave Porthos an indescribable happiness.

Chapter LI.

The Flight.

When D'Artagnan returned to the Palais Royal at five o'clock, it presented, in spite of the excitement which reigned in the town, a spectacle of the greatest rejoicing. Nor was that surprising. The queen had restored Broussel and Blancmesnil to the people and had therefore nothing to fear, since the people had nothing more just then to ask for. The return, also, of the conqueror of Lens was the pretext for giving a grand banquet. The princes and princesses were invited and their carriages had crowded the court since noon; then after dinner the queen was to have a play in her apartment. Anne of Austria had never appeared more brilliant than on that day—radiant with grace and wit. Mazarin disappeared as they rose from table. He found D'Artagnan waiting for him already at his post in the ante-room.

The cardinal advanced to him with a smile and taking him by the hand led him into his study.

"My dear M. d'Artagnan," said the minister, sitting down, "I am about to give you the greatest proof of confidence that a minister can give an officer."

"I hope," said D'Artagnan, bowing, "that you give it, my lord, without hesitation and with the conviction that I am worthy of it."

"More worthy than any one in Paris my dear friend; therefore I apply to you. We are about to leave this evening," continued Mazarin. "My dear M. d'Artagnan, the welfare of the state is deposited in your hands." He paused.

"Explain yourself, my lord, I am listening."

"The queen has resolved to make a little excursion with the king to Saint Germain."

"Aha!" said D'Artagnan, "that is to say, the queen wishes to leave Paris."

"A woman's caprice—you understand."

"Yes, I understand perfectly," said D'Artagnan.

"It was for this she summoned you this morning and that she told you to return at five o'clock."

"Was it worth while to wish me to swear this morning that I would mention the appointment to no one?" muttered D'Artagnan. "Oh, women! women! whether queens or not, they are always the same."

"Do you disapprove of this journey, my dear M. d'Artagnan?" asked Mazarin, anxiously.

"I, my lord?" said D'Artagnan; "why should I?"

"Because you shrug your shoulders."

"It is a way I have of speaking to myself. I neither approve nor disapprove, my lord; I merely await your commands."

"Good; it is you, accordingly, that I have pitched upon to conduct the king and the queen to Saint Germain."

"Liar!" thought D'Artagnan.

"You see, therefore," continued the cardinal, perceiving D'Artagnan's composure, "that, as I have told you, the welfare of the state is placed in your hands."

"Yes, my lord, and I feel the whole responsibility of such a charge."

"You accept, however?"

"I always accept."

"Do you think the thing possible?"

"Everything is possible."

"Shall you be attacked on the road?"

"Probably."

"And what will you do in that case?"

"I shall pass through those who attack me."

"And suppose you cannot pass through them?"

"So much the worse for them; I shall pass over them."

"And you will place the king and queen in safety also, at Saint Germain?"

"Yes."

"On your life?"

"On my life."

"You are a hero, my friend," said Mazarin, gazing at the musketeer with admiration.

D'Artagnan smiled.

"And I?" asked Mazarin, after a moment's silence.

"How? and you, my lord?"

"If I wish to leave?"

"That would be much more difficult."

"Why so?"

"Your eminence might be recognized."

"Even under this disguise?" asked Mazarin, raising a cloak which covered an arm-chair, upon which lay a complete dress for an officer, of pearl-gray and red, entirely embroidered with silver.

"If your eminence is disguised it will be almost easy."

"Ah!" said Mazarin, breathing more freely.

"But it will be necessary for your eminence to do what the other day you declared you should have done in our place—cry, 'Down with Mazarin!'"

"I will: 'Down with Mazarin'"

"In French, in good French, my lord, take care of your accent; they killed six thousand Angevins in Sicily because they pronounced Italian badly. Take care that the French do not take their revenge on you for the Sicilian vespers."

"I will do my best."

"The streets are full of armed men," continued D'Artagnan. "Are you sure that no one is aware of the queen's project?"

Mazarin reflected.

"This affair would give a fine opportunity for a traitor, my lord; the chance of being attacked would be an excuse for everything."

Mazarin shuddered, but he reflected that a man who had the least intention to betray would not warn first.

"And therefore," added he, quietly, "I have not confidence in every one; the proof of which is, that I have fixed upon you to escort me."

"Shall you not go with the queen?"

"No," replied Mazarin.

"Then you will start after the queen?"

"No," said Mazarin again.

"Ah!" said D'Artagnan, who began to understand.

"Yes," continued the cardinal. "I have my plan. With the queen I double her risk; after the queen her departure would double mine; then, the court once safe, I might be forgotten. The great are often ungrateful."

"Very true," said D'Artagnan, fixing his eyes, in spite of himself, on the queen's diamond, which Mazarin wore on his finger. Mazarin followed the direction of his eyes and gently turned the hoop of the ring inside.

"I wish," he said, with his cunning smile, "to prevent them from being ungrateful to me."

"It is but Christian charity," replied D'Artagnan, "not to lead one's neighbors into temptation."

"It is exactly for that reason," said Mazarin, "that I wish to start before them."

D'Artagnan smiled—he was just the man to understand the astute Italian. Mazarin saw the smile and profited by the moment.

"You will begin, therefore, by taking me first out of Paris, will you not, my dear M. d'Artagnan?"

"A difficult commission, my lord," replied D'Artagnan, resuming his serious manner.

"But," said Mazarin, "you did not make so many difficulties with regard to the king and queen."

"The king and the queen are my king and queen," replied the musketeer, "my life is theirs and I must give it for them. If they ask it what have I to say?"

"That is true," murmured Mazarin, in a low tone, "but as thy life is not mine I suppose I must buy it, must I not?" and sighing deeply he began to turn the hoop of his ring outside again. D'Artagnan smiled. These two men met at one point and that was, cunning; had they been actuated equally by courage, the one would have done great things for the other.

"But, also," said Mazarin, "you must understand that if I ask this service from you it is with the intention of being grateful."

"Is it still only an intention, your eminence?" asked D'Artagnan.

"Stay," said Mazarin, drawing the ring from his finger, "my dear D'Artagnan, there is a diamond which belonged to you formerly, it is but just it should return to you; take it, I pray."

D'Artagnan spared Mazarin the trouble of insisting, and after looking to see if the stone was the same and assuring himself of the purity of its water, he took it and passed it on his finger with indescribable pleasure.

"I valued it much," said Mazarin, giving a last look at it; "nevertheless, I give it to you with great pleasure."

"And I, my lord," said D'Artagnan, "accept it as it is given. Come, let us speak of your little affairs. You wish to leave before everybody and at what hour?"

"At ten o'clock."

"And the queen, at what time is it her wish to start?"

"At midnight."

"Then it is possible. I can get you out of Paris and leave you beyond the barriere, and can return for her."

"Capital; but how will you get me out of Paris?"

"Oh! as to that, you must leave it to me."

"I give you absolute power, therefore; take as large an escort as you like."

D'Artagnan shook his head.

"It seems to me, however," said Mazarin, "the safest method."

"Yes, for you, my lord, but not for the queen; you must leave it to me and give me the entire direction of the undertaking."

"Nevertheless——"

"Or find some one else," continued D'Artagnan, turning his back.

"Oh!" muttered Mazarin, "I do believe he is going off with the diamond! M. d'Artagnan, my dear M. d'Artagnan," he called out in a coaxing voice, "will you answer for everything?"

"I will answer for nothing. I will do my best."

"Well, then, let us go—I must trust to you."

"It is very fortunate," said D'Artagnan to himself.

"You will be here at half-past nine."

"And I shall find your eminence ready?"

"Certainly, quite ready."

"Well, then, it is a settled thing; and now, my lord, will you obtain for me an audience with the queen?"

"For what purpose?"

"I wish to receive her majesty's commands from her own lips."

"She desired me to give them to you."

"She may have forgotten something."

"You really wish to see her?"

"It is indispensable, my lord."

Mazarin hesitated for one instant, but D'Artagnan was firm.

"Come, then," said the minister; "I will conduct you to her, but remember, not one word of our conversation."

"What has passed between us concerns ourselves alone, my lord," replied D'Artagnan.

"Swear to be mute."

"I never swear, my lord, I say yes or no; and, as I am a gentleman, I keep my word."

"Come, then, I see that I must trust unreservedly to you."

"Believe me, my lord, it will be your best plan."

"Come," said Mazarin, conducting D'Artagnan into the queen's oratory and desiring him to wait there. He did not wait long, for in five minutes the queen entered in full gala costume. Thus dressed she scarcely appeared thirty-five years of age. She was still exceedingly handsome.

"It is you, Monsieur D'Artagnan," she said, smiling graciously; "I thank you for having insisted on seeing me."

"I ought to ask your majesty's pardon, but I wished to receive your commands from your own mouth."

"Do you accept the commission which I have intrusted to you?"

"With gratitude."

"Very well, be here at midnight."

"I will not fail."

"Monsieur d'Artagnan," continued the queen, "I know your disinterestedness too well to speak of my own gratitude at such a moment, but I swear to you that I shall not forget this second service as I forgot the first."

"Your majesty is free to forget or to remember, as it pleases you; and I know not what you mean," said D'Artagnan, bowing.

"Go, sir," said the queen, with her most bewitching smile, "go and return at midnight."

And D'Artagnan retired, but as he passed out he glanced at the curtain through which the queen had entered and at the bottom of the tapestry he remarked the tip of a velvet slipper.

"Good," thought he; "Mazarin has been listening to discover whether I betrayed him. In truth, that Italian puppet does not deserve the services of an honest man."

D'Artagnan was not less exact to his appointment and at half-past nine o'clock he entered the ante-room.

He found the cardinal dressed as an officer, and he looked very well in that costume, which, as we have already said, he wore elegantly; only he was very pale and trembled slightly.

"Quite alone?" he asked.

"Yes, my lord."

"And that worthy Monsieur du Vallon, are we not to enjoy his society?"

"Certainly, my lord; he is waiting in his carriage at the gate of the garden of the Palais Royal."

"And we start in his carriage, then?"

"Yes, my lord."

"And with us no other escort but you two?"

"Is it not enough? One of us would suffice."

"Really, my dear Monsieur d'Artagnan," said the cardinal, "your coolness startles me."

"I should have thought, on the contrary, that it ought to have inspired you with confidence."

"And Bernouin—do I not take him with me?"

"There is no room for him, he will rejoin your eminence."

"Let us go," said Mazarin, "since everything must be done as you wish."

"My lord, there is time to draw back," said D'Artagnan, "and your eminence is perfectly free."

"Not at all, not at all," said Mazarin; "let us be off."

And so they descended the private stair, Mazarin leaning on the arm of D'Artagnan a hand the musketeer felt trembling. At last, after crossing the courts of the Palais Royal, where there still remained some of the conveyances of late guests, they entered the garden and reached the little gate. Mazarin attempted to open it by a key which he took from his pocket, but with such shaking fingers that he could not find the keyhole.

"Give it to me," said D'Artagnan, who when the gate was open deposited the key in his pocket, reckoning upon returning by that gate.

The steps were already down and the door open. Mousqueton stood at the door and Porthos was inside the carriage.

"Mount, my lord," said D'Artagnan to Mazarin, who sprang into the carriage without waiting for a second bidding. D'Artagnan followed him, and Mousqueton, having closed the door, mounted behind the carriage with many groans. He had made some difficulties about going, under pretext that he still suffered from his wound, but D'Artagnan had said to him:

"Remain if you like, my dear Monsieur Mouston, but I warn you that Paris will be burnt down to-night;" upon which Mousqueton had declared, without asking anything further, that he was ready to follow his master and Monsieur d'Artagnan to the end of the world.

The carriage started at a measured pace, without betraying by the slightest sign that it contained people in a hurry. The cardinal wiped his forehead with his handkerchief and looked around him. On his left was Porthos, whilst D'Artagnan was on his right; each guarded a door and served as a rampart to him on either side. Before him, on the front seat, lay two pairs of pistols—one in front of Porthos and the other of D'Artagnan. About a hundred paces from the Palais Royal a patrol stopped the carriage.

"Who goes?" asked the captain.

"Mazarin!" replied D'Artagnan, bursting into a laugh. The cardinal's hair stood on end. But the joke appeared an excellent one to the citizens, who, seeing the conveyance without escort and unarmed, would never have believed in the possibility of so great an imprudence.

"A good journey to ye," they cried, allowing it to pass.

"Hem!" said D'Artagnan, "what does my lord think of that reply?"

"Man of talent!" cried Mazarin.

"In truth," said Porthos, "I understand; but now——"

About the middle of the Rue des Petits Champs they were stopped by a second patrol.

"Who goes there?" inquired the captain of the patrol.

"Keep back, my lord," said D'Artagnan. And Mazarin buried himself so far behind the two friends that he disappeared, completely hidden between them.

"Who goes there?" cried the same voice, impatiently whilst D'Artagnan perceived that they had rushed to the horses' heads. But putting his head out of the carriage:

"Eh! Planchet," said he.

The chief approached, and it was indeed Planchet; D'Artagnan had recognized the voice of his old servant.

"How, sir!" said Planchet, "is it you?"

"Eh! mon Dieu! yes, my good friend, this worthy Porthos has just received a sword wound and I am taking him to his country house at Saint Cloud."

"Oh! really," said Planchet.

"Porthos," said D'Artagnan, "if you can still speak, say a word, my dear Porthos, to this good Planchet."

"Planchet, my friend," said Porthos, in a melancholy voice, "I am very ill; should you meet a doctor you will do me a favor by sending him to me."

"Oh! good Heaven," said Planchet, "what a misfortune! and how did it happen?"

"I will tell you all about it," replied Mousqueton.

Porthos uttered a deep groan.

"Make way for us, Planchet," said D'Artagnan in a whisper to him, "or he will not arrive alive; the lungs are attacked, my friend."

Planchet shook his head with the air of a man who says, "In that case things look ill." Then he exclaimed, turning to his men:

"Let them pass; they are friends."

The carriage resumed its course, and Mazarin, who had held his breath, ventured to breathe again.

"Bricconi!" muttered he.

A few steps in advance of the gate of Saint Honore they met a third troop; this latter party was composed of ill-looking fellows, who resembled bandits more than anything else; they were the men of the beggar of Saint Eustache.

"Attention, Porthos!" cried D'Artagnan.

Porthos placed his hand on the pistols.

"What is it?" asked Mazarin.

"My lord, I think we are in bad company."

A man advanced to the door with a kind of scythe in his hand. "Qui vive?" he asked.

"Eh, rascal!" said D'Artagnan, "do you not recognize his highness the prince's carriage?"

"Prince or not," said the man, "open. We are here to guard the gate, and no one whom we do not know shall pass."

"What is to be done?" said Porthos.

"Pardieu! pass," replied D'Artagnan.

"But how?" asked Mazarin.

"Through or over; coachman, gallop on."

The coachman raised his whip.

"Not a step further," said the man, who appeared to be the captain, "or I will hamstring your horses."

"Peste!" said Porthos, "it would be a pity; animals which cost me a hundred pistoles each."

"I will pay you two hundred for them," said Mazarin.

"Yes, but when once they are hamstrung, our necks will be strung next."

"If one of them comes to my side," asked Porthos, "must I kill him?"

"Yes, by a blow of your fist, if you can; we will not fire but at the last extremity."

"I can do it," said Porthos.

"Come and open, then!" cried D'Artagnan to the man with the scythe, taking one of the pistols up by the muzzle and preparing to strike with the handle. And as the man approached, D'Artagnan, in order to have more freedom for his actions, leaned half out of the door; his eyes were fixed upon those of the mendicant, which were lighted up by a lantern. Without doubt he recognized D'Artagnan, for he became deadly pale; doubtless the musketeer knew him, for his hair stood up on his head.

"Monsieur d'Artagnan!" he cried, falling back a step; "it is Monsieur d'Artagnan! let him pass."

D'Artagnan was perhaps about to reply, when a blow, similar to that of a mallet falling on the head of an ox, was heard. The noise was caused by Porthos, who had just knocked down his man.

D'Artagnan turned around and saw the unfortunate man upon his back about four paces off.

"'Sdeath!" cried he to the coachman. "Spur your horses! whip! get on!"

The coachman bestowed a heavy blow of the whip upon his horses; the noble animals bounded forward; then cries of men who were knocked down were heard; then a double concussion was felt, and two of the wheels seemed to pass over a round and flexible body. There was a moment's silence, then the carriage cleared the gate.

"To Cours la Reine!" cried D'Artagnan to the coachman; then turning to Mazarin he said, "Now, my lord, you can say five paters and five aves, in thanks to Heaven for your deliverance. You are safe—you are free."

Mazarin replied only by a groan; he could not believe in such a miracle. Five minutes later the carriage stopped, having reached Cours la Reine.

"Is my lord pleased with his escort?" asked D'Artagnan.

"Enchanted, monsieur," said Mazarin, venturing his head out of one of the windows; "and now do as much for the queen."

"It will not be so difficult," replied D'Artagnan, springing to the ground. "Monsieur du Vallon, I commend his eminence to your care."

"Be quite at ease," said Porthos, holding out his hand, which D'Artagnan took and shook in his.

"Oh!" cried Porthos, as if in pain.

D'Artagnan looked with surprise at his friend.

"What is the matter, then?" he asked.

"I think I have sprained my wrist,' said Porthos.

"The devil! why, you strike like a blind or a deaf man."

"It was necessary; my man was going to fire a pistol at me; but you—how did you get rid of yours?"

"Oh, mine," replied D'Artagnan, "was not a man."

"What was it then?"

"It was an apparition."

"And——"

"I charmed it away."

Without further explanation D'Artagnan took the pistols which were upon the front seat, placed them in his belt, wrapped himself in his cloak, and not wishing to enter by the same gate as that through which they had left, he took his way toward the Richelieu gate.

Chapter LII.

The Carriage of Monsieur le Coadjuteur.

Instead of returning, then, by the Saint Honore gate, D'Artagnan, who had time before him, walked around and re-entered by the Porte Richelieu. He was approached to be examined, and when it was discovered by his plumed hat and his laced coat, that he was an officer of the musketeers, he was surrounded, with the intention of making him cry, "Down with Mazarin!" The demonstration did not fail to make him uneasy at first; but when he discovered what it meant, he shouted it in such a voice that even the most exacting were satisfied. He walked down the Rue Richelieu, meditating how he should carry off the queen in her turn, for to take her in a carriage bearing the arms of France was not to be thought of, when he perceived an equipage standing at the door of the hotel belonging to Madame de Guemenee.

He was struck by a sudden idea.

"Ah, pardieu!" he exclaimed; "that would be fair play."

And approaching the carriage, he examined the arms on the panels and the livery of the coachman on his box. This scrutiny was so much the more easy, the coachman being sound asleep.

"It is, in truth, monsieur le coadjuteur's carriage," said D'Artagnan; "upon my honor I begin to think that Heaven favors us."

He mounted noiselessly into the chariot and pulled the silk cord which was attached to the coachman's little finger.

"To the Palais Royal," he called out.

The coachman awoke with a start and drove off in the direction he was desired, never doubting but that the order had come from his master. The porter at the palace was about to close the gates, but seeing such a handsome equipage he fancied that it was some visit of importance and the carriage was allowed to pass and to stop beneath the porch. It was then only the coachman perceived the grooms were not behind the vehicle; he fancied monsieur le coadjuteur had sent them back, and without dropping the reins he sprang from his box to open the door. D'Artagnan, in his turn, sprang to the ground, and just at the moment when the coachman, alarmed at not seeing his master, fell back a step, he seized him by his collar with the left, whilst with the right hand he placed the muzzle of a pistol at his breast.

"Pronounce one single word," muttered D'Artagnan, "and you are a dead man."

The coachman perceived at once, by the expression of the man who thus addressed him, that he had fallen into a trap, and he remained with his mouth wide open and his eyes portentously staring.

Two musketeers were pacing the court, to whom D'Artagnan called by their names.

"Monsieur de Belliere," said he to one of them, "do me the favor to take the reins from the hands of this worthy man, mount upon the box and drive to the door of the private stair, and wait for me there; it is an affair of importance on the service of the king."

The musketeer, who knew that his lieutenant was incapable of jesting with regard to the service, obeyed without a word, although he thought the order strange. Then turning toward the second musketeer, D'Artagnan said:

"Monsieur du Verger, help me to place this man in a place of safety."

The musketeer, thinking that his lieutenant had just arrested some prince in disguise, bowed, and drawing his sword, signified that he was ready. D'Artagnan mounted the staircase, followed by his prisoner, who in his turn was followed by the soldier, and entered Mazarin's ante-room. Bernouin was waiting there, impatient for news of his master.

"Well, sir?" he said.

"Everything goes on capitally, my dear Monsieur Bernouin, but here is a man whom I must beg you to put in a safe place."

"Where, then, sir?"

"Where you like, provided that the place which you shall choose has iron shutters secured by padlocks and a door that can be locked."

"We have that, sir," replied Bernouin; and the poor coachman was conducted to a closet, the windows of which were barred and which looked very much like a prison.

"And now, my good friend," said D'Artagnan to him, "I must invite you to deprive yourself, for my sake, of your hat and cloak."

The coachman, as we can well understand, made no resistance; in fact, he was so astonished at what had happened to him that he stammered and reeled like a drunken man; D'Artagnan deposited his clothes under the arm of one of the valets.

"And now, Monsieur du Verger," he said, "shut yourself up with this man until Monsieur Bernouin returns to open the door. The duty will be tolerably long and not very amusing, I know; but," added he, seriously, "you understand, it is on the king's service."

"At your command, lieutenant," replied the musketeer, who saw the business was a serious one.

"By-the-bye," continued D'Artagnan, "should this man attempt to fly or to call out, pass your sword through his body."

The musketeer signified by a nod that these commands should be obeyed to the letter, and D'Artagnan went out, followed by Bernouin. Midnight struck.

"Lead me into the queen's oratory," said D'Artagnan, "announce to her I am here, and put this parcel, with a well-loaded musket, under the seat of the carriage which is waiting at the foot of the private stair."

Bernouin conducted D'Artagnan to the oratory, where he sat down pensively. Everything had gone on as usual at the Palais Royal. As we said before, by ten o'clock almost all the guests had dispersed; those who were to fly with the court had the word of command and they were each severally desired to be from twelve o'clock to one at Cours la Reine.

At ten o'clock Anne of Austria had entered the king's room. Monsieur had just retired, and the youthful Louis, remaining the last, was amusing himself by placing some lead soldiers in a line of battle, a game which delighted him much. Two royal pages were playing with him.

"Laporte," said the queen, "it is time for his majesty to go to bed."

The king asked to remain up, having, he said, no wish to sleep; but the queen was firm.

"Are you not going to-morrow morning at six o'clock, Louis, to bathe at Conflans? I think you wished to do so of your own accord?"

"You are right, madame," said the king, "and I am ready to retire to my room when you have kissed me. Laporte, give the light to Monsieur the Chevalier de Coislin."

The queen touched with her lips the white, smooth brow the royal child presented to her with a gravity which already partook of etiquette.

"Go to sleep soon, Louis," said the queen, "for you must be awakened very early."

"I will do my best to obey you, madame," said the youthful king, "but I have no inclination to sleep."

"Laporte," said Anne of Austria, in an undertone, "find some very dull book to read to his majesty, but do not undress yourself."

The king went out, accompanied by the Chevalier de Coislin, bearing the candlestick, and then the queen returned to her own apartment. Her ladies—that is to say Madame de Bregy, Mademoiselle de Beaumont, Madame de Motteville, and Socratine, her sister, so called on account of her sense—had just brought into her dressing-room the remains of the dinner, on which, according to her usual custom, she supped. The queen then gave her orders, spoke of a banquet which the Marquis de Villequier was to give to her on the day after the morrow, indicated the persons she would admit to the honor of partaking of it, announced another visit on the following day to Val-de-Grace, where she intended to pay her devotions, and gave her commands to her senior valet to accompany her. When the ladies had finished their supper the queen feigned extreme fatigue and passed into her bedroom. Madame de Motteville, who was on especial duty that evening, followed to aid and undress her. The queen then began to read, and after conversing with her affectionately for a few minutes, dismissed her.

It was at this moment D'Artagnan entered the courtyard of the palace, in the coadjutor's carriage, and a few seconds later the carriages of the ladies-in-waiting drove out and the gates were shut after them.

A few minutes after twelve o'clock Bernouin knocked at the queen's bedroom door, having come by the cardinal's secret corridor. Anne of Austria opened the door to him herself. She was dressed, that is to say, in dishabille, wrapped in a long, warm dressing-gown.

"It is you, Bernouin," she said. "Is Monsieur d'Artagnan there?"

"Yes, madame, in your oratory. He is waiting till your majesty is ready."

"I am. Go and tell Laporte to wake and dress the king, and then pass on to the Marechal de Villeroy and summon him to me."

Bernouin bowed and retired.

The queen entered her oratory, which was lighted by a single lamp of Venetian crystal, She saw D'Artagnan, who stood expecting her.

"Is it you?" she said.

"Yes, madame."

"Are you ready?"

"I am."

"And his eminence, the cardinal?"

"Has got off without any accident. He is awaiting your majesty at Cours la Reine."

"But in what carriage do we start?"

"I have provided for everything; a carriage below is waiting for your majesty."

"Let us go to the king."

D'Artagnan bowed and followed the queen. The young Louis was already dressed, with the exception of his shoes and doublet; he had allowed himself to be dressed, in great astonishment, overwhelming Laporte with questions, who replied only in these words, "Sire, it is by the queen's commands."

The bedclothes were thrown back, exposing the king's bed linen, which was so worn that here and there holes could be seen. It was one of the results of Mazarin's niggardliness.

The queen entered and D'Artagnan remained at the door. As soon as the child perceived the queen he escaped from Laporte and ran to meet her. Anne then motioned to D'Artagnan to approach, and he obeyed.

"My son," said Anne of Austria, pointing to the musketeer, calm, standing uncovered, "here is Monsieur d'Artagnan, who is as brave as one of those ancient heroes of whom you like so much to hear from my women. Remember his name well and look at him well, that his face may not be forgotten, for this evening he is going to render us a great service."

The young king looked at the officer with his large-formed eye, and repeated:

"Monsieur d'Artagnan."

"That is it, my son."

The young king slowly raised his little hand and held it out to the musketeer; the latter bent on his knee and kissed it.

"Monsieur d'Artagnan," repeated Louis; "very well, madame."

At this moment they were startled by a noise as if a tumult were approaching.

"What is that?" exclaimed the queen.

"Oh, oh!" replied D'Artagnan, straining both at the same time his quick ear and his intelligent glance, "it is the murmur of the populace in revolution."

"We must fly," said the queen.

"Your majesty has given me the control of this business; we had better wait and see what they want."

"Monsieur d'Artagnan!"

"I will answer for everything."

Nothing is so catching as confidence. The queen, full of energy and courage, was quickly alive to these two virtues in others.

"Do as you like," she said, "I rely upon you."

"Will your majesty permit me to give orders in your name throughout this business?"

"Command, sir."

"What do the people want this time?" demanded the king.

"We are about to ascertain, sire," replied D'Artagnan, as he rapidly left the room.

The tumult continued to increase and seemed to surround the Palais Royal entirely. Cries were heard from the interior, of which they could not comprehend the sense. It was evident that there was clamor and sedition.

The king, half dressed, the queen and Laporte remained each in the same state and almost in the same place, where they were listening and waiting. Comminges, who was on guard that night at the Palais Royal, ran in. He had about two hundred men in the courtyards and stables, and he placed them at the queen's disposal.

"Well," asked Anne of Austria, when D'Artagnan reappeared, "what does it mean?"

"It means, madame, that the report has spread that the queen has left the Palais Royal, carrying off the king, and the people ask to have proof to the contrary, or threaten to demolish the Palais Royal."

"Oh, this time it is too much!" exclaimed the queen, "and I will prove to them I have not left."

D'Artagnan saw from the expression of the queen's face that she was about to issue some violent command. He approached her and said in a low voice:

"Has your majesty still confidence in me?"

This voice startled her. "Yes, sir," she replied, "every confidence; speak."

"Will the queen deign to follow my advice?"

"Speak."

"Let your majesty dismiss M. de Comminges and desire him to shut himself up with his men in the guardhouse and in the stables."

Comminges glanced at D'Artagnan with the envious look with which every courtier sees a new favorite spring up.

"You hear, Comminges?" said the queen.

D'Artagnan went up to him; with his usual quickness he caught the anxious glance.

"Monsieur de Comminges," he said, "pardon me; we both are servants of the queen, are we not? It is my turn to be of use to her; do not envy me this happiness."

Comminges bowed and left.

"Come," said D'Artagnan to himself, "I have got one more enemy."

"And now," said the queen, addressing D'Artagnan, "what is to be done? for you hear that, instead of becoming calmer, the noise increases."

"Madame," said D'Artagnan, "the people want to see the king and they must see him."

"What! must see him! Where—on the balcony?"

"Not at all, madame, but here, sleeping in his bed."

"Oh, your majesty," exclaimed Laporte, "Monsieur d'Artagnan is right."

The queen became thoughtful and smiled, like a woman to whom duplicity is no stranger.

"Without doubt," she murmured.

"Monsieur Laporte," said D'Artagnan, "go and announce to the people through the grating that they are going to be satisfied and that in five minutes they shall not only see the king, but they shall see him in bed; add that the king sleeps and that the queen begs that they will keep silence, so as not to awaken him."

"But not every one; a deputation of two or four people."

"Every one, madame."

"But reflect, they will keep us here till daybreak."

"It shall take but a quarter of an hour, I answer for everything, madame; believe me, I know the people; they are like a great child, who only wants humoring. Before the sleeping king they will be mute, gentle and timid as lambs."

"Go, Laporte," said the queen.

The young king approached his mother and said, "Why do as these people ask?"

"It must be so, my son," said Anne of Austria.

"But if they say, 'it must be' to me, am I no longer king?"

The queen remained silent.

"Sire," said D'Artagnan, "will your majesty permit me to ask you a question?"

Louis XIV. turned around, astonished that any one should dare to address him. But the queen pressed the child's hand.

"Yes, sir." he said.

"Does your majesty remember, when playing in the park of Fontainebleau, or in the palace courts at Versailles, ever to have seen the sky grow suddenly dark and heard the sound of thunder?"

"Yes, certainly."

"Well, then, this noise of thunder, however much your majesty may have wished to continue playing, has said, 'go in, sire. You must do so.'"

"Certainly, sir; but they tell me that the noise of thunder is the voice of God."

"Well then, sire," continued D'Artagnan, "listen to the noise of the people; you will perceive that it resembles that of thunder."

In truth at that moment a terrible murmur was wafted to them by the night breeze; then all at once it ceased.

"Hold, sire," said D'Artagnan, "they have just told the people that you are asleep; you see, you still are king."

The queen looked with surprise at this strange man, whose brilliant courage made him the equal of the bravest, and who was, by his fine and quick intelligence, the equal of the most astute.

Laporte entered.

"Well, Laporte?" asked the queen.

"Madame," he replied, "Monsieur d'Artagnan's prediction has been accomplished; they are calm, as if by enchantment. The doors are about to be opened and in five minutes they will be here."

"Laporte," said the queen, "suppose you put one of your sons in the king's place; we might be off during the time."

"If your majesty desires it," said Laporte, "my sons, like myself, are at the queen's service."

"Not at all," said D'Artagnan; "should one of them know his majesty and discover but a substitute, all would be lost."

"You are right, sir, always right," said Anne of Austria. "Laporte, place the king in bed."

Laporte placed the king, dressed as he was, in the bed and then covered him as far as the shoulders with the sheet. The queen bent over him and kissed his brow.

"Pretend to sleep, Louis," said she.

"Yes," said the king, "but I do not wish to be touched by any of those men."

"Sire, I am here," said D'Artagnan, "and I give you my word, that if a single man has the audacity, his life shall pay for it."

"And now what is to be done?" asked the queen, "for I hear them."

"Monsieur Laporte, go to them and again recommend silence. Madame, wait at the door, whilst I shall be at the head of the king's bed, ready to die for him."

Laporte went out; the queen remained standing near the hangings, whilst D'Artagnan glided behind the curtains.

Then the heavy and collected steps of a multitude of men were heard, and the queen herself raised the tapestry hangings and put her finger on her lips.

On seeing the queen, the men stopped short, respectfully.

"Enter, gentlemen, enter," said the queen.

There was then amongst that crowd a moment's hesitation, which looked like shame. They had expected resistance, they had expected to be thwarted, to have to force the gates, to overturn the guards. The gates had opened of themselves, and the king, ostensibly at least, had no other guard at his bed-head but his mother. The foremost of them stammered and attempted to fall back.

"Enter, gentlemen," said Laporte, "since the queen desires you so to do."

Then one more bold than the rest ventured to pass the door and to advance on tiptoe. This example was imitated by the rest, until the room filled silently, as if these men had been the humblest, most devoted courtiers. Far beyond the door the heads of those who were not able to enter could be seen, all craning to their utmost height to try and see.

D'Artagnan saw it all through an opening he had made in the curtain, and in the very first man who entered he recognized Planchet.

"Sir," said the queen to him, thinking he was the leader of the band, "you wished to see the king and therefore I determined to show him to you myself. Approach and look at him and say if we have the appearance of people who wish to run away."

"No, certainly," replied Planchet, rather astonished at the unexpected honor conferred upon him.

"You will say, then, to my good and faithful Parisians," continued Anne, with a smile, the expression of which did not deceive D'Artagnan, "that you have seen the king in bed, asleep, and the queen also ready to retire."

"I shall tell them, madame, and those who accompany me will say the same thing; but——"

"But what?" asked Anne of Austria.

"Will your majesty pardon me," said Planchet, "but is it really the king who is lying there?"

Anne of Austria started. "If," she said, "there is one among you who knows the king, let him approach and say whether it is really his majesty lying there."

A man wrapped in a cloak, in the folds of which his face was hidden, approached and leaned over the bed and looked.

For one second, D'Artagnan thought the man had some evil design and he put his hand to his sword; but in the movement made by the man in stooping a portion of his face was uncovered and D'Artagnan recognized the coadjutor.

"It is certainly the king," said the man, rising again. "God bless his majesty!"

"Yes," repeated the leader in a whisper, "God bless his majesty!" and all these men, who had entered enraged, passed from anger to pity and blessed the royal infant in their turn.

"Now," said Planchet, "let us thank the queen. My friends, retire."

They all bowed, and retired by degrees as noiselessly as they had entered. Planchet, who had been the first to enter, was the last to leave. The queen stopped him.

"What is your name, my friend?" she said.

Planchet, much surprised at the inquiry, turned back.

"Yes," continued the queen, "I think myself as much honored to have received you this evening as if you had been a prince, and I wish to know your name."

"Yes," thought Planchet, "to treat me as a prince. No, thank you."

D'Artagnan trembled lest Planchet, seduced, like the crow in the fable, should tell his name, and that the queen, knowing his name, would discover that Planchet had belonged to him.

"Madame," replied Planchet, respectfully, "I am called Dulaurier, at your service."

"Thank you, Monsieur Dulaurier," said the queen; "and what is your business?"

"Madame, I am a clothier in the Rue Bourdonnais."

"That is all I wished to know," said the queen. "Much obliged to you, Monsieur Dulaurier. You will hear again from me."

"Come, come," thought D'Artagnan, emerging from behind the curtain, "decidedly Monsieur Planchet is no fool; it is evident he has been brought up in a good school."

The different actors in this strange scene remained facing one another, without uttering a single word; the queen standing near the door, D'Artagnan half out of his hiding place, the king raised on his elbow, ready to fall down on his bed again at the slightest sound that would indicate the return of the multitude, but instead of approaching, the noise became more and more distant and very soon it died entirely away.

The queen breathed more freely. D'Artagnan wiped his damp forehead and the king slid off his bed, saying, "Let us go."

At this moment Laporte reappeared.

"Well?" asked the queen

"Well, madame," replied the valet, "I followed them as far as the gates. They announced to all their comrades that they had seen the king and that the queen had spoken to them; and, in fact, they went away quite proud and happy."

"Oh, the miserable wretches!" murmured the queen, "they shall pay dearly for their boldness, and it is I who promise this."

Then turning to D'Artagnan, she said:

"Sir, you have given me this evening the best advice I have ever received. Continue, and say what we must do now."

"Monsieur Laporte," said D'Artagnan, "finish dressing his majesty."

"We may go, then?" asked the queen.

"Whenever your majesty pleases. You have only to descend by the private stairs and you will find me at the door."

"Go, sir," said the queen; "I will follow you."

D'Artagnan went down and found the carriage at its post and the musketeer on the box. D'Artagnan took out the parcel which he had desired Bernouin to place under the seat. It may be remembered that it was the hat and cloak belonging to Monsieur de Gondy's coachman.

He placed the cloak on his shoulders and the hat on his head, whilst the musketeer got off the box.

"Sir," said D'Artagnan, "you will go and release your companion, who is guarding the coachman. You must mount your horse and proceed to the Rue Tiquetonne, Hotel de la Chevrette, whence you will take my horse and that of Monsieur du Vallon, which you must saddle and equip as if for war, and then you will leave Paris, bringing them with you to Cours la Reine. If, when you arrive at Cours la Reine, you find no one, you must go on to Saint Germain. On the king's service."

The musketeer touched his cap and went away to execute the orders thus received.

D'Artagnan mounted the box, having a pair of pistols in his belt, a musket under his feet and a naked sword behind him.

The queen appeared, and was followed by the king and the Duke d'Anjou, his brother.

"Monsieur the coadjutor's carriage!" she exclaimed, falling back.

"Yes, madame," said D'Artagnan; "but get in fearlessly, for I myself will drive you."

The queen uttered a cry of surprise and entered the carriage, and the king and monsieur took their places at her side.

"Come, Laporte," said the queen.

"How, madame!" said the valet, "in the same carriage as your majesties?"

"It is not a matter of royal etiquette this evening, but of the king's safety. Get in, Laporte."

Laporte obeyed.

"Pull down the blinds," said D'Artagnan.

"But will that not excite suspicion, sir?" asked the queen.

"Your majesty's mind may be quite at ease," replied the officer; "I have my answer ready."

The blinds were pulled down and they started at a gallop by the Rue Richelieu. On reaching the gate the captain of the post advanced at the head of a dozen men, holding a lantern in his hand.

D'Artagnan signed to them to draw near.

"Do you recognize the carriage?" he asked the sergeant.

"No," replied the latter.

"Look at the arms."

The sergeant put the lantern near the panel.

"They are those of monsieur le coadjuteur," he said.

"Hush; he is enjoying a ride with Madame de Guemenee."

The sergeant began to laugh.

"Open the gate," he cried. "I know who it is!" Then putting his face to the lowered blinds, he said:

"I wish you joy, my lord!"

"Impudent fellow!" cried D'Artagnan, "you will get me turned off."

The gate groaned on its hinges, and D'Artagnan, seeing the way clear, whipped his horses, who started at a canter, and five minutes later they had rejoined the cardinal.

"Mousqueton!" exclaimed D'Artagnan, "draw up the blinds of his majesty's carriage."

"It is he!" cried Porthos.

"Disguised as a coachman!" exclaimed Mazarin.

"And driving the coadjutor's carriage!" said the queen.

"Corpo di Dio! Monsieur d'Artagnan!" said Mazarin, "you are worth your weight in gold."

Chapter LIII.

How D'Artagnan and Porthos earned by selling Straw.

Mazarin was desirous of setting out instantly for Saint Germain, but the queen declared that she should wait for the people whom she had appointed to meet her. However, she offered the cardinal Laporte's place, which he accepted and went from one carriage to the other.

It was not without foundation that a report of the king's intention to leave Paris by night had been circulated. Ten or twelve persons had been in the secret since six o'clock, and howsoever great their prudence might be, they could not issue the necessary orders for the departure without suspicion being generated. Besides, each individual had one or two others for whom he was interested; and as there could be no doubt but that the queen was leaving Paris full of terrible projects of vengeance, every one had warned parents and friends of what was about to transpire; so that the news of the approaching exit ran like a train of lighted gunpowder along the streets.

The first carriage which arrived after that of the queen was that of the Prince de Condé, with the princess and dowager princess. Both these ladies had been awakened in the middle of the night and did not know what it all was about. The second contained the Duke and Duchess of Orleans, the tall young Mademoiselle and the Abbé de la Riviere; and the third, the Duke de Longueville and the Prince de Conti, brother and brother-in-law of Condé. They all alighted and hastened to pay their respects to the king and queen in their coach. The queen fixed her eyes upon the carriage they had left, and seeing that it was empty, she said:

"But where is Madame de Longueville?"

"Ah, yes, where is my sister?" asked the prince.

"Madame de Longueville is ill," said the duke, "and she desired me to excuse her to your majesty."

Anne gave a quick glance to Mazarin, who answered by an almost imperceptible shake of his head.

"What do you say of this?" asked the queen.

"I say that she is a hostage for the Parisians," answered the cardinal.

"Why is she not come?" asked the prince in a low voice, addressing his brother.

"Silence," whispered the duke, "she has her reasons."

"She will ruin us!" returned the prince.

"She will save us," said Conti.

Carriages now arrived in crowds; those of the Marechal de Villeroy, Guitant, Villequier and Comminges came into the line. The two musketeers arrived in their turn, holding the horses of D'Artagnan and Porthos in their hands. These two instantly mounted, the coachman of the latter replacing D'Artagnan on the coach-box of the royal coach. Mousqueton took the place of the coachman, and drove standing, for reasons known to himself, like Automedon of antiquity.

The queen, though occupied by a thousand details, tried to catch the Gascon's eye; but he, with his wonted prudence, had mingled with the crowd.

"Let us be the avant guard," said he to Porthos, "and find good quarters at Saint Germain; nobody will think of us, and for my part I am greatly fatigued."

"As for me," replied Porthos, "I am falling asleep, which is strange, considering we have not had any fighting; truly the Parisians are idiots."

"Or rather, we are very clever," said D'Artagnan.

"Perhaps."

"And how is your wrist?"

"Better; but do you think that we've got them this time?"

"Got what?"

"You your command, and I my title?"

"I'faith! yes—I should expect so; besides, if they forget, I shall take the liberty of reminding them."

"The queen's voice! she is speaking," said Porthos; "I think she wants to ride on horseback."

"Oh, she would like it, but——"

"But what?"

"The cardinal won't allow it. Gentlemen," he said, addressing the two musketeers, "accompany the royal carriage, we are going forward to look for lodgings."

D'Artagnan started off for Saint Germain, followed by Porthos.

"We will go on, gentlemen," said the queen.

And the royal carriage drove on, followed by the other coaches and about fifty horsemen.

They reached Saint German without any accident; on descending, the queen found the prince awaiting her, bare-headed, to offer her his hand.

"What an awakening for the Parisians!" said the queen, radiant.

"It is war," said the prince.

"Well, then, let it be war! Have we not on our side the conqueror of Rocroy, of Nordlingen, of Lens?"

The prince bowed low.

It was then three o'clock in the morning. The queen walked first, every one followed her. About two hundred persons had accompanied her in her flight.

"Gentlemen," said the queen, laughing, "pray take up your abode in the chateau; it is large, and there will be no want of room for you all; but, as we never thought of coming here, I am informed that there are, in all, only three beds in the whole establishment, one for the king, one for me——"

"And one for the cardinal," muttered the prince.

"Am I—am I, then, to sleep on the floor?" asked Gaston d'Orleans, with a forced smile.

"No, my prince," replied Mazarin, "the third bed is intended for your highness."

"But your eminence?" replied the prince.

"I," answered Mazarin, "I shall not sleep at all; I have work to do."

Gaston desired that he should be shown into the room wherein he was to sleep, without in the least concerning himself as to where his wife and daughter were to repose.

"Well, for my part, I shall go to bed," said D'Artagnan; "come, Porthos."

Porthos followed the lieutenant with that profound confidence he ever had in the wisdom of his friend. They walked from one end of the chateau to the other, Porthos looking with wondering eyes at D'Artagnan, who was counting on his fingers.

"Four hundred, at a pistole each, four hundred pistoles."

"Yes," interposed Porthos, "four hundred pistoles; but who is to make four hundred pistoles?"

"A pistole is not enough," said D'Artagnan, "'tis worth a louis."

"What is worth a louis?"

"Four hundred, at a louis each, make four hundred louis."

"Four hundred?" said Porthos.

"Yes, there are two hundred of them, and each of them will need two, which will make four hundred."

"But four hundred what?"

"Listen!" cried D'Artagnan.

But as there were all kinds of people about, who were in a state of stupefaction at the unexpected arrival of the court, he whispered in his friend's ear.

"I understand," answered Porthos, "I understand you perfectly, on my honor; two hundred louis, each of us, would be making a pretty thing of it; but what will people say?"

"Let them say what they will; besides, how will they know that we are doing it?"

"But who will distribute these things?" asked Porthos.

"Isn't Mousqueton there?"

"But he wears my livery; my livery will be known," replied Porthos.

"He can turn his coat inside out."

"You are always in the right, my dear friend," cried Porthos; "but where the devil do you discover all the notions you put into practice?"

D'Artagnan smiled. The two friends turned down the first street they came to. Porthos knocked at the door of a house to the right, whilst D'Artagnan knocked at the door of a house to the left.

"Some straw," they said.

"Sir, we don't keep any," was the reply of the people who opened the doors; "but please ask at the hay dealer's."

"Where is the hay dealer's?"

"At the last large door in the street."

"Are there any other people in Saint Germain who sell straw?"

"Yes; there's the landlord of the Lamb, and Gros-Louis the farmer; they both live in the Rue des Ursulines."

"Very well."

D'Artagnan went instantly to the hay dealer and bargained with him for a hundred and fifty trusses of straw, which he obtained, at the rate of three pistoles each. He went afterward to the innkeeper and bought from him two hundred trusses at the same price. Finally, Farmer Louis sold them eighty trusses, making in all four hundred and thirty.

There was no more to be had in Saint Germain. This foraging did not occupy more than half an hour. Mousqueton, duly instructed, was put at the head of this sudden and new business. He was cautioned not to let a bit of straw out of his hands under a louis the truss, and they intrusted to him straw to the amount of four hundred and thirty louis. D'Artagnan, taking with him three trusses of straw, returned to the chateau, where everybody, freezing with cold and more than half asleep, envied the king, the queen, and the Duke of Orleans, on their camp beds. The lieutenant's entrance produced a burst of laughter in the great drawing-room; but he did not appear to notice that he was the object of general attention, but began to arrange, with so much cleverness, nicety and gayety, his straw bed, that the mouths of all these poor creatures, who could not go to sleep, began to water.

"Straw!" they all cried out, "straw! where is there any to be found?"

"I can show you," answered the Gascon.

And he conducted them to Mousqueton, who freely distributed the trusses at the rate of a louis apiece. It was thought rather dear, but people wanted to sleep, and who would not give even two or three louis for a few hours of sound sleep?

D'Artagnan gave up his bed to any one who wanted it, making it over about a dozen times; and since he was supposed to have paid, like the others, a louis for his truss of straw, he pocketed in that way thirty louis in less than half an hour. At five o'clock in the morning the straw was worth eighty francs a truss and there was no more to be had.

D'Artagnan had taken the precaution to set apart four trusses for his own use. He put in his pocket the key of the room where he had hidden them, and accompanied by Porthos returned to settle with Mousqueton, who, naively, and like the worthy steward that he was, handed them four hundred and thirty louis and kept one hundred for himself.

Mousqueton, who knew nothing of what was going on in the chateau, wondered that the idea had not occurred to him sooner. D'Artagnan put the gold in his hat, and in going back to the chateau settled the reckoning with Porthos, each of them had cleared two hundred and fifteen louis.

Porthos, however, found that he had no straw left for himself. He returned to Mousqueton, but the steward had sold the last wisp. He then repaired to D'Artagnan, who, thanks to his four trusses of straw, was in the act of making up and tasting, by anticipation, the luxury of a bed so soft, so well stuffed at the head, so well covered at the foot, that it would have excited the envy of the king himself, if his majesty had not been fast asleep in his own. D'Artagnan could on no account consent to pull his bed to pieces again for Porthos, but for a consideration of four louis that the latter paid him for it, he consented that Porthos should share his couch with him. He laid his sword at the head, his pistols by his side, stretched his cloak over his feet, placed his felt hat on the top of his cloak and extended himself luxuriously on the straw, which rustled under him. He was already enjoying the sweet dream engendered by the possession of two hundred and nineteen louis, made in a quarter of an hour, when a voice was heard at the door of the hall, which made him stir.

"Monsieur d'Artagnan!" it cried.

"Here!" cried Porthos, "here!"

Porthos foresaw that if D'Artagnan was called away he should remain the sole possessor of the bed. An officer approached.

"I am come to fetch you, Monsieur d'Artagnan."

"From whom?"

"His eminence sent me."

"Tell my lord that I'm going to sleep, and I advise him, as a friend, to do the same."

"His eminence is not gone to bed and will not go to bed, and wants you instantly."

"The devil take Mazarin, who does not know when to sleep at the proper time. What does he want with me? Is it to make me a captain? In that case I will forgive him."

And the musketeer rose, grumbling, took his sword, hat, pistols, and cloak, and followed the officer, whilst Porthos, alone and sole possessor of the bed, endeavored to follow the good example of falling asleep, which his predecessor had set him.

"Monsieur d'Artagnan," said the cardinal, on perceiving him, "I have not forgotten with what zeal you have served me. I am going to prove to you that I have not."

"Good," thought the Gascon, "this is a promising beginning."

"Monsieur d'Artagnan," he resumed, "do you wish to become a captain?"

"Yes, my lord."

"And your friend still longs to be made a baron?"

"At this very moment, my lord, he no doubt dreams that he is one already."

"Then," said Mazarin, taking from his portfolio the letter which he had already shown D'Artagnan, "take this dispatch and carry it to England."

D'Artagnan looked at the envelope; there was no address on it.

"Am I not to know to whom to present it?"

"You will know when you reach London; at London you may tear off the outer envelope."

"And what are my instructions?"

"To obey in every particular the man to whom this letter is addressed. You must set out for Boulogne. At the Royal Arms of England you will find a young gentleman named Mordaunt."

"Yes, my lord; and what am I to do with this young gentleman?"

"Follow wherever he leads you."

D'Artagnan looked at the cardinal with a stupefied air.

"There are your instructions," said Mazarin; "go!"

"Go! 'tis easy to say so, but that requires money, and I haven't any."

"Ah!" replied Mazarin, "so you have no money?"

"None, my lord."

"But the diamond I gave you yesterday?"

"I wish to keep it in remembrance of your eminence."

Mazarin sighed.

"'Tis very dear living in England, my lord, especially as envoy extraordinary."

"Zounds!" replied Mazarin, "the people there are very sedate, and their habits, since the revolution, simple; but no matter."

He opened a drawer and took out a purse.

"What do you say to a thousand crowns?"

D'Artagnan pouted out his lower lip in a most extraordinary manner.

"I reply, my lord, 'tis but little, as certainly I shall not go alone."

"I suppose not. Monsieur du Vallon, that worthy gentleman, for, with the exception of yourself, Monsieur d'Artagnan, there's not a man in France that I esteem and love so much as him——"

"Then, my lord," replied D'Artagnan, pointing to the purse which Mazarin still held, "if you love and esteem him so much, you—understand me?"

"Be it so! on his account I add two hundred crowns."

"Scoundrel!" muttered D'Artagnan. "But on our return," he said aloud, "may we, that is, my friend and I, depend on having, he his barony, and I my promotion?"

"On the honor of Mazarin."

"I should like another sort of oath better," said D'Artagnan to himself; then aloud, "May I not offer my duty to her majesty the queen?"

"Her majesty is asleep and you must set off directly," replied Mazarin; "go, pray, sir——"

"One word more, my lord; if there's any fighting where I'm going, must I fight?"

"You are to obey the commands of the personage to whom I have addressed the inclosed letter."

"'Tis well," said D'Artagnan, holding out his hand to receive the money. "I offer my best respects and services to you, my lord."

D'Artagnan then, returning to the officer, said:

"Sir, have the kindness also to awaken Monsieur du Vallon and to say 'tis by his eminence's order, and that I shall await him at the stables."

The officer went off with an eagerness that showed the Gascon that he had some personal interest in the matter.

Porthos was snoring most musically when some one touched him on the shoulder.

"I come from the cardinal," said the officer.

"Heigho!" said Porthos, opening his large eyes; "what have you got to say?"

"That his eminence has ordered you to England and that Monsieur d'Artagnan is waiting for you in the stables."

Porthos sighed heavily, arose, took his hat, his pistols, and his cloak, and departed, casting a look of regret upon the couch where he had hoped to sleep so well.

No sooner had he turned his back than the officer laid himself down in it, and he had scarcely crossed the threshold before his successor, in his turn, was snoring immoderately. It was very natural, he being the only person in the whole assemblage, except the king, the queen, and the Duke of Orleans, who slept gratuitously.

Chapter LIV.

In which we hear Tidings of Aramis.

D'Artagnan went straight to the stables; day was just dawning. He found his horse and that of Porthos fastened to the manger, but to an empty manger. He took pity on these poor animals and went to a corner of the stable, where he saw a little straw, but in doing so he struck his foot against a human body, which uttered a cry and arose on its knees, rubbing its eyes. It was Mousqueton, who, having no straw to lie upon, had helped himself to that of the horses.

"Mousqueton," cried D'Artagnan, "let us be off! Let us set off."

Mousqueton, recognizing the voice of his master's friend, got up suddenly, and in doing so let fall some louis which he had appropriated to himself illegally during the night.

"Ho! ho!" exclaimed D'Artagnan, picking up a louis and displaying it; "here's a louis that smells confoundedly of straw."

Mousqueton blushed so confusedly that the Gascon began to laugh at him and said:

"Porthos would be angry, my dear Monsieur Mousqueton, but I pardon you, only let us remember that this gold must serve us as a joke, so be gay—come along."

Mousqueton instantly assumed a jovial countenance, saddled the horses quickly and mounted his own without making faces over it.

Whilst this went on, Porthos arrived with a very cross look on his face, and was astonished to find the lieutenant resigned and Mousqueton almost merry.

"Ah, that's it!" he cried, "you have your promotion and I my barony."

"We are going to fetch our brevets," said D'Artagnan, "and when we come back, Master Mazarin will sign them."

"And where are we going?" asked Porthos.

"To Paris first; I have affairs to settle."

And they both set out for Paris.

On arriving at its gates they were astounded to see the threatening aspect of the capital. Around a broken-down carriage the people were uttering imprecations, whilst the persons who had attempted to escape were made prisoners—that is to say, an old man and two women. On the other hand, as the two friends approached to enter, they showed them every kind of civility, thinking them deserters from the royal party and wishing to bind them to their own.

"What is the king doing?" they asked.

"He is asleep."

"And the Spanish woman?"

"Dreaming."

"And the cursed Italian?"

"He is awake, so keep on the watch, as they are gone away; it's for some purpose, rely on it. But as you are the strongest, after all," continued D'Artagnan, "don't be furious with old men and women, and keep your wrath for more appropriate occasions."

The people listened to these words and let go the ladies, who thanked D'Artagnan with an eloquent look.

"Now! onward!" cried the Gascon.

And they continued their way, crossing the barricades, getting the chains about their legs, pushed about, questioning and questioned.

In the place of the Palais Royal D'Artagnan saw a sergeant, who was drilling six or seven hundred citizens. It was Planchet, who brought into play profitably the recollections of the regiment of Piedmont.

In passing before D'Artagnan he recognized his former master.

"Good-day, Monsieur d'Artagnan," said Planchet proudly.

"Good-day, Monsieur Dulaurier," replied D'Artagnan.

Planchet stopped short, staring at D'Artagnan. The first row, seeing their sergeant stop, stopped in their turn, and so on to the very last.

"These citizens are dreadfully ridiculous," observed D'Artagnan to Porthos and went on his way.

Five minutes afterward he entered the hotel of La Chevrette, where pretty Madeleine, the hostess, came to him.

"My dear Mistress Turquaine," said the Gascon, "if you happen to have any money, lock it up quickly; if you happen to have any jewels, hide them directly; if you happen to have any debtors, make them pay you, or any creditors, don't pay them."

"Why, prithee?" asked Madeleine.

"Because Paris is going to be reduced to dust and ashes like Babylon, of which you have no doubt heard tell."

"And are you going to leave me at such a time?"

"This very instant."

"And where are you going?"

"Ah, if you could tell me that, you would be doing me a service."

"Ah, me! ah, me!"

"Have you any letters for me?" inquired D'Artagnan, wishing to signify to the hostess that her lamentations were superfluous and that therefore she had better spare him demonstrations of her grief.

"There's one just arrived," and she handed the letter to D'Artagnan.

"From Athos!" cried D'Artagnan, recognizing the handwriting.

"Ah!" said Porthos, "let us hear what he says."

D'Artagnan opened the letter and read as follows:

"Dear D'Artagnan, dear Du Vallon, my good friends, perhaps this may be the last time that you will ever hear from me. Aramis and I are very unhappy; but God, our courage, and the remembrance of our friendship sustain us. Think often of Raoul. I intrust to you certain papers which are at Blois; and in two months and a half, if you do not hear of us, take possession of them.

"Embrace, with all your heart, the vicomte, for your devoted, friend,

"ATHOS."

"I believe, by Heaven," said D'Artagnan, "that I shall embrace him, since he's upon our road; and if he is so unfortunate as to lose our dear Athos, from that very day he becomes my son."

"And I," said Porthos, "shall make him my sole heir."

"Let us see, what more does Athos say?"

"Should you meet on your journey a certain Monsieur Mordaunt, distrust him, in a letter I cannot say more."

"Monsieur Mordaunt!" exclaimed the Gascon, surprised.

"Monsieur Mordaunt! 'tis well," said Porthos, "we shall remember that; but see, there is a postscript from Aramis."

"So there is," said D'Artagnan, and he read:

"We conceal the place where we are, dear friends, knowing your brotherly affection and that you would come and die with us were we to reveal it."

"Confound it," interrupted Porthos, with an explosion of passion which sent Mousqueton to the other end of the room; "are they in danger of dying?"

D'Artagnan continued:

"Athos bequeaths to you Raoul, and I bequeath to you my revenge. If by any good luck you lay your hand on a certain man named Mordaunt, tell Porthos to take him into a corner and to wring his neck. I dare not say more in a letter.

"ARAMIS."

"If that is all, it is easily done," said Porthos.

"On the contrary," observed D'Artagnan, with a vexed look; "it would be impossible."

"How so?"

"It is precisely this Monsieur Mordaunt whom we are going to join at Boulogne and with whom we cross to England."

"Well, suppose instead of joining this Monsieur Mordaunt we were to go and join our friends?" said Porthos, with a gesture fierce enough to have frightened an army.

"I did think of it, but this letter has neither date nor postmark."

"True," said Porthos. And he began to wander about the room like a man beside himself, gesticulating and half drawing his sword out of the scabbard.

As to D'Artagnan, he remained standing like a man in consternation, with the deepest affliction depicted on his face.

"Ah, this is not right; Athos insults us; he wishes to die alone; it is bad, bad, bad."

Mousqueton, witnessing this despair, melted into tears in a corner of the room.

"Come," said D'Artagnan, "all this leads to nothing. Let us go on. We will embrace Raoul, and perhaps he will have news of Athos."

"Stop—an idea!" cried Porthos; "indeed, my dear D'Artagnan, I don't know how you manage, but you are always full of ideas; let us go and embrace Raoul."

"Woe to that man who should happen to contradict my master at this moment," said Mousqueton to himself; "I wouldn't give a farthing for his life."

They set out. On arriving at the Rue Saint Denis, the friends found a vast concourse of people. It was the Duc de Beaufort, who was coming from the Vendomois and whom the coadjutor was showing to the Parisians, intoxicated with joy. With the duke's aid they already considered themselves invincible.

The two friends turned off into a side street to avoid meeting the prince, and so reached the Saint Denis gate.

"Is it true," said the guard to the two cavaliers, "that the Duc de Beaufort has arrived in Paris?"

"Nothing more certain; and the best proof of it is," said D'Artagnan, "that he has dispatched us to meet the Duc de Vendome, his father, who is coming in his turn."

"Long live De Beaufort!" cried the guards, and they drew back respectfully to let the two friends pass. Once across the barriers these two knew neither fatigue nor fear. Their horses flew, and they never ceased speaking of Athos and Aramis.

The camp had entered Saint Omer; the friends made a little detour and went to the camp, and gave the army an exact account of the flight of the king and queen. They found Raoul near his tent, reclining on a truss of hay, of which his horse stole some mouthfuls; the young man's eyes were red and he seemed dejected. The Marechal de Grammont and the Comte de Guiche had returned to Paris and he was quite lonely. And as soon as he saw the two cavaliers he ran to them with open arms.

"Oh, is it you, dear friends? Did you come here to fetch me? Will you take me away with you? Do you bring me tidings of my guardian?"

"Have you not received any?" said D'Artagnan to the youth.

"Alas! sir, no, and I do not know what has become of him; so that I am really so unhappy that I weep."

In fact, tears rolled down his cheeks.

Porthos turned aside, in order not to show by his honest round face what was passing in his mind.

"Deuce take it!" cried D'Artagnan, more moved than he had been for a long time, "don't despair, my friend, if you have not received any letters from the count, we have received one."

"Oh, really!" cried Raoul.

"And a comforting one, too," added D'Artagnan, seeing the delight that his intelligence gave the young man.

"Have you it?" asked Raoul.

"Yes—that is, I had it," repined the Gascon, making believe to find it. "Wait, it ought to be there in my pocket; it speaks of his return, does it not, Porthos?"

All Gascon as he was, D'Artagnan could not bear alone the weight of that falsehood.

"Yes," replied Porthos, coughing.

"Eh, give it to me!" said the young man.

"Eh! I read it a little while since. Can I have lost it? Ah! confound it! yes, my pocket has a hole in it."

"Oh, yes, Monsieur Raoul!" said Mousqueton, "the letter was very consoling. These gentlemen read it to me and I wept for joy."

"But at any rate, you know where he is, Monsieur d'Artagnan?" asked Raoul, somewhat comforted.

"Ah! that's the thing!" replied the Gascon. "Undoubtedly I know it, but it is a mystery."

"Not to me, I hope?"

"No, not to you, so I am going to tell you where he is."

Porthos devoured D'Artagnan with wondering eyes.

"Where the devil shall I say that he is, so that he cannot try to rejoin him?" thought D'Artagnan.

"Well, where is he, sir?" asked Raoul, in a soft and coaxing voice.

"He is at Constantinople."

"Among the Turks!" exclaimed Raoul, alarmed. "Good heavens! how can you tell me that?"

"Does that alarm you?" cried D'Artagnan. "Pooh! what are the Turks to such men as the Comte de la Fere and the Abbé d'Herblay?"

"Ah, his friend is with him?" said Raoul. "That comforts me a little."

"Has he wit or not—this demon D'Artagnan?" said Porthos, astonished at his friend's deception.

"Now, sir," said D'Artagnan, wishing to change the conversation, "here are fifty pistoles that the count has sent you by the same courier. I suppose you have no more money and that they will be welcome."

"I have still twenty pistoles, sir."

"Well, take them; that makes seventy."

"And if you wish for more," said Porthos, putting his hand to his pocket——

"Thank you, sir," replied Raoul, blushing; "thank you a thousand times."

At this moment Olivain appeared. "Apropos," said D'Artagnan, loud enough for the servant to hear him, "are you satisfied with Olivain?"

"Yes, in some respects, tolerably well."

Olivain pretended to have heard nothing and entered the tent.

"What fault do you find with the fellow?"

"He is a glutton."

"Oh, sir!" cried Olivain, reappearing at this accusation.

"And a little bit of a thief."

"Oh, sir! oh!"

"And, more especially, a notorious coward."

"Oh, oh! sir! you really vilify me!" cried Olivain.

"The deuce!" cried D'Artagnan. "Pray learn, Monsieur Olivain, that people like us are not to be served by cowards. Rob your master, eat his sweetmeats, and drink his wine; but, by Jove! don't be a coward, or I shall cut off your ears. Look at Monsieur Mouston, see the honorable wounds he has received, observe how his habitual valor has given dignity to his countenance."

Mousqueton was in the third heaven and would have embraced D'Artagnan had he dared; meanwhile he resolved to sacrifice his life for him on the next occasion that presented itself.

"Send away that fellow, Raoul," said the Gascon; "for if he's a coward he will disgrace thee some day."

"Monsieur says I am coward," cried Olivain, "because he wanted the other day to fight a cornet in Grammont's regiment and I refused to accompany him."

"Monsieur Olivain, a lackey ought never to disobey," said D'Artagnan, sternly; then taking him aside, he whispered to him: "Thou hast done right; thy master was in the wrong; here's a crown for thee, but should he ever be insulted and thou dost not let thyself be cut in quarters for him, I will cut out thy tongue. Remember that."

Olivain bowed and slipped the crown into his pocket.

"And now, Raoul," said the Gascon, "Monsieur du Vallon and I are going away as ambassadors, where, I know not; but should you want anything, write to Madame Turquaine, at La Chevrette, Rue Tiquetonne and draw upon her purse as on a banker—with economy; for it is not so well filled as that of Monsieur d'Emery."

And having, meantime, embraced his ward, he passed him into the robust arms of Porthos, who lifted him up from the ground and held him a moment suspended near the noble heart of the formidable giant.

"Come," said D'Artagnan, "let us go."

And they set out for Boulogne, where toward evening they arrived, their horses flecked with foam and dark with perspiration.

At ten steps from the place where they halted was a young man in black, who seemed waiting for some one, and who, from the moment he saw them enter the town, never took his eyes off them.

D'Artagnan approached him, and seeing him stare so fixedly, said:

"Well, friend! I don't like people to quiz me!"

"Sir," said the young man, "do you not come from Paris, if you please?"

D'Artagnan thought it was some gossip who wanted news from the capital.

"Yes, sir," he said, in a softened tone.

"Are you not going to put up at the 'Arms of England'?"

"Yes, sir."

"Are you not charged with a mission from his eminence, Cardinal Mazarin?"

"Yes, sir."

"In that case, I am the man you have to do with. I am M. Mordaunt."

"Ah!" thought D'Artagnan, "the man I am warned against by Athos."

"Ah!" thought Porthos, "the man Aramis wants me to strangle."

They both looked searchingly at the young man, who misunderstood the meaning of that inquisition.

"Do you doubt my word?" he said. "In that case I can give you proofs."

"No, sir," said D'Artagnan; "and we place ourselves at your orders."

"Well, gentlemen," resumed Mordaunt, "we must set out without delay, to-day is the last day granted me by the cardinal. My ship is ready, and had you not come I must have set off without you, for General Cromwell expects my return impatiently."

"So!" thought the lieutenant, "'tis to General Cromwell that our dispatches are addressed."

"Have you no letter for him?" asked the young man.

"I have one, the seal of which I am not to break till I reach London; but since you tell me to whom it is addressed, 'tis useless to wait till then."

D'Artagnan tore open the envelope of the letter. It was directed to "Monsieur Oliver Cromwell, General of the Army of the English Nation."

"Ah!" said D'Artagnan; "a singular commission."

"Who is this Monsieur Oliver Cromwell?" inquired Porthos.

"Formerly a brewer," replied the Gascon.

"Perhaps Mazarin wishes to make a speculation in beer, as we did in straw," said Porthos.

"Come, come, gentlemen," said Mordaunt, impatiently, "let us depart."

"What!" exclaimed Porthos "without supper? Cannot Monsieur Cromwell wait a little?"

"Yes, but I?" said Mordaunt.

"Well, you," said Porthos, "what then?"

"I cannot wait."

"Oh! as to you, that is not my concern, and I shall sup either with or without your permission."

The young man's eyes kindled in secret, but he restrained himself.

"Monsieur," said D'Artagnan, "you must excuse famished travelers. Besides, our supper can't delay you much. We will hasten on to the inn; you will meanwhile proceed on foot to the harbor. We will take a bite and shall be there as soon as you are."

"Just as you please, gentlemen, provided we set sail," he said.

"The name of your ship?" inquired D'Artagnan.

"The Standard."

"Very well; in half an hour we shall be on board."

And the friends, spurring on their horses, rode to the hotel, the "Arms of England."

"What do you say of that young man?" asked D'Artagnan, as they hurried along.

"I say that he doesn't suit me at all," said Porthos, "and that I feel a strong itching to follow Aramis's advice."

"By no means, my dear Porthos; that man is a messenger of General Cromwell; it would insure for us a poor reception, I imagine, should it be announced to him that we had twisted the neck of his confidant."

"Nevertheless," said Porthos, "I have always noticed that Aramis gives good advice."

"Listen," returned D'Artagnan, "when our embassy is finished——"

"Well?"

"If it brings us back to France——"

"Well?"

"Well, we shall see."

At that moment the two friends reached the hotel, "Arms of England," where they supped with hearty appetite and then at once proceeded to the port.

There they found a brig ready to set sail, upon the deck of which they recognized Mordaunt walking up and down impatiently.

"It is singular," said D'Artagnan, whilst the boat was taking them to the Standard, "it is astonishing how that young man resembles some one I must have known, but who it was I cannot yet remember."

A few minutes later they were on board, but the embarkation of the horses was a longer matter than that of the men, and it was eight o'clock before they raised anchor.

The young man stamped impatiently and ordered all sail to be spread.

Porthos, completely used up by three nights without sleep and a journey of seventy leagues on horseback, retired to his cabin and went to sleep.

D'Artagnan, overcoming his repugnance to Mordaunt, walked with him upon the deck and invented a hundred stories to make him talk.

Mousqueton was seasick.

Chapter LV.

The Scotchman.

And now our readers must leave the Standard to sail peaceably, not toward London, where D'Artagnan and Porthos believed they were going, but to Durham, whither Mordaunt had been ordered to repair by the letter he had received during his sojourn at Boulogne, and accompany us to the royalist camp, on this side of the Tyne, near Newcastle.

There, placed between two rivers on the borders of Scotland, but still on English soil, the tents of a little army extended. It was midnight. Some Highlanders were listlessly keeping watch. The moon, which was partially obscured by heavy clouds, now and then lit up the muskets of the sentinels, or silvered the walls, the roofs, and the spires of the town that Charles I. had just surrendered to the parliamentary troops, whilst Oxford and Newark still held out for him in the hopes of coming to some arrangement.

At one of the extremities of the camp, near an immense tent, in which the Scottish officers were holding a kind of council, presided over by Lord Leven, their commander, a man attired as a cavalier lay sleeping on the turf, his right hand extended over his sword.

About fifty paces off, another man, also appareled as a cavalier, was talking to a Scotch sentinel, and, though a foreigner, he seemed to understand without much difficulty the answers given in the broad Perthshire dialect.

As the town clock of Newcastle struck one the sleeper awoke, and with all the gestures of a man rousing himself out of deep sleep he looked attentively about him; perceiving that he was alone he rose and making a little circuit passed close to the cavalier who was speaking to the sentinel. The former had no doubt finished his questions, for a moment later he said good-night and carelessly followed the same path taken by the first cavalier.

In the shadow of a tent the former was awaiting him.

"Well, my dear friend?" said he, in as pure French as has ever been uttered between Rouen and Tours.

"Well, my friend, there is not a moment to lose; we must let the king know immediately."

"Why, what is the matter?"

"It would take too long to tell you, besides, you will hear it all directly and the least word dropped here might ruin all. We must go and find Lord Winter."

They both set off to the other end of the camp, but as it did not cover more than a surface of five hundred feet they quickly arrived at the tent they were looking for.

"Tony, is your master sleeping?" said one of the two cavaliers to a servant who was lying in the outer compartment, which served as a kind of ante-room.

"No, monsieur le comte," answered the servant, "I think not; or at least he has not long been so, for he was pacing up and down for more than two hours after he left the king, and the sound of his footsteps has only ceased during the last ten minutes. However, you may look and see," added the lackey, raising the curtained entrance of the tent.

Lord Winter was seated near an aperture, arranged as a window to let in the night air, his eyes mechanically following the course of the moon, intermittently veiled, as we before observed, by heavy clouds. The two friends approached Winter, who, with his head on his hands, was gazing at the heavens; he did not hear them enter and remained in the same attitude till he felt a hand upon his shoulder.

He turned around, recognized Athos and Aramis and held out his hand to them.

"Have you observed," said he to them, "what a blood-red color the moon has to-night?"

"No," replied Athos; "I thought it looked much the same as usual."

"Look, again, chevalier," returned Lord Winter.

"I must own," said Aramis, "I am like the Comte de la Fere—I can see nothing remarkable about it."

"My lord," said Athos, "in a position so precarious as ours we must examine the earth and not the heavens. Have you studied our Scotch troops and have you confidence in them?"

"The Scotch?" inquired Winter. "What Scotch?"

"Ours, egad!" exclaimed Athos. "Those in whom the king has confided—Lord Leven's Highlanders."

"No," said Winter, then he paused; "but tell me, can you not perceive the russet tint which marks the heavens?"

"Not the least in the world," said Aramis and Athos at once.

"Tell me," continued Winter, always possessed by the same idea, "is there not a tradition in France that Henry IV., the evening before the day he was assassinated, when he was playing at chess with M. de Bassompiere, saw clots of blood upon the chessboard?"

"Yes," said Athos, "and the marechal has often told me so himself."

"Then it was so," murmured Winter, "and the next day Henry IV. was killed."

"But what has this vision of Henry IV. to do with you, my lord?" inquired Aramis.

"Nothing; and indeed I am mad to trouble you with such things, when your coming to my tent at such an hour announces that you are the bearers of important news."

"Yes, my lord," said Athos, "I wish to speak to the king."

"To the king! but the king is asleep."

"I have something important to reveal to him."

"Can it not be put off till to-morrow?"

"He must know it this moment, and perhaps it is already too late."

"Come, then," said Lord Winter.

Lord Winter's tent was pitched by the side of the royal marquee, a kind of corridor communicating between the two. This corridor was guarded, not by a sentinel, but by a confidential servant, through whom, in case of urgency, Charles could communicate instantly with his faithful subject.

"These gentlemen are with me," said Winter.

The lackey bowed and let them pass. As he had said, on a camp bed, dressed in his black doublet, booted, unbelted, with his felt hat beside him, lay the king, overcome by sleep and fatigue. They advanced, and Athos, who was the first to enter, gazed a moment in silence on that pale and noble face, framed in its long and now untidy, matted hair, the blue veins showing through the transparent temples, his eyes seemingly swollen by tears.

Athos sighed deeply; the sigh woke the king, so lightly did he sleep.

He opened his eyes.

"Ah!" said he, raising himself on his elbow, "is it you, Comte de la Fere?"

"Yes, sire," replied Athos.

"You watch while I sleep and you have come to bring me some news?"

"Alas, sire," answered Athos, "your majesty has guessed aright."

"It is bad news?"

"Yes, sire."

"Never mind; the messenger is welcome. You never come to me without conferring pleasure. You whose devotion recognizes neither country nor misfortune, you who are sent to me by Henrietta; whatever news you bring, speak out."

"Sire, Cromwell has arrived this night at Newcastle."

"Ah!" exclaimed the king, "to fight?"

"No, sire, but to buy your majesty."

"What did you say?"

"I said, sire, that four hundred thousand pounds are owing to the Scottish army."

"For unpaid wages; yes, I know it. For the last year my faithful Highlanders have fought for honor alone."

Athos smiled.

"Well, sir, though honor is a fine thing, they are tired of fighting for it, and to-night they have sold you for two hundred thousand pounds—that is to say, for half what is owing them."

"Impossible!" cried the king, "the Scotch sell their king for two hundred thousand pounds! And who is the Judas who has concluded this infamous bargain?"

"Lord Leven."

"Are you certain of it, sir?"

"I heard it with my own ears."

The king sighed deeply, as if his heart would break, and then buried his face in his hands.

"Oh! the Scotch," he exclaimed, "the Scotch I called 'my faithful,' to whom I trusted myself when I could have fled to Oxford! the Scotch, my brothers! But are you well assured, sir?"

"Lying behind the tent of Lord Leven, I raised it and saw all, heard all!"

"And when is this to be consummated?"

"To-day—this morning; so your majesty must perceive there is no time to lose!"

"To do what? since you say I am sold."

"To cross the Tyne, reach Scotland and rejoin Lord Montrose, who will not sell you."

"And what shall I do in Scotland? A war of partisans, unworthy of a king."

"The example of Robert Bruce will absolve you, sire."

"No, no! I have fought too long; they have sold me, they shall give me up, and the eternal shame of treble treason shall fall on their heads."

"Sire," said Athos, "perhaps a king should act thus, but not a husband and a father. I have come in the name of your wife and daughter and of the children you have still in London, and I say to you, 'Live, sire,'—it is the will of Heaven."

The king raised himself, buckled on his belt, and passing his handkerchief over his moist forehead, said:

"Well, what is to be done?"

"Sire, have you in the army one regiment on which you can implicitly rely?"

"Winter," said the king, "do you believe in the fidelity of yours?"

"Sire, they are but men, and men are become both weak and wicked. I will not answer for them. I would confide my life to them, but I should hesitate ere I trusted them with your majesty's."

"Well!" said Athos, "since you have not a regiment, we are three devoted men. It is enough. Let your majesty mount on horseback and place yourself in the midst of us; we will cross the Tyne, reach Scotland, and you will be saved."

"Is this your counsel also, Winter?" inquired the king.

"Yes, sire."

"And yours, Monsieur d'Herblay?"

"Yes, sire."

"As you wish, then. Winter, give the necessary orders."

Winter then left the tent; in the meantime the king finished his toilet. The first rays of daybreak penetrated the aperture of the tent as Winter re-entered it.

"All is ready, sire," said he.

"For us, also?" inquired Athos.

"Grimaud and Blaisois are holding your horses, ready saddled."

"In that case," exclaimed Athos, "let us not lose an instant, but set off."

"Come," added the king.

"Sire," said Aramis, "will not your majesty acquaint some of your friends of this?"

"Friends!" answered Charles, sadly, "I have but three—one of twenty years, who has never forgotten me, and two of a week's standing, whom I shall never forget. Come, gentlemen, come!"

The king quitted his tent and found his horse ready waiting for him. It was a chestnut that the king had ridden for three years and of which he was very fond.

The horse neighed with pleasure at seeing him.

"Ah!" said the king, "I was unjust; here is a creature that loves me. You at least will be faithful to me, Arthur."

The horse, as if it understood these words, bent its red nostrils toward the king's face, and parting his lips displayed all its teeth, as if with pleasure.

"Yes, yes," said the king, caressing it with his hand, "yes, my Arthur, thou art a fond and faithful creature."

After this little scene Charles threw himself into the saddle, and turning to Athos, Aramis and Winter, said:

"Now, gentlemen, I am at your service."

But Athos was standing with his eyes fixed on a black line which bordered the banks of the Tyne and seemed to extend double the length of the camp.

"What is that line?" cried Athos, whose vision was still rather obscured by the uncertain shades and demi-tints of daybreak. "What is that line? I did not observe it yesterday."

"It must be the fog rising from the river," said the king.

"Sire, it is something more opaque than the fog."

"Indeed!" said Winter, "it appears to me like a bar of red color."

"It is the enemy, who have made a sortie from Newcastle and are surrounding us!" exclaimed Athos.

"The enemy!" cried the king.

"Yes, the enemy. It is too late. Stop a moment; does not that sunbeam yonder, just by the side of the town, glitter on the Ironsides?"

This was the name given the cuirassiers, whom Cromwell had made his body-guard.

"Ah!" said the king, "we shall soon see whether my Highlanders have betrayed me or not."

"What are you going to do?" exclaimed Athos.

"To give them the order to charge, and run down these miserable rebels."

And the king, putting spurs to his horse, set off to the tent of Lord Leven.

"Follow him," said Athos.

"Come!" exclaimed Aramis.

"Is the king wounded?" cried Lord Winter. "I see spots of blood on the ground." And he set off to follow the two friends.

He was stopped by Athos.

"Go and call out your regiment," said he; "I can foresee that we shall have need of it directly."

Winter turned his horse and the two friends rode on. It had taken but two minutes for the king to reach the tent of the Scottish commander; he dismounted and entered.

The general was there, surrounded by the more prominent chiefs.

"The king!" they exclaimed, as all rose in bewilderment.

Charles was indeed in the midst of them, his hat on his head, his brows bent, striking his boot with his riding whip.

"Yes, gentlemen, the king in person, the king who has come to ask for some account of what has happened."

"What is the matter, sire?" exclaimed Lord Leven.

"It is this, sir," said the king, angrily, "that General Cromwell has reached Newcastle; that you knew it and I was not informed of it; that the enemy have left the town and are now closing the passages of the Tyne against us; that our sentinels have seen this movement and I have been left unacquainted with it; that, by an infamous treaty you have sold me for two hundred thousand pounds to Parliament. Of this treaty, at least, I have been warned. This is the matter, gentlemen; answer and exculpate yourselves, for I stand here to accuse you."

"Sire," said Lord Leven, with hesitation, "sire, your majesty has been deceived by false reports."

"My own eyes have seen the enemy extend itself between myself and Scotland; and I can almost say that with my own ears I have heard the clauses of the treaty debated."

The Scotch chieftains looked at each other in their turn with frowning brows.

"Sire," murmured Lord Leven, crushed by shame, "sire, we are ready to give you every proof of our fidelity."

"I ask but one," said the king; "put the army in battle array and face the enemy."

"That cannot be, sire," said the earl.

"How, cannot be? What hinders it?" exclaimed the king.

"Your majesty is well aware that there is a truce between us and the English army."

"And if there is a truce the English army has broken it by quitting the town, contrary to the agreement which kept it there. Now, I tell you, you must pass with me through this army across to Scotland, and if you refuse you may choose betwixt two names, which the contempt of all honest men will brand you with—you are either cowards or traitors!"

The eyes of the Scotch flashed fire; and, as often happens on such occasions, from shame they passed to effrontery and two heads of clans advanced upon the king.

"Yes," said they, "we have promised to deliver Scotland and England from him who for the last five-and-twenty years has sucked the blood and gold of Scotland and England. We have promised and we will keep our promise. Charles Stuart, you are our prisoner."

And both extended their hands as if to seize the king, but before they could touch him with the tips of their fingers, both had fallen, one dead, the other stunned.

Aramis had passed his sword through the body of the first and Athos had knocked down the other with the butt end of his pistol.

Then, as Lord Leven and the other chieftains recoiled before this unexpected rescue, which seemed to come from Heaven for the prince they already thought was their prisoner, Athos and Aramis dragged the king from the perjured assembly into which he had so imprudently ventured, and throwing themselves on horseback all three returned at full gallop to the royal tent.

On their road they perceived Lord Winter marching at the head of his regiment. The king motioned him to accompany them.

Chapter LVI.

The Avenger.

They all four entered the tent; they had no plan ready—they must think of one.

The king threw himself into an arm-chair. "I am lost," said he.

"No, sire," replied Athos. "You are only betrayed."

The king sighed deeply.

"Betrayed! yes betrayed by the Scotch, amongst whom I was born, whom I have always loved better than the English. Oh, traitors that ye are!"

"Sire," said Athos, "this is not a moment for recrimination, but a time to show yourself a king and a gentleman. Up, sire! up! for you have here at least three men who will not betray you. Ah! if we had been five!" murmured Athos, thinking of D'Artagnan and Porthos.

"What do you say?" inquired Charles, rising.

"I say, sire, that there is now but one way open. Lord Winter answers for his regiment, or at least very nearly so—we will not split straws about words—let him place himself at the head of his men, we will place ourselves at the side of your majesty, and we will mow a swath through Cromwell's army and reach Scotland."

"There is another method," said Aramis. "Let one of us put on the dress and mount the king's horse. Whilst they pursue him the king might escape."

"It is good advice," said Athos, "and if the king will do one of us the honor we shall be truly grateful to him."

"What do you think of this counsel, Winter?" asked the king, looking with admiration at these two men, whose chief idea seemed to be how they could take on their shoulders all the dangers that assailed him.

"I think the only chance of saving your majesty has just been proposed by Monsieur d'Herblay. I humbly entreat your majesty to choose quickly, for we have not an instant to lose."

"But if I accept, it is death, or at least imprisonment, for him who takes my place."

"He will have had the glory of having saved his king," cried Winter.

The king looked at his old friend with tears in his eyes; undid the Order of the Saint Esprit which he wore, to honor the two Frenchmen who were with him, and passed it around Winter's neck, who received on his knees this striking proof of his sovereign's confidence and friendship.

"It is right," said Athos; "he has served your majesty longer than we have."

The king overheard these words and turned around with tears in his eyes.

"Wait a moment, sir," said he; "I have an order for each of you also."

He turned to a closet where his own orders were locked up, and took out two ribbons of the Order of the Garter.

"These cannot be for us," said Athos.

"Why not, sir?" asked Charles.

"Such are for royalty, and we are simple commoners."

"Speak not of crowns. I shall not find amongst them such great hearts as yours. No, no, you do yourselves injustice; but I am here to do you justice. On your knees, count."

Athos knelt down and the king passed the ribbon down from left to right as usual, raised his sword, and instead of pronouncing the customary formula, "I make you a knight. Be brave, faithful and loyal," he said, "You are brave, faithful and loyal. I knight you, monsieur le comte."

Then turning to Aramis, he said:

"It is now your turn, monsieur le chevalier."

The same ceremony recommenced, with the same words, whilst Winter unlaced his leather cuirass, that he might disguise himself like the king. Charles, having proceeded with Aramis as with Athos, embraced them both.

"Sire," said Winter, who in this trying emergency felt all his strength and energy fire up, "we are ready."

The king looked at the three gentlemen. "Then we must fly!" said he.

"Flying through an army, sire," said Athos, "in all countries in the world is called charging."

"Then I shall die, sword in hand," said Charles. "Monsieur le comte, monsieur le chevalier, if ever I am king——"

"Sire, you have already done us more honor than simple gentlemen could ever aspire to, therefore gratitude is on our side. But we must not lose time. We have already wasted too much."

The king again shook hands with all three, exchanged hats with Winter and went out.

Winter's regiment was ranged on some high ground above the camp. The king, followed by the three friends, turned his steps that way. The Scotch camp seemed as if at last awakened; the soldiers had come out of their tents and taken up their station in battle array.

"Do you see that?" said the king. "Perhaps they are penitent and preparing to march."

"If they are penitent," said Athos, "let them follow us."

"Well!" said the king, "what shall we do?"

"Let us examine the enemy's army."

At the same instant the eyes of the little group were fixed on the same line which at daybreak they had mistaken for fog and which the morning sun now plainly showed was an army in order of battle. The air was soft and clear, as it generally is at that early hour of the morning. The regiments, the standards, and even the colors of the horses and uniforms were now clearly distinct.

On the summit of a rising ground, a little in advance of the enemy, appeared a short and heavy looking man; this man was surrounded by officers. He turned a spyglass toward the little group amongst which the king stood.

"Does this man know your majesty personally?" inquired Aramis.

Charles smiled.

"That man is Cromwell," said he.

"Then draw down your hat, sire, that he may not discover the substitution."

"Ah!" said Athos, "how much time we have lost."

"Now," said the king, "give the word and let us start."

"Will you not give it, sire?" asked Athos.

"No; I make you my lieutenant-general," said the king.

"Listen, then, Lord Winter. Proceed, sire, I beg. What we are going to say does not concern your majesty."

The king, smiling, turned a few steps back.

"This is what I propose to do," said Athos. "We will divide our regiments into two squadrons. You will put yourself at the head of the first. We and his majesty will lead the second. If no obstacle occurs we will both charge together, force the enemy's line and throw ourselves into the Tyne, which we must cross, either by fording or swimming; if, on the contrary, any repulse should take place, you and your men must fight to the last man, whilst we and the king proceed on our road. Once arrived at the brink of the river, should we even find them three ranks deep, as long as you and your regiment do your duty, we will look to the rest."

"To horse!" said Lord Winter.

"To horse!" re-echoed Athos; "everything is arranged and decided."

"Now, gentlemen," cried the king, "forward! and rally to the old cry of France, 'Montjoy and St. Denis!' The war cry of England is too often in the mouths of traitors."

They mounted—the king on Winter's horse and Winter on that of the king; then Winter took his place at the head of the first squadron, and the king, with Athos on his right and Aramis on his left, at the head of the second.

The Scotch army stood motionless and silent, seized with shame at sight of these preparations.

Some of the chieftains left the ranks and broke their swords in two.

"There," said the king, "that consoles me; they are not all traitors."

At this moment Winter's voice was raised with the cry of "Forward!"

The first squadron moved off; the second followed, and descended from the plateau. A regiment of cuirassiers, nearly equal as to numbers, issued from behind the hill and came full gallop toward it.

The king pointed this out.

"Sire," said Athos, "we foresaw this; and if Lord Winter's men but do their duty, we are saved, instead of lost."

At this moment they heard above all the galloping and neighing of the horses Winter's voice crying out:

"Sword in hand!"

At these words every sword was drawn, and glittered in the air like lightning.

"Now, gentlemen," said the king in his turn, excited by this sight, "come, gentlemen, sword in hand!"

But Aramis and Athos were the only ones to obey this command and the king's example.

"We are betrayed," said the king in a low voice.

"Wait a moment," said Athos, "perhaps they do not recognize your majesty's voice, and await the order of their captain."

"Have they not heard that of their colonel? But look! look!" cried the king, drawing up his horse with a sudden jerk, which threw it on its haunches, and seizing the bridle of Athos's horse.

"Ah, cowards! traitors!" screamed Lord Winter, whose voice they heard, whilst his men, quitting their ranks, dispersed all over the plain.

About fifteen men were ranged around him and awaited the charge of Cromwell's cuirassiers.

"Let us go and die with them!" said the king.

"Let us go," said Athos and Aramis.

"All faithful hearts with me!" cried out Winter.

This voice was heard by the two friends, who set off, full gallop.

"No quarter!" cried a voice in French, answering to that of Winter, which made them tremble.

As for Winter, at the sound of that voice he turned pale, and was, as it were, petrified.

It was the voice of a cavalier mounted on a magnificent black horse, who was charging at the head of the English regiment, of which, in his ardor, he was ten steps in advance.

"'Tis he!" murmured Winter, his eyes glazed and he allowed his sword to fall to his side.

"The king! the king!" cried out several voices, deceived by the blue ribbon and chestnut horse of Winter; "take him alive."

"No! it is not the king!" exclaimed the cavalier. "Lord Winter, you are not the king; you are my uncle."

At the same moment Mordaunt, for it was he, leveled his pistol at Winter; it went off and the ball entered the heart of the old cavalier, who with one bound on his saddle fell back into the arms of Athos, murmuring: "He is avenged!"

"Think of my mother!" shouted Mordaunt, as his horse plunged and darted off at full gallop.

"Wretch!" exclaimed Aramis, raising his pistol as he passed by him; but the powder flashed in the pan and it did not go off.

At this moment the whole regiment came up and they fell upon the few men who had held out, surrounding the two Frenchmen. Athos, after making sure that Lord Winter was really dead, let fall the corpse and said:

"Come, Aramis, now for the honor of France!" and the two Englishmen who were nearest to them fell, mortally wounded.

At the same moment a fearful "hurrah!" rent the air and thirty blades glittered about their heads.

Suddenly a man sprang out of the English ranks, fell upon Athos, twined arms of steel around him, and tearing his sword from him, said in his ear:

"Silence! yield—you yield to me, do you not?"

A giant had seized also Aramis's two wrists, who struggled in vain to release himself from this formidable grasp.

"D'Art——" exclaimed Athos, whilst the Gascon covered his mouth with his hand.

"I am your prisoner," said Aramis, giving up his sword to Porthos.

"Fire, fire!" cried Mordaunt, returning to the group surrounding the two friends.

"And wherefore fire?" said the colonel; "every one has yielded."

"It is the son of Milady," said Athos to D'Artagnan.

"I recognize him."

"It is the monk," whispered Porthos to Aramis.

"I know it."

And now the ranks began to open. D'Artagnan held the bridle of Athos's horse and Porthos that of Aramis. Both of them attempted to lead his prisoner off the battle-field.

This movement revealed the spot where Winter's body had fallen. Mordaunt had found it out and was gazing on his dead relative with an expression of malignant hatred.

Athos, though now cool and collected, put his hand to his belt, where his loaded pistols yet remained.

"What are you about?" said D'Artagnan.

"Let me kill him."

"We are all four lost, if by the least gesture you discover that you recognize him."

Then turning to the young man he exclaimed:

"A fine prize! a fine prize, friend Mordaunt; we have both myself and Monsieur du Vallon, taken two Knights of the Garter, nothing less."

"But," said Mordaunt, looking at Athos and Aramis with bloodshot eyes, "these are Frenchmen, I imagine."

"I'faith, I don't know. Are you French, sir?" said he to Athos.

"I am," replied the latter, gravely.

"Very well, my dear sir, you are the prisoner of a fellow countryman."

"But the king—where is the king?" exclaimed Athos, anxiously.

D'Artagnan vigorously seized his prisoner's hand, saying:

"Eh! the king? We have secured him."

"Yes," said Aramis, "through an infamous act of treason."

Porthos pressed his friend's hand and said to him:

"Yes, sir, all is fair in war, stratagem as well as force; look yonder!"

At this instant the squadron, that ought to have protected Charles's retreat, was advancing to meet the English regiments. The king, who was entirely surrounded, walked alone in a great empty space. He appeared calm, but it was evidently not without a mighty effort. Drops of perspiration trickled down his face, and from time to time he put a handkerchief to his mouth to wipe away the blood that rilled from it.

"Behold Nebuchadnezzar!" exclaimed an old Puritan soldier, whose eyes flashed at the sight of the man they called the tyrant.

"Do you call him Nebuchadnezzar?" said Mordaunt, with a terrible smile; "no, it is Charles the First, the king, the good King Charles, who despoils his subjects to enrich himself."

Charles glanced a moment at the insolent creature who uttered this, but did not recognize him. Nevertheless, the calm religious dignity of his countenance abashed Mordaunt.

"Bon jour, messieurs!" said the king to the two gentlemen who were held by D'Artagnan and Porthos. "The day has been unfortunate, but it is not your fault, thank God! But where is my old friend Winter?"

The two gentlemen turned away their heads in silence.

"In Strafford's company," said Mordaunt, tauntingly.

Charles shuddered. The demon had known how to wound him. The remembrance of Strafford was a source of lasting remorse to him, the shadow that haunted him by day and night. The king looked around him. He saw a corpse at his feet. It was Winter's. He uttered not a word, nor shed a tear, but a deadly pallor spread over his face; he knelt down on the ground, raised Winter's head, and unfastening the Order of the Saint Esprit, placed it on his own breast.

"Lord Winter is killed, then?" inquired D'Artagnan, fixing his eyes on the corpse.

"Yes," said Athos, "by his own nephew."

"Come, he was the first of us to go; peace be to him! he was an honest man," said D'Artagnan.

"Charles Stuart," said the colonel of the English regiment, approaching the king, who had just put on the insignia of royalty, "do you yield yourself a prisoner?"

"Colonel Tomlison," said Charles, "kings cannot yield; the man alone submits to force."

"Your sword."

The king drew his sword and broke it on his knee.

At this moment a horse without a rider, covered with foam, his nostrils extended and eyes all fire, galloped up, and recognizing his master, stopped and neighed with pleasure; it was Arthur.

The king smiled, patted it with his hand and jumped lightly into the saddle.

"Now, gentlemen," said he, "conduct me where you will."

Turning back again, he said, "I thought I saw Winter move; if he still lives, by all you hold most sacred, do not abandon him."

"Never fear, King Charles," said Mordaunt, "the bullet pierced his heart."

"Do not breathe a word nor make the least sign to me or Porthos," said D'Artagnan to Athos and Aramis, "that you recognize this man, for Milady is not dead; her soul lives in the body of this demon."

The detachment now moved toward the town with the royal captive; but on the road an aide-de-camp, from Cromwell, sent orders that Colonel Tomlison should conduct him to Holdenby Castle.

At the same time couriers started in every direction over England and Europe to announce that Charles Stuart was the prisoner of Oliver Cromwell.

Chapter LVII.

Oliver Cromwell.

Have you been to the general?" said Mordaunt to D'Artagnan and Porthos; "you know he sent for you after the action."

"We want first to put our prisoners in a place of safety," replied D'Artagnan. "Do you know, sir, these gentlemen are each of them worth fifteen hundred pounds?"

"Oh, be assured," said Mordaunt, looking at them with an expression he vainly endeavoured to soften, "my soldiers will guard them, and guard them well, I promise you."

"I shall take better care of them myself," answered D'Artagnan; "besides, all they require is a good room, with sentinels, or their simple parole that they will not attempt escape. I will go and see about that, and then we shall have the honor of presenting ourselves to the general and receiving his commands for his eminence."

"You think of starting at once, then?" inquired Mordaunt.

"Our mission is ended, and there is nothing more to detain us now but the good pleasure of the great man to whom we were sent."

The young man bit his lips and whispered to his sergeant:

"You will follow these men and not lose sight of them; when you have discovered where they lodge, come and await me at the town gate."

The sergeant made a sign of comprehension.

Instead of following the knot of prisoners that were being taken into the town, Mordaunt turned his steps toward the rising ground from whence Cromwell had witnessed the battle and on which he had just had his tent pitched.

Cromwell had given orders that no one was to be allowed admission; but the sentinel, who knew that Mordaunt was one of the most confidential friends of the general, thought the order did not extend to the young man. Mordaunt, therefore, raised the canvas, and saw Cromwell seated before a table, his head buried in his hands, his back being turned.

Whether he heard Mordaunt or not as he entered, Cromwell did not move. Mordaunt remained standing near the door. At last, after a few moments, Cromwell raised his head, and, as if he divined that some one was there, turned slowly around.

"I said I wished to be alone," he exclaimed, on seeing the young man.

"They thought this order did not concern me, sir; nevertheless, if you wish it, I am ready to go."

"Ah! is it you, Mordaunt?" said Cromwell, the cloud passing away from his face; "since you are here, it is well; you may remain."

"I come to congratulate you."

"To congratulate me—what for?"

"On the capture of Charles Stuart. You are now master of England."

"I was much more really so two hours ago."

"How so, general?"

"Because England had need of me to take the tyrant, and now the tyrant is taken. Have you seen him?"

"Yes, sir." said Mordaunt.

"What is his bearing?"

Mordaunt hesitated; but it seemed as though he was constrained to tell the truth.

"Calm and dignified," said he.

"What did he say?"

"Some parting words to his friends."

"His friends!" murmured Cromwell. "Has he any friends?" Then he added aloud, "Did he make any resistance?"

"No, sir, with the exception of two or three friends every one deserted him; he had no means of resistance."

"To whom did he give up his sword?"

"He did not give it up; he broke it."

"He did well; but instead of breaking it, he might have used it to still more advantage."

There was a momentary pause.

"I heard that the colonel of the regiment that escorted Charles was killed," said Cromwell, staring very fixedly at Mordaunt.

"Yes, sir."

"By whom?" inquired Cromwell.

"By me."

"What was his name?"

"Lord Winter."

"Your uncle?" exclaimed Cromwell.

"My uncle," answered Mordaunt; "but traitors to England are no longer members of my family."

Cromwell observed the young man a moment in silence, then, with that profound melancholy Shakespeare describes so well:

"Mordaunt," he said, "you are a terrible servant."

"When the Lord commands," said Mordaunt, "His commands are not to be disputed. Abraham raised the knife against Isaac, and Isaac was his son."

"Yes," said Cromwell, "but the Lord did not suffer that sacrifice to be accomplished."

"I have looked around me," said Mordaunt, "and I have seen neither goat nor kid caught among the bushes of the plain."

Cromwell bowed. "You are strong among the strong, Mordaunt," he said; "and the Frenchmen, how did they behave?"

"Most fearlessly."

"Yes, yes," murmured Cromwell; "the French fight well; and if my glass was good and I mistake not, they were foremost in the fight."

"They were," replied Mordaunt.

"After you, however," said Cromwell.

"It was the fault of their horses, not theirs."

Another pause.

"And the Scotch?"

"They kept their word and never stirred," said Mordaunt.

"Wretched men!"

"Their officers wish to see you, sir."

"I have no time to see them. Are they paid?"

"Yes, to-night."

"Let them be off and return to their own country, there to hide their shame, if its hills are high enough; I have nothing more to do with them nor they with me. And now go, Mordaunt."

"Before I go," said Mordaunt, "I have some questions and a favor to ask you, sir."

"A favor from me?"

Mordaunt bowed.

"I come to you, my leader, my head, my father, and I ask you, master, are you contented with me?"

Cromwell looked at him with astonishment. The young man remained immovable.

"Yes," said Cromwell; "you have done, since I knew you, not only your duty, but more than your duty; you have been a faithful friend, a cautious negotiator, a brave soldier."

"Do you remember, sir it was my idea, the Scotch treaty, for giving up the king?"

"Yes, the idea was yours. I had no such contempt for men before."

"Was I not a good ambassador in France?"

"Yes, for Mazarin has granted what I desire."

"Have I not always fought for your glory and interests?"

"Too ardently, perhaps; it is what I have just reproached you for. But what is the meaning of all these questions?"

"To tell you, my lord, that the moment has now arrived when, with a single word, you may recompense all these services."

"Oh!" said Oliver, with a slight curl of his lip, "I forgot that every service merits some reward and that up to this moment you have not been paid."

"Sir, I can take my pay at this moment, to the full extent of my wishes."

"How is that?"

"I have the payment under my hand; I almost possess it."

"What is it? Have they offered you money? Do you wish a step, or some place in the government?"

"Sir, will you grant me my request?"

"Let us hear what it is, first."

"Sir, when you have told me to obey an order did I ever answer, 'Let me see that order'?"

"If, however, your wish should be one impossible to fulfill?"

"When you have cherished a wish and have charged me with its fulfillment, have I ever replied, 'It is impossible'?"

"But a request preferred with so much preparation——"

"Ah, do not fear, sir," said Mordaunt, with apparent simplicity: "it will not ruin you."

"Well, then," said Cromwell, "I promise, as far as lies in my power, to grant your request; proceed."

"Sir, two prisoners were taken this morning, will you let me have them?"

"For their ransom? have they then offered a large one?" inquired Cromwell.

"On the contrary, I think they are poor, sir."

"They are friends of yours, then?"

"Yes, sir," exclaimed Mordaunt, "they are friends, dear friends of mine, and I would lay down my life for them."

"Very well, Mordaunt," exclaimed Cromwell, pleased at having his opinion of the young man raised once more; "I will give them to you; I will not even ask who they are; do as you like with them."

"Thank you, sir!" exclaimed Mordaunt, "thank you; my life is always at your service, and should I lose it I should still owe you something; thank you; you have indeed repaid me munificently for my services."

He threw himself at the feet of Cromwell, and in spite of the efforts of the Puritan general, who did not like this almost kingly homage, he took his hand and kissed it.

"What!" said Cromwell, arresting him for a moment as he arose; "is there nothing more you wish? neither gold nor rank?"

"You have given me all you can give me, and from to-day your debt is paid."

And Mordaunt darted out of the general's tent, his heart beating and his eyes sparkling with joy.

Cromwell gazed a moment after him.

"He has slain his uncle!" he murmured. "Alas! what are my servants? Possibly this one, who asks nothing or seems to ask nothing, has asked more in the eyes of Heaven than those who tax the country and steal the bread of the poor. Nobody serves me for nothing. Charles, who is my prisoner, may still have friends, but I have none!"

And with a deep sigh he again sank into the reverie that had been interrupted by Mordaunt.

Chapter LVIII.

Jesus Seigneur.

Whilst Mordaunt was making his way to Cromwell's tent, D'Artagnan and Porthos had brought their prisoners to the house which had been assigned to them as their dwelling at Newcastle.

The order given by Mordaunt to the sergeant had been heard by D'Artagnan, who accordingly, by an expressive glance, warned Athos and Aramis to exercise extreme caution. The prisoners, therefore, had remained silent as they marched along in company with their conquerors—which they could do with the less difficulty since each of them had occupation enough in answering his own thoughts.

It would be impossible to describe Mousqueton's astonishment when from the threshold of the door he saw the four friends approaching, followed by a sergeant with a dozen men. He rubbed his eyes, doubting if he really saw before him Athos and Aramis; and forced at last to yield to evidence, he was on the point of breaking forth in exclamations when he encountered a glance from the eyes of Porthos, the repressive force of which he was not inclined to dispute.

Mousqueton remained glued to the door, awaiting the explanation of this strange occurrence. What upset him completely was that the four friends seemed to have no acquaintance with one another.

The house to which D'Artagnan and Porthos conducted Athos and Aramis was the one assigned to them by General Cromwell and of which they had taken possession on the previous evening. It was at the corner of two streets and had in the rear, bordering on the side street, stables and a sort of garden. The windows on the ground floor, according to a custom in provincial villages, were barred, so that they strongly resembled the windows of a prison.

The two friends made the prisoners enter the house first, whilst they stood at the door, desiring Mousqueton to take the four horses to the stable.

"Why don't we go in with them?" asked Porthos.

"We must first see what the sergeant wishes us to do," replied D'Artagnan.

The sergeant and his men took possession of the little garden.

D'Artagnan asked them what they wished and why they had taken that position.

"We have had orders," answered the man, "to help you in taking care of your prisoners."

There could be no fault to find with this arrangement; on the contrary, it seemed to be a delicate attention, to be gratefully received; D'Artagnan, therefore, thanked the man and gave him a crown piece to drink to General Cromwell's health.

The sergeant answered that Puritans never drank, and put the crown piece in his pocket.

"Ah!" said Porthos, "what a fearful day, my dear D'Artagnan!"

"What! a fearful day, when to-day we find our friends?"

"Yes; but under what circumstances?"

"'Tis true that our position is an awkward one; but let us go in and see more clearly what is to be done."

"Things look black enough," replied Porthos; "I understand now why Aramis advised me to strangle that horrible Mordaunt."

"Silence!" cried the Gascon; "do not utter that name."

"But," argued Porthos, "I speak French and they are all English."

D'Artagnan looked at Porthos with that air of wonder which a cunning man cannot help feeling at displays of crass stupidity.

But as Porthos on his side could not comprehend his astonishment, he merely pushed him indoors, saying, "Let us go in."

They found Athos in profound despondency; Aramis looked first at Porthos and then at D'Artagnan, without speaking, but the latter understood his meaningful look.

"You want to know how we came here? 'Tis easily guessed. Mazarin sent us with a letter to General Cromwell."

"But how came you to fall into company with Mordaunt, whom I bade you distrust?" asked Athos.

"And whom I advised you to strangle, Porthos," said Aramis.

"Mazarin again. Cromwell had sent him to Mazarin. Mazarin sent us to Cromwell. There is a certain fatality in it."

"Yes, you are right, D'Artagnan, a fatality that will separate and ruin us! So, my dear Aramis, say no more about it and let us prepare to submit to destiny."

"Zounds! on the contrary, let us speak about it; for it was agreed among us, once for all, that we should always hold together, though engaged on opposing sides."

"Yes," added Athos, "I now ask you, D'Artagnan, what side you are on? Ah! behold for what end the wretched Mazarin has made use of you. Do you know in what crime you are to-day engaged? In the capture of a king, his degradation and his murder."

"Oh! oh!" cried Porthos, "do you think so?"

"You are exaggerating, Athos; we are not so far gone as that," replied the lieutenant.

"Good heavens! we are on the very eve of it. I say, why is the king taken prisoner? Those who wish to respect him as a master would not buy him as a slave. Do you think it is to replace him on the throne that Cromwell has paid for him two hundred thousand pounds sterling? They will kill him, you may be sure of it."

"I don't maintain the contrary," said D'Artagnan. "But what's that to us? I am here because I am a soldier and have to obey orders—I have taken an oath to obey, and I do obey; but you who have taken no such oath, why are you here and what cause do you represent?"

"That most sacred in the world," said Athos; "the cause of misfortune, of religion, royalty. A friend, a wife, a daughter, have done us the honor to call us to their aid. We have served them to the best of our poor means, and God will recompense the will, forgive the want of power. You may see matters differently, D'Artagnan, and think otherwise. I will not attempt to argue with you, but I blame you."

"Heyday!" cried D'Artagnan, "what matters it to me, after all, if Cromwell, who's an Englishman, revolts against his king, who is a Scotchman? I am myself a Frenchman. I have nothing to do with these things—why hold me responsible?"

"Yes," said Porthos.

"Because all gentlemen are brothers, because you are a gentleman, because the kings of all countries are the first among gentlemen, because the blind populace, ungrateful and brutal, always takes pleasure in pulling down what is above them. And you, you, D'Artagnan, a man sprung from the ancient nobility of France, bearing an honorable name, carrying a good sword, have helped to give up a king to beersellers, shopkeepers, and wagoners. Ah! D'Artagnan! perhaps you have done your duty as a soldier, but as a gentleman, I say that you are very culpable."

D'Artagnan was chewing the stalk of a flower, unable to reply and thoroughly uncomfortable; for when turned from the eyes of Athos he encountered those of Aramis.

"And you, Porthos," continued the count, as if in consideration for D'Artagnan's embarrassment, "you, the best heart, the best friend, the best soldier that I know—you, with a soul that makes you worthy of a birth on the steps of a throne, and who, sooner or later, must receive your reward from an intelligent king—you, my dear Porthos, you, a gentleman in manners, in tastes and in courage, you are as culpable as D'Artagnan."

Porthos blushed, but with pleasure rather than with confusion; and yet, bowing his head, as if humiliated, he said:

"Yes, yes, my dear count, I feel that you are right."

Athos arose.

"Come," he said, stretching out his hand to D'Artagnan, "come, don't be sullen, my dear son, for I have said all this to you, if not in the tone, at least with the feelings of a father. It would have been easier to me merely to have thanked you for preserving my life and not to have uttered a word of all this."

"Doubtless, doubtless, Athos. But here it is: you have sentiments, the devil knows what, such as every one can't entertain. Who could suppose that a sensible man could leave his house, France, his ward—a charming youth, for we saw him in the camp—to fly to the aid of a rotten, worm-eaten royalty, which is going to crumble one of these days like an old hovel. The sentiments you air are certainly fine, so fine that they are superhuman."

"However that may be, D'Artagnan," replied Athos, without falling into the snare which his Gascon friend had prepared for him by an appeal to his parental love, "however that may be, you know in the bottom of your heart that it is true; but I am wrong to dispute with my master. D'Artagnan, I am your prisoner—treat me as such."

"Ah! pardieu!" said D'Artagnan, "you know you will not be my prisoner very long."

"No," said Aramis, "they will doubtless treat us like the prisoners of the Philipghauts."

"And how were they treated?" asked D'Artagnan.

"Why," said Aramis, "one-half were hanged and the other half were shot."

"Well, I," said D'Artagnan "I answer that while there remains a drop of blood in my veins you will be neither hanged nor shot. Sang Diou! let them come on! Besides—do you see that door, Athos?"

"Yes; what then?"

"Well, you can go out by that door whenever you please; for from this moment you are free as the air."

"I recognize you there, my brave D'Artagnan," replied Athos; "but you are no longer our masters. That door is guarded, D'Artagnan; you know that."

"Very well, you will force it," said Porthos. "There are only a dozen men at the most."

"That would be nothing for us four; it is too much for us two. No, divided as we now are, we must perish. See the fatal example: on the Vendomois road, D'Artagnan, you so brave, and you, Porthos, so valiant and so strong—you were beaten; to-day Aramis and I are beaten in our turn. Now that never happened to us when we were four together. Let us die, then, as De Winter has died; as for me, I will fly only on condition that we all fly together."

"Impossible," said D'Artagnan; "we are under Mazarin's orders."

"I know it and I have nothing more to say; my arguments lead to nothing; doubtless they are bad, since they have not determined minds so just as yours."

"Besides," said Aramis, "had they taken effect it would be still better not to compromise two excellent friends like D'Artagnan and Porthos. Be assured, gentlemen, we shall do you honor in our dying. As for myself, I shall be proud to face the bullets, or even the rope, in company with you, Athos; for you have never seemed to me so grand as you are to-day."

D'Artagnan said nothing, but, after having gnawed the flower stalk, he began to bite his nails. At last:

"Do you imagine," he resumed, "that they mean to kill you? And wherefore should they do so? What interest have they in your death? Moreover, you are our prisoners."

"Fool!" cried Aramis; "knowest thou not, then, Mordaunt? I have but exchanged with him one look, yet that look convinced me that we were doomed."

"The truth is, I'm very sorry that I did not strangle him as you advised me," said Porthos.

"Eh! I make no account of the harm Mordaunt can do!" cried D'Artagnan. "Cap de Diou! if he troubles me too much I will crush him, the insect! Do not fly, then. It is useless; for I swear to you that you are as safe here as you were twenty years, ago—you, Athos, in the Rue Ferou, and you, Aramis, in the Rue de Vaugirard."

"Stop," cried Athos, extending his hand to one of the grated windows by which the room was lighted; "you will soon know what to expect, for here he is."

"Who?"

"Mordaunt."

In fact, looking at the place to which Athos pointed, D'Artagnan saw a cavalier coming toward the house at full gallop.

It was Mordaunt.

D'Artagnan rushed out of the room.

Porthos wanted to follow him.

"Stay," said D'Artagnan, "and do not come till you hear me drum my fingers on the door."

When Mordaunt arrived opposite the house he saw D'Artagnan on the threshold and the soldiers lying on the grass here and there, with their arms.

"Halloo!" he cried, "are the prisoners still there?"

"Yes, sir," answered the sergeant, uncovering.

"'Tis well; order four men to conduct them to my lodging."

Four men prepared to do so.

"What is it?" said D'Artagnan, with that jeering manner which our readers have so often observed in him since they made his acquaintance. "What is the matter, if you please?"

"Sir," replied Mordaunt, "I have ordered the two prisoners we made this morning to be conducted to my lodging."

"Wherefore, sir? Excuse curiosity, but I wish to be enlightened on the subject."

"Because these prisoners, sir, are at my disposal and I choose to dispose of them as I like."

"Allow me—allow me, sir," said D'Artagnan, "to observe you are in error. The prisoners belong to those who take them and not to those who only saw them taken. You might have taken Lord Winter—who, 'tis said, was your uncle—prisoner, but you preferred killing him; 'tis well; we, that is, Monsieur du Vallon and I, could have killed our prisoners—we preferred taking them."

Mordaunt's very lips grew white with rage.

D'Artagnan now saw that affairs were growing worse and he beat the guard's march upon the door. At the first beat Porthos rushed out and stood on the other side of the door.

This movement was observed by Mordaunt.

"Sir!" he thus addressed D'Artagnan, "your resistance is useless; these prisoners have just been given me by my illustrious patron, Oliver Cromwell."

These words struck D'Artagnan like a thunderbolt. The blood mounted to his temples, his eyes became dim; he saw from what fountainhead the ferocious hopes of the young man arose, and he put his hand to the hilt of his sword.

As for Porthos, he looked inquiringly at D'Artagnan.

This look of Porthos's made the Gascon regret that he had summoned the brute force of his friend to aid him in an affair which seemed to require chiefly cunning.

"Violence," he said to himself, "would spoil all; D'Artagnan, my friend, prove to this young serpent that thou art not only stronger, but more subtle than he is."

"Ah!" he said, making a low bow, "why did you not begin by saying that, Monsieur Mordaunt? What! are you sent by General Oliver Cromwell, the most illustrious captain of the age?"

"I have this instant left him," replied Mordaunt, alighting, in order to give his horse to a soldier to hold.

"Why did you not say so at once, my dear sir! all England is with Cromwell; and since you ask for my prisoners, I bend, sir, to your wishes. They are yours; take them."

Mordaunt, delighted, advanced, Porthos looking at D'Artagnan with open-mouthed astonishment. Then D'Artagnan trod on his foot and Porthos began to understand that this was merely acting.

Mordaunt put his foot on the first step of the door and, with his hat in hand, prepared to pass by the two friends, motioning to the four men to follow him.

"But, pardon," said D'Artagnan, with the most charming smile and putting his hand on the young man's shoulder, "if the illustrious General Oliver Cromwell has disposed of our prisoners in your favour, he has, of course, made that act of donation in writing."

Mordaunt stopped short.

"He has given you some little writing for me—the least bit of paper which may show that you come in his name. Be pleased to give me that scrap of paper so that I may justify, by a pretext at least, my abandoning my countrymen. Otherwise, you see, although I am sure that General Oliver Cromwell can intend them no harm, it would have a bad appearance."

Mordaunt recoiled; he felt the blow and discharged a terrible look at D'Artagnan, who responded by the most amiable expression that ever graced a human countenance.

"When I tell you a thing, sir," said Mordaunt, "you insult me by doubting it."

"I!" cried D'Artagnan, "I doubt what you say! God keep me from it, my dear Monsieur Mordaunt! On the contrary, I take you to be a worthy and accomplished gentleman. And then, sir, do you wish me to speak freely to you?" continued D'Artagnan, with his frank expression.

"Speak out, sir," said Mordaunt.

"Monsieur du Vallon, yonder, is rich and has forty thousand francs yearly, so he does not care about money. I do not speak for him, but for myself."

"Well, sir? What more?"

"Well—I—I'm not rich. In Gascony 'tis no dishonor, sir, nobody is rich; and Henry IV., of glorious memory, who was the king of the Gascons, as His Majesty Philip IV. is the king of the Spaniards, never had a penny in his pocket."

"Go on, sir, I see what you wish to get at; and if it is simply what I think that stops you, I can obviate the difficulty."

"Ah, I knew well," said the Gascon, "that you were a man of talent. Well, here's the case, here's where the saddle hurts me, as we French say. I am an officer of fortune, nothing else; I have nothing but what my sword brings me in—that is to say, more blows than banknotes. Now, on taking prisoners, this morning, two Frenchmen, who seemed to me of high birth—in short, two knights of the Garter—I said to myself, my fortune is made. I say two, because in such circumstances, Monsieur du Vallon, who is rich, always gives me his prisoners."

Mordaunt, completely deceived by the wordy civility of D'Artagnan, smiled like a man who understands perfectly the reasons given him, and said:

"I shall have the order signed directly, sir, and with it two thousand pistoles; meanwhile, let me take these men away."

"No," replied D'Artagnan; "what signifies a delay of half an hour? I am a man of order, sir; let us do things in order."

"Nevertheless," replied Mordaunt, "I could compel you; I command here."

"Ah, sir!" said D'Artagnan, "I see that although we have had the honor of traveling in your company you do not know us. We are gentlemen; we are, both of us, able to kill you and your eight men—we two only. For Heaven's sake don't be obstinate, for when others are obstinate I am obstinate likewise, and then I become ferocious and headstrong, and there's my friend, who is even more headstrong and ferocious than myself. Besides, we are sent here by Cardinal Mazarin, and at this moment represent both the king and the cardinal, and are, therefore, as ambassadors, able to act with impunity, a thing that General Oliver Cromwell, who is assuredly as great a politician as he is a general, is quite the man to understand. Ask him then, for the written order. What will that cost you my dear Monsieur Mordaunt?"

"Yes, the written order," said Porthos, who now began to comprehend what D'Artagnan was aiming at, "we ask only for that."

However inclined Mordaunt was to have recourse to violence, he understood the reasons D'Artagnan had given him; besides, completely ignorant of the friendship which existed between the four Frenchmen, all his uneasiness disappeared when he heard of the plausible motive of the ransom. He decided, therefore, not only to fetch the order, but the two thousand pistoles, at which he estimated the prisoners. He therefore mounted his horse and disappeared.

"Good!" thought D'Artagnan; "a quarter of an hour to go to the tent, a quarter of an hour to return; it is more than we need." Then turning, without the least change of countenance, to Porthos, he said, looking him full in the face: "Friend Porthos, listen to this; first, not a syllable to either of our friends of what you have heard; it is unnecessary for them to know the service we are going to render them."

"Very well; I understand."

"Go to the stable; you will find Mousqueton there; saddle your horses, put your pistols in your saddle-bags, take out the horses and lead them to the street below this, so that there will be nothing to do but mount them; all the rest is my business."

Porthos made no remark, but obeyed, with the sublime confidence he had in his friend.

"I go," he said, "only, shall I enter the chamber where those gentlemen are?"

"No, it is not worth while."

"Well, do me the kindness to take my purse, which I left on the mantelpiece."

"All right."

He then proceeded, with his usual calm gait, to the stable and went into the very midst of the soldiery, who, foreigner as he was, could not help admiring his height and the enormous strength of his great limbs.

At the corner of the street he met Mousqueton and took him with him.

D'Artagnan, meantime, went into the house, whistling a tune which he had begun before Porthos went away.

"My dear Athos, I have reflected on your arguments and I am convinced. I am sorry to have had anything to do with this matter. As you say, Mazarin is a knave. I have resolved to fly with you, not a word—be ready. Your swords are in the corner; do not forget them, they are in many circumstances very useful; there is Porthos's purse, too."

He put it into his pocket. The two friends were perfectly stupefied.

"Well, pray, is there anything to be so surprised at?" he said. "I was blind; Athos has made me see, that's all; come here."

The two friends went near him.

"Do you see that street? There are the horses. Go out by the door, turn to the right, jump into your saddles, all will be right; don't be uneasy at anything except mistaking the signal. That will be the signal when I call out—Jesus Seigneur!"

"But give us your word that you will come too, D'Artagnan," said Athos.

"I swear I will, by Heaven."

"'Tis settled," said Aramis; "at the cry 'Jesus Seigneur' we go out, upset all that stands in our way, run to our horses, jump into our saddles, spur them; is that all?"

"Exactly."

"See, Aramis, as I have told you, D'Artagnan is first amongst us all," said Athos.

"Very true," replied the Gascon, "but I always run away from compliments. Don't forget the signal: 'Jesus Seigneur!'" and he went out as he came in, whistling the self-same air.

The soldiers were playing or sleeping; two of them were singing in a corner, out of tune, the psalm: "On the rivers of Babylon."

D'Artagnan called the sergeant. "My dear friend, General Cromwell has sent Monsieur Mordaunt to fetch me. Guard the prisoners well, I beg of you."

The sergeant made a sign, as much as to say he did not understand French, and D'Artagnan tried to make him comprehend by signs and gestures. Then he went into the stable; he found the five horses saddled, his own amongst the rest.

"Each of you take a horse by the bridle," he said to Porthos and Mousqueton; "turn to the left, so that Athos and Aramis may see you clearly from the window."

"They are coming, then?" said Porthos.

"In a moment."

"You didn't forget my purse?"

"No; be easy."

"Good."

Porthos and Mousqueton each took a horse by the bridle and proceeded to their post.

Then D'Artagnan, being alone, struck a light and lighted a small bit of tinder, mounted his horse and stopped at the door in the midst of the soldiers. There, caressing as he pretended, the animal with his hand, he put this bit of burning tinder in his ear. It was necessary to be as good a horseman as he was to risk such a scheme, for no sooner had the animal felt the burning tinder than he uttered a cry of pain and reared and jumped as if he had been mad.

The soldiers, whom he was nearly trampling, ran away.

"Help! help!" cried D'Artagnan; "stop—my horse has the staggers."

In an instant the horse's eyes grew bloodshot and he was white with foam.

"Help!" cried D'Artagnan. "What! will you let me be killed? Jesus Seigneur!"

No sooner had he uttered this cry than the door opened and Athos and Aramis rushed out. The coast, owing to the Gascon's stratagem, was clear.

"The prisoners are escaping! the prisoners are escaping!" cried the sergeant.

"Stop! stop!" cried D'Artagnan, giving rein to his famous steed, who, darting forth, overturned several men.

"Stop! stop!" cried the soldiers, and ran for their arms.

But the prisoners were in their saddles and lost no time hastening to the nearest gate.

In the middle of the street they saw Grimaud and Blaisois, who were coming to find their masters. With one wave of his hand Athos made Grimaud, who followed the little troop, understand everything, and they passed on like a whirlwind, D'Artagnan still directing them from behind with his voice.

They passed through the gate like apparitions, without the guards thinking of detaining them, and reached the open country.

All this time the soldiers were calling out, "Stop! stop!" and the sergeant, who began to see that he was the victim of an artifice, was almost in a frenzy of despair. Whilst all this was going on, a cavalier in full gallop was seen approaching. It was Mordaunt with the order in his hand.

"The prisoners!" he exclaimed, jumping off his horse.

The sergeant had not the courage to reply; he showed him the open door, the empty room. Mordaunt darted to the steps, understood all, uttered a cry, as if his very heart was pierced, and fell fainting on the stone steps.

Chapter LIX.

Noble Natures never lose Courage, nor good Stomachs their Appetites.

The little troop, without looking behind them or exchanging a word, fled at a rapid gallop, fording a little stream, of which none of them knew the name, and leaving on their left a town which Athos declared to be Durham. At last they came in sight of a small wood, and spurring their horses afresh, rode in its direction.

As soon as they had disappeared behind a green curtain sufficiently thick to conceal them from the sight of any one who might be in pursuit they drew up to hold a council together. The two grooms held the horses, that they might take a little rest without being unsaddled, and Grimaud was posted as sentinel.

"Come, first of all," said Athos to D'Artagnan, "my friend, that I may shake hands with you—you, our rescuer—you, the true hero of us all."

"Athos is right—you have my adoration," said Aramis, in his turn pressing his hand. "To what are you not equal, with your superior intelligence, infallible eye, your arm of iron and your enterprising mind!"

"Now," said the Gascon, "that is all well, I accept for Porthos and myself everything—thanks and compliments; we have plenty of time to spare."

The two friends, recalled by D'Artagnan to what was also due to Porthos, pressed his hand in their turn.

"And now," said Athos, "it is not our plan to run anywhere and like madmen, but we must map up our campaign. What shall we do?"

"What are we going to do, i'faith? It is not very difficult to say."

"Tell us, then, D'Artagnan."

"We are going to reach the nearest seaport, unite our little resources, hire a vessel and return to France. As for me I will give my last sou for it. Life is the greatest treasure, and speaking candidly, ours hangs by a thread."

"What do you say to this, Du Vallon?"

"I," said Porthos, "I am entirely of D'Artagnan's opinion; this is a 'beastly' country, this England."

"You are quite decided, then, to leave it?" asked Athos of D'Artagnan.

"Egad! I don't see what is to keep me here."

A glance was exchanged between Athos and Aramis.

"Go, then, my friends," said the former, sighing.

"How, go then?" exclaimed D'Artagnan. "Let us go, you mean?"

"No, my friend," said Athos, "you must leave us."

"Leave you!" cried D'Artagnan, quite bewildered at this unexpected announcement.

"Bah!" said Porthos, "why separate, since we are all together?"

"Because you can and ought to return to France; your mission is accomplished, but ours is not."

"Your mission is not accomplished?" exclaimed D'Artagnan, looking in astonishment at Athos.

"No, my friend," replied Athos, in his gentle but decided voice, "we came here to defend King Charles; we have but ill defended him—it remains for us to save him!"

"To save the king?" said D'Artagnan, looking at Aramis as he had looked at Athos.

Aramis contented himself by making a sign with his head.

D'Artagnan's countenance took an expression of the deepest compassion; he began to think he had to do with madmen.

"You cannot be speaking seriously, Athos!" said he; "the king is surrounded by an army, which is conducting him to London. This army is commanded by a butcher, or the son of a butcher—it matters little—Colonel Harrison. His majesty, I can assure you, will be tried on his arrival in London; I have heard enough from the lips of Oliver Cromwell to know what to expect."

A second look was exchanged between Athos and Aramis.

"And when the trial is ended there will be no delay in putting the sentence into execution," continued D'Artagnan.

"And to what penalty do you think the king will be condemned?" asked Athos.

"The penalty of death, I greatly fear; they have gone too far for him to pardon them, and there is nothing left to them but one thing, and that is to kill him. Have you never heard what Oliver Cromwell said when he came to Paris and was shown the dungeon at Vincennes where Monsieur de Vendome was imprisoned?"

"What did he say?" asked Porthos.

"'Princes must be knocked on the head.'"

"I remember it," said Athos.

"And you fancy he will not put his maxim into execution, now that he has got hold of the king?"

"On the contrary, I am certain he will do so. But then that is all the more reason why we should not abandon the august head so threatened."

"Athos, you are becoming mad."

"No, my friend," Athos gently replied, "but De Winter sought us out in France and introduced us, Monsieur d'Herblay and myself, to Madame Henrietta. Her majesty did us the honor to ask our aid for her husband. We engaged our word; our word included everything. It was our strength, our intelligence, our life, in short, that we promised. It remains now for us to keep our word. Is that your opinion, D'Herblay?"

"Yes," said Aramis, "we have promised."

"Then," continued Athos, "we have another reason; it is this—listen: In France at this moment everything is poor and paltry. We have a king ten years old, who doesn't yet know what he wants; we have a queen blinded by a belated passion; we have a minister who governs France as he would govern a great farm—that is to say, intent only on turning out all the gold he can by the exercise of Italian cunning and invention; we have princes who set up a personal and egotistic opposition, who will draw from Mazarin's hands only a few ingots of gold or some shreds of power granted as bribes. I have served them without enthusiasm—God knows that I estimated them at their real value, and that they are not high in my esteem—but on principle. To-day I am engaged in a different affair. I have encountered misfortune in a high place, a royal misfortune, a European misfortune; I attach myself to it. If we can succeed in saving the king it will be good; if we die for him it will be grand."

"So you know beforehand you must perish!" said D'Artagnan.

"We fear so, and our only regret is to die so far from both of you."

"What will you do in a foreign land, an enemy's country?"

"I traveled in England when I was young, I speak English like an Englishman, and Aramis, too, knows something of the language. Ah! if we had you, my friends! With you, D'Artagnan, with you, Porthos—all four reunited for the first time for twenty years—we would dare not only England, but the three kingdoms put together!"

"And did you promise the queen," resumed D'Artagnan, petulantly, "to storm the Tower of London, to kill a hundred thousand soldiers, to fight victoriously against the wishes of the nation and the ambition of a man, and when that man is Cromwell? Do not exaggerate your duty. In Heaven's name, my dear Athos, do not make a useless sacrifice. When I see you merely, you look like a reasonable being; when you speak, I seem to have to do with a madman. Come, Porthos, join me; say frankly, what do you think of this business?"

"Nothing good," replied Porthos.

"Come," continued D'Artagnan, who, irritated that instead of listening to him Athos seemed to be attending to his own thoughts, "you have never found yourself the worse for my advice. Well, then, believe me, Athos, your mission is ended, and ended nobly; return to France with us."

"Friend," said Athos, "our resolution is irrevocable."

"Then you have some other motive unknown to us?"

Athos smiled and D'Artagnan struck his hands together in anger and muttered the most convincing reasons that he could discover; but to all these reasons Athos contented himself by replying with a calm, sweet smile and Aramis by nodding his head.

"Very well," cried D'Artagnan, at last, furious, "very well, since you wish it, let us leave our bones in this beggarly land, where it is always cold, where fine weather is a fog, fog is rain, and rain a deluge; where the sun represents the moon and the moon a cream cheese; in truth, whether we die here or elsewhere matters little, since we must die."

"Only reflect, my good fellow," said Athos, "it is but dying rather sooner."

"Pooh! a little sooner or a little later, it isn't worth quarreling over."

"If I am astonished at anything," remarked Porthos, sententiously, "it is that it has not already happened."

"Oh, it will happen, you may be sure," said D'Artagnan. "So it is agreed, and if Porthos makes no objection——"

"I," said Porthos, "I will do whatever you please; and besides, I think what the Comte de la Fere said just now is very good."

"But your future career, D'Artagnan—your ambition, Porthos?"

"Our future, our ambition!" replied D'Artagnan, with feverish volubility. "Need we think of that since we are to save the king? The king saved—we shall assemble our friends together—we will head the Puritans—reconquer England; we shall re-enter London—place him securely on his throne——"

"And he will make us dukes and peers," said Porthos, whose eyes sparkled with joy at this imaginary prospect.

"Or he will forget us," added D'Artagnan.

"Oh!" said Porthos.

"Well, that has happened, friend Porthos. It seems to me that we once rendered Anne of Austria a service not much less than that which to-day we are trying to perform for Charles I.; but, none the less, Anne of Austria has forgotten us for twenty years."

"Well, in spite of that, D'Artagnan," said Athos, "you are not sorry that you were useful to her?"

"No, indeed," said D'Artagnan; "I admit even that in my darkest moments I find consolation in that remembrance."

"You see, then, D'Artagnan, though princes often are ungrateful, God never is."

"Athos," said D'Artagnan, "I believe that were you to fall in with the devil, you would conduct yourself so well that you would take him with you to Heaven."

"So, then?" said Athos, offering his hand to D'Artagnan.

"'Tis settled," replied D'Artagnan. "I find England a charming country, and I stay—but on one condition only."

"What is it?"

"That I am not forced to learn English."

"Well, now," said Athos, triumphantly, "I swear to you, my friend, by the God who hears us—I believe that there is a power watching over us, and that we shall all four see France again."

"So be it!" said D'Artagnan, "but I—I confess I have a contrary conviction."

"Our good D'Artagnan," said Aramis, "represents among us the opposition in parliament, which always says no, and always does aye."

"But in the meantime saves the country," added Athos.

"Well, now that everything is decided," cried Porthos, rubbing his hands, "suppose we think of dinner! It seems to me that in the most critical positions of our lives we have always dined."

"Oh! yes, speak of dinner in a country where for a feast they eat boiled mutton, and as a treat drink beer. What the devil did you come to such a country for, Athos? But I forgot," added the Gascon, smiling, "pardon, I forgot you are no longer Athos; but never mind, let us hear your plan for dinner, Porthos."

"My plan!"

"Yes, have you a plan?"

"No! I am hungry, that is all."

"Pardieu, if that is all, I am hungry, too; but it is not everything to be hungry, one must find something to eat, unless we browse on the grass, like our horses——"

"Ah!" exclaimed Aramis, who was not quite so indifferent to the good things of the earth as Athos, "do you remember, when we were at Parpaillot, the beautiful oysters that we ate?"

"And the legs of mutton of the salt marshes," said Porthos, smacking his lips.

"But," suggested D'Artagnan, "have we not our friend Mousqueton, who managed for us so well at Chantilly, Porthos?"

"Yes," said Porthos, "we have Mousqueton, but since he has been steward, he has become very heavy; never mind, let us call him, and to make sure that he will reply agreeably——

"Here! Mouston," cried Porthos.

Mouston appeared, with a most piteous face.

"What is the matter, my dear M. Mouston?" asked D'Artagnan. "Are you ill?"

"Sir, I am very hungry," replied Mouston.

"Well, it is just for that reason that we have called you, my good M. Mouston. Could you not procure us a few of those nice little rabbits, and some of those delicious partridges, of which you used to make fricassees at the hotel——? 'Faith, I do not remember the name of the hotel."

"At the hotel of——," said Porthos; "by my faith—nor do I remember it either."

"It does not matter; and a few of those bottles of old Burgundy wine, which cured your master so quickly of his sprain!"

"Alas! sir," said Mousqueton, "I much fear that what you ask for are very rare things in this detestable and barren country, and I think we should do better to go and seek hospitality from the owner of a little house we see on the fringe of the forest."

"How! is there a house in the neighborhood?" asked D'Artagnan.

"Yes, sir," replied Mousqueton.

"Well, let us, as you say, go and ask a dinner from the master of that house. What is your opinion, gentlemen, and does not M. Mouston's suggestion appear to you full of sense?"

"Oh!" said Aramis, "suppose the master is a Puritan?"

"So much the better, mordioux!" replied D'Artagnan; "if he is a Puritan we will inform him of the capture of the king, and in honor of the news he will kill for us his fatted hens."

"But if he should be a cavalier?" said Porthos.

"In that case we will put on an air of mourning and he will pluck for us his black fowls."

"You are very happy," exclaimed Athos, laughing, in spite of himself, at the sally of the irresistible Gascon; "for you see the bright side of everything."

"What would you have?" said D'Artagnan. "I come from a land where there is not a cloud in the sky."

"It is not like this, then," said Porthos stretching out his hand to assure himself whether a chill sensation he felt on his cheek was not really caused by a drop of rain.

"Come, come," said D'Artagnan, "more reason why we should start on our journey. Halloo, Grimaud!"

Grimaud appeared.

"Well, Grimaud, my friend, have you seen anything?" asked the Gascon.

"Nothing!" replied Grimaud.

"Those idiots!" cried Porthos, "they have not even pursued us. Oh! if we had been in their place!"

"Yes, they are wrong," said D'Artagnan. "I would willingly have said two words to Mordaunt in this little desert. It is an excellent spot for bringing down a man in proper style."

"I think, decidedly," observed Aramis, "gentlemen, that the son hasn't his mother's energy."

"What, my good fellow!" replied Athos, "wait awhile; we have scarcely left him two hours ago—he does not know yet in what direction we came nor where we are. We may say that he is not equal to his mother when we put foot in France, if we are not poisoned or killed before then."

"Meanwhile, let us dine," suggested Porthos.

"I'faith, yes," said Athos, "for I am hungry."

"Look out for the black fowls!" cried Aramis.

And the four friends, guided by Mousqueton, took up the way toward the house, already almost restored to their former gayety; for they were now, as Athos had said, all four once more united and of single mind.

Chapter LX.

Respect to Fallen Majesty.

As our fugitives approached the house, they found the ground cut up, as if a considerable body of horsemen had preceded them. Before the door the traces were yet more apparent; these horsemen, whoever they might be, had halted there.

"Egad!" cried D'Artagnan, "it's quite clear that the king and his escort have been by here."

"The devil!" said Porthos; "in that case they have eaten everything."

"Bah!" said D'Artagnan, "they will have left a chicken, at least." He dismounted and knocked on the door. There was no response.

He pushed open the door and found the first room empty and deserted.

"Well?" cried Porthos.

"I can see nobody," said D'Artagnan. "Aha!"

"What?"

"Blood!"

At this word the three friends leaped from their horses and entered. D'Artagnan had already opened the door of the second room, and from the expression of his face it was clear that he there beheld some extraordinary object.

The three friends drew near and discovered a young man stretched on the ground, bathed in a pool of blood. It was evident that he had attempted to regain his bed, but had not had sufficient strength to do so.

Athos, who imagined that he saw him move, was the first to go up to him.

"Well?" inquired D'Artagnan.

"Well, if he is dead," said Athos, "he has not been so long, for he is still warm. But no, his heart is beating. Ho, there, my friend!"

The wounded man heaved a sigh. D'Artagnan took some water in the hollow of his hand and threw it upon his face. The man opened his eyes, made an effort to raise his head, and fell back again. The wound was in the top of his skull and blood was flawing copiously.

Aramis dipped a cloth into some water and applied it to the gash. Again the wounded man opened his eyes and looked in astonishment at these strangers, who appeared to pity him.

"You are among friends," said Athos, in English; "so cheer up, and tell us, if you have the strength to do so, what has happened?"

"The king," muttered the wounded man, "the king is a prisoner."

"You have seen him?" asked Aramis, in the same language.

The man made no reply.

"Make your mind easy," resumed Athos, "we are all faithful servants of his majesty."

"Is what you tell me true?" asked the wounded man.

"On our honor as gentlemen."

"Then I may tell you all. I am brother to Parry, his majesty's lackey."

Athos and Aramis remembered that this was the name by which De Winter had called the man they had found in the passage of the king's tent.

"We know him," said Athos, "he never left the king."

"Yes, that is he. Well, he thought of me, when he saw the king was taken, and as they were passing before the house he begged in the king's name that they would stop, as the king was hungry. They brought him into this room and placed sentinels at the doors and windows. Parry knew this room, as he had often been to see me when the king was at Newcastle. He knew that there was a trap-door communicating with a cellar, from which one could get into the orchard. He made a sign, which I understood, but the king's guards must have noticed it and held themselves on guard. I went out as if to fetch wood, passed through the subterranean passage into the cellar, and whilst Parry was gently bolting the door, pushed up the board and beckoned to the king to follow me. Alas! he would not. But Parry clasped his hands and implored him, and at last he agreed. I went on first, fortunately. The king was a few steps behind me, when suddenly I saw something rise up in front of me like a huge shadow. I wanted to cry out to warn the king, but that very moment I felt a blow as if the house was falling on my head, and fell insensible. When I came to myself again, I was stretched in the same place. I dragged myself as far as the yard. The king and his escort were no longer there. I spent perhaps an hour in coming from the yard to this place; then my strength gave out and I fainted again."

"And now how are you feeling?"

"Very ill," replied the wounded man.

"Can we do anything for you?" asked Athos.

"Help to put me on the bed; I think I shall feel better there."

"Have you any one to depend on for assistance?"

"My wife is at Durham and may return at any moment. But you—is there nothing that you want?"

"We came here with the intention of asking for something to eat."

"Alas, they have taken everything; there isn't a morsel of bread in the house."

"You hear, D'Artagnan?" said Athos; "we shall have to look elsewhere for our dinner."

"It is all one to me now," said D'Artagnan; "I am no longer hungry."

"Faith! neither am I," said Porthos.

They carried the man to his bed and called Grimaud to dress the wound. In the service of the four friends Grimaud had had so frequent occasion to make lint and bandages that he had become something of a surgeon.

In the meantime the fugitives had returned to the first room, where they took counsel together.

"Now," said Aramis, "we know how the matter stands. The king and his escort have gone this way; we had better take the opposite direction, eh?"

Athos did not reply; he reflected.

"Yes," said Porthos, "let us take the opposite direction; if we follow the escort we shall find everything devoured and die of hunger. What a confounded country this England is! This is the first time I have gone without my dinner for ten years, and it is generally my best meal."

"What do you think, D'Artagnan?" asked Athos. "Do you agree with Aramis?"

"Not at all," said D'Artagnan; "I am precisely of the contrary opinion."

"What! you would follow the escort?" exclaimed Porthos, in dismay.

"No, I would join the escort."

Athos's eyes shone with joy.

"Join the escort!" cried Aramis.

"Let D'Artagnan speak," said Athos; "you know he always has wise advice to give."

"Clearly," said D'Artagnan, "we must go where they will not look for us. Now, they will be far from looking for us among the Puritans; therefore, with the Puritans we must go."

"Good, my friend, good!" said Athos. "It is excellent advice. I was about to give it when you anticipated me."

"That, then, is your opinion?" asked Aramis.

"Yes. They will think we are trying to leave England and will search for us at the ports; meanwhile we shall reach London with the king. Once in London we shall be hard to find—without considering," continued Athos, throwing a glance at Aramis, "the chances that may come to us on the way."

"Yes," said Aramis, "I understand."

"I, however, do not understand," said Porthos. "But no matter; since it is at the same time the opinion of D'Artagnan and of Athos, it must be the best."

"But," said Aramis, "shall we not be suspected by Colonel Harrison?"

"Egad!" cried D'Artagnan, "he's just the man I count upon. Colonel Harrison is one of our friends. We have met him twice at General Cromwell's. He knows that we were sent from France by Monsieur Mazarin; he will consider us as brothers. Besides, is he not a butcher's son? Well, then, Porthos shall show him how to knock down an ox with a blow of the fist, and I how to trip up a bull by taking him by the horns. That will insure his confidence."

Athos smiled. "You are the best companion that I know, D'Artagnan," he said, offering his hand to the Gascon; "and I am very happy in having found you again, my dear son."

This was, as we have seen, the term which Athos applied to D'Artagnan in his more expansive moods.

At this moment Grimaud came in. He had stanched the wound and the man was better.

The four friends took leave of him and asked if they could deliver any message for him to his brother.

"Tell him," answered the brave man, "to let the king know that they have not killed me outright. However insignificant I am, I am sure that his majesty is concerned for me and blames himself for my death."

"Be easy," said D'Artagnan, "he will know all before night."

The little troop recommenced their march, and at the end of two hours perceived a considerable body of horsemen about half a league ahead.

"My dear friends," said D'Artagnan, "give your swords to Monsieur Mouston, who will return them to you at the proper time and place, and do not forget you are our prisoners."

It was not long before they joined the escort. The king was riding in front, surrounded by troopers, and when he saw Athos and Aramis a glow of pleasure lighted his pale cheeks.

D'Artagnan passed to the head of the column, and leaving his friends under the guard of Porthos, went straight to Harrison, who recognized him as having met him at Cromwell's and received him as politely as a man of his breeding and disposition could. It turned out as D'Artagnan had foreseen. The colonel neither had nor could have any suspicion.

They halted for the king to dine. This time, however, due precautions were taken to prevent any attempt at escape. In the large room of the hotel a small table was placed for him and a large one for the officers.

"Will you dine with me?" asked Harrison of D'Artagnan.

"Gad, I should be very happy, but I have my companion, Monsieur du Vallon, and the two prisoners, whom I cannot leave. Let us manage it better. Have a table set for us in a corner and send us whatever you like from yours."

"Good," answered Harrison.

The matter was arranged as D'Artagnan had suggested, and when he returned he found the king already seated at his little table, where Parry waited on him, Harrison and his officers sitting together at another table, and, in a corner, places reserved for himself and his companions.

The table at which the Puritan officers were seated was round, and whether by chance or coarse intention, Harrison sat with his back to the king.

The king saw the four gentlemen come in, but appeared to take no notice of them.

They sat down in such a manner as to turn their backs on nobody. The officers, table and that of the king were opposite to them.

"I'faith, colonel," said D'Artagnan, "we are very grateful for your gracious invitation; for without you we ran the risk of going without dinner, as we have without breakfast. My friend here, Monsieur du Vallon, shares my gratitude, for he was particularly hungry."

"And I am so still," said Porthos bowing to Harrison.

"And how," said Harrison, laughing, "did this serious calamity of going without breakfast happen to you?"

"In a very simple manner, colonel," said D'Artagnan. "I was in a hurry to join you and took the road you had already gone by. You can understand our disappointment when, arriving at a pretty little house on the skirts of a wood, which at a distance had quite a gay appearance, with its red roof and green shutters, we found nothing but a poor wretch bathed—Ah! colonel, pay my respects to the officer of yours who struck that blow."

"Yes," said Harrison, laughing, and looking over at one of the officers seated at his table. "When Groslow undertakes this kind of thing there's no need to go over the ground a second time."

"Ah! it was this gentleman?" said D'Artagnan, bowing to the officer. "I am sorry he does not speak French, that I might tender him my compliments."

"I am ready to receive and return them, sir," said the officer, in pretty good French, "for I resided three years in Paris."

"Then, sir, allow me to assure you that your blow was so well directed that you have nearly killed your man."

"Nearly? I thought I had quite," said Groslow.

"No. It was a very near thing, but he is not dead."

As he said this, D'Artagnan gave a glance at Parry, who was standing in front of the king, to show him that the news was meant for him.

The king, too, who had listened in the greatest agony, now breathed again.

"Hang it," said Groslow, "I thought I had succeeded better. If it were not so far from here to the house I would return and finish him."

"And you would do well, if you are afraid of his recovering; for you know, if a wound in the head does not kill at once, it is cured in a week."

And D'Artagnan threw a second glance toward Parry, on whose face such an expression of joy was manifested that Charles stretched out his hand to him, smiling.

Parry bent over his master's hand and kissed it respectfully.

"I've a great desire to drink the king's health," said Athos.

"Let me propose it, then," said D'Artagnan.

"Do," said Aramis.

Porthos looked at D'Artagnan, quite amazed at the resources with which his companion's Gascon sharpness continually supplied him. D'Artagnan took up his camp tin cup, filled it with wine and arose.

"Gentlemen," said he, "let us drink to him who presides at the repast. Here's to our colonel, and let him know that we are always at his commands as far as London and farther."

And as D'Artagnan, as he spoke, looked at Harrison, the colonel imagined the toast was for himself. He arose and bowed to the four friends, whose eyes were fixed on Charles, while Harrison emptied his glass without the slightest misgiving.

The king, in return, looked at the four gentlemen and drank with a smile full of nobility and gratitude.

"Come, gentlemen," cried Harrison, regardless of his illustrious captive, "let us be off."

"Where do we sleep, colonel?"

"At Thirsk," replied Harrison.

"Parry," said the king, rising too, "my horse; I desire to go to Thirsk."

"Egad!" said D'Artagnan to Athos, "your king has thoroughly taken me, and I am quite at his service."

"If what you say is sincere," replied Athos, "he will never reach London."

"How so?"

"Because before then we shall have carried him off."

"Well, this time, Athos," said D'Artagnan, "upon my word, you are mad."

"Have you some plan in your head then?" asked Aramis.

"Ay!" said Porthos, "the thing would not be impossible with a good plan."

"I have none," said Athos; "but D'Artagnan will discover one."

D'Artagnan shrugged his shoulders and they proceeded.

Chapter LXI.

D'Artagnan hits on a Plan.

As night closed in they arrived at Thirsk. The four friends appeared to be entire strangers to one another and indifferent to the precautions taken for guarding the king. They withdrew to a private house, and as they had reason every moment to fear for their safety, they occupied but one room and provided an exit, which might be useful in case of an attack. The lackeys were sent to their several posts, except that Grimaud lay on a truss of straw across the doorway.

D'Artagnan was thoughtful and seemed for the moment to have lost his usual loquacity. Porthos, who could never see anything that was not self-evident, talked to him as usual. He replied in monosyllables and Athos and Aramis looked significantly at one another.

Next morning D'Artagnan was the first to rise. He had been down to the stables, already taken a look at the horses and given the necessary orders for the day, whilst Athos and Aramis were still in bed and Porthos snoring.

At eight o'clock the march was resumed in the same order as the night before, except that D'Artagnan left his friends and began to renew the acquaintance which he had already struck up with Monsieur Groslow.

Groslow, whom D'Artagnan's praises had greatly pleased, welcomed him with a gracious smile.

"Really, sir," D'Artagnan said to him, "I am pleased to find one with whom to talk in my own poor tongue. My friend, Monsieur du Vallon, is of a very melancholy disposition, so much so, that one can scarcely get three words out of him all day. As for our two prisoners, you can imagine that they are but little in the vein for conversation."

"They are hot royalists," said Groslow.

"The more reason they should be sulky with us for having captured the Stuart, for whom, I hope, you're preparing a pretty trial."

"Why," said Groslow, "that is just what we are taking him to London for."

"And you never by any chance lose sight of him, I presume?"

"I should think not, indeed. You see he has a truly royal escort."

"Ay, there's no fear in the daytime; but at night?"

"We redouble our precautions."

"And what method of surveillance do you employ?"

"Eight men remain constantly in his room."

"The deuce, he is well guarded, then. But besides these eight men, you doubtless place some guard outside?"

"Oh, no! Just think. What would you have two men without arms do against eight armed men?"

"Two men—how do you mean?"

"Yes, the king and his lackey."

"Oh! then they allow the lackey to remain with him?"

"Yes; Stuart begged this favor and Harrison consented. Under pretense that he's a king it appears he cannot dress or undress without assistance."

"Really, captain," said D'Artagnan, determined to continue on the laudatory tack on which he had commenced, "the more I listen to you the more surprised I am at the easy and elegant manner in which you speak French. You have lived three years in Paris? May I ask what you were doing there?"

"My father, who is a merchant, placed me with his correspondent, who in turn sent his son to join our house in London."

"Were you pleased with Paris, sir?"

"Yes, but you are much in want of a revolution like our own—not against your king, who is a mere child, but against that lazar of an Italian, the queen's favorite."

"Ah! I am quite of your opinion, sir, and we should soon make an end of Mazarin if we had only a dozen officers like yourself, without prejudices, vigilant and incorruptible."

"But," said the officer, "I thought you were in his service and that it was he who sent you to General Cromwell."

"That is to say I am in the king's service, and that knowing he wanted to send some one to England, I solicited the appointment, so great was my desire to know the man of genius who now governs the three kingdoms. So that when he proposed to us to draw our swords in honor of old England you see how we snapped up the proposition."

"Yes, I know that you charged by the side of Mordaunt."

"On his right and left, sir. Ah! there's another brave and excellent young man."

"Do you know him?" asked the officer.

"Yes, very well. Monsieur du Vallon and myself came from France with him."

"It appears, too, you kept him waiting a long time at Boulogne."

"What would you have? I was like you, and had a king in keeping."

"Aha!" said Groslow; "what king?"

"Our own, to be sure, the little one—Louis XIV."

"And how long had you to take care of him?"

"Three nights; and, by my troth, I shall always remember those three nights with a certain pleasure."

"How do you mean?"

"I mean that my friends, officers in the guards and mousquetaires, came to keep me company and we passed the night in feasting, drinking, dicing."

"Ah true," said the Englishman, with a sigh; "you Frenchmen are born boon companions."

"And don't you play, too, when you are on guard?"

"Never," said the Englishman.

"In that case you must be horribly bored, and have my sympathy."

"The fact is, I look to my turn for keeping guard with horror. It's tiresome work to keep awake a whole night."

"Yes, but with a jovial partner and dice, and guineas clinking on the cloth, the night passes like a dream. You don't like playing, then?"

"On the contrary, I do."

"Lansquenet, for instance?"

"Devoted to it. I used to play almost every night in France."

"And since your return to England?"

"I have not handled a card or dice-box."

"I sincerely pity you," said D'Artagnan, with an air of profound compassion.

"Look here," said the Englishman.

"Well?"

"To-morrow I am on guard."

"In Stuart's room?"

"Yes; come and pass the night with me."

"Impossible!"

"Impossible! why so?"

"I play with Monsieur du Vallon every night. Sometimes we don't go to bed at all!"

"Well, what of that?"

"Why, he would be annoyed if I did not play with him."

"Does he play well?"

"I have seen him lose as much as two thousand pistoles, laughing all the while till the tears rolled down."

"Bring him with you, then."

"But how about our prisoners?"

"Let your servants guard them."

"Yes, and give them a chance of escaping," said D'Artagnan. "Why, one of them is a rich lord from Touraine and the other a knight of Malta, of noble family. We have arranged the ransom of each of them—2,000 on arriving in France. We are reluctant to leave for a single moment men whom our lackeys know to be millionaires. It is true we plundered them a little when we took them, and I will even confess that it is their purse that Monsieur du Vallon and I draw on in our nightly play. Still, they may have concealed some precious stone, some valuable diamond; so that we are like those misers who are unable to absent themselves from their treasures. We have made ourselves the constant guardians of our men, and while I sleep Monsieur du Vallon watches."

"Ah! ah!" said Groslow.

"You see, then, why I must decline your polite invitation, which is especially attractive to me, because nothing is so wearisome as to play night after night with the same person; the chances always balance and at the month's end nothing is gained or lost."

"Ah!" said Groslow, sighing; "there is something still more wearisome, and that is not to play at all."

"I can understand that," said D'Artagnan.

"But, come," resumed the Englishman, "are these men of yours dangerous?"

"In what respect?"

"Are they capable of attempting violence?"

D'Artagnan burst out laughing at the idea.

"Jesus Dieu!" he cried; "one of them is trembling with fever, having failed to adapt himself to this charming country of yours, and the other is a knight of Malta, as timid as a young girl; and for greater security we have taken from them even their penknives and pocket scissors."

"Well, then," said Groslow, "bring them with you."

"But really——" said D'Artagnan.

"I have eight men on guard, you know. Four of them can guard the king and the other four your prisoners. I'll manage it somehow, you will see."

"But," said D'Artagnan, "now I think of it—what is to prevent our beginning to-night?"

"Nothing at all," said Groslow.

"Just so. Come to us this evening and to-morrow we'll return your visit."

"Capital! This evening with you, to-morrow at Stuart's, the next day with me."

"You see, that with a little forethought one can lead a merry life anywhere and everywhere," said D'Artagnan.

"Yes, with Frenchmen, and Frenchmen like you."

"And Monsieur du Vallon," added the other. "You will see what a fellow he is; a man who nearly killed Mazarin between two doors. They employ him because they are afraid of him. Ah, there he is calling me now. You'll excuse me, I know."

They exchanged bows and D'Artagnan returned to his companions.

"What on earth can you have been saying to that bulldog?" exclaimed Porthos.

"My dear fellow, don't speak like that of Monsieur Groslow. He's one of my most intimate friends."

"One of your friends!" cried Porthos, "this butcher of unarmed farmers!"

"Hush! my dear Porthos. Monsieur Groslow is perhaps rather hasty, it's true, but at bottom I have discovered two good qualities in him—he is conceited and stupid."

Porthos opened his eyes in amazement; Athos and Aramis looked at one another and smiled; they knew D'Artagnan, and knew that he did nothing without a purpose.

"But," continued D'Artagnan, "you shall judge of him for yourself. He is coming to play with us this evening."

"Oho!" said Porthos, his eyes glistening at the news. "Is he rich?"

"He's the son of one of the wealthiest merchants in London."

"And knows lansquenet?"

"Adores it."

"Basset?"

"His mania."

"Biribi?"

"Revels in it."

"Good," said Porthos; "we shall pass an agreeable evening."

"The more so, as it will be the prelude to a better."

"How so?"

"We invite him to play to-night; he has invited us in return to-morrow. But wait. To-night we stop at Derby; and if there is a bottle of wine in the town let Mousqueton buy it. It will be well to prepare a light supper, of which you, Athos and Aramis, are not to partake—Athos, because I told him you had a fever; Aramis, because you are a knight of Malta and won't mix with fellows like us. Do you understand?"

"That's no doubt very fine," said Porthos; "but deuce take me if I understand at all."

"Porthos, my friend, you know I am descended on the father's side from the Prophets and on the mother's from the Sybils, and that I only speak in parables and riddles. Let those who have ears hear and those who have eyes see; I can tell you nothing more at present."

"Go ahead, my friend," said Athos; "I am sure that whatever you do is well done."

"And you, Aramis, are you of that opinion?"

"Entirely so, my dear D'Artagnan."

"Very good," said D'Artagnan; "here indeed are true believers; it is a pleasure to work miracles before them; they are not like that unbelieving Porthos, who must see and touch before he will believe."

"The fact is," said Porthos, with an air of finesse, "I am rather incredulous."

D'Artagnan gave him playful buffet on the shoulder, and as they had reached the station where they were to breakfast, the conversation ended there.

At five in the evening they sent Mousqueton on before as agreed upon. Blaisois went with him.

In crossing the principal street in Derby the four friends perceived Blaisois standing in the doorway of a handsome house. It was there a lodging was prepared for them.

At the hour agreed upon Groslow came. D'Artagnan received him as he would have done a friend of twenty years' standing. Porthos scanned him from head to foot and smiled when he discovered that in spite of the blow he had administered to Parry's brother, he was not nearly so strong as himself. Athos and Aramis suppressed as well as they could the disgust they felt in the presence of such coarseness and brutality.

In short, Groslow seemed to be pleased with his reception.

Athos and Aramis kept themselves to their role. At midnight they withdrew to their chamber, the door of which was left open on the pretext of kindly consideration. Furthermore, D'Artagnan went with them, leaving Porthos at play with Groslow.

Porthos gained fifty pistoles from Groslow, and found him a more agreeable companion than he had at first believed him to be.

As to Groslow, he promised himself that on the following evening he would recover from D'Artagnan what he had lost to Porthos, and on leaving reminded the Gascon of his appointment.

The next day was spent as usual. D'Artagnan went from Captain Groslow to Colonel Harrison and from Colonel Harrison to his friends. To any one not acquainted with him he seemed to be in his normal condition; but to his friends—to Athos and Aramis—was apparent a certain feverishness in his gayety.

"What is he contriving?" asked Aramis.

"Wait," said Athos.

Porthos said nothing, but he handled in his pocket the fifty pistoles he had gained from Groslow with a degree of satisfaction which betrayed itself in his whole bearing.

Arrived at Ryston, D'Artagnan assembled his friends. His face had lost the expression of careless gayety it had worn like a mask the whole day. Athos pinched Aramis's hand.

"The moment is at hand," he said.

"Yes," returned D'Artagnan, who had overheard him, "to-night, gentlemen, we rescue the king."

"D'Artagnan," said Athos, "this is no joke, I trust? It would quite cut me up."

"You are a very odd man, Athos," he replied, "to doubt me thus. Where and when have you seen me trifle with a friend's heart and a king's life? I have told you, and I repeat it, that to-night we rescue Charles I. You left it to me to discover the means and I have done so."

Porthos looked at D'Artagnan with an expression of profound admiration. Aramis smiled as one who hopes. Athos was pale, and trembled in every limb.

"Speak," said Athos.

"We are invited," replied D'Artagnan, "to pass the night with M. Groslow. But do you know where?"

"No."

"In the king's room."

"The king's room?" cried Athos.

"Yes, gentlemen, in the king's room. Groslow is on guard there this evening, and to pass the time away he has invited us to keep him company."

"All four of us?" asked Athos.

"Pardieu! certainly, all four; we couldn't leave our prisoners, could we?"

"Ah! ah!" said Aramis.

"Tell us about it," said Athos, palpitating.

"We are going, then, we two with our swords, you with daggers. We four have got to master these eight fools and their stupid captain. Monsieur Porthos, what do you say to that?"

"I say it is easy enough," answered Porthos.

"We dress the king in Groslow's clothes. Mousqueton, Grimaud and Blaisois have our horses saddled at the end of the first street. We mount them and before daylight are twenty leagues distant."

Athos placed his two hands on D'Artagnan's shoulders, and gazed at him with his calm, sad smile.

"I declare, my friend," said he, "that there is not a creature under the sky who equals you in prowess and in courage. Whilst we thought you indifferent to our sorrows, which you couldn't share without crime, you alone among us have discovered what we were searching for in vain. I repeat it, D'Artagnan, you are the best one among us; I bless and love you, my dear son."

"And to think that I couldn't find that out," said Porthos, scratching his head; "it is so simple."

"But," said Aramis, "if I understand rightly we are to kill them all, eh?"

Athos shuddered and turned pale.

"Mordioux!" answered D'Artagnan, "I believe we must. I confess I can discover no other safe and satisfactory way."

"Let us see," said Aramis, "how are we to act?"

"I have arranged two plans. Firstly, at a given signal, which shall be the words 'At last,' you each plunge a dagger into the heart of the soldier nearest to you. We, on our side, do the same. That will be four killed. We shall then be matched, four against the remaining five. If these five men give themselves up we gag them; if they resist, we kill them. If by chance our Amphitryon changes his mind and receives only Porthos and myself, why, then, we must resort to heroic measures and each give two strokes instead of one. It will take a little longer time and may make a greater disturbance, but you will be outside with swords and will rush in at the proper time."

"But if you yourselves should be struck?" said Athos.

"Impossible!" said D'Artagnan; "those beer drinkers are too clumsy and awkward. Besides, you will strike at the throat, Porthos; it kills as quickly and prevents all outcry."

"Very good," said Porthos; "it will be a nice little throat cutting."

"Horrible, horrible," exclaimed Athos.

"Nonsense," said D'Artagnan; "you would do as much, Mr. Humanity, in a battle. But if you think the king's life is not worth what it must cost there's an end of the matter and I send to Groslow to say I am ill."

"No, you are right," said Athos.

At this moment a soldier entered to inform them that Groslow was waiting for them.

"Where?" asked D'Artagnan.

"In the room of the English Nebuchadnezzar," replied the staunch Puritan.

"Good," replied Athos, whose blood mounted to his face at the insult offered to royalty; "tell the captain we are coming."

The Puritan then went out. The lackeys had been ordered to saddle eight horses and to wait, keeping together and without dismounting, at the corner of a street about twenty steps from the house where the king was lodged.

It was nine o'clock in the evening; the sentinels had been relieved at eight and Captain Groslow had been on guard for an hour. D'Artagnan and Porthos, armed with their swords, and Athos and Aramis, each carrying a concealed poniard, approached the house which for the time being was Charles Stuart's prison. The two latter followed their captors in the humble guise of captives, without arms.

"Od's bodikins," said Groslow, as the four friends entered, "I had almost given you up."

D'Artagnan went up to him and whispered in his ear:

"The fact is, we, that is, Monsieur du Vallon and I, hesitated a little."

"And why?"

D'Artagnan looked significantly toward Athos and Aramis.

"Aha," said Groslow; "on account of political opinions? No matter. On the contrary," he added, laughing, "if they want to see their Stuart they shall see him.

"Are we to pass the night in the king's room?" asked D'Artagnan.

"No, but in the one next to it, and as the door will remain open it comes to the same thing. Have you provided yourself with money? I assure you I intend to play the devil's game to-night."

D'Artagnan rattled the gold in his pockets.

"Very good," said Groslow, and opened the door of the room. "I will show you the way," and he went in first.

D'Artagnan turned to look at his friends. Porthos was perfectly indifferent; Athos, pale, but resolute; Aramis was wiping a slight moisture from his brow.

The eight guards were at their posts. Four in the king's room, two at the door between the rooms and two at that by which the friends had entered. Athos smiled when he saw their bare swords; he felt it was no longer to be a butchery, but a fight, and he resumed his usual good humor.

Charles was perceived through the door, lying dressed upon his bed, at the head of which Parry was seated, reading in a low voice a chapter from the Bible.

A candle of coarse tallow on a black table lighted up the handsome and resigned face of the king and that of his faithful retainer, far less calm.

From time to time Parry stopped, thinking the king, whose eyes were closed, was really asleep, but Charles would open his eyes and say with a smile:

"Go on, my good Parry, I am listening."

Groslow advanced to the door of the king's room, replaced on his head the hat he had taken off to receive his guests, looked for a moment contemptuously at this simple, yet touching scene, then turning to D'Artagnan, assumed an air of triumph at what he had achieved.

"Capital!" cried the Gascon, "you would make a distinguished general."

"And do you think," asked Groslow, "that Stuart will ever escape while I am on guard?"

"No, to be sure," replied D'Artagnan; "unless, forsooth, the sky rains friends upon him."

Groslow's face brightened.

It is impossible to say whether Charles, who kept his eyes constantly closed, had noticed the insolence of the Puritan captain, but the moment he heard the clear tone of D'Artagnan's voice his eyelids rose, in spite of himself.

Parry, too, started and stopped reading.

"What are you thinking about?" said the king; "go on, my good Parry, unless you are tired."

Parry resumed his reading.

On a table in the next room were lighted candles, cards, two dice-boxes, and dice.

"Gentlemen," said Groslow, "I beg you will take your places. I will sit facing Stuart, whom I like so much to see, especially where he now is, and you, Monsieur d'Artagnan, opposite to me."

Athos turned red with rage. D'Artagnan frowned at him.

"That's it," said D'Artagnan; "you, Monsieur le Comte de la Fere, to the right of Monsieur Groslow. You, Chevalier d'Herblay, to his left. Du Vallon next me. You'll bet for me and those gentlemen for Monsieur Groslow."

By this arrangement D'Artagnan could nudge Porthos with his knee and make signs with his eyes to Athos and Aramis.

At the names Comte de la Fere and Chevalier d'Herblay, Charles opened his eyes, and raising his noble head, in spite of himself, threw a glance at all the actors in the scene.

At that moment Parry turned over several leaves of his Bible and read with a loud voice this verse in Jeremiah:

"God said, 'Hear ye the words of the prophets my servants, whom I have sent unto you.'"

The four friends exchanged glances. The words that Parry had read assured them that their presence was understood by the king and was assigned to its real motive. D'Artagnan's eyes sparkled with joy.

"You asked me just now if I was in funds," said D'Artagnan, placing some twenty pistoles upon the table. "Well, in my turn I advise you to keep a sharp lookout on your treasure, my dear Monsieur Groslow, for I can tell you we shall not leave this without robbing you of it."

"Not without my defending it," said Groslow.

"So much the better," said D'Artagnan. "Fight, my dear captain, fight. You know or you don't know, that that is what we ask of you."

"Oh! yes," said Groslow, bursting with his usual coarse laugh, "I know you Frenchmen want nothing but cuts and bruises."

Charles had heard and understood it all. A slight color mounted to his cheeks. The soldiers then saw him stretch his limbs, little by little, and under the pretense of much heat throw off the Scotch plaid which covered him.

Athos and Aramis started with delight to find that the king was lying with his clothes on.

The game began. The luck had turned, and Groslow, having won some hundred pistoles, was in the merriest possible humor.

Porthos, who had lost the fifty pistoles he had won the night before and thirty more besides, was very cross and questioned D'Artagnan with a nudge of the knee as to whether it would not soon be time to change the game. Athos and Aramis looked at him inquiringly. But D'Artagnan remained impassible.

It struck ten. They heard the guard going its rounds.

"How many rounds do they make a night?" asked D'Artagnan, drawing more pistoles from his pocket.

"Five," answered Groslow, "one every two hours."

D'Artagnan glanced at Athos and Aramis and for the first time replied to Porthos's nudge of the knee by a nudge responsive. Meanwhile, the soldiers whose duty it was to remain in the king's room, attracted by that love of play so powerful in all men, had stolen little by little toward the table, and standing on tiptoe, lounged, watching the game, over the shoulders of D'Artagnan and Porthos. Those on the other side had followed their example, thus favoring the views of the four friends, who preferred having them close at hand to chasing them about the chamber. The two sentinels at the door still had their swords unsheathed, but they were leaning on them while they watched the game.

Athos seemed to grow calm as the critical moment approached. With his white, aristocratic hands he played with the louis, bending and straightening them again, as if they were made of pewter. Aramis, less self-controlled, fumbled continually with his hidden poniard. Porthos, impatient at his continued losses, kept up a vigorous play with his knee.

D'Artagnan turned, mechanically looking behind him, and between the figures of two soldiers he could see Parry standing up and Charles leaning on his elbow with his hands clasped and apparently offering a fervent prayer to God.

D'Artagnan saw that the moment was come. He darted a preparatory glance at Athos and Aramis, who slyly pushed their chairs a little back so as to leave themselves more space for action. He gave Porthos a second nudge of the knee and Porthos got up as if to stretch his legs and took care at the same time to ascertain that his sword could be drawn smoothly from the scabbard.

"Hang it!" cried D'Artagnan, "another twenty pistoles lost. Really, Captain Groslow, you are too much in fortune's way. This can't last," and he drew another twenty from his pocket. "One more turn, captain; twenty pistoles on one throw—only one, the last."

"Done for twenty," replied Groslow.

And he turned up two cards as usual, a king for D'Artagnan and an ace for himself.

"A king," said D'Artagnan; "it's a good omen, Master Groslow—look out for the king."

And in spite of his extraordinary self-control there was a strange vibration in the Gascon's voice which made his partner start.

Groslow began turning the cards one after another. If he turned up an ace first he won; if a king he lost.

He turned up a king.

"At last!" cried D'Artagnan.

At this word Athos and Aramis jumped up. Porthos drew back a step. Daggers and swords were just about to shine, when suddenly the door was thrown open and Harrison appeared in the doorway, accompanied by a man enveloped in a large cloak. Behind this man could be seen the glistening muskets of half a dozen soldiers.

Groslow jumped up, ashamed at being surprised in the midst of wine, cards, and dice. But Harrison paid not the least attention to him, and entering the king's room, followed by his companion:

"Charles Stuart," said he, "an order has come to conduct you to London without stopping day or night. Prepare yourself, then, to start at once."

"And by whom is this order given?" asked the king.

"By General Oliver Cromwell. And here is Mr. Mordaunt, who has brought it and is charged with its execution."

"Mordaunt!" muttered the four friends, exchanging glances.

D'Artagnan swept up the money that he and Porthos had lost and buried it in his huge pocket. Athos and Aramis placed themselves behind him. At this movement Mordaunt turned around, recognized them, and uttered an exclamation of savage delight.

"I'm afraid we are prisoners," whispered D'Artagnan to his friend.

"Not yet," replied Porthos.

"Colonel, colonel," cried Mordaunt, "you are betrayed. These four Frenchmen have escaped from Newcastle, and no doubt want to carry off the king. Arrest them."

"Ah! my young man," said D'Artagnan, drawing his sword, "that is an order sooner given than executed. Fly, friends, fly!" he added, whirling his sword around him.

The next moment he darted to the door and knocked down two of the soldiers who guarded it, before they had time to cock their muskets. Athos and Aramis followed him. Porthos brought up the rear, and before soldiers, officers, or colonel had time to recover their surprise all four were in the street.

"Fire!" cried Mordaunt; "fire upon them!"

Three or four shots were fired, but with no other result than to show the four fugitives turning the corner of the street safe and sound.

The horses were at the place fixed upon, and they leaped lightly into their saddles.

"Forward!" cried D'Artagnan, "and spur for your dear lives!"

They galloped away and took the road they had come by in the morning, namely, in the direction toward Scotland. A few hundred yards beyond the town D'Artagnan drew rein.

"Halt!" he cried, "this time we shall be pursued. We must let them leave the village and ride after us on the northern road, and when they have passed we will take the opposite direction."

There was a stream close by and a bridge across it.

D'Artagnan led his horse under the arch of the bridge. The others followed. Ten minutes later they heard the rapid gallop of a troop of horsemen. A few minutes more and the troop passed over their heads.

Chapter LXII.

London.

As soon as the noise of the hoofs was lost in the distance D'Artagnan remounted the bank of the stream and scoured the plain, followed by his three friends, directing their course, as well as they could guess, toward London.

"This time," said D'Artagnan, when they were sufficiently distant to proceed at a trot, "I think all is lost and we have nothing better to do than to reach France. What do you say, Athos, to that proposition? Isn't it reasonable?"

"Yes, dear friend," Athos replied, "but you said a word the other day that was more than reasonable—it was noble and generous. You said, 'Let us die here!' I recall to you that word."

"Oh," said Porthos, "death is nothing: it isn't death that can disquiet us, since we don't know what it is. What troubles me is the idea of defeat. As things are turning out, I foresee that we must give battle to London, to the provinces, to all England, and certainly in the end we can't fail to be beaten."

"We ought to witness this great tragedy even to its last scene," said Athos. "Whatever happens, let us not leave England before the crisis. Don't you agree with me, Aramis?"

"Entirely, my dear count. Then, too, I confess I should not be sorry to come across Mordaunt again. It appears to me that we have an account to settle with him, and that it is not our custom to leave a place without paying our debts, of this kind, at least."

"Ah! that's another thing," said D'Artagnan, "and I should not mind waiting in London a whole year for a chance of meeting this Mordaunt in question. Only let us lodge with some one on whom we can count; for I imagine, just now, that Noll Cromwell would not be inclined to trifle with us. Athos, do you know any inn in the whole town where one can find white sheets, roast beef reasonably cooked, and wine which is not made of hops and gin?"

"I think I know what you want," replied Athos. "De Winter took us to the house of a Spaniard, who, he said, had become naturalized as an Englishman by the guineas of his new compatriots. What do you say to it, Aramis?"

"Why, the idea of taking quarters with Senor Perez seems to me very reasonable, and for my part I agree to it. We will invoke the remembrance of that poor De Winter, for whom he seemed to have a great regard; we will tell him that we have come as amateurs to see what is going on; we will spend with him a guinea each per day; and I think that by taking all these precautions we can be quite undisturbed."

"You forget, Aramis, one precaution of considerable importance."

"What is that?"

"The precaution of changing our clothes."

"Changing our clothes!" exclaimed Porthos. "I don't see why; we are very comfortable in those we wear."

"To prevent recognition," said D'Artagnan. "Our clothes have a cut which would proclaim the Frenchman at first sight. Now, I don't set sufficient store on the cut of my jerkin to risk being hung at Tyburn or sent for change of scene to the Indies. I shall buy a chestnut-colored suit. I've remarked that your Puritans revel in that color."

"But can you find your man?" said Aramis to Athos.

"Oh! to be sure, yes. He lives at the Bedford Tavern, Greenhall Street. Besides, I can find my way about the city with my eyes shut."

"I wish we were already there," said D'Artagnan; "and my advice is that we reach London before daybreak, even if we kill our horses."

"Come on, then," said Athos, "for unless I am mistaken in my calculations we have only eight or ten leagues to go."

The friends urged on their horses and arrived, in fact, at about five o'clock in the morning. They were stopped and questioned at the gate by which they sought to enter the city, but Athos replied, in excellent English, that they had been sent forward by Colonel Harrison to announce to his colleague, Monsieur Bridge, the approach of the king. That reply led to several questions about the king's capture, and Athos gave details so precise and positive that if the gatekeepers had any suspicions they vanished completely. The way was therefore opened to the four friends with all sorts of Puritan congratulations.

Athos was right. He went direct to the Bedford Tavern, and the host, who recognized him, was delighted to see him again with such a numerous and promising company.

Though it was scarcely daylight our four travelers found the town in a great bustle, owing to the reported approach of Harrison and the king.

The plan of changing their clothes was unanimously adopted. The landlord sent out for every description of garment, as if he wanted to fit up his wardrobe. Athos chose a black coat, which gave him the appearance of a respectable citizen. Aramis, not wishing to part with his sword, selected a dark-blue cloak of a military cut. Porthos was seduced by a wine-colored doublet and sea-green breeches. D'Artagnan, who had fixed on his color beforehand, had only to select the shade, and looked in his chestnut suit exactly like a retired sugar dealer.

"Now," said D'Artagnan, "for the actual man. We must cut off our hair, that the populace may not insult us. As we no longer wear the sword of the gentleman we may as well have the head of the Puritan. This, as you know, is the important point of distinction between the Covenanter and the Cavalier."

After some discussion this was agreed to and Mousqueton played the role of barber.

"We look hideous," said Athos.

"And smack of the Puritan to a frightful extent," said Aramis.

"My head feels actually cold," said Porthos.

"As for me, I feel anxious to preach a sermon," said D'Artagnan.

"Now," said Athos, "that we cannot even recognize one another and have therefore no fear of others recognizing us, let us go and see the king's entrance."

They had not been long in the crowd before loud cries announced the king's arrival. A carriage had been sent to meet him, and the gigantic Porthos, who stood a head above the entire rabble, soon announced that he saw the royal equipage approaching. D'Artagnan raised himself on tiptoe, and as the carriage passed, saw Harrison at one window and Mordaunt at the other.

The next day, Athos, leaning out of his window, which looked upon the most populous part of the city, heard the Act of Parliament, which summoned the ex-king, Charles I., to the bar, publicly cried.

"Parliament indeed!" cried Athos. "Parliament can never have passed such an act as that."

At this moment the landlord came in.

"Did parliament pass this act?" Athos asked of him in English.

"Yes, my lord, the pure parliament."

"What do you mean by 'the pure parliament'? Are there, then, two parliaments?"

"My friend," D'Artagnan interrupted, "as I don't understand English and we all understand Spanish, have the kindness to speak to us in that language, which, since it is your own, you must find pleasure in using when you have the chance."

"Ah! excellent!" said Aramis.

As to Porthos, all his attention was concentrated on the allurements of the breakfast table.

"You were asking, then?" said the host in Spanish.

"I asked," said Athos, in the same language, "if there are two parliaments, a pure and an impure?"

"Why, how extraordinary!" said Porthos, slowly raising his head and looking at his friends with an air of astonishment, "I understand English, then! I understand what you say!"

"That is because we are talking Spanish, my dear friend," said Athos.

"Oh, the devil!" said Porthos, "I am sorry for that; it would have been one language more."

"When I speak of the pure parliament," resumed the host, "I mean the one which Colonel Bridge has weeded."

"Ah! really," said D'Artagnan, "these people are very ingenious. When I go back to France I must suggest some such convenient course to Cardinal Mazarin and the coadjutor. One of them will weed the parliament in the name of the court, and the other in the name of the people; and then there won't be any parliament at all."

"And who is this Colonel Bridge?" asked Aramis, "and how does he go to work to weed the parliament?"

"Colonel Bridge," replied the Spaniard, "is a retired wagoner, a man of much sense, who made one valuable observation whilst driving his team, namely, that where there happened to be a stone on the road, it was much easier to remove the stone than try and make the wheel pass over it. Now, of two hundred and fifty-one members who composed the parliament, there were one hundred and ninety-one who were in the way and might have upset his political wagon. He took them up, just as he formerly used to take up the stones from the road, and threw them out of the house."

"Neat," remarked D'Artagnan. "Very!"

"And all these one hundred and ninety-one were Royalists?" asked Athos.

"Without doubt, senor; and you understand that they would have saved the king."

"To be sure," said Porthos, with majestic common sense; "they were in the majority."

"And you think," said Aramis, "he will consent to appear before such a tribunal?"

"He will be forced to do so," smiled the Spaniard.

"Now, Athos!" said D'Artagnan, "do you begin to believe that it's a ruined cause, and that what with your Harrisons, Joyces, Bridges and Cromwells, we shall never get the upper hand?"

"The king will be delivered at the tribunal," said Athos; "the very silence of his supporters indicates that they are at work."

D'Artagnan shrugged his shoulders.

"But," said Aramis, "if they dare to condemn their king, it can only be to exile or imprisonment."

D'Artagnan whistled a little air of incredulity.

"We shall see," said Athos, "for we shall go to the sittings, I presume."

"You will not have long to wait," said the landlord; "they begin to-morrow."

"So, then, they drew up the indictments before the king was taken?"

"Of course," said D'Artagnan; "they began the day he was sold."

"And you know," said Aramis, "that it was our friend Mordaunt who made, if not the bargain, at least the overtures."

"And you know," added D'Artagnan, "that whenever I catch him I will kill him, this Mordaunt."

"And I, too," exclaimed Porthos.

"And I, too," added Aramis.

"Touching unanimity!" cried D'Artagnan, "which well becomes good citizens like us. Let us take a turn around the town and imbibe a little fog."

"Yes," said Porthos, "'twill be at least a little change from beer."

Chapter LXIII.

The Trial.

The next morning King Charles I. was haled by a strong guard before the high court which was to judge him. All London was crowding to the doors of the house. The throng was terrific, and it was not till after much pushing and some fighting that our friends reached their destination. When they did so they found the three lower rows of benches already occupied; but being anxious not to be too conspicuous, all, with the exception of Porthos, who had a fancy to display his red doublet, were quite satisfied with their places, the more so as chance had brought them to the centre of their row, so that they were exactly opposite the arm-chair prepared for the royal prisoner.

Toward eleven o'clock the king entered the hall, surrounded by guards, but wearing his head covered, and with a calm expression turned to every side with a look of complete assurance, as if he were there to preside at an assembly of submissive subjects, rather than to meet the accusations of a rebel court.

The judges, proud of having a monarch to humiliate, evidently prepared to enjoy the right they had arrogated to themselves, and sent an officer to inform the king that it was customary for the accused to uncover his head.

Charles, without replying a single word, turned his head in another direction and pulled his felt hat over it. Then when the officer was gone he sat down in the arm-chair opposite the president and struck his boots with a little cane which he carried in his hand. Parry, who accompanied him, stood behind him.

D'Artagnan was looking at Athos, whose face betrayed all those emotions which the king, possessing more self-control, had banished from his own. This agitation in one so cold and calm as Athos, frightened him.

"I hope," he whispered to him, "that you will follow his majesty's example and not get killed for your folly in this den."

"Set your mind at rest," replied Athos.

"Aha!" continued D'Artagnan, "it is clear that they are afraid of something or other; for look, the sentinels are being reinforced. They had only halberds before, now they have muskets. The halberds were for the audience in the rear; the muskets are for us."

"Thirty, forty, fifty, sixty-five men," said Porthos, counting the reinforcements.

"Ah!" said Aramis, "but you forget the officer."

D'Artagnan grew pale with rage. He recognized Mordaunt, who with bare sword was marshalling the musketeers behind the king and opposite the benches.

"Do you think they have recognized us?" said D'Artagnan. "In that case I should beat a retreat. I don't care to be shot in a box."

"No," said Aramis, "he has not seen us. He sees no one but the king. Mon Dieu! how he stares at him, the insolent dog! Does he hate his majesty as much as he does us?"

"Pardi," answered Athos "we only carried off his mother; the king has spoiled him of his name and property."

"True," said Aramis; "but silence! the president is speaking to the king."

"Stuart," Bradshaw was saying, "listen to the roll call of your judges and address to the court any observations you may have to make."

The king turned his head away, as if these words had not been intended for him. Bradshaw waited, and as there was no reply there was a moment of silence.

Out of the hundred and sixty-three members designated there were only seventy-three present, for the rest, fearful of taking part in such an act, had remained away.

When the name of Colonel Fairfax was called, one of those brief but solemn silences ensued, which announced the absence of the members who had no wish to take a personal part in the trial.

"Colonel Fairfax," repeated Bradshaw.

"Fairfax," answered a laughing voice, the silvery tone of which betrayed it as that of a woman, "is not such a fool as to be here."

A loud laugh followed these words, pronounced with that boldness which women draw from their own weakness—a weakness which removes them beyond the power of vengeance.

"It is a woman's voice," cried Aramis; "faith, I would give a good deal if she is young and pretty." And he mounted on the bench to try and get a sight of her.

"By my soul," said Aramis, "she is charming. Look D'Artagnan; everybody is looking at her; and in spite of Bradshaw's gaze she has not turned pale."

"It is Lady Fairfax herself," said D'Artagnan. "Don't you remember, Porthos, we saw her at General Cromwell's?"

The roll call continued.

"These rascals will adjourn when they find that they are not in sufficient force," said the Comte de la Fere.

"You don't know them. Athos, look at Mordaunt's smile. Is that the look of a man whose victim is likely to escape him? Ah, cursed basilisk, it will be a happy day for me when I can cross something more than a look with you."

"The king is really very handsome," said Porthos; "and look, too, though he is a prisoner, how carefully he is dressed. The feather in his hat is worth at least five-and-twenty pistoles. Look at it, Aramis."

The roll call finished, the president ordered them to read the act of accusation. Athos turned pale. A second time he was disappointed in his expectation. Notwithstanding the judges were so few the trial was to continue; the king then, was condemned in advance.

"I told you so, Athos," said D'Artagnan, shrugging his shoulders. "Now take your courage in both hands and hear what this gentleman in black is going to say about his sovereign, with full license and privilege."

Never till then had a more brutal accusation or meaner insults tarnished kingly majesty.

Charles listened with marked attention, passing over the insults, noting the grievances, and, when hatred overflowed all bounds and the accuser turned executioner beforehand, replying with a smile of lofty scorn.

"The fact is," said D'Artagnan, "if men are punished for imprudence and triviality, this poor king deserves punishment. But it seems to me that that which he is just now undergoing is hard enough."

"In any case," Aramis replied, "the punishment should fall not on the king, but on his ministers; for the first article of the constitution is, 'The king can do no wrong.'"

"As for me," thought Porthos, giving Mordaunt his whole attention, "were it not for breaking in on the majesty of the situation I would leap down from the bench, reach Mordaunt in three bounds and strangle him; I would then take him by the feet and knock the life out of these wretched musketeers who parody the musketeers of France. Meantime, D'Artagnan, who is full of invention, would find some way to save the king. I must speak to him about it."

As to Athos, his face aflame, his fists clinched, his lips bitten till they bled, he sat there foaming with rage at that endless parliamentary insult and that long enduring royal patience; the inflexible arm and steadfast heart had given place to a trembling hand and a body shaken by excitement.

At this moment the accuser concluded with these words: "The present accusation is preferred by us in the name of the English people."

At these words there was a murmur along the benches, and a second voice, not that of a woman, but a man's, stout and furious, thundered behind D'Artagnan.

"You lie!" it cried. "Nine-tenths of the English people are horrified at what you say."

This voice was that of Athos, who, standing up with outstretched hand and quite out of his mind, thus assailed the public accuser.

King, judges, spectators, all turned their eyes to the bench where the four friends were seated. Mordaunt did the same and recognized the gentleman, around whom the three other Frenchmen were standing, pale and menacing. His eyes glittered with delight. He had discovered those to whose death he had devoted his life. A movement of fury called to his side some twenty of his musketeers, and pointing to the bench where his enemies were: "Fire on that bench!" he cried.

But with the rapidity of thought D'Artagnan seized Athos by the waist, and followed by Porthos with Aramis, leaped down from the benches, rushed into the passages, and flying down the staircase were lost in the crowd without, while the muskets within were pointed on some three thousand spectators, whose piteous cries and noisy alarm stopped the impulse already given to bloodshed.

Charles also had recognized the four Frenchmen. He put one hand on his heart to still its beating and the other over his eyes, that he might not witness the slaying of his faithful friends.

Mordaunt, pale and trembling with anger, rushed from the hall sword in hand, followed by six pikemen, pushing, inquiring and panting in the crowd; and then, having found nothing, returned.

The tumult was indescribable. More than half an hour passed before any one could make himself heard. The judges were looking for a new outbreak from the benches. The spectators saw the muskets leveled at them, and divided between fear and curiosity, remained noisy and excited.

Quiet was at length restored.

"What have you to say in your defense?" asked Bradshaw of the king.

Then rising, with his head still covered, in the tone of a judge rather than a prisoner, Charles began.

"Before questioning me," he said, "reply to my question. I was free at Newcastle and had there concluded a treaty with both houses. Instead of performing your part of this contract, as I performed mine, you bought me from the Scotch, cheaply, I know, and that does honor to the economic talent of your government. But because you have paid the price of a slave, do you imagine that I have ceased to be your king? No. To answer you would be to forget it. I shall only reply to you when you have satisfied me of your right to question me. To answer you would be to acknowledge you as my judges, and I only acknowledge you as my executioners." And in the middle of a deathlike silence, Charles, calm, lofty, and with his head still covered, sat down again in his arm-chair.

"Why are not my Frenchmen here?" he murmured proudly and turning his eyes to the benches where they had appeared for a moment; "they would have seen that their friend was worthy of their defense while alive, and of their tears when dead."

"Well," said the president, seeing that Charles was determined to remain silent, "so be it. We will judge you in spite of your silence. You are accused of treason, of abuse of power, and murder. The evidence will support it. Go, and another sitting will accomplish what you have postponed in this."

Charles rose and turned toward Parry, whom he saw pale and with his temples dewed with moisture.

"Well, my dear Parry," said he, "what is the matter, and what can affect you in this manner?"

"Oh, my king," said Parry, with tears in his eyes and in a tone of supplication, "do not look to the left as we leave the hall."

"And why, Parry?"

"Do not look, I implore you, my king."

"But what is the matter? Speak," said Charles, attempting to look across the hedge of guards which surrounded him.

"It is—but you will not look, will you?—it is because they have had the axe, with which criminals are executed, brought and placed there on the table. The sight is hideous."

"Fools," said Charles, "do they take me for a coward, like themselves? You have done well to warn me. Thank you, Parry."

When the moment arrived the king followed his guards out of the hall. As he passed the table on which the axe was laid, he stopped, and turning with a smile, said:

"Ah! the axe, an ingenious device, and well worthy of those who know not what a gentleman is; you frighten me not, executioner's axe," added he, touching it with the cane which he held in his hand, "and I strike you now, waiting patiently and Christianly for you to return the blow."

And shrugging his shoulders with unaffected contempt he passed on. When he reached the door a stream of people, who had been disappointed in not being able to get into the house and to make amends had collected to see him come out, stood on each side, as he passed, many among them glaring on him with threatening looks.

"How many people," thought he, "and not one true friend."

And as he uttered these words of doubt and depression within his mind, a voice beside him said:

"Respect to fallen majesty."

The king turned quickly around, with tears in his eyes and heart. It was an old soldier of the guards who could not see his king pass captive before him without rendering him this final homage. But the next moment the unfortunate man was nearly killed with heavy blows of sword-hilts, and among those who set upon him the king recognized Captain Groslow.

"Alas!" said Charles, "that is a severe chastisement for a very trifling fault."

He continued his walk, but he had scarcely gone a hundred paces, when a furious fellow, leaning between two soldiers, spat in the king's face, as once an infamous and accursed Jew spit in the face of Jesus of Nazareth. Loud roars of laughter and sullen murmurs arose together. The crowd opened and closed again, undulating like a stormy sea, and the king imagined that he saw shining in the midst of this living wave the bright eyes of Athos.

Charles wiped his face and said with a sad smile: "Poor wretch, for half a crown he would do as much to his own father."

The king was not mistaken. Athos and his friends, again mingling with the throng, were taking a last look at the martyr king.

When the soldier saluted Charles, Athos's heart bounded for joy; and that unfortunate, on coming to himself, found ten guineas that the French gentleman had slipped into his pocket. But when the cowardly insulter spat in the face of the captive monarch Athos grasped his dagger. But D'Artagnan stopped his hand and in a hoarse voice cried, "Wait!"

Athos stopped. D'Artagnan, leaning on Athos, made a sign to Porthos and Aramis to keep near them and then placed himself behind the man with the bare arms, who was still laughing at his own vile pleasantry and receiving the congratulations of several others.

The man took his way toward the city. The four friends followed him. The man, who had the appearance of being a butcher, descended a little steep and isolated street, looking on to the river, with two of his friends. Arrived at the bank of the river the three men perceived that they were followed, turned around, and looking insolently at the Frenchmen, passed some jests from one to another.

"I don't know English, Athos," said D'Artagnan; "but you know it and will interpret for me."

Then quickening their steps they passed the three men, but turned back immediately, and D'Artagnan walked straight up to the butcher and touching him on the chest with the tip of his finger, said to Athos:

"Say this to him in English: 'You are a coward. You have insulted a defenseless man. You have befouled the face of your king. You must die.'"

Athos, pale as a ghost, repeated these words to the man, who, seeing the bodeful preparations that were making, put himself in an attitude of defense. Aramis, at this movement, drew his sword.

"No," cried D'Artagnan, "no steel. Steel is for gentlemen."

And seizing the butcher by the throat:

"Porthos," said he, "kill this fellow for me with a single blow."

Porthos raised his terrible fist, which whistled through the air like a sling, and the portentous mass fell with a smothered crash on the insulter's skull and crushed it. The man fell like an ox beneath the poleaxe. His companions, horror-struck, could neither move nor cry out.

"Tell them this, Athos," resumed D'Artagnan; "thus shall all die who forget that a captive man is sacred and that a captive king doubly represents the Lord."

Athos repeated D'Artagnan's words.

The fellows looked at the body of their companion, swimming in blood, and then recovering voice and legs together, ran screaming off.

"Justice is done," said Porthos, wiping his forehead.

"And now," said D'Artagnan to Athos, "entertain no further doubts about me; I undertake all that concerns the king."

Chapter LXIV.

Whitehall.

The parliament condemned Charles to death, as might have been foreseen. Political judgments are generally vain formalities, for the same passions which give rise to the accusation ordain to the condemnation. Such is the atrocious logic of revolutions.

Although our friends were expecting that condemnation, it filled them with grief. D'Artagnan, whose mind was never more fertile in resources than in critical emergencies, swore again that he would try all conceivable means to prevent the dénouement of the bloody tragedy. But by what means? As yet he could form no definite plan; all must depend on circumstances. Meanwhile, it was necessary at all hazards, in order to gain time, to put some obstacle in the way of the execution on the following day—the day appointed by the judges. The only way of doing that was to cause the disappearance of the London executioner. The headsman out of the way, the sentence could not be executed. True, they could send for the headsman of the nearest town, but at least a day would be gained, and a day might be sufficient for the rescue. D'Artagnan took upon himself that more than difficult task.

Another thing, not less essential, was to warn Charles Stuart of the attempt to be made, so that he might assist his rescuers as much as possible, or at least do nothing to thwart their efforts. Aramis assumed that perilous charge. Charles Stuart had asked that Bishop Juxon might be permitted to visit him. Mordaunt had called on the bishop that very evening to apprise him of the religious desire expressed by the king and also of Cromwell's permission. Aramis determined to obtain from the bishop, through fear or by persuasion, consent that he should enter in the bishop's place, and clad in his sacerdotal robes, the prison at Whitehall.

Finally, Athos undertook to provide, in any event, the means of leaving England—in case either of failure or of success.

The night having come they made an appointment to meet at eleven o'clock at the hotel, and each started out to fulfill his dangerous mission.

The palace of Whitehall was guarded by three regiments of cavalry and by the fierce anxiety of Cromwell, who came and went or sent his generals or his agents continually. Alone in his usual room, lighted by two candles, the condemned monarch gazed sadly on the luxury of his past greatness, just as at the last hour one sees the images of life more mildly brilliant than of yore.

Parry had not quitted his master, and since his condemnation had not ceased to weep. Charles, leaning on a table, was gazing at a medallion of his wife and daughter; he was waiting first for Juxon, then for martyrdom.

At times he thought of those brave French gentlemen who had appeared to him from a distance of a hundred leagues fabulous and unreal, like the forms that appear in dreams. In fact, he sometimes asked himself if all that was happening to him was not a dream, or at least the delirium of a fever. He rose and took a few steps as if to rouse himself from his torpor and went as far as the window; he saw glittering below him the muskets of the guards. He was thereupon constrained to admit that he was indeed awake and that his bloody dream was real.

Charles returned in silence to his chair, rested his elbow on the table, bowed his head upon his hand and reflected.

"Alas!" he said to himself, "if I only had for a confessor one of those lights of the church, whose soul has sounded all the mysteries of life, all the littlenesses of greatness, perhaps his utterance would overawe the voice that wails within my soul. But I shall have a priest of vulgar mind, whose career and fortune I have ruined by my misfortune. He will speak to me of God and death, as he has spoken to many another dying man, not understanding that this one leaves his throne to an usurper, his children to the cold contempt of public charity."

And he raised the medallion to his lips.

It was a dull, foggy night. A neighboring church clock slowly struck the hour. The flickering light of the two candles showed fitful phantom shadows in the lofty room. These were the ancestors of Charles, standing back dimly in their tarnished frames.

An awful sadness enveloped the heart of Charles. He buried his brow in his hands and thought of the world, so beautiful when one is about to leave it; of the caresses of children, so pleasing and so sweet, especially when one is parting from his children never to see them again; then of his wife, the noble and courageous woman who had sustained him to the last moment. He drew from his breast the diamond cross and the star of the Garter which she had sent him by those generous Frenchmen; he kissed it, and then, as he reflected, that she would never again see those things till he lay cold and mutilated in the tomb, there passed over him one of those icy shivers which may be called forerunners of death.

Then, in that chamber which recalled to him so many royal souvenirs, whither had come so many courtiers, the scene of so much flattering homage, alone with a despairing servant, whose feeble soul could afford no support to his own, the king at last yielded to sorrow, and his courage sank to a level with that feebleness, those shadows, and that wintry cold. That king, who was so grand, so sublime in the hour of death, meeting his fate with a smile of resignation on his lips, now in that gloomy hour wiped away a tear which had fallen on the table and quivered on the gold embroidered cloth.

Suddenly the door opened, an ecclesiastic in episcopal robes entered, followed by two guards, to whom the king waved an imperious gesture. The guards retired; the room resumed its obscurity.

"Juxon!" cried Charles, "Juxon, thank you, my last friend; you come at a fitting moment."

The bishop looked anxiously at the man sobbing in the ingle-nook.

"Come, Parry," said the king, "cease your tears."

"If it's Parry," said the bishop, "I have nothing to fear; so allow me to salute your majesty and to tell you who I am and for what I am come."

At this sight and this voice Charles was about to cry out, when Aramis placed his finger on his lips and bowed low to the king of England.

"The chevalier!" murmured Charles.

"Yes, sire," interrupted Aramis, raising his voice, "Bishop Juxon, the faithful knight of Christ, obedient to your majesty's wishes."

Charles clasped his hands, amazed and stupefied to find that these foreigners, without other motive than that which their conscience imposed on them, thus combated the will of a people and the destiny of a king.

"You!" he said, "you! how did you penetrate hither? If they recognize you, you are lost."

"Care not for me, sire; think only of yourself. You see, your friends are wakeful. I know not what we shall do yet, but four determined men can do much. Meanwhile, do not be surprised at anything that happens; prepare yourself for every emergency."

Charles shook his head.

"Do you know that I die to-morrow at ten o'clock?"

"Something, your majesty, will happen between now and then to make the execution impossible."

The king looked at Aramis with astonishment.

At this moment a strange noise, like the unloading of a cart, and followed by a cry of pain, was heard beneath the window.

"Do you hear?" said the king.

"I hear," said Aramis, "but I understand neither the noise nor the cry of pain."

"I know not who can have uttered the cry," said the king, "but the noise is easily understood. Do you know that I am to be beheaded outside this window? Well, these boards you hear unloaded are the posts and planks to build my scaffold. Some workmen must have fallen underneath them and been hurt."

Aramis shuddered in spite of himself.

"You see," said the king, "that it is useless for you to resist. I am condemned; leave me to my death."

"My king," said Aramis, "they well may raise a scaffold, but they cannot make an executioner."

"What do you mean?" asked the king.

"I mean that at this hour the headsman has been got out of the way by force or persuasion. The scaffold will be ready by to-morrow, but the headsman will be wanting and they will put it off till the day after to-morrow."

"What then?" said the king.

"To-morrow night we shall rescue you."

"How can that be?" cried the king, whose face was lighted up, in spite of himself, by a flash of joy.

"Oh! sir," cried Parry, "may you and yours be blessed!"

"How can it be?" repeated the king. "I must know, so that I may assist you if there is any chance."

"I know nothing about it," continued Aramis, "but the cleverest, the bravest, the most devoted of us four said to me when I left him, 'Tell the king that to-morrow at ten o'clock at night, we shall carry him off.' He has said it and will do it."

"Tell me the name of that generous friend," said the king, "that I may cherish for him an eternal gratitude, whether he succeeds or not."

"D'Artagnan, sire, the same who had so nearly rescued you when Colonel Harrison made his untimely entrance."

"You are, indeed, wonderful men," said the king; "if such things had been related to me I should not have believed them."

"Now, sire," resumed Aramis, "listen to me. Do not forget for a single instant that we are watching over your safety; observe the smallest gesture, the least bit of song, the least sign from any one near you; watch everything, hear everything, interpret everything."

"Oh, chevalier!" cried the king, "what can I say to you? There is no word, though it should come from the profoundest depth of my heart, that can express my gratitude. If you succeed I do not say that you will save a king; no, in presence of the scaffold as I am, royalty, I assure you, is a very small affair; but you will save a husband to his wife, a father to his children. Chevalier, take my hand; it is that of a friend who will love you to his last sigh."

Aramis stooped to kiss the king's hand, but Charles clasped his and pressed it to his heart.

At this moment a man entered, without even knocking at the door. Aramis tried to withdraw his hand, but the king still held it. The man was one of those Puritans, half preacher and half soldier, who swarmed around Cromwell.

"What do you want, sir?" said the king.

"I desire to know if the confession of Charles Stuart is at an end?" said the stranger.

"And what is it to you?" replied the king; "we are not of the same religion."

"All men are brothers," said the Puritan. "One of my brothers is about to die and I come to prepare him."

"Bear with him," whispered Aramis; "it is doubtless some spy."

"After my reverend lord bishop," said the king to the man, "I shall hear you with pleasure, sir."

The man retired, but not before examining the supposed Juxon with an attention which did not escape the king.

"Chevalier," said the king, when the door was closed, "I believe you are right and that this man only came here with evil intentions. Take care that no misfortune befalls you when you leave."

"I thank your majesty," said Aramis, "but under these robes I have a coat of mail, a pistol and a dagger."

"Go, then, sir, and God keep you!"

The king accompanied him to the door, where Aramis pronounced his benediction upon him, and passing through the ante-rooms, filled with soldiers, jumped into his carriage and drove to the bishop's palace. Juxon was waiting for him impatiently.

"Well?" said he, on perceiving Aramis.

"Everything has succeeded as I expected; spies, guards, satellites, all took me for you, and the king blesses you while waiting for you to bless him."

"May God protect you, my son; for your example has given me at the same time hope and courage."

Aramis resumed his own attire and left Juxon with the assurance that he might again have recourse to him.

He had scarcely gone ten yards in the street when he perceived that he was followed by a man, wrapped in a large cloak. He placed his hand on his dagger and stopped. The man came straight toward him. It was Porthos.

"My dear friend," cried Aramis.

"You see, we had each our mission," said Porthos; "mine was to guard you and I am doing so. Have you seen the king?"

"Yes, and all goes well."

"We are to meet our friends at the hotel at eleven."

It was then striking half-past ten by St. Paul's.

Arrived at the hotel it was not long before Athos entered.

"All's well," he cried, as he entered; "I have hired a cedar wherry, as light as a canoe, as easy on the wing as any swallow. It is waiting for us at Greenwich, opposite the Isle of Dogs, manned by a captain and four men, who for the sum of fifty pounds sterling will keep themselves at our disposition three successive nights. Once on board we drop down the Thames and in two hours are on the open sea. In case I am killed, the captain's name is Roger and the skiff is called the Lightning. A handkerchief, tied at the four corners, is to be the signal."

Next moment D'Artagnan entered.

"Empty your pockets," said he; "I want a hundred pounds, and as for my own——" and he emptied them inside out.

The sum was collected in a minute. D'Artagnan ran out and returned directly after.

"There," said he, "it's done. Ough! and not without a deal of trouble, too."

"Has the executioner left London?" asked Athos.

"Ah, you see that plan was not sure enough; he might go out by one gate and return by another."

"Where is he, then?"

"In the cellar."

"The cellar—what cellar?"

"Our landlord's, to be sure. Mousqueton is propped against the door and here's the key."

"Bravo!" said Aramis, "how did you manage it?"

"Like everything else, with money; but it cost me dear."

"How much?" asked Athos.

"Five hundred pounds."

"And where did you get so much money?" said Athos. "Had you, then, that sum?"

"The queen's famous diamond," answered D'Artagnan, with a sigh.

"Ah, true," said Aramis. "I recognized it on your finger."

"You bought it back, then, from Monsieur des Essarts?" asked Porthos.

"Yes, but it was fated that I should not keep it."

"So, then, we are all right as regards the executioner," said Athos; "but unfortunately every executioner has his assistant, his man, or whatever you call him."

"And this one had his," said D'Artagnan; "but, as good luck would have it, just as I thought I should have two affairs to manage, our friend was brought home with a broken leg. In the excess of his zeal he had accompanied the cart containing the scaffolding as far as the king's window, and one of the crossbeams fell on his leg and broke it."

"Ah!" cried Aramis, "that accounts for the cry I heard."

"Probably," said D'Artagnan, "but as he is a thoughtful young man he promised to send four expert workmen in his place to help those already at the scaffold, and wrote the moment he was brought home to Master Tom Lowe, an assistant carpenter and friend of his, to go down to Whitehall, with three of his friends. Here's the letter he sent by a messenger, for sixpence, who sold it to me for a guinea."

"And what on earth are you going to do with it?" asked Athos.

"Can't you guess, my dear Athos? You, who speak English like John Bull himself, are Master Tom Lowe, we, your three companions. Do you understand it now?"

Athos uttered a cry of joy and admiration, ran to a closet and drew forth workmen's clothes, which the four friends immediately put on; they then left the hotel, Athos carrying a saw, Porthos a vise, Aramis an axe and D'Artagnan a hammer and some nails.

The letter from the executioner's assistant satisfied the master carpenter that those were the men he expected.

Chapter LXV.

The Workmen.

Toward midnight Charles heard a great noise beneath his window. It arose from blows of hammer and hatchet, clinking of pincers and cranching of saws.

Lying dressed upon his bed, the noise awoke him with a start and found a gloomy echo in his heart. He could not endure it, and sent Parry to ask the sentinel to beg the workmen to strike more gently and not disturb the last slumber of one who had been their king. The sentinel was unwilling to leave his post, but allowed Parry to pass.

Arriving at the window Parry found an unfinished scaffold, over which they were nailing a covering of black serge. Raised to the height of twenty feet, so as to be on a level with the window, it had two lower stories. Parry, odious as was this sight to him, sought for those among some eight or ten workmen who were making the most noise; and fixed on two men, who were loosening the last hooks of the iron balcony.

"My friends," said Parry, mounting the scaffold and standing beside them, "would you work a little more quietly? The king wishes to get a sleep."

One of the two, who was standing up, was of gigantic size and was driving a pick with all his might into the wall, whilst the other, kneeling beside him, was collecting the pieces of stone. The face of the first was lost to Parry in the darkness; but as the second turned around and placed his finger on his lips Parry started back in amazement.

"Very well, very well," said the workman aloud, in excellent English. "Tell the king that if he sleeps badly to-night he will sleep better to-morrow night."

These blunt words, so terrible if taken literally, were received by the other workmen with a roar of laughter. But Parry withdrew, thinking he was dreaming.

Charles was impatiently awaiting his return. At the moment he re-entered, the sentinel who guarded the door put his head through the opening, curious as to what the king was doing. The king was lying on his bed, resting on his elbow. Parry closed the door and approaching the king, his face radiant with joy:

"Sire," he said, in a low voice, "do you know who these workmen are who are making so much noise?"

"I? No; how would you have me know?"

Parry bent his head and whispered to the king: "It is the Comte de la Fere and his friends."

"Raising my scaffold!" cried the king, astounded.

"Yes, and at the same time making a hole in the wall."

The king clasped his hands and raised his eyes to Heaven; then leaping down from his bed he went to the window, and pulling aside the curtain tried to distinguish the figures outside, but in vain.

Parry was not wrong. It was Athos he had recognized, and Porthos who was boring a hole through the wall.

This hole communicated with a kind of loft—the space between the floor of the king's room and the ceiling of the one below it. Their plan was to pass through the hole they were making into this loft and cut out from below a piece of the flooring of the king's room, so as to form a kind of trap-door.

Through this the king was to escape the next night, and, hidden by the black covering of the scaffold, was to change his dress for that of a workman, slip out with his deliverers, pass the sentinels, who would suspect nothing, and so reach the skiff that was waiting for him at Greenwich.

Day gilded the tops of the houses. The aperture was finished and Athos passed through it, carrying the clothes destined for the king wrapped in black cloth, and the tools with which he was to open a communication with the king's room. He had only two hours' work to do to open communication with the king and, according to the calculations of the four friends, they had the entire day before them, since, the executioner being absent, another must be sent for to Bristol.

D'Artagnan returned to change his workman's clothes for his chestnut-colored suit, and Porthos to put on his red doublet. As for Aramis, he went off to the bishop's palace to see if he could possibly pass in with Juxon to the king's presence. All three agreed to meet at noon in Whitehall Place to see how things went on.

Before leaving the scaffold Aramis had approached the opening where Athos was concealed to tell him that he was about to make an attempt to gain another interview with the king.

"Adieu, then, and be of good courage," said Athos. "Report to the king the condition of affairs. Say to him that when he is alone it will help us if he will knock on the floor, for then I can continue my work in safety. Try, Aramis, to keep near the king. Speak loud, very loud, for they will be listening at the door. If there is a sentinel within the apartment, kill him without hesitation. If there are two, let Parry kill one and you the other. If there are three, let yourself be slain, but save the king."

"Be easy," said Aramis; "I will take two poniards and give one to Parry. Is that all?"

"Yes, go; but urge the king strongly not to stand on false generosity. While you are fighting if there is a fight, he must flee. The trap once replaced over his head, you being on the trap, dead or alive, they will need at least ten minutes to find the hole by which he has escaped. In those ten minutes we shall have gained the road and the king will be saved."

"Everything shall be done as you say, Athos. Your hand, for perhaps we shall not see each other again."

Athos put his arm around Aramis's neck and embraced him.

"For you," he said. "Now if I die, say to D'Artagnan that I love him as a son, and embrace him for me. Embrace also our good and brave Porthos. Adieu."

"Adieu," said Aramis. "I am as sure now that the king will be saved as I am sure that I clasp the most loyal hand in the world."

Aramis parted from Athos, went down from the scaffold in his turn and took his way to the hotel, whistling the air of a song in praise of Cromwell. He found the other two friends sitting at table before a good fire, drinking a bottle of port and devouring a cold chicken. Porthos was cursing the infamous parliamentarians; D'Artagnan ate in silence, revolving in his mind the most audacious plans.

Aramis related what had been agreed upon. D'Artagnan approved with a movement of the head and Porthos with his voice.

"Bravo!" he said; "besides, we shall be there at the time of the flight. What with D'Artagnan, Grimaud and Mousqueton, we can manage to dispatch eight of them. I say nothing about Blaisois, for he is only fit to hold the horses.

Two minutes a man makes four minutes. Mousqueton will lose another, that's five; and in five minutes we shall have galloped a quarter of a league."

Aramis swallowed a hasty mouthful, gulped a glass of wine and changed his clothes.

"Now," said he, "I'm off to the bishop's. Take care of the executioner, D'Artagnan."

"All right. Grimaud has relieved Mousqueton and has his foot on the cellar door."

"Well, don't be inactive."

"Inactive, my dear fellow! Ask Porthos. I pass my life upon my legs."

Aramis again presented himself at the bishop's. Juxon consented the more readily to take him with him, as he would require an assistant priest in case the king should wish to communicate. Dressed as Aramis had been the night before, the bishop got into his carriage, and the former, more disguised by his pallor and sad countenance than his deacon's dress, got in by his side. The carriage stopped at the door of the palace.

It was about nine o'clock in the morning.

Nothing was changed. The ante-rooms were still full of soldiers, the passages still lined by guards. The king was already sanguine, but when he perceived Aramis his hope turned to joy. He embraced Juxon and pressed the hand of Aramis. The bishop affected to speak in a loud voice, before every one, of their previous interview. The king replied that the words spoken in that interview had borne their fruit, and that he desired another under the same conditions. Juxon turned to those present and begged them to leave him and his assistant alone with the king. Every one withdrew. As soon as the door was closed:

"Sire," said Aramis, speaking rapidly, "you are saved; the London executioner has vanished. His assistant broke his leg last night beneath your majesty's window—the cry we heard was his—and there is no executioner nearer at hand than Bristol."

"But the Comte de la Fere?" asked the king.

"Two feet below you; take the poker from the fireplace and strike three times on the floor. He will answer you."

The king did so, and the moment after, three muffled knocks, answering the given signal, sounded beneath the floor.

"So," said Charles, "he who knocks down there——"

"Is the Comte de la Fere, sire," said Aramis. "He is preparing a way for your majesty to escape. Parry, for his part, will raise this slab of marble and a passage will be opened."

"Oh, Juxon," said the king, seizing the bishop's two hands in his own, "promise that you will pray all your life for this gentleman and for the other that you hear beneath your feet, and for two others also, who, wherever they may be, are on the watch for my safety."

"Sire," replied Juxon, "you shall be obeyed."

Meanwhile, the miner underneath was heard working away incessantly, when suddenly an unexpected noise resounded in the passage. Aramis seized the poker and gave the signal to stop; the noise came nearer and nearer. It was that of a number of men steadily approaching. The four men stood motionless. All eyes were fixed on the door, which opened slowly and with a kind of solemnity.

A parliamentary officer, clothed in black and with a gravity that augured ill, entered, bowed to the king, and unfolding a parchment, read the sentence, as is usually done to criminals before their execution.

"What is this?" said Aramis to Juxon.

Juxon replied with a sign which meant that he knew no more than Aramis about it.

"Then it is for to-day?" asked the king.

"Was not your majesty warned that it was to take place this morning?"

"Then I must die like a common criminal by the hand of the London executioner?"

"The London executioner has disappeared, your majesty, but a man has offered his services instead. The execution will therefore only be delayed long enough for you to arrange your spiritual and temporal affairs."

A slight moisture on his brow was the only trace of emotion that Charles evinced, as he learned these tidings. But Aramis was livid. His heart ceased beating, he closed his eyes and leaned upon the table. Charles perceived it and took his hand.

"Come, my friend," said he, "courage." Then he turned to the officer. "Sir, I am ready. There is but little reason why I should delay you. Firstly, I wish to communicate; secondly, to embrace my children and bid them farewell for the last time. Will this be permitted me?"

"Certainly," replied the officer, and left the room.

Aramis dug his nails into his flesh and groaned aloud.

"Oh! my lord bishop," he cried, seizing Juxon's hands, "where is Providence? where is Providence?"

"My son," replied the bishop, with firmness, "you see Him not, because the passions of the world conceal Him."

"My son," said the king to Aramis, "do not take it so to heart. You ask what God is doing. God beholds your devotion and my martyrdom, and believe me, both will have their reward. Ascribe to men, then, what is happening, and not to God. It is men who drive me to death; it is men who make you weep."

"Yes, sire," said Aramis, "yes, you are right. It is men whom I should hold responsible, and I will hold them responsible."

"Be seated, Juxon," said the king, falling upon his knees. "I have now to confess to you. Remain, sir," he added to Aramis, who had moved to leave the room. "Remain, Parry. I have nothing to say that cannot be said before all."

Juxon sat down, and the king, kneeling humbly before him, began his confession.

Chapter LXVI.

Remember!

The mob had already assembled when the confession terminated. The king's children next arrived—the Princess Charlotte, a beautiful, fair-haired child, with tears in her eyes, and the Duke of Gloucester, a boy eight or nine years old, whose tearless eyes and curling lip revealed a growing pride. He had wept all night long, but would not show his grief before the people.

Charles's heart melted within him at the sight of those two children, whom he had not seen for two years and whom he now met at the moment of death. He turned to brush away a tear, and then, summoning up all his firmness, drew his daughter toward him, recommending her to be pious and resigned. Then he took the boy upon his knee.

"My son," he said to him, "you saw a great number of people in the streets as you came here. These men are going to behead your father. Do not forget that. Perhaps some day they will want to make you king, instead of the Prince of Wales, or the Duke of York, your elder brothers. But you are not the king, my son, and can never be so while they are alive. Swear to me, then, never to let them put a crown upon your head unless you have a legal right to the crown. For one day—listen, my son—one day, if you do so, they will doom you to destruction, head and crown, too, and then you will not be able to die with a calm conscience, as I die. Swear, my son."

The child stretched out his little hand toward that of his father and said, "I swear to your majesty."

"Henry," said Charles, "call me your father."

"Father," replied the child, "I swear to you that they shall kill me sooner than make me king."

"Good, my child. Now kiss me; and you, too, Charlotte. Never forget me."

"Oh! never, never!" cried both the children, throwing their arms around their father's neck.

"Farewell," said Charles, "farewell, my children. Take them away, Juxon; their tears will deprive me of the courage to die."

Juxon led them away, and this time the doors were left open.

Meanwhile, Athos, in his concealment, waited in vain the signal to recommence his work. Two long hours he waited in terrible inaction. A deathlike silence reigned in the room above. At last he determined to discover the cause of this stillness. He crept from his hole and stood, hidden by the black drapery, beneath the scaffold. Peeping out from the drapery, he could see the rows of halberdiers and musketeers around the scaffold and the first ranks of the populace swaying and groaning like the sea.

"What is the matter, then?" he asked himself, trembling more than the wind-swayed cloth he was holding back. "The people are hurrying on, the soldiers under arms, and among the spectators I see D'Artagnan. What is he waiting for? What is he looking at? Good God! have they allowed the headsman to escape?"

Suddenly the dull beating of muffled drums filled the square. The sound of heavy steps was heard above his head. The next moment the very planks of the scaffold creaked with the weight of an advancing procession, and the eager faces of the spectators confirmed what a last hope at the bottom of his heart had prevented him till then believing. At the same moment a well-known voice above him pronounced these words:

"Colonel, I want to speak to the people."

Athos shuddered from head to foot. It was the king speaking on the scaffold.

In fact, after taking a few drops of wine and a piece of bread, Charles, weary of waiting for death, had suddenly decided to go to meet it and had given the signal for movement. Then the two wings of the window facing the square had been thrown open, and the people had seen silently advancing from the interior of the vast chamber, first, a masked man, who, carrying an axe in his hand, was recognized as the executioner. He approached the block and laid his axe upon it. Behind him, pale indeed, but marching with a firm step, was Charles Stuart, who advanced between two priests, followed by a few superior officers appointed to preside at the execution and attended by two files of partisans who took their places on opposite sides of the scaffold.

The sight of the masked man gave rise to a prolonged sensation. Every one was full of curiosity as to who that unknown executioner could be who presented himself so opportunely to assure to the people the promised spectacle, when the people believed it had been postponed until the following day. All gazed at him searchingly.

But they could discern nothing but a man of middle height, dressed in black, apparently of a certain age, for the end of a gray beard peeped out from the bottom of the mask that hid his features.

The king's request had undoubtedly been acceded to by an affirmative sign, for in firm, sonorous accents, which vibrated in the depths of Athos's heart, the king began his speech, explaining his conduct and counseling the welfare of the kingdom.

"Oh!" said Athos to himself, "is it indeed possible that I hear what I hear and that I see what I see? Is it possible that God has abandoned His representative on earth and left him to die thus miserably? And I have not seen him! I have not said adieu to him!"

A noise was heard like that the instrument of death would make if moved upon the block.

"Do not touch the axe," said the king, and resumed his speech.

At the end of his speech the king looked tenderly around upon the people. Then unfastening the diamond ornament which the queen had sent him, he placed it in the hands of the priest who accompanied Juxon. Then he drew from his breast a little cross set in diamonds, which, like the order, had been the gift of Henrietta Maria.

"Sir," said he to the priest, "I shall keep this cross in my hand till the last moment. Take it from me when I am—dead."

"Yes, sire," said a voice, which Athos recognized as that of Aramis.

He then took his hat from his head and threw it on the ground. One by one he undid the buttons of his doublet, took it off and deposited it by the side of his hat. Then, as it was cold, he asked for his gown, which was brought to him.

All the preparations were made with a frightful calmness. One would have thought the king was going to bed and not to his coffin.

"Will these be in your way?" he said to the executioner, raising his long locks; "if so, they can be tied up."

Charles accompanied these words with a look designed to penetrate the mask of the unknown headsman. His calm, noble gaze forced the man to turn away his head. But after the searching look of the king he encountered the burning eyes of Aramis.

The king, seeing that he did not reply, repeated his question.

"It will do," replied the man, in a tremulous voice, "if you separate them across the neck."

The king parted his hair with his hands, and looking at the block he said:

"This block is very low, is there no other to be had?"

"It is the usual block," answered the man in the mask.

"Do you think you can behead me with a single blow?" asked the king.

"I hope so," was the reply. There was something so strange in these three words that everybody, except the king, shuddered.

"I do not wish to be taken by surprise," added the king. "I shall kneel down to pray; do not strike then."

"When shall I strike?"

"When I shall lay my head on the block and say 'Remember!' then strike boldly."

"Gentlemen," said the king to those around him, "I leave you to brave the tempest; I go before you to a kingdom which knows no storms. Farewell."

He looked at Aramis and made a special sign to him with his head.

"Now," he continued, "withdraw a little and let me say my prayer, I beseech you. You, also, stand aside," he said to the masked man. "It is only for a moment and I know that I belong to you; but remember that you are not to strike till I give the signal."

Then he knelt down, made the sign of the cross, and lowering his face to the planks, as if he would have kissed them, said in a low tone, in French, "Comte de la Fere, are you there?"

"Yes, your majesty," he answered, trembling.

"Faithful friend, noble heart!" said the king, "I should not have been rescued. I have addressed my people and I have spoken to God; last of all I speak to you. To maintain a cause which I believed sacred I have lost the throne and my children their inheritance. A million in gold remains; it is buried in the cellars of Newcastle Keep. You only know that this money exists. Make use of it, then, whenever you think it will be most useful, for my eldest son's welfare. And now, farewell."

"Farewell, saintly, martyred majesty," lisped Athos, chilled with terror.

A moment's silence ensued and then, in a full, sonorous voice, the king exclaimed: "Remember!"

He had scarcely uttered the word when a heavy blow shook the scaffold and where Athos stood immovable a warm drop fell upon his brow. He reeled back with a shudder and the same moment the drops became a crimson cataract.

Athos fell on his knees and remained some minutes as if bewildered or stunned. At last he rose and taking his handkerchief steeped it in the blood of the martyred king. Then as the crowd gradually dispersed he leaped down, crept from behind the drapery, glided between two horses, mingled with the crowd and was the first to arrive at the inn.

Having gained his room he raised his hand to his face, and observing that his fingers were covered with the monarch's blood, fell down insensible.

Chapter LXVII.

The Man in the Mask.

The snow was falling thick and icy. Aramis was the next to come in and to discover Athos almost insensible. But at the first words he uttered the comte roused himself from the kind of lethargy in which he had sunk.

"Well," said Aramis, "beaten by fate!"

"Beaten!" said Athos. "Noble and unhappy king!"

"Are you wounded?" cried Aramis.

"No, this is his blood."

"Where were you, then?"

"Where you left me—under the scaffold."

"Did you see it all?"

"No, but I heard all. God preserve me from another such hour as I have just passed."

"Then you know that I did not leave him?"

"I heard your voice up to the last moment."

"Here is the order he gave me and the cross I took from his hand; he desired they should be returned to the queen."

"Then here is a handkerchief to wrap them in," replied Athos, drawing from his pocket the one he had steeped in the king's blood.

"And what," he continued, "has been done with the poor body?"

"By order of Cromwell royal honors will be accorded to it. The doctors are embalming the corpse, and when it is ready it will be placed in a lighted chapel."

"Mockery," muttered Athos, savagely; "royal honors to one whom they have murdered!"

"Well, cheer up!" said a loud voice from the staircase, which Porthos had just mounted. "We are all mortal, my poor friends."

"You are late, my dear Porthos."

"Yes, there were some people on the way who delayed me. The wretches were dancing. I took one of them by the throat and three-quarters throttled him. Just then a patrol rode up. Luckily the man I had had most to do with was some minutes before he could speak, so I took advantage of his silence to walk off."

"Have you seen D'Artagnan?"

"We got separated in the crowd and I could not find him again."

"Oh!" said Athos, satirically, "I saw him. He was in the front row of the crowd, admirably placed for seeing; and as on the whole the sight was curious, he probably wished to stay to the end."

"Ah Comte de la Fere," said a calm voice, though hoarse with running, "is it your habit to calumniate the absent?"

This reproof stung Athos to the heart, but as the impression produced by seeing D'Artagnan foremost in a coarse, ferocious crowd had been very strong, he contented himself with replying:

"I am not calumniating you, my friend. They were anxious about you here; I simply told them where you were. You didn't know King Charles; to you he was only a foreigner and you were not obliged to love him."

So saying, he stretched out his hand, but the other pretended not to see it and he let it drop again slowly by his side.

"Ugh! I am tired," cried D'Artagnan, sitting down.

"Drink a glass of port," said Aramis; "it will refresh you."

"Yes, let us drink," said Athos, anxious to make it up by hobnobbing with D'Artagnan, "let us drink and get away from this hateful country. The felucca is waiting for us, you know; let us leave to-night, we have nothing more to do here."

"You are in a hurry, sir count," said D'Artagnan.

"But what would you have us to do here, now that the king is dead?"

"Go, sir count," replied D'Artagnan, carelessly; "you see nothing to keep you a little longer in England? Well, for my part, I, a bloodthirsty ruffian, who can go and stand close to a scaffold, in order to have a better view of the king's execution—I remain."

Athos turned pale. Every reproach his friend uttered struck deeply in his heart.

"Ah! you remain in London?" said Porthos.

"Yes. And you?"

"Hang it!" said Porthos, a little perplexed between the two, "I suppose, as I came with you, I must go away with you. I can't leave you alone in this abominable country."

"Thanks, my worthy friend. So I have a little adventure to propose to you when the count is gone. I want to find out who was the man in the mask, who so obligingly offered to cut the king's throat."

"A man in a mask?" cried Athos. "You did not let the executioner escape, then?"

"The executioner is still in the cellar, where, I presume, he has had an interview with mine host's bottles. But you remind me. Mousqueton!"

"Sir," answered a voice from the depths of the earth.

"Let out your prisoner. All is over."

"But," said Athos, "who is the wretch that has dared to raise his hand against his king?"

"An amateur headsman," replied Aramis, "who however, does not handle the axe amiss."

"Did you not see his face?" asked Athos.

"He wore a mask."

"But you, Aramis, who were close to him?"

"I could see nothing but a gray beard under the fringe of the mask."

"Then it must be a man of a certain age."

"Oh!" said D'Artagnan, "that matters little. When one puts on a mask, it is not difficult to wear a beard under it."

"I am sorry I did not follow him," said Porthos.

"Well, my dear Porthos," said D'Artagnan, "that's the very thing it came into my head to do."

Athos understood all now.

"Pardon me, D'Artagnan," he said. "I have distrusted God; I could the more easily distrust you. Pardon me, my friend."

"We will see about that presently," said D'Artagnan, with a slight smile.

"Well, then?" said Aramis.

"Well, while I was watching—not the king, as monsieur le comte thinks, for I know what it is to see a man led to death, and though I ought to be accustomed to the sight it always makes me ill—while I was watching the masked executioner, the idea came to me, as I said, to find out who he was. Now, as we are wont to complete ourselves each by all the rest and to depend on one another for assistance, as one calls his other hand to aid the first, I looked around instinctively to see if Porthos was there; for I had seen you, Aramis, with the king, and you, count, I knew would be under the scaffold, and for that reason I forgive you," he added, offering Athos his hand, "for you must have suffered much. I was looking around for Porthos when I saw near me a head which had been broken, but which, for better or worse, had been patched with plaster and with black silk. 'Humph!' thought I, 'that looks like my handiwork; I fancy I must have mended that skull somewhere or other.' And, in fact, it was that unfortunate Scotchman, Parry's brother, you know, on whom Groslow amused himself by trying his strength. Well, this man was making signs to another at my left, and turning around I recognized the honest Grimaud. 'Oh!' said I to him. Grimaud turned round with a jerk, recognized me, and pointed to the man in the mask. 'Eh!' said he, which meant, 'Do you see him?' 'Parbleu!' I answered, and we perfectly understood one another. Well, everything was finished as you know. The mob dispersed. I made a sign to Grimaud and the Scotchman, and we all three retired into a corner of the square. I saw the executioner return into the king's room, change his clothes, put on a black hat and a large cloak and disappear. Five minutes later he came down the grand staircase."

"You followed him?" cried Athos.

"I should think so, but not without difficulty. Every few minutes he turned around, and thus obliged us to conceal ourselves. I might have gone up to him and killed him. But I am not selfish, and I thought it might console you all a little to have a share in the matter. So we followed him through the lowest streets in the city, and in half an hour's time he stopped before a little isolated house. Grimaud drew out a pistol. 'Eh?' said he, showing it. I held back his arm. The man in the mask stopped before a low door and drew out a key; but before he placed it in the lock he turned around to see if he was being followed. Grimaud and I got behind a tree, and the Scotchman having nowhere to hide himself, threw himself on his face in the road. Next moment the door opened and the man disappeared."

"The scoundrel!" said Aramis. "While you have been returning hither he will have escaped and we shall never find him."

"Come, now, Aramis," said D'Artagnan, "you must be taking me for some one else."

"Nevertheless," said Athos, "in your absence——"

"Well, in my absence haven't I put in my place Grimaud and the Scotchman? Before he had taken ten steps beyond the door I had examined the house on all sides. At one of the doors, that by which he had entered, I placed our Scotchman, making a sign to him to follow the man wherever he might go, if he came out again. Then going around the house I placed Grimaud at the other exit, and here I am. Our game is beaten up. Now for the tally-ho."

Athos threw himself into D'Artagnan's arms.

"Friend," he said, "you have been too good in pardoning me; I was wrong, a hundred times wrong. I ought to have known you better by this time; but we are all possessed of a malignant spirit, which bids us doubt."

"Humph!" said Porthos. "Don't you think the executioner might be Master Cromwell, who, to make sure of this affair, undertook it himself?"

"Ah! just so. Cromwell is stout and short, and this man thin and lanky, rather tall than otherwise."

"Some condemned soldier, perhaps," suggested Athos, "whom they have pardoned at the price of regicide."

"No, no," continued D'Artagnan, "it was not the measured step of a foot soldier, nor was it the gait of a horseman. If I am not mistaken we have to do with a gentleman."

"A gentleman!" exclaimed Athos. "Impossible! It would be a dishonor to all the nobility."

"Fine sport, by Jove!" cried Porthos, with a laugh that shook the windows. "Fine sport!"

"Are you still bent on departure, Athos?" asked D'Artagnan.

"No, I remain," replied Athos, with a threatening gesture that promised no good to whomsoever it was addressed.

"Swords, then!" cried Aramis, "swords! let us not lose a moment."

The four friends resumed their own clothes, girded on their swords, ordered Mousqueton and Blaisois to pay the bill and to arrange everything for immediate departure, and wrapped in their large cloaks left in search of their game.

The night was dark, snow was falling, the streets were silent and deserted. D'Artagnan led the way through the intricate windings and narrow alleys of the city and ere long they had reached the house in question. For a moment D'Artagnan thought that Parry's brother had disappeared; but he was mistaken. The robust Scotchman, accustomed to the snows of his native hills, had stretched himself against a post, and like a fallen statue, insensible to the inclemency of the weather, had allowed the snow to cover him. He rose, however, as they approached.

"Come," said Athos, "here's another good servant. Really, honest men are not so scarce as I thought."

"Don't be in a hurry to weave crowns for our Scotchman. I believe the fellow is here on his own account, for I have heard that these gentlemen born beyond the Tweed are very vindictive. I should not like to be Groslow, if he meets him."

"Well?" said Athos, to the man, in English.

"No one has come out," he replied.

"Then, Porthos and Aramis, will you remain with this man while we go around to Grimaud?"

Grimaud had made himself a kind of sentry box out of a hollow willow, and as they drew near he put his head out and gave a low whistle.

"Soho!" cried Athos.

"Yes," said Grimaud.

"Well, has anybody come out?"

"No, but somebody has gone in."

"A man or a woman?"

"A man."

"Ah! ah!" said D'Artagnan, "there are two of them, then!"

"I wish there were four," said Athos; "the two parties would then be equal."

"Perhaps there are four," said D'Artagnan.

"What do you mean?"

"Other men may have entered before them and waited for them."

"We can find out," said Grimaud. At the same time he pointed to a window, through the shutters of which a faint light streamed.

"That is true," said D'Artagnan, "let us call the others."

They returned around the house to fetch Porthos and Aramis.

"Have you seen anything?" they asked.

"No, but we are going to," replied D'Artagnan, pointing to Grimaud, who had already climbed some five or six feet from the ground.

All four came up together. Grimaud continued to climb like a cat and succeeded at last in catching hold of a hook, which served to keep one of the shutters back when opened. Then resting his foot on a small ledge he made a sign to show all was right.

"Well?" asked D'Artagnan.

Grimaud showed his closed hand, with two fingers spread out.

"Speak," said Athos; "we cannot see your signs. How many are there?"

"Two. One opposite to me, the other with his back to me."

"Good. And the man opposite to you is——"

"The man I saw go in."

"Do you know him?"

"I thought I recognized him, and was not mistaken. Short and stout."

"Who is it?" they all asked together in a low tone.

"General Oliver Cromwell."

The four friends looked at one another.

"And the other?" asked Athos.

"Thin and lanky."

"The executioner," said D'Artagnan and Aramis at the same time.

"I can see nothing but his back," resumed Grimaud. "But wait. He is moving; and if he has taken off his mask I shall be able to see. Ah——"

And as if struck in the heart he let go the hook and dropped with a groan.

"Did you see him?" they all asked.

"Yes," said Grimaud, with his hair standing on end.

"The thin, spare man?"

"Yes."

"The executioner, in short?" asked Aramis.

"Yes."

"And who is it?" said Porthos.

"He—he—is——" murmured Grimaud, pale as a ghost and seizing his master's hand.

"Who? He?" asked Athos.

"Mordaunt," replied Grimaud.

D'Artagnan, Porthos and Aramis uttered a cry of joy.

Athos stepped back and passed his hand across his brow.

"Fatality!" he muttered.

Chapter LXVIII.

Cromwell's House.

It was, in fact, Mordaunt whom D'Artagnan had followed, without knowing it. On entering the house he had taken off his mask and imitation beard, then, mounting a staircase, had opened a door, and in a room lighted by a single lamp found himself face to face with a man seated behind a desk.

This man was Cromwell.

Cromwell had two or three of these retreats in London, unknown except to the most intimate of his friends. Mordaunt was among these.

"It is you, Mordaunt," he said. "You are late."

"General, I wished to see the ceremony to the end, which delayed me."

"Ah! I scarcely thought you were so curious as that."

"I am always curious to see the downfall of your honor's enemies, and he was not among the least of them. But you, general, were you not at Whitehall?"

"No," said Cromwell.

There was a moment's silence.

"Have you had any account of it?"

"None. I have been here since the morning. I only know that there was a conspiracy to rescue the king."

"Ah, you knew that?" said Mordaunt.

"It matters little. Four men, disguised as workmen, were to get the king out of prison and take him to Greenwich, where a vessel was waiting."

"And knowing all that, your honor remained here, far from the city, tranquil and inactive."

"Tranquil, yes," replied Cromwell. "But who told you I was inactive?"

"But—if the plot had succeeded?"

"I wished it to do so."

"I thought your excellence considered the death of Charles I. as a misfortune necessary to the welfare of England."

"Yes, his death; but it would have been more seemly not upon the scaffold."

"Why so?" asked Mordaunt.

Cromwell smiled. "Because it could have been said that I had had him condemned for the sake of justice and had let him escape out of pity."

"But if he had escaped?"

"Impossible; my precautions were taken."

"And does your honor know the four men who undertook to rescue him?"

"The four Frenchmen, of whom two were sent by the queen to her husband and two by Mazarin to me."

"And do you think Mazarin commissioned them to act as they have done?"

"It is possible. But he will not avow it."

"How so?"

"Because they failed."

"Your honor gave me two of these Frenchmen when they were only guilty of fighting for Charles I. Now that they are guilty of a conspiracy against England will your honor give me all four of them?"

"Take them," said Cromwell.

Mordaunt bowed with a smile of triumphant ferocity.

"Did the people shout at all?" Cromwell asked.

"Very little, except 'Long live Cromwell!'"

"Where were you placed?"

Mordaunt tried for a moment to read in the general's face if this was simply a useless question, or whether he knew everything. But his piercing eyes could by no means penetrate the sombre depths of Cromwell's.

"I was so situated as to hear and see everything," he answered.

It was now Cromwell's turn to look fixedly at Mordaunt, and Mordaunt to make himself impenetrable.

"It appears," said Cromwell, "that this improvised executioner did his duty remarkably well. The blow, so they tell me at least, was struck with a master's hand."

Mordaunt remembered that Cromwell had told him he had had no detailed account, and he was now quite convinced that the general had been present at the execution, hidden behind some screen or curtain.

"In fact," said Mordaunt, with a calm voice and immovable countenance, "a single blow sufficed."

"Perhaps it was some one in that occupation," said Cromwell.

"Do you think so, sir? He did not look like an executioner."

"And who else save an executioner would have wished to fill that horrible office?"

"But," said Mordaunt, "it might have been some personal enemy of the king, who had made a vow of vengeance and accomplished it in this way. Perhaps it was some man of rank who had grave reasons for hating the fallen king, and who, learning that the king was about to flee and escape him, threw himself in the way, with a mask on his face and an axe in his hand, not as substitute for the executioner, but as an ambassador of Fate."

"Possibly."

"And if that were the case would your honor condemn his action?"

"It is not for me to judge. It rests between his conscience and his God."

"But if your honor knew this man?"

"I neither know nor wish to know him. Provided Charles is dead, it is the axe, not the man, we must thank."

"And yet, without the man, the king would have been rescued."

Cromwell smiled.

"They would have carried him to Greenwich," he said, "and put him on board a felucca with five barrels of powder in the hold. Once out to sea, you are too good a politician not to understand the rest, Mordaunt."

"Yes, they would have all been blown up."

"Just so. The explosion would have done what the axe had failed to do. Men would have said that the king had escaped human justice and been overtaken by God's. You see now why I did not care to know your gentleman in the mask; for really, in spite of his excellent intentions, I could not thank him for what he has done."

Mordaunt bowed humbly. "Sir," he said, "you are a profound thinker and your plan was sublime."

"Say absurd, since it has become useless. The only sublime ideas in politics are those which bear fruit. So to-night, Mordaunt, go to Greenwich and ask for the captain of the felucca Lightning. Show him a white handkerchief knotted at the four corners and tell the crew to disembark and carry the powder back to the arsenal, unless, indeed——"

"Unless?" said Mordaunt, whose face was lighted by a savage joy as Cromwell spoke:

"This skiff might be of use to you for personal projects."

"Oh, my lord, my lord!"

"That title," said Cromwell, laughing, "is all very well here, but take care a word like that does not escape your lips in public."

"But your honor will soon be called so generally."

"I hope so, at least," said Cromwell, rising and putting on his cloak.

"You are going, sir?"

"Yes," said Cromwell. "I slept here last night and the night before, and you know it is not my custom to sleep three times in the same bed."

"Then," said Mordaunt, "your honor gives me my liberty for to-night?"

"And even for all day to-morrow, if you want it. Since last evening," he added, smiling, "you have done enough in my service, and if you have any personal matters to settle it is just that I should give you time."

"Thank you, sir; it will be well employed, I hope."

Cromwell turned as he was going.

"Are you armed?" he asked.

"I have my sword."

"And no one waiting for you outside?"

"No."

"Then you had better come with me."

"Thank you, sir, but the way by the subterranean passage would take too much time and I have none to lose."

Cromwell placed his hand on a hidden handle and opened a door so well concealed by the tapestry that the most practiced eye could not have discovered it. It closed after him with a spring. This door communicated with a subterranean passage, leading under the street to a grotto in the garden of a house about a hundred yards from that of the future Protector.

It was just before this that Grimaud had perceived the two men seated together.

D'Artagnan was the first to recover from his surprise.

"Mordaunt," he cried. "Ah! by Heaven! it is God Himself who sent us here."

"Yes," said Porthos, "let us break the door in and fall upon him."

"No," replied D'Artagnan, "no noise. Now, Grimaud, you come here, climb up to the window again and tell us if Mordaunt is alone and whether he is preparing to go out or go to bed. If he comes out we shall catch him. If he stays in we will break in the window. It is easier and less noisy than the door."

Grimaud began to scale the wall again.

"Keep guard at the other door, Athos and Aramis. Porthos and I will stay here."

The friends obeyed.

"He is alone," said Grimaud.

"We did not see his companion come out."

"He may have gone by the other door."

"What is he doing?"

"Putting on his cloak and gloves."

"He's ours," muttered D'Artagnan.

Porthos mechanically drew his dagger from the scabbard.

"Put it up again, my friend," said D'Artagnan. "We must proceed in an orderly manner."

"Hush!" said Grimaud, "he is coming out. He has put out the lamp, I can see nothing now."

"Get down then and quickly."

Grimaud leaped down. The snow deadened the noise of his fall.

"Now go and tell Athos and Aramis to stand on each side of the door and clap their hands if they catch him. We will do the same."

The next moment the door opened and Mordaunt appeared on the threshold, face to face with D'Artagnan. Porthos clapped his hands and the other two came running around. Mordaunt was livid, but he uttered no cry nor called for assistance. D'Artagnan quietly pushed him in again, and by the light of a lamp on the staircase made him ascend the steps backward one by one, keeping his eyes all the time on Mordaunt's hands, who, however, knowing that it was useless, attempted no resistance. At last they stood face to face in the very room where ten minutes before Mordaunt had been talking to Cromwell.

Porthos came up behind, and unhooking the lamp on the staircase relit that in the room. Athos and Aramis entered last and locked the door behind them.

"Oblige me by taking a seat," said D'Artagnan, pushing a chair toward Mordaunt, who sat down, pale but calm. Aramis, Porthos and D'Artagnan drew their chairs near him. Athos alone kept away and sat in the furthest corner of the room, as if determined to be merely a spectator of the proceedings. He seemed to be quite overcome. Porthos rubbed his hands in feverish impatience. Aramis bit his lips till the blood came.

D'Artagnan alone was calm, at least in appearance.

"Monsieur Mordaunt," he said, "since, after running after one another so long, chance has at last brought us together, let us have a little conversation, if you please."

Chapter LXIX.

Conversational.

Though Mordaunt had been so completely taken by surprise and had mounted the stairs in such utter confusion, when once seated he recovered himself, as it were, and prepared to seize any possible opportunity of escape. His eye wandered to a long stout sword on his flank and he instinctively slipped it around within reach of his right hand.

D'Artagnan was waiting for a reply to his remark and said nothing. Aramis muttered to himself, "We shall hear nothing but the usual commonplace things."

Porthos sucked his mustache, muttering, "A good deal of ceremony to-night about crushing an adder." Athos shrunk into his corner, pale and motionless as a bas-relief.

The silence, however, could not last forever. So D'Artagnan began:

"Sir," he said, with desperate politeness, "it seems to me that you change your costume almost as rapidly as I have seen the Italian mummers do, whom the Cardinal Mazarin brought over from Bergamo and whom he doubtless took you to see during your travels in France."

Mordaunt did not reply.

"Just now," D'Artagnan continued, "you were disguised—I mean to say, attired—as a murderer, and now——"

"And now I look very much like a man who is going to be murdered."

"Oh! sir," said D'Artagnan, "how can you talk like that when you are in the company of gentlemen and have such an excellent sword at your side?"

"No sword is excellent enough to be of use against four swords and daggers."

"Well, that is scarcely the question. I had the honor of asking you why you altered your costume. The mask and beard became you very well, and as to the axe, I do not think it would be out of keeping even at this moment. Why, then, have you laid it aside?"

"Because, remembering the scene at Armentieres, I thought I should find four axes for one, as I was to meet four executioners."

"Sir," replied D'Artagnan, in the calmest manner possible, "you are very young; I shall therefore overlook your frivolous remarks. What took place at Armentieres has no connection whatever with the present occasion. We could scarcely have requested your mother to take a sword and fight us."

"Aha! It is a duel, then?" cried Mordaunt, as if disposed to reply at once to the provocation.

Porthos rose, always ready for this kind of adventure.

"Pardon me," said D'Artagnan. "Do not let us do things in a hurry. We will arrange the matter rather better. Confess, Monsieur Mordaunt, that you are anxious to kill some of us."

"All," replied Mordaunt.

"Then, my dear sir; I am convinced that these gentlemen return your kind wishes and will be delighted to kill you also. Of course they will do so as honorable gentlemen, and the best proof I can furnish is this——"

So saying, he threw his hat on the ground, pushed back his chair to the wall and bowed to Mordaunt with true French grace.

"At your service, sir," he continued. "My sword is shorter than yours, it's true, but, bah! I think the arm will make up for the sword."

"Halt!" cried Porthos coming forward. "I begin, and without any rhetoric."

"Allow me, Porthos," said Aramis.

Athos did not move. He might have been taken for a statue. Even his breathing seemed to be arrested.

"Gentlemen," said D'Artagnan, "you shall have your turn. Monsieur Mordaunt dislikes you sufficiently not to refuse you afterward. You can see it in his eye. So pray keep your places, like Athos, whose calmness is entirely laudable. Besides, we will have no words about it. I have particular business to settle with this gentleman and I shall and will begin."

Porthos and Aramis drew back, disappointed, and drawing his sword D'Artagnan turned to his adversary:

"Sir, I am waiting for you."

"And for my part, gentlemen, I admire you. You are disputing which shall fight me first, but you do not consult me who am most concerned in the matter. I hate you all, but not equally. I hope to kill all four of you, but I am more likely to kill the first than the second, the second than the third, and the third than the last. I claim, then, the right to choose my opponent. If you refuse this right you may kill me, but I shall not fight."

"It is but fair," said Porthos and Aramis, hoping he would choose one of them.

Athos and D'Artagnan said nothing, but their silence seemed to imply consent.

"Well, then," said Mordaunt, "I choose for my adversary the man who, not thinking himself worthy to be called Comte de la Fere, calls himself Athos."

Athos sprang up, but after an instant of motionless silence he said, to the astonishment of his friends, "Monsieur Mordaunt, a duel between us is impossible. Submit this honour to somebody else." And he sat down.

"Ah!" said Mordaunt, with a sneer, "there's one who is afraid."

"Zounds!" exclaimed D'Artagnan, bounding toward him, "who says that Athos is afraid?"

"Let him have his say, D'Artagnan," said Athos, with a smile of sadness and contempt.

"Is it your decision, Athos?" resumed the Gascon.

"Irrevocably."

"You hear, sir," said D'Artagnan, turning to Mordaunt. "The Comte de la Fere will not do you the honor of fighting with you. Choose one of us to replace the Comte de la Fere."

"As long as I don't fight with him it is the same to me with whom I fight. Put your names into a hat and draw lots."

"A good idea," said D'Artagnan.

"At least that will conciliate us all," said Aramis.

"I should never have thought of that," said Porthos, "and yet it is very simple."

"Come, Aramis," said D'Artagnan, "write this for us in those neat little characters in which you wrote to Marie Michon that the mother of this gentleman intended to assassinate the Duke of Buckingham."

Mordaunt sustained this new attack without wincing. He stood with his arms folded, apparently as calm as any man could be in such circumstances. If he had not courage he had what is very like it, namely, pride.

Aramis went to Cromwell's desk, tore off three bits of paper of equal size, wrote on the first his own name and on the others those of his two companions, and presented them open to Mordaunt, who by a movement of his head indicated that he left the matter entirely to Aramis. He then rolled them separately and put them in a hat, which he handed to Mordaunt.

Mordaunt put his hand into the hat, took out one of the three papers and disdainfully dropped it on the table without reading it.

"Ah! serpent," muttered D'Artagnan, "I would give my chance of a captaincy in the mousquetaires for that to be my name."

Aramis opened the paper, and in a voice trembling with hate and vengeance read "D'Artagnan."

The Gascon uttered a cry of joy and turning to Mordaunt:

"I hope, sir," said he, "you have no objection to make."

"None, whatever," replied the other, drawing his sword and resting the point on his boot.

The moment that D'Artagnan saw that his wish was accomplished and his man would not escape him, he recovered his usual tranquillity. He turned up his cuffs neatly and rubbed the sole of his right boot on the floor, but did not fail, however, to remark that Mordaunt was looking about him in a singular manner.

"Are you ready, sir?" he said at last.

"I was waiting for you, sir," said Mordaunt, raising his head and casting at his opponent a look it would be impossible to describe.

"Well, then," said the Gascon, "take care of yourself, for I am not a bad hand at the rapier."

"Nor I either."

"So much the better; that sets my mind at rest. Defend yourself."

"One minute," said the young man. "Give me your word, gentlemen, that you will not attack me otherwise than one after the other."

"Is it to have the pleasure of insulting us that you say that, my little viper?"

"No, but to set my mind at rest, as you observed just now."

"It is for something else than that, I imagine," muttered D'Artagnan, shaking his head doubtfully.

"On the honor of gentlemen," said Aramis and Porthos.

"In that case, gentlemen, have the kindness to retire into the corners, so as to give us ample room. We shall require it."

"Yes, gentlemen," said D'Artagnan, "we must not leave this person the slightest pretext for behaving badly, which, with all due respect, I fancy he is anxious still to do."

This new attack made no impression on Mordaunt. The space was cleared, the two lamps placed on Cromwell's desk, in order that the combatants might have as much light as possible; and the swords crossed.

D'Artagnan was too good a swordsman to trifle with his opponent. He made a rapid and brilliant feint which Mordaunt parried.

"Aha!" he cried with a smile of satisfaction.

And without losing a minute, thinking he saw an opening, he thrust his right in and forced Mordaunt to parry a counter en quarte so fine that the point of the weapon might have turned within a wedding ring.

This time it was Mordaunt who smiled.

"Ah, sir," said D'Artagnan, "you have a wicked smile. It must have been the devil who taught it you, was it not?"

Mordaunt replied by trying his opponent's weapon with an amount of strength which the Gascon was astonished to find in a form apparently so feeble; but thanks to a parry no less clever than that which Mordaunt had just achieved, he succeeded in meeting his sword, which slid along his own without touching his chest.

Mordaunt rapidly sprang back a step.

"Ah! you lose ground, you are turning? Well, as you please, I even gain something by it, for I no longer see that wicked smile of yours. You have no idea what a false look you have, particularly when you are afraid. Look at my eyes and you will see what no looking-glass has ever shown you—a frank and honorable countenance."

To this flow of words, not perhaps in the best taste, but characteristic of D'Artagnan, whose principal object was to divert his opponent's attention, Mordaunt did not reply, but continuing to turn around he succeeded in changing places with D'Artagnan.

He smiled more and more sarcastically and his smile began to make the Gascon anxious.

"Come, come," cried D'Artagnan, "we must finish with this," and in his turn he pressed Mordaunt hard, who continued to lose ground, but evidently on purpose and without letting his sword leave the line for a moment. However, as they were fighting in a room and had not space to go on like that forever, Mordaunt's foot at last touched the wall, against which he rested his left hand.

"Ah, this time you cannot lose ground, my fine friend!" exclaimed D'Artagnan. "Gentlemen, did you ever see a scorpion pinned to a wall? No. Well, then, you shall see it now."

In a second D'Artagnan had made three terrible thrusts at Mordaunt, all of which touched, but only pricked him. The three friends looked on, panting and astonished. At last D'Artagnan, having got up too close, stepped back to prepare a fourth thrust, but the moment when, after a fine, quick feint, he was attacking as sharply as lightning, the wall seemed to give way, Mordaunt disappeared through the opening, and D'Artagnan's blade, caught between the panels, shivered like a sword of glass. D'Artagnan sprang back; the wall had closed again.

Mordaunt, in fact, while defending himself, had manoeuvred so as to reach the secret door by which Cromwell had left, had felt for the knob with his left hand, pressed it and disappeared.

The Gascon uttered a furious imprecation, which was answered by a wild laugh on the other side of the iron panel.

"Help me, gentlemen," cried D'Artagnan, "we must break in this door."

"It is the devil in person!" said Aramis, hastening forward.

"He escapes us," growled Porthos, pushing his huge shoulder against the hinges, but in vain. "'Sblood! he escapes us."

"So much the better," muttered Athos.

"I thought as much," said D'Artagnan, wasting his strength in useless efforts. "Zounds, I thought as much when the wretch kept moving around the room. I thought he was up to something."

"It's a misfortune, to which his friend, the devil, treats us," said Aramis.

"It's a piece of good fortune sent from Heaven," said Athos, evidently much relieved.

"Really!" said D'Artagnan, abandoning the attempt to burst open the panel after several ineffectual attempts, "Athos, I cannot imagine how you can talk to us in that way. You cannot understand the position we are in. In this kind of game, not to kill is to let one's self be killed. This fox of a fellow will be sending us a hundred iron-sided beasts who will pick us off like sparrows in this place. Come, come, we must be off. If we stay here five minutes more there's an end of us."

"Yes, you are right."

"But where shall we go?" asked Porthos.

"To the hotel, to be sure, to get our baggage and horses; and from there, if it please God, to France, where, at least, I understand the architecture of the houses."

So, suiting the action to the word, D'Artagnan thrust the remnant of his sword into its scabbard, picked up his hat and ran down the stairs, followed by the others.

Chapter LXX.

The Skiff "Lightning."

D'Artagnan had judged correctly; Mordaunt felt that he had no time to lose, and he lost none. He knew the rapidity of decision and action that characterized his enemies and resolved to act with reference to that. This time the musketeers had an adversary who was worthy of them.

After closing the door carefully behind him Mordaunt glided into the subterranean passage, sheathing on the way his now useless sword, and thus reached the neighboring house, where he paused to examine himself and to take breath.

"Good!" he said, "nothing, almost nothing—scratches, nothing more; two in the arm and one in the breast. The wounds that I make are better than that—witness the executioner of Bethune, my uncle and King Charles. Now, not a second to lose, for a second lost will perhaps save them. They must die—die all together—killed at one stroke by the thunder of men in default of God's. They must disappear, broken, scattered, annihilated. I will run, then, till my legs no longer serve, till my heart bursts in my bosom but I will arrive before they do."

Mordaunt proceeded at a rapid pace to the nearest cavalry barracks, about a quarter of a league distant. He made that quarter of a league in four or five minutes. Arrived at the barracks he made himself known, took the best horse in the stables, mounted and gained the high road. A quarter of an hour later he was at Greenwich.

"There is the port," he murmured. "That dark point yonder is the Isle of Dogs. Good! I am half an hour in advance of them, an hour, perhaps. Fool that I was! I have almost killed myself by my needless haste. Now," he added, rising in the stirrups and looking about him, "which, I wonder, is the Lightning?"

At this moment, as if in reply to his words, a man lying on a coil of cables rose and advanced a few steps toward him. Mordaunt drew a handkerchief from his pocket, and tying a knot at each corner—the signal agreed upon—waved it in the air and the man came up to him. He was wrapped in a large rough cape, which concealed his form and partly his face.

"Do you wish to go on the water, sir?" said the sailor.

"Yes, just so. Along the Isle of Dogs."

"And perhaps you have a preference for one boat more than another. You would like one that sails as rapidly as——"

"Lightning," interrupted Mordaunt.

"Then mine is the boat you want, sir. I'm your man."

"I begin to think so, particularly if you have not forgotten a certain signal."

"Here it is, sir," and the sailor took from his coat a handkerchief, tied at each corner.

"Good, quite right!" cried Mordaunt, springing off his horse. "There's not a moment to lose; now take my horse to the nearest inn and conduct me to your vessel."

"But," asked the sailor, "where are your companions? I thought there were four of you."

"Listen to me, sir. I'm not the man you take me for; you are in Captain Rogers's post, are you not? under orders from General Cromwell. Mine, also, are from him!"

"Indeed, sir, I recognize you; you are Captain Mordaunt."

Mordaunt was startled.

"Oh, fear nothing," said the skipper, showing his face. "I am a friend."

"Captain Groslow!" cried Mordaunt.

"Himself. The general remembered that I had formerly been a naval officer and he gave me the command of this expedition. Is there anything new in the wind?"

"Nothing."

"I thought, perhaps, that the king's death——"

"Has only hastened their flight; in ten minutes they will perhaps be here."

"What have you come for, then?"

"To embark with you."

"Ah! ah! the general doubted my fidelity?"

"No, but I wish to have a share in my revenge. Haven't you some one who will relieve me of my horse?"

Groslow whistled and a sailor appeared.

"Patrick," said Groslow, "take this horse to the stables of the nearest inn. If any one asks you whose it is you can say that it belongs to an Irish gentleman."

The sailor departed without reply.

"Now," said Mordaunt, "are you not afraid that they will recognize you?"

"There is no danger, dressed as I am in this pilot coat, on a night as dark as this. Besides even you didn't recognize me; they will be much less likely to."

"That is true," said Mordaunt, "and they will be far from thinking of you. Everything is ready, is it not?"

"Yes."

"The cargo on board?"

"Yes."

"Five full casks?"

"And fifty empty ones."

"Good."

"We are carrying port wine to Anvers."

"Excellent. Now take me aboard and return to your post, for they will soon be here."

"I am ready."

"It is important that none of your crew should see me."

"I have but one man on board, and I am as sure of him as I am of myself. Besides, he doesn't know you; like his mates he is ready to obey our orders knowing nothing of our plan."

"Very well; let us go."

They then went down to the Thames. A boat was fastened to the shore by a chain fixed to a stake. Groslow jumped in, followed by Mordaunt, and in five minutes they were quite away from that world of houses which then crowded the outskirts of London; and Mordaunt could discern the little vessel riding at anchor near the Isle of Dogs. When they reached the side of this felucca, Mordaunt, dexterous in his eagerness for vengeance, seized a rope and climbed up the side of the vessel with a coolness and agility very rare among landsmen. He went with Groslow to the captain's berth, a sort of temporary cabin of planks, for the chief apartment had been given up by Captain Rogers to the passengers, who were to be accommodated at the other end of the boat.

"They will have nothing to do, then at this end?" said Mordaunt.

"Nothing at all."

"That's a capital arrangement. Return to Greenwich and bring them here. I shall hide myself in your cabin. You have a longboat?"

"That in which we came."

"It appeared light and well constructed."

"Quite a canoe."

"Fasten it to the poop with a rope; put the oars into it, so that it may follow in the track and there will be nothing to do except to cut the cord. Put a good supply of rum and biscuit in it for the seamen; should the night happen to be stormy they will not be sorry to find something to console themselves with."

"Consider all this done. Do you wish to see the powder-room?"

"No. When you return I will set the fuse myself, but be careful to conceal your face, so that you cannot be recognized by them."

"Never fear."

"There's ten o'clock striking at Greenwich."

Groslow, then, having given the sailor on duty an order to be on the watch with more than usual vigilance, went down into the longboat and soon reached Greenwich. The wind was chilly and the jetty was deserted, as he approached it; but he had no sooner landed than he heard a noise of horses galloping upon the paved road.

These horsemen were our friends, or rather, an avant garde, composed of D'Artagnan and Athos. As soon as they arrived at the spot where Groslow stood they stopped, as if guessing that he was the man they wanted. Athos alighted and calmly opened the handkerchief tied at each corner, whilst D'Artagnan, ever cautious, remained on horseback, one hand upon his pistol, leaning forward watchfully.

On seeing the appointed signal, Groslow, who had at first crept behind one of the cannons planted on that spot, walked straight up to the gentlemen. He was so well wrapped up in his cloak that it would have been impossible to see his face even if the night had not been so dark as to render precaution superfluous; nevertheless, the keen glance of Athos perceived at once it was not Rogers who stood before them.

"What do you want with us?" he asked of Groslow.

"I wish to inform you, my lord," replied Groslow, with an Irish accent, feigned of course, "that if you are looking for Captain Rogers you will not find him. He fell down this morning and broke his leg. But I'm his cousin; he told me everything and desired me to watch instead of him, and in his place to conduct, wherever they wished to go, the gentlemen who should bring me a handkerchief tied at each corner, like that one which you hold and one which I have in my pocket."

And he drew out the handkerchief.

"Was that all he said?" inquired Athos.

"No, my lord; he said you had engaged to pay seventy pounds if I landed you safe and sound at Boulogne or any other port you choose in France."

"What do you think of all this?" said Athos, in a low tone to D'Artagnan, after explaining to him in French what the sailor had said in English.

"It seems a likely story to me."

"And to me, too."

"Besides, we can but blow out his brains if he proves false," said the Gascon; "and you, Athos, you know something of everything and can be our captain. I dare say you know how to navigate, should he fail us."

"My dear friend, you guess well. My father meant me for the navy and I have some vague notions about navigation."

"You see!" cried D'Artagnan.

They then summoned their friends, who, with Blaisois, Mousqueton and Grimaud, promptly joined them, leaving Parry behind them, who was to take back to London the horses of the gentlemen and of their lackeys, which had been sold to the host in settlement of their account with him. Thanks to this stroke of business the four friends were able to take away with them a sum of money which, if not large, was sufficient as a provision against delays and accidents.

Parry parted from his friends regretfully; they had proposed his going with them to France, but he had straightway declined.

"It is very simple," Mousqueton had said; "he is thinking of Groslow."

It was Captain Groslow, the reader will remember, who had broken Parry's head.

D'Artagnan resumed immediately the attitude of distrust that was habitual with him. He found the wharf too completely deserted, the night too dark, the captain too accommodating. He had reported to Aramis what had taken place, and Aramis, not less distrustful than he, had increased his suspicions. A slight click of the tongue against his teeth informed Athos of the Gascon's uneasiness.

"We have no time now for suspicions," said Athos. "The boat is waiting for us; come."

"Besides," said Aramis, "what prevents our being distrustful and going aboard at the same time? We can watch the skipper."

"And if he doesn't go straight I will crush him, that's all."

"Well said, Porthos," replied D'Artagnan. "Let us go, then. You first, Mousqueton," and he stopped his friends, directing the valets to go first, in order to test the plank leading from the pier to the boat.

The three valets passed without accident. Athos followed them, then Porthos, then Aramis. D'Artagnan went last, still shaking his head.

"What in the devil is the matter with you, my friend?" said Porthos. "Upon my word you would make Caesar afraid."

"The matter is," replied D'Artagnan, "that I can see upon this pier neither inspector nor sentinel nor exciseman."

"And you complain of that!" said Porthos. "Everything goes as if in flowery paths."

"Everything goes too well, Porthos. But no matter; we must trust in God."

As soon as the plank was withdrawn the captain took his place at the tiller and made a sign to one of the sailors, who, boat-hook in hand, began to push out from the labyrinth of boats in which they were involved. The other sailor had already seated himself on the port side and was ready to row. As soon as there was room for rowing, his companion rejoined him and the boat began to move more rapidly.

"At last we are off!" exclaimed Porthos.

"Alas," said Athos, "we depart alone."

"Yes; but all four together and without a scratch; which is a consolation."

"We are not yet at our destination," observed the prudent D'Artagnan; "beware of misadventure."

"Ah, my friend!" cried Porthos, "like the crows, you always bring bad omens. Who could intercept us on such a night as this, pitch dark, when one does not see more than twenty yards before one?"

"Yes, but to-morrow morning——"

"To-morrow we shall be at Boulogne."

"I hope so, with all my heart," said the Gascon, "and I confess my weakness. Yes, Athos, you may laugh, but as long as we were within gunshot of the pier or of the vessels lying by it I was looking for a frightful discharge of musketry which would crush us."

"But," said Porthos, with great wisdom, "that was impossible, for they would have killed the captain and the sailors."

"Bah! much Monsieur Mordaunt would care. You don't imagine he would consider a little thing like that?"

"At any rate," said Porthos, "I am glad to hear D'Artagnan admit that he is afraid."

"I not only confess it, but am proud of it," returned the Gascon; "I'm not such a rhinoceros as you are. Oho! what's that?"

"The Lightning," answered the captain, "our felucca."

"So far, so good," laughed Athos.

They went on board and the captain instantly conducted them to the berth prepared for them—a cabin which was to serve for all purposes and for the whole party; he then tried to slip away under pretext of giving orders to some one.

"Stop a moment," cried D'Artagnan; "pray how many men have you on board, captain?"

"I don't understand," was the reply.

"Explain it, Athos."

Groslow, on the question being interpreted, answered, "Three, without counting myself."

D'Artagnan understood, for while replying the captain had raised three fingers. "Oh!" he exclaimed, "I begin to be more at my ease, however, whilst you settle yourselves, I shall make the round of the boat."

"As for me," said Porthos, "I will see to the supper."

"A very good idea, Porthos," said the Gascon. "Athos lend me Grimaud, who in the society of his friend Parry has perhaps picked up a little English, and can act as my interpreter."

"Go, Grimaud," said Athos.

D'Artagnan, finding a lantern on the deck, took it up and with a pistol in his hand he said to the captain, in English, "Come," (being, with the classic English oath, the only English words he knew), and so saying he descended to the lower deck.

This was divided into three compartments—one which was covered by the floor of that room in which Athos, Porthos and Aramis were to pass the night; the second was to serve as the sleeping-room for the servants, the third, under the prow of the ship, was under the temporary cabin in which Mordaunt was concealed.

"Oho!" cried D'Artagnan, as he went down the steps of the hatchway, preceded by the lantern, "what a number of barrels! one would think one was in the cave of Ali Baba. What is there in them?" he added, putting his lantern on one of the casks.

The captain seemed inclined to go upon deck again, but controlling himself he answered:

"Port wine."

"Ah! port wine! 'tis a comfort," said the Gascon, "since we shall not die of thirst. Are they all full?"

Grimaud translated the question, and Groslow, who was wiping the perspiration from off his forehead, answered:

"Some full, others empty."

D'Artagnan struck the barrels with his hand, and having ascertained that he spoke the truth, pushed his lantern, greatly to the captain's alarm, into the interstices between the barrels, and finding that there was nothing concealed in them:

"Come along," he said; and he went toward the door of the second compartment.

"Stop!" said the Englishman, "I have the key of that door;" and he opened the door, with a trembling hand, into the second compartment, where Mousqueton and Blaisois were preparing supper.

Here there was evidently nothing to seek or to apprehend and they passed rapidly to examine the third compartment.

This was the room appropriated to the sailors. Two or three hammocks hung upon the ceiling, a table and two benches composed the entire furniture. D'Artagnan picked up two or three old sails hung on the walls, and meeting nothing to suspect, regained by the hatchway the deck of the vessel.

"And this room?" he asked, pointing to the captain's cabin.

"That's my room," replied Groslow.

"Open the door."

The captain obeyed. D'Artagnan stretched out his arm in which he held the lantern, put his head in at the half opened door, and seeing that the cabin was nothing better than a shed:

"Good," he said. "If there is an army on board it is not here that it is hidden. Let us see what Porthos has found for supper." And thanking the captain, he regained the state cabin, where his friends were.

Porthos had found nothing, and with him fatigue had prevailed over hunger. He had fallen asleep and was in a profound slumber when D'Artagnan returned. Athos and Aramis were beginning to close their eyes, which they half opened when their companion came in again.

"Well!" said Aramis.

"All is well; we may sleep tranquilly."

On this assurance the two friends fell asleep; and D'Artagnan, who was very weary, bade good-night to Grimaud and laid himself down in his cloak, with naked sword at his side, in such a manner that his body barricaded the passage, and it should be impossible to enter the room without upsetting him.

Chapter LXXI.

Port Wine.

In ten minutes the masters slept; not so the servants—-hungry, and more thirsty than hungry.

Blaisois and Mousqueton set themselves to preparing their bed which consisted of a plank and a valise. On a hanging table, which swung to and fro with the rolling of the vessel, were a pot of beer and three glasses.

"This cursed rolling!" said Blaisois. "I know it will serve me as it did when we came over."

"And to think," said Mousqueton, "that we have nothing to fight seasickness with but barley bread and hop beer. Pah!"

"But where is your wicker flask, Monsieur Mousqueton? Have you lost it?" asked Blaisois.

"No," replied Mousqueton, "Parry kept it. Those devilish Scotchmen are always thirsty. And you, Grimaud," he said to his companion, who had just come in after his round with D'Artagnan, "are you thirsty?"

"As thirsty as a Scotchman!" was Grimaud's laconic reply.

And he sat down and began to cast up the accounts of his party, whose money he managed.

"Oh, lackadaisy! I'm beginning to feel queer!" cried Blaisois.

"If that's the case," said Mousqueton, with a learned air, "take some nourishment."

"Do you call that nourishment?" said Blaisois, pointing to the barley bread and pot of beer upon the table.

"Blaisois," replied Mousqueton, "remember that bread is the true nourishment of a Frenchman, who is not always able to get bread, ask Grimaud."

"Yes, but beer?" asked Blaisois sharply, "is that their true drink?"

"As to that," answered Mousqueton, puzzled how to get out of the difficulty, "I must confess that to me beer is as disagreeable as wine is to the English."

"What! Monsieur Mousqueton! The English—do they dislike wine?"

"They hate it."

"But I have seen them drink it."

"As a punishment. For example, an English prince died one day because they had put him into a butt of Malmsey. I heard the Chevalier d'Herblay say so."

"The fool!" cried Blaisois, "I wish I had been in his place."

"Thou canst be," said Grimaud, writing down his figures.

"How?" asked Blaisois, "I can? Explain yourself."

Grimaud went on with his sum and cast up the whole.

"Port," he said, extending his hand in the direction of the first compartment examined by D'Artagnan and himself.

"Eh? eh? ah? Those barrels I saw through the door?"

"Port!" replied Grimaud, beginning a fresh sum.

"I have heard," said Blaisois, "that port is a very good wine."

"Excellent!" exclaimed Mousqueton, smacking his lips. "Excellent; there is port wine in the cellar of Monsieur le Baron de Bracieux."

"Suppose we ask these Englishmen to sell us a bottle," said the honest Blaisois.

"Sell!" cried Mousqueton, about whom there was a remnant of his ancient marauding character left. "One may well perceive, young man, that you are inexperienced. Why buy what one can take?"

"Take!" said Blaisois; "covet the goods of your neighbor? That is forbidden, it seems to me."

"Where forbidden?" asked Mousqueton.

"In the commandments of God, or of the church, I don't know which. I only know it says, 'Thou shalt not covet thy neighbor's goods, nor yet his wife.'"

"That is a child's reason, Monsieur Blaisois," said Mousqueton in his most patronizing manner. "Yes, you talk like a child—I repeat the word.

Where have you read in the Scriptures, I ask you, that the English are your neighbors?"

"Where, that is true," said Blaisois; "at least, I can't now recall it."

"A child's reason—I repeat it," continued Mousqueton. "If you had been ten years engaged in war, as Grimaud and I have been, my dear Blaisois, you would know the difference there is between the goods of others and the goods of enemies. Now an Englishman is an enemy; this port wine belongs to the English, therefore it belongs to us."

"And our masters?" asked Blaisois, stupefied by this harangue, delivered with an air of profound sagacity, "will they be of your opinion?"

Mousqueton smiled disdainfully.

"I suppose that you think it necessary that I should disturb the repose of these illustrious lords to say, 'Gentlemen, your servant, Mousqueton, is thirsty.' What does Monsieur Bracieux care, think you, whether I am thirsty or not?"

"'Tis a very expensive wine," said Blaisois, shaking his head.

"Were it liquid gold, Monsieur Blaisois, our masters would not deny themselves this wine. Know that Monsieur de Bracieux is rich enough to drink a tun of port wine, even if obliged to pay a pistole for every drop." His manner became more and more lofty every instant; then he arose and after finishing off the beer at one draught he advanced majestically to the door of the compartment where the wine was. "Ah! locked!" he exclaimed; "these devils of English, how suspicious they are!"

"Locked!" said Blaisois; "ah! the deuce it is; unlucky, for my stomach is getting more and more upset."

"Locked!" repeated Mousqueton.

"But," Blaisois ventured to say, "I have heard you relate, Monsieur Mousqueton, that once on a time, at Chantilly, you fed your master and yourself by taking partridges in a snare, carp with a line, and bottles with a slipnoose."

"Perfectly true; but there was an airhole in the cellar and the wine was in bottles. I cannot throw the loop through this partition nor move with a packthread a cask of wine which may perhaps weigh two hundred pounds."

"No, but you can take out two or three boards of the partition," answered Blaisois, "and make a hole in the cask with a gimlet."

Mousqueton opened his great round eyes to the utmost, astonished to find in Blaisois qualities for which he did not give him credit.

"'Tis true," he said; "but where can I get a chisel to take the planks out, a gimlet to pierce the cask?"

"Trousers," said Grimaud, still squaring his accounts.

"Ah, yes!" said Mousqueton.

Grimaud, in fact, was not only the accountant, but the armorer of the party; and as he was a man full of forethought, these trousers, carefully rolled up in his valise, contained every sort of tool for immediate use.

Mousqueton, therefore, was soon provided with tools and he began his task. In a few minutes he had extracted three boards. He tried to pass his body through the aperture, but not being like the frog in the fable, who thought he was larger than he really was, he found he must take out three or four more before he could get through.

He sighed and set to work again.

Grimaud had now finished his accounts. He arose and stood near Mousqueton.

"I," he said.

"What?" said Mousqueton.

"I can pass."

"That is true," said Mousqueton, glancing at his friend's long and thin body, "you will pass easily."

"And he knows the full casks," said Blaisois, "for he has already been in the hold with Monsieur le Chevalier d'Artagnan. Let Monsieur Grimaud go in, Monsieur Mouston."

"I could go in as well as Grimaud," said Mousqueton, a little piqued.

"Yes, but that would take too much time and I am thirsty. I am getting more and more seasick."

"Go in, then, Grimaud," said Mousqueton, handing him the beer pot and gimlet.

"Rinse the glasses," said Grimaud. Then with a friendly gesture toward Mousqueton, that he might forgive him for finishing an enterprise so brilliantly begun by another, he glided like a serpent through the opening and disappeared.

Blaisois was in a state of great excitement; he was in ecstasies. Of all the exploits performed since their arrival in England by the extraordinary men with whom he had the honor to be associated, this seemed without question to be the most wonderful.

"You are about to see," said Mousqueton, looking at Blaisois with an expression of superiority which the latter did not even think of questioning, "you are about to see, Blaisois, how we old soldiers drink when we are thirsty."

"My cloak," said Grimaud, from the bottom of the hold.

"What do you want?" asked Blaisois.

"My cloak—stop up the aperture with it."

"Why?" asked Blaisois.

"Simpleton!" exclaimed Mousqueton; "suppose any one came into the room."

"Ah, true," cried Blaisois, with evident admiration; "but it will be dark in the cellar."

"Grimaud always sees, dark or light, night as well as day," answered Mousqueton.

"That is lucky," said Blaisois. "As for me, when I have no candle I can't take two steps without knocking against something."

"That's because you haven't served," said Mousqueton. "Had you been in the army you would have been able to pick up a needle on the floor of a closed oven. But hark! I think some one is coming."

Mousqueton made, with a low whistling sound, the sign of alarm well known to the lackeys in the days of their youth, resumed his place at the table and made a sign to Blaisois to follow his example.

Blaisois obeyed.

The door of their cabin was opened. Two men, wrapped in their cloaks, appeared.

"Oho!" said they, "not in bed at a quarter past eleven. That's against all rules. In a quarter of an hour let every one be in bed and snoring."

These two men then went toward the compartment in which Grimaud was secreted; opened the door, entered and shut it after them.

"Ah!" cried Blaisois, "he is lost!"

"Grimaud's a cunning fellow," murmured Mousqueton.

They waited for ten minutes, during which time no noise was heard that might indicate that Grimaud was discovered, and at the expiration of that anxious interval the two men returned, closed the door after them, and repeating their orders that the servants should go to bed and extinguish their lights, disappeared.

"Shall we obey?" asked Blaisois. "All this looks suspicious."

"They said a quarter of an hour. We still have five minutes," replied Mousqueton.

"Suppose we warn the masters."

"Let's wait for Grimaud."

"But perhaps they have killed him."

"Grimaud would have cried out."

"You know he is almost dumb."

"We should have heard the blow, then."

"But if he doesn't return?"

"Here he is."

At that very moment Grimaud drew back the cloak which hid the aperture and came in with his face livid, his eyes staring wide open with terror, so that the pupils were contracted almost to nothing, with a large circle of white around them. He held in his hand a tankard full of a dark substance, and approaching the gleam of light shed by the lamp he uttered this single monosyllable: "Oh!" with such an expression of extreme terror that Mousqueton started, alarmed, and Blaisois was near fainting from fright.

Both, however, cast an inquisitive glance into the tankard—it was full of gunpowder.

Convinced that the ship was full of powder instead of having a cargo of wine, Grimaud hastened to awake D'Artagnan, who had no sooner beheld him than he perceived that something extraordinary had taken place. Imposing silence, Grimaud put out the little night lamp, then knelt down and poured into the lieutenant's ear a recital melodramatic enough not to require play of feature to give it pith.

This was the gist of his strange story:

The first barrel that Grimaud had found on passing into the compartment he struck—it was empty. He passed on to another—it, also, was empty, but the third which he tried was, from the dull sound it gave out, evidently full. At this point Grimaud stopped and was preparing to make a hole with his gimlet, when he found a spigot; he therefore placed his tankard under it and turned the spout; something, whatever it was the cask contained, fell silently into the tankard.

Whilst he was thinking that he should first taste the liquor which the tankard contained before taking it to his companions, the door of the cellar opened and a man with a lantern in his hands and enveloped in a cloak, came and stood just before the hogshead, behind which Grimaud, on hearing him come in, instantly crept. This was Groslow. He was accompanied by another man, who carried in his hand something long and flexible rolled up, resembling a washing line. His face was hidden under the wide brim of his hat. Grimaud, thinking that they had come, as he had, to try the port wine, effaced himself behind his cask and consoled himself with the reflection that if he were discovered the crime was not a great one.

"Have you the wick?" asked the one who carried the lantern.

"Here it is," answered the other.

At the voice of this last speaker, Grimaud started and felt a shudder creeping through his very marrow. He rose gently, so that his head was just above the round of the barrel, and under the large hat he recognized the pale face of Mordaunt.

"How long will this fuse burn?" asked this person.

"About five minutes," replied the captain.

That voice also was known to Grimaud. He looked from one to the other and after Mordaunt he recognized Groslow.

"Then tell the men to be in readiness—don't tell them why now. When the clock strikes a quarter after midnight collect your men. Get down into the longboat."

"That is, when I have lighted the match?"

"I will undertake that. I wish to be sure of my revenge. Are the oars in the boat?"

"Everything is ready."

"'Tis well."

Mordaunt knelt down and fastened one end of the train to the spigot, in order that he might have nothing to do but to set it on fire at the opposite end with the match.

He then arose.

"You hear me—at a quarter past midnight—in fact, in twenty minutes."

"I understand all perfectly, sir," replied Groslow; "but allow me to say there is great danger in what you undertake; would it not be better to intrust one of the men to set fire to the train?"

"My dear Groslow," answered Mordaunt, "you know the French proverb, 'Nothing one does not do one's self is ever well done.' I shall abide by that rule."

Grimaud had heard all this, if he had not understood it. But what he saw made good what he lacked in perfect comprehension of the language. He had seen the two mortal enemies of the musketeers, had seen Mordaunt adjust the fuse; he had heard the proverb, which Mordaunt had given in French. Then he felt and felt again the contents of the tankard he held in his hand; and, instead of the lively liquor expected by Blaisois and Mousqueton, he found beneath his fingers the grains of some coarse powder.

Mordaunt went away with the captain. At the door he stopped to listen.

"Do you hear how they sleep?" he asked.

In fact, Porthos could be heard snoring through the partition.

"'Tis God who gives them into our hands," answered Groslow.

"This time the devil himself shall not save them," rejoined Mordaunt.

And they went out together.

Chapter LXXII.

End of the Port Wine Mystery.

Grimaud waited till he heard the bolt grind in the lock and when he was satisfied that he was alone he slowly rose from his recumbent posture.

"Ah!" he said, wiping with his sleeve large drops of sweat from his forehead, "how lucky it was that Mousqueton was thirsty!"

He made haste to pass out by the opening, still thinking himself in a dream; but the sight of the gunpowder in the tankard proved to him that his dream was a fatal nightmare.

It may be imagined that D'Artagnan listened to these details with increasing interest; before Grimaud had finished he rose without noise and putting his mouth to Aramis's ear, and at the same time touching him on the shoulder to prevent a sudden movement:

"Chevalier," he said, "get up and don't make the least noise."

Aramis awoke. D'Artagnan, pressing his hand, repeated his call. Aramis obeyed.

"Athos is near you," said D'Artagnan; "warn him as I have warned you."

Aramis easily aroused Athos, whose sleep was light, like that of all persons of a finely organized constitution. But there was more difficulty in arousing Porthos. He was beginning to ask full explanation of that breaking in on his sleep, which was very annoying to him, when D'Artagnan, instead of explaining, closed his mouth with his hand.

Then our Gascon, extending his arms, drew to him the heads of his three friends till they almost touched one another.

"Friends," he said, "we must leave this craft at once or we are dead men."

"Bah!" said Athos, "are you still afraid?"

"Do you know who is captain of this vessel?"

"No."

"Captain Groslow."

The shudder of the three musketeers showed to D'Artagnan that his words began to make some impression on them.

"Groslow!" said Aramis; "the devil!"

"Who is this Groslow?" asked Porthos. "I don't remember him."

"Groslow is the man who broke Parry's head and is now getting ready to break ours."

"Oh! oh!"

"And do you know who is his lieutenant?"

"His lieutenant? There is none," said Athos. "They don't have lieutenants in a felucca manned by a crew of four."

"Yes, but Monsieur Groslow is not a captain of the ordinary kind; he has a lieutenant, and that lieutenant is Monsieur Mordaunt."

This time the musketeers did more than shudder—they almost cried out. Those invincible men were subject to a mysterious and fatal influence which that name had over them; the mere sound of it filled them with terror.

"What shall we do?" said Athos.

"We must seize the felucca," said Aramis.

"And kill him," said Porthos.

"The felucca is mined," said D'Artagnan. "Those casks which I took for casks of port wine are filled with powder. When Mordaunt finds himself discovered he will destroy all, friends and foes; and on my word he would be bad company in going either to Heaven or to hell."

"You have some plan, then?" asked Athos.

"Yes."

"What is it?"

"Have you confidence in me?"

"Give your orders," said the three musketeers.

"Very well; come this way."

D'Artagnan went toward a very small, low window, just large enough to let a man through. He turned it gently on its hinges.

"There," he said, "is our road."

"The deuce! it is a very cold one, my dear friend," said Aramis.

"Stay here, if you like, but I warn you 'twill be rather too warm presently."

"But we cannot swim to the shore."

"The longboat is yonder, lashed to the felucca. We will take possession of it and cut the cable. Come, my friends."

"A moment's delay," said Athos; "our servants?"

"Here we are!" they cried.

Meantime the three friends were standing motionless before the awful sight which D'Artagnan, in raising the shutters, had disclosed to them through the narrow opening of the window.

Those who have once beheld such a spectacle know that there is nothing more solemn, more striking, than the raging sea, rolling, with its deafening roar, its dark billows beneath the pale light of a wintry moon.

"Gracious Heaven, we are hesitating!" cried D'Artagnan; "if we hesitate what will the servants do?"

"I do not hesitate, you know," said Grimaud.

"Sir," interposed Blaisois, "I warn you that I can only swim in rivers."

"And I not at all," said Mousqueton.

But D'Artagnan had now slipped through the window.

"You have decided, friend?" said Athos.

"Yes," the Gascon answered; "Athos! you, who are a perfect being, bid spirit triumph over body. Do you, Aramis, order the servants. Porthos, kill every one who stands in your way."

And after pressing the hand of Athos, D'Artagnan chose a moment when the ship rolled backward, so that he had only to plunge into the water, which was already up to his waist.

Athos followed him before the felucca rose again on the waves; the cable which tied the boat to the vessel was then seen plainly rising out of the sea.

D'Artagnan swam to it and held it, suspending himself by this rope, his head alone out of water.

In one second Athos joined him.

Then they saw, as the felucca turned, two other heads peeping, those of Aramis and Grimaud.

"I am uneasy about Blaisois," said Athos; "he can, he says, only swim in rivers."

"When people can swim at all they can swim anywhere. To the boat! to the boat!"

"But Porthos, I do not see him."

"Porthos is coming—he swims like Leviathan."

In fact, Porthos did not appear; for a scene, half tragedy and half comedy, had been performed by him with Mousqueton and Blaisois, who, frightened by the noise of the sea, by the whistling of the wind, by the sight of that dark water yawning like a gulf beneath them, shrank back instead of going forward.

"Come, come!" said Porthos; "jump in."

"But, monsieur," said Mousqueton, "I can't swim; let me stay here."

"And me, too, monsieur," said Blaisois.

"I assure you, I shall be very much in the way in that little boat," said Mousqueton.

"And I know I shall drown before reaching it," continued Blaisois.

"Come along! I shall strangle you both if you don't get out," said Porthos at last, seizing Mousqueton by the throat. "Forward, Blaisois!"

A groan, stifled by the grasp of Porthos, was all the reply of poor Blaisois, for the giant, taking him neck and heels, plunged him into the water headforemost, pushing him out of the window as if he had been a plank.

"Now, Mousqueton," he said, "I hope you don't mean to desert your master?"

"Ah, sir," replied Mousqueton, his eyes filling with tears, "why did you re-enter the army? We were all so happy in the Chateau de Pierrefonds!"

And without any other complaint, passive and obedient, either from true devotion to his master or from the example set by Blaisois, Mousqueton leaped into the sea headforemost. A sublime action, at all events, for Mousqueton looked upon himself as dead. But Porthos was not a man to abandon an old servant, and when Mousqueton rose above the water, blind as a new-born puppy, he found he was supported by the large hand of Porthos and that he was thus enabled, without having occasion even to move, to advance toward the cable with the dignity of a very triton.

In a few minutes Porthos had rejoined his companions, who were already in the boat; but when, after they had all got in, it came to his turn, there was great danger that in putting his huge leg over the edge of the boat he would upset the little vessel. Athos was the last to enter.

"Are you all here?" he asked.

"Ah! have you your sword, Athos?" cried D'Artagnan.

"Yes."

"Cut the cable, then."

Athos drew a sharp poniard from his belt and cut the cord. The felucca went on, the boat continued stationary, rocked only by the swashing waves.

"Come, Athos!" said D'Artagnan, giving his hand to the count; "you are going to see something curious," added the Gascon.

Chapter LXXIII.

Fatality.

Scarcely had D'Artagnan uttered these words when a ringing and sudden noise was heard resounding through the felucca, which had now become dim in the obscurity of the night.

"That, you may be sure," said the Gascon, "means something."

They then at the same instant perceived a large lantern carried on a pole appear on the deck, defining the forms of shadows behind it.

Suddenly a terrible cry, a cry of despair, was wafted through space; and as if the shrieks of anguish had driven away the clouds, the veil which hid the moon was cleated away and the gray sails and dark shrouds of the felucca were plainly visible beneath the silvery light.

Shadows ran, as if bewildered, to and fro on the vessel, and mournful cries accompanied these delirious walkers. In the midst of these screams they saw Mordaunt upon the poop with a torch in hand.

The agitated figures, apparently wild with terror, consisted of Groslow, who at the hour fixed by Mordaunt had collected his men and the sailors. Mordaunt, after having listened at the door of the cabin to hear if the musketeers were still asleep, had gone down into the cellar, convinced by their silence that they were all in a deep slumber. Then he had run to the train, impetuous as a man who is excited by revenge, and full of confidence, as are those whom God blinds, he had set fire to the wick of nitre.

All this while Groslow and his men were assembled on deck.

"Haul up the cable and draw the boat to us," said Groslow.

One of the sailors got down the side of the ship, seized the cable, and drew it; it came without the least resistance.

"The cable is cut!" he cried, "no boat!"

"How! no boat!" exclaimed Groslow; "it is impossible."

"'Tis true, however," answered the sailor; "there's nothing in the wake of the ship; besides, here's the end of the cable."

"What's the matter?" cried Mordaunt, who, coming up out of the hatchway, rushed to the stern, waving his torch.

"Only that our enemies have escaped; they have cut the cord and gone off with the boat."

Mordaunt bounded with one step to the cabin and kicked open the door.

"Empty!" he exclaimed; "the infernal demons!"

"We must pursue them," said Groslow, "they can't be gone far, and we will sink them, passing over them."

"Yes, but the fire," ejaculated Mordaunt; "I have lighted it."

"Ten thousand devils!" cried Groslow, rushing to the hatchway; "perhaps there is still time to save us."

Mordaunt answered only by a terrible laugh, threw his torch into the sea and plunged in after it. The instant Groslow put his foot upon the hatchway steps the ship opened like the crater of a volcano. A burst of flame rose toward the skies with an explosion like that of a hundred cannon; the air burned, ignited by flaming embers, then the frightful lightning disappeared, the brands sank, one after another, into the abyss, where they were extinguished, and save for a slight vibration in the air, after a few minutes had elapsed one would have thought that nothing had happened.

Only—the felucca had disappeared from the surface of the sea and Groslow and his three sailors were consumed.

The four friends saw all this—not a single detail of this fearful scene escaped them. At one moment, bathed as they were in a flood of brilliant light, which illumined the sea for the space of a league, they might each be seen, each by his own peculiar attitude and manner expressing the awe which, even in their hearts of bronze, they could not help experiencing. Soon a torrent of vivid sparks fell around them—then, at last, the volcano was extinguished—then all was dark and still—the floating bark and heaving ocean.

They sat silent and dejected.

"By Heaven!" at last said Athos, the first to speak, "by this time, I think, all must be over."

"Here, my lords! save me! help!" cried a voice, whose mournful accents, reaching the four friends, seemed to proceed from some phantom of the ocean.

All looked around; Athos himself stared.

"'Tis he! it is his voice!"

All still remained silent, the eyes of all were turned in the direction where the vessel had disappeared, endeavoring in vain to penetrate the darkness. After a minute or two they were able to distinguish a man, who approached them, swimming vigorously.

Athos extended his arm toward him, pointing him out to his companions.

"Yes, yes, I see him well enough," said D'Artagnan.

"He—again!" cried Porthos, who was breathing like a blacksmith's bellows; "why, he is made of iron."

"Oh, my God!" muttered Athos.

Aramis and D'Artagnan whispered to each other.

Mordaunt made several strokes more, and raising his arm in sign of distress above the waves: "Pity, pity on me, gentlemen, in Heaven's name! my strength is failing me; I am dying."

The voice that implored aid was so piteous that it awakened pity in the heart of Athos.

"Poor fellow!" he exclaimed.

"Indeed!" said D'Artagnan, "monsters have only to complain to gain your sympathy. I believe he's swimming toward us. Does he think we are going to take him in? Row, Porthos, row." And setting the example he plowed his oar into the sea; two strokes took the bark on twenty fathoms further.

"Oh! you will not abandon me! You will not leave me to perish! You will not be pitiless!" cried Mordaunt.

"Ah! ah!" said Porthos to Mordaunt, "I think we have you now, my hero! and there are no doors by which you can escape this time but those of hell."

"Oh! Porthos!" murmured the Comte de la Fere.

"Oh, pray, for mercy's sake, don't fly from me. For pity's sake!" cried the young man, whose agony-drawn breath at times, when his head went under water, under the wave, exhaled and made the icy waters bubble.

D'Artagnan, however, who had consulted with Aramis, spoke to the poor wretch. "Go away," he said; "your repentance is too recent to inspire confidence. See! the vessel in which you wished to fry us is still smoking; and the situation in which you are is a bed of roses compared to that in which you wished to place us and in which you have placed Monsieur Groslow and his companions."

"Sir!" replied Mordaunt, in a tone of deep despair, "my penitence is sincere. Gentlemen, I am young, scarcely twenty-three years old. I was drawn on by a very natural resentment to avenge my mother. You would have done what I did."

Mordaunt wanted now only two or three fathoms to reach the boat, for the approach of death seemed to give him supernatural strength.

"Alas!" he said, "I am then to die? You are going to kill the son, as you killed the mother! Surely, if I am culpable and if I ask for pardon, I ought to be forgiven."

Then, as if his strength failed him, he seemed unable to sustain himself above the water and a wave passed over his head, which drowned his voice.

"Oh! this is torture to me," cried Athos.

Mordaunt reappeared.

"For my part," said D'Artagnan, "I say this must come to an end; murderer, as you were, of your uncle! executioner, as you were, of King Charles! incendiary! I recommend you to sink forthwith to the bottom of the sea; and if you come another fathom nearer, I'll stave your wicked head in with this oar."

"D'Artagnan! D'Artagnan!" cried Athos, "my son, I entreat you; the wretch is dying, and it is horrible to let a man die without extending a hand to save him. I cannot resist doing so; he must live."

"Zounds!" replied D'Artagnan, "why don't you give yourself up directly, feet and hands bound, to that wretch? Ah! Comte de la Fere, you wish to perish by his hands! I, your son, as you call me—I will not let you!"

'Twas the first time D'Artagnan had ever refused a request from Athos.

Aramis calmly drew his sword, which he had carried between his teeth as he swam.

"If he lays his hand on the boat's edge I will cut it off, regicide that he is."

"And I," said Porthos. "Wait."

"What are you going to do?" asked Aramis.

"Throw myself in the water and strangle him."

"Oh, gentlemen!" cried Athos, "be men! be Christians! See! death is depicted on his face! Ah! do not bring on me the horrors of remorse! Grant me this poor wretch's life. I will bless you—I——"

"I am dying!" cried Mordaunt, "come to me! come to me!"

D'Artagnan began to be touched. The boat at this moment turned around, and the dying man was by that turn brought nearer Athos.

"Monsieur the Comte de la Fere," he cried, "I supplicate you! pity me! I call on you—where are you? I see you no longer—I am dying—help me! help me!"

"Here I am, sir!" said Athos, leaning and stretching out his arm to Mordaunt with that air of dignity and nobility of soul habitual to him; "here I am, take my hand and jump into our boat."

Mordaunt made a last effort—rose—seized the hand thus extended to him and grasped it with the vehemence of despair.

"That's right," said Athos; "put your other hand here." And he offered him his shoulder as another stay and support, so that his head almost touched that of Mordaunt; and these two mortal enemies were in as close an embrace as if they had been brothers.

"Now, sir," said the count, "you are safe—calm yourself."

"Ah! my mother," cried Mordaunt, with eyes on fire with a look of hate impossible to paint, "I can only offer thee one victim, but it shall at any rate be the one thou wouldst thyself have chosen!"

And whilst D'Artagnan uttered a cry, Porthos raised the oar, and Aramis sought a place to strike, a frightful shake given to the boat precipitated Athos into the sea; whilst Mordaunt, with a shout of triumph, grasped the neck of his victim, and in order to paralyze his movements, twined arms and legs around the musketeer. For an instant, without an exclamation, without a cry for help, Athos tried to sustain himself on the surface of the waters, but the weight dragged him down; he disappeared by degrees; soon nothing was to be seen except his long, floating hair; then both men disappeared and the bubbling of the water, which, in its turn, was soon effaced, alone indicated the spot where these two had sunk.

Mute with horror, the three friends had remained open-mouthed, their eyes dilated, their arms extended like statues, and, motionless as they were, the beating of their hearts was audible. Porthos was the first who came to himself. He tore his hair.

"Oh!" he cried, "Athos! Athos! thou man of noble heart; woe is me! I have let thee perish!"

At this instant, in the midst of the silver circle illumined by the light of the moon the same whirlpool which had been made by the sinking men was again obvious, and first were seen, rising above the waves, a wisp of hair, then a pale face with open eyes, yet, nevertheless, the eyes of death; then a body, which, after rising of itself even to the waist above the sea, turned gently on its back, according to the caprice of the waves, and floated.

In the bosom of this corpse was plunged a poniard, the gold hilt of which shone in the moonbeams.

"Mordaunt! Mordaunt!" cried the three friends; "'tis Mordaunt!"

"But Athos!" exclaimed D'Artagnan.

Suddenly the boat leaned on one side beneath a new and unexpected weight and Grimaud uttered a shout of joy; every one turned around and beheld Athos, livid, his eyes dim and his hands trembling, supporting himself on the edge of the boat. Eight vigorous arms lifted him up immediately and laid him in the boat, where directly Athos was warmed and reanimated, reviving with the caresses and cares of his friends, who were intoxicated with joy.

"You are not hurt?" asked D'Artagnan.

"No," replied Athos; "and he——"

"Oh, he! now we may say at last, thank Heaven! he is really dead. Look!" and D'Artagnan, obliging Athos to look in the direction he pointed, showed him the body of Mordaunt floating on its back, which, sometimes submerged, sometimes rising, seemed still to pursue the four friends with looks of insult and mortal hatred.

At last he sank. Athos had followed him with a glance in which the deepest melancholy and pity were expressed.

"Bravo! Athos!" cried Aramis, with an emotion very rare in him.

"A capital blow you gave!" cried Porthos.

"I have a son. I wished to live," said Athos.

"In short," said D'Artagnan, "this has been the will of God."

"It was not I who killed him," said Athos in a soft, low tone, "'twas destiny."

Chapter LXXIV.

How Mousqueton had a Narrow Escape of being eaten.

A deep silence reigned for a long time in the boat after the fearful scene described.

The moon, which had shone for a short time, disappeared behind the clouds; every object was again plunged in the obscurity that is so awful in the deserts and still more so in that liquid desert, the ocean, and nothing was heard save the whistling of the west wind driving along the tops of the crested billows.

Porthos was the first to speak.

"I have seen," he said, "many dreadful things, but nothing that ever agitated me so much as what I have just witnessed. Nevertheless, even in my present state of perturbation, I protest that I feel happy. I have a hundred pounds' weight less upon my chest. I breathe more freely." In fact, Porthos breathed so loud as to do credit to the free play of his powerful lungs.

"For my part," observed Aramis, "I cannot say the same as you do, Porthos. I am still terrified to such a degree that I scarcely believe my eyes. I look around the boat, expecting every moment to see that poor wretch holding between his hands the poniard plunged into his heart."

"Oh! I feel easy," replied Porthos. "The poniard was pointed at the sixth rib and buried up to the hilt in his body. I do not reproach you, Athos, for what you have done. On the contrary, when one aims a blow that is the regulation way to strike. So now, I breathe again—I am happy!"

"Don't be in haste to celebrate a victory, Porthos," interposed D'Artagnan; "never have we incurred a greater danger than we are now encountering. Men may subdue men—they cannot overcome the elements. We are now on the sea, at night, without any pilot, in a frail bark; should a blast of wind upset the boat we are lost."

Mousqueton heaved a deep sigh.

"You are ungrateful, D'Artagnan," said Athos; "yes, ungrateful to Providence, to whom we owe our safety in the most miraculous manner. Let us sail before the wind, and unless it changes we shall be drifted either to Calais or Boulogne. Should our bark be upset we are five of us good swimmers, able enough to turn it over again, or if not, to hold on by it. Now we are on the very road which all the vessels between Dover and Calais take, 'tis impossible but that we should meet with a fisherman who will pick us up."

"But should we not find any fisherman and should the wind shift to the north?"

"That," said Athos, "would be quite another thing; and we should nevermore see land until we were upon the other side of the Atlantic."

"Which implies that we may die of hunger," said Aramis.

"'Tis more than possible," answered the Comte de la Fere.

Mousqueton sighed again, more deeply than before.

"What is the matter? what ails you?" asked Porthos.

"I am cold, sir," said Mousqueton.

"Impossible! your body is covered with a coating of fat which preserves it from the cold air."

"Ah! sir, 'tis this very coating of fat that makes me shiver."

"How is that, Mousqueton?

"Alas! your honor, in the library of the Chateau of Bracieux there are a lot of books of travels."

"What then?"

"Amongst them the voyages of Jean Mocquet in the time of Henry IV."

"Well?"

"In these books, your honor, 'tis told how hungry voyagers, drifting out to sea, have a bad habit of eating each other and beginning with——"

"The fattest among them!" cried D'Artagnan, unable in spite of the gravity of the occasion to help laughing.

"Yes, sir," answered Mousqueton; "but permit me to say I see nothing laughable in it. However," he added, turning to Porthos, "I should not regret dying, sir, were I sure that by doing so I might still be useful to you."

"Mouston," replied Porthos, much affected, "should we ever see my castle of Pierrefonds again you shall have as your own and for your descendants the vineyard that surrounds the farm."

"And you should call it 'Devotion,'" added Aramis; "the vineyard of self-sacrifice, to transmit to latest ages the recollection of your devotion to your master."

"Chevalier," said D'Artagnan, laughing, "you could eat a piece of Mouston, couldn't you, especially after two or three days of fasting?"

"Oh, no," replied Aramis, "I should much prefer Blaisois; we haven't known him so long."

One may readily conceive that during these jokes which were intended chiefly to divert Athos from the scene which had just taken place, the servants, with the exception of Grimaud, were not silent. Suddenly Mousqueton uttered a cry of delight, taking from beneath one of the benches a bottle of wine; and on looking more closely in the same place he discovered a dozen similar bottles, bread, and a monster junk of salted beef.

"Oh, sir!" he cried, passing the bottle to Porthos, "we are saved—the bark is supplied with provisions."

This intelligence restored every one save Athos to gayety.

"Zounds!" exclaimed Porthos, "'tis astonishing how empty violent agitation makes the stomach."

And he drank off half a bottle at a draught and bit great mouthfuls of the bread and meat.

"Now," said Athos, "sleep, or try to sleep, my friends, and I will watch."

In a few moments, notwithstanding their wet clothes, the icy blast that blew and the previous scene of terror, these hardy adventurers, with their iron frames, inured to every hardship, threw themselves down, intending to profit by the advice of Athos, who sat at the helm, pensively wakeful, guiding the little bark the way it was to go, his eyes fixed on the heavens, as if he sought to verify not only the road to France, but the benign aspect of protecting Providence. After some hours of repose the sleepers were aroused by Athos.

Dawn was shedding its pallid, placid glimmer on the purple ocean, when at the distance of a musket shot from them was seen a dark gray mass, above which gleamed a triangular sail; then masters and servants joined in a fervent cry to the crew of that vessel to hear them and to save.

"A bark!" all cried together.

It was, in fact, a small craft from Dunkirk bound for Boulogne.

A quarter of an hour afterward the rowboat of this craft took them all aboard. Grimaud tendered twenty guineas to the captain, and at nine o'clock in the morning, having a fair wind, our Frenchmen set foot on their native land.

"Egad! how strong one feels here!" said Porthos, almost burying his large feet in the sands. "Zounds! I could defy a nation!"

"Be quiet, Porthos," said D'Artagnan, "we are observed."

"We are admired, i'faith," answered Porthos.

"These people who are looking at us are only merchants," said Athos, "and are looking more at the cargo than at us."

"I shall not trust to that," said the lieutenant, "and I shall make for the Dunes* as soon as possible."

* Sandy hills about Dunkirk, from which it derives its name.

The party followed him and soon disappeared with him behind the hillocks of sand unobserved. Here, after a short conference, they proposed to separate.

"And why separate?" asked Athos.

"Because," answered the Gascon, "we were sent, Porthos and I, by Cardinal Mazarin to fight for Cromwell; instead of fighting for Cromwell we have served Charles I.—not the same thing by any means. In returning with the Comte de la Fere and Monsieur d'Herblay our crime would be confirmed. We have circumvented Cromwell, Mordaunt, and the sea, but we shall find a certain difficulty in circumventing Mazarin."

"You forget," replied Athos, "that we consider ourselves your prisoners and not free from the engagement we entered into."

"Truly, Athos," interrupted D'Artagnan, "I am vexed that such a man as you are should talk nonsense which schoolboys would be ashamed of. Chevalier," he continued, addressing Aramis, who, leaning proudly on his sword, seemed to agree with his companion, "Chevalier, Porthos and I run no risk; besides, should any ill-luck happen to two of us, will it not be much better that the other two should be spared to assist those who may be apprehended? Besides, who knows whether, divided, we may not obtain a pardon—you from the queen, we from Mazarin—which, were we all four together, would never be granted. Come, Athos and Aramis, go to the right; Porthos, come with me to the left; these gentlemen should file off into Normandy, whilst we, by the nearest road, reach Paris."

He then gave his friends minute directions as to their route.

"Ah! my dear friend," exclaimed Athos, "how I should admire the resources of your mind did I not stop to adore those of your heart."

And he gave him his hand.

"Isn't this fox a genius, Athos?" asked the Gascon. "No! he knows how to crunch fowls, to dodge the huntsman and to find his way home by day or by night, that's all. Well, is all said?"

"All."

"Then let's count our money and divide it. Ah! hurrah! there's the sun! A merry morning to you, Sunshine. 'Tis a long time since I saw thee!"

"Come, come, D'Artagnan," said Athos, "do not affect to be strong-minded; there are tears in your eyes. Let us be open with each other and sincere."

"What!" cried the Gascon, "do you think, Athos, we can take leave, calmly, of two friends at a time not free from danger to you and Aramis?"

"No," answered Athos; "embrace me, my son."

"Zounds!" said Porthos, sobbing, "I believe I'm crying; but how foolish all this is!"

Then they embraced. At that moment their fraternal bond of union was closer than ever, and when they parted, each to take the route agreed on, they turned back to utter affectionate expressions, which the echoes of the Dunes repeated. At last they lost sight of each other.

"Sacrebleu! D'Artagnan," said Porthos, "I must out with it at once, for I can't keep to myself anything I have against you; I haven't been able to recognize you in this matter."

"Why not?" said D'Artagnan, with his wise smile.

"Because if, as you say, Athos and Aramis are in real danger, this is not the time to abandon them. For my part, I confess to you that I was all ready to follow them and am still ready to rejoin them, in spite of all the Mazarins in the world."

"You would be right, Porthos, but for one thing, which may change the current of your ideas; and that is, that it is not those gentlemen who are in the greatest danger, it is ourselves; it is not to abandon them that we have separated, but to avoid compromising them."

"Really?" said Porthos, opening his eyes in astonishment.

"Yes, no doubt. If they are arrested they will only be put in the Bastile; if we are arrested it is a matter of the Place de Greve."

"Oh! oh!" said Porthos, "there is quite a gap between that fate and the baronial coronet you promised me, D'Artagnan."

"Bah! perhaps not so great as you think, Porthos; you know the proverb, 'All roads lead to Rome.'"

"But how is it that we are incurring greater risks than Athos and Aramis?" asked Porthos.

"Because they have but fulfilled the mission confided to them by Queen Henrietta and we have betrayed that confided to us by Mazarin; because, going hence as emissaries to Cromwell, we became partisans of King Charles; because, instead of helping cut off the royal head condemned by those fellows called Mazarin, Cromwell, Joyce, Bridge, Fairfax, etc., we very nearly succeeded in saving it."

"Upon my word that is true," said Porthos; "but how can you suppose, my dear friend, that in the midst of his great preoccupations General Cromwell has had time to think——"

"Cromwell thinks of everything; Cromwell has time for everything; and believe me, dear friend, we ought not to lose our time—it is precious. We shall not be safe till we have seen Mazarin, and then——"

"The devil!" said Porthos; "what can we say to Mazarin?"

"Leave that to me—I have my plan. He laughs best who laughs last. Cromwell is mighty, Mazarin is tricky, but I would rather have to do with them than with the late Monsieur Mordaunt."

"Ah!" said Porthos, "it is very pleasant to be able to say 'the late Monsieur Mordaunt.'"

"My faith, yes," said D'Artagnan. "But we must be going."

The two immediately started across country toward the road to Paris, followed by Mousqueton, who, after being too cold all night, at the end of a quarter of an hour found himself too warm.

Chapter LXXV.

The Return.

During the six weeks that Athos and Aramis had been absent from France, the Parisians, finding themselves one morning without either queen or king, were greatly annoyed at being thus deserted, and the absence of Mazarin, a thing so long desired, did not compensate for that of the two august fugitives.

The first feeling that pervaded Paris on hearing of the flight to Saint Germain, was that sort of affright which seizes children when they awake in the night and find themselves alone. A deputation was therefore sent to the queen to entreat her to return to Paris; but she not only declined to receive the deputies, but sent an intimation by Chancellor Seguier, implying that if the parliament did not humble itself before her majesty by negativing all the questions that had been the cause of the quarrel, Paris would be besieged the very next day.

This threatening answer, unluckily for the court, produced quite a different effect to that which was intended. It wounded the pride of the parliament, which, supported by the citizens, replied by declaring that Cardinal Mazarin was the cause of all the discontent; denounced him as the enemy both of the king and the state, and ordered him to retire from the court that same day and from France within a week afterward; enjoining, in case of disobedience on his part, all the subjects of the king to pursue and take him.

Mazarin being thus placed beyond the pale of the protection of the law, preparations on both sides were commenced—by the queen, to attack Paris, by the citizens, to defend it. The latter were occupied in breaking up the pavement and stretching chains across the streets, when, headed by the coadjutor, appeared the Prince de Conti (the brother of the Prince de Condé) and the Duc de Longueville, his brother-in-law. This unexpected band of auxiliaries arrived in Paris on the tenth of January and the Prince of Conti was named, but not until after a stormy discussion, generalissimo of the army of the king, out of Paris.

As for the Duc de Beaufort, he arrived from Vendome, according to the annals of the day, bringing with him his high bearing and his long and beautiful hair, qualifications which gained him the sovereignty of the marketplaces.

The Parisian army had organized with the promptness characteristic of the bourgeois whenever they are moved by any sentiment whatever to disguise themselves as soldiers. On the nineteenth the impromptu army had attempted a sortie, more to assure itself and others of its actual existence than with any more serious intention. They carried a banner, on which could be read this strange device: "We are seeking our king."

The next following days were occupied in trivial movements which resulted only in the carrying off of a few herds of cattle and the burning of two or three houses.

That was still the situation of affairs up to the early days of February. On the first day of that month our four companions had landed at Boulogne, and, in two parties, had set out for Paris. Toward the end of the fourth day of the journey Athos and Aramis reached Nanterre, which place they cautiously passed by on the outskirts, fearing that they might encounter some troop from the queen's army.

It was against his will that Athos took these precautions, but Aramis had very judiciously reminded him that they had no right to be imprudent, that they had been charged by King Charles with a supreme and sacred mission, which, received at the foot of the scaffold, could be accomplished only at the feet of Queen Henrietta. Upon that, Athos yielded.

On reaching the capital Athos and Aramis found it in arms. The sentinel at the gate refused even to let them pass, and called his sergeant.

The sergeant, with the air of importance which such people assume when they are clad with military dignity, said:

"Who are you, gentlemen?"

"Two gentlemen."

"And where do you come from?"

"From London."

"And what are you going to do in Paris?"

"We are going with a mission to Her Majesty, the Queen of England."

"Ah, every one seems to be going to see the queen of England. We have already at the station three gentlemen whose passports are under examination, who are on their way to her majesty. Where are your passports?"

"We have none; we left England, ignorant of the state of politics here, having left Paris before the departure of the king."

"Ah!" said the sergeant, with a cunning smile, "you are Mazarinists, who are sent as spies."

"My dear friend," here Athos spoke, "rest assured, if we were Mazarinists we should come well prepared with every sort of passport. In your situation distrust those who are well provided with every formality."

"Enter the guardroom," said the sergeant; "we will lay your case before the commandant of the post."

The guardroom was filled with citizens and common people, some playing, some drinking, some talking. In a corner, almost hidden from view, were three gentlemen, who had preceded Athos and Aramis, and an officer was examining their passports. The first impulse of these three, and of those who last entered, was to cast an inquiring glance at each other. The first arrivals wore long cloaks, in whose drapery they were carefully enveloped; one of them, shorter than the rest, remained pertinaciously in the background.

When the sergeant on entering the room announced that in all probability he was bringing in two Mazarinists, it appeared to be the unanimous opinion of the officers on guard that they ought not to pass.

"Be it so," said Athos; "yet it is probable, on the contrary, that we shall enter, because we seem to have to do with sensible people. There seems to be only one thing to do, which is, to send our names to Her Majesty the Queen of England, and if she engages to answer for us I presume we shall be allowed to enter."

On hearing these words the shortest of the other three men seemed more attentive than ever to what was going on, wrapping his cloak around him more carefully than before.

"Merciful goodness!" whispered Aramis to Athos, "did you see?"

"What?" asked Athos.

"The face of the shortest of those three gentlemen?"

"No."

"He looked to me—but 'tis impossible."

At this instant the sergeant, who had been for his orders, returned, and pointing to the three gentlemen in cloaks, said:

"The passports are in order; let these three gentlemen pass."

The three gentlemen bowed and hastened to take advantage of this permission.

Aramis looked after them, and as the last of them passed close to him he pressed the hand of Athos.

"What is the matter with you, my friend?" asked the latter.

"I have—doubtless I am dreaming; tell me, sir," he said to the sergeant, "do you know those three gentlemen who are just gone out?"

"Only by their passports; they are three Frondists, who are gone to rejoin the Duc de Longueville."

"'Tis strange," said Aramis, almost involuntarily; "I fancied that I recognized Mazarin himself."

The sergeant burst into a fit of laughter.

"He!" he cried; "he venture himself amongst us, to be hung! Not so foolish as all that."

"Ah!" muttered Athos, "I may be mistaken, I haven't the unerring eye of D'Artagnan."

"Who is speaking of Monsieur D'Artagnan?" asked an officer who appeared at that moment upon the threshold of the room.

"What!" cried Aramis and Athos, "what! Planchet!"

"Planchet," added Grimaud; "Planchet, with a gorget, indeed!"

"Ah, gentlemen!" cried Planchet, "so you are back again in Paris. Oh, how happy you make us! no doubt you come to join the princes!"

"As thou seest, Planchet," said Aramis, whilst Athos smiled on seeing what important rank was held in the city militia by the former comrade of Mousqueton, Bazin and Grimaud.

"And Monsieur d'Artagnan, of whom you spoke just now, Monsieur d'Herblay; may I ask if you have any news of him?"

"We parted from him four days ago and we have reason to believe that he has reached Paris before us."

"No, sir; I am sure he hasn't yet arrived. But then he may have stopped at Saint Germain."

"I don't think so; we appointed to meet at La Chevrette."

"I was there this very day."

"And had the pretty Madeleine no news?" asked Aramis, smiling.

"No, sir, and it must be admitted that she seemed very anxious."

"In fact," said Aramis, "there is no time lost and we made our journey quickly. Permit me, then, my dear Athos, without inquiring further about our friend, to pay my respects to M. Planchet."

"Ah, monsieur le chevalier," said Planchet, bowing.

"Lieutenant?" asked Aramis.

"Lieutenant, with a promise of becoming captain."

"'Tis capital; and pray, how did you acquire all these honors?"

"In the first place, gentlemen, you know that I was the means of Monsieur de Rochefort's escape; well, I was very near being hung by Mazarin and that made me more popular than ever."

"So, owing to your popularity——"

"No; thanks to something better. You know, gentlemen, that I served the Piedmont regiment and had the honor of being a sergeant?"

"Yes."

"Well, one day when no one could drill a mob of citizens, who began to march, some with the right foot, others with the left, I succeeded, I did, in making them all begin with the same foot, and I was made lieutenant on the spot."

"So I presume," said Athos, "that you have a large number of the nobles with you?"

"Certainly. There are the Prince de Conti, the Duc de Longueville, the Duc de Beaufort, the Duc de Bouillon, the Marechal de la Mothe, the Marquis de Sevigne, and I don't know who, for my part."

"And the Vicomte Raoul de Bragelonne?" inquired Athos, in a tremulous voice. "D'Artagnan told me that he had recommended him to your care, in parting."

"Yes, count; nor have I lost sight of him for a single instant since."

"Then," said Athos in a tone of delight, "he is well? no accident has happened to him?"

"None, sir."

"And he lives?"

"Still at the Hotel of the Great Charlemagne."

"And passes his time?"

"Sometimes with the queen of England, sometimes with Madame de Chevreuse. He and the Count de Guiche are like each other's shadows."

"Thanks, Planchet, thanks!" cried Athos, extending his hand to the lieutenant.

"Oh, sir!" Planchet only touched the tips of the count's fingers.

"Well, what are you doing, count—to a former lackey?"

"My friend," said Athos, "he has given me news of Raoul."

"And now, gentlemen," said Planchet, who had not heard what they were saying, "what do you intend to do?"

"Re-enter Paris, if you will let us, my good Planchet."

"Let you, sir? Now, as ever, I am nothing but your servant." Then turning to his men:

"Allow these gentlemen to pass," he said; "they are friends of the Duc de Beaufort."

"Long live the Duc de Beaufort!" cried the sentinels.

The sergeant drew near to Planchet.

"What! without passports?" he murmured.

"Without passports," said Planchet.

"Take notice, captain," he continued, giving Planchet his expected title, "take notice that one of the three men who just now went out from here told me privately to distrust these gentlemen."

"And I," said Planchet, with dignity, "I know them and I answer for them."

As he said this, he pressed Grimaud's hand, who seemed honored by the distinction.

"Farewell till we meet again," said Aramis, as they took leave of Planchet; "if anything happens to us we shall blame you for it."

"Sir," said Planchet, "I am in all things at your service."

"That fellow is no fool," said Aramis, as he got on his horse.

"How should he be?" replied Athos, whilst mounting also, "seeing he was used so long to brush your hats."

Chapter LXXVI.

The Ambassadors.

The two friends rode rapidly down the declivity of the Faubourg, but on arriving at the bottom were surprised to find that the streets of Paris had become rivers, and the open places lakes; after the great rains which fell in January the Seine had overflowed its banks and the river inundated half the capital. The two gentlemen were obliged, therefore, to get off their horses and take a boat; and in that strange manner they approached the Louvre.

Night had closed in, and Paris, seen thus, by the light of lanterns flickering on the pools of water, crowded with ferry-boats of every kind, including those that glittered with the armed patrols, with the watchword, passing from post to post—Paris presented such an aspect as to strongly seize the senses of Aramis, a man most susceptible to warlike impressions.

They reached the queen's apartments, but were compelled to stop in the ante-chamber, since her majesty was at that moment giving audience to gentlemen bringing her news from England.

"We, too," said Athos, to the footman who had given him that answer, "not only bring news from England, but have just come from there."

"What? then, are your names, gentlemen?"

"The Comte de la Fere and the Chevalier d'Herblay," said Aramis.

"Ah! in that case, gentlemen," said the footman, on hearing the names which the queen had so often pronounced with hope, "in that case it is another thing, and I think her majesty will pardon me for not keeping you here a moment. Please follow me," and he went on before, followed by Athos and Aramis.

On arriving at the door of the room where the queen was receiving he made a sign for them to wait and opening the door:

"Madame," he said, "I hope your majesty will forgive me for disobeying your orders, when you learn that the gentlemen I have come to announce are the Comte de la Fere and the Chevalier d'Herblay."

On hearing those two names the queen uttered a cry of joy, which the two gentlemen heard.

"Poor queen!" murmured Athos.

"Oh, let them come in! let them come in," cried the young princess, bounding to the door.

The poor child was constant in her attendance on her mother and sought by her filial attentions to make her forget the absence of her two sons and her other daughter.

"Come in, gentlemen," repeated the princess, opening the door herself.

The queen was seated on a fauteuil and before her were standing two or three gentlemen, and among them the Duc de Chatillon, the brother of the nobleman killed eight or nine years previously in a duel on account of Madame de Longueville, on the Place Royale. All these gentlemen had been noticed by Athos and Aramis in the guardhouse, and when the two friends were announced they started and exchanged some words in a low tone. "Well, sirs!" cried the queen, on perceiving the two friends, "you have come, faithful friends! But the royal couriers have been more expeditious than you, and here are Monsieur de Flamarens and Monsieur de Chatillon, who bring me from Her Majesty the Queen Anne of Austria, the very latest intelligence."

Aramis and Athos were astounded by the calmness, even the gayety of the queen's manner.

"Go on with your recital, sirs," said the queen, turning to the Duc de Chatillon. "You said that His Majesty, King Charles, my august consort, had been condemned to death by a majority of his subjects!"

"Yes, madame," Chatillon stammered out.

Athos and Aramis were more and more astonished.

"And that being conducted to the scaffold," resumed the queen—"oh, my lord! oh, my king!—and that being led to the scaffold he had been saved by an indignant people."

"Just so madame," replied Chatillon, in so low a voice that though the two friends were listening eagerly they could hardly hear this affirmation.

The queen clasped her hands in enthusiastic gratitude, whilst her daughter threw her arms around her mother's neck and kissed her—her own eyes streaming with tears.

"Now, madame, nothing remains to me except to proffer my respectful homage," said Chatillon, who felt confused and ashamed beneath the stern gaze of Athos.

"One moment, yes," answered the queen. "One moment—I beg—for here are the Chevalier d'Herblay and the Comte de la Fere, just arrived from London, and they can give you, as eye-witnesses, such details as you can convey to the queen, my royal sister. Speak, gentlemen, speak—I am listening; conceal nothing, gloss over nothing. Since his majesty still lives, since the honor of the throne is safe, everything else is a matter of indifference to me."

Athos turned pale and laid his hand on his heart.

"Well!" exclaimed the queen, who remarked this movement and his paleness. "Speak, sir! I beg you to do so."

"I beg you to excuse me, madame; I wish to add nothing to the recital of these gentlemen until they perceive themselves that they have perhaps been mistaken."

"Mistaken!" cried the queen, almost suffocated by emotion; "mistaken! what has happened, then?"

"Sir," interposed Monsieur de Flamarens to Athos, "if we are mistaken the error has originated with the queen. I do not suppose you will have the presumption to set it to rights—that would be to accuse Her Majesty, Queen Anne, of falsehood."

"With the queen, sir?" replied Athos, in his calm, vibrating voice.

"Yes," murmured Flamarens, lowering his eyes.

Athos sighed deeply.

"Or rather, sir," said Aramis, with his peculiar irritating politeness, "the error of the person who was with you when we met you in the guardroom; for if the Comte de la Fere and I are not mistaken, we saw you in the company of a third gentleman."

Chatillon and Flamarens started.

"Explain yourself, count!" cried the queen, whose anxiety grew greater every moment. "On your brow I read despair—your lips falter ere you announce some terrible tidings—your hands tremble. Oh, my God! my God! what has happened?"

"Lord!" ejaculated the young princess, falling on her knees, "have mercy on us!"

"Sir," said Chatillon, "if you bring bad tidings it will be cruel in you to announce them to the queen."

Aramis went so close to Chatillon as almost to touch him.

"Sir," said he, with compressed lips and flashing eyes, "you have not the presumption to instruct the Comte de la Fere and myself what we ought to say here?"

During this brief altercation Athos, with his hands on his heart, his head bent low, approached the queen and in a voice of deepest sorrow said:

"Madame, princes—who by nature are above other men—receive from Heaven courage to support greater misfortunes than those of lower rank, for their hearts are elevated as their fortunes. We ought not, therefore, I think, to act toward a queen so illustrious as your majesty as we should act toward a woman of our lowlier condition. Queen, destined as you are to endure every sorrow on this earth, hear the result of our unhappy mission."

Athos, kneeling down before the queen, trembling and very cold, drew from his bosom, inclosed in the same case, the order set in diamonds which the queen had given to Lord de Winter and the wedding ring which Charles I. before his death had placed in the hands of Aramis. Since the moment he had first received these two mementoes Athos had never parted with them.

He opened the case and offered them to the queen with deep and silent anguish.

The queen stretched out her hand, seized the ring, pressed it convulsively to her lips—and without being able to breathe a sigh, to give vent to a sob, she extended her arms, became deadly pale, and fell senseless in the arms of her attendants and her daughter.

Athos kissed the hem of the robe of the widowed queen and rising, with a dignity that made a deep impression on those around:

"I, the Comte de la Fere, a gentleman who has never deceived any human being, swear before God and before this unhappy queen, that all that was possible to save the king of England was done whilst we were on English ground. Now, chevalier," he added, turning to Aramis, "let us go. Our duty is fulfilled."

"Not yet." said Aramis; "we have still a word to say to these gentlemen."

And turning to Chatillon: "Sir, be so good as not to go away without giving me an opportunity to tell you something I cannot say before the queen."

Chatillon bowed in token of assent and they all went out, stopping at the window of a gallery on the ground floor.

"Sir," said Aramis, "you allowed yourself just now to treat us in a most extraordinary manner. That would not be endurable in any case, and is still less so on the part of those who came to bring the queen the message of a liar."

"Sir!" cried De Chatillon.

"What have you done with Monsieur de Bruy? Has he by any possibility gone to change his face which was too like that of Monsieur de Mazarin? There is an abundance of Italian masks at the Palais Royal, from harlequin even to pantaloon."

"Chevalier! chevalier!" said Athos.

"Leave me alone," said Aramis impatiently. "You know well that I don't like to leave things half finished."

"Conclude, then, sir," answered De Chatillon, with as much hauteur as Aramis.

"Gentlemen," resumed Aramis, "any one but the Comte de la Fere and myself would have had you arrested—for we have friends in Paris—but we are contented with another course. Come and converse with us for just five minutes, sword in hand, upon this deserted terrace."

"One moment, gentlemen," cried Flamarens. "I know well that the proposition is tempting, but at present it is impossible to accept it."

"And why not?" said Aramis, in his tone of raillery. "Is it Mazarin's proximity that makes you so prudent?"

"Oh, you hear that, Flamarens!" said Chatillon. "Not to reply would be a blot on my name and my honor."

"That is my opinion," said Aramis.

"You will not reply, however, and these gentlemen, I am sure, will presently be of my opinion."

Aramis shook his head with a motion of indescribable insolence.

Chatillon saw the motion and put his hand to his sword.

"Willingly," replied De Chatillon.

"Duke," said Flamarens, "you forget that to-morrow you are to command an expedition of the greatest importance, projected by the prince, assented to by the queen. Until to-morrow evening you are not at your own disposal."

"Let it be then the day after to-morrow," said Aramis.

"To-morrow, rather," said De Chatillon, "if you will take the trouble of coming so far as the gates of Charenton."

"How can you doubt it, sir? For the pleasure of a meeting with you I would go to the end of the world."

"Very well, to-morrow, sir."

"I shall rely on it. Are you going to rejoin your cardinal? Swear first, on your honor, not to inform him of our return."

"Conditions?"

"Why not?"

"Because it is for victors to make conditions, and you are not yet victors, gentlemen."

"Then let us draw on the spot. It is all one to us—to us who do not command to-morrow's expedition."

Chatillon and Flamarens looked at each other. There was such irony in the words and in the bearing of Aramis that the duke had great difficulty in bridling his anger, but at a word from Flamarens he restrained himself and contented himself with saying:

"You promise, sir—that's agreed—that I shall find you to-morrow at Charenton?"

"Oh, don't be afraid, sir," replied Aramis; and the two gentlemen shortly afterward left the Louvre.

"For what reason is all this fume and fury?" asked Athos. "What have they done to you?"

"They—did you not see what they did?"

"No."

"They laughed when we swore that we had done our duty in England. Now, if they believed us, they laughed in order to insult us; if they did not believe it they insulted us all the more. However, I'm glad not to fight them until to-morrow. I hope we shall have something better to do to-night than to draw the sword."

"What have we to do?"

"Egad! to take Mazarin."

Athos curled his lip with disdain.

"These undertakings do not suit me, as you know, Aramis."

"Why?"

"Because it is taking people unawares."

"Really, Athos, you would make a singular general. You would fight only by broad daylight, warn your foe before an attack, and never attempt anything by night lest you should be accused of taking advantage of the darkness."

Athos smiled.

"You know one cannot change his nature," he said. "Besides, do you know what is our situation, and whether Mazarin's arrest wouldn't be rather an encumbrance than an advantage?"

"Say at once you disapprove of my proposal."

"I think you ought to do nothing, since you exacted a promise from these gentlemen not to let Mazarin know that we were in France."

"I have entered into no engagement and consider myself quite free. Come, come."

"Where?"

"Either to seek the Duc de Beaufort or the Duc de Bouillon, and to tell them about this."

"Yes, but on one condition—that we begin by the coadjutor. He is a priest, learned in cases of conscience, and we will tell him ours."

It was then agreed that they were to go first to Monsieur de Bouillon, as his house came first; but first of all Athos begged that he might go to the Hotel du Grand Charlemagne, to see Raoul.

They re-entered the boat which had brought them to the Louvre and thence proceeded to the Halles; and taking up Grimaud and Blaisois, they went on foot to the Rue Guenegaud.

But Raoul was not at the Hotel du Grand Charlemagne. He had received a message from the prince, to whom he had hastened with Olivain the instant he had received it.

Chapter LXXVII.

The three Lieutenants of the Generalissimo.

The night was dark, but still the town resounded with those noises that disclose a city in a state of siege. Athos and Aramis did not proceed a hundred steps without being stopped by sentinels placed before the barricades, who demanded the watchword; and on their saying that they were going to Monsieur de Bouillon on a mission of importance a guide was given them under pretext of conducting them, but in fact as a spy over their movements.

On arriving at the Hotel de Bouillon they came across a little troop of three cavaliers, who seemed to know every possible password; for they walked without either guide or escort, and on arriving at the barricades had nothing to do but to speak to those who guarded them, who instantly let them pass with evident deference, due probably to their high birth.

On seeing them Athos and Aramis stood still.

"Oh!" cried Aramis, "do you see, count?"

"Yes," said Athos.

"Who do these three cavaliers appear to you to be?"

"What do you think, Aramis?"

"Why, they are our men."

"You are not mistaken; I recognize Monsieur de Flamarens."

"And I, Monsieur de Chatillon."

"As to the cavalier in the brown cloak——"

"It is the cardinal."

"In person."

"How the devil do they venture so near the Hotel de Bouillon?"

Athos smiled, but did not reply. Five minutes afterward they knocked at the prince's door.

This door was guarded by a sentinel and there was also a guard placed in the courtyard, ready to obey the orders of the Prince de Conti's lieutenant.

Monsieur de Bouillon had the gout, but notwithstanding his illness, which had prevented his mounting on horseback for the last month—-that is, since Paris had been besieged—he was ready to receive the Comte de la Fere and the Chevalier d'Herblay.

He was in bed, but surrounded with all the paraphernalia of war. Everywhere were swords, pistols, cuirasses, and arquebuses, and it was plain that as soon as his gout was better Monsieur de Bouillon would give a pretty tangle to the enemies of the parliament to unravel. Meanwhile, to his great regret, as he said, he was obliged to keep his bed.

"Ah, gentlemen," he cried, as the two friends entered, "you are very happy! you can ride, you can go and come and fight for the cause of the people. But I, as you see, am nailed to my bed—ah! this demon, gout—this demon, gout!"

"My lord," said Athos, "we are just arrived from England and our first concern is to inquire after your health."

"Thanks, gentlemen, thanks! As you see, my health is but indifferent. But you come from England. And King Charles is well, as I have just heard?"

"He is dead, my lord!" said Aramis.

"Pooh!" said the duke, too much astonished to believe it true.

"Dead on the scaffold; condemned by parliament."

"Impossible!"

"And executed in our presence."

"What, then, has Monsieur de Flamarens been telling me?"

"Monsieur de Flamarens?"

"Yes, he has just gone out."

Athos smiled. "With two companions?" he said.

"With two companions, yes," replied the duke. Then he added with a certain uneasiness, "Did you meet them?"

"Why, yes, I think so—in the street," said Athos; and he looked smilingly at Aramis, who looked at him with an expression of surprise.

"The devil take this gout!" cried Monsieur de Bouillon, evidently ill at ease.

"My lord," said Athos, "we admire your devotion to the cause you have espoused, in remaining at the head of the army whilst so ill, in so much pain."

"One must," replied Monsieur de Bouillon, "sacrifice one's comfort to the public good; but I confess to you I am now almost exhausted. My spirit is willing, my head is clear, but this demon, the gout, o'ercrows me. I confess, if the court would do justice to my claims and give the head of my house the title of prince, and if my brother De Turenne were reinstated in his command I would return to my estates and leave the court and parliament to settle things between themselves as they might."

"You are perfectly right, my lord."

"You think so? At this very moment the court is making overtures to me; hitherto I have repulsed them; but since such men as you assure me that I am wrong in doing so, I've a good mind to follow your advice and to accept a proposition made to me by the Duc de Chatillon just now."

"Accept it, my lord, accept it," said Aramis.

"Faith! yes. I am even sorry that this evening I almost repulsed—but there will be a conference to-morrow and we shall see."

The two friends saluted the duke.

"Go, gentlemen," he said; "you must be much fatigued after your voyage. Poor King Charles! But, after all, he was somewhat to blame in all that business and we may console ourselves with the reflection that France has no cause of reproach in the matter and did all she could to serve him."

"Oh! as to that," said Aramis, "we are witnesses. Mazarin especially——"

"Yes, do you know, I am very glad to hear you give that testimony; the cardinal has some good in him, and if he were not a foreigner—well, he would be more justly estimated. Oh! the devil take this gout!"

Athos and Aramis took their leave, but even in the ante-chamber they could still hear the duke's cries; he was evidently suffering the tortures of the damned.

When they reached the street, Aramis said:

"Well, Athos, what do you think?"

"Of whom?"

"Pardieu! of Monsieur de Bouillon."

"My friend, I think that he is much troubled with gout."

"You noticed that I didn't breathe a word as to the purpose of our visit?"

"You did well; you would have caused him an access of his disease. Let us go to Monsieur de Beaufort."

The two friends went to the Hotel de Vendome. It was ten o'clock when they arrived. The Hotel de Vendome was not less guarded than the Hotel de Bouillon, and presented as warlike an appearance. There were sentinels, a guard in the court, stacks of arms, and horses saddled. Two horsemen going out as Athos and Aramis entered were obliged to give place to them.

"Ah! ah! gentlemen," said Aramis, "decidedly it is a night for meetings. We shall be very unfortunate if, after meeting so often this evening, we should not succeed in meeting to-morrow."

"Oh, as to that, sir," replied Chatillon (for it was he who, with Flamarens, was leaving the Duc de Beaufort), "you may be assured; for if we meet by night without seeking each other, much more shall we meet by day when wishing it."

"I hope that is true," said Aramis.

"As for me, I am sure of it," said the duke.

De Flamarens and De Chatillon continued on their way and Athos and Aramis dismounted.

Hardly had they given the bridles of their horses to their lackeys and rid themselves of their cloaks when a man approached them, and after looking at them for an instant by the doubtful light of the lantern hung in the centre of the courtyard he uttered an exclamation of joy and ran to embrace them.

"Comte de la Fere!" the man cried out; "Chevalier d'Herblay! How does it happen that you are in Paris?"

"Rochefort!" cried the two friends.

"Yes! we arrived four or five days ago from the Vendomois, as you know, and we are going to give Mazarin something to do. You are still with us, I presume?"

"More than ever. And the duke?"

"Furious against the cardinal. You know his success—our dear duke? He is really king of Paris; he can't go out without being mobbed by his admirers."

"Ah! so much the better! Can we have the honor of seeing his highness?"

"I shall be proud to present you," and Rochefort walked on. Every door was opened to him. Monsieur de Beaufort was at supper, but he rose quickly on hearing the two friends announced.

"Ah!" he cried, "by Jove! you're welcome, sirs. You are coming to sup with me, are you not? Boisgoli, tell Noirmont that I have two guests. You know Noirmont, do you not? The successor of Father Marteau who makes the excellent pies you know of. Boisgoli, let him send one of his best, but not such a one as he made for La Ramee. Thank God! we don't want either rope ladders or gag-pears now."

"My lord," said Athos, "do not let us disturb you. We came merely to inquire after your health and to take your orders."

"As to my health, since it has stood five years of prison, with Monsieur de Chavigny to boot, 'tis excellent! As to my orders, since every one gives his own commands in our party, I shall end, if this goes on, by giving none at all."

"In short, my lord," said Athos, glancing at Aramis, "your highness is discontented with your party?"

"Discontented, sir! say my highness is furious! To such a degree, I assure you, though I would not say so to others, that if the queen, acknowledging the injuries she has done me, would recall my mother and give me the reversion of the admiralty, which belonged to my father and was promised me at his death, well! it would not be long before I should be training dogs to say that there were greater traitors in France than the Cardinal Mazarin!"

At this Athos and Aramis could not help exchanging not only a look but a smile; and had they not known it for a fact, this would have told them that De Chatillon and De Flamarens had been there.

"My lord," said Athos, "we are satisfied; we came here only to express our loyalty and to say that we are at your lordship's service and his most faithful servants."

"My most faithful friends, gentlemen, my most faithful friends; you have proved it. And if ever I am reconciled with the court I shall prove to you, I hope, that I remain your friend, as well as that of—what the devil are their names—D'Artagnan and Porthos?"

"D'Artagnan and Porthos."

"Ah, yes. You understand, then, Comte de la Fere, you understand, Chevalier d'Herblay, that I am altogether and always at your service."

Athos and Aramis bowed and went out.

"My dear Athos," cried Aramis, "I think you consented to accompany me only to give me a lesson—God forgive me!"

"Wait a little, Aramis; it will be time for you to perceive my motive when we have paid our visit to the coadjutor."

"Let us then go to the archiepiscopal palace," said Aramis.

They directed their horses to the city. On arriving at the cradle from which Paris sprang they found it inundated with water, and it was again necessary to take a boat. The palace rose from the bosom of the water, and to see the number of boats around it one would have fancied one's self not in Paris, but in Venice. Some of these boats were dark and mysterious, others noisy and lighted up with torches. The friends slid in through this congestion of embarkation and landed in their turn. The palace was surrounded with water, but a kind of staircase had been fixed to the lower walls; and the only difference was, that instead of entering by the doors, people entered by the windows.

Thus did Athos and Aramis make their appearance in the ante-chamber, where about a dozen noblemen were collected in waiting.

"Good heavens!" said Aramis to Athos, "does the coadjutor intend to indulge himself in the pleasure of making us cool our hearts off in his ante-chamber?"

"My dear friend, we must take people as we find them. The coadjutor is at this moment one of the seven kings of Paris, and has a court. Let us send in our names, and if he does not send us a suitable message we will leave him to his own affairs or those of France. Let us call one of these lackeys, with a demi-pistole in the left hand."

"Exactly so," cried Aramis. "Ah! if I'm not mistaken here's Bazin. Come here, fellow."

Bazin, who was crossing the ante-chamber majestically in his clerical dress, turned around to see who the impertinent gentleman was who thus addressed him; but seeing his friends he went up to them quickly and expressed delight at seeing them.

"A truce to compliments," said Aramis; "we want to see the coadjutor, and instantly, as we are in haste."

"Certainly, sir—it is not such lords as you are who are allowed to wait in the ante-chamber, only just now he has a secret conference with Monsieur de Bruy."

"De Bruy!" cried the friends, "'tis then useless our seeing monsieur the coadjutor this evening," said Aramis, "so we give it up."

And they hastened to quit the palace, followed by Bazin, who was lavish of bows and compliments.

"Well," said Athos, when Aramis and he were in the boat again, "are you beginning to be convinced that we should have done a bad turn to all these people in arresting Mazarin?"

"You are wisdom incarnate, Athos," Aramis replied.

What had especially been observed by the two friends was the little interest taken by the court of France in the terrible events which had occurred in England, which they thought should have arrested the attention of all Europe.

In fact, aside from a poor widow and a royal orphan who wept in the corner of the Louvre, no one appeared to be aware that Charles I. had ever lived and that he had perished on the scaffold.

The two friends made an appointment for ten o'clock on the following day; for though the night was well advanced when they reached the door of the hotel, Aramis said that he had certain important visits to make and left Athos to enter alone.

At ten o'clock the next day they met again. Athos had been out since six o'clock.

"Well, have you any news?" Athos asked.

"Nothing. No one has seen D'Artagnan and Porthos has not appeared. Have you anything?"

"Nothing."

"The devil!" said Aramis.

"In fact," said Athos, "this delay is not natural; they took the shortest route and should have arrived before we did."

"Add to that D'Artagnan's rapidity in action and that he is not the man to lose an hour, knowing that we were expecting him."

"He expected, you will remember, to be here on the fifth."

"And here we are at the ninth. This evening the margin of possible delay expires."

"What do you think should be done," asked Athos, "if we have no news of them to-night?"

"Pardieu! we must go and look for them."

"All right," said Athos.

"But Raoul?" said Aramis.

A light cloud passed over the count's face.

"Raoul gives me much uneasiness," he said. "He received yesterday a message from the Prince de Condé; he went to meet him at Saint Cloud and has not returned."

"Have you seen Madame de Chevreuse?"

"She was not at home. And you, Aramis, you were going, I think, to visit Madame de Longueville."

"I did go there."

"Well?"

"She was no longer there, but she had left her new address."

"Where was she?"

"Guess; I give you a thousand chances."

"How should I know where the most beautiful and active of the Frondists was at midnight? for I presume it was when you left me that you went to visit her."

"At the Hotel de Ville, my dear fellow."

"What! at the Hotel de Ville? Has she, then, been appointed provost of merchants?"

"No; but she has become queen of Paris, ad interim, and since she could not venture at once to establish herself in the Palais Royal or the Tuileries, she is installed at the Hotel de Ville, where she is on the point of giving an heir or an heiress to that dear duke."

"You didn't tell me of that, Aramis."

"Really? It was my forgetfulness then; pardon me."

"Now," asked Athos, "what are we to do with ourselves till evening? Here we are without occupation, it seems to me."

"You forget, my friend, that we have work cut out for us in the direction of Charenton; I hope to see Monsieur de Chatillon, whom I've hated for a long time, there."

"Why have you hated him?"

"Because he is the brother of Coligny."

"Ah, true! he who presumed to be a rival of yours, for which he was severely punished; that ought to satisfy you."

"'Yes, but it does not; I am rancorous—the only stigma that proves me to be a churchman. Do you understand? You understand that you are in no way obliged to go with me."

"Come, now," said Athos, "you are joking."

"In that case, my dear friend, if you are resolved to accompany me there is no time to lose; the drum beats; I observed cannon on the road; I saw the citizens in order of battle on the Place of the Hotel de Ville; certainly the fight will be in the direction of Charenton, as the Duc de Chatillon said."

"I supposed," said Athos, "that last night's conferences would modify those warlike arrangements."

"No doubt; but they will fight, none the less, if only to mask the conferences."

"Poor creatures!" said Athos, "who are going to be killed, in order that Monsieur de Bouillon may have his estate at Sedan restored to him, that the reversion of the admiralty may be given to the Duc de Beaufort, and that the coadjutor may be made a cardinal."

"Come, come, dear Athos, confess that you would not be so philosophical if your Raoul were to be involved in this affair."

"Perhaps you speak the truth, Aramis."

"Well, let us go, then, where the fighting is, for that is the most likely place to meet with D'Artagnan, Porthos, and possibly even Raoul. Stop, there are a fine body of citizens passing; quite attractive, by Jupiter! and their captain—see! he has the true military style."

"What, ho!" said Grimaud.

"What?" asked Athos.

"Planchet, sir."

"Lieutenant yesterday," said Aramis, "captain to-day, colonel, doubtless, to-morrow; in a fortnight the fellow will be marshal of France."

"Question him about the fight," said Athos.

Planchet, prouder than ever of his new duties, deigned to explain to the two gentlemen that he was ordered to take up his position on the Place Royale with two hundred men, forming the rear of the army of Paris, and to march on Charenton when necessary.

"This day will be a warm one," said Planchet, in a warlike tone.

"No doubt," said Aramis, "but it is far from here to the enemy."

"Sir, the distance will be diminished," said a subordinate.

Aramis saluted, then turning toward Athos:

"I don't care to camp on the Place Royale with all these people," he said. "Shall we go forward? We shall see better what is going on."

"And then Monsieur de Chatillon will not come to the Place Royale to look for you. Come, then, my friend, we will go forward."

"Haven't you something to say to Monsieur de Flamarens on your own account?"

"My friend," said Athos, "I have made a resolution never to draw my sword save when it is absolutely necessary."

"And how long ago was that?"

"When I last drew my poniard."

"Ah! Good! another souvenir of Monsieur Mordaunt. Well, my friend, nothing now is lacking except that you should feel remorse for having killed that fellow."

"Hush!" said Athos, putting a finger on his lips, with the sad smile peculiar to him; "let us talk no more of Mordaunt—it will bring bad luck." And Athos set forward toward Charenton, followed closely by Aramis.

Chapter LXXVIII.

The Battle of Charenton.

As Athos and Aramis proceeded, and passed different companies on the road, they became aware that they were arriving near the field of battle.

"Ah! my friend!" cried Athos, suddenly, "where have you brought us? I fancy I perceive around us faces of different officers in the royal army; is not that the Duc de Chatillon himself coming toward us with his brigadiers?"

"Good-day, sirs," said the duke, advancing; "you are puzzled by what you see here, but one word will explain everything. There is now a truce and a conference. The prince, Monsieur de Retz, the Duc de Beaufort, the Duc de Bouillon, are talking over public affairs. Now one of two things must happen: either matters will not be arranged, or they will be arranged, in which last case I shall be relieved of my command and we shall still meet again."

"Sir," said Aramis, "you speak to the point. Allow me to ask you a question: Where are the plenipotentiaries?"

"At Charenton, in the second house on the right on entering from the direction of Paris."

"And was this conference arranged beforehand?"

"No, gentlemen, it seems to be the result of certain propositions which Mazarin made last night to the Parisians."

Athos and Aramis exchanged smiles; for they well knew what those propositions were, to whom they had been made and who had made them.

"And that house in which the plenipotentiaries are," asked Athos, "belongs to——"

"To Monsieur de Chanleu, who commands your troops at Charenton. I say your troops, for I presume that you gentlemen are Frondeurs?"

"Yes, almost," said Aramis.

"We are for the king and the princes," added Athos.

"We must understand each other," said the duke. "The king is with us and his generals are the Duke of Orleans and the Prince de Condé, although I must add 'tis almost impossible now to know to which party any one belongs."

"Yes," answered Athos, "but his right place is in our ranks, with the Prince de Conti, De Beaufort, D'Elbeuf, and De Bouillon; but, sir, supposing that the conference is broken off—are you going to try to take Charenton?"

"Such are my orders."

"Sir, since you command the cavalry——"

"Pardon me, I am commander-in-chief."

"So much the better. You must know all your officers—I mean those more distinguished."

"Why, yes, very nearly."

"Will you then kindly tell me if you have in your command the Chevalier d'Artagnan, lieutenant in the musketeers?"

"No, sir, he is not with us; he left Paris more than six weeks ago and is believed to have gone on a mission to England."

"I knew that, but I supposed he had returned."

"No, sir; no one has seen him. I can answer positively on that point, for the musketeers belong to our forces and Monsieur de Cambon, the substitute for Monsieur d'Artagnan, still holds his place."

The two friends looked at each other.

"You see," said Athos.

"It is strange," said Aramis.

"It is absolutely certain that some misfortune has happened to them on the way."

"If we have no news of them this evening, to-morrow we must start."

Athos nodded affirmatively, then turning:

"And Monsieur de Bragelonne, a young man fifteen years of age, attached to the Prince de Condé—has he the honor of being known to you?" diffident in allowing the sarcastic Aramis to perceive how strong were his paternal feelings.

"Yes, surely, he came with the prince; a charming young man; he is one of your friends then, monsieur le comte?"

"Yes, sir," answered Athos, agitated; "so much so that I wish to see him if possible."

"Quite possible, sir; do me the favor to accompany me and I will conduct you to headquarters."

"Halloo, there!" cried Aramis, turning around; "what a noise behind us!"

"A body of cavaliers is coming toward us," said Chatillon.

"I recognize the coadjutor by his Frondist hat."

"And I the Duc de Beaufort by his white plume of ostrich feathers."

"They are coming, full gallop; the prince is with them—ah! he is leaving them!"

"They are beating the rappel!" cried Chatillon; "we must discover what is going on."

In fact, they saw the soldiers running to their arms; the trumpets sounded; the drums beat; the Duc de Beaufort drew his sword. On his side the prince sounded a rappel and all the officers of the royalist army, mingling momentarily with the Parisian troops, ran to him.

"Gentlemen," cried Chatillon, "the truce is broken, that is evident; they are going to fight; go, then, into Charenton, for I shall begin in a short time—there's a signal from the prince!"

The cornet of a troop had in fact just raised the standard of the prince.

"Farewell, till the next time we meet," cried Chatillon, and he set off, full gallop.

Athos and Aramis turned also and went to salute the coadjutor and the Duc de Beaufort. As to the Duc de Bouillon, he had such a fit of gout as obliged him to return to Paris in a litter; but his place was well filled by the Duc d'Elbeuf and his four sons, ranged around him like a staff. Meantime, between Charenton and the royal army was left a space which looked ready to serve as a last resting place for the dead.

"Gentlemen," cried the coadjutor, tightening his sash, which he wore, after the fashion of the ancient military prelates, over his archiepiscopal simar, "there's the enemy approaching. Let us save them half of their journey."

And without caring whether he were followed or not he set off; his regiment, which bore the name of the regiment of Corinth, from the name of his archbishopric, darted after him and began the fight. Monsieur de Beaufort sent his cavalry, toward Etampes and Monsieur de Chanleu, who defended the place, was ready to resist an assault, or if the enemy were repulsed, to attempt a sortie.

The battle soon became general and the coadjutor performed miracles of valor. His proper vocation had always been the sword and he was delighted whenever he could draw it from the scabbard, no matter for whom or against whom.

Chanleu, whose fire at one time repulsed the royal regiment, thought that the moment was come to pursue it; but it was reformed and led again to the charge by the Duc de Chatillon in person. This charge was so fierce, so skillfully conducted, that Chanleu was almost surrounded. He commanded a retreat, which began, step by step, foot by foot; unhappily, in an instant he fell, mortally wounded. De Chatillon saw him fall and announced it in a loud voice to his men, which raised their spirits and completely disheartened their enemies, so that every man thought only of his own safety and tried to gain the trenches, where the coadjutor was trying to reform his disorganized regiment.

Suddenly a squadron of cavalry galloped up to encounter the royal troops, who were entering, pele-mele, the intrenchments with the fugitives. Athos and Aramis charged at the head of their squadrons; Aramis with sword and pistol in his hands, Athos with his sword in his scabbard, his pistol in his saddle-bags; calm and cool as if on the parade, except that his noble and beautiful countenance became sad as he saw slaughtered so many men who were sacrificed on the one side to the obstinacy of royalty and on the other to the personal rancor of the princes. Aramis, on the contrary, struck right and left and was almost delirious with excitement. His bright eyes kindled, and his mouth, so finely formed, assumed a wicked smile; every blow he aimed was sure, and his pistol finished the deed—annihilated the wounded wretch who tried to rise again.

On the opposite side two cavaliers, one covered with a gilt cuirass, the other wearing simply a buff doublet, from which fell the sleeves of a vest of blue velvet, charged in front. The cavalier in the gilt cuirass fell upon Aramis and struck a blow that Aramis parried with his wonted skill.

"Ah! 'tis you, Monsieur de Chatillon," cried the chevalier; "welcome to you—I expected you."

"I hope I have not made you wait too long, sir," said the duke; "at all events, here I am."

"Monsieur de Chatillon," cried Aramis, taking from his saddle-bags a second pistol, "I think if your pistols have been discharged you are a dead man."

"Thank God, sir, they are not!"

And the duke, pointing his pistol at Aramis, fired. But Aramis bent his head the instant he saw the duke's finger press the trigger and the ball passed without touching him.

"Oh! you've missed me," cried Aramis, "but I swear to Heaven! I will not miss you."

"If I give you time!" cried the duke, spurring on his horse and rushing upon him with his drawn sword.

Aramis awaited him with that terrible smile which was peculiar to him on such occasions, and Athos, who saw the duke advancing toward Aramis with the rapidity of lightning, was just going to cry out, "Fire! fire, then!" when the shot was fired. De Chatillon opened his arms and fell back on the crupper of his horse.

The ball had entered his breast through a notch in the cuirass.

"I am a dead man," he said, and fell from his horse to the ground.

"I told you this, I am now grieved I have kept my word. Can I be of any use to you?"

Chatillon made a sign with his hand and Aramis was about to dismount when he received a violent shock; 'twas a thrust from a sword, but his cuirass turned aside the blow.

He turned around and seized his new antagonist by the wrist, when he started back, exclaiming, "Raoul!"

"Raoul?" cried Athos.

The young man recognized at the same instant the voices of his father and the Chevalier d'Herblay; two officers in the Parisian forces rushed at that instant on Raoul, but Aramis protected him with his sword.

"My prisoner!" he cried.

Athos took his son's horse by the bridle and led him forth out of the melee.

At this crisis of the battle, the prince, who had been seconding De Chatillon in the second line, appeared in the midst of the fight; his eagle eye made him known and his blows proclaimed the hero.

On seeing him, the regiment of Corinth, which the coadjutor had not been able to reorganize in spite of all his efforts, threw itself into the midst of the Parisian forces, put them into confusion and re-entered Charenton flying. The coadjutor, dragged along with his fugitive forces, passed near the group formed by Athos, Raoul and Aramis. Aramis could not in his jealousy avoid being pleased at the coadjutor's misfortune, and was about to utter some bon mot more witty than correct, when Athos stopped him.

"On, on!" he cried, "this is no moment for compliments; or rather, back, for the battle seems to be lost by the Frondeurs."

"It is a matter of indifference to me," said Aramis; "I came here only to meet De Chatillon; I have met him, I am contented; 'tis something to have met De Chatillon in a duel!"

"And besides, we have a prisoner," said Athos, pointing to Raoul.

The three cavaliers continued their road on full gallop.

"What were you doing in the battle, my friend?" inquired Athos of the youth; "'twas not your right place, I think, as you were not equipped for an engagement!"

"I had no intention of fighting to-day, sir; I was charged, indeed, with a mission to the cardinal and had set out for Rueil, when, seeing Monsieur de Chatillon charge, an invincible desire possessed me to charge at his side. It was then that he told me two cavaliers of the Parisian army were seeking me and named the Comte de la Fere."

"What! you knew we were there and yet wished to kill your friend the chevalier?"

"I did not recognize the chevalier in armor, sir!" said Raoul, blushing; "though I might have known him by his skill and coolness in danger."

"Thank you for the compliment, my young friend," replied Aramis, "we can see from whom you learned courtesy. Then you were going to Rueil?"

"Yes! I have a despatch from the prince to his eminence."

"You must still deliver it," said Athos.

"No false generosity, count! the fate of our friends, to say nothing of our own, is perhaps in that very despatch."

"This young man must not, however, fail in his duty," said Athos.

"In the first place, count, this youth is our prisoner; you seem to forget that. What I propose to do is fair in war; the vanquished must not be dainty in the choice of means. Give me the despatch, Raoul."

The young man hesitated and looked at Athos as if seeking to read in his eyes a rule of conduct.

"Give him the despatch, Raoul! you are the chevalier's prisoner."

Raoul gave it up reluctantly; Aramis instantly seized and read it.

"You," he said, "you, who are so trusting, read and reflect that there is something in this letter important for us to see."

Athos took the letter, frowning, but an idea that he should find something in this letter about D'Artagnan conquered his unwillingness to read it.

"My lord, I shall send this evening to your eminence in order to reinforce the troop of Monsieur de Comminges, the ten men you demand. They are good soldiers, fit to confront the two violent adversaries whose address and resolution your eminence is fearful of."

"Oh!" cried Athos.

"Well," said Aramis, "what think you about these two enemies whom it requires, besides Comminges's troop, ten good soldiers to confront; are they not as like as two drops of water to D'Artagnan and Porthos?"

"We'll search Paris all day long," said Athos, "and if we have no news this evening we will return to the road to Picardy; and I feel no doubt that, thanks to D'Artagnan's ready invention, we shall then find some clew which will solve our doubts."

"Yes, let us search Paris and especially inquire of Planchet if he has yet heard from his former master."

"That poor Planchet! You speak of him very much at your ease, Aramis; he has probably been killed. All those fighting citizens went out to battle and they have been massacred."

It was, then, with a sentiment of uneasiness whether Planchet, who alone could give them information, was alive or dead, that the friends returned to the Place Royale; to their great surprise they found the citizens still encamped there, drinking and bantering each other, although, doubtless, mourned by their families, who thought they were at Charenton in the thickest of the fighting.

Athos and Aramis again questioned Planchet, but he had seen nothing of D'Artagnan; they wished to take Planchet with them, but he could not leave his troop, who at five o'clock returned home, saying that they were returning from the battle, whereas they had never lost sight of the bronze equestrian statue of Louis XIII.

Chapter LXXIX.

The Road to Picardy.

On leaving Paris, Athos and Aramis well knew that they would be encountering great danger; but we know that for men like these there could be no question of danger. Besides, they felt that the *dénouement* of this second Odyssey was at hand and that there remained but a single effort to make.

Besides, there was no tranquillity in Paris itself. Provisions began to fail, and whenever one of the Prince de Conti's generals wished to gain more influence he got up a little popular tumult, which he put down again, and thus for the moment gained a superiority over his colleagues.

In one of these risings, the Duc de Beaufort pillaged the house and library of Mazarin, in order to give the populace, as he put it, something to gnaw at. Athos and Aramis left Paris after this coup-d'etat, which took place on the very evening of the day in which the Parisians had been beaten at Charenton.

They quitted Paris, beholding it abandoned to extreme want, bordering on famine; agitated by fear, torn by faction. Parisians and Frondeurs as they were, the two friends expected to find the same misery, the same fears, the same intrigue in the enemy's camp; but what was their surprise, after passing Saint Denis, to hear that at Saint Germain people were singing and laughing, and leading generally cheerful lives. The two gentlemen traveled by byways in order not to encounter the Mazarinists scattered about the Isle of France, and also to escape the Frondeurs, who were in possession of Normandy and who never failed to conduct captives to the Duc de Longueville, in order that he might ascertain whether they were friends or foes. Having escaped these dangers, they returned by the main road to Boulogne, at Abbeville, and followed it step by step, examining every track.

Nevertheless, they were still in a state of uncertainty. Several inns were visited by them, several innkeepers questioned, without a single clew being given to guide their inquiries, when at Montreuil Athos felt upon the table that something rough was touching his delicate fingers. He turned up the cloth and found these hieroglyphics carved upon the wood with a knife:

"Port.... D'Art.... 2d February."

"This is capital!" said Athos to Aramis, "we were to have slept here, but we cannot—we must push on." They rode forward and reached Abbeville. There the great number of inns puzzled them; they could not go to all; how could they guess in which those whom they were seeking had stayed?

"Trust me," said Aramis, "do not expect to find anything in Abbeville. If we had only been looking for Porthos, Porthos would have stationed himself in one of the finest hotels and we could easily have traced him. But D'Artagnan is devoid of such weaknesses. Porthos would have found it very difficult even to make him see that he was dying of hunger; he has gone on his road as inexorable as fate and we must seek him somewhere else."

They continued their route. It had now become a weary and almost hopeless task, and had it not been for the threefold motives of honor, friendship and gratitude, implanted in their hearts, our two travelers would have given up many a time their rides over the sand, their interrogatories of the peasantry and their close inspection of faces.

They proceeded thus to Peronne.

Athos began to despair. His noble nature felt that their ignorance was a sort of reflection upon them. They had not looked carefully enough for their lost friends. They had not shown sufficient pertinacity in their inquiries. They were willing and ready to retrace their steps, when, in crossing the suburb which leads to the gates of the town, upon a white wall which was at the corner of a street turning around the rampart, Athos cast his eyes upon a drawing in black chalk, which represented, with the awkwardness of a first attempt, two cavaliers riding furiously; one of them carried a roll of paper on which were written these words: "They are following us."

"Oh!" exclaimed Athos, "here it is, as clear as day; pursued as he was, D'Artagnan would not have tarried here five minutes had he been pressed very closely, which gives us hopes that he may have succeeded in escaping."

Aramis shook his head.

"Had he escaped we should either have seen him or have heard him spoken of."

"You are right, Aramis, let us travel on."

To describe the impatience and anxiety of these two friends would be impossible. Uneasiness took possession of the tender, constant heart of Athos, and fearful forecasts were the torment of the impulsive Aramis. They galloped on for two or three hours as furiously as the cavaliers on the wall. All at once, in a narrow pass, they perceived that the road was partially barricaded by an enormous stone. It had evidently been rolled across the pass by some arm of giant strength.

Aramis stopped.

"Oh!" he said, looking at the stone, "this is the work of either Hercules or Porthos. Let us get down, count, and examine this rock."

They both alighted. The stone had been brought with the evident intention of barricading the road, but some one having perceived the obstacle had partially turned it aside.

With the assistance of Blaisois and Grimaud the friends succeeded in turning the stone over. Upon the side next the ground were scratched the following words:

"Eight of the light dragoons are pursuing us. If we reach Compiegne we shall stop at the Peacock. It is kept by a friend of ours."

"At last we have something definite," said Athos; "let us go to the Peacock."

"Yes," answered Aramis, "but if we are to get there we must rest our horses, for they are almost broken-winded."

Aramis was right; they stopped at the first tavern and made each horse swallow a double quantity of corn steeped in wine; they gave them three hours' rest and then set off again. The men themselves were almost dead with fatigue, but hope supported them.

In six hours they reached Compiegne and alighted at the Peacock. The host proved to be a worthy man, as bald as a Chinaman. They asked him if some time ago he had not received in his house two gentlemen who were pursued by dragoons; without answering he went out and brought in the blade of a rapier.

"Do you know that?" he asked.

Athos merely glanced at it.

"'Tis D'Artagnan's sword," he said.

"Does it belong to the smaller or to the larger of the two?" asked the host.

"To the smaller."

"I see that you are the friends of these gentlemen."

"Well, what has happened to them?"

"They were pursued by eight of the light dragoons, who rode into the courtyard before they had time to close the gate."

"Eight!" said Aramis; "it surprises me that two such heroes as Porthos and D'Artagnan should have allowed themselves to be arrested by eight men."

"The eight men would doubtless have failed had they not been assisted by twenty soldiers of the regiment of Italians in the king's service, who are in garrison in this town so that your friends were overpowered by numbers."

"Arrested, were they?" inquired Athos; "is it known why?"

"No, sir, they were carried off instantly, and had not even time to tell me why; but as soon as they were gone I found this broken sword-blade, as I was helping to raise two dead men and five or six wounded ones."

"'Tis still a consolation that they were not wounded," said Aramis.

"Where were they taken?" asked Athos.

"Toward the town of Louvres," was the reply.

The two friends having agreed to leave Blaisois and Grimaud at Compiegne with the horses, resolved to take post horses; and having snatched a hasty dinner they continued their journey to Louvres. Here they found only one inn, in which was consumed a liqueur which preserves its reputation to our time and which is still made in that town.

"Let us alight here," said Athos. "D'Artagnan will not have let slip an opportunity of drinking a glass of this liqueur, and at the same time leaving some trace of himself."

They went into the town and asked for two glasses of liqueur, at the counter—as their friends must have done before them. The counter was covered with a plate of pewter; upon this plate was written with the point of a large pin: "Rueil... D.."

"They went to Rueil," cried Aramis.

"Let us go to Rueil," said Athos.

"It is to throw ourselves into the wolf's jaws," said Aramis.

"Had I been as great a friend of Jonah as I am of D'Artagnan I should have followed him even into the inside of the whale itself; and you would have done the same, Aramis."

"Certainly—but you make me out better than I am, dear count. Had I been alone I should scarcely have gone to Rueil without great caution. But where you go, I go."

They then set off for Rueil. Here the deputies of the parliament had just arrived, in order to enter upon those famous conferences which were to last three weeks, and produced eventually that shameful peace, at the conclusion of which the prince was arrested. Rueil was crowded with advocates, presidents and councillors, who came from the Parisians, and, on the side of the court, with officers and guards; it was therefore easy, in the midst of this confusion, to remain as unobserved as any one might wish; besides, the conferences implied a truce, and to arrest two gentlemen, even Frondeurs, at this time, would have been an attack on the rights of the people.

The two friends mingled with the crowd and fancied that every one was occupied with the same thought that tormented them. They expected to hear some mention made of D'Artagnan or of Porthos, but every one was engrossed by articles and reforms. It was the advice of Athos to go straight to the minister.

"My friend," said Aramis, "take care; our safety lies in our obscurity. If we were to make ourselves known we should be sent to rejoin our friends in some deep ditch, from which the devil himself could not take us out. Let us try not to find them out by accident, but from our notions. Arrested at Compiegne, they have been carried to Rueil; at Rueil they have been questioned by the cardinal, who has either kept them near him or sent them to Saint Germain. As to the Bastile, they are not there, though the Bastile is especially for the Frondeurs. They are not dead, for the death of D'Artagnan would make a sensation. As for Porthos, I believe him to be eternal, like God, although less patient. Do not let us despond, but wait at Rueil, for my conviction is that they are at Rueil. But what ails you? You are pale."

"It is this," answered Athos, with a trembling voice.

"I remember that at the Castle of Rueil the Cardinal Richelieu had some horrible 'oubliettes' constructed."

"Oh! never fear," said Aramis. "Richelieu was a gentleman, our equal in birth, our superior in position. He could, like the king, touch the greatest of us on the head, and touching them make such heads shake on their shoulders. But Mazarin is a low-born rogue, who can at the most take us by the collar, like an archer. Be calm—for I am sure that D'Artagnan and Porthos are at Rueil, alive and well."

"But," resumed Athos, "I recur to my first proposal. I know no better means than to act with candor. I shall seek, not Mazarin, but the queen, and say to her, 'Madame, restore to us your two servants and our two friends.'"

Aramis shook his head.

"'Tis a last resource, but let us not employ it till it is imperatively called for; let us rather persevere in our researches."

They continued their inquiries and at last met with a light dragoon who had formed one of the guard which had escorted D'Artagnan to Rueil.

Athos, however, perpetually recurred to his proposed interview with the queen.

"In order to see the queen," said Aramis, "we must first see the cardinal; and when we have seen the cardinal—remember what I tell you, Athos—we shall be reunited to our friends, but not in the way you wish. Now, that way of joining them is not very attractive to me, I confess. Let us act in freedom, that we may act well and quickly."

"I shall go," he said, "to the queen."

"Well, then," answered Aramis, "pray tell me a day or two beforehand, that I may take that opportunity of going to Paris."

"To whom?"

"Zounds! how do I know? perhaps to Madame de Longueville. She is all-powerful yonder; she will help me. But send me word should you be arrested, for then I will return directly."

"Why do you not take your chance and be arrested with me?"

"No, I thank you."

"Should we, by being arrested, be all four together again, we should not, I am not sure, be twenty-four hours in prison without getting free."

"My friend, since I killed Chatillon, adored of the ladies of Saint Germain, I am too great a celebrity not to fear a prison doubly. The queen is likely to follow Mazarin's counsels and to have me tried."

"Do you think she loves this Italian so much as they say she does?"

"Did she not love an Englishman?"

"My friend, she is a woman."

"No, no, you are deceived—she is a queen."

"Dear friend, I shall sacrifice myself and go and see Anne of Austria."

"Adieu, Athos, I am going to raise an army."

"For what purpose?"

"To come back and besiege Rueil."

"Where shall we meet again?"

"At the foot of the cardinal's gallows."

The two friends departed—Aramis to return to Paris, Athos to take measures preparatory to an interview with the queen.

Chapter LXXX.

The Gratitude of Anne of Austria.

Athos found much less difficulty than he had expected in obtaining an audience of Anne of Austria. It was granted, and was to take place after her morning's "levee," at which, in accordance with his rights of birth, he was entitled to be present. A vast crowd filled the apartments of Saint Germain. Anne had never at the Louvre had so large a court; but this crowd represented chiefly the second class of nobility, while the Prince de Conti, the Duc de Beaufort and the coadjutor assembled around them the first nobility of France.

The greatest possible gayety prevailed at court. The particular characteristic of this was that more songs were made than cannons fired during its continuance. The court made songs on the Parisians and the Parisians on the court; and the casualties, though not mortal, were painful, as are all wounds inflicted by the weapon of ridicule.

In the midst of this seeming hilarity, nevertheless, people's minds were uneasy. Was Mazarin to remain the favorite and minister of the queen? Was he to be carried back by the wind which had blown him there? Every one hoped so, so that the minister felt that all around him, beneath the homage of the courtiers, lay a fund of hatred, ill disguised by fear and interest. He felt ill at ease and at a loss what to do.

Condé himself, whilst fighting for him, lost no opportunity of ridiculing, of humbling him. The queen, on whom he threw himself as sole support, seemed to him now not much to be relied upon.

When the hour appointed for the audience arrived Athos was obliged to stay until the queen, who was waited upon by a new deputation from Paris, had consulted with her minister as to the propriety and manner of receiving them. All were fully engrossed with the affairs of the day; Athos could not therefore have chosen a more inauspicious moment to speak of his friends— poor atoms, lost in that raging whirlwind.

But Athos was a man of inflexible determination; he firmly adhered to a purpose once formed, when it seemed to him to spring from conscience and to be prompted by a sense of duty. He insisted on being introduced, saying that although he was not a deputy from Monsieur de Conti, or Monsieur de Beaufort, or Monsieur de Bouillon, or Monsieur d'Elbeuf, or the coadjutor, or Madame de Longueville, or Broussel, or the Parliament, and although he had come on his own private account, he nevertheless had things to say to her majesty of the utmost importance.

The conference being finished, the queen summoned him to her cabinet.

Athos was introduced and announced by name. It was a name that too often resounded in her majesty's ears and too often vibrated in her heart for Anne of Austria not to recognize it; yet she remained impassive, looking at him with that fixed stare which is tolerated only in women who are queens, either by the power of beauty or by the right of birth.

"It is then a service which you propose to render us, count?" asked Anne of Austria, after a moment's silence.

"Yes, madame, another service," said Athos, shocked that the queen did not seem to recognize him.

Athos had a noble heart, and made, therefore, but a poor courtier.

Anne frowned. Mazarin, who was sitting at a table folding up papers, as if he had only been a secretary of state, looked up.

"Speak," said the queen.

Mazarin turned again to his papers.

"Madame," resumed Athos, "two of my friends, named D'Artagnan and Monsieur du Vallon, sent to England by the cardinal, suddenly disappeared when they set foot on the shores of France; no one knows what has become of them."

"Well?" said the queen.

"I address myself, therefore, first to the benevolence of your majesty, that I may know what has become of my friends, reserving to myself, if necessary, the right of appealing hereafter to your justice."

"Sir," replied Anne, with a degree of haughtiness which to certain persons became impertinence, "this is the reason that you trouble me in the midst of so many absorbing concerns! an affair for the police! Well, sir, you ought to know that we no longer have a police, since we are no longer at Paris."

"I think your majesty will have no need to apply to the police to know where my friends are, but that if you will deign to interrogate the cardinal he can reply without any further inquiry than into his own recollections."

"But, God forgive me!" cried Anne, with that disdainful curl of the lips peculiar to her, "I believe that you are yourself interrogating."

"Yes, madame, here I have a right to do so, for it concerns Monsieur d'Artagnan---d'Artagnan," he repeated, in such a manner as to bow the regal brow with recollections of the weak and erring woman.

The cardinal saw that it was now high time to come to the assistance of Anne.

"Sir," he said, "I can tell you what is at present unknown to her majesty. These individuals are under arrest. They disobeyed orders."

"I beg of your majesty, then," said Athos, calmly and not replying to Mazarin, "to quash these arrests of Messieurs d'Artagnan and du Vallon."

"What you ask is merely an affair of discipline and does not concern me," said the queen.

"Monsieur d'Artagnan never made such an answer as that when the service of your majesty was concerned," said Athos, bowing with great dignity. He was going toward the door when Mazarin stopped him.

"You, too, have been in England, sir?" he said, making a sign to the queen, who was evidently going to issue a severe order.

"I was a witness of the last hours of Charles I. Poor king! culpable, at the most, of weakness, how cruelly punished by his subjects! Thrones are at this time shaken and it is to little purpose for devoted hearts to serve the interests of princes. This is the second time that Monsieur d'Artagnan has been in England. He went the first time to save the honor of a great queen; the second, to avert the death of a great king."

"Sir," said Anne to Mazarin, with an accent from which daily habits of dissimulation could not entirely chase the real expression, "see if we can do something for these gentlemen."

"I wish to do, madame, all that your majesty pleases."

"Do what Monsieur de la Fere requests; that is your name, is it not, sir?"

"I have another name, madame—I am called Athos."

"Madame," said Mazarin, with a smile, "you may rest easy; your wishes shall be fulfilled."

"You hear, sir?" said the queen.

"Yes, madame, I expected nothing less from the justice of your majesty. May I not go and see my friends?"

"Yes, sir, you shall see them. But, apropos, you belong to the Fronde, do you not?"

"Madame, I serve the king."

"Yes, in your own way."

"My way is the way of all gentlemen, and I know only one way," answered Athos, haughtily.

"Go, sir, then," said the queen; "you have obtained what you wish and we know all we desire to know."

Scarcely, however, had the tapestry closed behind Athos when she said to Mazarin:

"Cardinal, desire them to arrest that insolent fellow before he leaves the court."

"Your majesty," answered Mazarin, "desires me to do only what I was going to ask you to let me do. These bravoes who resuscitate in our epoch the traditions of another reign are troublesome; since there are two of them already there, let us add a third."

Athos was not altogether the queen's dupe, but he was not a man to run away on suspicion—above all, when distinctly told that he should see his friends again. He waited, then, in the ante-chamber with impatience, till he should be conducted to them.

He walked to the window and looked into the court. He saw the deputation from the Parisians enter it; they were coming to assign the definitive place for the conference and to make their bow to the queen. A very imposing escort awaited them without the gates.

Athos was looking on attentively, when some one touched him softly on the shoulder.

"Ah! Monsieur de Comminges," he said.

"Yes, count, and charged with a commission for which I beg of you to accept my excuses."

"What is it?"

"Be so good as to give me up your sword, count."

Athos smiled and opened the window.

"Aramis!" he cried.

A gentleman turned around. Athos fancied he had seen him among the crowd. It was Aramis. He bowed with great friendship to the count.

"Aramis," cried Athos, "I am arrested."

"Good," replied Aramis, calmly.

"Sir," said Athos, turning to Comminges and giving him politely his sword by the hilt, "here is my sword; have the kindness to keep it safely for me until I quit my prison. I prize it—it was given to my ancestor by King Francis I. In his time they armed gentlemen, not disarmed them. Now, whither do you conduct me?"

"Into my room first," replied Comminges; "the queen will ultimately decide your place of domicile."

Athos followed Comminges without saying a single word.

Chapter LXXXI.

Cardinal Mazarin as King.

The arrest produced no sensation, indeed was almost unknown, and scarcely interrupted the course of events. To the deputation it was formally announced that the queen would receive it.

Accordingly, it was admitted to the presence of Anne, who, silent and lofty as ever, listened to the speeches and complaints of the deputies; but when they had finished their harangues not one of them could say, so calm remained her face, whether or no she had heard them.

On the other hand, Mazarin, present at that audience, heard very well what those deputies demanded. It was purely and simply his removal, in terms clear and precise.

The discourse being finished, the queen remained silent.

"Gentlemen," said Mazarin, "I join with you in supplicating the queen to put an end to the miseries of her subjects. I have done all in my power to ameliorate them and yet the belief of the public, you say, is that they proceed from me, an unhappy foreigner, who has been unable to please the French. Alas! I have never been understood, and no wonder. I succeeded a man of the most sublime genius that ever upheld the sceptre of France. The memory of Richelieu annihilates me. In vain—were I an ambitious man—should I struggle against such remembrances as he has left; but that I am not ambitious I am going to prove to you. I own myself conquered. I shall obey the wishes of the people. If Paris has injuries to complain of, who has not some wrongs to be redressed? Paris has been sufficiently punished; enough blood has flowed, enough misery has humbled a town deprived of its king and of justice. 'Tis not for me, a private individual, to disunite a queen from her kingdom. Since you demand my resignation, I retire."

"Then," said Aramis, in his neighbor's ear, "the conferences are over. There is nothing to do but to send Monsieur Mazarin to the most distant frontier and to take care that he does not return even by that, nor any other entrance into France."

"One instant, sir," said the man in a gown, whom he addressed; "a plague on't! how fast you go! one may soon see that you're a soldier. There's the article of remunerations and indemnifications to be discussed and set to rights."

"Chancellor," said the queen, turning to Seguier, our old acquaintance, "you will open the conferences. They can take place at Rueil. The cardinal has said several things which have agitated me, therefore I will not speak more fully now. As to his going or staying, I feel too much gratitude to the cardinal not to leave him free in all his actions; he shall do what he wishes to do."

A transient pallor overspread the speaking countenance of the prime minister; he looked at the queen with anxiety. Her face was so passionless, that he, as every one else present, was incapable of reading her thoughts.

"But," added the queen, "in awaiting the cardinal's decision let there be, if you please, a reference to the king only."

The deputies bowed and left the room.

"What!" exclaimed the queen, when the last of them had quitted the apartment, "you would yield to these limbs of the law—these advocates?"

"To promote your majesty's welfare, madame," replied Mazarin, fixing his penetrating eyes on the queen, "there is no sacrifice that I would not make."

Anne dropped her head and fell into one of those reveries so habitual with her. A recollection of Athos came into her mind. His fearless deportment, his words, so firm, yet dignified, the shades which by one word he had evoked, recalled to her the past in all its intoxication of poetry and romance, youth, beauty, the eclat of love at twenty years of age, the bloody death of Buckingham, the only man whom she had ever really loved, and the heroism of those obscure champions who had saved her from the double hatred of Richelieu and the king.

Mazarin looked at her, and whilst she deemed herself alone and freed from the world of enemies who sought to spy into her secret thoughts, he read her thoughts in her countenance, as one sees in a transparent lake clouds pass—reflections, like thoughts, of the heavens.

"Must we, then," asked Anne of Austria, "yield to the storm, buy peace, and patiently and piously await better times?"

Mazarin smiled sarcastically at this speech, which showed that she had taken the minister's proposal seriously.

Anne's head was bent down—she had not seen the Italian's smile; but finding that her question elicited no reply she looked up.

"Well, you do not answer, cardinal, what do you think about it?"

"I am thinking, madame, of the allusion made by that insolent gentleman, whom you have caused to be arrested, to the Duke of Buckingham—to him whom you allowed to be assassinated—to the Duchess de Chevreuse, whom you suffered to be exiled—to the Duc de Beaufort, whom you imprisoned; but if he made allusion to me it was because he is ignorant of the relation in which I stand to you."

Anne drew up, as she always did, when anything touched her pride. She blushed, and that she might not answer, clasped her beautiful hands till her sharp nails almost pierced them.

"That man has sagacity, honor and wit, not to mention likewise that he is a man of undoubted resolution. You know something about him, do you not, madame? I shall tell him, therefore, and in doing so I shall confer a personal favor on him, how he is mistaken in regard to me. What is proposed to me would be, in fact, almost an abdication, and an abdication requires reflection."

"An abdication?" repeated Anne; "I thought, sir, that it was kings alone who abdicated!"

"Well," replied Mazarin, "and am I not almost a king—king, indeed, of France? Thrown over the foot of the royal bed, my simar, madame, looks not unlike the mantle worn by kings."

This was one of the humiliations which Mazarin made Anne undergo more frequently than any other, and one that bowed her head with shame. Queen Elizabeth and Catherine II. of Russia are the only two monarchs of their set on record who were at once sovereigns and lovers. Anne of Austria looked with a sort of terror at the threatening aspect of the cardinal—his physiognomy in such moments was not destitute of a certain grandeur.

"Sir," she replied, "did I not say, and did you not hear me say to those people, that you should do as you pleased?"

"In that case," said Mazarin, "I think it must please me best to remain; not only on account of my own interest, but for your safety."

"Remain, then, sir; nothing can be more agreeable to me; only do not allow me to be insulted."

"You are referring to the demands of the rebels and to the tone in which they stated them? Patience! They have selected a field of battle on which I am an abler general than they—that of a conference. No, we shall beat them by merely temporizing. They want food already. They will be ten times worse off in a week."

"Ah, yes! Good heavens! I know it will end in that way; but it is not they who taunt me with the most wounding reproaches, but——"

"I understand; you mean to allude to the recollections perpetually revived by these three gentlemen. However, we have them safe in prison, and they are just sufficiently culpable for us to keep them in prison as long as we find it convenient. One only is still not in our power and braves us. But, devil take him! we shall soon succeed in sending him to join his boon companions. We have accomplished more difficult things than that. In the first place I have as a precaution shut up at Rueil, near me, under my own eyes, within reach of my hand, the two most intractable ones. To-day the third will be there also."

"As long as they are in prison all will be well," said Anne, "but one of these days they will get out."

"Yes, if your majesty releases them."

"Ah!" exclaimed Anne, following the train of her own thoughts on such occasions, "one regrets Paris!"

"Why so?"

"On account of the Bastile, sir, which is so strong and so secure."

"Madame, these conferences will bring us peace; when we have peace we shall regain Paris; with Paris, the Bastile, and our four bullies shall rot therein."

Anne frowned slightly when Mazarin, in taking leave, kissed her hand.

Mazarin, after this half humble, half gallant attention, went away. Anne followed him with her eyes, and as he withdrew, at every step he took, a disdainful smile was seen playing, then gradually burst upon her lips.

"I once," she said, "despised the love of a cardinal who never said 'I shall do,' but, 'I have done so and so.' That man knew of retreats more secure than Rueil, darker and more silent even than the Bastile. Degenerate world!"

Chapter LXXXII.

Precautions.

After quitting Anne, Mazarin took the road to Rueil, where he usually resided; in those times of disturbance he went about with numerous followers and often disguised himself. In military dress he was, indeed, as we have stated, a very handsome man.

In the court of the old Chateau of Saint Germain he entered his coach, and reached the Seine at Chatou. The prince had supplied him with fifty light horse, not so much by way of guard as to show the deputies how readily the queen's generals dispersed their troops and to prove that they might be safely scattered at pleasure. Athos, on horseback, without his sword and kept in sight by Comminges, followed the cardinal in silence. Grimaud, finding that his master had been arrested, fell back into the ranks near Aramis, without saying a word and as if nothing had happened.

Grimaud had, indeed, during twenty-two years of service, seen his master extricate himself from so many difficulties that nothing less than Athos's imminent death was likely to make him uneasy.

At the branching off of the road toward Paris, Aramis, who had followed in the cardinal's suite, turned back. Mazarin went to the right hand and Aramis could see the prisoner disappear at the turning of the avenue. Athos, at the same moment, moved by a similar impulse, looked back also. The two friends exchanged a simple inclination of the head and Aramis put his finger to his hat, as if to bow, Athos alone comprehending by that signal that he had some project in his head.

Ten minutes afterward Mazarin entered the court of that chateau which his predecessor had built for him at Rueil; as he alighted, Comminges approached him.

"My lord," he asked, "where does your eminence wish Monsieur Comte de la Fere to be lodged?"

"In the pavilion of the orangery, of course, in front of the pavilion where the guard is. I wish every respect to be shown the count, although he is the prisoner of her majesty the queen."

"My lord," answered Comminges, "he begs to be taken to the place where Monsieur d'Artagnan is confined—that is, in the hunting lodge, opposite the orangery."

Mazarin thought for an instant.

Comminges saw that he was undecided.

"'Tis a very strong post," he resumed, "and we have forty good men, tried soldiers, having no connection with Frondeurs nor any interest in the Fronde."

"If we put these three men together, Monsieur Comminges," said Mazarin, "we must double the guard, and we are not rich enough in fighting men to commit such acts of prodigality."

Comminges smiled; Mazarin read and construed that smile.

"You do not know these men, Monsieur Comminges, but I know them, first personally, also by hearsay. I sent them to carry aid to King Charles and they performed prodigies to save him; had it not been for an adverse destiny, that beloved monarch would this day have been among us."

"But since they served your eminence so well, why are they, my lord cardinal, in prison?"

"In prison?" said Mazarin, "and when has Rueil been a prison?"

"Ever since there were prisoners in it," answered Comminges.

"These gentlemen, Comminges, are not prisoners," returned Mazarin, with his ironical smile, "only guests; but guests so precious that I have put a grating before each of their windows and bolts to their doors, that they may not refuse to continue my visitors. So much do I esteem them that I am going to make the Comte de la Fere a visit, that I may converse with him tete-a-tete, and that we may not be disturbed at our interview you must conduct him, as I said before, to the pavilion of the orangery; that, you know, is my daily promenade. Well, while taking my walk I will call on him and we will talk. Although he professes to be my enemy I have sympathy for him, and if he is reasonable perhaps we shall arrange matters."

Comminges bowed, and returned to Athos, who was awaiting with apparent calmness, but with real anxiety, the result of the interview.

"Well?" he said to the lieutenant.

"Sir," replied Comminges, "it seems that it is impossible."

"Monsieur de Comminges," said Athos, "I have been a soldier all my life and I know the force of orders; but outside your orders there is a service you can render me."

"I will do it with all my heart," said Comminges; "for I know who you are and what service you once performed for her majesty; I know, too, how dear to you is the young man who came so valiantly to my aid when that old rogue of a Broussel was arrested. I am entirely at your service, except only for my orders."

"Thank you, sir; what I am about to ask will not compromise you in any degree."

"If it should even compromise me a little," said Monsieur de Comminges, with a smile, "still make your demand. I don't like Mazarin any better than you do. I serve the queen and that draws me naturally into the service of the cardinal; but I serve the one with joy and the other against my will. Speak, then, I beg of you; I wait and listen."

"Since there is no harm," said Athos, "in my knowing that D'Artagnan is here, I presume there will be none in his knowing that I am here."

"I have received no orders on that point."

"Well, then, do me the kindness to give him my regards and tell him that I am his neighbor. Tell him also what you have just told me—that Mazarin has placed me in the pavilion of the orangery in order to make me a visit, and assure him that I shall take advantage of this honor he proposes to accord to me to obtain from him some amelioration of our captivity."

"Which cannot last," interrupted Comminges; "the cardinal said so; there is no prison here."

"But there are oubliettes!" replied Athos, smiling.

"Oh! that's a different thing; yes, I know there are traditions of that sort," said Comminges. "It was in the time of the other cardinal, who was a great nobleman; but our Mazarin—impossible! an Italian adventurer would not dare to go such lengths with such men as ourselves. Oubliettes are employed as a means of kingly vengeance, and a low-born fellow such as he is would not have recourse to them. Your arrest is known, that of your friends will soon be known; and all the nobility of France would demand an explanation of your disappearance. No, no, be easy on that score. I will, however, inform Monsieur d'Artagnan of your arrival here."

Comminges then led the count to a room on the ground floor of a pavilion, at the end of the orangery. They passed through a courtyard as they went, full of soldiers and courtiers. In the centre of this court, in the form of a horseshoe, were the buildings occupied by Mazarin, and at each wing the pavilion (or smaller building), where D'Artagnan was confined, and that, level with the orangery, where Athos was to be. From the ends of these two wings extended the park.

Athos, when he reached his appointed room, observed through the gratings of his window, walls and roofs; and was told, on inquiry, by Comminges, that he was looking on the back of the pavilion where D'Artagnan was confined.

"Yes, 'tis too true," said Comminges, "'tis almost a prison; but what a singular fancy this is of yours, count—you, who are the very flower of our nobility—to squander your valor and loyalty amongst these upstarts, the Frondists! Really, count, if ever I thought that I had a friend in the ranks of the royal army, it was you. A Frondeur! you, the Comte de la Fere, on the side of Broussel, Blancmesnil and Viole! For shame! you, a Frondeur!"

"On my word of honor," said Athos, "one must be either a Mazarinist or a Frondeur. For a long time I had these words whispered in my ears, and I chose the latter; at any rate, it is a French word. And now, I am a Frondeur—not of Broussel's party, nor of Blancmesnil's, nor am I with Viole; but with the Duc de Beaufort, the Ducs de Bouillon and d'Elbeuf; with princes, not with presidents, councillors and low-born lawyers. Besides, what a charming outlook it would have been to serve the cardinal! Look at that wall—without a single window—which tells you fine things about Mazarin's gratitude!"

"Yes," replied De Comminges, "more especially if it could reveal how Monsieur d'Artagnan for this last week has been anathematizing him."

"Poor D'Artagnan'" said Athos, with the charming melancholy that was one of the traits of his character, "so brave, so good, so terrible to the enemies of those he loves. You have two unruly prisoners there, sir."

"Unruly," Comminges smiled; "you wish to terrify me, I suppose. When he came here, Monsieur D'Artagnan provoked and braved the soldiers and inferior officers, in order, I suppose, to have his sword back. That mood lasted some time; but now he's as gentle as a lamb and sings Gascon songs, which make one die of laughing."

"And Du Vallon?" asked Athos.

"Ah, he's quite another sort of person—a formidable gentleman, indeed. The first day he broke all the doors in with a single push of his shoulder; and

I expected to see him leave Rueil in the same way as Samson left Gaza. But his temper cooled down, like his friend's; he not only gets used to his captivity, but jokes about it."

"So much the better," said Athos.

"Do you think anything else was to be expected of them?" asked Comminges, who, putting together what Mazarin had said of his prisoners and what the Comte de la Fere had said, began to feel a degree of uneasiness.

Athos, on the other hand, reflected that this recent gentleness of his friends most certainly arose from some plan formed by D'Artagnan. Unwilling to injure them by praising them too highly, he replied: "They? They are two hotheads—the one a Gascon, the other from Picardy; both are easily excited, but they quiet down immediately. You have had a proof of that in what you have just related to me."

This, too, was the opinion of Comminges, who withdrew somewhat reassured. Athos remained alone in the vast chamber, where, according to the cardinal's directions, he was treated with all the courtesy due to a nobleman. He awaited Mazarin's promised visit to get some light on his present situation.

Chapter LXXXIII.

Strength and Sagacity.

Now let us pass the orangery to the hunting lodge. At the extremity of the courtyard, where, close to a portico formed of Ionic columns, were the dog kennels, rose an oblong building, the pavilion of the orangery, a half circle, inclosing the court of honor. It was in this pavilion, on the ground floor, that D'Artagnan and Porthos were confined, suffering interminable hours of imprisonment in a manner suitable to each different temperament.

D'Artagnan was pacing to and fro like a caged tiger; with dilated eyes, growling as he paced along by the bars of a window looking upon the yard of servant's offices.

Porthos was ruminating over an excellent dinner he had just demolished.

The one seemed to be deprived of reason, yet he was meditating. The other seemed to meditate, yet he was more than half asleep. But his sleep was a nightmare, which might be guessed by the incoherent manner in which he sometimes snored and sometimes snorted.

"Look," said D'Artagnan, "day is declining. It must be nearly four o'clock. We have been in this place nearly eighty-three hours."

"Hem!" muttered Porthos, with a kind of pretense of answering.

"Did you hear, eternal sleeper?" cried D'Artagnan, irritated that any one could doze during the day, when he had the greatest difficulty in sleeping during the night.

"What?" said Porthos.

"I say we have been here eighty-three hours."

"'Tis your fault," answered Porthos.

"How, my fault?"

"Yes, I offered you escape."

"By pulling out a bar and pushing down a door?"

"Certainly."

"Porthos, men like us can't go out from here purely and simply."

"Faith!" said Porthos, "as for me, I could go out with that purity and that simplicity which it seems to me you despise too much."

D'Artagnan shrugged his shoulders.

"And besides," he said, "going out of this chamber isn't all."

"Dear friend," said Porthos, "you appear to be in a somewhat better humor to-day than you were yesterday. Explain to me why going out of this chamber isn't everything."

"Because, having neither arms nor password, we shouldn't take fifty steps in the court without knocking against a sentinel."

"Very well," said Porthos, "we will kill the sentinel and we shall have his arms."

"Yes, but before we can kill him—and he will be hard to kill, that Swiss—he will shriek out and the whole picket will come, and we shall be taken like foxes, we, who are lions, and thrown into some dungeon, where we shall not even have the consolation of seeing this frightful gray sky of Rueil, which no more resembles the sky of Tarbes than the moon is like the sun. Lack-a-day! if we only had some one to instruct us about the physical and moral topography of this castle. Ah! when one thinks that for twenty years, during which time I did not know what to do with myself, it never occurred to me to come to study Rueil."

"What difference does that make?" said Porthos. "We shall go out all the same."

"Do you know, my dear fellow, why master pastrycooks never work with their hands?"

"No," said Porthos, "but I should be glad to be informed."

"It is because in the presence of their pupils they fear that some of their tarts or creams may turn out badly cooked."

"What then?"

"Why, then they would be laughed at, and a master pastrycook must never be laughed at."

"And what have master pastrycooks to do with us?"

"We ought, in our adventures, never to be defeated or give any one a chance to laugh at us. In England, lately, we failed, we were beaten, and that is a blemish on our reputation."

"By whom, then, were we beaten?" asked Porthos.

"By Mordaunt."

"Yes, but we have drowned Monsieur Mordaunt."

"That is true, and that will redeem us a little in the eyes of posterity, if posterity ever looks at us. But listen, Porthos: though Monsieur Mordaunt was a man not to be despised, Mazarin is not less strong than he, and we shall not easily succeed in drowning him. We must, therefore, watch and play a close game; for," he added with a sigh, "we two are equal, perhaps, to eight others; but we are not equal to the four that you know of."

"That is true," said Porthos, echoing D'Artagnan's sigh.

"Well, Porthos, follow my examples; walk back and forth till some news of our friends reaches us or till we are visited by a good idea. But don't sleep as you do all the time; nothing dulls the intellect like sleep. As to what may lie before us, it is perhaps less serious than we at first thought. I don't believe that Monsieur de Mazarin thinks of cutting off our heads, for heads are not taken off without previous trial; a trial would make a noise, and a noise would get the attention of our friends, who would check the operations of Monsieur de Mazarin."

"How well you reason!" said Porthos, admiringly.

"Well, yes, pretty well," replied D'Artagnan; "and besides, you see, if they put us on trial, if they cut off our heads, they must meanwhile either keep us here or transfer us elsewhere."

"Yes, that is inevitable," said Porthos.

"Well, it is impossible but that Master Aramis, that keen-scented bloodhound, and Athos, that wise and prudent nobleman, will discover our retreat. Then, believe me, it will be time to act."

"Yes, we will wait. We can wait the more contentedly, that it is not absolutely bad here, but for one thing, at least."

"What is that?"

"Did you observe, D'Artagnan, that three days running they have brought us braised mutton?"

"No; but if it occurs a fourth time I shall complain of it, so never mind."

"And then I feel the loss of my house, 'tis a long time since I visited my castles."

"Forget them for a time; we shall return to them, unless Mazarin razes them to the ground."

"Do you think that likely?"

"No, the other cardinal would have done so, but this one is too mean a fellow to risk it."

"You reconcile me, D'Artagnan."

"Well, then, assume a cheerful manner, as I do; we must joke with the guards, we must gain the good-will of the soldiers, since we can't corrupt them. Try, Porthos, to please them more than you are wont to do when they are under our windows. Thus far you have done nothing but show them your fist; and the more respectable your fist is, Porthos, the less attractive it is. Ah, I would give much to have five hundred louis, only."

"So would I," said Porthos, unwilling to be behind D'Artagnan in generosity; "I would give as much as a hundred pistoles."

The two prisoners were at this point of their conversation when Comminges entered, preceded by a sergeant and two men, who brought supper in a basket with two handles, filled with basins and plates.

"What!" exclaimed Porthos, "mutton again?"

"My dear Monsieur de Comminges," said D'Artagnan, "you will find that my friend, Monsieur du Vallon, will go to the most fatal lengths if Cardinal Mazarin continues to provide us with this sort of meat; mutton every day."

"I declare," said Porthos, "I shall eat nothing if they do not take it away."

"Remove the mutton," cried Comminges; "I wish Monsieur du Vallon to sup well, more especially as I have news to give him that will improve his appetite."

"Is Mazarin dead?" asked Porthos.

"No; I am sorry to tell you he is perfectly well."

"So much the worse," said Porthos.

"What is that news?" asked D'Artagnan. "News in prison is a fruit so rare that I trust, Monsieur de Comminges, you will excuse my impatience—the more eager since you have given us to understand that the news is good."

"Should you be glad to hear that the Comte de la Fere is well?" asked De Comminges.

D'Artagnan's penetrating gray eyes were opened to the utmost.

"Glad!" he cried; "I should be more than glad! Happy—beyond measure!"

"Well, I am desired by him to give you his compliments and to say that he is in good health."

D'Artagnan almost leaped with joy. A quick glance conveyed his thought to Porthos: "If Athos knows where we are, if he opens communication with us, before long Athos will act."

Porthos was not very quick to understand the language of glances, but now since the name of Athos had suggested to him the same idea, he understood.

"Do you say," asked the Gascon, timidly, "that the Comte de la Fere has commissioned you to give his compliments to Monsieur du Vallon and myself?"

"Yes, sir."

"Then you have seen him?"

"Certainly I have."

"Where? if I may ask without indiscretion."

"Near here," replied De Comminges, smiling; "so near that if the windows which look on the orangery were not stopped up you could see him from where you are."

"He is wandering about the environs of the castle," thought D'Artagnan. Then he said aloud:

"You met him, I dare say, in the park—hunting, perhaps?"

"No; nearer, nearer still. Look, behind this wall," said De Comminges, knocking against the wall.

"Behind this wall? What is there, then, behind this wall? I was brought here by night, so devil take me if I know where I am."

"Well," said Comminges, "suppose one thing."

"I will suppose anything you please."

"Suppose there were a window in this wall."

"Well?"

"From that window you would see Monsieur de la Fere at his."

"The count, then, is in the chateau?"

"Yes."

"For what reason?"

"The same as yourself."

"Athos—a prisoner?"

"You know well," replied De Comminges, "that there are no prisoners at Rueil, because there is no prison."

"Don't let us play upon words, sir. Athos has been arrested."

"Yesterday, at Saint Germain, as he came out from the presence of the queen."

The arms of D'Artagnan fell powerless by his side. One might have supposed him thunderstruck; a paleness ran like a cloud over his dark skin, but disappeared immediately.

"A prisoner?" he reiterated.

"A prisoner," repeated Porthos, quite dejected.

Suddenly D'Artagnan looked up and in his eyes there was a gleam which scarcely even Porthos observed; but it died away and he appeared more sorrowful than before.

"Come, come," said Comminges, who, since D'Artagnan, on the day of Broussel's arrest, had saved him from the hands of the Parisians, had entertained a real affection for him, "don't be unhappy; I never thought of bringing you bad news. Laugh at the chance which has brought your friend near to you and Monsieur du Vallon, instead of being in the depths of despair about it."

But D'Artagnan was still in a desponding mood.

"And how did he look?" asked Porthos, who, perceiving that D'Artagnan had allowed the conversation to drop, profited by it to put in a word or two.

"Very well, indeed, sir," replied Comminges; "at first, like you, he seemed distressed; but when he heard that the cardinal was going to pay him a visit this very evening——"

"Ah!" cried D'Artagnan, "the cardinal is about to visit the Comte de la Fere?"

"Yes; and the count desired me to tell you that he should take advantage of this visit to plead for you and for himself."

"Ah! our dear count!" said D'Artagnan.

"A fine thing, indeed!" grunted Porthos. "A great favor! Zounds! Monsieur the Comte de la Fere, whose family is allied to the Montmorency and the Rohan, is easily the equal of Monsieur de Mazarin."

"No matter," said D'Artagnan, in his most wheedling tone. "On reflection, my dear Du Vallon, it is a great honor for the Comte de la Fere, and gives good reason to hope. In fact, it seems to me so great an honor for a prisoner that I think Monsieur de Comminges must be mistaken."

"What? I am mistaken?"

"Monsieur de Mazarin will not come to visit the Comte de la Fere, but the Comte de la Fere will be sent for to visit him."

"No, no, no," said Comminges, who made a point of having the facts appear exactly as they were, "I clearly understood what the cardinal said to me. He will come and visit the Comte de la Fere."

D'Artagnan tried to gather from the expression of his eyes whether Porthos understood the importance of that visit, but Porthos did not even look toward him.

"It is, then, the cardinal's custom to walk in his orangery?" asked D'Artagnan.

"Every evening he shuts himself in there. That, it seems, is where he meditates on state affairs."

"In that case," said D'Artagnan, "I begin to believe that Monsieur de la Fere will receive the visit of his eminence; he will, of course, have an escort."

"Yes—two soldiers."

"And will he talk thus of affairs in presence of two strangers?"

"The soldiers are Swiss, who understand only German. Besides, according to all probability they will wait at the door."

D'Artagnan made a violent effort over himself to keep his face from being too expressive.

"Let the cardinal take care of going alone to visit the Comte de la Fere," said D'Artagnan; "for the count must be furious."

Comminges began to laugh. "Oh, oh! why, really, one would say that you four were anthropaphagi! The count is an affable man; besides, he is unarmed; at the first word from his eminence the two soldiers about him would run to his assistance."

"Two soldiers," said D'Artagnan, seeming to remember something, "two soldiers, yes; that, then, is why I hear two men called every evening and see them walking sometimes for half an hour, under my window."

"That is it; they are waiting for the cardinal, or rather for Bernouin, who comes to call them when the cardinal goes out."

"Fine-looking men, upon my word!" said D'Artagnan.

"They belong to the regiment that was at Lens, which the prince assigned to the cardinal."

"Ah, monsieur," said D'Artagnan, as if to sum up in a word all that conversation, "if only his eminence would relent and grant to Monsieur de la Fere our liberty."

"I wish it with all my heart," said Comminges.

"Then, if he should forget that visit, you would find no inconvenience in reminding him of it?"

"Not at all."

"Ah, that gives me more confidence."

This skillful turn of the conversation would have seemed a sublime manoeuvre to any one who could have read the Gascon's soul.

"Now," said D'Artagnan, "I've one last favor to ask of you, Monsieur de Comminges."

"At your service, sir."

"You will see the count again?"

"To-morrow morning."

"Will you remember us to him and ask him to solicit for me the same favor that he will have obtained?"

"You want the cardinal to come here?"

"No; I know my place and am not so presumptuous. Let his eminence do me the honor to give me a hearing; that is all I want."

"Oh!" muttered Porthos, shaking his head, "never should I have thought this of him! How misfortune humbles a man!"

"I promise you it shall be done," answered De Comminges.

"Tell the count that I am well; that you found me sad, but resigned."

"I am pleased, sir, to hear that."

"And the same, also, for Monsieur du Vallon——"

"Not for me," cried Porthos; "I am not by any means resigned."

"But you will be resigned, my friend."

"Never!"

"He will become so, monsieur; I know him better than he knows himself. Be silent, dear Du Vallon, and resign yourself."

"Adieu, gentlemen," said De Comminges; "sleep well!"

"We will try."

De Comminges went away, D'Artagnan remaining apparently in the same attitude of humble resignation; but scarcely had he departed when he turned and clasped Porthos in his arms with an expression not to be doubted.

"Oh!" cried Porthos; "what's the matter now? Have you gone mad, my dear friend?"

"What is the matter?" returned D'Artagnan; "we are saved!"

"I don't see that at all," answered Porthos. "I think we are all taken prisoners, except Aramis, and that our chances of getting out are lessened since one more of us is caught in Mazarin's mousetrap."

"Which is far too strong for two of us, but not strong enough for three of us," returned D'Artagnan.

"I don't understand," said Porthos.

"Never mind; let's sit down to table and take something to strengthen us for the night."

"What are we to do, then, to-night?"

"To travel—perhaps."

"But——"

"Sit down, dear friend, to table. When one is eating, ideas flow easily. After supper, when they are perfected, I will communicate my plans to you."

So Porthos sat down to table without another word and ate with an appetite that did honor to the confidence that was ever inspired in him by D'Artagnan's inventive imagination.

Chapter LXXXIV.

Strength and Sagacity—Continued.

Supper was eaten in silence, but not in sadness; for from time to time one of those sweet smiles which were habitual to him in moments of good-humor illumined the face of D'Artagnan. Not a scintilla of these was lost on Porthos; and at every one he uttered an exclamation which betrayed to his friend that he had not lost sight of the idea which possessed his brain.

At dessert D'Artagnan reposed in his chair, crossed one leg over the other and lounged about like a man perfectly at his ease.

Porthos rested his chin on his hands, placed his elbows on the table and looked at D'Artagnan with an expression of confidence which imparted to that colossus an admirable appearance of good-fellowship.

"Well?" said D'Artagnan, at last.

"Well!" repeated Porthos.

"You were saying, my dear friend——"

"No; I said nothing."

"Yes; you were saying you wished to leave this place."

"Ah, indeed! the will was never wanting."

"To get away you would not mind, you added, knocking down a door or a wall."

"'Tis true—I said so, and I say it again."

"And I answered you, Porthos, that it was not a good plan; that we couldn't go a hundred steps without being recaptured, because we were without clothes to disguise ourselves and arms to defend ourselves."

"That is true; we should need clothes and arms."

"Well," said D'Artagnan, rising, "we have them, friend Porthos, and even something better."

"Bah!" said Porthos, looking around.

"Useless to look; everything will come to us when wanted. At about what time did we see the two Swiss guards walking yesterday?"

"An hour after sunset."

"If they go out to-day as they did yesterday we shall have the honor, then, of seeing them in half an hour?"

"In a quarter of an hour at most."

"Your arm is still strong enough, is it not, Porthos?"

Porthos unbuttoned his sleeve, raised his shirt and looked complacently on his strong arm, as large as the leg of any ordinary man.

"Yes, indeed," said he, "I believe so."

"So that you could without trouble convert these tongs into a hoop and yonder shovel into a corkscrew?"

"Certainly." And the giant took up these two articles, and without any apparent effort produced in them the metamorphoses suggested by his companion.

"There!" he cried.

"Capital!" exclaimed the Gascon. "Really, Porthos, you are a gifted individual!"

"I have heard speak," said Porthos, "of a certain Milo of Crotona, who performed wonderful feats, such as binding his forehead with a cord and bursting it—of killing an ox with a blow of his fist and carrying it home on his shoulders, et cetera. I used to learn all these feat by heart yonder, down at Pierrefonds, and I have done all that he did except breaking a cord by the corrugation of my temples."

"Because your strength is not in your head, Porthos," said his friend.

"No; it is in my arms and shoulders," answered Porthos with gratified naivete.

"Well, my dear friend, let us approach the window and there you can match your strength against that of an iron bar."

Porthos went to the window, took a bar in his hands, clung to it and bent it like a bow; so that the two ends came out of the sockets of stone in which for thirty years they had been fixed.

"Well! friend, the cardinal, although such a genius, could never have done that."

"Shall I take out any more of them?" asked Porthos.

"No; that is sufficient; a man can pass through that."

Porthos tried, and passed the upper portion of his body through.

"Yes," he said.

"Now pass your arm through this opening."

"Why?"

"You will know presently—pass it."

Porthos obeyed with military promptness and passed his arm through the opening.

"Admirable!" said D'Artagnan.

"The scheme goes forward, it seems."

"On wheels, dear friend."

"Good! What shall I do now?"

"Nothing."

"It is finished, then?"

"No, not yet."

"I should like to understand," said Porthos.

"Listen, my dear friend; in two words you will know all. The door of the guardhouse opens, as you see."

"Yes, I see."

"They are about to send into our court, which Monsieur de Mazarin crosses on his way to the orangery, the two guards who attend him."

"There they are, coming out."

"If only they close the guardhouse door! Good! They close it."

"What, then?"

"Silence! They may hear us."

"I don't understand it at all."

"As you execute you will understand."

"And yet I should have preferred——"

"You will have the pleasure of the surprise."

"Ah, that is true."

"Hush!"

Porthos remained silent and motionless.

In fact, the two soldiers advanced on the side where the window was, rubbing their hands, for it was cold, it being the month of February.

At this moment the door of the guardhouse was opened and one of the soldiers was summoned away.

"Now," said D'Artagnan, "I am going to call this soldier and talk to him. Don't lose a word of what I'm going to say to you, Porthos. Everything lies in the execution."

"Good, the execution of plots is my forte."

"I know it well. I depend on you. Look, I shall turn to the left, so that the soldier will be at your right, as soon as he mounts on the bench to talk to us."

"But supposing he doesn't mount?"

"He will; rely upon it. As soon as you see him get up, stretch out your arm and seize him by the neck. Then, raising him up as Tobit raised the fish by the gills, you must pull him into the room, taking care to squeeze him so tight that he can't cry out."

"Oh!" said Porthos. "Suppose I happen to strangle him?"

"To be sure there would only be a Swiss the less in the world; but you will not do so, I hope. Lay him down here; we'll gag him and tie him—no matter where—somewhere. So we shall get from him one uniform and a sword."

"Marvelous!" exclaimed Porthos, looking at the Gascon with the most profound admiration.

"Pooh!" replied D'Artagnan.

"Yes," said Porthos, recollecting himself, "but one uniform and one sword will not suffice for two."

"Well; but there's his comrade."

"True," said Porthos.

"Therefore, when I cough, stretch out your arm."

"Good!"

The two friends then placed themselves as they had agreed, Porthos being completely hidden in an angle of the window.

"Good-evening, comrade," said D'Artagnan in his most fascinating voice and manner.

"Good-evening, sir," answered the soldier, in a strong provincial accent.

"'Tis not too warm to walk," resumed D'Artagnan.

"No, sir."

"And I think a glass of wine will not be disagreeable to you?"

"A glass of wine will be extremely welcome."

"The fish bites—the fish bites!" whispered the Gascon to Porthos.

"I understand," said Porthos.

"A bottle, perhaps?"

"A whole bottle? Yes, sir."

"A whole bottle, if you will drink my health."

"Willingly," answered the soldier.

"Come, then, and take it, friend," said the Gascon.

"With all my heart. How convenient that there's a bench here. Egad! one would think it had been placed here on purpose."

"Get on it; that's it, friend."

And D'Artagnan coughed.

That instant the arm of Porthos fell. His hand of iron grasped, quick as lightning, firm as a pair of blacksmith's pincers, the soldier's throat. He raised him, almost stifling him as he drew him through the aperture, at the risk of flaying him in the passage. He then laid him down on the floor, where D'Artagnan, after giving him just time enough to draw his breath, gagged him with his long scarf; and the moment he had done so began to undress him with the promptitude and dexterity of a man who had learned his business on the field of battle. Then the soldier, gagged and bound, was placed upon the hearth, the fire of which had been previously extinguished by the two friends.

"Here's a sword and a dress," said Porthos.

"I take them," said D'Artagnan, "for myself. If you want another uniform and sword you must play the same trick over again. Stop! I see the other soldier issue from the guardroom and come toward us."

"I think," replied Porthos, "it would be imprudent to attempt the same manoeuvre again; it is said that no man can succeed twice in the same way, and a failure would be ruinous. No; I will go down, seize the man unawares and bring him to you ready gagged."

"That is better," said the Gascon.

"Be ready," said Porthos, as he slipped through the opening.

He did as he said. Porthos seized his opportunity, caught the next soldier by his neck, gagged him and pushed him like a mummy through the bars into the room, and entered after him. Then they undressed him as they had done the first, laid him on their bed and bound him with the straps which composed the bed—the bedstead being of oak. This operation proved as great a success as the first.

"There," said D'Artagnan, "this is capital! Now let me try on the dress of yonder chap. Porthos, I doubt if you can wear it; but should it be too tight, never mind, you can wear the breastplate and the hat with the red feathers."

It happened, however, that the second soldier was a Swiss of gigantic proportions, so, save that some few of the seams split, his uniform fitted Porthos perfectly.

They then dressed themselves.

"'Tis done!" they both exclaimed at once. "As to you, comrades," they said to the men, "nothing will happen to you if you are discreet; but if you stir you are dead men."

The soldiers were complaisant; they had found the grasp of Porthos pretty powerful and that it was no joke to fight against it.

"Now," said D'Artagnan, "you wouldn't be sorry to understand the plot, would you, Porthos?"

"Well, no, not very."

"Well, then, we shall go down into the court."

"Yes."

"We shall take the place of those two fellows."

"Well?"

"We will walk back and forth."

"That's a good idea, for it isn't warm."

"In a moment the valet-de-chambre will call the guard, as he did yesterday and the day before."

"And we shall answer?"

"No, on the contrary, we shall not answer."

"As you please; I don't insist on answering."

"We will not answer, then; we will simply settle our hats on our heads and we will escort his eminence."

"Where shall we escort him?"

"Where he is going—to visit Athos. Do you think Athos will be sorry to see us?"

"Oh!" cried Porthos, "oh! I understand."

"Wait a little, Porthos, before crying out; for, on my word, you haven't reached the end," said the Gascon, in a jesting tone.

"What is to happen?" said Porthos.

"Follow me," replied D'Artagnan. "The man who lives to see shall see."

And slipping through the aperture, he alighted in the court. Porthos followed him by the same road, but with more difficulty and less diligence. They could hear the two soldiers shivering with fear, as they lay bound in the chamber.

Scarcely had the two Frenchmen touched the ground when a door opened and the voice of the valet-de-chambre called out:

"Make ready!"

At the same moment the guardhouse was opened and a voice called out:

"La Bruyere and Du Barthois! March!"

"It seems that I am named La Bruyere," remarked D'Artagnan.

"And I, Du Barthois," added Porthos.

"Where are you?" asked the valet-de-chambre, whose eyes, dazzled by the light, could not clearly distinguish our heroes in the gloom.

"Here we are," said the Gascon.

"What say you to that, Monsieur du Vallon?" he added in a low tone to Porthos.

"If it but lasts, most capital," responded Porthos.

These two newly enlisted soldiers marched gravely after the valet-de-chambre, who opened the door of the vestibule, then another which seemed to be that of a waiting-room, and showing them two stools:

"Your orders are very simple," he said; "don't allow anybody, except one person, to enter here. Do you hear—not a single creature! Obey that person implicitly. On your return you cannot make a mistake. You have only to wait here till I release you."

D'Artagnan was known to this valet-de-chambre, who was no other than Bernouin, and he had during the last six or eight months introduced the Gascon a dozen times to the cardinal. The Gascon, therefore, instead of answering, growled out "Ja! Ja!" in the most German and the least Gascon accent possible.

As for Porthos, on whom D'Artagnan had impressed the necessity of absolute silence and who did not even now begin to comprehend the scheme of his friend, which was to follow Mazarin in his visit to Athos, he was simply mute. All that he was allowed to say, in case of emergencies, was the proverbial Der Teufel!

Bernouin shut the door and went away. When Porthos heard the key turn in the lock he began to be alarmed, lest they should only have exchanged one prison for another.

"Porthos, my friend," said D'Artagnan, "don't distrust Providence! Let me meditate and consider."

"Meditate and consider as much as you like," replied Porthos, who was now quite out of humor at seeing things take this turn.

"We have walked eight paces," whispered D'Artagnan, "and gone up six steps, so hereabouts is the pavilion called the pavilion of the orangery. The Comte de la Fere cannot be far off, only the doors are locked."

"That is a slight difficulty," said Porthos, "and a good push with the shoulders——"

"For God's sake, Porthos my friend, reserve your feats of strength, or they will not have, when needed, the honor they deserve. Have you not heard that some one is coming here?"

"Yes."

"Well, that some one will open the doors."

"But, my dear fellow, if that some one recognizes us, if that some one cries out, we are lost; for you don't propose, I imagine, that I shall kill that man of the church. That might do if we were dealing with Englishmen or Germans."

"Oh, may God keep me from it, and you, too!" said D'Artagnan. "The young king would, perhaps, show us some gratitude; but the queen would never forgive us, and it is she whom we have to consider. And then, besides, the useless blood! never! no, never! I have my plan; let me carry it out and we shall laugh."

"So much the better," said Porthos; "I feel some need of it."

"Hush!" said D'Artagnan; "the some one is coming."

The sound of a light step was heard in the vestibule. The hinges of the door creaked and a man appeared in the dress of a cavalier, wrapped in a brown cloak, with a lantern in one hand and a large beaver hat pulled down over his eyes.

Porthos effaced himself against the wall, but he could not render himself invisible; and the man in the cloak said to him, giving him his lantern:

"Light the lamp which hangs from the ceiling."

Then addressing D'Artagnan:

"You know the watchword?" he said.

"Ja!" replied the Gascon, determined to confine himself to this specimen of the German tongue.

"Tedesco!" answered the cavalier; "va bene."

And advancing toward the door opposite to that by which he came in, he opened it and disappeared behind it, shutting it as he went.

"Now," asked Porthos, "what are we to do?"

"Now we shall make use of your shoulder, friend Porthos, if this door proves to be locked. Everything in its proper time, and all comes right to those who know how to wait patiently. But first barricade the first door well; then we will follow yonder cavalier."

The two friends set to work and crowded the space before the door with all the furniture in the room, as not only to make the passage impassable, but so to block the door that by no means could it open inward.

"There!" said D'Artagnan, "we can't be overtaken. Come! forward!"

Chapter LXXXV.

The Oubliettes of Cardinal Mazarin.

At first, on arriving at the door through which Mazarin had passed, D'Artagnan tried in vain to open it, but on the powerful shoulder of Porthos being applied to one of the panels, which gave way, D'Artagnan introduced the point of his sword between the bolt and the staple of the lock. The bolt gave way and the door opened.

"As I told you, everything can be attained, Porthos, women and doors, by proceeding with gentleness."

"You're a great moralist, and that's the fact," said Porthos.

They entered; behind a glass window, by the light of the cardinal's lantern, which had been placed on the floor in the midst of the gallery, they saw the orange and pomegranate trees of the Castle of Rueil, in long lines, forming one great alley and two smaller side alleys.

"No cardinal!" said D'Artagnan, "but only his lantern; where the devil, then, is he?"

Exploring, however, one of the side wings of the gallery, after making a sign to Porthos to explore the other, he saw, all at once, at his left, a tub containing an orange tree, which had been pushed out of its place and in its place an open aperture.

Ten men would have found difficulty in moving that tub, but by some mechanical contrivance it had turned with the flagstone on which it rested.

D'Artagnan, as we have said, perceived a hole in that place and in this hole the steps of a winding staircase.

He called Porthos to look at it.

"Were our object money only," he said, "we should be rich directly."

"How's that?"

"Don't you understand, Porthos? At the bottom of that staircase lies, probably, the cardinal's treasury of which folk tell such wonders, and we should only have to descend, empty a chest, shut the cardinal up in it, double lock it, go away, carrying off as much gold as we could, put back this orange-tree over the place, and no one in the world would ever ask us where our fortune came from—not even the cardinal."

"It would be a happy hit for clowns to make, but as it seems to be unworthy of two gentlemen——" said Porthos.

"So I think; and therefore I said, 'Were our object money only;' but we want something else," replied the Gascon.

At the same moment, whilst D'Artagnan was leaning over the aperture to listen, a metallic sound, as if some one was moving a bag of gold, struck on his ear; he started; instantly afterward a door opened and a light played upon the staircase.

Mazarin had left his lamp in the gallery to make people believe that he was walking about, but he had with him a waxlight, to help him to explore his mysterious strong box.

"Faith," he said, in Italian, as he was reascending the steps and looking at a bag of reals, "faith, there's enough to pay five councillors of parliament, and two generals in Paris. I am a great captain—that I am! but I make war in my own way."

The two friends were crouching down, meantime, behind a tub in the side alley.

Mazarin came within three steps of D'Artagnan and pushed a spring in the wall; the slab turned and the orange tree resumed its place.

Then the cardinal put out the waxlight, slipped it into his pocket, and taking up the lantern: "Now," he said, "for Monsieur de la Fere."

"Very good," thought D'Artagnan, "'tis our road likewise; we will go together."

All three set off on their walk, Mazarin taking the middle alley and the friends the side ones.

The cardinal reached a second door without perceiving he was being followed; the sand with which the alleys were covered deadened the sound of footsteps.

He then turned to the left, down a corridor which had escaped the attention of the two friends, but as he opened the door he paused, as if in thought.

"Ah! Diavolo!" he exclaimed, "I forgot the recommendation of De Comminges, who advised me to take a guard and place it at this door, in order not to put myself at the mercy of that four-headed combination of devils." And with a movement of impatience he turned to retrace his steps.

"Do not give yourself the trouble, my lord," said D'Artagnan, with his right foot forward, his beaver in his hand, a smile on his face, "we have followed your eminence step by step and here we are."

"Yes—here we are," said Porthos.

And he made the same friendly salute as D'Artagnan.

Mazarin gazed at each of them with an affrighted stare, recognized them, and let drop his lantern, uttering a cry of terror.

D'Artagnan picked it up; by good luck it had not been extinguished.

"Oh, what imprudence, my lord," said D'Artagnan; "'tis not good to be about just here without a light. Your eminence might knock against something, or fall into a hole."

"Monsieur d'Artagnan!" muttered Mazarin, unable to recover from his astonishment.

"Yes, my lord, it is I. I have the honor to present to you Monsieur du Vallon, that excellent friend of mine, in whom your eminence had the kindness to interest yourself formerly."

And D'Artagnan held the lamp before the merry face of Porthos, who now began to comprehend the affair and be very proud of the whole undertaking.

"You were going to visit Monsieur de la Fere?" said D'Artagnan. "Don't let us disarrange your eminence. Be so good as to show us the way and we will follow you."

Mazarin was by degrees recovering his senses.

"Have you been long in the orangery?" he asked in a trembling voice, remembering the visits he had been paying to his treasury.

Porthos opened his mouth to reply; D'Artagnan made him a sign, and his mouth, remaining silent, gradually closed.

"This moment come, my lord," said D'Artagnan.

Mazarin breathed again. His fears were now no longer for his hoard, but for himself. A sort of smile played on his lips.

"Come," he said, "you have me in a snare, gentlemen. I confess myself conquered. You wish to ask for liberty, and—I give it you."

"Oh, my lord!" answered D'Artagnan, "you are too good; as to our liberty, we have that; we want to ask something else of you."

"You have your liberty?" repeated Mazarin, in terror.

"Certainly; and on the other hand, my lord, you have lost it, and now, in accordance with the law of war, sir, you must buy it back again."

Mazarin felt a shiver run through him—a chill even to his heart's core. His piercing look was fixed in vain on the satirical face of the Gascon and the unchanging countenance of Porthos. Both were in shadow and the Sybil of Cuma herself could not have read them.

"To purchase back my liberty?" said the cardinal.

"Yes, my lord."

"And how much will that cost me, Monsieur d'Artagnan?"

"Zounds, my lord, I don't know yet. We must ask the Comte de la Fere the question. Will your eminence deign to open the door which leads to the count's room, and in ten minutes all will be settled."

Mazarin started.

"My lord," said D'Artagnan, "your eminence sees that we wish to act with all formality and due respect; but I must warn you that we have no time to lose; open the door then, my lord, and be so good as to remember, once for all, that on the slightest attempt to escape or the faintest cry for help, our position being very critical indeed, you must not be angry with us if we go to extremities."

"Be assured," answered Mazarin, "that I shall attempt nothing; I give you my word of honor."

D'Artagnan made a sign to Porthos to redouble his watchfulness; then turning to Mazarin:

"Now, my lord, let us enter, if you please."

Chapter LXXXVI.

Conferences.

Mazarin turned the lock of a double door, on the threshold of which they found Athos ready to receive his illustrious guests according to the notice Comminges had given him.

On perceiving Mazarin he bowed.

"Your eminence," he said, "might have dispensed with your attendants; the honor bestowed on me is too great for me to be unmindful of it."

"And so, my dear count," said D'Artagnan, "his eminence didn't actually insist on our attending him; it is Du Vallon and I who have insisted, and even in a manner somewhat impolite, perhaps, so great was our longing to see you."

At that voice, that mocking tone, and that familiar gesture, accenting voice and tone, Athos made a bound of surprise.

"D'Artagnan! Porthos!" he exclaimed.

"My very self, dear friend."

"Me, also!" repeated Porthos.

"What means this?" asked the count.

"It means," replied Mazarin, trying to smile and biting his lips in the attempt, "that our parts are changed, and that instead of these gentlemen being my prisoners I am theirs; but, gentlemen, I warn you, unless you kill me, your victory will be of very short duration; people will come to the rescue."

"Ah! my lord!" cried the Gascon, "don't threaten! 'tis a bad example. We are so good and gentle to your eminence. Come, let us put aside all rancor and talk pleasantly."

"There's nothing I wish more," replied Mazarin. "But don't think yourselves in a better position than you are. In ensnaring me you have fallen into the trap yourselves. How are you to get away from here? remember the soldiers and sentinels who guard these doors. Now, I am going to show you how sincere I am."

"Good," thought D'Artagnan; "we must look about us; he's going to play us a trick."

"I offered you your liberty," continued the minister; "will you take it? Before an hour has passed you will be discovered, arrested, obliged to kill me, which would be a crime unworthy of loyal gentlemen like you."

"He is right," thought Athos.

And, like every other reflection passing in a mind that entertained none but noble thoughts, this feeling was expressed in his eyes.

"And therefore," said D'Artagnan, to clip the hope which Athos's tacit adhesion had imparted to Mazarin, "we shall not proceed to that violence save in the last extremity."

"If on the contrary," resumed Mazarin, "you accept your liberty——"

"Why you, my lord, might take it away from us in less than five minutes afterward; and from my knowledge of you I believe you will so take it away from us."

"No—on the faith of a cardinal. You do not believe me?"

"My lord, I never believe cardinals who are not priests."

"Well, on the faith of a minister."

"You are no longer a minister, my lord; you are a prisoner."

"Then, on the honor of a Mazarin, as I am and ever shall be, I hope," said the cardinal.

"Hem," replied D'Artagnan. "I have heard speak of a Mazarin who had not much religion when his oaths were in question. I fear he may have been an ancestor of your eminence."

"Monsieur d'Artagnan, you are a great wit and I am really sorry to be on bad terms with you."

"My lord, let us come to terms; I ask nothing better."

"Very well," said Mazarin, "if I place you in security, in a manner evident, palpable——"

"Ah! that is another thing," said Porthos.

"Let us see," said Athos.

"Let us see," said D'Artagnan.

"In the first place, do you accept?" asked the cardinal.

"Unfold your plan, my lord, and we will see."

"Take notice that you are shut up—captured."

"You well know, my lord, that there always remains to us a last resource."

"What?"

"That of dying together."

Mazarin shuddered.

"Listen," he said; "at the end of yonder corridor is a door, of which I have the key, it leads into the park. Go, and take this key with you; you are active, vigorous, and you have arms. At a hundred steps, on turning to the left, you will find the wall of the park; get over it, and in three leaps you will be on the road and free."

"Ah! by Jove, my lord," said D'Artagnan, "you have well said, but these are only words. Where is the key you speak of?"

"Here it is."

"Ah, my lord! You will conduct us yourself, then, to that door?"

"Very willingly, if it be necessary to reassure you," answered the minister, and Mazarin, who was delighted to get off so cheaply, led the way, in high spirits, to the corridor and opened the door.

It led into the park, as the three fugitives perceived by the night breeze which rushed into the corridor and blew the wind into their faces.

"The devil!" exclaimed the Gascon, "'tis a dreadful night, my lord. We don't know the locality, and shall never find the wall. Since your eminence has come so far, come a few steps further; conduct us, my lord, to the wall."

"Be it so," replied the cardinal; and walking in a straight line he went to the wall, at the foot of which they all four arrived at the same instant.

"Are you satisfied, gentlemen?" asked Mazarin.

"I think so, indeed; we should be hard to please if we were not. Deuce take it! three poor gentlemen escorted by a prince of the church! Ah! apropos, my lord! you remarked that we were all active, vigorous and armed."

"Yes."

"You are mistaken. Monsieur du Vallon and I are the only two who are armed. The count is not; and should we meet with one of your patrol we must defend ourselves."

"'Tis true."

"Where can we find another sword?" asked Porthos.

"My lord," said D'Artagnan, "will lend his, which is of no use to him, to the Comte de la Fere."

"Willingly," said the cardinal; "I will even ask the count to keep it for my sake."

"I promise you, my lord, never to part with it," replied Athos.

"Well, well," cried D'Artagnan, "this reconciliation is truly touching; have you not tears in your eyes, Porthos?"

"Yes," said Porthos; "but I do not know if it is feeling or the wind that makes me weep; I think it is the wind."

"Now climb up, Athos, quickly," said D'Artagnan. Athos, assisted by Porthos, who lifted him up like a feather, arrived at the top.

"Now, jump down, Athos."

Athos jumped and disappeared on the other side of the wall.

"Are you on the ground?" asked D'Artagnan.

"Yes."

"Without accident?"

"Perfectly safe and sound."

"Porthos, whilst I get up, watch the cardinal. No, I don't want your help, watch the cardinal."

"I am watching," said Porthos. "Well?"

"You are right; it is more difficult than I thought. Lend me your back—but don't let the cardinal go."

Porthos lent him his back and D'Artagnan was soon on the summit of the wall, where he seated himself.

Mazarin pretended to laugh.

"Are you there?" asked Porthos.

"Yes, my friend; and now——"

"Now, what?" asked Porthos.

"Now give me the cardinal up here; if he makes any noise stifle him."

Mazarin wished to call out, but Porthos held him tight and passed him to D'Artagnan, who seized him by the neck and made him sit down by him; then in a menacing tone, he said:

"Sir! jump directly down, close to Monsieur de la Fere, or, on the honor of a gentleman, I'll kill you!"

"Monsieur, monsieur," cried Mazarin, "you are breaking your word to me!"

"I—did I promise you anything, my lord?"

Mazarin groaned.

"You are free," he said, "through me; your liberty was my ransom."

"Agreed; but the ransom of that immense treasure buried under the gallery, to which one descends on pushing a spring hidden in the wall, which causes a tub to turn, revealing a staircase—must not one speak of that a little, my lord?"

"Diavolo!" cried Mazarin, almost choked, and clasping his hands; "I am a lost and ruined man!"

But without listening to his protestations of alarm, D'Artagnan slipped him gently down into the arms of Athos, who stood immovable at the bottom of the wall.

Porthos next made an effort which shook the solid wall, and by the aid of his friend's hand gained the summit.

"I didn't understand it all," he said, "but I understand now; how droll it is!"

"You think so? so much the better; but that it may prove laughter-worthy even to the end, let us not lose time." And he jumped off the wall.

Porthos did the same.

"Attend to monsieur le cardinal, gentlemen," said D'Artagnan; "for myself, I will reconnoitre."

The Gascon then drew his sword and marched as avant guard.

"My lord," he said, "which way do we go? Think well of your reply, for should your eminence be mistaken, there might ensue most grave results for all of us."

"Along the wall, sir," said Mazarin, "there will be no danger of losing yourselves."

The three friends hastened on, but in a short time were obliged to slacken the pace. The cardinal could not keep up with them, though with every wish to do so.

Suddenly D'Artagnan touched something warm, which moved.

"Stop! a horse!" he cried; "I have found a horse!"

"And I, likewise," said Athos.

"I, too," said Porthos, who, faithful to the instructions, still held the cardinal's arm.

"There's luck, my lord! just as you were complaining of being tired and obliged to walk."

But as he spoke the barrel of a pistol was presented at his breast and these words were pronounced:

"Touch it not!"

"Grimaud!" he cried; "Grimaud! what art thou about? Why, thou art posted here by Heaven!"

"No, sir," said the honest servant, "it was Monsieur Aramis who posted me here to take care of the horses."

"Is Aramis here?"

"Yes, sir; he has been here since yesterday."

"What are you doing?"

"On the watch——"

"What! Aramis here?" cried Athos.

"At the lesser gate of the castle; he's posted there."

"Are you a large party?"

"Sixty."

"Let him know."

"This moment, sir."

And believing that no one could execute the commission better than himself, Grimaud set off at full speed; whilst, enchanted at being all together again, the friends awaited his return.

There was no one in the whole group in a bad humor except Cardinal Mazarin.

Chapter LXXXVII.

Thinking that Porthos will be at last a Baron, and D'Artagnan a Captain.

At the expiration of ten minutes Aramis arrived, accompanied by Grimaud and eight or ten followers. He was excessively delighted and threw himself into his friends' arms.

"You are free, my brothers! free without my aid! and I shall have succeeded in doing nothing for you in spite of all my efforts."

"Do not be unhappy, dear friend, on that account; if you have done nothing as yet, you will do something soon," replied Athos.

"I had well concerted my plans," pursued Aramis; "the coadjutor gave me sixty men; twenty guard the walls of the park, twenty the road from Rueil to Saint Germain, twenty are dispersed in the woods. Thus I was able, thanks to the strategic disposition of my forces, to intercept two couriers from Mazarin to the queen."

Mazarin listened intently.

"But," said D'Artagnan, "I trust that you honorably sent them back to monsieur le cardinal!"

"Ah, yes!" said Aramis, "toward him I should be very likely to practice such delicacy of sentiment! In one of the despatches the cardinal declares to the queen that the treasury is empty and that her majesty has no more money. In the other he announces that he is about to transport his prisoners to Melun, since Rueil seemed to him not sufficiently secure. You can understand, dear friend, with what hope I was inspired by that last letter. I placed myself in ambuscade with my sixty men; I encircled the castle; the riding horses I entrusted to Grimaud and I awaited your coming out, which I did not expect till to-morrow, and I didn't hope to free you without a skirmish. You are free to-night, without fighting; so much the better! How did you manage to escape that scoundrel Mazarin? You must have much reason to complain of him."

"Not very much," said D'Artagnan.

"Really!"

"I might even say that we have some reason to praise him."

"Impossible!"

"Yes, really; it is owing to him that we are free."

"Owing to him?"

"Yes, he had us conducted into the orangery by Monsieur Bernouin, his valet-de-chambre, and from there we followed him to visit the Comte de la Fere. Then he offered us our liberty and we accepted it. He even went so far as to show us the way out; he led us to the park wall, which we climbed over without accident, and then we fell in with Grimaud."

"Well!" exclaimed Aramis, "this will reconcile me to him; but I wish he were here that I might tell him that I did not believe him capable of so noble an act."

"My lord," said D'Artagnan, no longer able to contain himself, "allow me to introduce to you the Chevalier d'Herblay, who wishes—as you may have heard—to offer his congratulations to your eminence."

And he retired, discovering Mazarin, who was in great confusion, to the astonished gaze of Aramis.

"Ho! ho!" exclaimed the latter, "the cardinal! a glorious prize! Halloo! halloo! friends! to horse! to horse!"

Several horsemen ran quickly to him.

"Zounds!" cried Aramis, "I may have done some good; so, my lord, deign to receive my most respectful homage! I will lay a wager that 'twas that Saint Christopher, Porthos, who performed this feat! Apropos! I forgot——" and he gave some orders in a low voice to one of the horsemen.

"I think it will be wise to set off," said D'Artagnan.

"Yes; but I am expecting some one, a friend of Athos."

"A friend!" exclaimed the count.

"And here he comes, by Jupiter! galloping through the bushes."

"The count! the count!" cried a young voice that made Athos start.

"Raoul! Raoul!" he ejaculated.

For one moment the young man forgot his habitual respect—he threw himself on his father's neck.

"Look, my lord cardinal," said Aramis, "would it not have been a pity to have separated men who love each other as we love? Gentlemen," he continued, addressing the cavaliers, who became more and more numerous every instant; "gentlemen, encircle his eminence, that you may show him the greater honor. He will, indeed give us the favor of his company; you will, I hope, be grateful for it; Porthos, do not lose sight of his eminence."

Aramis then joined Athos and D'Artagnan, who were consulting together.

"Come," said D'Artagnan, after a conference of five minutes' duration, "let us begin our journey."

"Where are we to go?" asked Porthos.

"To your house, dear Porthos, at Pierrefonds; your fine chateau is worthy of affording its princely hospitality to his eminence; it is, likewise, well situated—neither too near Paris, nor too far from it; we can establish a communication between it and the capital with great facility. Come, my lord, you shall be treated like a prince, as you are."

"A fallen prince!" exclaimed Mazarin, piteously.

"The chances of war," said Athos, "are many, but be assured we shall take no improper advantage of them."

"No, but we shall make use of them," said D'Artagnan.

The rest of the night was employed by these cavaliers in traveling with the wonderful rapidity of former days. Mazarin, still sombre and pensive, permitted himself to be dragged along in this way; it looked a race of phantoms. At dawn twelve leagues had been passed without drawing rein; half the escort were exhausted and several horses fell down.

"Horses, nowadays, are not what they were formerly," observed Porthos; "everything degenerates."

"I have sent Grimaud to Dammartin," said Aramis. "He is to bring us five fresh horses—one for his eminence, four for us. We, at least, must keep close to monseigneur; the rest of the start will rejoin us later. Once beyond Saint Denis we shall have nothing to fear."

Grimaud, in fact, brought back five horses. The nobleman to whom he applied, being a friend of Porthos, was very ready, not to sell them, as was proposed, but to lend them. Ten minutes later the escort stopped at Ermenonville, but the four friends went on with well sustained ardor, guarding Mazarin carefully. At noon they rode into the avenue of Pierrefonds.

"Ah!" said Mousqueton, who had ridden by the side of D'Artagnan without speaking a word on the journey, "you may think what you will, sir, but I can breathe now for the first time since my departure from Pierrefonds;" and he put his horse to a gallop to announce to the other servants the arrival of Monsieur du Vallon and his friends.

"We are four of us," said D'Artagnan; "we must relieve each other in mounting guard over my lord and each of us must watch three hours at a time. Athos is going to examine the castle, which it will be necessary to render impregnable in case of siege; Porthos will see to the provisions and Aramis to the troops of the garrison. That is to say, Athos will be chief engineer, Porthos purveyor-in-general, and Aramis governor of the fortress."

Meanwhile, they gave up to Mazarin the handsomest room in the chateau.

"Gentlemen," he said, when he was in his room, "you do not expect, I presume, to keep me here a long time incognito?"

"No, my lord," replied the Gascon; "on the contrary, we think of announcing very soon that we have you here."

"Then you will be besieged."

"We expect it."

"And what shall you do?"

"Defend ourselves. Were the late Cardinal Richelieu alive he would tell you a certain story of the Bastion Saint Gervais, which we four, with our four lackeys and twelve dead men, held out against a whole army."

"Such feats, sir, are done once—and never repeated."

"However, nowadays there's no need of so much heroism. To-morrow the army of Paris will be summoned, the day after it will be here! The field of battle, instead, therefore, of being at Saint Denis or at Charenton, will be near Compiegne or Villars-Cotterets."

"The prince will vanquish you, as he has always done."

"'Tis possible; my lord; but before an engagement ensues we shall move your eminence to another castle belonging to our friend Du Vallon, who has three. We will not expose your eminence to the chances of war."

"Come," answered Mazarin, "I see it will be necessary for me to capitulate."

"Before a siege?"

"Yes; the conditions will be better than afterward."

"Ah, my lord! as to conditions, you would soon see how moderate and reasonable we are!"

"Come, now, what are your conditions?"

"Rest yourself first, my lord, and we—we will reflect."

"I do not need rest, gentlemen; I need to know whether I am among enemies or friends."

"Friends, my lord! friends!"

"Well, then, tell me at once what you want, that I may see if any arrangement be possible. Speak, Comte de la Fere!"

"My lord," replied Athos, "for myself I have nothing to demand. For France, were I to specify my wishes, I should have too much. I beg you to excuse me and propose to the chevalier."

And Athos, bowing, retired and remained leaning against the mantelpiece, a spectator of the scene.

"Speak, then, chevalier!" said the cardinal. "What do you want? Nothing ambiguous, if you please. Be clear, short and precise."

"As for me," replied Aramis, "I have in my pocket the very programme of the conditions which the deputation—of which I formed one—went yesterday to Saint Germain to impose on you. Let us consider first the ancient rights. The demands in that programme must be granted."

"We were almost agreed on those," replied Mazarin; "let us pass on to private and personal stipulations."

"You suppose, then, that there are some?" said Aramis, smiling.

"I do not suppose that you will all be quite so disinterested as Monsieur de la Fere," replied the cardinal, bowing to Athos.

"My lord, you are right, and I am glad to see that you do justice to the count at last. The count has a mind above vulgar desires and earthly passions. He is a proud soul—he is a man by himself! You are right—he is worth us all, and we avow it to you!"

"Aramis," said Athos, "are you jesting?"

"No, no, dear friend; I state only what we all know. You are right; it is not you alone this matter concerns, but my lord and his unworthy servant, myself."

"Well, then, what do you require besides the general conditions before recited?"

"I require, my lord, that Normandy should be given to Madame de Longueville, with five hundred thousand francs and full absolution. I require that his majesty should deign to be godfather to the child she has just borne;

and that my lord, after having been present at the christening, should go to proffer his homage to our Holy Father the Pope."

"That is, you wish me to lay aside my ministerial functions, to quit France and be an exile."

"I wish his eminence to become pope on the first opportunity, allowing me then the right of demanding full indulgences for myself and my friends."

Mazarin made a grimace which was quite indescribable, and then turned to D'Artagnan.

"And you, sir?" he said.

"I, my lord," answered the Gascon, "I differ from Monsieur d'Herblay entirely as to the last point, though I agree with him on the first. Far from wishing my lord to quit Paris, I hope he will stay there and continue to be prime minister, as he is a great statesman. I shall try also to help him to down the Fronde, but on one condition—that he sometimes remembers the king's faithful servants and gives the first vacant company of musketeers to a man that I could name. And you, Monsieur du Vallon——"

"Yes, you, sir! Speak, if you please," said Mazarin.

"As for me," answered Porthos, "I wish my lord cardinal, in order to do honor to my house, which gives him an asylum, would in remembrance of this adventure erect my estate into a barony, with a promise to confer that order on one of my particular friends, whenever his majesty next creates peers."

"You know, sir, that before receiving the order one must submit proofs."

"My friends will submit them. Besides, should it be necessary, monseigneur will show him how that formality may be avoided."

Mazarin bit his lips; the blow was direct and he replied rather dryly:

"All this appears to me to be ill conceived, disjointed, gentlemen; for if I satisfy some I shall displease others. If I stay in Paris I cannot go to Rome; if I became pope I could not continue to be prime minister; and it is only by continuing prime minister that I can make Monsieur d'Artagnan a captain and Monsieur du Vallon a baron."

"True," said Aramis, "so, as I am in a minority, I withdraw my proposition, so far as it relates to the voyage to Rome and monseigneur's resignation."

"I am to remain minister, then?" said Mazarin.

"You remain minister; that is understood," said D'Artagnan; "France needs you."

"And I desist from my pretensions," said Aramis. "His eminence will continue to be prime minister and her majesty's favorite, if he will grant to me and my friends what we demand for France and for ourselves."

"Occupy yourselves with your own affairs, gentlemen, and let France settle matters as she will with me," resumed Mazarin.

"Ho! ho!" replied Aramis. "The Frondeurs will have a treaty and your eminence must sign it before us, promising at the same time to obtain the queen's consent to it."

"I can answer only for myself," said Mazarin. "I cannot answer for the queen. Suppose her majesty refuses?"

"Oh!" said D'Artagnan, "monseigneur knows very well that her majesty refuses him nothing."

"Here, monseigneur," said Aramis, "is the treaty proposed by the deputation of Frondeurs. Will your eminence please read and examine?"

"I am acquainted with it."

"Sign it, then."

"Reflect, gentlemen, that a signature given under circumstances like the present might be regarded as extorted by violence."

"Monseigneur will be at hand to testify that it was freely given."

"Suppose I refuse?"

"Then," said D'Artagnan, "your eminence must expect the consequences of a refusal."

"Would you dare to touch a cardinal?"

"You have dared, my lord, to imprison her majesty's musketeers."

"The queen will revenge me, gentlemen."

"I do not think so, although inclination might lead her to do so, but we shall take your eminence to Paris, and the Parisians will defend us."

"How uneasy they must be at this moment at Rueil and Saint Germain," said Aramis. "How they must be asking, 'Where is the cardinal?' 'What has become of the minister?' 'Where has the favorite gone?' How they must be looking for monseigneur in all corners! What comments must be made; and if the Fronde knows that monseigneur has disappeared, how the Fronde must triumph!"

"It is frightful," murmured Mazarin.

"Sign the treaty, then, monseigneur," said Aramis.

"Suppose the queen should refuse to ratify it?"

"Ah! nonsense!" cried D'Artagnan, "I can manage so that her majesty will receive me well; I know an excellent method."

"What?"

"I shall take her majesty the letter in which you tell her that the finances are exhausted."

"And then?" asked Mazarin, turning pale.

"When I see her majesty embarrassed, I shall conduct her to Rueil, make her enter the orangery and show her a certain spring which turns a box."

"Enough, sir," muttered the cardinal, "you have said enough; where is the treaty?"

"Here it is," replied Aramis. "Sign, my lord," and he gave him a pen.

Mazarin arose, walked some moments, thoughtful, but not dejected.

"And when I have signed," he said, "what is to be my guarantee?"

"My word of honor, sir," said Athos.

Mazarin started, turned toward the Comte de la Fere, and looking for an instant at that grand and honest countenance, took the pen.

"It is sufficient, count," he said, and signed the treaty.

"And now, Monsieur d'Artagnan," he said, "prepare to set off for Saint Germain and take a letter from me to the queen."

Chapter LXXXVIII.

Shows how with Threat and Pen more is effected than by the Sword.

D'Artagnan knew his part well; he was aware that opportunity has a forelock only for him who will take it and he was not a man to let it go by him without seizing it. He soon arranged a prompt and certain manner of traveling, by sending relays of horses to Chantilly, so that he might be in Paris in five or six hours. But before setting out he reflected that for a lad of intelligence and experience he was in a singular predicament, since he was proceeding toward uncertainty and leaving certainty behind him.

"In fact," he said, as he was about to mount and start on his dangerous mission, "Athos, for generosity, is a hero of romance; Porthos has an excellent disposition, but is easily influenced; Aramis has a hieroglyphic countenance, always illegible. What will come out of those three elements when I am no longer present to combine them? The deliverance of the cardinal, perhaps. Now, the deliverance of the cardinal would be the ruin of our hopes; and our hopes are thus far the only recompense we have for labors in comparison with which those of Hercules were pygmean."

He went to find Aramis.

"You, my dear Chevalier d'Herblay," he said, "are the Fronde incarnate. Mistrust Athos, therefore, who will not prosecute the affairs of any one, even his own. Mistrust Porthos, especially, who, to please the count whom he regards as God on earth, will assist him in contriving Mazarin's escape, if Mazarin has the wit to weep or play the chivalric."

Aramis smiled; his smile was at once cunning and resolute.

"Fear nothing," he said; "I have my conditions to impose. My private ambition tends only to the profit of him who has justice on his side."

"Good!" thought D'Artagnan: "in this direction I am satisfied." He pressed Aramis's hand and went in search of Porthos.

"Friend," he said, "you have worked so hard with me toward building up our fortune, that, at the moment when we are about to reap the fruits of our labours, it would be a ridiculous piece of silliness in you to allow yourself to be controlled by Aramis, whose cunning you know—a cunning which, we may say between ourselves, is not always without egotism; or by Athos, a noble and disinterested man, but blasé, who, desiring nothing further for himself, doesn't sympathize with the desires of others. What should you say if either of these two friends proposed to you to let Mazarin go?"

"Why, I should say that we had too much trouble in taking him to let him off so easily."

"Bravo, Porthos! and you would be right, my friend; for in losing him you would lose your barony, which you have in your grasp, to say nothing of the fact that, were he once out of this, Mazarin would have you hanged."

"Do you think so?"

"I am sure of it."

"Then I would kill him rather than let him go."

"And you would act rightly. There is no question, you understand, provided we secure our own interests, of securing those of the Frondeurs; who, besides, don't understand political matters as we old soldiers do."

"Never fear, dear friend," said Porthos. "I shall see you through the window as you mount your horse; I shall follow you with my eyes as long as you are in sight; then I shall place myself at the cardinal's door—a door with glass windows. I shall see everything, and at the least suspicious sign I shall begin to exterminate."

"Bravo!" thought D'Artagnan; "on this side I think the cardinal will be well guarded." He pressed the hand of the lord of Pierrefonds and went in search of Athos.

"My dear Athos," he said, "I am going away. I have only one thing to say to you. You know Anne of Austria; the captivity of Mazarin alone guarantees my life; if you let him go I am a dead man."

"I needed nothing less than that consideration, my dear D'Artagnan, to persuade myself to adopt the role of jailer. I give you my word that you will find the cardinal where you leave him."

"This reassures me more than all the royal signatures," thought D'Artagnan. "Now that I have the word of Athos I can set out."

D'Artagnan started alone on his journey, without other escort than his sword, and with a simple passport from Mazarin to secure his admission to the queen's presence. Six hours after he left Pierrefonds he was at Saint Germain.

The disappearance of Mazarin was not as yet generally known. Anne of Austria was informed of it and concealed her uneasiness from every one. In the chamber of D'Artagnan and Porthos the two soldiers had been found bound and gagged. On recovering the use of their limbs and tongues they could, of course, tell nothing but what they knew—that they had been seized, stripped and bound. But as to what had been done by Porthos and D'Artagnan afterward they were as ignorant as all the inhabitants of the chateau.

Bernouin alone knew a little more than the others. Bernouin, seeing that his master did not return and hearing the stroke of midnight, had made an examination of the orangery. The first door, barricaded with furniture, had aroused in him certain suspicions, but without communicating his suspicions to any one he had patiently worked his way into the midst of all that confusion. Then he came to the corridor, all the doors of which he found open; so, too, was the door of Athos's chamber and that of the park. From the latter point it was easy to follow tracks on the snow. He saw that these tracks tended toward the wall; on the other side he found similar tracks, then footprints of horses and then signs of a troop of cavalry which had moved away in the direction of Enghien. He could no longer cherish any doubt that the cardinal had been carried off by the three prisoners, since the prisoners had disappeared at the same time; and he had hastened to Saint Germain to warn the queen of that disappearance.

Anne had enforced the utmost secrecy and had disclosed the event to no one except the Prince de Condé, who had sent five or six hundred horsemen into the environs of Saint Germain with orders to bring in any suspicious person who was going away from Rueil, in whatsoever direction it might be.

Now, since D'Artagnan did not constitute a body of horsemen, since he was alone, since he was not going away from Rueil and was going to Saint Germain, no one paid any attention to him and his journey was not obstructed in any way.

On entering the courtyard of the old chateau the first person seen by our ambassador was Maitre Bernouin in person, who, standing on the threshold, awaited news of his vanished master.

At the sight of D'Artagnan, who entered the courtyard on horseback, Bernouin rubbed his eyes and thought he must be mistaken. But D'Artagnan made a friendly sign to him with his head, dismounted, and throwing his bridle to a lackey who was passing, he approached the valet-de-chambre with a smile on his lips.

"Monsieur d'Artagnan!" cried the latter, like a man who has the nightmare and talks in his sleep, "Monsieur d'Artagnan!"

"Himself, Monsieur Bernouin."

"And why have you come here?"

"To bring news of Monsieur de Mazarin—the freshest news there is."

"What has become of him, then?"

"He is as well as you and I."

"Nothing bad has happened to him, then?"

"Absolutely nothing. He felt the need of making a trip in the Ile de France, and begged us—the Comte de la Fere and Monsieur du Vallon—to accompany him. We were too devoted servants to refuse him a request of that sort. We set out last evening and here we are."

"Here you are."

"His eminence had something to communicate to her majesty, something secret and private—a mission that could be confided only to a sure man—and so has sent me to Saint Germain. And therefore, my dear Monsieur Bernouin, if you wish to do what will be pleasing to your master, announce to her majesty that I have come, and tell her with what purpose."

Whether he spoke seriously or in jest, since it was evident that under existing circumstances D'Artagnan was the only man who could relieve the queen's uneasiness, Bernouin went without hesitation to announce to her this strange embassy; and as he had foreseen, the queen gave orders to introduce Monsieur d'Artagnan at once.

D'Artagnan approached the sovereign with every mark of profound respect, and having fallen on his knees presented to her the cardinal's letter.

It was, however, merely a letter of introduction. The queen read it, recognized the writing, and, since there were no details in it of what had occurred, asked for particulars. D'Artagnan related everything with that simple and ingenuous air which he knew how to assume on occasions. The queen, as he went on, looked at him with increasing astonishment. She could not comprehend how a man could conceive such an enterprise and still less how he could have the audacity to disclose it to her whose interest and almost duty it was to punish him.

"How, sir!" she cried, as D'Artagnan finished, "you dare to tell me the details of your crime—to give me an account of your treason!"

"Pardon, madame, but I think that either I have expressed myself badly or your majesty has imperfectly understood me. There is here no question of crime or treason. Monsieur de Mazarin held us in prison, Monsieur du Vallon and myself, because we could not believe that he had sent us to England to quietly look on while they cut off the head of Charles I., brother-in-law of the late king, your husband, the consort of Madame Henrietta, your sister and your guest, and because we did all that we could do to save the life of the royal martyr. We were then convinced, my friend and I, that there was some error of which we were the victims, and that an explanation was called for between his eminence and ourselves. Now, that an explanation may bear fruit, it is necessary that it should be quietly conducted, far from noise and interruption. We have therefore taken away monsieur le cardinal to my friend's chateau and there we have come to an understanding. Well, madame, it proved to be as we had supposed; there was a mistake. Monsieur de Mazarin had thought that we had rendered service to General Cromwell, instead of King Charles, which would have been a disgrace, rebounding from us to him, and from him to your majesty—a dishonor which would have tainted the royalty of your illustrious son. We were able to prove the contrary, and that proof we are ready to give to your majesty, calling in support of it the august widow weeping in the Louvre, where your royal munificence has provided for her a home. That proof satisfied him so completely that, as a sign of satisfaction, he has sent me, as your majesty may see, to consider with you what reparation should be made to gentlemen unjustly treated and wrongfully persecuted."

"I listen to you, and I wonder at you, sir," said the queen. "In fact, I have rarely seen such excess of impudence."

"Your majesty, on your side," said D'Artagnan, "is as much mistaken as to our intentions as the Cardinal Mazarin has always been."

"You are in error, sir," answered the queen. "I am so little mistaken that in ten minutes you shall be arrested, and in an hour I shall set off at the head of my army to release my minister."

"I am sure your majesty will not commit such an act of imprudence, first, because it would be useless and would produce the most disastrous results. Before he could be possibly set free the cardinal would be dead; and indeed, so convinced is he of this, that he entreated me, should I find your majesty disposed to act in this way, to do all I could to induce you to change your resolution."

"Well, then, I will content myself with arresting you!"

"Madame, the possibility of my arrest has been foreseen, and should I not have returned by to-morrow, at a certain hour the next day the cardinal will be brought to Paris and delivered to the parliament."

"It is evident, sir, that your position has kept you out of relation to men and affairs; otherwise you would know that since we left Paris monsieur le cardinal has returned thither five or six times; that he has there met De Beaufort, De Bouillon, the coadjutor and D'Elbeuf and that not one of them had any desire to arrest him."

"Your pardon, madame, I know all that. And therefore my friends will conduct monsieur le cardinal neither to De Beaufort, nor to De Bouillon, nor to the coadjutor, nor to D'Elbeuf. These gentlemen wage war on private account, and in buying them up, by granting them what they wished, monsieur le cardinal has made a good bargain. He will be delivered to the parliament, members of which can, of course, be bought, but even Monsieur de Mazarin is not rich enough to buy the whole body."

"I think," returned Anne of Austria, fixing upon him a glance, which in any woman's face would have expressed disdain, but in a queen's, spread terror to those she looked upon, "nay, I perceive you dare to threaten the mother of your sovereign."

"Madame," replied D'Artagnan, "I threaten simply and solely because I am obliged to do so. Believe me, madame, as true a thing as it is that a heart beats in this bosom—a heart devoted to you—believe that you have been the idol of our lives; that we have, as you well know—good Heaven!—risked our lives twenty times for your majesty. Have you, then, madame, no compassion for your servants who for twenty years have vegetated in obscurity, without betraying in a single sigh the solemn and sacred secrets they have had the honor to share with you? Look at me, madame—at me, whom you accuse of speaking loud and threateningly. What am I? A poor officer, without fortune, without protection, without a future, unless the eye of my queen, which I have sought so long, rests on me for a moment. Look at the Comte de la Fere, a type of nobility, a flower of chivalry. He has taken part against his queen, or rather, against her minister. He has not been unreasonably exacting, it seems to me. Look at Monsieur du Vallon, that faithful soul, that arm of steel, who for twenty years has awaited the word from your lips which will make him in rank what he is in sentiment and in courage. Consider, in short, your people who love you and who yet are famished, who have no other wish than to bless you, and who, nevertheless—no, I am wrong, your subjects, madame, will never curse you; say one word to them and all will be ended—peace succeed war, joy tears, and happiness to misfortune!"

Anne of Austria looked with wonderment on the warlike countenance of D'Artagnan, which betrayed a singular expression of deep feeling.

"Why did you not say all this before you took action, sir?" she said.

"Because, madame, it was necessary to prove to your majesty one thing of which you doubted—-that is, that we still possess amongst us some valor and are worthy of some consideration at your hands."

"And that valor would shrink from no undertaking, according to what I see."

"It has hesitated at nothing in the past; why, then, should it be less daring in the future?"

"Then, in case of my refusal, this valor, should a struggle occur, will even go the length of carrying me off in the midst of my court, to deliver me into the hands of the Fronde, as you propose to deliver my minister?"

"We have not thought about it yet, madame," answered D'Artagnan, with that Gascon effrontery which had in him the appearance of naivete; "but if we four had resolved upon it we should do it most certainly."

"I ought," muttered Anne to herself, "by this time to remember that these men are giants."

"Alas, madame!" exclaimed D'Artagnan, "this proves to me that not till to-day has your majesty had a just idea of us."

"Perhaps," said Anne; "but that idea, if at last I have it——"

"Your majesty will do us justice. In doing us justice you will no longer treat us as men of vulgar stamp. You will see in me an ambassador worthy of the high interests he is authorized to discuss with his sovereign."

"Where is the treaty?"

"Here it is."

Anne of Austria cast her eyes upon the treaty that D'Artagnan presented to her.

"I do not see here," she said, "anything but general conditions; the interests of the Prince de Conti or of the Ducs de Beaufort, de Bouillon and d'Elbeuf and of the coadjutor, are herein consulted; but with regard to yours?"

"We do ourselves justice, madame, even in assuming the high position that we have. We do not think ourselves worthy to stand near such great names."

"But you, I presume, have decided to assert your pretensions viva voce?"

"I believe you, madame, to be a great and powerful queen, and that it will be unworthy of your power and greatness if you do not recompense the arms which will bring back his eminence to Saint Germain."

"It is my intention so to do; come, let us hear you. Speak."

"He who has negotiated these matters (forgive me if I begin by speaking of myself, but I must claim that importance which has been given to me, not assumed by me) he who has arranged matters for the return of the cardinal, ought, it appears to me, in order that his reward may not be unworthy of your majesty, to be made commandant of the guards—an appointment something like that of captain of the musketeers."

"'Tis the appointment Monsieur de Tréville held, you ask of me."

"The place, madame, is vacant, and although 'tis a year since Monsieur de Tréville has left it, it has not been filled."

"But it is one of the principal military appointments in the king's household."

"Monsieur de Tréville was but a younger son of a simple Gascon family, like me, madame; he occupied that post for twenty years."

"You have an answer ready for everything," replied the queen, and she took from her bureau a document, which she filled up and signed.

"Undoubtedly, madame," said D'Artagnan, taking the document and bowing, "this is a noble reward; but everything in the world is unstable, and the man who happened to fall into disgrace with your majesty might lose this office to-morrow."

"What more do you want?" asked the queen, coloring, as she found that she had to deal with a mind as subtle as her own.

"A hundred thousand francs for this poor captain of musketeers, to be paid whenever his services shall no longer be acceptable to your majesty."

Anne hesitated.

"To think of the Parisians," soliloquized D'Artagnan, "offering only the other day, by an edict of the parliament, six hundred thousand francs to any man soever who would deliver up the cardinal to them, dead or alive—if alive, in order to hang him; if dead, to deny him the rites of Christian burial!"

"Come," said Anne, "'tis reasonable, since you only ask from a queen the sixth of what the parliament has proposed;" and she signed an order for a hundred thousand francs.

"Now, then," she said, "what next?"

"Madame, my friend Du Vallon is rich and has therefore nothing in the way of fortune to desire; but I think I remember that there was a question between him and Monsieur Mazarin as to making his estate a barony. Nay, it must have been a promise."

"A country clown," said Anne of Austria, "people will laugh."

"Let them," answered D'Artagnan. "But I am sure of one thing—that those who laugh at him in his presence will never laugh a second time."

"Here goes the barony." said the queen; she signed a patent.

"Now there remains the chevalier, or the Abbé d'Herblay, as your majesty pleases."

"Does he wish to be a bishop?"

"No, madame, something easier to grant."

"What?"

"It is that the king should deign to stand godfather to the son of Madame de Longueville."

The queen smiled.

"Monsieur de Longueville is of royal blood, madame," said D'Artagnan.

"Yes," said the queen; "but his son?"

"His son, madame, must be, since the husband of the son's mother is."

"And your friend has nothing more to ask for Madame de Longueville?"

"No, madame, for I presume that the king, standing godfather to him, could do no less than present him with five hundred thousand francs, giving his father, also, the government of Normandy."

"As to the government of Normandy," replied the queen, "I think I can promise; but with regard to the present, the cardinal is always telling me there is no more money in the royal coffers."

"We shall search for some, madame, and I think we can find a little, and if your majesty approves, we will seek for some together."

"What next?"

"What next, madame?"

"Yes."

"That is all."

"Haven't you, then, a fourth companion?"

"Yes, madame, the Comte de la Fere."

"What does he ask?"

"Nothing."

"There is in the world, then, one man who, having the power to ask, asks—nothing!"

"There is the Comte de la Fere, madame. The Comte de la Fere is not a man."

"What is he, then?"

"The Comte de la Fere is a demi-god."

"Has he not a son, a young man, a relative, a nephew, of whom Comminges spoke to me as being a brave boy, and who, with Monsieur de Chatillon, brought the standards from Lens?"

"He has, as your majesty has said, a ward, who is called the Vicomte de Bragelonne."

"If that young man should be appointed to a regiment what would his guardian say?"

"Perhaps he would accept."

"Perhaps?"

"Yes, if your majesty herself should beg him to accept."

"He must be indeed a strange man. Well, we will reflect and perhaps we will beg him. Are you satisfied, sir?"

"There is one thing the queen has not signed—her assent to the treaty."

"Of what use to-day? I will sign it to-morrow."

"I can assure her majesty that if she does not sign to-day she will not have time to sign to-morrow. Consent, then, I beg you, madame, to write at the bottom of this schedule, which has been drawn up by Mazarin, as you see:

"'I consent to ratify the treaty proposed by the Parisians.'"

Anne was caught, she could not draw back—she signed; but scarcely had she done so when pride burst forth and she began to weep.

D'Artagnan started on seeing these tears. Since that period of history queens have shed tears, like other women.

The Gascon shook his head, these tears from royalty melted his heart.

"Madame," he said, kneeling, "look upon the unhappy man at your feet. He begs you to believe that at a gesture of your majesty everything will be possible to him. He has faith in himself; he has faith in his friends; he wishes also to have faith in his queen. And in proof that he fears nothing, that he counts on nothing, he will restore Monsieur de Mazarin to your majesty without conditions. Behold, madame! here are the august signatures of your majesty's hand; if you think you are right in giving them to me, you shall do so, but from this very moment you are free from any obligation to keep them."

And D'Artagnan, full of splendid pride and manly intrepidity, placed in Anne's hands, in a bundle, the papers that he had one by one won from her with so much difficulty.

There are moments—for if everything is not good, everything in this world is not bad—in which the most rigid and the coldest soul is softened by the tears of strong emotion, heart-arraigning sentiment: one of these momentary impulses actuated Anne. D'Artagnan, when he gave way to his own feelings—which were in accordance with those of the queen—had accomplished more than the most astute diplomacy could have attempted. He was therefore instantly recompensed, either for his address or for his sensibility, whichever it might be termed.

"You were right, sir," said Anne. "I misunderstood you. There are the acts signed; I deliver them to you without compulsion. Go and bring me back the cardinal as soon as possible."

"Madame," faltered D'Artagnan, "'tis twenty years ago—I have a good memory—since I had the honor behind a piece of tapestry in the Hotel de Ville, of kissing one of those lovely hands."

"There is the other," replied the queen; "and that the left hand should not be less liberal than the right," she drew from her finger a diamond similar to the one formerly given to him, "take and keep this ring in remembrance of me."

"Madame," said D'Artagnan, rising, "I have only one thing more to wish, which is, that the next thing you ask from me, shall be—my life."

And with this conclusion—a way peculiar to himself—he rose and left the room.

"I never rightly understood those men," said the queen, as she watched him retiring from her presence; "and it is now too late, for in a year the king will be of age."

In twenty-four hours D'Artagnan and Porthos conducted Mazarin to the queen; and the one received his commission, the other his patent of nobility.

On the same day the Treaty of Paris was signed, and it was everywhere announced that the cardinal had shut himself up for three days in order to draw it up with the greatest care.

Here is what each of the parties concerned gained by that treaty:

Monsieur de Conti received Damvilliers, and having made his proofs as general, he succeeded in remaining a soldier, instead of being made cardinal. Moreover, something had been said of a marriage with Mazarin's niece. The idea was welcomed by the prince, to whom it was of little importance whom he married, so long as he married some one.

The Duc de Beaufort made his entrance at court, receiving ample reparation for the wrongs he had suffered, and all the honor due to his rank. Full pardon was accorded to those who had aided in his escape. He received also the office of admiral, which had been held by his father, the Duc de Vendome and an indemnity for his houses and castles, demolished by the Parliament of Bretagne.

The Duc de Bouillon received domains of a value equal to that of his principality of Sedan, and the title of prince, granted to him and to those belonging to his house.

The Duc de Longueville gained the government of Pont-de-l'Arche, five hundred thousand francs for his wife and the honor of seeing her son held at the baptismal font by the young king and Henrietta of England.

Aramis stipulated that Bazin should officiate at that ceremony and that Planchet should furnish the christening sugar plums.

The Duc d'Elbeuf obtained payment of certain sums due to his wife, one hundred thousand francs for his eldest son and twenty-five thousand for each of the three others.

The coadjutor alone obtained nothing. They promised, indeed, to negotiate with the pope for a cardinal's hat for him; but he knew how little reliance should be placed on such promises, made by the queen and Mazarin. Quite contrary to the lot of Monsieur de Conti, unable to be cardinal, he was obliged to remain a soldier.

And therefore, when all Paris was rejoicing in the expected return of the king, appointed for the next day, Gondy alone, in the midst of the general happiness, was dissatisfied; he sent for the two men whom he was wont to summon when in especially bad humor. Those two men were the Count de Rochefort and the mendicant of Saint Eustache. They came with their usual promptness, and the coadjutor spent with them a part of the night.

Chapter LXXXIX.

Difficult for Kings to return to the Capitals of their Kingdoms.

Whilst D'Artagnan and Porthos were engaged in conducting the cardinal to Saint Germain, Athos and Aramis returned to Paris.

Each had his own particular visit to make.

Aramis rushed to the Hotel de Ville, where Madame de Longueville was sojourning. The duchess loudly lamented the announcement of peace. War had made her a queen; peace brought her abdication. She declared that she would never assent to the treaty and that she wished eternal war.

But when Aramis had presented that peace to her in a true light—that is to say, with all its advantages; when he had pointed out to her, in exchange for the precarious and contested royalty of Paris, the viceroyalty of Font-de-l'Arche, in other words, of all Normandy; when he had rung in her ears the five hundred thousand francs promised by the cardinal; when he had dazzled her eyes with the honor bestowed on her by the king in holding her child at the baptismal font, Madame de Longueville contended no longer, except as is the custom with pretty women to contend, and defended herself only to surrender at last.

Aramis made a presence of believing in the reality of her opposition and was unwilling to deprive himself in his own view of the credit of her conversion.

"Madame," he said, "you have wished to conquer the prince your brother—that is to say, the greatest captain of the age; and when women of genius wish anything they always succeed in attaining it. You have succeeded; the prince is beaten, since he can no longer fight. Now attach him to our party. Withdraw him gently from the queen, whom he does not like, from Mazarin, whom he despises. The Fronde is a comedy, of which the first act only is played. Let us wait for a dénouement—for the day when the prince, thanks to you, shall have turned against the court."

Madame de Longueville was persuaded. This Frondist duchess trusted so confidently to the power of her fine eyes, that she could not doubt their influence even over Monsieur de Condé; and the chronicles of the time aver that her confidence was justified.

Athos, on quitting Aramis, went to Madame de Chevreuse. Here was another frondeuse to persuade, and she was even less open to conviction than her younger rival. There had been no stipulation in her favor. Monsieur de Chevreuse had not been appointed governor of a province, and if the queen should consent to be godmother it could be only of her grandson or granddaughter. At the first announcement of peace Madame de Chevreuse frowned, and in spite of all the logic of Athos to show her that a prolonged war would have been impracticable, contended in favor of hostilities.

"My fair friend," said Athos, "allow me to tell you that everybody is tired of war. You will get yourself exiled, as you did in the time of Louis XIII. Believe me, we have passed the time of success in intrigue, and your fine eyes are not destined to be eclipsed by regretting Paris, where there will always be two queens as long as you are there."

"Oh," cried the duchess, "I cannot make war alone, but I can avenge myself on that ungrateful queen and most ambitious favorite-on the honor of a duchess, I will avenge myself."

"Madame," replied Athos, "do not injure the Vicomte de Bragelonne—do not ruin his prospects. Alas! excuse my weakness! There are moments when a man grows young again in his children."

The duchess smiled, half tenderly, half ironically.

"Count," she said, "you are, I fear, gained over to the court. I suppose you have a blue ribbon in your pocket?"

"Yes, madame; I have that of the Garter, which King Charles I. gave me some days before he died."

"Come, I am growing an old woman!" said the duchess, pensively.

Athos took her hand and kissed it. She sighed, as she looked at him.

"Count," she said, "Bragelonne must be a charming place. You are a man of taste. You have water—woods—flowers there?"

She sighed again and leaned her charming head, gracefully reclined, on her hand, still beautiful in form and color.

"Madame!" exclaimed Athos, "what were you saying just now about growing old? Never have I seen you look so young, so beautiful!"

The duchess shook her head.

"Does Monsieur de Bragelonne remain in Paris?" she inquired.

"What think you of it?" inquired Athos.

"Leave him with me," replied the duchess.

"No, madame; if you have forgotten the history of Oedipus, I, at least, remember it."

"Really, sir, you are delightful, and I should like to spend a month at Bragelonne."

"Are you not afraid of making people envious of me, duchess?" replied Athos.

"No, I shall go incognito, count, under the name of Marie Michon."

"You are adorable, madame."

"But do not keep Raoul with you."

"Why not?"

"Because he is in love."

"He! he is quite a child!"

"And 'tis a child he loves."

Athos became thoughtful.

"You are right, duchess. This singular passion for a child of seven may some day make him very unhappy. There is to be war in Flanders. He shall go thither."

"And at his return you will send him to me. I will arm him against love."

"Alas, madame!" exclaimed Athos, "to-day love is like war—the breastplate is becoming useless."

Raoul entered at this moment; he came to announce that the solemn entrance of the king, queen, and her ministers was to take place on the ensuing day.

The next day, in fact, at daybreak, the court made preparations to quit Saint Germain.

Meanwhile, the queen every hour had been sending for D'Artagnan.

"I hear," she said, "that Paris is not quiet. I am afraid for the king's safety; place yourself close to the coach door on the right."

"Reassure yourself, madame, I will answer for the king's safety."

As he left the queen's presence Bernouin summoned him to the cardinal.

"Sir," said Mazarin to him "an emeute is spoken of in Paris. I shall be on the king's left and as I am the chief person threatened, remain at the coach door to the left."

"Your eminence may be perfectly easy," replied D'Artagnan; "they will not touch a hair of your head."

"Deuce take it!" he thought to himself, "how can I take care of both? Ah! plague on't, I will guard the king and Porthos shall guard the cardinal."

This arrangement pleased every one. The queen had confidence in the courage of D'Artagnan, which she knew, and the cardinal in the strength of Porthos, which he had experienced.

The royal procession set out for Paris. Guitant and Comminges, at the head of the guards, marched first; then came the royal carriage, with D'Artagnan on one side, Porthos on the other; then the musketeers, for two and twenty years staunch friends of D'Artagnan. During twenty he had been lieutenant, their captain since the night before.

The cortege proceeded to Notre Dame, where a Te Deum was chanted. All Paris were in the streets. The Swiss were drawn up along the road, but as the road was long, they were placed at six or eight feet distant from each other and one deep only. This force was therefore wholly insufficient, and from time to time the line was broken through by the people and was formed again with difficulty. Whenever this occurred, although it proceeded only from goodwill and a desire to see the king and queen, Anne looked at D'Artagnan anxiously.

Mazarin, who had dispensed a thousand louis to make the people cry "Long live Mazarin," and who had accordingly no confidence in acclamations bought at twenty pistoles each, kept one eye on Porthos; but that gigantic body-guard replied to the look with his great bass voice, "Be tranquil, my lord," and Mazarin became more and more composed.

At the Palais Royal, the crowd, which had flowed in from the adjacent street was still greater; like an impetuous mob, a wave of human beings came to meet the carriage and rolled tumultuously into the Rue Saint Honore.

When the procession reached the palace, loud cries of "Long live their majesties!" resounded. Mazarin leaned out of the window. One or two shouts of "Long live the cardinal" saluted his shadow; but instantly hisses and yells stifled them remorselessly. Mazarin turned pale and shrank back in the coach.

"Low-born fellows!" ejaculated Porthos.

D'Artagnan said nothing, but twirled his mustache with a peculiar gesture which showed that his fine Gascon humor was awake.

Anne of Austria bent down and whispered in the young king's ear:

"Say something gracious to Monsieur d'Artagnan, my son."

The young king leaned toward the door.

"I have not said good-morning to you, Monsieur d'Artagnan," he said; "nevertheless, I have remarked you. It was you who were behind my bed-curtains that night the Parisians wished to see me asleep."

"And if the king permits me," returned the Gascon, "I shall be near him always when there is danger to be encountered."

"Sir," said Mazarin to Porthos, "what would you do if the crowd fell upon us?"

"Kill as many as I could, my lord."

"Hem! brave as you are and strong as you are, you could not kill them all."

"'Tis true," answered Porthos, rising on his saddle, in order that he might appraise the immense crowd, "there are a lot of them."

"I think I should like the other fellow better than this one," said Mazarin to himself, and he threw himself back in his carriage.

The queen and her minister, more especially the latter, had reason to feel anxious. The crowd, whilst preserving an appearance of respect and even of affection for the king and queen regent, began to be tumultuous. Reports were whispered about, like certain sounds which announce, as they whistle from wave to wave, the coming storm—and when they pass athwart a multitude, presage an emeute.

D'Artagnan turned toward the musketeers and made a sign imperceptible to the crowd, but very easily understood by that chosen regiment, the flower of the army.

The ranks closed firmly in and a kind of majestic tremor ran from man to man.

At the Barriere des Sergents the procession was obliged to stop. Comminges left the head of the escort and went to the queen's carriage. Anne questioned D'Artagnan by a look. He answered in the same language.

"Proceed," she said.

Comminges returned to his post. An effort was made and the living barrier was violently broken through.

Some complaints arose from the crowd and were addressed this time to the king as well as the minister.

"Onward!" cried D'Artagnan, in a loud voice.

"Onward!" cried Porthos.

But as if the multitude had waited only for this demonstration to burst out, all the sentiments of hostility that possessed it exploded simultaneously. Cries of "Down with Mazarin!" "Death to the cardinal!" resounded on all sides.

At the same time through the streets of Grenelle, Saint Honore, and Du Coq, a double stream of people broke the feeble hedge of Swiss guards and came like a whirlwind even to the very legs of Porthos's horse and that of D'Artagnan.

This new eruption was more dangerous than the others, being composed of armed men. It was plain that it was not the chance combination of those who had collected a number of the malcontents at the same spot, but a concerted organized attack.

Each of these mobs was led by a chief, one of whom appeared to belong, not to the people, but to the honorable corporation of mendicants, and the other, notwithstanding his affected imitation of the people, might easily be discerned to be a gentleman. Both were evidently stimulated by the same impulse.

There was a shock which was perceived even in the royal carriage. Myriads of hoarse cries, forming one vast uproar, were heard, mingled with guns firing.

"Ho! Musketeers!" cried D'Artagnan.

The escort divided into two files. One of them passed around to the right of the carriage, the other to the left. One went to support D'Artagnan, the other Porthos. Then came a skirmish, the more terrible because it had no definite object; the more melancholy, because those engaged in it knew not for whom they were fighting. Like all popular movements, the shock given by the rush of this mob was formidable. The musketeers, few in number, not being able, in the midst of this crowd, to make their horses wheel around, began to give way. D'Artagnan offered to lower the blinds of the royal carriage, but the young king stretched out his arm, saying:

"No, sir! I wish to see everything."

"If your majesty wishes to look out—well, then, look!" replied D'Artagnan. And turning with that fury which made him so formidable, he rushed toward the chief of the insurgents, a man who, with a huge sword in his hand, was trying to hew a passage to the coach door through the musketeers.

"Make room!" cried D'Artagnan. "Zounds! give way!"

At these words the man with a pistol and sword raised his head, but it was too late. The blow was sped by D'Artagnan; the rapier had pierced his bosom.

"Ah! confound it!" cried the Gascon, trying in vain, too late, to retract the thrust. "What the devil are you doing here, count?"

"Accomplishing my destiny," replied Rochefort, falling on one knee. "I have already got up again after three stabs from you, I shall never rise after this fourth."

"Count!" said D'Artagnan, with some degree of emotion, "I struck without knowing that it was you. I am sorry, if you die, that you should die with sentiments of hatred toward me."

Rochefort extended his hand to D'Artagnan, who took it. The count wished to speak, but a gush of blood stifled him. He stiffened in the last convulsions of death and expired.

"Back, people!" cried D'Artagnan, "your leader is dead; you have no longer any business here."

Indeed, as if De Rochefort had been the very soul of the attack, the crowd who had followed and obeyed him took to flight on seeing him fall. D'Artagnan charged, with a party of musketeers, up the Rue du Coq, and the portion of the mob he assailed disappeared like smoke, dispersing near the Place Saint Germain-l'Auxerrois and taking the direction of the quays.

D'Artagnan returned to help Porthos, if Porthos needed help; but Porthos, for his part, had done his work as conscientiously as D'Artagnan. The left of the carriage was as well cleared as the right, and they drew up the blind of the window which Mazarin, less heroic than the king, had taken the precaution to lower.

Porthos looked very melancholy.

"What a devil of a face you have, Porthos! and what a strange air for a victor!"

"But you," answered Porthos, "seem to me agitated."

"There's a reason! Zounds! I have just killed an old friend."

"Indeed!" replied Porthos, "who?"

"That poor Count de Rochefort."

"Well! exactly like me! I have just killed a man whose face is not unknown to me. Unluckily, I hit him on the head and immediately his face was covered with blood."

"And he said nothing as he died?"

"Yes; he exclaimed, 'Oh!'"

"I suppose," answered D'Artagnan, laughing, "if he only said that, it did not enlighten you much."

"Well, sir!" cried the queen.

"Madame, the passage is quite clear and your majesty can continue your road."

In fact, the procession arrived, in safety at Notre Dame, at the front gate of which all the clergy, with the coadjutor at their head, awaited the king, the queen and the minister, for whose happy return they chanted a Te Deum.

As the service was drawing to a close a boy entered the church in great excitement, ran to the sacristy, dressed himself quickly in the choir robes, and cleaving, thanks to that uniform, the crowd that filled the temple, approached Bazin, who, clad in his blue robe, was standing gravely in his place at the entrance to the choir.

Bazin felt some one pulling his sleeve. He lowered to earth his eyes, beatifically raised to Heaven, and recognized Friquet.

"Well, you rascal, what is it? How do you dare to disturb me in the exercise of my functions?" asked the beadle.

"Monsieur Bazin," said Friquet, "Monsieur Maillard—you know who he is, he gives holy water at Saint Eustache——"

"Well, go on."

"Well, he received in the scrimmage a sword stroke on the head. That great giant who was there gave it to him."

"In that case," said Bazin, "he must be pretty sick."

"So sick that he is dying, and he wants to confess to the coadjutor, who, they say, has power to remit great sins."

"And does he imagine that the coadjutor will put himself out for him?"

"To be sure; the coadjutor has promised."

"Who told you that?"

"Monsieur Maillard himself."

"You have seen him, then?"

"Certainly; I was there when he fell."

"What were you doing there?"

"I was shouting, 'Down with Mazarin!' 'Death to the cardinal!' 'The Italian to the gallows!' Isn't that what you would have me shout?"

"Be quiet, you rascal!" said Bazin, looking uneasily around.

"So that he told me, that poor Monsieur Maillard, 'Go find the coadjutor, Friquet, and if you bring him to me you shall be my heir.' Say, then, Father Bazin—the heir of Monsieur Maillard, the giver of holy water at Saint Eustache! Hey! I shall have nothing to do but to fold my arms! All the same, I should like to do him that service—what do you say to it?"

"I will tell the coadjutor," said Bazin.

In fact, he slowly and respectfully approached the prelate and spoke to him privately a few words, to which the latter responded by an affirmative sign. He then returned with the same slow step and said:

"Go and tell the dying man that he must be patient. Monseigneur will be with him in an hour."

"Good!" said Friquet, "my fortune is made."

"By the way," said Bazin, "where was he carried?"

"To the tower Saint Jacques la Boucherie;" and delighted with the success of his embassy, Friquet started off at the top of his speed.

When the Te Deum was over, the coadjutor, without stopping to change his priestly dress, took his way toward that old tower which he knew so well. He arrived in time. Though sinking from moment to moment, the wounded man was not yet dead. The door was opened to the coadjutor of the room in which the mendicant was suffering.

A moment later Friquet went out, carrying in his hand a large leather bag; he opened it as soon as he was outside the chamber and to his great astonishment found it full of gold. The mendicant had kept his word and made Friquet his heir.

"Ah! Mother Nanette!" cried Friquet, suffocating; "ah! Mother Nanette!"

He could say no more; but though he hadn't strength to speak he had enough for action. He rushed headlong to the street, and like the Greek from Marathon who fell in the square at Athens, with his laurel in his hand, Friquet reached Councillor Broussel's threshold, and then fell exhausted, scattering on the floor the louis disgorged by his leather bag.

Mother Nanette began by picking up the louis; then she picked up Friquet.

In the meantime the cortege returned to the Palais Royal.

"That Monsieur d'Artagnan is a very brave man, mother," said the young king.

"Yes, my son; and he rendered very important services to your father. Treat him kindly, therefore, in the future."

"Captain," said the young king to D'Artagnan, on descending from the carriage, "the queen has charged me to invite you to dinner to-day—you and your friend the Baron du Vallon."

That was a great honor for D'Artagnan and for Porthos. Porthos was delighted; and yet during the entire repast he seemed to be preoccupied.

"What was the matter with you, baron?" D'Artagnan said to him as they descended the staircase of the Palais Royal. "You seemed at dinner to be anxious about something."

"I was trying," said Porthos, "to recall where I had seen that mendicant whom I must have killed."

"And you couldn't remember?"

"No."

"Well, search, my friend, search; and when you have found, you will tell me, will you not?"

"Pardieu!" said Porthos.

Chapter XC.

Conclusion.

On going home, the two friends found a letter from Athos, who desired them to meet him at the Grand Charlemagne on the following day.

The friends went to bed early, but neither of them slept. When we arrive at the summit of our wishes, success has usually the power to drive away sleep on the first night after the fulfilment of long cherished hopes.

The next day at the appointed hour they went to see Athos and found him and Aramis in traveling costume.

"What!" cried Porthos, "are we all going away, then? I also have made my preparations this morning."

"Oh, heavens! yes," said Aramis. "There's nothing to do in Paris now there's no Fronde. The Duchess de Longueville has invited me to pass a few days in Normandy, and has deputed me, while her son is being baptized, to go and prepare her residence at Rouen; after which, if nothing new occurs, I shall go and bury myself in my convent at Noisy-le-Sec."

"And I," said Athos, "am returning to Bragelonne. You know, dear D'Artagnan, I am nothing more than a good honest country gentleman. Raoul has no fortune other than I possess, poor child! and I must take care of it for him, since I only lend him my name."

"And Raoul—what shall you do with him?"

"I leave him with you, my friend. War has broken out in Flanders. You shall take him with you there. I am afraid that remaining at Blois would be dangerous to his youthful mind. Take him and teach him to be as brave and loyal as you are yourself."

"Then," replied D'Artagnan, "though I shall not have you, Athos, at all events I shall have that dear fair-haired head by me; and though he's but a boy, yet, since your soul lives again in him, dear Athos, I shall always fancy that you are near me, sustaining and encouraging me."

The four friends embraced with tears in their eyes.

Then they departed, without knowing whether they would ever see each other again.

D'Artagnan returned to the Rue Tiquetonne with Porthos, still possessed by the wish to find out who the man was that he had killed. On arriving at the Hotel de la Chevrette they found the baron's equipage all ready and Mousqueton on his saddle.

"Come, D'Artagnan," said Porthos, "bid adieu to your sword and go with me to Pierrefonds, to Bracieux, or to Du Vallon. We will grow old together and talk of our companions."

"No!" replied D'Artagnan, "deuce take it, the campaign is going to begin; I wish to be there, I expect to get something by it."

"What do you expect to get?"

"Why, I expect to be made Marechal of France!"

"Ha! ha!" cried Porthos, who was not completely taken in by D'Artagnan's Gasconades.

"Come my brother, go with me," added D'Artagnan, "and I will see that you are made a duke!"

"No," answered Porthos, "Mouston has no desire to fight; besides, they have erected a triumphal arch for me to enter my barony, which will kill my neighbors with envy."

"To that I can say nothing," returned D'Artagnan, who knew the vanity of the new baron. "Then, here's to our next merry meeting!"

"Adieu, dear captain," said Porthos, "I shall always be happy to welcome you to my barony."

"Yes, yes, when the campaign is over," replied the Gascon.

"His honor's equipage is waiting," said Mousqueton.

The two friends, after a cordial pressure of the hands, separated. D'Artagnan was standing at the door looking after Porthos with a mournful gaze, when the baron, after walking scarcely more than twenty paces, returned—stood still—struck his forehead with his finger and exclaimed:

"I recollect!"

"What?" inquired D'Artagnan.

"Who the beggar was that I killed."

"Ah! indeed! and who was he?"

"'Twas that low fellow, Bonacieux."

And Porthos, enchanted at having relieved his mind, rejoined Mousqueton and they disappeared around an angle of the street. D'Artagnan stood for an instant, mute, pensive and motionless; then, as he went in, he saw the fair Madeleine, his hostess, standing on the threshold.

"Madeleine," said the Gascon, "give me your apartment on the first floor; now that I am a captain in the royal musketeers I must make an appearance; nevertheless, reserve my old room on the fifth story for me; one never knows what may happen."